Bed & Breakfast

Great Britain & Ireland 1998

Top: Yalbury Cottage, Dorchester

Right: Polraen Country House, Looe

Below: Woodlands, Keswick

RAC

© West One (Trade) Publishing Ltd. 1997

This book is sold subject to the condition that it shall not, by way of trade, or otherwise, be lent, re-sold, hired out or otherwise circulated without the publisher's prior consent in any form of binding or cover other than that in which it is published.

All rights reserved. No parts of this work may be reproduced, stored in a retrieval system or transmitted by any means without permission. Whilst every effort has been made to ensure that the information contained in this publication is accurate and up to date, the publisher does not accept any responsibility for any error, omission, or misrepresentation. All liability for loss, disappointment, negligence or other damage caused by reliance on the information contained in this guide, or in the event of bankruptcy, or liquidation, or cessation of trade of any company, individual or firm mentioned is hereby excluded.

ISBN 1-900327-15-5 paperback

A CIP catalogue record for this book is available from the British Library.

Cartography: The Map Room, London

Production: Sino Publishing House Ltd, Hong Kong
Printed and bound in China

Published by West One (Trade) Publishing Ltd, Portland House, 4 Great Portland Street, London, W1N 5AA. Tel: 0171 580 6886

Publisher — Alan Wakeford

Managing Editor — Stan Dover

Production Manager — Ted Timberlake

Production Team — Tim Price
John Jones
Matthias Thaler
Elaine Pate
Tim Wheatley
Louise Coleman

Advertising
Sales Director — Marcia Smythe

Sales Executives — Yeside Akiwowo
Virginie Bellivier
David Kemp
Robert Case

Finance Director — Kevin Fitzgerald

Finance and Administration Team
Sarah Browne
Freddie Brexendorff
Katya Skaff
Eddie Malone
Margarita Guerra

Chief Executive Officer — Martin Coleman
P.A. to C.E.O. — Jan Gale

Contents

Leonard's Croft, Stafford

Introduction	4
How to use the guide	5
Small Hotels of the Year Awards 1997	6
Symbols and abbreviations	10

Directory of Hotels

England	12
Scotland	291
Wales	333
Northern Ireland	366
Republic of Ireland	368
Isle of Man	392
Channel Islands	393
Great Britain & Ireland Maps	397

Introduction

The Redland, Chester

The bed & breakfast sector is the most diverse in the hotel industry, Not only does it include guest houses with a welcoming home-from-home atmosphere, but small hotels and sometimes pubs and restaurants with rooms. The one common factor is that almost without exception, they are run by an owner and partner who take a constant and personal interest in the business. Indeed, business may be a misnomer; for many owners, the establishment is also their home. Their guests become their friends who return frequently.

It follows that many of the establishments in this book are small with as few as half a dozen rooms and rarely more than twenty. As often as not, the proprietor is responsible for the cooking as well, so "home cooking" is a phrase which really does menu something. In the best of these establishments, the food is delicious and substantial. Even if lunch and dinner is not always served, breakfast is invariably a highly enjoyable, traditionally cooked meal which will set you up for the day- hence the title of our guide.

In it, you will see the best of bed and breakfast in Britain and Ireland, where the discerning traveller is able to enjoy personal caring hospitality of the highest order.

Rose & Crown, Stroud

An Entry Explained

1. Town, county and map reference
2. A guest house or hotel name in blue indicates an RAC inspected establishment
3. Short description with a picture of the hotel or guest house.
4. Bedroon information and facilities;
   10 bedrs - number of bedrooms;
   1 ⊷ - number of public bathrooms;
   TCF - tea/coffee making facilities in at least some bedrooms;
   TV - TV in at least some bedrooms;
   ⊶ - dogs allowed;
   P12 - number of parking places.
5. Child restrictions - some restrictions on the age of child guests. Please phone for details.
6. Details of prices and credit cards accepted.

ALNMOUTH Northumberland 13F3

Marine House *Highly Acclaimed*
1 Marine Road, Alnmouth NE66 2RW
☎ 01665-830349

A 200 year old building of considerable charm, facing the sea. Ten individually appointed ensuite bedrooms..
10 bedrs, all ensuite, 1 ⊷ **TCF TV** ⊶ **P**12
No children under 7
HB £227-£240 **D** £13 **CC** MC Visa

How to use this guide

Price information

SB £30-£34: range of prices for one night bed & breakfast for one person.
DB £48: price for one night bed & breakfast for two people in a double room.
HB £260-£290: cost of dinner, bed & breakfast for 7 nights for one person.
D £16.95: price of table d'hôte dinner or evening meal.
CC: credit cards accepted
   MC: Mastercard
   Visa: Visa
   Amex: American Express
   DC: Diners Club
   JCB: Japan Card Bank

Prices

Prices given in the guide are forecasts by hoteliers of what they can expect to charge in 1998. Check with the hotel or guest house beforehand. All prices quoted should include VAT where applicable. The prices range from that for low season in standard rooms to that for superior rooms in high season.

Arrival times

Small hotels, guest houses and inns may close for part of the afternoon. It is wise to inform then of your expected arrival time when booking, and courteous to telephone them if you are delayed.

Cancellation of reservations

Should it become necessary to cancel reserved accommodation, guests are advised to telephone at once to the hotel or guest house, followed by written confirmation. If rooms which are reserved and not occupied cannot be re-let, the hotel proprietor may suffer loss, and guests may be held legally responsible for part of the cost.

Maps

Map references in the guide are to the relevant square on the maps at the end of the guide.

Disabled facilities

Establishment entries shown with ♿ are, in the opinion of the owner or manager, suitable for disabled people. Please check with the manager before you book.

RAC Awards

The RAC recognises the very high standards reached by some of the Listed hotels we inspect by the award of 'Highly Acclaimed' and 'Acclaimed' status. To gain such recognition, a hotel or guest house must have a proportion of rooms with ensuite bathrooms, have decor and furnishings with a certain degree of elegance and above average fittings and equipment. In addition, each year RAC Inspectors choose a hotel or guest house to receive the regional 'Small Hotel of the Year Award.'

SMALL HOTELS of the YEAR

EASTERN ENGLAND

CAMBRIDGE LODGE HOTEL
139 Huntingdon Road
Cambridge
CB3 0DQ

Sheila Hipwell and Darren Chamberlain

Every year we select one establishment from each of our regions which epitomises all those qualities which make for an outstanding bed & breakfast establishment. Not only does this include great style and comfort in the decor, furnishings and furniture, but it also includes original, high quality cooking and warm and caring hospitality. We believe that the seven establishments we have selected are truly the small hotels of the year.

Just minutes from the historic centre of Cambridge on the A1307, the Cambridge Lodge Hotel, occupying a spacious and impressive mock-Tudor house built at the turn of the century, radiates an aura of quiet elegance, long forgotten in larger establishments.

The proprietors are dedicated to making their guests totally at home in a hotel whose staff take a pride at making each visit a memorable one. Attention to detail is the motto of this intimate establishment, with its 13 well-appointed bedrooms, some oak-beamed, and charming bar lounge.

Chef Peter Reynolds and his talented team work behind the scenes creating imaginative and exciting dishes generally reflecting a classic style of cooking. The meals are served in a beautiful 50 seat oak beamed restaurant overlooking large mature gardens and terraced area, where pre-dinner drinks can be taken in the summer months. Flexibility is the keyword in the hotel kitchens and the chef is happy to prepare special dishes on request.

Being so near to the historic city centre of Cambridge, the hotel is an ideal base from which to explore the sights of this great seat of learning. The delights of Cambridge are varied, with impressive architecture, narrow winding streets, punting on the river and a host of museums, colleges and galleries. Ely, famous for its cathedral, is less than 15 miles away.

SOUTH WEST ENGLAND

BARN HAYES
Brim Hill
Maidencombe
Torquay
Devon   TQ1 4TR

Fran and Geoff Gownes

Barn Hayes is a delightful country hotel, combining a warm and friendly country home atmosphere with all the modern facilities expected in a quality hotel. Your comfort and relaxation are guaranteed by the lovely surroundings and the proprietors' personal attention to the smallest detail, complemented by excellently prepared, fresh food, with a choice of menu, good wines and a well stocked bar.

The hotel is hidden away down a Devon country lane in an officially designated area of outstanding natural beauty. The garden setting is in a natural valley sheltered on three sides by lovely folding hills and overlooking Lyme Bay on the fourth side - a vista of deep blue sea on an English summers day - and yet the centre of Torquay, England's most famous riviera resort beloved by generations of visitors, is only three miles away.

Maidencombe itself is a truly rural unspoilt magical hamlet on the very edge of the town. Whatever your interests there is a complete range of activities to please. The Torbay coastal path runs a few yards from the hotel and the local beach is just a five minute walk away and steps lead down to a small sandy cove with safe bathing. There are several good golf courses nearby.

Barn Hayes is the perfect place to introduce children to a countryside holiday. Close by is Dartmoor with its fascinating legends and wild natural beauty to explore, and the lovely valleys of the South Devon rivers are not to be missed. Olde worlde thatched villages like picturesque Cockington, with traditional crafts in abundance, are all within easy reach.

THE MIDLANDS

LEASOW HOUSE
Laverton Meadows
Broadway
Worcestershire
WR12 7NA

Barbara and Gordon Meekings

Situated in the heart of the Cotswolds close to the village of Broadway, this Costwold stone farm house, dating back to the 17th century, has been sympathetically renovated to provide guests with every modern comfort. The hosts like visitors to think of themselves as 'guests' in a traditional country house and the atmosphere is relaxed and convivial. A complimentary sherry awaits you on arrival and you are provided with your own front door key and encouraged to come and go as you please. At the end of the day you are welcome to unwind in the comfortable library which is used as a sitting room.

The bedrooms are spacious and furnished to a high standard. In the main house all have ensuite bath or shower rooms, plus central heating, tea and coffee making facilities, colour television and direct dial telephones. In the immaculately converted barn there are two more ensuite rooms, one of which has been specially equipped for disabled guests.

For those who enjoy the superb countryside of the Cotswolds or touring historic towns and stately houses, Leasow House is the ideal base. Shakespeare's Stratford, and the cathedral cities of Gloucester and Worcester are within easy reach. Blenheim Palace and Warwick and Sudeley castles make for fascinating visits as do the gardens of Hidecote and Kingsgate.

NORTH of ENGLAND

THE DOWNCLIFFE HOUSE HOTEL
The Beach
Filey
North Yorkshire
YO14 9LA

David and Elsie Garland

Situated directly overlooking Filey's six miles of golden sands, with views from Filey Brigg to Flamborough Head, this impressive Victorian detached hotel really does possess the perfect setting. Not the place for night clubs and noise, people who come to the elegant and unspoilt resort of Filey come here to relax.

Guests staying at Downcliffe House can expect the highest standards of service from its team of friendly staff. Quality, value for money and attention to detail make this hotel the perfect place for those seeking something a little special.

Recently refurbished by the owners, each of Downcliffe House's ten bedrooms are furnished to exacting high standards and have all the facilities expected by today's discerning customer - complimentary toiletries, television with radio and satellite channels, direct dial telephones, hair dryer and tea and coffee making facilities.

Breakfast offers an extensive cold buffet as well as a full English breakfast. Evening meal is served in the restaurant which overlooks Filey Bay. Guests select from the extensive, expertly prepared, a la carte menu. The reasonably priced wine list has a very interesting range, reputedly selected *and tested* by the owners. And while you savour the food you can also savour spectacular sea views.

SCOTLAND

ARBOR LODGE
Ballater Road
Aboyne
AB34 5HY

Mrs Sheena Buchan

Visit Arbor Lodge and you will understand immediately why it has won our top Small Hotel Award for Scotland.

This large luxury home is beautifully set in over and acre of grounds. A formal garden at the front greets the visitor, giving way to natural woodland at the rear. All the bedrooms have walk in dressing rooms and ensuite bathrooms containing baths and separate shower units. The rooms also have colour television and tea making facilities. Guests also have exclusive use of a lounge and reading room.

Arbor Lodge is ideally situated for touring Royal Deeside and for visiting the many castles in the area. Balmoral, the Queen's summer residence, is nearby. For those who enjoy a more active holiday, the village of Aboyne has a wide range of sporting facilities including golf, gliding, tennis, lawn bowling, fishing, shooting, swimming, water-skiing and golf. And in the picturesque valley there are also many areas for hill walking.

Small Hotels of the Year

WALES

MAES-y-GWERNEN HOTEL
School Road
Abercraf
Swansea Valley
SA9 1XD

Mr & Mrs Jim Moore

Over the last 20 years Maes-y-Gwernen has built an enviable reputation for good food, efficient and friendly service, comfort and all round excellent value, which has been recognised by the number of awards and commendations it has received.

This well appointed country hotel is set in private grounds in the village of Abercraf in the Upper Swansea Valley. The grounds also contain a Finnish chalet with a sauna, spa, solarium and fitness facility. Two garden suites with private patios are available and amongst the other special options are fourposter and waterbeds.

Being on the southern edge of the Brecon Beacons National Park, the hotel is within easy reach of many of the region's tourist attractions, the surrounding hills and river valleys offering the walker an abundance of waterfalls, caves and unspoilt countryside to explore. The hotel is also an ideal base for those journeying to the lower Swansea Valley on business.

REPUBLIC OF IRELAND

GREENMOUNT HOUSE
Gortonora
Dingle
County Kerry

John and Mary Curran

Greenmount House is a luxury guest house situated on an elevated site with panoramic views overlooking Dingle town and harbour.

The Curran family home has been extended over the years to incorporate six top class ensuite rooms and six newly developed superior rooms with sea views. Each room has a full bathroom and large sitting area. They also have direct dial phones, televisions, tea and coffee making facilities and many more extras.

Breakfast, which is served in a conservatory, again taking advantage of the fabulous view, is a feast for which the Curran's are famous.

Greenmount House is an ideal base to tour the beautiful Kerry countryside and its numerous archaeological and historic sites.

The town centre and the Conor Pass are only five minutes away, and within easy reach are golf, fishing, cycling, sailing, water sports, horse riding, tennis. There are organised trips to The Blaskets, local archaeological sights and by boat to see 'Fungi' the Dolphin.

Symbols and Abbreviations

English	Français	Deutsch
facilities for the disabled	Aménagements pour handicapés	Einrichtungen für Behinderte
dogs permitted	chiens acceptés	Hunde erlaubt
no smoking anywhere in hotel	Interdiction de fumer dans l'hôtel	Rauchverbot im ganzen Hotel
lift	ascenseur	Fahrstuhl
P parking	Parking	Parken
TCF tea/coffee making facilities	Équipment pour faire du thé/café dans les chambres	Tee/Kaffee Aufgusseinrichtungen
SB single room & breakfast	chambre d'une personne + petit déjeuner	Preis für Einzelzimmer und Frühstück
DB double room & breakfast	chambre pour deux personnes + petit déjeuner	Preis für Doppelzimmer und Frühstück
HB halfboard	demi-pension	Halb Pension
D dinner	Dîner	Abendessen
CC credit cards	Cartes de crédit	Kreditkarten
MC MasterCard/Access	MasterCard	MasterCard
Visa Visa Barclaycard	Visa	Visa
Amex American Express	American Express	American Express
DC Diners Club	Diners Club	Diners Club
JCB Japan Card Bank	Japan Card Bank	Japan Card Bank

Sporting facilities

English	Français	Deutsch
indoor swimming pool	Piscine couverte	Hallenbad
outdoor swimming pool	Piscine en extérieur	Freibad
golf course	Terrain de Golf	Golfplatz
tennis	Tennis	Tennis
fishing	Pêche	Angeln
squash	Squash	Squash
riding	Equatation	Reiten
gymnasium	Gymnase	Sporthalle
billiards/snooker	Billard	Billard
sauna	Sauna	Sauna

England

Top: Bird in Hand,
High Wycombe

Right: Widbrook Grange,
Bradford upon Avon

Below: Dorset Westbury,
Bournemouth

ADSTOCK Buckinghamshire 8B4

Folly Inn Listed
Buckingham Road, Adstock MK18 2HS
☎ 01296-712671
5 bedrs, all ensuite, TCF TV ⚡ P 40 CC MC Visa Amex ♿

ALDERSHOT Hampshire 4C3

George Listed
Wellington Street, Aldershot GU11 1DX
☎ 01252-330800 Fax 01252-330800
9 bedrs, 1 ensuite, SB £20 DB £40 CC MC Visa Amex

ALDERTON Gloucestershire 7E4

Moors Farm House
32 Beckford Road, Alderton GL20 8NL
☎ 01242-620523

An 18th century Cotswold family farmhouse in a quiet village setting, close to local places to eat and the Cotswolds.

ALKMONTON Derbyshire 8A2

Dairy House
Alkmonton DE6 3DG
☎ 01335-330359 Fax 01335-330359

Old oak beamed farmhouse with inglenook fireplace and guests' own lounge and dining room. Tranquil location, good food, comfortable rooms, close to many historical properties - Chatsworth, Calke Abbey and others.

7 bedrs, 4 ensuite, 1 ⚡ TCF ⚡ P 8 No children SB £17-£24 DB £34-£40 HB £217-£266 D £12

ALLONBY Cumbria 10A1

Ship Listed
Main Street, Allonby CA15 6PD
☎ 01900-881017
7 bedrs, 4 ensuite, 2 ⚡ TCF TV ⚡ P 6 SB £16-£20 DB £50-£70 HB £200-£300 D £10 CC MC Visa

ALMONDSBURY Gloucestershire 3E1

Abbotts Way Highly Acclaimed
Gloucester Road, Almondsbury BS12 4JB
☎ 01454-613134 Fax 01454-613134

Situated in 12 acres of outstanding natural beauty offering guests panoramic views of the Severn Vale and both bridges. All rooms ensuite, central heating, separate dining room, TV lounge with log fire, conservatory, conference facilities, ample parking.

6 bedrs, all ensuite, TCF TV P 10 SB £25 DB £40 HB £160 CC MC Visa Amex DC 🏊 ⚡

ALNMOUTH Northumberland 13F3

★★ Famous Schooner
Northumberland Street, Alnmouth NE66 2RS
☎ 01665-830216 Fax 01665-830216
26 bedrs, all ensuite, 1 ⚡ TCF TV ⚡ P 60 SB £29.50-£34.50 DB £59-£69 D £12

Marine House Highly Acclaimed
1 Marine Road, Alnmouth NE66 2RW
☎ 01665-830349

A 200 year old building of considerable charm, facing the sea. Ten individually appointed ensuite bedrooms, warm, homely atmosphere, delicious imaginative cooking, pets welcome, parking.

10 bedrs, all ensuite, 1 ⇌ TCF TV ⊢ P 12 No children under 7 HB £227-£240 D £13 CC MC Visa

ALNWICK Northumberland 13F3

★★ Hotspur
Bondgate Without, Alnwick NE66 1PR
📞 01665-510101 Fax 01665-605033

Town centre coaching inn offering warm hospitality and comfortable ensuite accommodation. Excellent standard of food, good selection of wines and fine ales.

25 bedrs, all ensuite, 1 ⇌ TCF TV P 20 SB £35-£40 DB £60-£70 HB £262.50 D £12 CC MC Visa JCB

Bondgate House *Acclaimed*
20 Bondgate Without, Alnwick NE66 1PN
📞 01665-602025 Fax 01665-602554
8 bedrs, 5 ensuite, 1 ⇌ TV P 8 SB £23-£26 DB £40-£42 HB £133-£140 D £12 CC MC Visa JCB

ALSTON Cumbria 10B1

★★ Lovelady Shield Country House
Hospitality, Comfort, Restaurant merit awards
Nenthead Road, Alston CA9 3LF
📞 01434-381203 Fax 01434-381515
Closed 4 Jan-4 Feb
12 bedrs, all ensuite, TV ⊢ P 25 SB £56 DB £112-£132 HB £438-£492 D £26 CC MC Visa Amex DC

★★ Lowbyer Manor Country House
Hexham Road, Alston CA9 3JX
📞 01434-381230 Fax 01434-382937
12 bedrs, all ensuite, TCF TV ⊢ P 14 SB £35 DB £70 HB £330 D £17 CC MC Visa Amex DC

ALTON Hampshire 4B3

White Hart
London Road, Hollybourne, Alton GU34 4EY
📞 01420-87654 Fax 01420-543982

A traditional public house situated in the beautiful village of Holybourne, boasting an a la carte restaurant, a play area for children and garden.

4 bedrs, 1 ⇌ TCF TV ⊢ P 40 SB £21 DB £35 D £1.75 CC MC Visa Amex DC

ALTRINCHAM Cheshire 10C4

Ash Farm *Highly Acclaimed*
Park Lane, Little Bollington, Altrincham WA14 4JJ
📞 0161-929 9290

Situated in the heart of National Trust countryside, this beautiful licensed country guest house features exposed beams, open fires and a full a la carte menu.

3 bedrs, all ensuite, TCF TV P 6 No children under 9 SB £40-£45 DB £56-£62 D £17 CC MC Visa Amex DC

Old Packet House *Highly Acclaimed*
Navigation Road, Broadheath, Altrincham WA14 1LW
📞 0161-929 1331 Fax 0161-929 1331

A delightful olde worlde inn with four ensuite bedrooms, providing the ultimate in comfort and decor, complemented by home cooking and real ales.

4 bedrs, all ensuite, TCF TV P 12 SB £37.50-£47.50 DB £57.50-£67.50 D £14 CC MC Visa

Beech Mount *Listed*
46 Barrington Road, Altrincham WA14 1HN
📞 **0161-928 4523** Fax **0161-928 1055**
35 bedrs, all ensuite, 2 ⇌ **TCF TV P** 30 **SB** £25-£30 **DB** £45 **D** £12 **CC** MC Visa

Lodge at the Bull's Head *Lodge*
Wicker Lane, Hale Barns, Altrincham WA15 0HG
📞 **0161-903 1300** Fax **0161-903 1300**

AMBLESIDE Cumbria   10B2

★★ Borrans Park
Comfort, Restaurant merit awards
Borrans Road, Ambleside LA22 0EN
📞 **015394-33454** Fax **015394-33003**
12 bedrs, all ensuite, **TCF TV P** 15 No children under 7 **SB** £30-£50 **DB** £60-£80 **HB** £255-£330 **D** £17.50 **CC** MC Visa JCB ♿

★★ Fisherbeck
Hospitality, Comfort merit awards
Old Lake Road, Ambleside LA22 0DH
📞 **015394-33215** Fax **015394-33600**
Closed Jan
20 bedrs, 18 ensuite, 2 🛏, 2 ⇌ **TCF TV P** 20 **SB** £25-£39 **DB** £50-£74 **HB** £231-£353 **D** £16.95 **CC** MC Visa

★★ Kirkstone Foot
Hospitality, Comfort merit awards
Kirkstone Pass Road, Ambleside LA22 9EH
📞 **01539-432232** Fax **01539-432232**
Closed Jan
31 bedrs, all ensuite, **TCF TV P** 30 **SB** £35-£42 **DB** £62-£80 **HB** £330-£365 **D** £20.95 **CC** MC Visa Amex DC JCB ♿

★★ Nanny Brow Country House
Hospitality, Comfort, Restaurant merit awards
Clappersgate, Ambleside LA22 9NF
📞 **01539-432036** Fax **01539-432450**
18 bedrs, 17 ensuite, 1 🛏, **TV** 🐾 **P** 25 **SB** £55-£65 **DB** £110-£130 **HB** £378-£478 **D** £18.50 **CC** MC Visa Amex DC JCB 📧

★★ Queen's
Market Place, Ambleside LA22 9BU
📞 **01539-432206** Fax **01539-432721**
26 bedrs, all ensuite, **TCF TV P** 11 **SB** £25-£31 **DB** £50-£62 **HB** £244-£300 **D** £14 **CC** MC Visa Amex DC

★★ Skelwith Bridge
Restaurant merit award
Skelwith Bridge, Ambleside LA22 9NJ
📞 **01539-432115** Fax **01539-434254**
Closed 11-26 Dec

Set in the heart of the Lake District, ideal for walking, exploring or simply relaxing.

29 bedrs, all ensuite, **TCF TV** 🐾 **P** 60 **SB** £28-£50 **DB** £56-£90 **HB** £195-£325 **D** £18.95 **CC** MC Visa JCB

★★ Waterhead
Lake Road, Ambleside LA22 0ER
📞 **01539-432566** Fax **01539-431255**
28 bedrs, all ensuite, **TCF TV** 🐾 **P** 50 **SB** £42 **DB** £88-£94 **D** £18 **CC** MC Visa Amex DC JCB

Elder Grove *Highly Acclaimed*
Lake Road, Ambleside LA22 0DB
📞 **015394-32504** Fax **015394-32504**
Closed Nov-Feb
12 bedrs, all ensuite, **TCF TV** 🐾 **P** 12 No children under 5 **SB** £22-£28 **DB** £44-£56 **HB** £252-£294 **D** £16.50 **CC** MC Visa JCB

ELDER GROVE HOTEL

A delightful hotel owned and managed by the Haywood family to a high standard. Comfortable bedrooms with ensuite bath/shower. Renowned for delicious food. Bar. Parking.

**LAKE ROAD,
AMBLESIDE LA22 0DB
Tel: 015394–32504**

ANDOVER – ENGLAND

Grey Friar Lodge *Highly Acclaimed*
Brathay, Ambleside LA22 9NE
☎ 01539-433158 Fax 01539-433158
Closed Nov-Feb
8 bedrs, all ensuite, TCF TV P 12 No children under 12
SB £29-£32 DB £43-£64 HB £230-£300 D £16.50

Rowanfield Country House *Highly Acclaimed*
Kirkstone Road, Ambleside LA22 9ET
☎ 015394-33686 Fax 015394-31569
Closed Dec-Mar
7 bedrs, all ensuite, TCF TV P 7 No children under 5
SB £56-£60 HB £267-£277 D £17 CC MC Visa

Rysdale *Highly Acclaimed*
Rothay Road, Ambleside LA22 0EE
☎ 01539-432140 Fax 01539-431111
9 bedrs, 6 ensuite, 2 TCF TV P 2 CC MC Visa

Anchorage *Acclaimed*
Rydal Road, Ambleside LA22 9AY
☎ 015394-32046
Closed Dec-Jan
5 bedrs, 3 ensuite, 1 TCF TV P 7 No children
DB £36-£48

Lyndhurst *Acclaimed*
Wansfell Road, Ambleside LA22 0EG
☎ 01539-432421 Fax 01539-432421

Attractive lakeland stone house delightfully situated with private car park, scrumptious breakfast, cosy bar, fourposter beds, warm and friendly and all facilities. Special breaks available.

8 bedrs, all ensuite, TCF TV P 8 SB £30-£40 DB £39-£45 HB £210-£245 D £14

Lyndale *Listed*
Lake Road, Ambleside LA22 0DN
☎ 01539-434244
Closed Christmas
6 bedrs, 2 ensuite, 2 TCF TV SB £16-£17 DB £31-£40

Britannia Inn
Elterwater, Nr. Ambleside LA22 9HP
☎ 015394-37210

A traditional village inn with very comfortable ensuite guest accommodation, serving home cooked bar meals and real ales in cosy bars with log fires.

13 bedrs, 9 ensuite, 2 TCF TV P 12 CC MC Visa

Easedale
Compston Road, Ambleside LA22 9DJ
☎ 015394-32112

Victorian house, recently extended and lovingly refurbished to a high standard. Attractive lounge with TV overlooking putting and bowling greens and fells beyond. Central position. Advice given for walking and sightseeing. Own car park.

7 bedrs, 5 ensuite, 1 TCF TV P 7 DB £32-£52

AMERSHAM Buckinghamshire 4C2

Chequers *Listed*
London Road, Amersham HP7 9DA
☎ 01494-727866
4 bedrs, 3 ensuite, TCF TV P 27

ANDOVER Hampshire 4B3

★★ Danebury
High Street, Andover SP10 1NX
☎ 01264-323332 Fax 01264-334021
23 bedrs, all ensuite, TCF TV P 40 SB £50 DB £60 D £8.65 CC MC Visa Amex DC

APPLEBY-IN-WESTMORLAND Cumbria 10B2

★★ Royal Oak
Restaurant merit award
Bondgate, Appleby-in-Westmorland CA16 6UN
☎ 01768-351463 Fax 017683-52300
Closed 25 Dec
9 bedrs, 7 ensuite, 2 ⇌ TCF TV ✝ P 12 SB £30-£50
DB £63-£80 CC MC Visa Amex DC JCB

★★ White Hart
34 Boroughgate, Appleby-in-Westmorland CA16 6XG
☎ 01768-351598 Fax 01768-351598
9 bedrs, 5 ensuite, 2 ⌂, 2 ⇌ TCF TV ✝ SB £25-£32.50
DB £45-£60 D £14 CC MC Visa Amex DC

★ Courtfield
Bongate, Appleby-in-Westmorland CA16 6UP
☎ 017683-51394
11 bedrs, 4 ensuite, 1 ⇌ ✝

Bongate House
Bongate, Appleby-in-Westmorland CA16 6UE
☎ 017683-51245 Fax 017683-51423
Closed Christmas & New Year

Enjoy a relaxed atmosphere and good home cooking in a family run Georgian guest house set in an acre of secluded gardens.

8 bedrs, 5 ensuite, 1 ⇌ TCF TV ✝ P 10 No children under 5 SB £17.50 DB £35-£40 HB £170-£190 D £9

APPLETON-LE-MOORS North Yorkshire 11E2

★★ Appleton Hall
Hospitality, Comfort merit awards
Appleton-le-Moors YO6 6TF
☎ 01751-417227 Fax 01751-417540
10 bedrs, all ensuite, TCF TV ✝ 🗎 P 20 No children under 12 SB £45-£50 DB £90-£100 HB £350 D £20 CC MC Visa Amex JCB

RAC Hotel Reservations Service
0870 603 9109
(Calls charged at national call rate)

ARNSIDE Cumbria 10B3

Willowfield *Acclaimed*
The Promenade, Arnside LA5 0AD
☎ 01524-761354

Non-smoking, relaxed, family run private hotel with superb outlook over estuary to lakeland hills. Warm welcome, good home cooking (table licence) and quiet situation.

10 bedrs, 7 ensuite, 2 ⇌ TCF TV ⌂ ✝ P 8 SB £19 DB £48 HB £210 D £11 CC MC Visa JCB

ARUNDEL West Sussex 4C4

★★ Comfort Friendly Inn
Junction A27/A284, Crossbush, Arundel
☎ 01903-840840
35 bedrs, all ensuite

Arundel Park Inn & Travel Lodge *Highly Acclaimed*
The Causeway, Station Approach, Arundel BN18 9JL
☎ 01903-882588 Fax 01903-883808
12 bedrs, all ensuite, TCF TV P 60 SB £34-£38 DB £44-£48 D £11 CC MC Visa Amex ♿

ASCOT Berkshire 4C2

★★ Highclere
19 Kings Road, Sunninghill, Ascot SL5 9AD
☎ 01344-25220 Fax 01344-872528
11 bedrs, all ensuite, TCF TV P 14 SB £60-£80 DB £70-£100 D £15 CC MC Visa Amex JCB

ASHBOURNE Derbyshire 8A2

★★ Dog & Partridge
Swinscoe, Ashbourne DE6 2HS
☎ 01335-343183 Fax 01335-342742
30 bedrs, ✝ P 55 SB £35-£45 DB £60-£65 HB £265-£285 D £11.95 CC MC Visa Amex DC 🖪 ♿

Lichfield *Highly Acclaimed*
Bridgeview, Mayfield, Ashbourne DE6 2HN
📞 01335-344422 Fax 01335-344422
Closed 25-26 Dec

A family run, non-smoking Georgian guest house, standing in two acres of grounds on the Derbyshire/Staffordshire border and overlooking the River Dove and valleys beyond.

4 bedrs, 2 ensuite, 2 🛏, 1 🚻 TCF TV 🖼 P 10 SB £20 DB £27-£42

ASHBURTON Devon   3D3

★★ Dartmoor Lodge
Peartree Cross, Ashburton TQ13 7JW
📞 01364-652232 Fax 01364-653990
30 bedrs, all ensuite, TCF TV 🐕 🍽 P 100 SB £39 DB £55 HB £240 D £7 CC MC Visa Amex JCB ♿

Gages Mill *Acclaimed*
Buckfastleigh Road, Ashburton TQ13 7JW
📞 01364-652391
Closed Dec-Feb

Carefully converted former 14th century woollen mill, set in 1¼ acres on the edge of Dartmoor National Park. Delightful ensuite rooms, all with country views; home cooked food to a very high standard, licensed, ample parking.

8 bedrs, 7 ensuite, 1 🛏, TCF TV P 8 No children under 10 SB £22-£23 DB £44-£46 HB £210-£220.50 D £12

New Cott Farm
Poundsgate, Newton Abbot TQ13 7PD
📞 01364-631421 Fax 01364-631421
Closed 25 Dec

Enjoy the freedom, peace and tranquillity of moorland and valleys in the Dartmoor National Park. Warm welcome and lovely homemade food. Less able guests welcome.

4 bedrs, all ensuite, TCF 🖼 P 4 No children under 5 SB £25 DB £36 HB £182 D £10.50 ♿

ASHFORD Kent   5E3

Croft *Highly Acclaimed*
Canterbury Road, Ashford TN25 4DU
📞 01233-622140 Fax 01233-622140
28 bedrs, all ensuite, TCF TV 🐕 P 30 SB £37.50-£43.50 DB £48.50-£58.50 D £11 CC MC Visa Amex

Warren Cottage *Highly Acclaimed*
136 The Street, Willesborough, Ashford TN24 0NB
📞 01233-621905 Fax 01233-623400

A privately owned hotel in two acres of gardens. The bedrooms all have private facilities and TV. Restaurant open 6:30-8:00. Just off M20 (jn10), take the B2164 Kennington Road going toward Canterbury, after a few hundred yards turn right into The Street.

11 bedrs, 10 ensuite, 1 🚻 TCF TV 🐕 P 15 SB £34.90-£39.90 DB £42-£59.90 HB £314.30-£489.30 D £10 CC MC Visa

Elvey Farm
Pluckley, Ashford TN27 0SU
📞 01233-840442 Fax 01233-840726

A luxury country hotel in the midst of a working farm offering all modern facilities in a peaceful location. Licensed bar, dining room. Families welcome.

9 bedrs, all ensuite, TCF TV ⊁ P 15 SB £35.50-£49.50 DB £49.50-£59.50 D £14.50 CC MC Visa ♿

ASHOVER Derbyshire 8A2

Old School Farm *Listed*
Uppertown, Ashover S45 0JF
📞 01246-590813
4 bedrs, 2 ensuite, 1 ⇥ TCF TV P 10 SB £20 DB £40 HB £140 D £8

ASHTON-UNDER-LYNE Lancashire 10C4

Welbeck House *Acclaimed*
324 Katharine Street, Ashton-under-Lyne OL6 7BD
📞 0161-344 0751 Fax 0161-343 4278
8 bedrs, all ensuite, TCF TV ⊁ P 20 SB £33 DB £45 D £6.75 CC MC Visa DC 🖼 ♿

ASHURST Hampshire 4B4

★★ Busketts Lawn
174 Woodlands Road, Woodlands, Ashurst SO4 2GL
📞 01703-292272 Fax 01703-292487
14 bedrs, all ensuite, TCF TV ⊁ P 50 SB £38.50-£50 DB £70-£80 HB £287-£297.50 D £16.50 CC MC Visa Amex DC 🏊

ASKRIGG North Yorkshire 10C2

★★ King's Arms
Hospitality, Restaurant merit awards
Askrigg DL8 3HQ
📞 01969-650258 Fax 01969-650635
E Mail rayliz@kahaskrigg.prestel.co.uk
11 bedrs, all ensuite, TCF TV ⊁ P 12 SB £55-£75 DB £79-£120 HB £275-£495 D £27.50 CC MC Visa Amex JCB

AUSTWICK North Yorkshire 10C3

★★ Traddock
Hospitality, Comfort, Restaurant merit awards
Austwick, Settle LA2 8BY
📞 015242-51224 Fax 015242-51224
11 bedrs, all ensuite, 1 ⇥ TCF TV P 20 SB £35-£40 DB £65-£75 HB £300-£320 D £19.50 CC MC Visa

AXBRIDGE Somerset 3E1

Mill House *Listed*
Tarnock, Axbridge BS26 2SN
📞 01934-750545
Closed Jan
3 bedrs, 2 ensuite, 1 🐾, 4 ⇥ TV 🚭 P 16 CC MC Visa

AYLESBURY Buckinghamshire 4C2

★★ Horse and Jockey
Buckingham Road, Aylesbury HP19 3QL
📞 01296-23803 Fax 01296-395142
24 bedrs, all ensuite, TCF TV P 60 CC MC Visa Amex DC

BADMINTON, GREAT Gloucestershire 3F1

Chestnut Farm
Tolmarton, Badminton GL9 1HS
📞 01454-218563

An 18th century farmhouse situated on the edge of the Cotswolds, a quarter of a mile from the M4 (jn 18), 12 miles from Bath and Bristol and 6 miles from Castle Combe. French, Italian and Spanish spoken.

5 bedrs, all ensuite, TCF TV ⊁ P 10

BAINBRIDGE North Yorkshire 10C2

★★ Rose & Crown
Bainbridge, Wensleydale DL8 3EE
📞 01969-650225 Fax 01969-650735
12 bedrs, all ensuite, TCF TV ⊁ P 65 SB £31.50-£38.50 DB £51-£65 HB £276.50-£325.50 D £17 CC MC Visa 🎵

Riverdale House *Highly Acclaimed*
Bainbridge DL8 3EW
☎ 01969-650311
Closed Nov-Jan
12 bedrs, 11 ensuite, 1 ⇌ TCF TV P 4 DB £52 D £16.50

BAKEWELL Derbyshire 8A2

★★ Milford House
Mill Street, Bakewell DE45 1DA
☎ 01629-812130
Closed Nov-Mar
12 bedrs, all ensuite, TCF TV P 10 No children under 10
SB £36-£40 DB £67-£75 HB £319-£340 D £16 CC MC Visa

BALSALL COMMON West Midlands 8A4

★★ Haigs
Hospitality merit award
273 Kenilworth Road, Balsall Common CV7 7EL
☎ 01676-533004 Fax 01676-535132
15 bedrs, all ensuite, TCF TV ⇌ P 25 SB £47.50-£52.50
DB £62.50-£67.50 D £15.50 CC MC Visa ♿

BAMBURGH Northumberland 13F3

★★ Lord Crewe Arms
Hospitality, Comfort merit awards
Front Street, Bamburgh NE69 7BL
☎ 01668-214243 Fax 01668-214273
Closed 31 Oct
25 bedrs, 20 ensuite, 3 ⇌ TCF TV ⇌ P 34 No children under 5 CC MC Visa

★★ Mizen Head
Lucker Road, Bamburgh NE69 7BS
☎ 01668-214254
15 bedrs, 11 ensuite, 2 ⇌ TCF TV ⇌ P 30 SB £22.50-£444 DB £45-£74 HB £231-£300 D £13 CC MC Visa

BAMFORD Derbyshire 8A1

Ye Derwent
Main Road, Bamford S30 2AY
☎ 01433-651395

Set amongst the rolling hills of the Peak National Park, the Derwent Hotel is a traditional 100 year old inn, noted for its food, ale and country friendliness.

10 bedrs, 3 ensuite, 2 ⇌ TCF TV ⇌ P 40 SB £25-£35
DB £40-£48 HB £195-£205 D £8 CC MC Visa Amex DC JCB

BAMPTON Oxfordshire 4A2

Farmhouse *Highly Acclaimed*
University Farm, Lew, Bampton OX18 2AU
☎ 01993-850297 Fax 01993-850938
6 bedrs, all ensuite, TCF TV P 30 No children under 5
SB £39 DB £50 CC MC Visa ♿

BAMPTON Devon 3D2

★★ Bark House
Hospitality, Comfort merit awards
Oakford Bridge, Bampton EX16 9HZ
☎ 01398-351236
Closed Dec-Feb
6 bedrs, 4 ensuite, 1 ⇌ ⇌ P 16 No children under 8
SB £29 DB £50 HB £280 D £14.50 CC MC Visa

BANBURY Oxfordshire 4B1

★★ Lismore
61 Oxford Road, Banbury OX16 9AJ
☎ 01295-267661 Fax 01295-269010
Closed Christmas-New Year
22 bedrs, all ensuite, TCF TV ⇌ P 23 SB £40-£75 DB £60-£90 D £13.95 CC MC Visa Amex DC ♿

Easington House *Highly Acclaimed*
50 Oxford Road, Banbury OX16 9AN
☎ 01295-270181 Fax 01295-269527
12 bedrs, 10 ensuite, 1 ⇌, 12 ⇌ TV ⇌ P 27 SB £49
DB £70 D £12 CC MC Visa Amex DC

La Madonette *Highly Acclaimed*
North Newington, Banbury OX15 6AA
☎ 01295-730212 Fax 01295-730363

Peacefully situated 17th century mill house, set in rural surroundings. Well located for the Cotswolds, Stratford-upon-Avon, Oxford and Blenheim. Gardens and swimming pool. Licensed.

5 bedrs, all ensuite, TCF TV P 20 SB £32-£36 DB £52-£68
CC MC Visa DC JCB

BARHAM Kent — 5F3

★★ Old Coach House
Restaurant merit award
Dover Road (A2), Barham CT4 6JA
☎ 01227-831218 Fax 01227-831932
7 bedrs, all ensuite, TCF TV P 60 SB £40-£49 DB £50-£62
HB £262.50 D £16.50 CC MC Visa JCB

BARNARD CASTLE Co. Durham — 10C2

West Roods Working Farm *Listed*
Boldron, Barnard Castle DL12 9SW
☎ 01833-690116
Closed Nov-Apr
3 bedrs, 2 ensuite, 1 ⇌ TCF TV P 6 SB £18 DB £36 CC Amex DC

BARNSTAPLE Devon — 2C2

Home Park Farm *Acclaimed*
Lower Blakewell, Muddiford, Barnstaple EX31 4ET
☎ 01271-42955 Fax 01271-42955
Closed Christmas

Paradise for country garden lovers, 2 miles north of Barnstaple. All ensuite, tea trays, colour TV, peaceful tranquil atmosphere. Central heating, excellent accomodation. Convenient touring base for Moors, beaches, Lynton etc.

3 bedrs, all ensuite, TCF TV P 3 SB £18 DB £30
HB £150 D £8.50

Yeo Dale *Acclaimed*
Pilton Bridge, Barnstaple EX31 1PG
☎ 01271-42954 Fax 01271-42954
10 bedrs, 6 ensuite, 2 ⇌ TCF TV SB £20-£26 DB £38-£50
HB £214-£256 D £10 CC MC Visa

RAC Hotel Reservations Service
0870 603 9109
(Calls charged at national call rate)

Cedars Lodge Inn *Lodge*
Bickington Road, Barnstaple EX31 2HP
☎ 01271-71784 Fax 01271-25733

Former country house, with elegant bars, restaurant, conference centre and secluded bedroom accommodation, set in three acres of landscaped grounds.

30 bedrs, all ensuite, TCF TV P 120 SB £46 DB £62 D £9
CC MC Visa Amex ✈ ♿

West View Guest House
Pilton Causeway, Barnstaple EX32 7AA
☎ 01271-42079 Fax 01271-42079

Situated on the A39, overlooking Pilton Park. 23 bedrooms, many ensuite. Close to the town centre, convenient for both business and pleasure. Licensed with function room.

BARTON ON SEA Hampshire — 4A4

★★ Cliff House
Hospitality, Comfort, Restaurant merit awards
Marine Drive East, Barton on Sea BH25 7QL
☎ 01425-619333 Fax 01425-612462
9 bedrs, all ensuite, 1 ⇌ TCF TV ✉ P 50 No children under 14 SB £37.50-£50 DB £70-£90 HB £325-£392
D £17.95 CC MC Visa Amex ♿

BASILDON Essex — 5E2

Campanile Basildon *Lodge*
A127 Southend Arterial Road, Pipps Hill, SS14 3AE
☎ 01268-530810 Fax 01268-286710
98 bedrs, all ensuite, TCF TV ⚑ P 98 SB £42.50 DB £47
D £10.55 CC MC Visa Amex DC ♿

BASINGSTOKE Hampshire — 4B3

★★ Red Lion
London Street, Basingstoke RG21 7NY
☎ 01256-328525 Fax 01256-844056
58 bedrs, all ensuite, ⚑ ✉ P 50 SB £70-£75 DB £90-£110 CC MC Visa Amex DC ✈

BATH – ENGLAND

BASSENTHWAITE Cumbria 10A1

Lakeside *Highly Acclaimed*
Bassenthwaite Lake, Cockermouth CA13 9YD
☎ 017687-76358
Closed Jan-Nov
8 bedrs, 7 ensuite, TCF TV P 8 SB £25-£30 DB £40-£50
HB £202-£235 D £13

Ravenstone *Highly Acclaimed*
Bassenthwaite CA12 4QG
☎ 017687-76240
20 bedrs, all ensuite, TCF TV P 24

BATH Somerset 3F1

★★ Bath Tasburgh
Warminster Road, Bath BA2 6SH
☎ 01225-425096 Fax 01225-463842

Beautiful Victorian mansion standing in lovely gardens with spectacular views. Ideal country comfort in a city setting and convenient for Bath city centre. Well appointed ensuite bedrooms. Elegant drawing room and stunning conservatory.

12 bedrs, all ensuite, TCF TV P 15 SB £43-£48 DB £58-£78 D £15 CC MC Visa Amex

★★ George's
2-3 South Parade, Bath BA2 4AA
☎ 01225-464923 Fax 01225-425471
Closed 25-26 Dec
19 bedrs, all ensuite, TCF TV SB £35-£45 DB £55-£65
D £14 CC MC Visa Amex

★★ Limpley Stoke
Lower Limpley Stoke, Bath BA3 6HZ
☎ 01225-723333 Fax 01225-722406
67 bedrs, all ensuite, 4 TCF TV P 60 SB £45-£49
DB £60-£70 CC MC Visa Amex DC

★★ Old Mill
Tollbridge Road, Batheaston, Bath BA1 7DE
☎ 01225-858476 Fax 01225-852600
26 bedrs, all ensuite, TCF TV P 40 SB £35-£43 DB £46-£65 D £12 CC MC Visa Amex JCB

Ashley Villa *Highly Acclaimed*
26 Newbridge Road, Bath BA1 3JZ
☎ 01225-421683 Fax 01225-313604
14 bedrs, all ensuite, TCF TV P 10 SB £49-£55 DB £59-£79 CC MC Visa

Ashley Villa
HOTEL

Comfortably furnished licensed hotel with relaxing, informal atmosphere. Situated close to the city centre.

All bedrooms have ensuite facilities, colour television, direct dial telephone, tea/coffee making facilities.

26 NEWBRIDGE ROAD, BATH, SOMERSET BA1 3JZ
Tel: 01225-421683 Fax: 01225-313604

BATH – ENGLAND

Badminton Villa *Highly Acclaimed*
10 Upper Oldfield Park, Bath BA2 3JZ
☎ 01225-426347 Fax 01225-420393
Closed 24 Dec-2 Jan

Large Victorian family house, recently renovated, situated in a quiet residential road a ten minute walk from the city centre. Gardens and rooms with magnificent views over the city.

4 bedrs, all ensuite, 1 ⇌ TCF TV ✉ P 5 No children under 6 SB £38-£40 DB £52-£56 CC MC Visa JCB

Bailbrook Lodge *Highly Acclaimed*
35-37 London Road West, Bath BA1 7HZ
☎ 01225-859090 Fax 01225-859090
Closed Christmas

An imposing Georgian hotel, 1½ miles from Bath. All rooms ensuite, lounge bar and dining room. Ample car parking.

12 bedrs, all ensuite, TCF TV P 14 SB £32-£35 DB £52-£70 D £13 CC MC Visa Amex DC

Bloomfield House *Highly Acclaimed*
146 Bloomfield Road, Bath BA2 2AS
☎ 01225-420105 Fax 01225-481958 8 bedrs, 5 ensuite, 3 🕭, TCF TV ✉ P 8 No children under 10 SB £35-£40 DB £56-£95 CC MC Visa

RAC Hotel Reservations Service
0870 603 9109
(Calls charged at national call rate)

146 Bloomfield Road, Bath BA2 2AS

Tel: 01225 420105
Fax: 01225 481958

THE FINEST, THE FRIENDLIEST, THE BEST.

Elegant GEORGIAN COUNTRY HOUSE in peaceful setting with glorious views over the City and ample parking. Antique furniture, French crystal chandeliers. Breakfast is served against a candlelit and open fire background. Rooms have an ensuite bath or shower, direct dial telephone, remote control colour television and canopied/FOUR POSTER BEDS including the lavish Principal Bedroom of the Mayor and Mayoress of Bath (1902/3). A spacious 2 bedroomed apartment is available for family use.

BLOOMFIELD HOUSE

BATH – ENGLAND

BROMPTON HOUSE

Elegant Georgian residence (former Rectory 1777). Family owned and run. Car Park and beautiful secluded gardens. Only 6 minutes level walk to main historic sights. Tastefully furnished and fully equipped en-suite bedrooms. Delicious breakfasts. No smoking.

ETB 2 Crowns Highly Commended. RAC Highly Acclaimed. Les Routiers Guest House of the Year 1996.

Resident proprietors: David, Sue, Belinda & Tim Selby

ST JOHN'S ROAD, BATH BA2 6PT
Tel: 01225 420972 Fax: 01225 420505
Email: BROMPTON_HOUSE@compuserve.com

Cheriton House

Situated on the southern slope of Bath with splendid views of the city, we have carefully restored and redecorated the house and our rooms are individually and attractively furnished.
All of our bedrooms have private bathrooms (ensuite), colour TV and hot drink making facilities.
We offer a choice of delicious breakfasts including traditional English and a warm welcome is extended to all of our guests. Guests are welcome to enjoy our beautiful peaceful garden.
RAC Highly Acclaimed.
9 UPPER OLDFIELD PARK, BATH, AVON BA2 3JX
Tel: 01225 429862 Fax: 01225 428403

Brompton House *Highly Acclaimed*
St Johns Road, Bath BA2 6PT
☎ 01225-420972 Fax 01225-420505
E Mail bromptonhouse@compuserve.com
Closed Christmas-New Year
18 bedrs, all ensuite, TCF TV P 18 No children under 10 SB £32-£50 DB £55-£80 CC MC Visa Amex JCB

Burghope Manor *Highly Acclaimed*
Winsley, Bradford-on-Avon, Bath BA15 2LA
☎ 01225-723557 Fax 01225-723113
Closed Christmas-New Year

A historic 13th century country home set in beautiful countryside on the edge of the village of Winsley. Steeped in history, first and foremost a living family home, carefully modernised. A wealth of historical features complement present day comforts.

8 bedrs, all ensuite, TCF TV P 20 No children under 10
SB £50-£55 DB £65-£70 D £25 CC MC Visa Amex JCB

Cheriton House *Highly Acclaimed*
9 Upper Oldfield Park, Bath BA2 3JX
☎ 01225-429862 Fax 01225-428403
9 bedrs, all ensuite, TCF TV P 9 No children under 12
SB £37-£42 DB £54-£62 CC MC Visa Amex DC

Dorian House
Bath

A well appointed gracious Victorian house on southern slopes overlooking the historic city of Bath.

Only a ten minute stroll to the city attractions.

Highly acclaimed.

1 UPPER OLDFIELD PARK, BATH BA2 3JX
Tel: 01225 426336 Fax: 01225 444699

BATH – ENGLAND

Dorian House *Highly Acclaimed*
1 Upper Oldfield Park, Bath BA2 3JX
☎ 01225-426336 Fax 01225-444699

A well appointed gracious Victorian house on the southern slopes overlooking the historic city centre of Bath. Only a ten minute stroll to the city attractions.

8 bedrs, all ensuite, TCF TV P 8 SB £40-£45 DB £58-£64
CC MC Visa Amex DC
See advert on previous page

Don't forget to mention the guide
When booking direct, please remember to tell the hotel that you chose it from RAC Bed & Breakfast 1998.

Fern Cottage *Highly Acclaimed*
Monkton Farleigh, Bradford-on-Avon BA15 2QJ
☎ 01225-859412 Fax 01225-859018

Delightful stone-built 17th century cottage, set in fine gardens in a peaceful conservation village, midway between Bath and Bradford-on-Avon. Well appointed comfortable rooms.

3 bedrs, all ensuite, TCF TV P 5 SB £30-£36 DB £48-£58

Gainsborough *Highly Acclaimed*
Weston Lane, Bath BA1 4AB
☎ 01225-311380 Fax 01225-447411
16 bedrs, all ensuite, TCF TV P 16 SB £32-£45 DB £50-£72 CC MC Visa Amex

---

RAC Highly Acclaimed

The Gainsborough Hotel
BATH

A spacious comfortable country house hotel in own attractive grounds near the Botanical gardens, Municipal golf course and park. The Abbey, Roman Baths and Pump Room are all within walking distance via the park, so most guests leave their cars and walk into town.

We provide a relaxing, friendly and informal atmosphere for our guests' stay. All of our tastefully furnished bedrooms are ensuite with colour TV, Satellite TV, tea/coffee facilities, telephones, hairdryers etc. The hotel has a small friendly bar, two sun terraces and our own large private car park. A warm welcome awaits.

WESTON LANE, BATH, AVON BA1 4AB
Tel: (01225) 311380 Fax: (01225) 447411

Haute Combe *Highly Acclaimed*
174-176 Newbridge Road, Bath BA1 3LE
📞 01225-420061 Fax 01225-420061
E Mail 101352.42@compuserve.com

Delightful Victorian house with original features and modern facilities. Non-smoking ensuite rooms have Sky TV, phone, radio alarm, tea & coffee, iron & board, hairdryer & trouser press. Lounge bar and separate smoking lounge. A la carte evening meals.

11 bedrs, all ensuite, **TCF TV** 🐾 **P** 11 **SB** £39-£49 **DB** £49-£69 **D** £15 **CC** MC Visa Amex DC JCB ♿

Haydon House *Highly Acclaimed*
9 Bloomfield Park, Bath BA2 2BY
📞 01225-427351 Fax 01225-444919

Hayden House is an oasis of tranquillity and elegance. Superb Laura Ashley decorated ensuite bedrooms with a generous hospitality tray and sherry decanter. Innovative breakfasts are stylishly served.

5 bedrs, all ensuite, **TCF TV** **P** 5 **SB** £45-£55 **DB** £60-£80 **CC** MC Visa Amex JCB

Highways House *Highly Acclaimed*
143 Wells Road, Bath BA2 3AL
📞 01225-421238 Fax 01225-481169
Closed Christmas

Sample the hospitality offered at this Victorian house. All rooms have private facilities, colour TV, and tea/coffee facilities. Full English breakfasts are available. Private parking.

7 bedrs, 6 ensuite, **TCF TV P** 8 No children under 5 **SB** £35-£38 **DB** £52-£62 **CC** MC Visa

Laura Place *Highly Acclaimed*
3 Laura Place, Great Pulteney Street, Bath BA2 4BH
📞 01225-463815 Fax 01225-310222
Closed 22 Dec-28 Feb

A Georgian town house centrally situated overlooking a fountain. Tastefully furnished with antiques and works of art. Brass and fourposter beds available. Rooms on four floors.

8 bedrs, 7 ensuite, 1 🛏 **TCF TV P** 8 No children under 8 **SB** £50-£55 **DB** £66-£88 **CC** MC Visa Amex

Leighton House *Highly Acclaimed*
139 Wells Road, Bath BA2 3AL
📞 01225-314769 Fax 01225-443079
Closed Christmas & New Year

Spacious, detached, Victorian house tastefully furnished and decorated, offering high standards of comfort, service and a warm, friendly atmosphere. Ten minutes walk to city attractions.

8 bedrs, all ensuite, **TCF TV P** 8 **SB** £47-£55 **DB** £62-£75 **CC** MC Visa

Meadowland *Highly Acclaimed*
36 Bloomfield Park, Bath BA2 2BX
📞 01225-311079 Fax 01452-304507
3 bedrs, all ensuite, **P** 3 **SB** £40-£45 **DB** £58-£65 **CC** MC Visa

OAKLEIGH

A warm welcome awaits you at Oakleigh, a quietly situated Victorian home only 10 minutes walk from the city centre, with splendid views over Georgian Bath. All luxury rooms are en suite with those little extras that make your stay special. A tempting choice of breakfast greets you in the morning.

Private car park. Credit cards accepted.

19 Upper Oldfield Park, Bath BA2 3JX
Tel: 01225 315698   Fax: 01225 448223

Oakleigh House *Highly Acclaimed*
19 Upper Oldfield Park, Bath BA2 3JX
📞 01225-315698 Fax 01225-448223
4 bedrs, all ensuite, TCF TV P 4 No children under 18
SB £35-£45 DB £50-£60 CC MC Visa Amex

Old School House *Highly Acclaimed*
Church Street, Bathford, Bath BA1 7RR
📞 01225-859593 Fax 01225-859590
4 bedrs, all ensuite, 1 ♿ TCF TV ⌨ P 6 CC MC Visa ♿

Oldfields *Highly Acclaimed*
102 Wells Road, Bath BA2 3AL
📞 01225-317984 Fax 01225-444471
Closed Christmas, Jan

Elegant and traditional B&B in Victorian mansion with views. English and wholefood breakfasts available. Ample parking in own grounds. Ten minutes walk to town centre.

14 bedrs, all ensuite, 1 ♿ TCF TV P 12 SB £48 DB £58-£70 CC MC Visa JCB ♿

OLDFIELDS
PRIVATE HOTEL

Elegant and traditional B&B in Victorian mansion with views. English and wholefood breakfast available.

Ample parking in own grounds.

10 minutes walk to city centre.

102 WELLS ROAD, BATH, SOMERSET BA2 3AL
Tel: 01225 317984   Fax: 01225 444471

BATH – ENGLAND

Orchard Lodge *Highly Acclaimed*
Warminster Road, Bathampton, Bath BA2 6XG
☎ 01225-466115 Fax 01225-446050

A modern purpose-built hotel, situated 1½ miles from Bath city centre, enjoying panoramic views of the Avon Valley.

14 bedrs, all ensuite, 4 🐕 TCF TV 🛏 P 14 CC   MC Visa Amex DC 📷

Paradise House *Highly Acclaimed*
88 Holloway, Bath BA2 4PX
☎ 01225-317723 Fax 01225-482005
8 bedrs, all ensuite, 1 🐕 TCF TV P 6 SB £45-£60 DB £65-£80 CC   MC Visa Amex

Siena *Highly Acclaimed*
24-25 Pulteney Road, Bath BA2 4EZ
☎ 01225-425495 Fax 01225-469029
15 bedrs, all ensuite, TCF TV 🛏 P 15 SB £43-£58 DB £70-£85 CC   MC Visa Amex DC JCB ♿

Sydney Gardens *Highly Acclaimed*
Sydney Road, Bath BA2 6NT
☎ 01225-464818
6 bedrs, all ensuite, TCF TV 🚭 🛏 P 6 SB £49-£59 DB £59-£75 CC   MC Visa Amex

Villa Magdala *Highly Acclaimed*
Henrietta Road, Bath BA2 6LX
☎ 01225-466329 Fax 01225-483207
E Mail villa@btinternet.com

Elegant town house hotel enjoying a peaceful location opposite Henrietta Park and with ample parking in own grounds. Just five minutes level walk to city centre.

17 bedrs, all ensuite, TCF TV P 16 SB £49-£65 DB £60-£95 CC   MC Visa Amex JCB

PARADISE HOUSE
BATH

Paradise House is a listed Georgian (1735) Bath stone house perfectly situated in a quiet cul-de-sac, only five minutes' walk from the centre of Bath. The rear-facing rooms and beautiful gardens command the most magnificent views of the city and surrounding countryside. Long established and highly recommended. For fully illustrated brochure contact the resident owners, David and Janet Cutting.

86/88 HOLLOWAY, BATH BA2 4PX
Tel: 01225 317723 Fax: 01225 482005

THE SIENA HOTEL
Comfort Merit Award

An elegant Victorian Villa within a few minutes level walk of the City Centre. Set in landscaped gardens and overlooking Bath's medieval Abbey the Siena Hotel offers quality accommodation, excellent home cuisine, licensed bar, use of gardens and private car park.

24-25 Pulteney Road
Bath BA2 4EX
Tel: 01225 425495 Fax: 01225 469029

WENTWORTH HOUSE
106 Bloomfield Road, Bath BA2 2AP
Tel: (01225) 339193 Fax: (01225) 310460

Built as a family home in 1887 Wentworth House is an imposing Victorian Mansion enjoying a peaceful location in secluded gardens with stunning views and is within walking distance of Bath centre. The tastefully decorated ensuite rooms, some with 4 poster beds offer colour TV, alarm, telephones, hairdryers and tea/coffee. Delicious breakfasts. Outdoor swimming pool.

LARGE FREE CAR PARK.
PRICES PER ROOM, PER NIGHT
£60 TO £80

Wentworth House *Highly Acclaimed*
106 Bloomfield Road, Bath BA2 2AP
☎ 01225-339193 Fax 01225-310460
Closed Christmas-New Year
18 bedrs, 17 ensuite, 1 ®, TCF TV P 19 No children under 5 SB £38-£45 DB £50-£70 CC MC Visa Amex

CHESTERFIELD HOTEL

A Grade 1 listed Georgian town house in one of Europe's finest streets. Centrally located and only a five minute level walk to the Roman Baths.

11 GREAT PULTENEY STREET, BATH, AVON. BA2 4BR.
Tel: (01225) 460953
Fax: (01225) 448770

Chesterfield *Acclaimed*
11 Great Pulteney Street, Bath BA2 4BR
☎ 01225-460953 Fax 01225-448770

Grade I Listed Georgian town house in one of Europe's finest streets. Centrally located and only a five minute level walk to the Roman Baths

20 bedrs, all ensuite, TCF TV P 8 CC MC Visa Amex DC

Devonshire House *Acclaimed*
143 Wellsway, Bath BA2 4RZ
☎ 01225-312495 Fax 01225-335534
3 bedrs, all ensuite, TCF TV ✉ P 6 SB £35-£40 DB £48-£55 HB £273-£297.50 D £15 CC MC Visa Amex

Dorset Villa *Acclaimed*
14 Newbridge Road, Bath BA1 3JX
☎ 01225-425975
8 bedrs, 5 ensuite, 1 ➡ TCF TV ✠ P 6 CC MC Visa

Kennard *Acclaimed*
11 Henrietta Street, Bath BA2 6LL
☎ 01225-310472 Fax 01225-460054
E Mail kennard@dircon.co.uk

A Georgian town house hotel of charm and character quietly situated within minutes of the city centre and Roman Baths.

13 bedrs, 11 ensuite, 1 ➡ TCF TV ✉ No children
SB £38-£45 DB £65-£85 CC MC Visa Amex DC JCB

Lamp Post Villa *Acclaimed*
3 Crescent Gardens, Bath BA1 2NA
☎ 01225-331221 Fax 01225-426783
Closed Christmas
4 bedrs, all ensuite, TCF TV ✉ ✠ P 4 SB £35-£40 DB £40-£50 CC MC Visa JCB

BATH – ENGLAND

Bonheur *Listed*
52 Box Road, Bathford, Bath BA1 7QH
☎ 01225-859537
6 bedrs, 4 ensuite, 2 🐾, 1 ⟶ TCF TV P 12 SB £20-£24
DB £38-£45

County *Listed*
18/19 Pulteney Road, Bath BA2 4EZ
☎ 01225-425003 Fax 01225-469845
22 bedrs, 12 ensuite, 3 ⟶ TCF TV 🐾 P 50 SB £45-£49
DB £58-£63 CC MC Visa

Edgar *Listed*
64 Great Pulteney Street, Bath BA2 4DN
☎ 01225-420619 Fax 01225-466916
E Mail snoo@netgates.co.uk
Closed Nov-Feb
16 bedrs, all ensuite, SB £25-£35 DB £35-£55 CC MC Visa Amex

Grove Lodge *Listed*
11 Lambridge, Bath BA1 6BJ
☎ 01225-310860 Fax 01225-429630
6 bedrs, 2 ⟶ TCF TV 🔲 DB £42-£48

Hotel St Clair *Listed*
1 Crescent Gardens, Upper Bristol Road, BA1 2NA
☎ 01225-425543 Fax 01225-425543
10 bedrs, 7 ensuite, 1 ⟶ TCF TV No children under 3
SB £22-£38 DB £35-£54 CC MC Visa

Millers *Listed*
69 Great Pulteney Street, Bath BA2 4DL
☎ 01225-465798 Fax 01225-461892
Closed Christmas
14 bedrs, 6 ensuite, 3 ⟶ TV SB £25-£28 DB £38-£56 CC MC Visa JCB ♿

Old Malt House *Listed*
Radford, Timsbury, Bath BA3 1QF
☎ 01761-470106 Fax 01761-472726
Closed Christmas
12 bedrs, all ensuite, TCF TV 🐾 P 50 SB £38-£39.50
DB £66 HB £281.75-£292.75 D £16.50 CC MC Visa Amex DC ♿

Waltons *Listed*
17 Crescent Gardens, Upper Bristol Road, BA1 2NA
☎ 01225-426528 Fax 01225-420350
15 bedrs, 1 🐾, 3 ⟶ TV

Bridge Cottage
Northfield End, Ashley Road, Bathford, Bath BA1 7TT
☎ 01225-852399

Two luxury ground floor ensuites with private entrances, set in a beautiful garden close to the city of Bath, Bradford-on-Avon, Lacock, and Castle Combe. A peaceful location with warm hospitality.

3 bedrs, all ensuite, TCF TV 🔲 SB £25 DB £40-£50 ♿

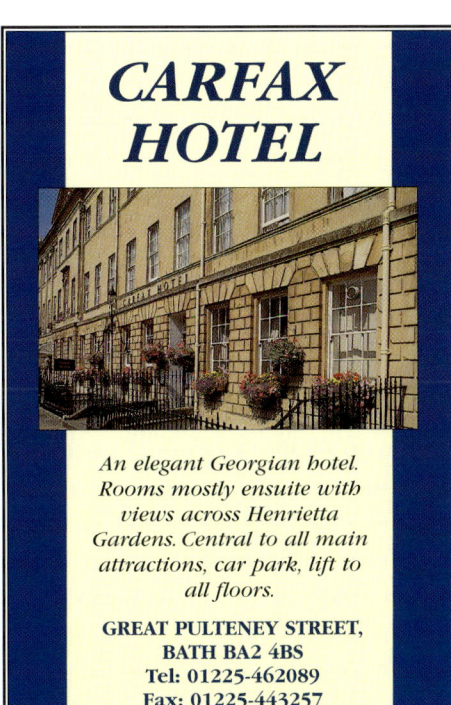

CARFAX HOTEL

An elegant Georgian hotel. Rooms mostly ensuite with views across Henrietta Gardens. Central to all main attractions, car park, lift to all floors.

GREAT PULTENEY STREET, BATH BA2 4BS
Tel: 01225-462089
Fax: 01225-443257

THE HOLLIES

Built in 1850 the Hollies is a Grade II Listed family-run guesthouse, within walking distance of city and overlooking Parish church and gardens. All rooms have ensuite/private facilities, colour TV, hairdryer, and hostess trays. Pretty secluded garden with apple trees and shrub roses.
• Private off-street parking. • No smoking.
ETB Grade II Commended.
THE HOLLIES, HATFIELD ROAD, BATH BA2 2BD
Tel: (01225) 313366

BATH – ENGLAND

Carfax
Great Pulteney Street, Bath BA2 4BS
☎ 01225-462089 Fax 01225-443257
38 bedrs, 33 ensuite, 2 ⇌ TCF TV ☒ P 13 SB £26.75-£47
DB £49.50-£76 HB £217-£269.50 D £13.50 CC MC Visa Amex ♿
See advert on previous page

Flaxley Villa
9 Newbridge Hill, Bath BA1 3LE
☎ 01255-313237

Flaxley Villa is a comfortable Victorian house, situated in a pleasant residential area with ten minutes walk to the Royal Crescent. Some ensuite rooms / showers. TV's and off street parking.

3 bedrs, all ensuite, TCF TV SB £18-£22

Hollies
Hatfield Road, Bath BA2 2BD
☎ 01225-313366 Fax 01225-313366
Closed Christmas-New Year
3 bedrs, 2 ensuite, 1 ⌂, 1 ⇌ TCF TV ☒ P 3 SB £25-£32
DB £40-£48 CC MC Visa
See advert on previous page

Monkshill
Shaft Road, Monkton Combe, Bath BA2 7HL
☎ 01225-833028 Fax 01225-833028

A majestic Edwardian mansion enjoying the finest English countryside views and gardens. Only 5 minutes from Bath city centre.

3 bedrs, 2 ensuite, 1 ⇌ TCF TV ☒ 🐕 P 8 SB £35-£45
DB £55-£70 CC MC Visa

Serendipity
19F Bradford Road, Winsley, Bath BA15 2HW
☎ 01225-722380

Ground floor accommodation in peaceful village, five minutes from Bath, set in beautiful gardens. Ideal for touring West Country. Wild badger feeding in garden. Excellent walking area.

2 bedrs, both ensuite, TCF TV ☒ P 5 SB £25-£33 DB £33-£39 ♿

BATLEY West Yorkshire 11D4

★★ **Alder House**
Towngate Road, Healey Lane, Batley WF17 7HR
☎ 01924-444777 Fax 01924-442644
20 bedrs, all ensuite, TCF TV 🐕 P 52 SB £48.50-£58.50
DB £65-£75 D £16.50 CC MC Visa Amex DC

BATTLE East Sussex 5E4

★★ **George**
23 High Street, Battle TN33 0EA
☎ 01424-774466 Fax 01424-774853
22 bedrs, all ensuite, TCF TV 🐕 P 20 SB £38-£50 DB £56-£70 D £8 CC MC Visa Amex DC

Brakes Coppice Farm *Highly Acclaimed*
Telham Lane, Battle TN33 0SJ
☎ 01424-830347 Fax 01424-830347
3 bedrs, all ensuite, TCF TV ☒ P 6 No children under 12 SB £30-£35 DB £45-£50

Moonshill Farm *Highly Acclaimed*
The Green, Moons Hill, Ninefield, Battle TN33 9JL
☎ 01424-892645 Fax 01424-892645
Closed Dec

In the heart of '1066 Country'. Comfortable rooms, three ensuite, central heating, electric heaters, hospitality tray, TV lounge, large car park. Every comfort in this safe, quiet and peaceful home.

3 bedrs, all ensuite, 1 ⇌ TCF TV ⊢ P 6 SB £15-£17.50 DB £30-£35

Little Hemingfold Hotel *Acclaimed*
Telham, Battle TN33 0TT
📞 01424-774338 Fax 01424-775351
Closed 5 Jan-12 Feb
13 bedrs, 10 ensuite, 2 ⇌ TCF TV ⊢ P 50 SB £35-£63 DB £65-£80 HB £315-£350 D £22 CC MC Visa Amex DC JCB 🖸 🖻 🖉

Netherfield Hall *Listed*
Netherfield, Battle TN33 9PQ
📞 01424-774450
Closed Feb

Coach house style, single storey, 'L' shaped building, with large garden set in Forestry Commission woodland.

4 bedrs, 2 ensuite, 1 🛏, 2 ⇌ TCF TV ⊢ P 7 No children SB £30-£35 DB £40-£50 ♿

BEACONSFIELD Buckinghamshire   4C2

★★ Chequers Inn
Comfort, Restaurant merit awards
Kiln Lane, Wooburn Common, Beaconsfield HP10 0JQ
📞 01628-529575 Fax 01628-850124
17 bedrs, all ensuite, TCF TV P 60 SB £83 DB £88 D £19 CC MC Visa Amex DC

Facilities for the disabled ♿
Hotels do their best to cater for disabled visitors. However, it is advisable to contact the hotel direct to ensure it can provide a particular requirement. For further information on accommodation facilities for the disabled why not order a copy of *RAC On the Move – The Guide for the Disabled Traveller*.

Highclere Farm
New Barn Lane, Seer Green, Nr Beaconsfield HP9 2QZ
📞 01494-875665 Fax 01494-875238
Closed Feb

Two tasteful farm conversions set amidst stunning countryside and overlooking a horse paddock. Peaceful, yet only 30 minutes from London Marylebone. All rooms now smoking and ensuite.

9 bedrs, all ensuite, TCF TV 🖂 P 15 SB £40-£56 DB £50-£56 CC MC Visa 🖻 🗙 🖻

BEAFORD Devon   2C2

Beaford House *Listed*
Winkleigh, Beaford EX19 8AB
📞 01805-603305

Five minutes walk from Rosemoor Gardens and Tarka Trail.

9 bedrs, all ensuite, TCF TV ⊢ P 50 SB £26-£29 DB £52-£58 HR £199-£250 D £12 CC MC Visa Amex 🖸 🖻

BEDALE North Yorkshire   11D2

Elmfield Country House *Highly Acclaimed*
Arrathorne, Bedale DL8 1NE
📞 01677-450558 Fax 01677-450557
9 bedrs, all ensuite, TCF TV P 14 SB £30.50 DB £42-£46 HB £221-£234 D £12 CC MC Visa 🖻 ♿
See advert on next page

Elmfield COUNTRY HOUSE HOTEL

A country house situated in its own grounds, between Richmond and Bedale in 'Herriot Country'. All rooms are ensuite with TV, tea/coffee facilities and telephone. Two rooms are available for the disabled. Excellent home cooked meals.

ARRATHORNE, BEDALE, NORTH YORKSHIRE DL8 1NE
Tel: 01677 450558 Fax: 01677 450557

BEDFORD OAK HOUSE

Mock Tudor style house near the town centre and railway station, offering motel style accommodation with a private car park.

33 SHAKESPEARE ROAD, BEDFORD MK40 2DX
Tel: 01234-266972
Fax: 01234-266972

BEDFORD Bedfordshire   4C1

★★ Knife & Cleaver
Restaurant merit award
The Grove, Houghton Conquest, Bedford MK45 3LA
📞 01234-740387 Fax 01234-740900
Closed 27-30 Dec
9 bedrs, all ensuite, TCF TV ⚐ P 26 SB £45-£55 DB £59-£69 D £18.50 CC MC Visa Amex DC

Bedford Oak House
33 Shakespeare Road, Bedford MK40 2DX
📞 01234-266972 Fax 01234-266972
14 bedrs, all ensuite, 1 ⚐, 1 ⚐ TCF TV P 15 No children under 10 SB £32-£35 DB £40-£42 CC MC Visa Amex DC

Hertford House
57 De Parys Avenue, Bedford MK40 2TP
📞 01234-350007 Fax 01234-353468
A family run hotel from basic to ensuite with full central heating, courtesy trays and satellite TV in every room. Close to the town centre and Bedford Park.

17 bedrs, 9 ensuite, 2 ⚐ TCF TV P 17 SB £25-£34.50 DB £37.50-£45 CC MC Visa DC ♿

BEER Devon   3E3

Bay View
Fore Street, Beer EX12 3EE
📞 01297-20489
Closed Nov-Mar

A traditional guest house with wonderful views and on seafront. A warm welcome, large well furnished rooms, great breakfasts and a perfect location.

10 bedrs, 3 ensuite, 4 ⚐ TCF TV ⚐ No children under 5 SB £15.50-£20 DB £31-£40

BEETHAM Cumbria   10B3

★ Wheatsheaf
A6 Road, Beetham LA7 7AL
📞 01539-562123
6 bedrs, all ensuite, TCF TV ⚐ P 40 SB £30 DB £40 D £9.25 CC MC Visa

---

RAC Hotel Reservations Service
0870 603 9109
(Calls charged at national call rate)

BELPER – ENGLAND

BELFORD Northumberland 13F3

Purdy Lodge *Lodge*
Adderstone Services, Belford NE70 7JU
☎ 01668-213000 Fax 01668-213111
20 bedrs, all ensuite, TCF TV ⚑ P 60 SB £41 DB £51
D £10 CC MC Visa Amex DC JCB ♿

BELLINGHAM Northumberland 13E3

★★ Riverdale Hall
Hospitality, Restaurant merit awards
Hexham, Bellingham NE48 2JT
☎ 01434-220254 Fax 01434-220457

A stone-built 19th century mansion with a modern wing set in five acres of grounds alongside the North Tyne River.

20 bedrs, all ensuite, 4 ⚑ TCF TV ⚑ P 40 SB £40-£45
DB £69-£80 HB £275-£335 D £18.50 CC MC Visa Amex
DC

Lyndale *Acclaimed*
Bellingham NE48 2AW
☎ 01434-220361
Closed Christmas
6 bedrs, 3 ensuite, 2 ⚑ TCF TV ⚑ P 5

BELPER Derbyshire 8B2

Dannah Farm Country *Highly Acclaimed*
Bowmans Lane, Shottle, Belper DE56 2DR
☎ 01773-550273 Fax 01773-550590
9 bedrs, all ensuite, TCF TV P 30 SB £39.50-£55 DB £64-£75 D £17 CC MC Visa

Shottle Hall *Acclaimed*
Shottle, Belper DE56 2EB
☎ 01773-550203 Fax 01773-550276
Closed Nov-Christmas

Built c.1850, and set in three acres of grounds in the picturesque Ecclebourne Valley, Shottle Hall is ideally situated for touring the spectacular countryside.

10 bedrs, 6 ensuite, 2 ⚑ TCF TV P 30 SB £25-£35
DB £42-£60 D £13

Dannah Farm
Country Guest House

Relax and unwind in our lovely Georgian farmhouse set amidst beautiful countryside, perfect for walking, touring and discovering the myriad beauties of Derbyshire. Superb, award winning, licensed dining room where we aim to serve the very best in farmhouse cooking.
All rooms ensuite.
4 poster available.
SAE brochure.

*RAC Highly Acclaimed.
Awarded Derbyshire Life Golden Goblet for our food.
Winners top national award for excellence and innovation.
1994 Best of Tourism Award.*

**Dannah Farm, Bowmans Lane,
Shottle, Nr. Belper,
Derbyshire DE56 2DR
Tel: (01773) 550273
Fax: (01773) 550590**

Ye Olde Bear Inn
Alderwasley, Belper DE4 4GD
☎ 01629-822585

The inn retains the charm and character that takes you back in time whilst providing the faciliites that 20th century man deserves, good food, good wine, a comfortable bed and a friendly relaxed atmosphere.

9 bedrs, all ensuite, 1 ➡ TCF TV P 200 SB £20 DB £40 D £4.50 CC MC Visa DC

BERKELEY Gloucestershire   7E4

★★ Prince of Wales
Berkeley Road, Berkeley GL13 9HD
☎ 01453-810474 Fax 01453-511370
41 bedrs, all ensuite, TCF TV ➡ P 150 SB £44.95-£49.95 DB £49.95-£55.90 D £6.95 CC MC Visa Amex DC 🐕

BERWICK-UPON-TWEED Northumberland 13F2

★ Queens Head
Sandgate, Berwick-upon-Tweed TD15 1EP
☎ 01289-307852 Fax 01289 307852
6 bedrs, all ensuite, 1 ➡ TCF TV ➡ SB £25-£35 DB £50-£55 HB £245 D £15 CC MC Visa JCB

Dervaig
1 North Road, Berwick-upon-Tweed TD15 1PW
☎ 01289-307378

An immaculate Victorian residence, retaining many original features and an elegant dining room, and set in beautiful gardens. Situated close to the railway station and a five minute stroll to the town.

5 bedrs, all ensuite, 1 ➡ TCF TV ➡ P 8 SB £25-£40 DB £40-£54

BEVERLEY East Yorkshire   11E3

★★ Lairgate
30 Lairgate, Beverley HU17 8EP
☎ 01482-882141 Fax 01482-861067

A Georgian building on the main road out of Beverley, behind the market.

22 bedrs, 18 ensuite, 1 🛁, 2 ➡ TCF TV ➡ P 20 SB £45 DB £65 D £14 CC MC Visa

Manor House *Highly Acclaimed*
Restaurant merit award
Northlands, Walkington, Beverley HU17 8RT
☎ 01482-881645 Fax 01482-866501

An award winning hotel and restaurant set in a lovely old house with three acres of tree-lined gardens.

7 bedrs, all ensuite, TV P 50 SB £74 DB £93 D £16.50 CC MC Visa

Eastgate *Listed*
7 Eastgate, Beverley HU17 0DR
☎ 01482-868464 Fax 01482-871899
18 bedrs, 7 ensuite, 3 ➡ TCF TV ➡ SB £19.50-£30 DB £32-£44

BEWDLEY Worcestershire   7E3

★★ George
Restaurant merit award
Load Street, Bewdley DY12 2AW
☎ 01299-402117 Fax 01299-401269
13 bedrs, 10 ensuite, 1 ➡ TV P 50 SB £45 DB £58 HB £252 D £9.50 CC MC Visa Amex JCB

Lightmarsh Farm
Crundalls Lane, Bewdley DY12 1NE
📞 **01299-404027**

A small pasture farm one mile from Bewdley. Noted for outstanding views, tranquillity, pleasant garden, hospitality, quality breakfasts and every comfort.

2 bedrs, both ensuite, **TCF P** 4 No children under 10 **SB** £25 **DB** £40

BEXHILL-ON-SEA East Sussex   5E4

Park Lodge *Acclaimed*
16 Egerton Road, Bexhill-on-Sea TN39 3HH
📞 **01424-216547**

Family run, informal hotel with character. Located in a quiet area of Bexhill but near shops, park and sea front. Rooms are very comfortable with ensuite, CTV, telephone and tea making.

10 bedrs, 8 ensuite, 2 🛁, 1 ♨ **TCF TV** ✈ **SB** £22-£28 **DB** £45-£49 **HB** £175-£195 **D** £8 **CC** MC Visa Amex DC

BIBURY Gloucestershire   7F4

★★ Bibury Court
Comfort, Restaurant merit awards
Bibury GL7 5NT
📞 **01285-740337 Fax 01285-740660**
Closed 21-30 Dec
20 bedrs, all ensuite, **TCF TV** ✈ **P** 100 **SB** £60 **DB** £84 **D** £21.50 **CC** MC Visa Amex DC

BICKLEY Kent   5D2

Glendevon House *Listed*
80 Southborough Road, Bickley BR1 2EN
📞 **0181-467 2183**
11 bedrs, 3 ensuite, 3 🛁, 1 ♨ **TCF TV** ✈ **P** 6 **SB** £24 **DB** £42 **CC** MC Visa

BIDEFORD Devon   2C2

★★ Hoops Inn
Horns Cross, Clovelly, Bideford EX39 5DL
📞 **01237-451222 Fax 01237-451247**
12 bedrs, all ensuite, **TCF TV** ✈ **P** 100 No children under 10 **SB** £38 **DB** £56-£112 **HB** £284-£454 **D** £19.50 **CC** MC Visa Amex DC JCB

★★ Riversford
Hospitality merit award
Limers Lane, Bideford EX39 2RG
📞 **01237-474239 Fax 01237-421661**
14 bedrs, all ensuite, **TCF TV** ✈ **P** 16 **SB** £40 **DB** £60-£82 **HB** £266-£298 **D** £16 **CC** MC Visa Amex DC JCB

★★ Yeoldon House
Durrant Lane, Northam, Bideford EX39 2RL
📞 **01237-474400 Fax 01237-476618**
Closed Christmas week
10 bedrs, all ensuite, **TCF TV** ✈ **P** 20 **SB** £42-£52 **DB** £75-£92 **D** £19 **CC** MC Visa Amex DC

Pines at Eastleigh *Highly Acclaimed*
Eastleigh, Bideford EX39 4PA
📞 **01271-860561 Fax 01271-861248**
E Mail barry@barpines.demon.co.uk
7 bedrs, all ensuite, 1 ♨ **TCF TV** ✈ **P** 20 **SB** £25-£40 **DB** £50-£80 **HB** £235-£300 **D** £14 **CC** MC Visa

Sunset
Landcross, Bideford EX39 5JA
📞 **01237-472962**

A small country hotel in a peaceful, picturesque location overlooking spectacular scenery. Highly recommended quality accommodation. Superb food, everything homemade. Special diets catered for. Private parking.

4 bedrs, all ensuite, **TCF TV** **P** 10 **SB** £25-£30 **DB** £47-£50 **HB** £222.50-£225 **D** £11.50 **CC** MC Visa

BIGBURY-ON-SEA Devon   2C4

★ Henley
Folly Hill, Bigbury-on-Sea TQ7 4AR
📞 01548-810240 Fax 01548-810240
7 bedrs, all ensuite, TCF TV 🖂 🐕 P 9 SB £25-£31 DB £57-£62 HB £245-£283 D £16 CC MC Visa Amex

BIGGLESWADE Bedfordshire   4C1

Old Warden
Shop & Post Office, Old Warden, Sandy SG18 9HQ
📞 01767-627201

Set in the centre of a small, quiet village, two miles from the A1 between Biggleswade and Bedford. All rooms ensuite with televisions.

3 bedrs, all ensuite, TCF TV P 5 SB £18-£22 DB £36

BINGLEY West Yorkshire   10C3

Five Rise Locks *Highly Acclaimed*
Beck Lane, Bingley BD16 4DD
📞 01274-565296 Fax 01274-568828
Closed Christmas-New Year
9 bedrs, all ensuite, TCF TV 🐕 P 15 SB £45-£50 DB £45-£55 D £12 CC MC Visa 🐾 &

March Cote Farm
Cottingley, Bingley BD16 1UB
📞 01274-487433 Fax 01274-488153
Closed Christmas

Your comfort our aim and satisfaction when you stay on our dairy / sheep farm. Fully modernised 17th century farmhouse. Colour TV and drink making facilities in all rooms. Lots of repeat bookings.

3 bedrs, 1 ensuite, 1 🐾 TCF TV SB £18-£20 DB £36-£40 HB £182-£196 D £8

BIRKENHEAD Merseyside   7D1

★★ Riverhill
Talbot Road, Oxton, Birkenhead L43 2HJ
📞 0151-653 3773 Fax 0151-653 7162
16 bedrs, all ensuite, TCF TV P 25 SB £30-£44 DB £39-£49 D £15 CC MC Visa Amex DC &

BIRMINGHAM West Midlands   8A3

★★ Bailey House
21 Sandon Road, Edgbaston, Birmingham B17 8DR
📞 0121-429 1929
15 bedrs, 6 ensuite, 5 🛁, 2 🐾 TCF TV P 14 No children under 5 SB £30 DB £40.12 D £12.50 CC MC Visa Amex

★★ Beechwood
201 Bristol Road, Edgbaston, Birmingham B5 7UB
📞 0121-440 2133 Fax 0121-446 4549
18 bedrs, 16 ensuite, 1 🐾 🐕 P 30 CC MC Visa Amex DC

★★ Hagley Court
229 Hagley Rd, Edgbaston, Birmingham B16 9RP
📞 0121-454 6514 Fax 0121-456 2722
Closed Christmas-New Year
27 bedrs, all ensuite, TCF TV P 30
SB £28-£49 DB £40-£64 D £16 CC MC Visa Amex DC JCB

★★ Norwood
Hospitality merit award
87/89 Bunbury Road, Northfield, Birmingham B31 2ET
📞 0121-411 2202 Fax 0121-411 2200
Closed Christmas
18 bedrs, all ensuite, TCF TV 🐕 P 11 SB £55 DB £60 CC MC Visa Amex DC JCB

★★ Woodlands Hotel & Restaurant
379/381 Hagley Road, Edgbaston, Birmingham B17 8DL
📞 0121-420 2341 Fax 0121-429 3935
21 bedrs, 17 ensuite, 3 🛁, 1 🐾 TCF TV P 20 SB £38 DB £49 D £13 CC MC Visa Amex JCB 🐾

Bridge House *Highly Acclaimed*
49 Sherbourne Road, Acocks Green, Birmingham B27 6DX
📞 0121-706 5900 Fax 0121-624 5900
50 bedrs, all ensuite, 1 🐾 TCF TV P 60 SB £37.60 DB £47 CC MC Visa Amex DC JCB 🐾

Chamberlain *Highly Acclaimed*
Alcester Road, Birmingham B12 0TJ
📞 0121-627 0627 Fax 0121-627 0628
250 bedrs, all ensuite, TCF TV 🖂 P 200 SB £35 DB £40 D £9 CC MC Visa Amex DC &

Greswolde Park *Highly Acclaimed*
980 Warwick Road, Acocks Green, Birmingham B27 6QG
☎ 0121-706 4068 Fax 0121-706 0649
11 bedrs, 10 ensuite, 1 ⌂, TCF TV ⚹ P 9 SB £33 DB £38 D £6.50 CC MC Visa JCB ⚹

Alexander *Acclaimed*
44 Bunbury Road, Northfield, Birmingham B31 2DW
☎ 0121-475 4341 Fax 0121-475 4341

Family owned and managed. All rooms ensuite, with Sky TV and tea and coffee making facilities. Off road parking. For a brochure and tarriff phone 0121-475 4341.

10 bedrs, all ensuite, 2 ⚹ TCF TV ⚹ P 10 SB £28-£43.65 DB £40-£58.75 HB £246-£375.55 D £10 CC MC Visa

Central *Acclaimed*
1637 Coventry Road, South Yardley, Birmingham B26 1DD
☎ 0121-706 7757 Fax 0121-706 7757
Closed 1 week at Christmas

Well established, family run. Close to NEC, airport, city centre. All rooms ensuite. Coffee/tea making facilities. Full English breakfast. Warm friendly atmosphere, home from home.

5 bedrs, all ensuite, TCF TV ⚹ P 4 SB £17.50 DB £35-£45

Heath Lodge *Acclaimed*
117 Coleshill Road, Marston Green, Birmingham B37 7HT
☎ 0121-779 2218 Fax 0121-779 2218
18 bedrs, 13 ensuite, 1 ⌂, 1 ⚹ TCF TV ⚹ P 20 No children under 6 SB £30 DB £42 CC MC Visa Amex DC

Lyndhurst *Acclaimed*
135 Kingsbury Road, Erdington, Birmingham B24 8QT
☎ 0121-373 5695 Fax 0121-373 5695
Closed Christmas

A large, well maintained Victorian building, with modern furnishings and equipment. The spacious restaurant offers an a la carte menu. Situated off the M6 (jn 6), only three miles to the city and close to Aston University, science park and leisure centre.

14 bedrs, 13 ensuite, 1 ⚹ TCF TV P 15 SB £38-£42 DB £50-£54 HB £275-£295 D £12 CC MC Visa Amex DC JCB

Tri-Star *Acclaimed*
Coventry Road, Elmdon, Birmingham B26 3QR
☎ 0121-782 1010 Fax 0121-782 6131

This licenced hotel is ideally situated on the A45, aprox 1.5 miles from NEC, airport and international station and 2 miles to jnct 6 M42. A modern hotel with homely atmosphere.

Wentworth *Acclaimed*
103 Wentworth Road, Harborne, Birmingham B17 9SU
☎ 0121-427 2839

Bristol Court *Listed*
250 Bristol Road, Edgbaston, Birmingham B5 7SL
☎ 0121-472 0078 Fax 0121-471 2823
25 bedrs, all ensuite, TCF TV ⚹ P 24 SB £35-£39 DB £49.50-£55 D £11.50 ⚹

Fairview *Listed*
1639 Coventry Road, South Yardley, B26 1DD
☎ 0121-708 2712
4 bedrs, all ensuite, TCF TV P 5 DB £32

BIRMINGHAM – ENGLAND

Remwick House Listed
13 Bournbrook Road, Selly Oak, Birmingham B29 7BL
☎ 0121-472 4640 Fax 0121-472 1098
P 6 SB £20-£25 DB £40-£42

Rollason Wood Listed
Wood End Road, Erdington, Birmingham B24 8BJ
☎ 0121-373 1230 Fax 0121-382 2578
35 bedrs, 11 ensuite, 5 ☏, 6 ⇌ TCF TV ⚲ P 40 SB £17-£35.50 DB £30-£50 D £8 CC MC Visa Amex DC

Royceland Listed
33 Elmdon Road, Marston Green, Birmingham B37 7BU
☎ 0121-779 4343 Fax 0121-779 4343
5 bedrs, all ensuite, TCF TV ✉ P 8 SB £25-£35 DB £35-£40

Campanile Birmingham Lodge
55 Irving Street, Birmingham B1 1DH
☎ 0121-622 4925 Fax 0121-622 4195
50 bedrs, all ensuite, TCF TV ⚲ P 50 SB £41 DB £45.50 D £10.55 CC MC Visa Amex DC ♿

Cape Race
929 Chester Rd, Erdington, Birmingham B24 0HJ
☎ 0121-373 3085

Friendly hotel run by resident proprietor. Licensed bar. Ten minutes from the NEC and city. Ensuite rooms with telephones. On A452, two minutes from M6 (junctions 5 and 6).

9 bedrs, 8 ensuite, 1 ☏, ⚲ P 11 CC MC Visa

Clover
775 Chester Road, Erdington, Birmingham B24 0BY
☎ 0121-382 8212 Fax 0121-382 2664

A small, friendly, licensed hotel, conveniently located in a pleasant area and offering quality service, ensuite and budget rooms, evening meals and exceptional value.

10 bedrs, all ensuite, TCF TV P 15 SB £29.50 DB £42-£48 D £6.95 CC MC Visa

Elston
751 Washwood Heath Road, Birmingham B8 2JY
☎ 0121-327 3338

A popular guest house with a relaxed friendly atmosphere. Located on the A47, four miles from the city.

11 bedrs, 6 ensuite, 4 ☏, 3 ⇌ TCF TV ♿

Grove
409-411 Hagley Road, Edgbaston, Birmingham B17 8BL
☎ 0121-429 2502 Fax 0121-420 1207

The Grove is a commercial hotel, ideally situated for the city centre, NIA, ICC and all major motorways. Fully licensed with restaurant facilities.

36 bedrs, all ensuite, 3 ⇌ TCF TV ⚲ P 30 SB £30 DB £45 D £5.95 CC MC Visa Amex DC ⚑ ♿

Don't forget to mention the guide
When booking direct, please remember to tell the hotel that you chose it from RAC Bed & Breakfast 1998.

Highfield House
Holly Road, Rowley Regis, Birmingham B65 0BH
☎ 0121-559 1066

Small, private, family run commercial hotel which takes great pride in the cleanliness and ambience of the establishment. Home cooked meals.

14 bedrs, 2 ensuite, 2 ➥ TCF TV ✕ P 10 SB £18-£22 DB £38 D £5.25 CC MC Visa ♿

BISHOP AUCKLAND Co. Durham   10C1

Greenhead Country House *Highly Acclaimed*
Fir Tree, Bishop Auckland DL15 8BL
☎ 01388-763143 Fax 01388-763143
7 bedrs, all ensuite, 1 ➥ TV P 10 No children under 14 SB £35-£40 DB £50-£55 CC MC Visa

BISHOP'S CASTLE Shropshire   7D3

Boars Head *Acclaimed*
Church Street, Bishop's Castle SY9 5AE
☎ 01588-638521 Fax 01588-630126
E Mail 101327.1457@compuserve.com

A former 16th century coaching inn, that has been restored to provide ensuite accommodation as well as the traditional bar and restaurant facilities.

4 bedrs, all ensuite, TCF TV ✕ P 20
SB £33-£38 DB £25-£28 HB £135-£150 D £6 CC MC Visa Amex DC JCB ♿

RAC Hotel Reservations Service
0870 603 9109
(Calls charged at national call rate)

BISHOP'S STORTFORD Hertfordshire   5D1

Cottage *Acclaimed*
71 Birchanger Lane, Birchanger, Bishop's Stortford CM23 5QA
☎ 01279-812349 Fax 01279-812349
Closed 4 days at Christmas

A 17th century listed property in a quiet village setting, yet near the M11 (jn 8) and Stansted Airport. Panelled reception rooms with wood burning stove and ensuite guest rooms. Conservatory dining room overlooks large mature garden.

15 bedrs, 13 ensuite, 1 ➥ TCF TV ✉ P 15 SB £40 DB £50 CC MC Visa JCB

George *Listed*
North Street, Bishop's Stortford HP4 2DF
☎ 01279-504128 Fax 01279-655135

The George Hotel is the oldest inn in Bishops Stortford and the third oldest in Hertfordshire.

27 bedrs, 9 ☏, 6 ➥ TCF TV ✕ P 6 SB £20.30 DB £40.10 D £9.95 CC MC Visa

BISHOPS TAWTON Devon   2C2

★★ Downrew House
Bishops Tawton, Barnstaple EX32 0DY
☎ 01271-42497 Fax 01271-23947
Closed Jan
12 bedrs, all ensuite, TCF TV ✕ P 20 SB £39.50-£48.50 DB £63-£81 HB £280-£329 D £17.50 CC MC Visa Amex

BLACKPOOL Lancashire   10B3

★★ Brabyns
Shaftesbury Avenue, North Shore, FY2 9QQ
☎ 01253-354263 Fax 01253-352915
25 bedrs, all ensuite, TCF TV ⛔ P 12 No children
SB £25-£35 DB £45-£60 D £12 CC MC Visa Amex DC

★★ Carlton
North Promenade, Blackpool FY1 2EZ
☎ 01253-28966 Fax 01253-752587
58 bedrs, all ensuite, TCF TV ▣ P 45 SB £25-£35 DB £60-£90 HB £210-£315 D £7.50 CC MC Visa Amex DC

★★ Gables Balmoral
Balmoral Road, Blackpool FY4 1HP
☎ 01253-345432 Fax 01253-406058

The nearest two star hotel to Blackpool Pleasure Beach. All rooms with private facilities. Other facilities include swimming pool, jacuzzi and lounge bar. Five course buffet breakfast/dinner served.

63 bedrs, all ensuite, TCF TV ⛔ ▣ P 7 SB £36-£49
DB £60-£64 HB £195-£234 D £14 CC MC Visa Amex DC

★★ Headlands
New South Promenade, Blackpool FY4 1NJ
☎ 01253-341179 Fax 01253-342047
Closed 3-10 Jan
42 bedrs, all ensuite, ⛔ ▣ P 38 SB £26.80-£39.35
DB £53.60-£72.70 D £13.50 CC MC Visa Amex DC

★★ Kimberley
New South Promenade, Blackpool FY4 1NQ
☎ 01253-341184 Fax 01253-408737
Closed 2-14 Jan
54 bedrs, 37 ensuite, 4 ⛔ TCF TV ⛔ ▣ P 32 SB £26-£28
DB £48-£56 HB £201-£210 D £12 CC MC Visa

★★ Revills
192 North Promenade, Blackpool FY1 1RJ
☎ 01253-25768 Fax 01253-24736
47 bedrs, all ensuite, TCF TV ▣ P 22 SB £25-£30 DB £40-£52 D £9 CC MC Visa

★★ Sheraton
54 Queen's Promenade, Blackpool FY2 9RP
☎ 01253-352723 Fax 01253-359549

Gables Balmoral
BLACKPOOL

Use this Blackpool Hotel as a centre to tour the Lakes and Lancashire. Value for money.

All rooms with private facilities. Other facilities include a swimming pool, jacuzzi and lounge bar. Five course buffet breakfast/dinner served.

BALMORAL ROAD, SOUTH SHORE, BLACKPOOL FY4 1HR
Tel: (01253) 345432 Fax: (01253) 406058

★★ Stretton
206 North Promenade, Blackpool FY1 1RU
☎ 01253-25688 Fax 01253-24075
51 bedrs, 43 ensuite, 3 ⛔ ⛔ ▣ P 10
DB £43-£59 HB £148.75-£217 D £7.50 CC MC Visa Amex DC

★★ Warwick
603 New South Promenade, Blackpool FY4 1NG
☎ 01253-342192 Fax 01253-405776
50 bedrs, all ensuite, TCF TV ⛔ ▣ P 30 SB £40-£46
DB £68-£78 HB £204-£276 D £13 CC MC Visa Amex DC JCB

★★ Windsor & Westmorland
256-258 Queens Promenade, Blackpool FY2 9HB
☎ ff: 0500 657807
30 bedrs, all ensuite, TCF TV ▣ P 12 SB £26 DB £44
HB £27 CC MC Visa Amex DC

Arosa *Highly Acclaimed*
18/20 Empress Drive, Blackpool FY2 9SD
☎ 01253-352555

Brooklands *Highly Acclaimed*
28-30 King Edward Avenue, North Shore, Blackpool FY2 9TA
☎ 01253-351479 Fax 01253-500311
Closed Jan-Mar
17 bedrs, all ensuite, TV P 5 SB £18-£21 DB £36-£42
HB £154-£161 D £6

BLACKPOOL – ENGLAND

Burlees *Highly Acclaimed*
40 Knowle Avenue, North Shore, Blackpool FY2 9TQ
☎ 01253-354535
Closed Nov-Feb
9 bedrs, all ensuite, 1 ⇌ **TCF TV P** 5 **SB** £21-£23.50
DB £42-£47 **HB** £180-£205 **D** £9 **CC** MC Visa

Cliff Head *Highly Acclaimed*
174 Queens Promenade, Bispham, Blackpool FY2 9JN
☎ 01253-591086 Fax 01253-590952

A warm welcome awaits you at the Cliff Head. Our intention is that you enjoy the relaxed and friendly atmosphere to help in making your stay one to remember. Easy walking distance of shopping amenities. Tram stops directly opposite the hotel.

10 bedrs, all ensuite, **TCF TV ⇌ P** 5 **SB** £16.50-£21.50 **DB** £33-£43 **HB** £117-£145 **D** £5.75 ♿

Hartshead *Highly Acclaimed*
17 King Edward Avenue, Blackpool FY2 9TA
☎ 01253-353133
Closed Nov-Mar
10 bedrs, all ensuite, **TCF TV ⇌ P** 6 **SB** £17-£21 **DB** £34-£42 **HB** £130-£143 **D** £4 **CC** MC Visa

Lynstead *Highly Acclaimed*
40 King Edward Avenue, Blackpool FY2 9TA
☎ 01253-351050
Closed 1-14 Jan

An Edwardian terrace house in a spacious avenue adjacent to the sea front.

10 bedrs, all ensuite, **TCF** No children under 3 **SB** £18-£21 **DB** £36-£42 **HB** £125 **D** £5

Lynwood *Highly Acclaimed*
38 Osborne Road, Blackpool FY4 1HQ
☎ 01253-344628
Closed Christmas-New Year
8 bedrs, 6 ensuite, 1 ⇌ **TCF TV P** 1 **DB** £30-£48 **HB** £120-£145 **D** £6

Old Coach House *Highly Acclaimed*
50 Dean Street, Blackpool FY4 1BP
☎ 01253-349195 Fax 01253-344330

Detached Tudor style building set in an award winning garden.

7 bedrs, all ensuite, 7 ⇌ **TCF TV P** 10 **SB** £20-£31 **DB** £39-£62 **HB** £230.65-£328.65 **D** £8.95 **CC** MC Visa Amex

Sunray *Highly Acclaimed*
42 Knowle Avenue, North Shore, Blackpool FY2 9TQ
☎ 01253-351937 Fax 01253-593307
Closed Christmas-New Year
9 bedrs, all ensuite, 1 ⇌ **TCF TV ⇌ P** 6 **SB** £25-£28 **DB** £50-£56 **HB** £222-£240 **D** £12 **CC** MC Visa Amex

Windsor *Highly Acclaimed*
21 King Edward Avenue, Blackpool FY2 9TA
☎ 01253-353735
Closed Nov-Mar
9 bedrs, all ensuite, **TCF TV P** 4 No children under 7 **SB** £20 **DB** £39 **HB** £119-£149 **D** £6

Windsor Park *Highly Acclaimed*
96 Queens Promenade, Blackpool FY2 9NS
☎ 01253-357025
Closed 3 Nov-23 Dec, 2 Jan-Easter

The Windsor Park Hotel is situated in one of the most sought after areas of the Fylde coast. Queens Promenade overlooks the north shore cliffs and looks out over the Irish Sea.

11 bedrs, all ensuite, **TCF TV P** 8 **SB** £16-£23 **DB** £36 **HB** £136-£140 **D** £5 **CC** MC Visa

BLACKPOOL – ENGLAND

Woodleigh *Highly Acclaimed*
32 King Edward Avenue, North Shore, Blackpool FY2 9TA
☎ 01253-593624
Closed Nov-Mar
10 bedrs, all ensuite, TCF TV SB £17-£19 DB £34-£38 HB £133-£140

Beaucliffe *Acclaimed*
20-22 Holmfield Road, North Shore, Blackpool FY2 9TB
☎ 01253-351663
13 bedrs, all ensuite, TCF TV 🐕 P 10 SB £16-£28 DB £32-£55 HB £129-£149 D £5 ♿

Claytons *Acclaimed*
28 Northumberland Avenue, Blackpool FY2 9SA
☎ 01253-355397 Fax 01253-500142
6 bedrs, all ensuite, TCF TV No children under 5
SB £16-£20 DB £32-£40 D £5 CC MC Visa Amex DC

Cliftonville *Acclaimed*
14 Empress Drive, Blackpool FY2 9SE
☎ 01253-351052

All rooms offer ensuite showers and toilets, remote controlled colour satellite TV. Lift to all floors, licensed bar and separate sun lounge. B&B from £18.

Derwent *Acclaimed*
8 Gynn Avenue, North Shore, Blackpool FY1 2LD
☎ 01253-355194
11 bedrs, 6 ensuite, 2 🐕 TCF 🐕 SB £18-£23 DB £30-£40
CC MC Visa

Garville *Acclaimed*
3 Beaufort Avenue, Bispham, Blackpool FY2 9HQ
☎ 01253-351004 Fax 01253-351004
Closed Jan, 2 weeks in May
7 bedrs, all ensuite, TCF TV P 5 No children under 3
SB £21-£25 DB £32-£44

Don't forget to mention the guide
When booking direct, please remember to tell the hotel that you chose it from RAC Bed & Breakfast 1998.

Sunny Cliff *Acclaimed*
98 Queens Promenade, Blackpool FY2 9NS
☎ 01253-351155
Closed Nov-Easter

Ample parking. Quiet area overlooking sea half a mile along Queens Promenade. Attractive ensuite rooms. Pleasant lounges, lovely homemade soups and puddings etc.

9 bedrs, all ensuite, TCF TV 🐕 P 6 SB £18-£22 DB £36-£44 HB £140-£150 D £6

Surrey House *Acclaimed*
9 Northumberland Avenue, Blackpool FY2 9SB
☎ 01253-351743
11 bedrs, 10 ensuite, 2 🐕 TCF 🐕 P 7 SB £19-£23
DB £38-£46 HB £175-£203 D £6 ♿

Villa *Acclaimed*
9-11 Withnell Road, Blackpool FY4 1HF
☎ 01253-343314
18 bedrs, 14 ensuite, 2 🐕 TCF TV 🐕 P 10 SB £15-£18
DB £30-£36 HB £116 CC MC Visa Amex DC

Denely *Listed*
15 King Edward Avenue, Blackpool FY2 9TA
☎ 01253-352757
Closed Christmas
9 bedrs, 2 ensuite, 2 🚭, 1 🐕 TCF P 6 SB £15.75-£17
DB £31.50-£34 HB £120.65

Knowsley *Listed*
68 Dean Street, Blackpool FY4 1BP
☎ 01253-343414

A friendly, family run hotel in a quiet area. Close to the Pleasure Beach, shops, M55 and the airport.

12 bedrs, 7 ensuite, 1 🐕 TCF TV P 14 SB £15-£20
DB £30-£40 HB £140-£175 D £6 CC MC Visa

BLAKENEY – ENGLAND

Langwood Listed
250 Queens Promenade, Blackpool FY2 9HA
☎ 01253-351370
Closed Jan-Easter
27 bedrs, 16 ensuite, 1 ➡ TCF ✱ 🅳 P 12

Roker Listed
563 New South Promenade, Blackpool FY4 1NF
☎ 01253-341853
17 bedrs, 12 ensuite, 1 ➡ TCF TV P 14 SB £36
HB £157.50 D £5

Westdean Listed
59 Dean Street, Blackpool FY4 1BP
☎ 01253-342904 Fax 01253-342904
E Mail unite@compuserve.com

A family run hotel ideally situated close to the Promenade, Pleasure Beach, Sandcastle, South Pier and shopping centre. Comfortable furnished lounge with colour television and a well appointed dining room with separate tables. Cosy cellar bar.

11 bedrs, all ensuite, TCF TV P 2 SB £18-£23 DB £36-£46
HB £149 D £6.50 CC Visa JCB ✱

Windsor Hotel Listed
53 Dean Street, Blackpool FY4 1BP
☎ 01253-400232 Fax 01253-346886
12 bedrs, all ensuite, TCF TV P 8 SB £18-£25 DB £32-£46
HB £126-£144 D £5 CC MC Visa JCB

North Crest
22 King Edward Ave, Blackpool FY2 9TD
☎ 01253-355937

Adjacent Queens Promenade, North Shore, this small homely licensed hotel offers ensuite facilities in most rooms and tea and coffee facilities in all rooms. Sky TV in lounge.

7 bedrs, all ensuite, TCF TV ✱ P 3 SB £14-£20 DB £28-£40 HB £118-£140 D £4 CC MC Visa

BLAKENEY Gloucestershire   7E4

Viney Hill Country Guesthouse
Blakeney, Gloucester GL15 4LT
☎ 01594-516000 Fax 01594-516018

A spacious period house just west of Gloucester in an area of outstanding natural beauty.

6 bedrs, all ensuite, TCF TV ☑ P 8 SB £32 DB £44
HB £226 D £14 CC MC Visa

BLAKENEY Norfolk   9E2

★★ **Manor**
Holt, Blakeney NR25 7ND
☎ 01263-740376 Fax 01263-741116
Closed 3-23 Jan

Previously a 16th century manor house which now provides all modern facilities. Converted flint faced barns and stables, flanking well kept gardens, enhance the inherent period charm and character.

37 bedrs, all ensuite, TCF TV ✱ P 60 No children under 14 SB £30 DB £56 HB £266-£343 D £16 ♿

RAC Hotel Reservations Service
0870 603 9109
(Calls charged at national call rate)

Flintstones *Acclaimed*
Wiveton, Blakeney NR25 7TL
☎ 01263-740337

A guest house situated in picturesque rural surroundings near the village green. Located one mile from Blakeney on the Blakeney to Holt road.

5 bedrs, all ensuite, TCF TV 🐾 P 5 SB £22 DB £36-£38
HB £196-£199

BLANCHLAND Northumberland   10C1

★★ Lord Crewe Arms
Hospitality, Restaurant merit awards
Blanchland, Consett DH8 9SP
☎ 01434-675251 Fax 01434-675371
20 bedrs, all ensuite, TCF TV 🐾 P 6 SB £80 DB £110
D £27 CC MC Visa Amex DC JCB

BLANDFORD FORUM Dorset   3F2

Anvil
Salisbury Road, Pimperne, Blandford Forum DT11 8UQ
☎ 01258-453431 Fax 01258-480182

Picturesque thatched inn, dating back to 1535, in Pimperne village, 2 miles north east of Blandford on A354.

11 bedrs, all ensuite, TCF TV 🐾 P 24 SB £47.50 DB £75
CC MC Visa Amex DC

BLOCKLEY Gloucestershire   7F4

Lower Brook House *Highly Acclaimed*
Moreton in Marsh, Blockley GL56 9DS
☎ 01386-700286 Fax 01386-700286
3 bedrs, all ensuite, TV 🐾 P 10

BODMIN Cornwall   2B3

Lanhydrock House
BODMIN, CORNWALL PL30 5AD

A largely Victorian House with 49 rooms open to the public, set in glorious gardens surrounded by park and woodland. Disabled facilities/Access wheelchairs/Batricar available. Closed Mondays except bank holidays.

TELEPHONE: 01208 73320

★★ Westberry
Rhind Street, Bodmin PL31 2EL
☎ 01208-72772 Fax 01208-72212
21 bedrs, 15 ensuite, 2 🚿 TCF TV 🐾 P 20 SB £42 DB £50
HB £250 D £12 CC MC Visa Amex DC 🚭 🚭

Treswalloch Farm
St Breward, Bodmin PL30 4PL
☎ 01208-850255
Closed Nov-Apr

Enjoy the tranquillity, fresh air and outstanding natural views of Bodmin Moor from this working beef and sheep farm. Many attractions close but not too close.

2 bedrs, 1 🚿 SB £16 DB £30

BOSCASTLE – ENGLAND

BOGNOR REGIS West Sussex — 4C4

★★ Black Mill House
Princess Avenue, Aldwick, Bognor Regis PO21 2QU
☎ 01243-821945 Fax 01243-821316
26 bedrs, 18 ensuite, 1, 4 P 13 CC MC Visa Amex DC

BOLTON Lancashire — 10B4

Quarlton Manor Farm *Awaiting Inspection*
Plantation Road, Edgworth, Turton, Bolton BL7 0DD
☎ 01204-852277 Fax 01204-852286

Experience wonderful farmhouse cooking in various unique settings. Catering for small parties in our galleried dining hall or your discreet anniversary celebration on the patio.

5 bedrs, 2 ensuite, 1 TCF TV P 20 SB £32-£50 DB £49-£65 HB £320 D £10 CC MC Visa Amex DC

Broomfield
33-35 Wigan Road, Deane, Bolton BL3 5PX
☎ 01204-61570 Fax 01204-650932

Comfortable family run hotel, situated conviently for the town centre, with excellent connections to the motorway network.

15 bedrs, all ensuite, TCF TV P 15 SB £26-£30 DB £42-£44 D £9.50 CC MC Visa Amex

BOOT Cumbria — 10A2

Stanley Ghyll House
Boot, Holmrook CA19 1TF
☎ 019467-23327
Closed mid Jan-mid Feb

Informal guest house in unspoilt Western Lakes, surrounded by woodland on banks of the River Esk. Ideal for walking, touring and relaxing. The single track Ratty Railway stops just outside.

24 bedrs, 11 TCF P 10 SB £19.50 DB £39 D £9.50 CC MC Visa

BOROUGHBRIDGE North Yorkshire — 11D3

★★ (Inn) Crown
Roecliffe, Boroughbridge YO5 9LY
☎ 01423-322578 Fax 01423-324060
13 bedrs, 11 ensuite, 1 TCF TV P 70 SB £35 DB £54 HB £266 D £10 CC MC Visa DC JCB

BORROWDALE Cumbria — 10B2

★★ Leathes Head
Borrowdale, Keswick CA12 5UY
☎ 017687-77247

BOSCASTLE Cornwall — 2B3

★★ Wellington
The Harbour, Boscastle PL35 0AQ
☎ 01840-250202 Fax 01840-250621
E Mail vtobutt@enterprise.net.
18 bedrs, 16 ensuite, 2 TCF TV P 20 No children under 7 SB £28.50-£39 DB £51-£68 HB £249-£320 D £19.50 CC MC Visa Amex DC

Short Breaks

Many hotels provide special rates for weekend and mid-week breaks - sometimes these are quoted in the hotel's entry, otherwise ring direct for the latest offers.

Old Coach House *Listed*
Tintagel Road, Boscastle PL35 OAS
☎ 01840-250398 Fax 01840-250346
Closed Nov-Mar

Relax in beautiful 300 year old former coach house. Ensuite rooms with colour TV's, tea makers etc. Area of outstanding natural beauty. Friendly and helpful owners.

8 bedrs, all ensuite, TCF TV ✉ P 9 No children under 6 SB £17-£24 DB £34-£48 CC MC Visa Amex ♿

BOSTON Lincolnshire   9D2

★★ Comfort Friendly Inn
Bicker Bar Roundabout (A17/A52 junction), Boston PE20 3AN
☎ 01205-820118 Fax 01205-820228
E Mail admin@gb607.u-net.com
55 bedrs, all ensuite, TCF TV ★ P 50 SB £47-£59 DB £54-£65 D £9.75 CC MC Visa Amex DC JCB ✈ ♿

★★ White Hart
1-5 High Street, Bridgefoot, Boston PE21 8SH
☎ 01205-364877

★ King's Arms
Horncastle Road, Boston PE21 9BU
☎ 01205-364296
4 bedrs, 3 ensuite, 1 ★ P 30

Admiral Nelson *Listed*
Bennington, Boston PE22 0BT
☎ 01205-760460

Castle Inn *Listed*
Haltoft End, Freiston, Boston PE22 0MY
☎ 01205-760393

BOURNE Lincolnshire   8C3

★★ Angel
Market Place, Bourne PE10 9AE
☎ 01778-422346 Fax 01778-426113
14 bedrs, all ensuite, TCF TV P 100 SB £40 DB £50 D £14 CC MC Visa Amex DC JCB

★★ Black Horse Inn
Grimsthorpe, Bourne PE10 0LY
☎ 01778-591247 Fax 01778-591373
6 bedrs, all ensuite, TCF TV P 20 No children under 10 SB £40-£49 DB £55-£69 D £15 CC MC Visa

BOURNEMOUTH & BOSCOMBE Dorset   3F3

★★ Arlington
Hospitality, Comfort merit awards
Exeter Park Road, Lower Gardens, BH2 5BD
☎ 01202-552879 Fax 01202-298317
29 bedrs, 28 ensuite, 1 ★ TCF TV ▣ P 21 No children under 2 SB £28-£35 DB £54-£69 HB £190-£245 D £10 CC MC Visa

★★ Chequers
West Cliff Road, Bournemouth BH2 5EX
☎ 01202-553900
23 bedrs, 21 ensuite, 3 ★ TCF TV ★ P 24 SB £18-£29 DB £36-£58 HB £150-£210 D £8.50 CC MC Visa Amex ✈

★★ Chinehurst
Hospitality, Comfort merit awards
Studland Road, Westbourne, Bournemouth BH4 8JA
☎ 01202-764583 Fax 01202-762854
30 bedrs, all ensuite, 1 ★ TCF TV ★ P 14 SB £22-£32 DB £44-£64 HB £140-£240 D £15 CC MC Visa Amex DC JCB ♿

★★ County
Westover Road, Bournemouth BH1 2BT
☎ 01202-552385 Fax 01202-297255
50 bedrs, 46 ensuite, 4 ★ ★ ▣ P 9 SB £19-£35 DB £35-£68 HB £126-£238 D £12 CC MC Visa Amex JCB

★★ Croham Hurst
9 Durley Road South, West Cliff, Bournemouth BH2 5JH
☎ 01202-552353 Fax 01202-311484
Closed 2 Jan-2 Feb
40 bedrs, all ensuite, TCF TV ▣ P 30 SB £23-£33 DB £50-£70 HB £145-£235 D £12 CC MC Visa JCB

★★ Diplomat
6-8 Durley Chine Road, West Cliff, Bournemouth BH2 5JY
☎ 01202-555025 Fax 01202-559019
60 bedrs, all ensuite, 1 ★ TCF TV ★ ▣ P 55 SB £29-£35 HB £180.50-£235.50 D £9 CC MC Visa

★★ Durley Chine
Hospitality, Comfort merit awards
Chine Crescent, West Cliff, Bournemouth BH2 5LB
☎ 01202-551926

★★ Durley Grange
Hospitality merit award
6 Durley Road, West Cliff, Bournemouth BH2 5JL
☎ 01202-554473 Fax 01202-293774
50 bedrs, all ensuite, TCF TV ▣ P 30 No children under 5 CC MC Visa ✈ ▣

BOURNEMOUTH & BOSCOMBE – ENGLAND

★★ Fircroft
Owls Road, Bournemouth BH5 1AE
☎ 01202-309771 Fax 01202-395644
50 bedrs, all ensuite, TCF ⌂ P 50 SB £18-£27 DB £36-£54 HB £175-£224 D £13 CC MC Visa Amex DC

★★ Fountain
13 Durley Road South, West Cliff, Bournemouth BH2 5JH
☎ 01202-551074 Fax 01202-553948
26 bedrs, 16 ensuite, 6, 2 TCF P 26 SB £30-£35 DB £30-£35 HB £180-£210 D £12.50 CC MC Visa JCB

★★ Grange
Overcliffe Drive, Southbourne, Bournemouth BH6 3NL
☎ 01202-433093 Fax 01202-424228
31 bedrs, all ensuite, TCF ⌂ P 37 SB £30 DB £59 HB £195 D £16 CC MC Visa

★★ Hotel Riviera
Hospitality, Comfort merit awards
West Cliff Gardens, Bournemouth BH2 5HL
☎ 01202-552845 Fax 01202-317717
Closed Nov-Mar
34 bedrs, all ensuite, TCF TV P 24 SB £24-£30 DB £48-£60 HB £190-£230 D £11 CC MC Visa

★★ Melford Hall
St Peters Road, Bournemouth BH1 2LS
☎ 551516 Fax 292533
65 bedrs, all ensuite, TCF TV ⌂ P 60 SB £30-£37 DB £52-£66 HB £210-£310 D £12 CC MC Visa Amex

★★ Montague
Durley Road South, Bournemouth BH2 5JE
☎ 01202-551074
26 bedrs, 22 ensuite, 2 TCF TV P 30 SB £23-£28 DB £45-£55 HB £182-£227 D £9.95 CC MC Visa

★★ Pinehurst
West Cliff Gardens, Bournemouth BH2 5HR
☎ 01202-556218 Fax 01202-551051
73 bedrs, all ensuite, 2 TCF TV P 40 SB £21-£31 DB £42-£62 HB £172-£247 D £14 CC MC Visa Amex DC

★★ Russell Court
Bath Road, Bournemouth BH1 2EP
☎ 01202-295819 Fax 01202-293457
62 bedrs, 56 ensuite, 3 TCF TV P 60 SB £29.50-£49.50 DB £49.50-£99.50 HB £259-£359 D £12.95 CC MC Visa Amex DC

★★ St George
West Cliff Gardens, Bournemouth BH2 5HL
☎ 01202-556075 Fax 01202-557330
22 bedrs, 20 ensuite, 2, TCF TV ⌂ P 10 SB £22-£29 DB £46-£62 HB £160-£235 D £4 CC MC Visa

★★ Sun Court
West Hill Road, Bournemouth BH2 5PH
☎ 01202-551343 Fax 01202-316747
36 bedrs, all ensuite, TCF TV ⌂ P 50 SB £22-£33 DB £52-£76 HB £162-£224 D £14 CC MC Visa Amex DC

★★ Taurus Park
Hospitality merit award
16 Knyveton Road, Bournemouth BH1 3QN
☎ 01202-557374
42 bedrs, 40 ensuite, 3 TCF TV ⌂ P 20 No children under 5 SB £20.50-£22 DB £38-£42 HB £135-£168 D £6 CC MC Visa

★★ Tower House
Hospitality merit award
West Cliff Gardens, Bournemouth BH2 5HP
☎ 01202-290742
34 bedrs, 32 ensuite, 1 ⌂ ⌂ P 38 CC MC Visa

★★ Ullswater
Hospitality, Comfort merit awards
West Cliff Gardens, Bournemouth BH2 5HW
☎ 01202-555181 Fax 01202-317896
42 bedrs, all ensuite, TCF TV ⌂ P 10 SB £25-£30 DB £50-£60 HB £140-£220 D £11 CC MC Visa Amex

★★ Westleigh
26 West Hill Road, Bournemouth BH2 5PG
☎ 01202-296989 Fax 01202-296989
30 bedrs, 28 ensuite, 2 TCF TV ⌂ P 20 SB £29-£40 DB £48-£64 HB £-£230 D £8 CC MC Visa

★★ Whitehall
Hospitality, Comfort merit awards
Exeter Park Road, Bournemouth BH2 5AX
☎ 01202-554682 Fax 01202-554682
49 bedrs, 44 ensuite, 5, 3 TCF TV ⌂ P 25 SB £27-£29 DB £54-£58 HB £190-£250 D £12 CC MC Visa Amex DC JCB

★★ Winterbourne
Hospitality merit award
Priory Road, West Cliff, Bournemouth BH2 5DJ
☎ 01202-296366 Fax 01202-780073
41 bedrs, all ensuite, TCF TV ⌂ P 31 SB £29-£39 DB £50-£70 HB £175-£270 D £10 CC MC Visa Amex

Boltons *Highly Acclaimed*
9 Durley Chine Road South, Westcliff, BH2 5JT
☎ 01202-751517 Fax 01202-751629
Closed Nov-Mar
12 bedrs, all ensuite, TV P 12 No children under 5 SB £25-£28 DB £50-£58 HB £165-£200 D £10.50 CC MC Visa

Tudor Grange *Highly Acclaimed*
31 Gervis Road, Bournemouth BH1 3EE
☎ 01202-291472
12 bedrs, 11 ensuite, 1 TCF TV ⌂ P 11 SB £19-£27 DB £38-£60 HB £170-£240 D £10 CC MC Visa

BOURNEMOUTH & BOSCOMBE – ENGLAND

Borodale *Acclaimed*
10 St Johns Road, Boscombe, Bournemouth BH5 1EL
📞 01202-395285
15 bedrs, 7 ensuite, 1 🛁, 1 🛏 TV P 12 CC   MC Visa

Carisbrooke *Acclaimed*
42 Tregonwell Road, Bournemouth BH2 5NT
📞 01202-290432 Fax 01202-310499
22 bedrs, 19 ensuite, 2 🛏 TCF TV 🐾 P 18 SB £18-£27 DB £36-£54 HB £169-£220 D £11 CC   MC Visa Amex DC ♿

Cherry View *Acclaimed*
66 Alum Chine Road, Bournemouth BH4 8DZ
📞 01202-760910
11 bedrs, all ensuite, TCF TV P 12 No children under 7 SB £27-£30 DB £38-£42 HB £165-£185 D £7 CC   MC Visa Amex DC

Cransley *Acclaimed*
11 Knyveton Road, East Cliff, Bournemouth BH1 3QG
📞 01202-290067
Closed Oct-Easter
12 bedrs, all ensuite, TCF TV 🚭 P 10 SB £17-£21 DB £34-£42 HB £140-£180 D £8.50

Dene Court *Acclaimed*
19 Boscombe Spa Road, Bournemouth BH5 1AR
📞 01202-394874
20 bedrs, 18 ensuite, 1 🛏 TCF TV P 12 No children under 2 SB £14-£25 DB £28-£49 HB £115-£150 D £6 CC   MC Visa

---

Holmcroft Hotel

Subtly elegant, with the familiarities of home. A friendly family run hotel, south facing, quietly situated just a few minutes stroll from the wooded chines and sandy beaches.

**5 EARLE ROAD,
ALUM CHINE WESTBOURNE,
BOURNEMOUTH, DORSET BH4 8JQ
Tel: 01202-761289 Fax: 01202-761289**

East Cliff Cottage *Acclaimed*
57 Grove Road, Bournemouth BH1 3AT
📞 01202-552788 Fax 01202-556400

A private hotel of character and comfort. Located within 300 yards of the East Cliff.

10 bedrs, 7 ensuite, 1 🛏 TCF TV 🐾 P 8 SB £19.50-£27 DB £40-£55 HB £179-£210 D £9.50 CC   MC Visa Amex DC

Highclere *Acclaimed*
15 Burnaby Road, Alum Chine, Bournemouth BH4 8JF
📞 01202-761350
Closed 1 Nov-31 Mar

A charming and welcoming family hotel with many original Victorian features. A choice of excellent, plentiful food at all meals. Four minutes walk from the beach.

9 bedrs, all ensuite, TCF TV 🐾 P 6 No children under 3 SB £19-£23 DB £38-£46 HB £150-£168 D £5 CC   MC Visa Amex DC JCB

Holmcroft *Acclaimed*
5 Earle Road, Alum Chine Westbourne, Bournemouth BH4 8JQ
📞 01202-761289 Fax 01202-761289
19 bedrs, all ensuite, TCF TV 🚭 P 12 No children under 8 SB £18-£25 DB £36-£50 HB £168-£210 D £10 CC   MC Visa

Hotel Cavendish *Acclaimed*
20 Durley Chine Road, West Cliff, Bournemouth BH2 5JG
📞 01202-290489
Closed Nov-Easter

BOURNEMOUTH & BOSCOMBE – ENGLAND

A 16 bedroom hotel, privately owned and personally managed with a reputation for comfort and relaxed friendly service, situated near beach and town.

16 bedrs, 15 ensuite, 1 ↦ TCF TV P 14 No children under 5 SB £19-£26 DB £38-£52 HB £150-£190 D £6

Linwood House *Acclaimed*
11 Wilfred Road, Boscombe, Bournemouth BH5 1ND
☎ 01202-397818
Closed Nov-Mar
10 bedrs, 8 ensuite, 1 ↦ TV ⚓ P 7 No children under 6 SB £17-£22 DB £32-£40 HB £142-£174

Oak Hall *Acclaimed*
9 Wilfred Road, Boscombe, Bournemouth BH5 1ND
☎ 01202-395062
13 bedrs, 9 ensuite, 1 ↦ TV ⚓ P 80 CC MC Visa Amex ♿

Ravenstone *Acclaimed*
36 Burnaby Road, Alum Chine Westbourne, Bournemouth BH4 8JG
☎ 01202-761047 Fax 01202-761047
Closed Dec-Feb

Situated close to a wooded chine and beach yet near to both Bournemouth and Poole town centres. All rooms ensuite with TV and tea making facilities. Four course dinner with a choice.

9 bedrs, all ensuite, TCF TV P 5 SB £16-£22 DB £32-£44 HB £126-£175 D £7 CC MC Visa

Silver Trees *Acclaimed*
57 Wimborne Road, Bournemouth BH3 7AL
☎ 01202-556040 Fax 01202-556040
E Mail billsmith@zetnet.co.uk
5 bedrs, all ensuite, 2 ↦ TV P 10 No children under 5 DB £40-£42 CC MC Visa Amex

Thanet *Acclaimed*
2 Drury Road, Alum Chine, Bournemouth BH4 8HA
☎ 01202-761135 Fax 01202-761135
Closed Nov-Easter
8 bedrs, 5 ensuite, 2 ↦ TCF TV P 6 No children under 7 SB £16.25-£19.75 DB £32.50-£43.50 HB £132-£169 D £5.75 CC MC Visa JCB

West Dene *Acclaimed*
117 Alumhurst Road, Alum Chine, BH4 8HS
☎ 01202-764843 Fax 01202-764843
Closed Dec-Jan
17 bedrs, 12 ensuite, 3 ↦ TCF TV P 17 No children under 5 SB £24-£27 DB £47-£53 HB £189-£238 D £15 CC MC Visa Amex DC

Wood Lodge *Acclaimed*
10 Manor Road, East Cliff, Bournemouth BH1 3EY
☎ 01202-290891
15 bedrs, 14 ensuite, TCF TV ⚓ P 14 SB £22-£30.50 DB £44-£61 D £12.75 CC Visa ♿

Wychcote *Acclaimed*
2 Somerville Road, West Cliff, BH2 5LH
☎ 01202-557898
Closed Jan-Feb
12 bedrs, 11 ensuite, TCF TV P 15 No children under 5 SB £20-£30 DB £40-£60 HB £144-£225 D £8 CC MC Visa

Amitie *Listed*
1247 Christchurch Road, Bournemouth BH7 6BP
☎ 01202-427255
8 bedrs, 5 ensuite, 2 ↦ TCF TV P 8 No children SB £16 DB £32-£40

Avonwood *Listed*
20 Owls Road, Boscombe, Bournemouth BH5 1AF
☎ 01202-394704 Fax 01202-309906
19 bedrs, 12 ensuite, 4 ↦ TCF TV P 14 No children under 2 SB £16.50-£21.50 DB £33-£43 HB £150-£190 D £8 CC MC Visa

Dorset Westbury *Listed*
62 Lansdowne Road, Bournemouth BH1 1RS
☎ 01202-551811 Fax 01202-551811

Friendly and comfortable family run hotel with secluded garden and large car park within easy reach of the town centre, sea, shops, golf course and public transport.

15 bedrs, 10 ensuite, 2 ↦ TCF TV ⚓ P 16 SB £20-£25 DB £34-£44 HB £162-£174 D £8 CC MC Visa JCB

Durley Court *Listed*
5 Durley Road, West Cliff, Bournemouth BH2 5JQ
☎ 01202-556857 Fax 01202-556857
Closed winter
16 bedrs, 13 ensuite, 1 🛁, 1 ⇌ TCF TV P 16

Hotel Sorrento *Listed*
16 Owls Road, Boscombe, Bournemouth BH5 1AG
☎ 01202-394019
Closed Jan
19 bedrs, 17 ensuite, 1 ⇌ TCF TV 🐾 P 19 SB £15-£22
DB £30-£44 HB £135-£195 D £6 CC MC Visa 🏊

Ingledene *Listed*
20 Derby Road, Bournemouth BH1 3QA
☎ 01202-555433
Closed Nov-Mar
8 bedrs, 7 ensuite, 1 ⇌ TCF TV 🐾 P 3 No children under 4 SB £14-£20 DB £28-£40 HB £120-£159 D £4.95

Mae Mar *Listed*
91-95 West Hill Road, Bournemouth BH2 5PQ
☎ 01202-553167 Fax 01202-311919
39 bedrs, 33 ensuite, 2 ⇌ TCF TV 🐾 ⊞ SB £18.50-£25
DB £37-£50 HB £140-£185 CC MC Visa 🏊 ♿

Northover *Listed*
10 Earle Road, Alum Chine, Bournemouth BH4 8JQ
☎ 01202-767349
10 bedrs, 7 ensuite, 2 ⇌ TV ⊠ 🐾 P 10 SB £21-£28
DB £42-£56 HB £159-£210 D £9

Valberg *Listed*
1a Wollenstonecraft Road, Boscombe, Bournemouth BH5 1JQ
☎ 01202-394644
10 bedrs, all ensuite, TV P 7 No children under 3

Gervis Court
38 Gervis Road, Bournemouth BH1 3DH
☎ 01202-556871 Fax 01202-556871

A hotel of character, centrally located for all local amenities including conference centre, beach and shops. All rooms are ensuite, with TV, tea and coffee making facilities. Ample private parking.

12 bedrs, all ensuite, TCF TV ⊠ P 20 SB £20-£25 DB £36-£44 CC MC Visa

---

BOURTON-ON-THE-WATER Gloucestershire 4A1

★★ Chester House
Bourton-on-the-Water GL54 2BU
☎ 01451-820286 Fax 01451-820471
22 bedrs, all ensuite, 1 ⇌ TCF TV 🐾 P 20 SB £49 DB £79
HB £252-£442 D £16.50 CC MC Visa Amex DC JCB ♿

★★ Old New Inn
Hospitality merit award
High Street, Bourton-on-the-Water GL54 2AF
☎ 01451-820467 Fax 01451-810236
E Mail 106206.2571@compuserve.com
Closed 25 Dec
17 bedrs, 12 ensuite, 3 ⇌ 🐾 P 24 SB £30 DB £60 D £18
CC MC Visa

Ridge *Highly Acclaimed*
Whiteshoots, Bourton-on-the-Water GL54 2LE
☎ 01451-820660

Large country house set in two acres of mature grounds. Spacious bedrooms (two on the ground floor) are available with all facilities. Good pubs and restaurants nearby.

5 bedrs, all ensuite, 1 ⇌ TCF TV ⊠ No children under 6
SB £20-£30 DB £35-£40

Polly Perkins *Listed*
1 The Chestnuts, High Street, Bourton-on-the-Water
GL54 2AN
☎ 01451-820244 Fax 01451-820558

This 300 year old building is ideally situated in the centre of this beautiful village. You are assured of a warm welcome all year round.

8 bedrs, all ensuite, TCF TV P 15 No children under 5
SB £30 DB £35-£45 D £12 CC MC Visa JCB

BRAITHWAITE – ENGLAND

BOVEY TRACEY Devon   3D3

★★ Coombe Cross
Bovey Tracey TQ13 9EY
📞 01626-832476 Fax 01626-835298
23 bedrs, all ensuite, 2 🛏 TCF TV 🐕 P 28 SB £39 DB £56-£64 HB £240-£290 D £19 CC MC Visa Amex DC JCB 🛎

★★ Riverside Inn
Fore Street, Bovey Tracey TQ13 9AF
📞 01626-832293 Fax 01626-833880
10 bedrs, all ensuite, TCF TV 🐕 P 100 SB £30 DB £40 CC MC Visa 🅿

BOWBURN Co. Durham   11D1

Roadchef Lodge *Lodge*
Motorway Service Area, Thursdale Road, Bowburn DH6 5NP
📞 0191-377 3666 Fax 0191-377 1448
Closed 25 Dec-2 Jan
38 bedrs, all ensuite, TCF TV P 130 **Room only rate** £43.50 D £4.50 CC MC Visa Amex DC ♿

BRACKLEY Northamptonshire   8B4

★★ (Inn) Crown
20/22 Market Place, Brackley NN13 7DP
📞 01280-702210 Fax 01280-701840
19 bedrs, all ensuite, TCF TV 🐕 P 100 SB £56 DB £77 D £6 CC MC Visa Amex DC

BRADFORD West Yorkshire   10C3

Park Grove *Acclaimed*
28 Park Grove, Frizinghall, Bradford BD9 4JY
📞 01274-543444 Fax 01274-495619

Quietly positioned, two miles from the city centre. All rooms ensuite with satellite TV and all the latest facilities. Ample car parking, award winning food. Gateway to the Dales.

12 bedrs, all ensuite, TCF TV P 9 No children under 2 SB £40-£46 DB £58-£60 D £10 CC MC Visa Amex DC

BRADFORD-ON-AVON Wiltshire   3F1

Widbrook Grange *Highly Acclaimed*
Trowbridge Road, Bradford-on-Avon BA15 1UH
📞 01225-863173 Fax 01225-862890

A warm welcome to an elegant, peaceful home in its own grounds of 11 acres. The house and courtyard rooms have been lovingly restored, with ensuite facilities, colour TV, and telephone with fourposter rooms. Indoor swimming pool and gymnasium.

19 bedrs, all ensuite, 1 🛏 TCF TV P 50 SB £55-£79 DB £89-£95 D £22.50 CC MC Visa Amex DC JCB 🛎 ♿

BRAINTREE Essex   5E1

Nags Head *Listed*
Market Place, Braintree CM7 6HG
📞 01376-323348
3 bedrs, 1 🛏 TV

BRAITHWAITE Cumbria   10A2

★★ Cottage in the Wood
Whinlatter Pass, Braithwaite CA12 5TW
📞 01768-778409
Closed Nov-Mar

An oasis of peace perched high on the Malvern Hills and enjoying 'the best view in England' (Daily Mail). Whether staying for pleasure or on business, the emphasis is on relaxation, good food and good wine. Owned and run by the Pattin family for 10 years

7 bedrs, all ensuite, TCF 🅿 🐕 P 15 DB £60-£62 D £17 CC MC Visa Amex JCB

BRAMHOPE West Yorkshire 11D3

Cottages
Moor Road, Bramhope, Leeds LS16 9HH
☎ 0113-284 2754 Fax 0113-284 2754

Set in rural surroundings, yet convenient for Leeds, Bradford, Harrogate and the airport. ETB 2 crowns highly commended. Ensuite rooms furnished to a high standard.

5 bedrs, all ensuite, **TCF** TV P 5 No children under 10 **SB** £30 **DB** £44

BRAMPTON Cumbria 10B1

Oakwood Park *Highly Acclaimed*
Longtown Road, Brampton CA8 2AP
☎ 01697-72436
5 bedrs, all ensuite, 1 ⇌ **TCF** TV P 10 **SB** £27 **DB** £42 **HB** £142 **D** £11 **CC** MC Visa

Abbey Bridge Inn *Acclaimed*
Lanercost, Brampton CA8 2HG
☎ 016977-2224 Fax 016977-2224
Closed 25 Dec

A family run country hotel in a peaceful riverside setting. The 17th century Blacksmiths Restaurant offers excellent food and real ales. A good touring centre for Hadrian's Wall and Lakes.

7 bedrs, 4 ensuite, 1 ⌂, 2 ⇌ **TCF** ✝ P 20 **SB** £22 **DB** £60 **CC** MC Visa Amex

BRAUNTON Devon 2C2

Denham Farm & Country House *Acclaimed*
North Buckland, Braunton EX33 1HY
☎ 01271-890297 Fax 01271-890297

A place for all seasons, this lovely farmhouse is situated amidst rolling Devon hills only two miles from the glorious coastline of Croyde and Woolacombe.

10 bedrs, all ensuite, 1 ⇌ **TCF** TV P 10 **DB** £44-£54 **HB** £210-£237 **CC** MC Visa ✈

BREDWARDINE Herefordshire 7D4

Bredwardine Hall *Highly Acclaimed*
Bredwardine HR3 6DB
☎ 01981-500596
4 bedrs, all ensuite, 1 ⇌ **TCF** TV ✈ P 7 No children under 10 **SB** £33 **DB** £46-£50 **HB** £231-£245 **D** £12

BRENT KNOLL Somerset 3E2

★★ **Battleborough Grange**
Bristol Road, Brent Knoll TA9 4HJ
☎ 01278-760208 Fax 01278-760208
16 bedrs, 14 ensuite, 1 ⇌ **TCF** TV P 50 No children **CC** MC Visa Amex DC

BRERETON Staffordshire 7F2

★★ **Cedar Tree**
Main Road, Rugeley, Brereton WS15 1DY
☎ 01889-584241 Fax 01889-575823
34 bedrs, all ensuite, **TCF** TV P 200 **SB** £25-£40 **DB** £40-£57.50 **D** £11 **CC** MC Visa Amex DC ✈ ♿

BRIDGNORTH Shropshire 7E3

★★ **Falcon**
St John Street, Lowton, Bridgnorth WV15 6AS
☎ 01746-763134 Fax 01746-765401
14 bedrs, all ensuite, 1 ⇌ **TCF** TV ✝ P 200 **SB** £35-£40 **DB** £46 **D** £10 **CC** MC Visa Amex

★★ Parlors Hall
Hospitality, Comfort merit awards
Mill Street, Bridgnorth WV15 5AL
☎ 01746-761931 Fax 01746-767058
15 bedrs, all ensuite, TCF TV 🐕 P 25 SB £39 DB £48 D £9 CC MC Visa

Middleton Lodge *Acclaimed*
Middleton Priors, Bridgnorth WV16 6UR
☎ 01746-712228
3 bedrs, all ensuite, TCF TV ✍ P 4 No children

BRIDGWATER Somerset   3E2

Castle of Comfort *Acclaimed*
Dodington, Nether Stowey, Bridgwater TA5 1LE
☎ 01278-741264
5 bedrs, all ensuite, 1 🐕 TCF TV 🐕 P 14 SB £34 DB £44 D £10 CC MC Visa Amex

Woodlands
35 Durleigh Rd, Bridgwater TA6 7HX
☎ 01278-423442

A beautiful listed house in landscaped gardens, convenient for the the Quantock Hills and Somerset Levels. Occupies a secluded location, yet is close to the town centre.

4 bedrs, 3 ensuite, 1 🐕 TCF TV P 4 No children under 10 SB £20-£30 DB £40-£46 HB £210-£260 D £12 CC MC Visa

BRIDLINGTON East Yorkshire   11F3

★★ Monarch
South Marine Drive, Bridlington YO15 3JJ
☎ 01262-674447 Fax 01262-670060
Closed winter
40 bedrs, all ensuite, TCF TV 🍽 P 10 No children SB £28-£30 DB £56-£60 HB £225-£240 D £11 CC MC Visa 🅁 ♿

★ Langdon
Pembroke Terrace, Bridlington YO15 3BX
☎ 01262-400124 Fax 01262-400124
27 bedrs, 24 ensuite, 2 🐕 TCF TV 🍽 P 3 SB £22 DB £44 HB £152.50-£162.50 D £7.50

Bay Ridge *Acclaimed*
Summerfield Road, Bridlington YO15 3LF
☎ 01262-673425
14 bedrs, 12 ensuite, 1 🐕 TCF TV 🐕 P 7 SB £21-£22 DB £42-£44 HB £155-£165 D £7 CC MC Visa 🅁

Glencoe *Listed*
43-45 Marshall Avenue, Bridlington YO15 2DT
☎ 01262-676818
18 bedrs, 6 ensuite, 4 🐕 TCF TV SB £20-£22 DB £32-£36 HB £125-£150 CC MC Visa

Park View *Listed*
9-11 Tennyson Avenue, Bridlington YO15 2EU
☎ 01262-672140 Fax 01262-672140

A small hotel situated only 250 yards from the beach and near a park and a leisure centre.

16 bedrs, 4 ensuite, 3 🐕 TCF TV 🐕 P 8 SB £15 DB £30 HB £130 D £5 CC MC Visa Amex

BRIDPORT Dorset   3E3

★★ Eype's Mouth
Eype, Bridport DT6 6AL
☎ 01308-423300 Fax 01308-420033
18 bedrs, all ensuite, TCF TV 🐕 P 50 SB £25-£57 DB £50-£64 D £15 CC MC Visa

★★ Roundham House
Hospitality, Comfort merit awards
Roundham Gardens, West Bay Road, Bridport DT6 4BD
☎ 01308-422753 Fax 01308-421145
Closed Jan-Feb
8 bedrs, all ensuite, TCF TV 🐕 P 12 SB £33-£35 DB £55-£65 HB £275-£280 D £17 CC MC Visa JCB ♿

★ Bridport Arms
West Bay, Bridport DT6 4EN
☎ 01308-422994 Fax 01308-425141
13 bedrs, 6 ensuite, 3 🐕 TCF TV 🐕 P 10 SB £24-£30 DB £45-£60 HB £220-£245 D £11 CC MC Visa

BRIDPORT – ENGLAND

Britmead House *Acclaimed*
West Bay Road, Bridport DT6 4EG
📞 01308-422941 Fax 01308-422516

Twixt Bridport and West Bay Harbour. Ensuite rooms (including one ground floor), all with many thoughtful extras. South facing lounge and dining room overlooking the garden to open countryside beyond.

7 bedrs, all ensuite, **TCF TV** 🐾 **P** 8 No children under 5 **SB** £25-£36 **DB** £40-£58 **HB** £206.50-£241.50 **D** £13.50 **CC** MC Visa Amex DC JCB &

Park Farmhouse *Acclaimed*
Main Street, Chideock, Bridport DT6 6JD
📞 01297-489157
Closed Christmas
6 bedrs, all ensuite, **TCF TV** 🐾 **P** 12 **SB** £25 **DB** £40 **HB** £140 **D** £14 **CC** MC Visa

Frogmore Farm
Chideock, Bridport DT6 6HT
📞 01308-456159

A 17th century farmhouse offering traditional country hospitality and views across Lyme Bay. Ideal for coast walks or to explore the interesting places of Dorset.

3 bedrs, 2 ensuite, 1 ➡ **TCF TV** 🐾 **P** 6 **SB** £16-£17 **DB** £30-£34 **HB** £-£161 **D** £9

BRIGHTON East Sussex   5D4

Adelaide *Highly Acclaimed*
51 Regency Square, Brighton BN1 2FF
📞 01273-205286 Fax 01273-220904
12 bedrs, all ensuite, 1 ➡ **TCF TV SB** £39-£55 **DB** £65-£78 **D** £19 **CC** MC Visa Amex

Ainsley House *Highly Acclaimed*
28 New Steine, Marine Parade, Brighton BN2 1PD
📞 01273-605310 Fax 01273-688604
Closed Christmas
11 bedrs, 9 ensuite, **TCF TV SB** £25-£30 **DB** £46-£68 **D** £10 **CC** MC Visa Amex DC JCB

Amblecliffe *Highly Acclaimed*
35 Upper Rock Gardens, Brighton BN2 1QF
📞 01273-681161 Fax 01273-676945
8 bedrs, all ensuite, 1 ➡ **TCF TV** ⊠ **P** 3 No children under 5 **DB** £47-£60 **CC** MC Visa Amex

Arlanda *Highly Acclaimed*
20 New Steine, Brighton BN2 1PD
📞 01273-699300 Fax 01273-600930
12 bedrs, all ensuite, **TCF TV SB** £22-£40 **DB** £46-£80 **D** £12 **CC** MC Visa Amex DC JCB

Ascott House *Highly Acclaimed*
21 New Steine, Marine Parade, Brighton BN2 1PD
📞 01273-688085 Fax 01273-623733

Grade II Listed Georgian hotel in seafront garden square close to all amenities, where high standards and personal attention are paramount.

12 bedrs, 10 ensuite, 1 🛁, 1 ➡ **TCF TV** No children under 3 **SB** £22-£40 **DB** £42-£80 **D** £18 **CC** MC Visa Amex DC

Kempton House *Highly Acclaimed*
33-34 Marine Parade, Brighton BN2 1TR
📞 01273-570248
12 bedrs, all ensuite, **TCF TV** 🐾 **SB** £30-£45 **DB** £40-£58 **HB** £245-£295 **D** £15.50 **CC** MC Visa

21 CHARLOTTE STREET BRIGHTON BN2 1AG

Tel: 01273 686450/681617
Fax: 01273 695560/681617
E-mail: the21@pavilion.co.uk
Web site: http://www.chelsoft.demon.co.uk/21.htm

This distinguished hotel is the **Charm of Brighton**. Just off the sea front, The Twenty One is ideally situated for all major attractions. All rooms are fully *en-suite and exquisitely* furnished and contain biscuits, chocolates, sweets and toiletries. A mouth watering breakfast menu, catering for Vegans, Vegetarians, continental and of course the full English.

- Stay on Sunday at **50% off** our normal tariff *(not including single occupancy, conferences, or bank holiday weekends)* as part of a three nights stay.

- Stay any 2 nights and claim a **10% discount** off our normal tariff.

- Stay any 4 nights and claim a **20% discount** off our normal tariff.

- Stay any 7 nights and claim a **30% discount** off our normal tariff.

- **Valentine offer:** Romantic offer.

- **Bank Holidays**: Stay **Four** nights for the price of **Three** over any Bank Holiday weekend.

- **Christmas**: Special lunch offer.

- **France**: Visit France on a Day Trip.

En suite rooms from
ONLY £17.50
per person sharing a room including breakfast minimum 7 nights

OUR COLLECTIONS OF "CLASSIC ROOMS" INCLUDE

The **"Bridal Suite"** contains a double vanity wash area, a cosy little conservatory which, in turn, leads on to a charming ivy-clad patio.
The double **"Executive Victorian"** room with balcony.
The twin **"Executive Green"** room.
The double **"Oak"** room.
The double **"Champagne"** room.

"A Perfect surrounding for a refreshing and memorable stay"

New Steine *Highly Acclaimed*
12a New Steine, Marine Parade, Brighton BN2 1PB
📞 01273-681546
Closed Jan-Feb
11 bedrs, 7 ensuite, 2 🐾, 2 ➡ TCF TV 🐕 No children under 8 SB £19-£27 DB £39-£48

Twenty One *Highly Acclaimed*
21 Charlotte Street, Marine Parade, Brighton BN2 1AG
📞 01273-686450 Fax 01273-695560
E Mail the21@pavilion.co.uk
6 bedrs, all ensuite, 1 ➡ TCF TV No children under 1 SB £39 DB £56-£86 HB £202-£300 D £18 CC MC Visa Amex DC JCB

Allendale *Acclaimed*
3 New Steine, Brighton BN2 1PB
📞 01273-675436 Fax 01273-602603
Closed Christmas

A Grade II Listed, privately owned, small hotel which has built its reputation on personal service, good food and a homely atmosphere. Ensuite rooms available. Central to all amenities.

13 bedrs, 9 ensuite, 1 🐾, 2 ➡ TCF TV SB £25-£36 DB £44-£70 D £13 CC MC Visa Amex

Brighton Marina House *Acclaimed*
8 Charlotte Street, Marine Parade, Brighton BN2 1AG
📞 01273-605349 Fax 01273-679484
E Mail the21@pavilion.co.uk
10 bedrs, 7 ensuite, 1 ➡ TCF TV SB £15-£31 DB £35-£59 HB £177-£270 D £12 CC MC Visa Amex DC JCB

Cavalaire House *Acclaimed*
34 Upper Rock Gardens, Brighton BN2 1QF
📞 01273-696899 Fax 01273-600504
Closed Christmas-New Year
9 bedrs, 3 ensuite, 3 🐾, 1 ➡ TCF TV No children under 5 SB £16-£18 DB £38-£44 CC MC Visa

Fyfield House *Acclaimed*
26 New Steine, Brighton BN2 1PD
📞 01273-602770 Fax 01273-602770
Closed Christmas

Homely, family run hotel with all rooms individually furnished. Peter and Anna are an English/Swiss combination and assure a nice stay.

9 bedrs, 6 ensuite, 1 ➡ TCF TV 🐕 SB £15-£30 DB £32-£60 HB £150-£250 D £10 CC MC Visa Amex DC JCB

Gullivers *Acclaimed*
10 New Steine, Brighton BN2 1PB
📞 01273-695415
9 bedrs, 5 ensuite, 1 ➡ TCF TV 🐕 SB £15-£22 DB £36-£54 CC MC Visa Amex DC

Malvern *Acclaimed*
33 Regency Square, Brighton BN1 2GG
📞 01273-324302 Fax 01273-324302
12 bedrs, all ensuite, 1 ➡ TCF TV No children CC MC Visa Amex DC JCB

MELFORD HALL HOTEL

Seafront hotel overlooking the Palace Pier at the corner of a garden square. Furnished to a high standard, with the majority of rooms enjoying sea views. Forecourt parking.

**41 MARINE PARADE,
BRIGHTON BN2 1PE**
Tel: 01273 681435   Fax: 01273 624186

BRIGHTON – ENGLAND

Melford Hall *Acclaimed*
41 Marine Parade, Brighton BN2 1PE
📞 01273-681435 Fax 01273-624186
Closed Christmas
25 bedrs, 23 ensuite, 2, 2 ⇌ TCF TV P 12 No children under 2 SB £30-£34 DB £44-£54 CC MC Visa Amex DC JCB

Regency *Acclaimed*
28 Regency Square, Brighton BN1 2FH
📞 01273-202690 Fax 01273-220438

A hotel with history: once owned by a Marlborough, Churchill's great-grandmother. Smart, comfortable. Family owned, professionally run. Licensed bar, direct sea views, children welcomed. Short breaks.

13 bedrs, 9 ensuite, 1 ⇌ TCF TV SB £38-£44 DB £65-£68 D £11 CC MC Visa Amex DC

AMBASSADOR

Family run licensed hotel situated in a sea-front Regency square with beautiful view of the sea and Palace Pier. Close to Royal Pavilion, shops, conference centre and all entertainment.

**22 NEW STEINE
MARINE PARADE
BRIGHTON BN2 1PD**
Tel: 01273 676869
Fax: 01273 689988

Trouville *Acclaimed*
11 New Steine, Marine Parade, Brighton BN2 1PB
📞 01273-697384
Closed Jan

The Trouville is a Regency town house, tastefully restored and furnished.

9 bedrs, 4 ensuite, 2 ⇌ TCF TV SB £20 DB £45 CC MC Visa Amex JCB

Ambassador *Listed*
22-23 New Steine, Marine Parade, Brighton BN2 1PD
📞 01273-676869 Fax 01273-689988
22 bedrs, all ensuite, TCF TV SB £25-£35 DB £42-£65 CC MC Visa Amex DC JCB

Dudley *Listed*
10 Madeira Place, Brighton BN2 1TN
📞 01273-676794

Kimberley *Listed*
17 Atlingworth Street, Brighton BN2 1PL
📞 01273-603504 Fax 01273-603504
15 bedrs, 4 ensuite, 11, 1 ⇌ TCF TV No children under 2 SB £20-£25 DB £35-£45 CC MC Visa Amex DC JCB

Rowland House *Listed*
21 St George Terrace, Marine Parade, BN2 1JJ
📞 01273-603639
11 bedrs, 11, TV SB £17-£19 DB £34-£38 HB £110-£120 CC MC Visa Amex

Paskins Town House
19 Charlotte Street, Brighton BN2 1AG
📞 01273-601203 Fax 01273-621973
E Mail welcome@paskins.co.uk

Set in a Regency terrace and sympathetically converted. Individually designed rooms, most ensuite, with TV, tea and coffee facilities and telephone.

19 bedrs, 16 ensuite, 1 ⇌ TCF TV SB £20-£35 DB £35-£70 CC MC Visa Amex DC

BRISTOL 3E1

★★ Clifton
St Pauls Road, Bristol BS8 1LX
☎ 0117-973 6882 Fax 0117-974 1082
60 bedrs, 48 ensuite, 4 ➡ TCF TV ☂ 🖃 P 12 SB £38-£64 DB £55-£71 D £15 CC MC Visa Amex DC

★★ Glenroy
Victoria Square, Clifton, Bristol BS8 4EW
☎ 0117-973 9058 Fax 0117-973 9058
E Mail admin@glenroyhotel.demon.co.uk
Closed Christmas
44 bedrs, all ensuite, TCF TV ☂ P 16 SB £53 DB £73 HB £325 D £10 CC MC Visa Amex DC ♿

★★ Parkside
470 Bath Road, Bristol BS4 3HQ
☎ 0117-971 1461 Fax 0117-971 5507
27 bedrs, 17 ensuite, 4 ➡ TCF TV P 300 No children under 5 SB £52.50-£67.50 DB £64.50-£77 D £9.95 CC MC Visa Amex DC 🈁

★★ Rodney
Rodney Place, Clifton, Bristol BS8 4HY
☎ 0117-973 5422 Fax 0117-946 7092
Closed Christmas
31 bedrs, all ensuite, ☂ SB £61.50 DB £76 D £15 CC MC Visa Amex DC

★★ Seeley's
Comfort merit award
17/27 St Paul's Road, Clifton, Bristol BS8 1LX
☎ 0117-973 8544 Fax 0117-973 2406
54 bedrs, all ensuite, TCF TV P 30 SB £55 DB £64 D £12 CC MC Visa Amex DC 🈁 📶

Westbury Park *Highly Acclaimed*
37 Westbury Road, Bristol BS9 3AU
☎ 0117-962 0465 Fax 0117-962 8607
8 bedrs, all ensuite, 1 ➡ TCF TV ☂ P 5 SB £29-£39 DB £45-£50 CC MC Visa Amex DC

Downlands *Acclaimed*
33 Henleaze Gardens, Bristol BS9 4HH
☎ 0117-962 1639 Fax 0117-962 1639
9 bedrs, 2 ensuite, 2 ➡ TCF TV ☂ CC MC Visa

Washington *Acclaimed*
11-15 St Paul's Road, Bristol BS8 1LX
☎ 0117-973 3980 Fax 0117-974 1082
Closed Christmas-New Year
46 bedrs, 37 ensuite, 5 ➡ TCF TV ☂ P 20 SB £45 DB £62 CC MC Visa Amex DC

Alcove *Listed*
508-510 Fishponds Road, Fishponds, Bristol BS16 3DT
☎ 0117-965 2436 Fax 0177-965 3886
9 bedrs, 3 ensuite, 4 ➡ TCF TV ☂ P 7 SB £25-£28 DB £38-£42 ♿

Downs View *Listed*
38 Upper Belgrave Road, Clifton, Bristol BS8 2XN
☎ 0117-973 7046

A Victorian guest house overlooking Durdham Down. Near Bristol Zoo and Clifton Suspension Bridge. Close to restaurants and buses. 1½ miles from the city centre. Panoramic views. ETB 1 Crown.

9 bedrs, 4 ensuite, 2 ➡ TCF TV ☂ SB £26 DB £40 CC MC Visa

Oakfield *Listed*
52/54 Oakfield Road, Bristol BS8 2BG
☎ 0117-973 5556 Fax 0117-974 4141
Closed 24 Dec-2 Jan

A well-established immaculate hotel with high standards and personal attention. Set in a convenient location close to the BBC, the University and Clifton.

27 bedrs, 8 ➡ TCF TV ☂ P 9 SB £27 DB £37 HB £234.50 D £6.50

Travelodge *Lodge*
Granada Severn View, M4, Severn Bridge, Bristol BS12 3BJ
☎ 0800-850950
51 bedrs, all ensuite, TCF TV ☂ P 200 SB £42.95 CC MC Visa Amex DC ♿

Mayfair
5 Henleaze Road, Westbury-on-Trym, Bristol BS9 4EX
☎ 01272-962 2008
Closed Christmas

Situated in a quiet residential area, close to the Downs, two and a half miles from the city centre.

9 bedrs, 3 ensuite, 2 ➡ TCF TV ☂ P 9 SB £23-£35 DB £42-£46 CC MC Visa

BRIXHAM Devon 3D4

Harbour View *Listed*
65 King Street, Brixham TQ5 9TH
☎ 01803-853052

A quaint hotel of character, formerly the harbour master's house, occupying an enviable position on the seafront road with panoramic views of the harbour and Torbay.

9 bedrs, 5 ensuite, 1, 1 TCF TV P 4 SB £19 DB £31-£39 CC MC Visa

Sampford House *Listed*
57-59 King Street, Brixham TQ5 9TH
☎ 01803-857761
Closed 25 Dec
6 bedrs, all ensuite, TCF TV P 2 SB £18-£20 DB £32-£40 D £7

Raddicombe Lodge
Kingswear Road, Brixham TQ5 0EX
☎ 01803-882125
Closed Nov-Jan

A charming country house in peaceful surroundings, overlooking National Trust land and the sea between the picturesque harbour towns of Brixham and Dartmouth. Scrumptious breakfasts. Log fires in winter.

8 bedrs, 3 ensuite, 2 TCF TV P 10 SB £15.80-£22.30 DB £31.60-£44.60 CC MC Visa DC

Richmond House
Higher Manor Road, Brixham TQ5 8HA
☎ 01803-882391 Fax 01803-882391
Closed Jan-Feb

Victorian hotel of character, central to historic harbour, shops and restaurants, yet quietly located with residents' car park and south facing sun terrace. Rooms equipped with television and tea and coffee making facilities. Dogs accepted by arrangement.

6 bedrs, 5 ensuite, 1 TCF TV P 5 DB £36-£40 CC MC Visa

Woodlands
Parkham Road, Brixham TQ5 9BU
☎ 01803-852040

All rooms ensuite with colour TV and tea and coffee making facilities, some have sea views. Non-smoking. Private car park. A five minute walk to the harbour.

BROADSTAIRS Kent 5F2

★★ Castlemere
Western Esplanade, Broadstairs CT10 1TD
☎ 01843-861566 Fax 01843-866379
Closed Christmas-5 Jan

Large red-brick building in gardens on cliff with lovely sea views.

37 bedrs, 31 ensuite, 2 P 20 CC MC Visa

BROADSTAIRS – ENGLAND

★★ Royal Albion
Albion Street, Broadstairs CT10 1LU
☎ 01843-868071 Fax 01843-861509
18 bedrs, all ensuite, **P** 20 **SB** £46.50-£51.50 **DB** £53-£58 **HB** £390-£400 **D** £17 **CC** MC Visa Amex DC

Oakfield *Highly Acclaimed*
11 The Vale, Broadstairs CT10 1RB
☎ 01843-862506 Fax 01843-862506
10 bedrs, all ensuite, 1 ⇨ **TCF TV P** 12 No children under 1 **SB** £22-£24 **DB** £44-£48 **HB** £175-£184 **D** £9 **CC** MC Visa Amex DC JCB

Bay Tree *Acclaimed*
12 Eastern Esplanade, Broadstairs CT10 1DR
☎ 01843-862502 Fax 01843-860589

Quiet family run hotel with panoramic sea views, in the quaint olde worlde Dickensian town of Broadstairs.

11 bedrs, all ensuite, **TCF TV P** 11 No children under 10 **SB** £22-£25 **DB** £44-£50 **HB** £186-£204 **D** £9 **CC** MC Visa

Devonhurst *Acclaimed*
13 Eastern Esplanade, Broadstairs CT10 1DR
☎ 01843-863010 Fax 01843-868940
9 bedrs, all ensuite, **TCF TV** No children under 5 **SB** £23-£25 **DB** £42-£50 **HB** £174-£197 **D** £10 **CC** MC Visa Amex DC JCB

Gull Cottage *Acclaimed*
5 Eastern Esplanade, Broadstairs CT10 1DP
☎ 01843-861936
Closed Nov-Feb

Detached Victorian property, overlooking the sea and sandy beaches. Close to the town, harbour and amenities. Ample parking on forecourt. Fully ensuite. A non smoking hotel.

8 bedrs, 7 ensuite, 1 ⇨ **TCF TV P** 6 No children under 6 **SB** £20-£23 **DB** £40-£46

East Horndon *Listed*
4 Eastern Esplanade, Broadstairs CT10 1DP
☎ 01843-868306
Closed Nov-Mar
10 bedrs, 4 ensuite, 2 ⇨ **TCF TV** 🐾 ⊡ **P** 4 **SB** £20 **DB** £44 **HB** £160 **D** £8 **CC** MC Visa

BROADWAY Worcestershire 7F4

Leasow House *Highly Acclaimed*
Laverton Meadows, Broadway WR12 7NA
☎ 01386-584526 Fax 01386 584596

A 17th century Cotswold stone farm house in a peaceful countryside setting close to Broadway village. An ideal base for touring the Cotswolds, Oxford, Stratford-upon-Avon and Warwick.

7 bedrs, all ensuite, **TCF TV** ⊡ 🐾 **P** 14 **SB** £35-£45 **DB** £52-£65 **CC** MC Visa Amex ♿

Old Rectory *Highly Acclaimed*
Church Street, Willersey, Broadway WR12 7PN
☎ 01386-853729 Fax 01386-858061
E Mail beauvoisin@btinternet.com
Closed Christmas

A Georgian rectory in an idyllic position with a beautiful walled garden. Immaculately furnished rooms, fourposters. Elegant dining room with a real log fire. All amenities and ideal for honeymooners.

8 bedrs, 6 ensuite, 1 🛏, 2 ⇨ **TCF TV** ⊡ **P** 10 No children under 8 **SB** £40-£80 **DB** £60-£95 **CC** MC Visa ♿

Olive Branch *Acclaimed*
78/80 High Street, Broadway WR12 7AJ
☎ 01386-853440 Fax 01386-853440
E Mail mark@olivebr.u-net.com
8 bedrs, 6 ensuite, 1 ⇨ **TCF TV P** 10 **SB** £20 **DB** £48 **CC** Amex ♿

BUCKFASTLEIGH – ENGLAND

BROCKENHURST Hampshire 4B4

★★ Watersplash
The Rise, Brockenhurst SO42 7ZP
☎ 01590-622344 Fax 01590-624047
23 bedrs, all ensuite, ⚑ P 25 SB £45-£48 DB £70-£80
HB £275-£295 D £18 CC MC Visa Amex

Cottage *Highly Acclaimed*
Sway Road, Brockenhurst SO42 7SH
☎ 01590-622296 Fax 01590-623014
Closed Dec-Jan

A delightfully converted 300 year old oak beamed forester's cottage with pretty gardens and residents cosy 'snug bar'. In summer, cream teas are served on the terrace.

7 bedrs, 6 ensuite, 1 ⚑, TCF TV ⚑ P 12 No children under 10 SB £45-£64 DB £64-£82 CC MC Visa

BROMSGROVE Worcestershire 8A4

Lower Bentley Farm
Lower Bentley Lane, Lower Bentley, B60 4JB
☎ 01527-821286 Fax 01527-821286

An elegant Victorian farmhouse set in tranquil countryside with spacious bedrooms, all with colour TV and tea/coffee facilities. Full central heating. Separate lounge and dining room overlooking the garden. Ample safe parking.

3 bedrs, 2 ensuite, 1 ⚑ TCF TV ⚑ P 5 SB £20-£22.50
DB £36

BROSELEY Shropshire 7E2

Cumberland *Listed*
Jackson Avenue, Broseley TF12 5NB
☎ 01952-882301 Fax 01952-884438
25 bedrs, 7 ensuite, 3 ⚑ TCF TV ⚑ P 30 CC Visa DC

BROUGH Cumbria 10C2

Augill House Farm *Highly Acclaimed*
Brough, Kirkby Stephen CA17 4DX
☎ 01768-341305
3 bedrs, all ensuite, TCF TV P 4 No children under 12 DB £40-£44 HB £190-£210 D £10

BROUGHTON-IN-FURNESS Cumbria 10A2

★ Old Kings Head
Church Street, Broughton-in-Furness LA20 6HJ
☎ 01229-716293
6 bedrs, 3 ensuite, 1 ⚑ ⚑ P 20

BUCKDEN Cambridgeshire 8C4

★★ George Coaching Inn
Great North Road, Buckden, Huntingdon PE18 9XA
☎ 01480-810307 Fax 01480-811274
22 bedrs, all ensuite, TCF TV ⚑ P 50 SB £58 DB £76
D £12 CC MC Visa Amex DC

★★ Lion
Comfort, Restaurant merit awards
High Street, Buckden, Huntingdon PE18 9XA
☎ 01480-810313 Fax 01480-811070
15 bedrs, all ensuite, TCF TV ⚑ P 20 SB £60 DB £75
D £16 CC MC Visa Amex DC JCB

BUCKFASTLEIGH Devon 2C3

FURZELEIGH MILL HOTEL

Superb Central Location for Moor and Coast

Charming character 16th Century former Mill House on edge of Dartmoor, comfortable ensuite bedrooms all with views of the beautiful River Dart valley. Lovely restaurant, varied menu, fine food and wines served with care and attention. Privately owned and personally run, you are always assured of a very warm welcome.

ETB 3 Crowns Commended   AA 3 Q's
Member of Dartmoor Tourist Association

**DARTBRIDGE, BUCKFASTLEIGH, SOUTH DEVON TQ11 0JP
Tel: 01364 643476**

Dartbridge Manor *Listed*
Dartbridge Road, Buckfastleigh TQ11 0SZ
☎ 01364-643575

Furzleigh Mill
Dartbridge, Buckfastleigh TQ11 0JP
☎ 01364-643476 Fax 01364-643476
15 bedrs, 14 ensuite, 2 🐕 TCF TV 🍴 P 30 CC MC Visa DC
See advert on previous page

BUDE Cornwall 2B3

★★ Camelot
Downs View, Bude EX23 8RE
☎ 01288-352361 Fax 01288-355470
21 bedrs, all ensuite, P 21 SB £22-£26 DB £44-£52
HB £199-£239 D £14 CC MC Visa

★★ Maer Lodge
Maer Down Road, Bude EX23 8NG
☎ 01288-353306 Fax 01288-354005
E Mail maerlodgehotel@btinternet.com.
16 bedrs, all ensuite, 1 🐕 TCF TV 🍴 P 20 SB £28.50-£33.50 DB £50-£60 HB £210-£250 D £13.50 CC MC Visa Amex DC ♿

★★ St Margarets
Killerton Road, Bude EX23 8EN
☎ 01288-352252 Fax 01288-355995
10 bedrs, all ensuite, TCF TV 🍴 P 4 SB £25-£30 DB £40-£50 HB £210-£280 D £12 CC MC Visa JCB ♿

★ Edgcumbe
Summerleaze Crescent, Bude EX23 8HJ
☎ 01288-353846 Fax 01288-355256
15 bedrs, 8 ensuite, 1 🐾, 2 🐕 TCF TV 🍴 P 7 SB £17-£22.25 DB £34-£44.50 HB £157-£189.50 D £9 CC MC Visa Amex DC 🎱 ♿

★ Meva Gwin
Upton, Bude EX23 0LY
☎ 01288-352347 Fax 01288-352347
Closed Oct-Apr
12 bedrs, 11 ensuite, 1 🐕 TCF TV P 44 SB £23-£34 DB £44-£48 HB £185-£195 D £8.95 CC MC Visa

Cliff *Highly Acclaimed*
Maer Down Road, Bude EX23 8NG
☎ 01288-353110 Fax 01288-353110
Closed Oct-Apr

Small top class family hotel with fabulous location, offering Bude's best facilities, including an indoor pool, all weather bowling and tennis. All bedrooms ensuite. Superb food.

15 bedrs, all ensuite, TCF TV 🍴 P 15 SB £24-£30 DB £48-£60 HB £210-£260 D £8 CC MC Visa JCB 🎱 🎾

Pencarrol *Listed*
21 Downs View, Bude EX23 8RF
☎ 01288-352478
Closed Christmas
8 bedrs, 2 ensuite, 2 🐕 TCF TV SB £14.50-£15.50 DB £29-£31 HB £152.50 D £9

BUDLEIGH SALTERTON Devon 3D3

Long Range *Acclaimed*
Vales Road, Budleigh Salterton EX9 6HS
☎ 01395-443321 Fax 01395-445220
6 bedrs, all ensuite, TCF TV P 7
SB £25-£35 DB £45-£60 HB £230-£270 D £15

BULPHAN Essex 5D2

★★ Ye Olde Plough House
Brentwood Road, Bulphan RM14 3SR
☎ 01375-891592 Fax 01375-892256
78 bedrs, all ensuite, 🍴 P 180 CC MC Visa Amex DC 🎱 🏊 🎾 ♿

LONG RANGE HOTEL

Personal service ensures your comfort and relaxation in this tranquil setting close to the sea, riverside nature reserve and open country. All suites with colour TV and beverage tray.

Vales Road, Budleigh Salterton, Devon EX9 6HS
Tel: 01395-443321
Fax: 01395-445220

BUNWELL Norfolk — 9E3

★★ Bunwell Manor
Bunwell, Nr Norwich NR16 1QU
☎ 01953-788304
10 bedrs, all ensuite, TCF TV ✻ P 30 SB £45 DB £65
HB £199-£235 D £13 CC MC Visa Amex

BURFORD Oxfordshire — 4A2

★★ Maytime
Asthall, Burford OX8 4HW
☎ 01993-822068 Fax 01993-822635
6 bedrs, all ensuite, TCF TV ✻ P 100 SB £47.50
DB £57.50 D £6 CC MC Visa Amex ♿

Elm House *Highly Acclaimed*
Meadow Lane, Fulbrook, Burford OX18 4BW
☎ 01993-823611 Fax 01993-823937

Cotswold country manor style house, with Stonesfield slate roof, gables, deep mullioned windows, Minster stone fireplaces and an elegant wide staircase, set in tranquil walled grounds.

7 bedrs, 6 ensuite, 1 ✻ TCF TV ✻ P 10 No children under 16 SB £41-£70 DB £50-£75 D £18 CC MC Visa JCB

BURNHAM-ON-CROUCH Essex — 5E2

★ Ye Olde White Harte
The Quay, Burnham-on-Crouch CM0 8AS
☎ 01621-782106 Fax 01621-782106
18 bedrs, 11 ensuite, 3 ✻ ✻ P 18 SB £20-£37 DB £36-£59 D £12.50 CC MC Visa

Anchor *Listed*
The Quay, Burnham-on-Crouch CM0 8AT
☎ 01621-782117
4 bedrs, all ensuite, TCF TV ✻ P 30 CC MC Visa DC 🅿 🅧

BURNHAM-ON-SEA Somerset — 3E2

★★ Royal Clarence
31 Esplanade, Burnham-on-Sea TA8 1BQ
☎ 01278-783138 Fax 01278-792965
19 bedrs, 18 ensuite, 1 ✻ TV ✻ P 18 CC MC Visa Amex DC

BURNLEY Lancashire — 10C3

★★ Comfort Friendly Inn
Keirby Walk, Burnley BB11 2DH
☎ 01282-427611 Fax 01282-436370
E Mail admin@gb608.u-net.com
50 bedrs, all ensuite, TCF TV ✻ 🅴 P 60 SB £47-£59
DB £54-£65 D £9.75 CC MC Visa Amex DC 🅧 ♿

★★ Rosehill House
Hospitality, Comfort merit awards
Rosehill Avenue, Burnley BB11 2PW
☎ 01282-453931 Fax 01282-455628
E Mail rhhotel@provider.co.uk
23 bedrs, all ensuite, TCF TV ✻ P 60 SB £27.50-£40
DB £39.50-£65 D £13 CC MC Visa Amex DC JCB 🅧

BURNSALL North Yorkshire — 10C3

★★ Fell
Burnsall BD23 6BT
☎ 01756-720209 Fax 01756-720605
14 bedrs, 13 ensuite, 1 ﾠ, 1 ✻ TCF TV P 65 SB £30.50-£33.50 DB £49-£55 HB £213.50-£234.50 D £14.95 CC MC Visa

★★ Red Lion
Burnsall BD23 6BU
☎ 01756-720204 Fax 01756-720292
E Mail redlion@daelnet.co.uk

Lovely 16th century ferryman's inn on the banks of the River Wharfe.

12 bedrs, 11 ensuite, 1 ✻ TCF TV P 40 SB £43-£52
DB £79-£86 HB £380 D £22.50 CC MC Visa Amex 🅿 ♿

BURTON IN KENDAL Cumbria — 10B3

★★ Clawthorpe Hall
Burton in Kendal LA6 1NU
☎ 01524-781166

RAC Hotel Reservations Service
0870 603 9109
(Calls charged at national call rate)

BURTON-UPON-TRENT Staffordshire 7F2

THE BASS MUSEUM

Horninglow St.,
Burton upon Trent,
Staffs DE14
Tel: 01283 511000

Museum of the history of Bass, Brewing and Beer. Features include a working 'N' Gauge model of Burton upon Trent dated 1921. An Edwardian Bar, "The Story of Brewing", historical fleet of horse drawn and motorised vehicles. Also the home of the famous "Bass Shire Horses". Fully licensed bars, restaurant and souvenir shop.
Open everyday except Christmas, Boxing and New Years day from 4pm-5pm (last admission 4pm).

Delter *Acclaimed*
5 Derby Road, Burton-upon-Trent DE14 1RU
☎ 01283-535115 Fax 01283-535115
5 bedrs, all ensuite, TCF TV P 8 SB £28.50 DB £39.50
D £10.50 CC MC Visa

BURWASH East Sussex 5D3

Woodlands Farm
Etchingham, Burwash TN19 7LA
☎ 01435-882794

A warm welcome awaits at this peaceful 16th century farmhouse, lying one third mile off the road surrounded by fields and wood. Fourposter ensuite, double, twin rooms, comfy beds, good breakfasts.

4 bedrs, 1 ensuite, 2 ⟶ P 5 SB £17.50-£25 DB £35-£40 D £8 ♿

BURY Lancashire 10C4

★★ **Bolholt**
Hospitality merit award
Walshaw Road, Bury BL8 1PU
☎ 0161-764 3888 Fax 0161-763 1789
57 bedrs, all ensuite, TCF TV P 250 SB £58 DB £58-£69
D £14.50 CC MC Visa Amex DC

BURY ST EDMUNDS Suffolk 9E4

Twelve Angel Hill *Highly Acclaimed*
12 Angel Hill, Bury St Edmunds IP33 1UZ
☎ 01284-704088 Fax 01284-725549
Closed Jan

Award winning hotel set in a Georgian terrace on the north side of Angel Hill, close to the cathedral and Abbey Gardens. Individually decorated rooms and a walled garden.

6 bedrs, all ensuite, TCF TV P 3 No children under 16 SB £45-£50 DB £70-£80 CC MC Visa Amex DC

Don't forget to mention the guide
When booking direct, please remember to tell the hotel that you chose it from
RAC Bed & Breakfast 1998.

BOLHOLT HOTEL

Exquisite 59 bedroom hotel set in 50 acres of parkland and lakes. Impressive leisure centre including swimming pool. Private fishing. Superb wedding venue.

WALSHAW ROAD,
BURY BL8 1PU
Tel: 0161-764 3888
Fax: 0161-763 1789

BUXTON – ENGLAND

Abbey *Acclaimed*
35 Southgate Street, Bury St Edmunds IP33 2AZ
☎ **01284-762020** Fax **01284-762020**
12 bedrs, all ensuite, 1 ➡ TCF TV P 12 SB £45 DB £65 CC
MC Visa Amex DC

Chantry *Acclaimed*
8 Sparhawk Street, Bury St Edmunds IP33 1RY
☎ **01284-767427** Fax **01284-760946**
16 bedrs, all ensuite, TCF TV ➤ P 16 SB £39.50 DB £58
D £15 CC MC Visa DC

BUTTERMERE Cumbria   10A2

★★ Bridge
Hospitality merit award
Buttermere CA13 9UZ
☎ **01768-770252** Fax **01768-770252**
22 bedrs, all ensuite, 1 ➡ TCF ➤ P 60 SB £34-£40
DB £69-£79 HB £315 D £20 CC MC Visa

BUXTON Derbyshire   8A1

★★ Grove
Grove Parade, Buxton SK17 6AJ
☎ **01298-79919** Fax **01298-77906**
21 bedrs, 11 ensuite, 6 ➡ TCF TV SB £27.50-£32.50
DB £40-£55 D £20 CC MC Visa JCB

★★ Portland
32 St John's Road, Buxton SK17 6XQ
☎ **01298-71493** Fax **01298-27464**
25 bedrs, all ensuite, TCF TV ➤ P 12 SB £35-£52 DB £58-£65 HB £292-£300 D £19.95
CC MC Visa Amex DC

★ Hartington
Hospitality merit award
18 Broad Walk, Buxton SK17 6JR
☎ **01298-22638** Fax **01298-22638**
Closed Christmas-New Year
16 bedrs, 9 ensuite, 3 ➡ TCF TV P 15 SB £22-£44
DB £44-£60 HB £205-£245 D £11
CC MC Visa Amex ♿

Brookfield On Longhill
Highly Acclaimed
Brookfield Hall, Longhill, Buxton SK17 6SU
☎ **01298-24151** Fax **01298-72231**

Coningsby *Highly Acclaimed*
6 Macclesfield Road, Buxton SK17 9AH
☎ **01298-26735** Fax **01298-26735**
Closed Nov-Jan
3 bedrs, all ensuite, TCF TV P 6 No children DB £45-£55 D £15

Netherdale *Highly Acclaimed*
16 Green Lane, Buxton SK17 9DP
☎ **01298-23896**
Closed Christmas-New Year

Quietly situated, stone-built Victorian house in a residential area, close to Pooles Cavern country park and Buxton town centre.

10 bedrs, 8 ensuite, 1 ⌂, 1 ➡ TCF TV P 12 No children under 4 SB £20-£21 DB £40-£42 HB £207-£220
D £12

Staden Grange Country House *Highly Acclaimed*
Ashbourne Road, Buxton SK17 9RZ
☎ **01298-24965** Fax **01298-72067**
Closed Christmas & New Year

A carefully extended spacious residence enjoying magnificent uninterrupted views over open farmland, one and a half miles from Buxton.

11 bedrs, 10 ensuite, 1 ⌂, 1 ➡ TCF TV ➤ P 20 SB £40-£50 DB £50-£65 D £18 CC MC Visa Amex DC

Thorn Heyes *Highly Acclaimed*
137 London Road, Buxton SK17 9NW
☎ **01298-23539**

Victorian elegance in family run hotel set in lovely grounds. Centrally heated rooms, TV, trouser press, tea and coffee facilities. Licenced. Also holiday apartments available.

11 bedrs, 10 ensuite, TCF TV P 12

BUXTON – ENGLAND

Westminster *Highly Acclaimed*
21 Broad Walk, Buxton SK17 6JR
☎ 01298-23929 Fax 01298-71121
12 bedrs, all ensuite, TCF TV P 12 SB £30 DB £47
HB £225 D £12 CC MC Visa Amex

Hawthorn Farm *Acclaimed*
Fairfield Road, Buxton SK17 7ED
☎ 01298-23230
Closed winter
12 bedrs, 5 ensuite, 2 TCF TV P 12 SB £22 DB £42-£50

Roseleigh *Listed*
19 Broad Walk, Buxton SK17 6JR
☎ 01298-24904
Closed Dec-Jan
14 bedrs, 10 ensuite, 3 TCF TV P 12 SB £20 DB £42-£44 HB £210-£220 D £11 CC MC Visa

Grosvenor House
1 Broad Walk, Buxton SK17 6JE
☎ 01298-72439 Fax 01298-72439

A privately run, licensed Victorian residence overlooking Broad Walk Promenade and Pavilion Gardens/Opera House. Light and airy, tastefully decorated and furnished throughout. Excellent home-cooked traditional cuisine. Which? recommended.

8 bedrs, all ensuite, TCF TV No children under 8
SB £42.50-£47.50 DB £50-£70 HB £250-£300 D £15

CADNAM Hampshire   4B4

Old Well *Listed*
Romsey Road, Copythorne, Cadnam SO40 2PE
☎ 01703-812321 Fax 01703-812700

The Old Well is situated on the edge of the New Forest at Copythorne. We are within easy reach of Southampton, Bournemouth, Salisbury, Winchester and Portsmouth.

6 bedrs, 3 ensuite, 2 TV P 10 CC MC Visa

CALLINGTON Cornwall   2C3

Manor House Inn *Listed*
Rilla Mill, Callington PL17 7NT
☎ 01579-362354 Fax 01579-363305
12 bedrs, all ensuite, TCF TV P 41 SB £25 DB £50 D £4.50
CC MC Visa JCB

CALNE Wiltshire   4A2

★★ **Lansdowne Strand**
The Strand, Calne SN11 0EH
☎ 01249-812488 Fax 01249-815323
E Mail ish@ukbusiness.com
26 bedrs, all ensuite, TCF TV P 25 SB £53-£57 DB £68-£74 HB £245-£294 D £11.75 CC MC Visa Amex DC

CAMBERLEY Surrey   4C3

Camberley *Listed*
116 London Road, Camberley GU15 3TJ
☎ 01276-24410 Fax 01276-65409
Closed Christmas
6 bedrs, 4 ensuite, 2 TCF TV P 10 SB £45 DB £55
CC MC Visa

CAMBRIDGE Cambridgeshire   9D4

★★ **Arundel House**
Comfort, Restaurant merit awards
Chesterton Road, Cambridge CB4 3AN
☎ 01223-367701 Fax 01223-367721
Closed Christmas

Beautifully located overlooking the River Cam and open parkland, this elegant terrace hotel offers some of the best food in the area. Close to city centre.

105 bedrs, 99 ensuite, 5 TCF TV P 70 SB £39.50-£67.50 DB £62.50-£89 D £15.95 CC MC Visa Amex DC

★★ Bridge
Clayhythe, Nr Waterbeach, Cambridge CB5 9ND
📞 01223-860252 Fax 01223-440448

An old world inn on the banks of the River Cam, set in countryside some four miles from Cambridge.

30 bedrs, 20 ensuite, 10 🛏, **TCF TV ⛔ P** 70 **SB** £30-£35 **DB** £45-£55 **D** £15 **CC** MC Visa Amex

★★ Centennial
Comfort merit award
63/71 Hills Road, Cambridge CB2 1PG
📞 01223-314652 Fax 01223-315443
Closed Christmas-New Year
39 bedrs, all ensuite, **TCF TV P** 32 **SB** £65-£70 **DB** £80-£88 **D** £15 **CC** MC Visa Amex DC

Aylesbray Lodge *Highly Acclaimed*
5 Mowbray Road, Cambridge CB1 4RS
📞 01223-240089 Fax 01223-240089

Comfort is our priority at Aylesbray Lodge. High standards of cleanliness and decoration throughout. All rooms ensuite with complimentry extras, incoming telephones.

6 bedrs, all ensuite, **TCF TV P** 6 **SB** £28 **DB** £40-£45 **CC** MC Visa Amex DC

Brooklands *Highly Acclaimed*
95 Cherry Hinton Road, Cambridge CB1 4BS
📞 01223-242035 Fax 01223-242035
5 bedrs, all ensuite, **TCF TV P** 5 **SB** £28-£30 **DB** £38-£45 **CC** MC Visa Amex DC JCB

Cambridge Lodge *Highly Acclaimed*
139 Huntingdon Road, Cambridge CB3 0DQ
📞 01223-352833 Fax 01223-355166
13 bedrs, 10 ensuite, 3 🛏, 1 ⛔ **TCF TV ⛔ P** 23 **SB** £56 **DB** £70 **D** £20 **CC** MC Visa Amex DC

ASSISI GUEST HOUSE

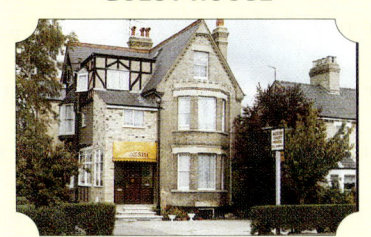

Fine detached Victorian house ideally situated for the city centre and the famous Addenbrookes Hospital. Family run guest house offering personal service. Spacious rooms with all modern facilities including showers and colour TV in all rooms.
Full English breakfast, ample garden with large car park.

Single £27-£30; Double £37-£40; Family £51

193 CHERRY HINTON, CAMBRIDGE CB1 4BX
Tel: 01223 246648/211466   Fax: 01223 412900

Lensfield *Highly Acclaimed*
53 Lensfield Road, Cambridge CR2 1GH
📞 01223-355017 Fax 01223-312022
32 bedrs, 27 ensuite, 1 🛏, 2 ⛔ **TCF TV P** 5 **SB** £42-£45 **DB** £55-£65 **HB** £350-£371 **D** £7 **CC** MC Visa Amex DC

Assisi *Acclaimed*
193 Cherry Hinton Road, Cambridge CB1 4BX
📞 01223-211466 Fax 01223-412900
Closed 17 Dec-8 Jan
17 bedrs, all ensuite, **TCF TV ⛔ P** 15 **SB** £28-£31 **DB** £39-£42 **CC** MC Visa

Bon Accord House *Acclaimed*
20 St Margarets Square, (off Cherry Hinton Road), Cambridge CB1 4AP
📞 01223-411188
E Mail bon.accord.house@dial.pipex.com
Closed Christmas-New Year
9 bedrs, 1 ensuite, 2 ⛔ **TCF TV ⛔ P** 9 **SB** £21-£30 **DB** £36-£44 **CC** MC Visa

Cristinas *Acclaimed*
47 St Andrews Road, Cambridge CB4 1DL
📞 01223-327700 Fax 01223-365855
Closed 24-26 Dec
9 bedrs, 7 ensuite, **TCF TV P** 8 **SB** £32-£47 **DB** £40-£48

De Freville House *Acclaimed*
166 Chesterton Road, Cambridge CB4 1DA
📞 01223-354993 Fax 01223-321890
9 bedrs, 5 ensuite, 2 ⛔ **TV** ⛔ No children under 6 **SB** £26-£30 **DB** £45-£50

CAMBRIDGE – ENGLAND

Suffolk House *Acclaimed*
69 Milton Road, Cambridge CB4 1XA
📞 01223-352016 Fax 01223-566816
8 bedrs, all ensuite, **TCF TV P** 9 No children under 7
SB £40-£50 **DB** £50-£68 **CC** MC Visa Amex JCB

Arbury Lodge *Listed*
82 Arbury Road, Cambridge CB4 2JE
📞 01223-364319 Fax 01223-566988

Comfortably furnished family run guest house. Situated north east of the city with easy access to the town centre and A14. Garden and private parking.

5 bedrs, 2 ensuite, 3 **TCF TV P** 9 **SB** £20-£24 **DB** £26-£45

Ashtrees *Listed*
128 Perne Road, Cambridge CB1 3RR
📞 01223-411233
Closed Christmas & New year

A small family run guest house on a main bus route. Convenient for the city centre, railway station and Addenbrooke's Hospital. A small garden is available for guests' use.

7 bedrs, 1 ensuite, 1 **TCF TV P** 6 **SB** £19 **DB** £36-£42 **D** £9 **CC** MC Visa JCB

Avimore *Listed*
310 Cherry Hinton Road, Cambridge CB1 4AU
📞 01223-410956 Fax 01223-576957
4 bedrs, 3 ensuite, 2 **TCF TV P** 5 **SB** £18 **DB** £34 **CC** MC Visa DC

Acorn
154 Chesterton Road, Cambridge CB4 1DA
📞 01223-353888 Fax 01223-350527

Hamden
89 High Street, Cherryhinton, Cambridge CB1 4LU
📞 01223-413263

The owner of this guest house guarantees that you will not be disappointed with our comfortable ensuite bedrooms. Most of the rooms have a garden view. Pubs and restaurants within walking distance.

5 bedrs, all ensuite, **TCF TV P** 7 **SB** £25-£28 **DB** £40-£45

Home From Home
39 Milton Road, Cambridge CB4 1XA
📞 01223-323555 Fax 01223-323555

Welcome to our comfortably furnished family home situated 10 minutes walk from the city centre. All bedrooms are spacious, with colour TV and tea/coffee facilities.

3 bedrs, all ensuite, **TCF TV P** 3 **DB** £40-£50

Manor Farm
Landbeach, Cambridge CB4 4ED
📞 01223-860165

Grade II Listed farmhouse with secluded walled gardens and ample parking. The rooms are individually decorated and are ensuite or with private bath, equipped with TV, tea/coffee facilities and radio.

3 bedrs, all ensuite, **TCF TV P** 10 **SB** £25 **DB** £38

CANTERBURY — ENGLAND 69

SLEEPERZ HOTEL
CAMBRIDGE

Located in a converted warehouse Sleeperz is a new hotel which has been designed in a contemporary manner to provide comfort and style for the independently minded traveller. Sleeperz is situated in the beautiful and historic City of Cambridge, which is readily accessible by road from London (M11) to the east by road and rail from Harwick and by air via Stansted. Sleeperz is conveniently near Cambridge Railway Station and has free car parking. From £36 per room Sleeperz is outstanding value for money.

STATION ROAD, CAMBRIDGE CB1 2TZ
Telephone: 01223 304050 Fax: 01223 357286

Sleeperz Hotel
Station Road, Cambridge CB1 2TZ
☏ 01223-304050 Fax 01223-357286
25 bedrs, all ensuite, TCF TV P 10 DB £36-£49

CANTERBURY Kent 5E3

THANINGTON HOTEL

Spacious Georgian Bed and Breakfast Hotel ideally situated 10 minutes stroll from the City centre. 15 en-suite bedrooms, beautifully decorated and furnished, all in immaculate condition with modern day extras. King-size 4 poster beds, antique bedsteads and 2 large family rooms. Walled garden with patio, indoor heated swimming pool, intimate bar, guest lounge and snooker/games room. Delicious breakfast served in the elegant dining room. Secure private car park. An oasis in a busy tourist city, convenient for channel ports, tunnel and historic houses of Kent. Gatwick 60 minutes.

140 Wincheap, Canterbury, Kent CT1 3RY
Tel: 01227-453227 Fax: 01227-453225

WALTHAM COURT HOTEL
AND
CHIVES RESTAURANT

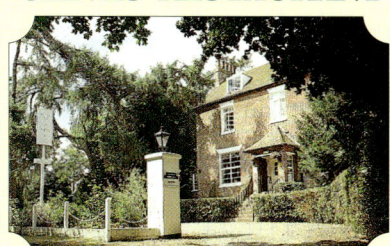

Built in 1796 as a Poorhouse, Waltham Court became a Hotel in 1984. Set amidst beautiful gardens in the Kent Weald, only 12 mins from Canterbury and 20 from the Channel Tunnel. All rooms are en-suite and fully equipped. The Restaurant 'Chives', has a good reputation for quality, creative food, offering Game, meat, fish, vegetarian and vegan dishes.

KAKE STREET, PETHAM,
CANTERBURY CT4 5BS
Tel: 01227 700413 Fax: 01227 700127

★★ Canterbury
71 New Dover Road, Canterbury CT1 3DZ
📞 **01227-450551 Fax 01227-780145**
26 bedrs, all ensuite, TCF TV 🐕 ⓘ P 40 SB £45-£48
DB £58-£68 D £13.50 CC MC Visa Amex DC JCB

★★ Ebury
Hospitality, Comfort merit awards
65-67 New Dover Road, Canterbury CT1 3DX
📞 **01227-768433 Fax 01227-459187**
Closed 15 Dec-15 Jan
15 bedrs, all ensuite, TCF TV 🐕 P 30 SB £45-£50 DB £60-£68 HB £250-£275 D £13 CC MC Visa Amex 🆔

Thanington *Highly Acclaimed*
140 Wincheap, Canterbury CT1 3RY
📞 **01227-453227 Fax 01227-453225**

Georgian Grade II Listed building linked to ten purpose built ensuite bedrooms by a conservatory in 1987. The distinctive black cowls over the first floor were added in 1837.

15 bedrs, all ensuite, 2 🐾 TCF TV 🐕 P 10 SB £43-£50
DB £65-£75 CC MC Visa Amex DC JCB 🆔 🐾
See advert on previous page

Waltham Court *Highly Acclaimed*
Kake Street, Petham, Canterbury CT4 5BS
📞 **01227-700413 Fax 01227-700127**
4 bedrs, all ensuite, TCF TV P 60 SB £40-£45 DB £60-£65
HB £230-£250 D £15 CC MC Visa Amex
See advert on previous page

Ersham Lodge *Acclaimed*
12 New Dover Road, Canterbury CT1 3AP
📞 **01227-463174 Fax 01227-455482**
Closed Jan, Feb
13 bedrs, 12 ensuite, 1 🐾 TCF TV P 11 SB £38-£47
DB £52-£61 CC MC Visa Amex

Oriel Lodge *Acclaimed*
3 Queens Avenue, Canterbury CT2 8AY
📞 **01227-462845 Fax 01227-462845**

Attractive Edwardian house in a tree-lined residential avenue near city centre. Afternoon tea in the garden or in lounge, log fire, parking.

6 bedrs, 2 ensuite, 2 🐾 TCF TV P 6 No children under 6 SB £22-£28 DB £38-£58 CC MC Visa JCB

Woodpeckers Country *Acclaimed*
Womenswold, Canterbury CT4 6HB
📞 **01227-831319 Fax 01227-831403**
11 bedrs, all ensuite, 2 🐾 TCF TV 🐕 P 40 CC MC Visa
🆔 🐾 ♿

Castle Court *Listed*
8 Castle Street, Canterbury CT1 2QF
📞 **01227-463441 Fax 01227-463441**
10 bedrs, 5 ensuite, 3 🐾 TV 🐕 P 4 SB £18-£25 DB £32-£48 CC MC Visa

Pointers *Listed*
1 London Road, Canterbury CT2 8LR
📞 **01227-456846 Fax 01227-831131**
E Mail pointers.hotel@pop.dial.pipex.com
Closed 23 Dec-14 Jan
12 bedrs, 11 ensuite, 1 🐾 TCF TV 🐕 P 8 SB £35-£40
DB £50-£60 HB £256-£280 D £14 CC MC Visa Amex DC JCB

Cathedral Gate
36 Burgate, Canterbury CT1 2HA
📞 **01227-464381 Fax 01227-462800**

Family run medieval hotel in the heart of Canterbury with cathedral and Burgate premium shops at its doorstep. Massive beams, sloping floors, winding corridors and a warm welcome await. Parking 500 yards away.

24 bedrs, 12 ensuite, 3 🐾 TCF TV 🐕 P 8 SB £22-£55
DB £40-£85 D £10 CC MC Visa Amex DC

Chaucer Lodge
62 New Dover Road, Canterbury CT1 3DT
📞 01227-459141 Fax 01227-459141

All rooms with private facilities. Family run with high standards of accommodation and service. Very close to cricket ground and hospitals. Ten minutes walk to city centre and cathedral. Secure parking

6 bedrs, 5 ensuite, 1 🐕, TCF TV P 10 SB £20-£25 DB £40-£48

Crockshard Farmhouse
Wingham, Canterbury CT3 1NY
📞 01227-720464 Fax 01227-721125

Exceptionally attractive large period farmhouse in beautiful gardens and countryside. Close to the Channel and centrally located for visiting the whole of Kent.

5 bedrs, 2 ensuite, 3 🐕 TCF 🐾 P 20 DB £35-£45

Magnolia House
36 St Dunstan's Terrace, Canterbury CT2 8AX
📞 01227-765121 Fax 01227-765121

A special bed & breakfast in quiet pleasant surroundings, ten minutes walk from the city centre. 1995 Gold winner of the 'Welcome to Kent' Hospitality Award sponsored by Hoverspeed. Evening meals by prior arrangement November to February.

7 bedrs, all ensuite, TCF TV ✉ P 5 No children under 12 SB £36-£45 DB £60-£80 D £18 CC MC Visa Amex

Pilgrims
18 The Friars, Canterbury CT1 2AS
📞 01227-464531 Fax 01227-762514

All bedrooms have ensuite bathrooms, central heating, colour television, direct dial telephones, electric shaver points and tea & coffee making facilities. Also coach parties welcome for dinners up to 70 people.

14 bedrs, all ensuite, TCF TV SB £35-£45 DB £50-£55 D £4.95 CC MC Visa

Renville Oast
Bridge, Canterbury CT4 5AD
📞 01227-830215 Fax 01227-764844
Closed Christmas

A 150 year old oasthouse in beautiful Kent countryside, only two miles from the cathedral city of Canterbury. Comfortable rooms. Tea and coffee making facilities. TV lounge. Open all year. A friendly welcome.

3 bedrs, all ensuite, TCF ✉ P 6 SB £25-£30 DB £45-£50

RAC Hotel Reservations Service
0870 603 9109
(Calls charged at national call rate)

CANTERBURY – ENGLAND

South Wootton House
Capel Lane, Perham, Canterbury CT4 5RG
☎ 01227-700643 Fax 01227-700613

A beautiful farmhouse with conservatory, set in extensive garden, surrounded by fields and woodland. Fully fitted co-ordinated bedrooms with private bathroom. Tea/coffee facilities. Children and dogs welcome.

2 bedrs, both ensuite, **TCF** TV 🐕 **SB** £20 **DB** £38

CARBIS BAY Cornwall   2A4

★★ **Boskerris**
Hospitality, Comfort merit awards
Boskerris Road, Carbis Bay TR26 2NQ
☎ 01736-795295 Fax 01736-798632
19 bedrs, 17 ensuite, 2 ⬅ 🐕 **P** 20 **CC** MC Visa Amex DC

CARLISLE Cumbria   10B1

★★ **Pinegrove**
262 London Road, Carlisle CA1 2QS
☎ 01228-524828 Fax 01228-810941
32 bedrs, 29 ensuite, 4 ⬅ **TCF** TV 🐕 **P** 50 **SB** £44 **DB** £56 **D** £14 **CC** MC Visa Amex DC 🐕 ♿

★★ **Tarn End House**
Talkin Tarn, Brampton, Carlisle CA8 1LS
☎ 01697-72340 Fax 01697-72089
7 bedrs, all ensuite, **TCF** TV 🐕 **P** 40 **SB** £39-£48 **DB** £55-£69 **HB** £237-£275 **D** £14 **CC** MC Visa Amex ♿

★ **Vallum House**
Burgh Road, Carlisle CA2 7NB
☎ 01228-521860
9 bedrs, 5 ensuite, 2 ⬅ **TCF** TV 🐕 **P** 18 **SB** £25-£35 **DB** £40-£50 **HB** £220-£250 **D** £5 **CC** MC Visa ♿

Bessiestown Farm Country Guest House
Highly Acclaimed
Catlowdy, Nr Longtown, Carlisle CA6 5QP
☎ 01228-577219 Fax 01228-577219

Pretty, well appointed ensuite bedrooms, with family and ground floor bedrooms in comfortable courtyard cottages. Delightful dining room and lounge bar. Delicious food. Indoor pool (open May-September).

4 bedrs, all ensuite, **TCF** TV **P** 10 **SB** £27-£30 **DB** £43-£47 **HB** £140-£150 **D** £11 **CC** MC Visa

Angus *Acclaimed*
14 Scotland Road, Carlisle CA3 9DG
☎ 01228-523546 Fax 01228-531895
E Mail england.angus@world-traveler.com
12 bedrs, 9 ensuite, 1 ⬅ **TCF** TV 🐕 **P** 6 **SB** £38-£42 **DB** £49-£54 **D** £12 **CC** MC Visa Amex

Avondale *Acclaimed*
3 St Aidans Road, Carlisle CA1 1LT
☎ 01228-523012

Attractive Edwardian house in quiet situation, yet close to M6 (jn43) and city centre. Well appointed and spacious rooms. Private parking.

3 bedrs, 1 ensuite, 1 ⬅ **TCF** TV **P** 3 **SB** £20-£25 **DB** £38-£40 **D** £8

Corner House *Acclaimed*
4 Grey Street, London Road, Carlisle CA1 2JP
☎ 01228-533239 Fax 01228-546678

Open all year with family and fourposter rooms available. A good base for golf, racing, walking, city attractions, touring lakes and Roman wall. Easy access for bus and trains. M6 j42 or j43.

10 bedrs, 8 ensuite, 2 🛁, 1 🐕 TCF TV 🍴 SB £20-£30 DB £38-£42 HB £210 D £7 CC MC Visa JCB 🍽

Courtfield *Acclaimed*
169 Warwick Road, Carlisle CA1 1LP
📞 01228-522767
Closed Christmas
4 bedrs, all ensuite, TV 🗹 🐕 P 4 DB £32-£35

East View *Acclaimed*
110 Warwick Road, Carlisle CA1 1JU
📞 01228-522112

Friendly family run guest house, centrally situated. Private facilities, welcome tray and colour televisions in all rooms. Hair dryers available. Walking distance from city centre. 1 mile from M6 (j43).

8 bedrs, all ensuite, TCF TV P 4 SB £18-£20 DB £32-£35

Royal *Acclaimed*
9 Lowther Street, Carlisle CA3 8ES
📞 01228-522103 Fax 01228-523904
23 bedrs, 15 ensuite, 3 🐕 TCF TV 🍴 SB £21-£30 DB £35-£51 D £6 CC MC Visa 🍽

Warren *Listed*
368 Warwick Road, Carlisle CA1 2RU
📞 01228-533663 Fax 01228-533663
6 bedrs, 5 ensuite, 3 🐕 TCF TV P 6 SB £20-£24 DB £34-£36 D £6.50 ♿

Craigburn Farm
Catlowdy, Nr Longtown, Carlisle CA6 5QP
📞 01228-577214 Fax 01228-577014

One of the best farmhouses for delicious food, deserts a speciality. Cosy and friendly, beautiful bedrooms, some fourposter. Stop over to and from Scotland and Northern Ireland.

6 bedrs, all ensuite, TCF TV 🍴 P 20 SB £26-£28 DB £42-£46 HB £180 D £11 CC MC Visa

Kingstown
246 Kingstown Road, Carlisle CA3 0DE
📞 01228-515292 Fax 01228-515292

Small family hotel, conveniently situated a quarter mile from the M6 (jn 44), offering well priced standard and ensuite accommodation. Licensed restaurant. Car park. Convenient for the Lakes and Hadrian's Wall.

8 bedrs, 7 ensuite, TCF TV 🍴 P 12 SB £35 DB £42 D £7.95 CC MC Visa Amex ♿

CARLTON-IN-COVERDALE North Yorkshire 10C2

Foresters Arms *Acclaimed*
Carlton-in-Coverdale, Leyburn DL8 4BB
📞 01969-640272 Fax 01969-640272
3 bedrs, all ensuite, TCF TV 🍴 P 10 SB £35 DB £60 D £25 CC MC Visa

CARNFORTH Lancashire 10B3

★★ Royal Station
Market Street, Carnforth LA5 9BT
📞 01524-733636 Fax 01524-720267
12 bedrs, all ensuite, 4 🐕 TCF TV 🍴 P 7 SB £28 DB £43 CC MC Visa Amex DC 🍽

CASTLE CARY Somerset 3E2

★★ George
Restaurant merit award
Market Place, Castle Cary BA7 7AH
📞 01963-350761 Fax 01963-350035
15 bedrs, all ensuite, TCF TV 🍴 P 10 SB £45 DB £75-£85 D £18 CC MC Visa Amex JCB ♿

CASTLE DONINGTON Leicestershire　　　7F2

Donington Park Farmhouse *Highly Acclaimed*
Melbourne Road, Isley Walton, Castle Donington DE74 2RN
☎ 01332-862409 Fax 01332-862364
Closed Christmas
11 bedrs, all ensuite, TCF TV P 15 SB £46-£50 DB £60-£70 D £15 CC MC Visa Amex DC JCB

Four Poster *Listed*
73 Clapgun Street, Castle Donington DE7 2LF
☎ 01332-810335 Fax 01332-812418
11 bedrs, 5 ensuite, 2 TCF TV P 20 SB £15-£25 DB £36-£50

CATTERICK North Yorkshire　　　11D2

★★ Bridge House
Catterick DL10 7PE
☎ 01748-818331 Fax 01748-818331
16 bedrs, 13 ensuite, 2 TCF TV P 72 SB £36-£40 DB £52-£55 HB £250-£300 D £12.50 CC MC Visa Amex DC

CHAGFORD Devon　　　2C3

★★ Three Crowns
High Street, Chagford TQ13 8AJ
☎ 01647-433444 Fax 01647-433117
16 bedrs, 15 ensuite, 3 TCF TV P 20 CC MC Visa Amex DC

Blackaller *Highly Acclaimed*
North Bovey, Chagford TQ13 8QY
☎ 01647-640322 Fax 01647-640322
Closed Jan-Feb
6 bedrs, all ensuite, TCF TV P 7 No children under 13

CHARMOUTH Dorset　　　3E3

★★ Hensleigh
Lower Sea Lane, Charmouth DT6 6LW
☎ 01297-560830
Closed Nov-Feb
11 bedrs, all ensuite, TCF TV P 30 No children under 3 SB £25-£27 DB £50-£54 HB £245-£260 D £14 CC MC Visa Amex

★★ Queens Armes
The Street, Charmouth DT6 6QF
☎ 01297-560339
Closed Nov-mid Feb
11 bedrs, 10 ensuite, TCF TV P 20 SB £30 HB £250 D £7 CC MC Visa

Newlands House *Acclaimed*
Stonebarrow Lane, Charmouth DT6 6RA
☎ 01297-560212
Closed Nov-Feb

A house of character set in its own grounds and garden on the eastern fringe of Charmouth village, offering excellent food and an ambience of quiet relaxation. The hotel is set in an area of outstanding natural beauty near the coastal footpaths.

12 bedrs, 11 ensuite, 1 TCF TV P 15 No children under 6 SB £23.75-£27 DB £47.50-£54 HB £241-£261 D £14.50

CHATTERIS Cambridgeshire　　　9D3

★ Cross Keys
16 Market Hill, Chatteris PE16 6BA
☎ 01354-692644 Fax 01354-693036
7 bedrs, 5 ensuite, 1 TCF TV P 10 SB £22 DB £33 D £15 CC MC Visa Amex DC JCB

CROSS KEYS

This delightful 16th century inn offers old world charm, traditional hospitality and friendly service. Situated at the junction of the A141 and A142 in the heart of the Fens, it is ideally placed for touring East Anglia.

**16 MARKET HILL,
CHATTERIS PE16 6BA
Tel: 01354-692644
Fax: 01354-693036**

CHELMSFORD – ENGLAND

CHEADLE Staffordshire　7E1

Manor Guest House & Restaurant *Listed*
Watt Place, Cheadle ST10 1NZ
☎ 01538-753450

Royal Oak *Listed*
69 High Street, Cheadle ST10 1AN
☎ 01538-753116 Fax 01538-753116
10 bedrs, 9 ensuite, 1 ➤ TCF TV ✱ CC   MC Visa

Mucelli's Restaurant & Guest Rooms
2 Charles Street, Cheadle ST10 1ED
☎ 01538-753836 Fax 01538-754650

Next to a Pugin church and ideal for couples or single occupants, Mucelli's Tuscan restaurant and guest rooms offers high standards in food and accommodation.

2 bedrs, both ensuite, TCF TV No children under 16
SB £30 DB £40 D £10

CHEDDAR Somerset　3E1

★ Gordon's
Cliff Street, Cheddar BS27 3PT
☎ 01934-742497 Fax 01934-744965
Closed mid Dec-mid Jan
15 bedrs, 9 ensuite, 2 ☎, 2 ➤ TCF TV ✱ P 8 SB £19-£20
DB £37-£38 D £9 CC   MC Visa DC

RAC Hotel Reservations Service

Use the RAC Reservations Service and you'll never have another sleepless night worrying about accommodation.
We can guarantee you a room almost anywhere in the UK and Ireland.
The price of a national call is all it takes.
The service is free to RAC Members.

0870 603 9109

Market Cross *Acclaimed*
Church Street, The Cross, Cheddar BS27 3RA
☎ 01934-742264
Closed Nov

An elegant Regency hotel with an original flagstone hallway and marble fireplaces, offering a high standard of accommodation. Situated minutes from the Cheddar Gorge and caves.

6 bedrs, 3 ensuite, 1 ➤ TCF TV P 6 SB £19.50-£21.50
DB £39-£47 D £12 CC   MC Visa

CHELMSFORD Essex　5E2

★★ Saracens Head
3-5 High Street, Chelmsford CM1 1BE
☎ 01245-262368 Fax 01245-062418
18 bedrs, all ensuite, TCF TV ✱ CC   MC Visa Amex DC

Snows Oaklands *Highly Acclaimed*
240 Springfield Road, Chelmsford CM2 6BP
☎ 01245-352004
16 bedrs, 14 ensuite, 1 ☎, 1 ➤ P 14 ♿

Boswell House *Acclaimed*
118-120 Springfield Road, Chelmsford CM2 6LF
☎ 01245-287587 Fax 01245-287587
Closed Christmas-New Year
13 bedrs, all ensuite, TCF TV P 13 SB £45-£48 DB £60
D £12 CC   MC Visa Amex DC JCB

Beechcroft *Listed*
211 New London Road, Chelmsford CM2 0AJ
☎ 01245-352462 Fax 01245-347833
Closed Christmas-New Year
20 bedrs, 10 ensuite, 4 ➤ TCF TV ✱ P 15 SB £31-£39
DB £44-£54 CC   MC Visa

Tanunda *Listed*
217-219 New London Road, Chelmsford CM2 0AJ
☎ 01245-354295 Fax 01245-345503
20 bedrs, 11 ensuite, 3 ➤ TCF TV P 20 SB £30-£45
DB £43.50-£53 CC   MC Visa Amex DC JCB

CHELTENHAM – ENGLAND

CHELTENHAM Gloucestershire   7E4

★★ **Allards Hotel & Restaurant**
Shurdington Road, Cheltenham GL51 5XA
☎ 01242-862498 Fax 01242-863017
12 bedrs, all ensuite, 1 ⇨ TCF TV P 50 SB £39-£41
DB £57-£62 HB £210-£320 D £14 CC MC Visa Amex JCB

Beaumont House *Highly Acclaimed*
Shurdington Road, Cheltenham GL53 0JE
☎ 01242-245986 Fax 01242-520044
Closed Christmas

Excellently situated where Cheltenham meets the Cotswolds. Close to good restaurants, the Montpellier antique area and secluded Cotswold walks. Enjoy gentle relaxation in our elegant surroundings, garden, private parking.

15 bedrs, all ensuite, 1 ⇨ TCF TV P 20 No children under 10 SB £37 DB £48-£62 HB £280 D £18 CC MC Visa Amex

LYPIATT HOUSE

Lypiatt Road, Cheltenham,
Glos. GL50 2QW
Tel: 01242 224994 Fax: 01242 224996
Proprietors: Jane & Michael Medforth

Lypiatt House is a charming Victorian villa set in its grounds with private parking. It is situated in Montpelier – the most attractive area of Cheltenham – offering a variety of good restaurants and fine shops. There is an elegant drawing room and a delightful conservatory with an 'honesty bar'. The emphasis is on relaxation with a professional, personal and friendly service. Ideally situated to explore the Cotswolds and surrounding areas.

Cotswold Grange *Highly Acclaimed*
Pittville Circus Road, Cheltenham GL52 2QH
☎ 01242-515119 Fax 01242-241537
Closed Christmas
25 bedrs, all ensuite, TCF TV ⇥ P 20 SB £45-£70 DB £54-£70 D £8 CC MC Visa Amex DC

Hannaford's *Highly Acclaimed*
20 Evesham Road, Cheltenham GL52 2AB
☎ 01242-515181 Fax 01242-257571
Closed 24 Dec-1 Jan
8 bedrs, all ensuite, TCF TV SB £35-£45 DB £55-£65 CC MC Visa Amex

Hilden Lodge *Highly Acclaimed*
271 London Road, Charlton Kings, Cheltenham GL52 6YL
☎ 01242-583242 Fax 01242-263511

An elegant Regency style hotel set in its own grounds within easy reach of Cheltenham town centre, the Cotswold Way and the many beautiful villages. Bar and restaurant serving fresh English cuisine.

10 bedrs, all ensuite, 1 ⇨ TCF TV ⇥ P 10 SB £30-£35 DB £40-£50 HB £220-£245 D £10 CC MC Visa Amex JCB ♿

Hollington House *Highly Acclaimed*
115 Hales Road, Cheltenham GL52 6ST
☎ 01242-256652 Fax 01242-570280

A spacious, well equipped Victorian house, where excellent standards are maintained by the resident proprietors. Large garden. Conveniently situated near the town centre and 700 yards from the A40 with ample free parking. German and French spoken.

9 bedrs, 8 ensuite, 1 ⇨ TCF TV P 16 No children under 3 SB £35-£45 DB £45-£60 D £12 CC MC Visa Amex

CHELTENHAM – ENGLAND

Lypiatt House *Highly Acclaimed*
Lypiatt Road, Cheltenham GL50 2QW
☎ 01242-224994 Fax 01242-224996
10 bedrs, all ensuite, TCF TV P 14 No children under 12
CC MC Visa Amex

Milton House *Highly Acclaimed*
12 Royal Parade, Bayshill Road, Cheltenham GL50 3AY
☎ 01242-582601 Fax 01242-222326
Closed Christmas & New Year

Relax in elegance and comfort in this beautiful Grade II Listed Regency hotel in the charming, peaceful Montpellier area, a short walk from the shops of the Promenade.

8 bedrs, all ensuite, TCF TV P 6 SB £39 DB £52-£68 CC MC Visa Amex DC

Moorend Park *Highly Acclaimed*
Moorend Park Road, Cheltenham GL53 0LA
☎ 01242-224441 Fax 01242-572413
10 bedrs, all ensuite, TCF TV P 30 SB £36-£43 DB £46-£55 D £15 CC MC Visa Amex JCB

Abbey *Acclaimed*
16 Bath Parade, Cheltenham GL53 7HN
☎ 01242-516053 Fax 01242-513034
13 bedrs, 7 ensuite, 6, 1 TCF TV SB £35-£40 DB £58-£65 HB £280 D £17.50 CC MC Visa Amex

Hallery House *Acclaimed*
48 Shurdington Road, Cheltenham GL53 0JE
☎ 01242-578450 Fax 01242-529730
E Mail hallery.house@bigfoot.com
15 bedrs, 10 ensuite, 2 TCF TV P 20 SB £23-£38 DB £42-£68 D £13.50 CC MC Visa Amex DC JCB

Willoughby House *Acclaimed*
1 Suffolk Square, Cheltenham GL50 2DR
☎ 01242-522798 Fax 01242-256369
15 bedrs, all ensuite, TCF TV P 15 CC Visa

Broomhill *Listed*
218 London Road, Cheltenham GL52 6HW
☎ 01242-513086 Fax 01242-513086
3 bedrs, 2 ensuite, 2 TCF TV P 4 SB £18-£19 DB £34-£36 CC MC Visa Amex DC JCB

Colesbourne Inn *Listed*
Colesbourne GL53 9NP
☎ 01242-870376 Fax 01242-870397
9 bedrs, all ensuite, TCF TV P 50 SB £38-£42 DB £56-£62 CC MC Visa JCB

Cleeve Hill Hotel

GOOD HOTEL GUIDE
CHARMING SMALL HOTEL GUIDE

TOTALLY NON SMOKING

ETB DELUXE

WHICH HOTEL GUIDE 1995 COUNTY HOTEL OF THE YEAR

This award-winning hotel offers the ultimate in bed and breakfast situated near the summit of the highest hill in the Cotswolds. All rooms have superb views to the Malvern Hills or Cleeve Common, yet we are only 10 mins from Cheltenham. Bedrooms are extremely comfortable and elegantly furnished with co-ordinating designer fabrics and all have ensuite facilities.

CLEEVE HILL, CHELTENHAM, GLOS GL52 3PR
Tel: 01242 672052 Fax: 01242 679969

Ivy Dene House *Listed*
145 Hewlett Road, Cheltenham GL52 6TS
☎ **01242-521726**

A charming house in its own grounds which is within walking distance of both the park and the town centre.

9 bedrs, 5 ensuite, 2 🛁 **TCF TV** 🐾 **P** 4 **SB** £20-£25 **DB** £40-£50

Leeswood *Listed*
14 Montpellier Drive, Cheltenham GL50 1TX
☎ **01242-524813 Fax 01242-524813**
8 bedrs, 2 ensuite, 2 🛁 **TCF TV** **P** 7 No children under 10 **SB** £17-£25 **DB** £34-£38 **CC** MC Visa

Montpellier *Listed*
33 Montpellier Terrace, Cheltenham GL50 1UX
☎ **01242-526009**
5 bedrs, 4 ensuite, 1 🐾, 1 🛁 **TCF TV SB** £21-£26 **DB** £38-£45

North Hall *Listed*
Pittville Circus Road, Cheltenham GL52 2PZ
☎ **01242-520589 Fax 01242-261953**
20 bedrs, 16 ensuite, 3 🛁 **TCF TV** 🐾 **P** 20 **SB** £20-£35 **DB** £48-£55 **HB** £183-£228 **D** £9 **CC** MC Visa

Cleeve Hill *Awaiting Inspection*
Cleeve Hill, Cheltenham GL52 3PR
☎ **01242-672052 Fax 01242-679969**
Closed Christmas, New Year
9 bedrs, all ensuite, **TCF TV P** 12 No children under 8 **SB** £45 **DB** £60-£75 **CC** MC Visa Amex
See advert on previous page

Cotswold Spa *Awaiting Inspection*
Cleeve Hill, Cheltenham GL52 3QE
☎ **01242-582727 Fax 01242-257327**
12 bedrs, all ensuite, **TCF TV** 🐾 **P** 10 **SB** £35-£55 **DB** £65-£80 **D** £17.50 **CC** MC Visa

Parkview
4 Pittville Crescent, Cheltenham GL52 2QZ
☎ **01242-575567**

We offer accommodation in a fine Regency house in Cheltenhams nicest area. Tourist Authority 'Commended'. Ideal for Cotswolds, Stratford, Heart of England.

3 bedrs, 1 🛁 **TCF TV** 🐾 **SB** £17.50-£18.50 **DB** £35-£37

CHELWOOD Gloucestershire	3E1

★★ Chelwood House
Chelwood BS18 4NH
☎ **01761-490730 Fax 01761-490730**
11 bedrs, all ensuite, **P** 20 No children under 8 **CC** MC Visa Amex DC JCB

CHESTER Cheshire	7D1

★★ Brookside
Brook Lane, Chester CH2 2AN
☎ **01244-381943 Fax 01244-379701**
26 bedrs, all ensuite, 2 🛁 **TCF TV** 🐾 **P** 16 **SB** £37 **DB** £52 **D** £10 **CC** MC Visa JCB

★★ Chester Court
48 Hoole Road, Chester CH2 3NL
☎ **01244-320779 Fax 01244-344795**
20 bedrs, all ensuite, **TCF TV** 🐾 **P** 30 **SB** £36-£40 **DB** £46-£50 **D** £12.95 **CC** MC Visa Amex DC JCB

★★ Dene
Hospitality merit award
95 Hoole Road, Chester CH2 3ND
☎ **01244-321165 Fax 01244-350277**
48 bedrs, all ensuite, **TCF TV** 🐾 **P** 55 **SB** £39.50 **DB** £52 **HB** £219 **D** £13 **CC** MC Visa Amex

★★ Green Bough
60 Hoole Road, Hoole, Chester CH2 3NL
☎ **01244-326241 Fax 01244-326265**
20 bedrs, 15 ensuite, 5 🐾, **TCF TV P** 21 **SB** £40-£44 **DB** £50-£60 **D** £13 **CC** MC Visa Amex JCB

Cavendish *Highly Acclaimed*
42-44 Hough Green, Chester CH4 8JQ
☎ 01244-675100 Fax 01244-678844
16 bedrs, 15 ensuite, TCF TV P 32 SB £45-£50 DB £55-£65 D £20 CC MC Visa Amex

Green Gables *Highly Acclaimed*
11 Eversley Park, Chester CH2 2AJ
☎ 01244-372243 Fax 01244-376352

Quietly situated, yet less than a mile from the town centre, Green Gables provides high standards of accommodation and service. Non-smoking throughout. Ample off-street parking.

4 bedrs, all ensuite, TCF TV P 8 SB £22-£23 DB £36

Redland *Highly Acclaimed*
64 Hough Green, Chester CH4 8JY
☎ 01244-671024 Fax 01244-681309

A delightful hotel, with a unique Victorian ambience, conveniently situated only one mile from the city centre of Chester and with the advantage of ample parking.

12 bedrs, all ensuite, TCF TV P 12 SB £40 DB £55

Bawn Park *Listed*
10 Hoole Road, Hoole, Chester CH2 3NH
☎ 01244-324971 Fax 01244-310951
7 bedrs, all ensuite, 1 TCF TV P 12 DB £28-£38 CC MC Visa Amex JCB

Devonia *Listed*
33-35 Hoole Road, Chester CH2 3NH
☎ 01244-322236 Fax 01244-310881
10 bedrs, 3 TCF TV P 20 SB £18-£20 DB £28-£30 D £7

Eaton *Listed*
29 City Road, Chester CH1 3AE
☎ 01244-320840 Fax 01244-320850

In the heart of Chester with secure parking and convenient for the station, offering traditional standards of service in a friendly atmosphere.

18 bedrs, 13 ensuite, 5, TCF TV P 9 SB £32.50 DB £42.50 D £9 CC MC Visa Amex DC JCB

Edwards House *Listed*
61-63 Hoole Road, Chester CH2 3NJ
☎ 01244-319888 Fax 01244-318055
10 bedrs, all ensuite, TCF TV P 10 SB £22-£30 DB £35-£50 D £9.50 CC MC Visa

Egerton Lodge *Listed*
57 Hoole Road, Hoole, Chester CH2 3NJ
☎ 01244-320712
Closed 19 Dec-3 Jan
7 bedrs, all ensuite, TCF TV P 5 No children under 9 SB £20 DB £36-£40

Eversley *Listed*
9 Eversley Park, off Liverpool Road, Chester CH2 2AJ
☎ 01244-373744
Closed Christmas-New Year
11 bedrs, 8 ensuite, 2, 1 TCF TV P 17 SB £23 DB £43 HB £186 D £5.25 CC MC Visa

Gables *Listed*
5 Vicarage Road, Hoole, Chester CH2 3HZ
☎ 01244-323969
Closed Christmas-New Year
6 bedrs, 2, TV P 6

Hamilton Court *Listed*
5-7 Hamilton Street, Hoole, Chester CH2 3JG
☎ 01244-345387 Fax 01244-317404
12 bedrs, 10 ensuite, 2, 2 TCF TV P 10 SB £23-£25 DB £46-£50 HB £450 D £15 CC MC Visa Amex DC JCB

Malvern *Listed*
21 Victoria Road, Chester CH2 2AX
☎ 01244-380865
6 bedrs, 2 No children under 2 SB £13 DB £25 D £5

Riverside Hotel & Recorder *Listed*
22 City Walls, off Lower Bridge Street, CH1 1SB
☎ 01244-326580 Fax 01244-311567
22 bedrs, all ensuite, 1 CC MC Visa Amex

Vicarage Lodge *Listed*
11 Vicarage Road, Chester CH2 3HZ
☎ 01244-319533
4 bedrs, 3 ensuite, 1 🐕, 1 ➡ TCF TV P 7 SB £18-£22 DB £28-£36

Cotton Farmhouse
Cotton Edmunds, Chester CH3 7PT
☎ 01244-336699 Fax 01244-336699

Our peaceful farmhouse has recently been completely renovated and lies in a glorious location deep in the Cheshire countryside, yet only 4 miles from historic Roman Chester.

3 bedrs, all ensuite, TCF TV 🐕 SB £25 DB £46-£50

Golborne Manor
Platts Lane, Hatton Heath, Chester CH3 9AN
☎ 01829-770310 Fax 01244-318084

An elegant, manor house set in three and a half acres of grounds with glorious views over peaceful rural surroundings. Beautifully decorated, spacious ensuite bedrooms. 5 miles south of Chester.

2 bedrs, all ensuite, TCF TV ✉ SB £25-£28 DB £42-£50 🐕

Grove House
Holme Street, Tarvin, Chester CH3 8EQ
☎ 01829-740893 Fax 01829-741769

A warm welcome in a relaxing spacious, comfortable family home. Ideal for Chester, North Wales, Liverpool, Manchester and the Potteries. Attractive walled garden. Excellent pubs and restaurants nearby.

3 bedrs, 1 ensuite, 1 ➡ TCF TV P 6 No children under 12 SB £23-£35 DB £46-£56

CHESTERFIELD Derbyshire   8B1

★★ Abbeydale
Cross Street, Chesterfield S40 4TD
☎ 01246-277849 Fax 01246-558223
11 bedrs, TCF TV P 15 SB £47 DB £60 D £15 CC MC Visa Amex DC JCB ♿

★★ Portland
West Bars, Chesterfield S40 1AY
☎ 01246-234502 Fax 01246-550915
24 bedrs, all ensuite, TCF TV P 40 SB £44-£55 DB £55-£66 D £12.75 CC MC Visa Amex DC

CHICHESTER West Sussex   4C4

Globe *Listed*
1 Southgate, Chichester PO19 2DH
☎ 01243-782035
11 bedrs, 5 ensuite, 2 ➡ TCF TV P 14 No children under 10 CC MC Visa Amex

Woolpack *Listed*
Main Road, Fishbourne, Chichester PO19 3JJ
☎ 01243-782792
4 bedrs, 2 ➡ TCF TV 🐕 P 20 CC MC Visa Amex

CHINLEY Derbyshire   7F1

Squirrels *Listed*
1 Green Lane, Chinley, Chapel-en-le-Frith SK23 6AA
☎ 01663-751200 Fax 01663-750210
6 bedrs, all ensuite, TCF TV 🐕 P 20 SB £28 DB £35 D £7.95 CC MC Visa Amex DC 🐕

CHINNOR Oxfordshire   4B2

★★ Peacock
Comfort merit award
Henton, Chinnor OX9 4AH
☎ 01844-353519 Fax 01844-353891
22 bedrs, all ensuite, TCF TV 🐕 P 55 SB £40-£65 DB £45-£75 D £15 CC MC Visa Amex DC JCB 🐕 ♿

CHIPPENHAM Wiltshire   3F1

★★ Angel
Market Place, Chippenham SN15 3HD
☎ 01249-652615 Fax 01249-443210
48 bedrs, all ensuite, TCF TV 🐕 P 50 SB £48-£88 DB £58-£106 D £17 CC MC Visa Amex DC JCB

★★ White Hart Inn
13 Clifton Crescent, Ford, Chippenham SN14 8RP
☎ 01249-782213 Fax 01249-783075
11 bedrs, all ensuite, TCF TV 🐕 P 100 SB £45-£65 DB £70-£90 D £14.25 CC MC Visa Amex DC 🐕

CHURCH STRETTON – ENGLAND

Oxford *Acclaimed*
32-36 Langley Road, Chippenham SN15 1BX
📞 01249-652542
13 bedrs, 7 ensuite, 1 🐾, 1 ⇨ TCF TV ★ P 9

CHIPPING CAMPDEN Gloucestershire   7F4

Orchard Hill House *Highly Acclaimed*
Broad Campden, Chipping Campden GL55 6UU
📞 01386-841473 Fax 01386-841030

A restored 17th century farmhouse with flagstone floors, beamed ceilings, open fire, huge breakfasts and friendly hosts! All rooms with their own facilities. Apologies no smoking. Set in a beautiful area for walking.

4 bedrs, all ensuite, TCF TV ☒ P 6 No children under 4
SB £41-£43 DB £45-£57

Holly House
Ebrington, Chipping Campden GL55 6NL
📞 01386-593213

Spacious well appointed ensuite rooms. Ground floor, TV, parking. Located in centre of picturesque Cotswold village two miles from Hidcote Gardens, ten miles from Stratford upon Avon. Village pub serves meals.

3 bedrs, all ensuite, TCF TV ★ P 6 SB £18-£34 DB £36-£40 D £12 ♿

CHIPPING NORTON Oxfordshire   4B1

★★ Crown & Cushion
23 High Street, Chipping Norton OX7 5AD
📞 01608-642533 Fax 01608-642926
40 bedrs, all ensuite, TCF TV ★ P 30 SB £43-£49 DB £60-£73 D £18 CC MC Visa Amex DC 🖺 🛆 🛌 🎿 ♿

★★ White Hart
High Street, Chipping Norton OX7 5AD
📞 01608-642572 Fax 01608-644143
21 bedrs, all ensuite, TCF TV ★ P 15 CC MC Visa Amex DC ♿

Southcombe Lodge *Listed*
Southcombe, Chipping Norton OX7 5QH
📞 01608-643068
6 bedrs, 3 ensuite, 2 ⇨ TCF TV ☒ ★ P 10 SB £22-£27 DB £40-£46 HB £210-£220 D £10

CHOLDERTON Wiltshire   4A3

Fayre Deal *Lodge*
Parkhouse Cross, Cholderton SP4 0EG
📞 01980-629542 Fax 01980-629481
35 bedrs, all ensuite, TCF TV ★ P 200 SB £42-£45 DB £50-£60 D £11 CC MC Visa Amex DC

CHRISTCHURCH Dorset   3F3

★★ Fisherman's Haunt
Hospitality merit award
Winkton, Christchurch BH23 7AS
📞 01202-477283 Fax 01202-478883
18 bedrs, 17 ensuite, 1 ⇨ TCF TV ★ P 75 SB £42-£50 DB £60 D £11 CC MC Visa ♿

CHURCH STRETTON Shropshire   7D3

★★ Denehurst
Shrewsbury Road, Church Stretton SY6 6EU
📞 01694-722699 Fax 01694-724110
16 bedrs, all ensuite, 1 ⇨ TV P 100 SB £35 DB £55 HB £220 D £13 CC MC Visa 🖺 🛆

★★ Mynd House
Hospitality, Comfort merit awards
Little Stretton, Church Stretton SY6 6RB
📞 01694-722212 Fax 01694-724180
Closed Jan
7 bedrs, all ensuite, TCF TV ★ P 16 SB £40-£50 DB £50-£90 D £26 CC MC Visa Amex

RAC Hotel Reservations Service
0870 603 9109
(Calls charged at national call rate)

CHURCH STRETTON – ENGLAND

Belvedere *Acclaimed*
Burway Road, Church Stretton SY6 6DP
📞 01694-722232 Fax 01694-722232
Closed Christmas week

Belvedere is a quiet guest house set in its own gardens, convenient for the town yet only 100 yards from 6,000 acres of National Trust hills.

12 bedrs, 6 ensuite, 3 🛏 TCF TV 🐾 P 9 SB £23-£25 DB £46-£50 HB £215-£227 D £10 CC MC Visa

Brookfields *Acclaimed*
Watling Street North, Church Stretton SY6 7AR
📞 01694-722314
4 bedrs, all ensuite, TCF TV 🐾 P 8

Court Farm *Acclaimed*
Gretton, Church Stretton SY6 7HU
📞 01694-771219
Closed Nov-Feb
5 bedrs, all ensuite, TCF TV ☒ P 10 No children under 14 SB £25-£30 DB £42-£45 HB £140-£145 D £13

Travellers Rest Inn *Listed*
Upper Affcot, Church Stretton SY6 6RL
📞 01694-781275 Fax 01694-781555
10 bedrs, 4 ensuite, 1 🛏 TCF TV 🐾 P 30 SB £22-£30 DB £44-£50 D £4 CC MC Visa Amex DC 🐾

Hope Bowdler Hall
Hope Bowdler, Church Stretton SY6 7DD
📞 01694-722041
Closed Nov-Feb

Peaceful manor house in the south Shropshire hills, 1½ miles from the A49. Ample secluded parking. Superb scenery and walking. Central for Shrewsbury, Ludlow and the Welsh borders.

2 bedrs, 2 🛏 ☒ P 4 No children SB £22 DB £40 🔍

Strefford Hall
Strefford, Cravens Arms, Church Stretton SY7 8DE
📞 01588-672383 Fax 01588-672383
Closed Christmas-New Year

Spacious farmhouse in peaceful setting with panoramic views of Wenlock Edge and Long Mynd Hills. Tastefully decorated ensuite bedrooms offering every comfort. Non-smoking household.

3 bedrs, all ensuite, TCF TV ☒ P 3 SB £20-£25 DB £38-£40

CIRENCESTER Gloucestershire 7F4

★★ **Corinium Court**
Hospitality merit award
Gloucester Street, Cirencester GL7 2DG
📞 01285-659711 Fax 01285-885807
16 bedrs, all ensuite, 🐾 P 40 CC MC Visa Amex ♿

Wimborne *Highly Acclaimed*
91 Victoria Road, Cirencester GL7 1ES
📞 01285-653890 Fax 01285-653890
Closed Christmas

Victorian Cotswold stone house with warm and friendly atmosphere, and spacious rooms. Fourposter room available. Non smokers only please.

5 bedrs, all ensuite, TCF TV ☒ P 6 No children under 7 SB £20-£40 DB £30-£40 D £7

Bungalow *Acclaimed*
93 Victoria Road, Cirencester GL7 1ES
📞 01285-654179
6 bedrs, all ensuite, TCF TV P 6 SB £20-£22 DB £30-£33

Smerrill Barns *Acclaimed*
Kemble, Cirencester GL7 6BW
📞 01285-770907 Fax 01285-770706

An ideal touring base at the heart of the Cotswolds, offering modern facilities in a building dating back to the 18th century.

7 bedrs, all ensuite, 1 ⚬ TCF TV ⌨ P 7 No children under 3 **SB** £35 **DB** £45-£55 **HB** £280-£315 **CC** MC Visa JCB

La Ronde *Listed*
52/54 Ashcroft Road, Cirencester GL7 1QX
📞 01285-654611
10 bedrs, all ensuite, ⌨ ⚬ **CC** MC Visa

CLACTON-ON-SEA Essex   5E1

Chudleigh *Acclaimed*
Agate Road, Marine Parade West, Clacton-on-Sea CO15 1RA
📞 01255-425407 Fax 01255-425407

Conveniently situated in a quiet side road near the central seafront gardens, pier and shopping centre, Chudleigh assures you of every comfort and personal attention. Renowned for its excellent cuisine. Fluent Italian and French spoken. Ample parking.

10 bedrs, all ensuite, 1 ⚬ TCF TV ⌨ P 7 No children under 1 **SB** £27.50-£32.50 **DB** £45-£50 **HB** £210-£215 **D** £11 **CC** MC Visa Amex DC JCB ♿

Sandrock *Acclaimed*
1 Penfold Road, Marine Parade West, Clacton-on-Sea CO15 1JN
📞 01255-428215 Fax 01255-428215

Private licensed hotel, 50 yards from the seafront, gardens and town centre. Some sea views, relaxed friendly atmosphere and high standards of accommodation and food. Free car park.

8 bedrs, all ensuite, TCF TV ⌨ P 7 **SB** £22-£24.50 **DB** £44-£49 **HB** £185-£200 **D** £10 **CC** MC Visa DC JCB

CLARE Suffolk   9E4

★ Clare
Nethergate Street, Clare CO10 8NP
📞 01787-277449 Fax 01787-278270
5 bedrs, 3 ensuite, 1 ⚬ ⌨ P 10 No children under 10 **CC** MC Visa ♿

CLEETHORPES Lincolnshire   11F4

★★ Wellow
Kings Road, Cleethorpes DN35 0AQ
📞 01472-695589 Fax 01472-200016

Mallow View *Listed*
9/11 Albert Road, Cleethorpes DN35 8LX
📞 01472-691297
20 bedrs, 3 ensuite, 5 ⌨, 3 ⚬ ▣ ♿

CLEOBURY MORTIMER Shropshire   7E3

★★ Redfern
Hospitality, Restaurant merit awards
Lower Street, Cleobury Mortimer DY14 8AA
📞 01299-270395 Fax 01299-271011
E Mail jon@red-fern.demon.co.uk
11 bedrs, all ensuite, ⚬ P 20 **SB** £48 **DB** £70 **HB** £280 **D** £17 **CC** MC Visa Amex DC

CLEVEDON Somerset   3E1

Salthouse Inn & Restaurant *Listed*
Salthouse Road, Clevedon BS21 7TY
📞 01275-871482
2 bedrs, both ensuite, 1 ⚬ TCF TV P 50 No children under 12 **SB** £30 **DB** £60 **HB** £350 **D** £6.75 **CC** MC Visa

CLIFTONVILLE Kent 5F2

Falcon Holiday *Acclaimed*
4 Ethelbert Road, Cliftonville CT9 1RY
☎ 01843-223846 Fax 01843-223846
Closed Nov-Feb ex Christmas
30 bedrs, 22 ensuite, 3 ⇌ TCF TV ▣ P 6 SB £21 HB £150-£162 D £8 🛏 🖼 ▣

Greswolde *Acclaimed*
20 Surrey Road, Cliftonville CT9 2LA
☎ 01843-223956
6 bedrs, all ensuite, 1 ⇌ TCF TV 🐾 CC MC Visa

CLITHEROE Lancashire 10C3

Brooklyn *Highly Acclaimed*
32 Pimlico Road, Clitheroe BB7 2AH
☎ 01200-428268
4 bedrs, all ensuite, TCF TV SB £25 DB £40 HB £168-£199 D £10 CC MC Visa JCB

CLOUGHTON North Yorkshire 11E2

★★ Blacksmiths Arms
Comfort merit award
High Street, Cloughton, Scarborough YO13 0AE
☎ 01723-870244
6 bedrs, all ensuite, TCF TV ▣ P 30 SB £25 DB £40 D £11 CC MC Visa

CLOVELLY Devon 2C2

Lower Waytown
Horns Cross, Bideford EX39 5DN
☎ 01237-451787 Fax 01237-451787
Closed Christmas & New Year

Situated within half a mile of the coastal footpath and four miles from Clovelly. Set in lovely grounds, this unique roundhouse offers superb ensuite rooms, fully equipped for every comfort.

3 bedrs, all ensuite, TCF TV ▣ P 8 No children under 12 SB £32-£35 DB £45-£50

CLUN Shropshire 7D3

New House Farm
Clun SY7 8NJ
☎ 01588-638314

Peaceful and isolated 18th century farmhouse, set high in the Clun Hills, near the Welsh Border. Walks from the doorstep, books to browse in, large country garden. Ring for brochure.

3 bedrs, TCF TV ▣ 🐾 P 6 SB £20 D £10.50

COALVILLE Leicestershire 8B3

★★ Charnwood Arms
Beveridge Lane, Bardon Hill, Coalville LE67 1TB
☎ 01530-813644 Fax 01530-815425
34 bedrs, all ensuite, TCF TV P 150 SB £44.45 DB £49.50 CC MC Visa Amex DC ♿

COCKERMOUTH Cumbria 10A1

★★ Globe
Main Street, Cockermouth CA13 9LE
☎ 01900-822126 Fax 01900-823705
Closed 25 Dec

Handsome three storey Georgian building in the centre of this market town.

30 bedrs, 20 ensuite, 2 ⇌ TCF TV 🐾 P 12 SB £25 DB £48-£50 HB £210-£250 D £16 CC MC Visa DC

COLESHILL – ENGLAND

CODSALL Staffordshire   7E2

Moors Farm Country Restaurant *Acclaimed*
Chillington Lane, Codsall WV8 1QF
01902-842330 Fax 01902-847878

Moos Farm is in a quiet picturesque valley one mile from Cotswold village. The attractively decorated, comfortable bedrooms have lovely views. Cosy lounge and bar. Superb lounge.

6 bedrs, 3 ensuite, 2 🛏 TCF TV 🖂 P 20 No children under 4 **SB** £25-£30 **DB** £42-£50 **D** £11 **CC** MC Visa DC JCB

COLCHESTER Essex   5E1

Bauble
Higham, Colchester CO7 6LA
01206-337254 Fax 01206-337263

In the heart of Constable country and ideal for touring East Anglia, a quiet country home on the edge of a picturesque village, set in 1½ acres of gardens with tennis and swimming.

3 bedrs, all ensuite, TCF TV 🖂 P 5 No children under 12 **SB** £25-£30 **DB** £40-£45

Four Sevens
28 Inglis Road, Colchester CO3 3HU
01206-546093 Fax 01206-546093

Large house offering genuinely warm hospitality near the town centre. All spacious bedrooms have colour Sky TV & video channels. Tea/coffee facilities. Generous breakfast and evening meals. Two Crowns English Tourist Board.

6 bedrs, 2 ensuite, 4 🛏 TCF TV P 2 No children under 2
SB £30-£35 **DB** £35-£45 **D** £15

Riverside Inn Motel
42 Lower Holt Street, Earls Colne, Colchester CO6 2PH
01787-223487 Fax 01787-223487

Friendly, family run, single storey accommodation in converted farm buildings on the banks of the River Colne. Ensuite rooms with TV, hairdryer and tea and coffee tray.

11 bedrs, all ensuite, TCF TV 🐾 P 35 **SB** £31.50-£33.50 **DB** £42-£46 **D** £5 **CC** MC Visa ♿

COLEFORD Gloucestershire   7E4

★★ Orepool Inn
St Briavels Road, Sling, Coleford GL16 8LH
01594-833277 Fax 01594-833785
10 bedrs, all ensuite, P 100 **CC** MC Visa Amex ♿

COLESHILL Warwickshire   8A3

★★ Coleshill
High Street, Coleshill B46 3BG
01675-465527 Fax 01675-464013
23 bedrs, all ensuite, TCF TV P 49 **SB** £65-£69 **DB** £75-£79 **D** £13.50 **CC** MC Visa Amex DC

Old Barn *Acclaimed*
Birmingham Road, Coleshill B46 1DP
☎ 01675-463692 Fax 01675-463692

Small, family run guest house close to the NEC. All rooms are ensuite, TV, tea/coffee making facilities. Lounge with bar. Indoor heated swimming pool.

9 bedrs, all ensuite, TCF TV P 25 SB £40 DB £65 D £3
CC MC Visa DC JCB

COLYTON Devon   3D3

★★ White Cottage
Dolphin Street, Colyton EX13 6NA
☎ 01297-552401 Fax 01297-553897
9 bedrs, all ensuite, 4 TCF TV P 16 No children under 14 SB £35.90 DB £62.90 HB £304.50 D £18.75 CC MC Visa

COMBE MARTIN Devon   2C2

★★ White Gates
Woodlands, Combe Martin EX34 0AT
☎ 01271-883511
17 bedrs, all ensuite, P 70 CC MC Visa Amex DC

Blair Lodge *Acclaimed*
Moory Meadow, Seaside, Combe Martin EX34 0DG
☎ 01271-882294
Closed end Oct-Easter
10 bedrs, 6 ensuite, 2 TCF TV P 10 No children under 8 SB £20 DB £22 HB £179-£198 D £10.50

Saffron House *Acclaimed*
King Street, Combe Martin EX34 0BX
☎ 01271-883521
9 bedrs, 7 ensuite, 1 TCF TV P 10 SB £21-£23 DB £36-£40 HB £165-£189 D £9 CC MC Visa JCB

Woodlands *Listed*
2 The Woodlands, Combe Martin EX34 0AT
☎ 01271-882769
8 bedrs, 4, 1 P 8 No children under 3

CONISTON Cumbria   10B2

★★ Black Bull
Yewdale Road, Coniston LA21 8DU
☎ 01539-441335 Fax 01539-441168
15 bedrs, all ensuite, 1 TCF TV P 16
SB £35 DB £50-£58 CC MC Visa

SUN HOTEL
and Coaching Inn

Magnificent family run Hotel standing at the foot of the Coniston Old Man. Own gardens and patio area. Warm welcome. Good home made food served in Restaurant or 16th C. adjacent Inn. Most rooms en suite and most with excellent views. Direct access to fells making an ideal walkers location.

CONISTON, CUMBRIA LA21 8HQ
Tel: (015394) 41248

★★ Sun
Coniston LA21 8HQ
☎ 01539-441248
11 bedrs, all ensuite, TCF TV P 15 SB £25-£35 DB £50-£70 D £15 CC MC Visa JCB

★★ Yewdale
Yewdale Road, Coniston LA21 8LU
☎ 01539-441662 Fax 01539-441662
10 bedrs, 8 ensuite, 2 P 6
CC MC Visa

Coniston Lodge *Highly Acclaimed*
Sunny Brow, Coniston LA21 8HH
☎ 01539-441201

An 'RAC Small Hotel of the Year' winner. Beautiful scenery, peaceful surroundings, fine home cooking and a very warm welcome.

6 bedrs, all ensuite, TCF TV P 9 No children under 10 SB £27.50-£41 DB £55-£72 D £17.50 CC MC Visa Amex

CORFE CASTLE – ENGLAND

Crown Inn *Listed*
Coniston LA21 8EA
☎ 01539-441243 Fax 015394-41804

Situated in the picturesque village of Coniston, within easy reach of the famous lake (which Donald Campbell used for his world speed record) and the mountains including Coniston Old Man (2633 feet) making it a good centre for walking.

8 bedrs, 1 ensuite, 2 🐕 **TCF TV P** 30 **SB** £20-£35 **DB** £35-£50 **HB** £320-£400 **D** £9 **CC** MC Visa Amex DC

Arrowfield Country Guest House
Little Arrow / Torver, Coniston LA21 8AU
☎ 015394-41741
Closed Dec-Jan

Elegant Victorian house in peaceful location with lovely garden and views. Breakfasts include homemade bread, preserves, home-produced eggs and honey. Ideal for walking, with immediate access to fells.

5 bedrs, all ensuite, **TCF TV** 🚭 **P** 6 **SB** £20-£23 **DB** £40-£46

COOKHAM DEAN Berkshire   4C2

Don't forget to mention the guide
When booking direct, please remember to tell the hotel that you chose it from RAC Bed & Breakfast 1998.

Inn on the Green
The Old Cricket Common, Cookham Dean SL6 9NZ
☎ 01628-482638

Charming country inn with renowned gourmet restaurant in a secluded setting overlooking the old cricket common. Sunny courtyard, log fires, comfortable rooms and friendly service.

6 bedrs, all ensuite, **TCF TV P** 6 **SB** £45-£70 **DB** £80-£90 **D** £15.95 **CC** MC Visa Amex

CORBRIDGE ON TYNE Northumberland   10C1

★★ Angel Inn
Hospitality, Restaurant merit awards
Main Street, Corbridge on Tyne NE45 5LA
☎ 01434-632119
5 bedrs, all ensuite, **P** 34 **CC** MC Visa Amex DC

Tynedale *Acclaimed*
Market Place, Corbridge on Tyne NE45 5AW
☎ 01434-632149
7 bedrs, all ensuite, 🛗 No children under 12

CORFE CASTLE Dorset   3F3

Bradle Farmhouse
Bradle, Church Knowle, Wareham, BH20 5NL
☎ 01929-480712 Fax 01929-481144
Closed 24-27 Dec

A picturesque farmhouse built in 1862 in the heart of Purbeck on a 550 acre mixed farm, with fine views of Corfe Castle just two miles away. Arrangement with local pub for meals.

3 bedrs, all ensuite, **TCF TV P** 3
SB £20-£30 **DB** £38-£40

CORNHILL-ON-TWEED Northumberland   13E2

★★ Collingwood Arms
Cornhill-on-Tweed TD12 4UH
📞 01890-882424 Fax 01890-883644
16 bedrs, all ensuite, TCF TV ⚑ P 30 SB £37.50 DB £60
HB £315 D £13 CC MC Visa ♿

CORSHAM Wiltshire   3F1

★★ Methuen Arms
High Street, Corsham SN13 0HB
📞 01249-714867 Fax 01249-712004
24 bedrs, all ensuite, TCF TV ⚑ P 60 SB £41-£47 DB £50-£59 D £12.50 CC MC Visa DC ♿

COVENTRY West Midlands   8B3

★ Falcon
13-19 Manor Road, Coventry CV1 2LH
📞 01203-258615 Fax 01203-520680
16 bedrs, all ensuite, TCF TV P 50 SB £45-£55 DB £60-£69 D £12 CC MC Visa Amex ♿

Croft *Listed*
23 Stoke Green, Coventry CV3 1FP
📞 01203-457846 Fax 01203-457846
Closed Christmas
11 bedrs, 5 ensuite, 2 ⌘, 2 ⚑ TCF TV ⚑ P 15 SB £24.75
DB £57.75 D £9 CC MC Visa

Hearsall Lodge *Listed*
1 Broad Lane, Coventry CV5 7AA
📞 01203-674543
12 bedrs, 1 ensuite, 9 ⌘, 2 ⚑ TCF TV ⚑ P 19 SB £25
DB £36 D £7 CC MC Visa ♿

Campanile Coventry North *Lodge*
4 Wigston Road, Walsgrave, Coventry CV2 2SD
📞 01203-622311 Fax 01203-602362
50 bedrs, all ensuite, TCF TV ⚑ P 50 SB £41 DB £45.50
D £10.55 CC MC Visa Amex DC ♿

Campanile Coventry South *Lodge*
Abbey Road, Whitley, Coventry CV3 4BJ
📞 01203-639922 Fax 01203-306898
50 bedrs, all ensuite, TCF TV ⚑ P 50 SB £41 DB £42.50
D £10.55 CC MC Visa Amex DC ♿

CRACKINGTON HAVEN Cornwall   2B3

Coombe Barton Inn *Listed*
Crackington Haven EX23 0JG
📞 01840-230345 Fax 01840-230788
5 bedrs, 3 ensuite, 2 ⚑ ⚑ P 40 SB £19-£22 DB £39-£60
D £10.25 CC MC Visa Amex

CRANBROOK Kent   5E3

Hancocks Farmhouse
Tilsden Lane, Cranbrook TN17 3PH
📞 01580-714645
Closed Christmas, 2 weeks in August

Hancocks is a listed 16th century house surrounded by farmland quietly set in a lovely garden. Inside are fine fabrics and antiques and log fires on cooler evenings.

3 bedrs, all ensuite, TCF TV ⚑ ⚑ P 3 No children under 12 SB £35-£45 DB £58-£65 D £22

CRANTOCK Cornwall   2A4

★★ Crantock Bay
Hospitality merit award
West Pentire, Crantock TR8 5SE
📞 01637-830229 Fax 01637-831111
Closed Dec-Jan
34 bedrs, all ensuite, 1 ⚑ TCF TV ⚑ P 36 SB £33-£49
HB £300-£385 D £17 CC MC Visa Amex DC JCB 🖼 ⚑
⚑ ⚑ ⚑ ⚑

CRAWLEY West Sussex   5D3

Waterhall Country House *Acclaimed*
Prestwood Lane, Ifield Wood, Crawley RH11 0LA
📞 01293-520002 Fax 01293-539905
Closed Christmas
6 bedrs, all ensuite, 1 ⚑ TCF TV ⚑ P 25 SB £25 DB £40

CREWE Cheshire   7E1

Clayhanger Hall Farm *Highly Acclaimed*
Maw Lane, Haslington, Crewe CW1 1SH
📞 01270-583952 Fax 01270-251685
4 bedrs, all ensuite

CREWKERNE Somerset   3E2

RAC Hotel Reservations Service
0870 603 9109
(Calls charged at national call rate)

CROWBOROUGH – ENGLAND

Broadview Gardens
East Crewkerne, Crewkerne TA18 7AG
☎ 01460-73424 Fax 01460-73424

Unusual Colonial bungalow - a winner of top awards for quality, friendliness and traditional English cooking. Ensuite rooms overlooking an acre of beautiful secluded gardens. Dorset border. Perfect touring base.

3 bedrs, all ensuite, **TCF TV** 🚭 🐕 **P** 6 **SB** £25-£46 **DB** £50-£56 **HB** £273-£294 **D** £12.50 **CC** MC Visa

CRICKLADE Wiltshire — 4A2

★★ White Hart
High Street, Cricklade SN6 6AA
☎ 01793-750206 Fax 01793-750650
14 bedrs, 12 ensuite, 1 ➔ **TCF TV** 🐕 **P** 20 **SB** £35 **DB** £45 **CC** MC Visa Amex 🍴

CROMER Norfolk — 9F2

★ Anglia Court
5 Runton Road, Cromer NR27 9AR
☎ 01263-512443 Fax 01263-513104
28 bedrs, 24 ensuite, 4 ➔ **TCF TV** 🐕 **P** 18 **SB** £19.50-£33.50 **DB** £39-£67 **HB** £210-£315 **D** £12 **CC** MC Visa Amex DC

Westgate Lodge *Highly Acclaimed*
Macdonald Road, Cromer NR27 9AP
☎ 01263-512840 Fax 01263-512840
Closed Christmas-New Year
11 bedrs, all ensuite, 1 ➔ **TCF TV P** 11 No children under 3 **DB** £42.30-£49.36 **HB** £197-£199.75

Beachcomber *Acclaimed*
17 MacDonald Road, Cromer NR27 9AP
☎ 01263-513398
7 bedrs, 5 ensuite, 1 ➔ **TCF TV SB** £15-£18 **DB** £18-£20 **D** £8

Brightside *Acclaimed*
19 Macdonald Road, Cromer NR27 9AP
☎ 01263-513408
Closed Dec-Feb
6 bedrs, all ensuite, **TCF TV** 🚭 No children under 4 **DB** £36-£39 **D** £8

Chellow Dene *Acclaimed*
23 Macdonald Road, Cromer NR27 9AP
☎ 01263-513251
7 bedrs, 5 ensuite, 1 ➔ **TCF TV** 🐕 **P** 6 No children under 3 **SB** £17-£18 **DB** £34-£36 **HB** £115-£142 **D** £6

Birch House *Listed*
34 Cabbell Road, Cromer NR27 9HX
☎ 01263-512521

Sandcliff *Listed*
Runton Road, Cromer NR27 9AS
☎ 01263-512888 Fax 01263-512888
23 bedrs, 16 ensuite, 2 ➔ **TCF TV** 🐕 **P** 14 **SB** £21-£26 **DB** £42-£52 **HB** £170-£200 ♿

Cliftonville
Seafront, Cromer NR27 9AS
☎ 01263-512543 Fax 01263-515700

Beautifully restored Edwardian hotel set in historic North Norfolk. All with sea view. Bolton's Seafood Bistro and excellent a la carte restaurant. All day coffee shop and bar.

30 bedrs, all ensuite, 1 ➔ **TCF TV** 🐕 **P** 20 **D** £15.95 **CC** MC Visa Amex ♿

CROWBOROUGH East Sussex — 5D3

★★ Plough & Horses
Walshes Road, Crowborough TN6 3RE
☎ 01892-652614

Traditional inn offering excellent value accommodation in ensuite double/twin rooms. Near Ashdown Forest. Crowborough & East Sussex national golf clubs within easy reach.

8 bedrs, all ensuite, **TCF TV P** 50 **SB** £-£23 **DB** £-£40 **D** £2.50 **CC** MC Visa

WEST WINDS GUEST HOUSE

ETB 3 Crown Commended
AA 3 Q Recommended

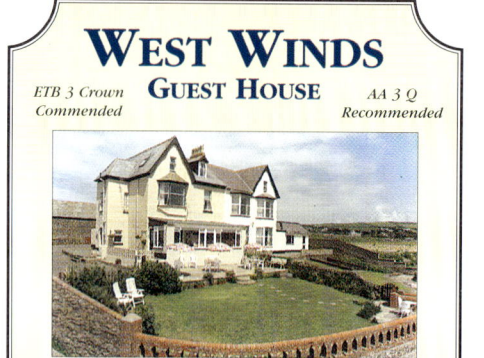

Small guest house, located on water's edge overlooking Croyde Bay beach, adjacent to Baggy Point NT coastal path. Private steps on to the beach. Ensuite rooms, with TV, radio, tea/coffee facilities.
Residential bar and separate sun lounge overlooking sea.

Open March – November
B & B from £23 p.p.

Telephone or write for brochure.

MOOR LANE, CROYDE BAY, CROYDE, BRAUNTON EX33 1PA
Tel: 01271-890489 Fax: 01271-890489

CROYDE Devon — 2C2

★★ Croyde Bay House
Hospitality, Comfort merit awards
Moor Lane, Croyde EX33 1PA
☏ 01271-890270
Closed Nov-Feb
7 bedrs, all ensuite, TCF TV ✻ P 7 SB £32-£42 DB £64-£84 HB £285-£335 D £18.50 CC MC Visa Amex JCB ♿

★★ Kittiwell
Hospitality, Restaurant merit awards
St Marys Road, Croyde EX33 1PG
☏ 01271-890247 Fax 01271-890469
Closed Jan-Feb
12 bedrs, all ensuite, TCF TV ✻ P 20 SB £39-£46 DB £70-£78 HB £329-£357 D £17.90 CC MC Visa Amex JCB

West Winds
Moor Lane, Croyde Bay, Croyde, Braunton EX33 1PA
☏ 01271-890489 Fax 01271-890489
Closed Nov-Feb
5 bedrs, 3 ensuite, 1 ✻ TCF TV ✻ P 7 SB £25-£38 DB £50-£56 HB £248-£262 CC MC Visa

---

CROYDON Surrey — 5D3

★★ Briarley
8 Outram Road, Croydon CR0 6XE
☏ 0181-654 1000 Fax 0181-656 6084
38 bedrs, all ensuite, TCF TV ✻ P 20 SB £54.50 DB £64.50 D £10.50 CC MC Visa Amex DC

★★ Central
3-5 South Park Hill Road, Croydon CR2 7DY
☏ 0181-688 5644 Fax 0181-760 0861
19 bedrs, all ensuite, 1 ✻ TCF TV P 12 SB £47.50 DB £55 D £12 CC MC Visa Amex JCB

★★ Hayesthorpe
48-52 St Augustines Avenue, Croydon CR2 6JJ
☏ 0181-688 8120 Fax 0181-688 8120
25 bedrs, all ensuite, 2 ✻ TCF TV P 10 SB £40 DB £50 D £7 CC MC Visa Amex DC JCB

★★ Markington
9 Haling Park Road, Croydon CR2 6NG
☏ 0181-681 6494 Fax 0818-688 6530
22 bedrs, all ensuite, 3 ✻ TCF TV P 17 SB £45-£52 DB £50-£55 D £7 CC MC Visa Amex JCB

Kirkdale *Acclaimed*
22 St Peters Road, Croydon CR0 1HD
☏ 0181-688 5898 Fax 0181-680 6001
19 bedrs, all ensuite, TCF TV ✉ P 12 SB £37 DB £50 CC MC Visa Amex DC

Alpine
16-18 Moreton Road, Croydon CR2 7DL
☏ 0181-688 6116 Fax 0818-667 1822

A friendly family run hotel, situated close to Croydon's shopping and business centre within easy commuting to London or Gatwick Airport 15 minutes away. The Alpine Hotel stands in a quiet area.

35 bedrs, all ensuite, 2 ✻ ✉ P 30

CULLOMPTON Devon — 3D2

★★ Manor House
2/4 Fore Street, Cullompton EX15 1JL
☏ 01884-32281 Fax 01884-38344
10 bedrs, all ensuite, TCF TV ✻ P 30 SB £42.50 DB £55 D £13 CC MC Visa

---

DARLINGTON Co. Durham — 11D2

Clow Beck House *Highly Acclaimed*
Monk End Farm, Croft on Tees, Darlington DL2 2SW
☏ 01325-721075 Fax 01325-720419
11 bedrs, all ensuite, 1 ✻ TCF TV P 30 SB £35 DB £50 CC MC Visa ✉ ♿

DARRINGTON West Yorkshire — 11D4

★★ Darrington
Great North Road, Pontefract, Darrington WF8 3BL
☎ 01977-791458
26 bedrs, all ensuite, TCF TV P 120 CC MC Visa Amex DC

DARTMOUTH Devon — 3D4

Ford House *Highly Acclaimed*
44 Victoria Road, Dartmouth TQ6 9DX
☎ 01803-834047 Fax 01803-834047
Closed Nov-Feb
3 bedrs, all ensuite, TCF TV ⚭ P 5 SB £40-£70 DB £50-£70 HB £350-£370 D £25 CC MC Visa Amex

Captains House *Acclaimed*
18 Clarence Street, Dartmouth TQ6 9NW
☎ 01803-832133
Closed Jan-Feb
5 bedrs, all ensuite, TCF TV ⚭ No children under 5 SB £30-£35 DB £42-£55

Victoria Cote
105 Victoria Road, Dartmouth TQ6 9DY
☎ 01803-832997

A comfortable Victorian house set in a lovely garden with ample parking in its grounds, but only 5 minutes stroll from Dartmouth town centre.

3 bedrs, all ensuite, TCF TV ⚭ P 5 SB £24-£26 DB £40-£50 HB £217-£234 D £12

DAWLISH Devon — 3D3

West Hatch *Highly Acclaimed*
34 West Cliff, Dawlish EX7 9DN
☎ 01626-864211
10 bedrs, all ensuite, 1 ⚭ TCF TV P 11 SB £30-£36 DB £44-£64 CC MC Visa Amex JCB

Walton House
Plantation Terrace, Dawlish EX7 9DR
☎ 01626-862760 Fax 01626-862760

Grade II Listed property quietly situated but centrally located in the pretty town of Dawlish. Fourposter bedroom. Quality accommodation, 'Which?' recommended.

6 bedrs, all ensuite, TCF TV P 6 No children DB £32-£42

DEAL Kent — 5F3

Royal *Awaiting Inspection*
Beach Street, Deal CT14 6JG
☎ 01304-375555 Fax 01304-372270
12 bedrs, all ensuite, TCF TV P 5 SB £40-£50 DB £60-£75 D £9.50 CC MC Visa Amex

DEDHAM Essex — 5E1

Marlborough Head *Listed*
Mill Lane, Dedham CM7 6HG
☎ 01206-323124
3 bedrs, all ensuite, TCF TV ⚭ P 25 CC MC Visa

DERBY Derbyshire — 8B2

★★ Hotel La Gondola
Hospitality, Comfort, Restaurant merit awards
220 Osmaston Road, Derby DE23 8JX
☎ 01332-332895 Fax 01332-384512
20 bedrs, all ensuite, TCF TV P 70 SB £48 DB £54 D £10 CC MC Visa Amex DC ♿

★★ Kedleston Country House
Kedleston Road, Derby DE22 5JD
☎ 01332-556507 Fax 01332-558822
14 bedrs, all ensuite, 1 ⚭ TCF TV P 70 SB £45-£50 DB £60-£70 D £17 CC MC Visa Amex DC ♿

Short Breaks

Many hotels provide special rates for weekend and mid-week breaks – sometimes these are quoted in the hotel's entry, otherwise ring direct for the latest offers.

Rangemoor Park *Acclaimed*
67 Macklin Street, Derby DE1 1LF
📞 01332-347252 Fax 01332-369319
Closed Christmas

A small hotel close to amenities.

20 bedrs, 13 ensuite, 2 ⇌ TCF TV ⚑ P 40 SB £25-£36
DB £40-£50 CC MC Visa Amex DC

Longlands *Listed*
Longlands Lane, Findern, Derby DE65 6AH
📞 01283-702320

European Inn *Lodge*
Midland Road, Derby DE1 2SL
📞 01332-292000 Fax 01332-293940
88 bedrs, all ensuite, TCF TV ⚑ 🛗 P 88 SB £49 DB £55
CC MC Visa Amex DC ♿

Dalby House
100 Radbourne St, Off Windmill Hill Lane, Derby DE22 3BU
📞 01332-342353

Popular, family run hotel in a splendid Georgian style property, situated in a quiet residential area, very convenient for the city centre, local historical attractions and Derby University.

9 bedrs, 2 ⇌ TCF TV ⚑ P 12 SB £17-£19 DB £31-£35

DEREHAM Norfolk   9E3

Bartles Lodge
Church Farm, Church Street, Elsing, East Dereham NR20 3EA
📞 01362-637177

7 bedrs, all ensuite, TCF TV ⚑ P 30 No children under 10 SB £27-£35 DB £45-£56 CC MC 🍴 ♿

Clinton House
Well Hill, Clint Green, Dereham NR19 1RX
📞 01362-692079

A charming 18th century country house full of character in a peaceful location. Recommended by the 'Which?' guide and highly commended by the ETB. Excellent facilities including tennis and croquet.

3 bedrs, 2 ⇌ TCF TV 🚭 P 8 SB £20-£22 DB £32-£34 🗝

DERSINGHAM Norfolk   9D2

Westdene House *Acclaimed*
60 Hunstanton Road, Dersingham PE31 6HQ
📞 01485-540395
5 bedrs, 1 ensuite, 1 ⇌ TCF TV ⚑ P 10

DISS Norfolk   9E3

★★ Hamblyn House
Rickinghall, Diss IP22 1BN
📞 01986-782322

Chippenhall Hall
Fressingfield, Eye IP21 5TD
☎ 01379-588180 Fax 01379-586272

Listed Tudor manor in rural seclusion, heavily beamed with inglenook log fires. Fine food and wines served by candlelight. Heated outdoor pool. Phone for brochure.

5 bedrs, all ensuite, TCF P 15 No children under 15
SB £53-£58 DB £59-£65 D £24 CC MC Visa

DONCASTER South Yorkshire 8B1

★★ Regent
Regent Square, Doncaster DN1 2DS
☎ 01302-364180 Fax 01302-322331
50 bedrs, all ensuite, TCF TV P 20 SB £52-£68.50
DB £65-£75 D £10 CC MC Visa Amex DC JCB

Almel *Acclaimed*
20/24 Christchurch Road, Doncaster DN1 2QL
☎ 01302-365230 Fax 01302-341434
30 bedrs, 14 ensuite, 10, 3 TCF TV P 8
SB £21.50-£27.50 DB £37-£41 D £3.50 CC MC Visa Amex DC

Campanile Doncaster *Lodge*
Bawtry Road, Doncaster Leisure Park, Doncaster DN4 7PD
☎ 01302-370770 Fax 01302-370813
50 bedrs, all ensuite, TCF TV P 60 SB £41 DB £45.50
D £10.55 CC MC Visa Amex DC

Formule 1 *Lodge*
Ten Pound Walk, Doncaster DN4 5HX
☎ 01302-761050 Fax 01302-328317
128 bedrs, 13 TV P 64 SB £22.50 DB £25 CC MC Visa Amex

Facilities for the disabled

Hotels do their best to cater for disabled visitors. However, it is advisable to contact the hotel direct to ensure it can provide a particular requirement. For further information on accommodation facilities for the disabled why not order a copy of *RAC On the Move – The Guide for the Disabled Traveller*.

DORCHESTER Dorset 3E3

Casterbridge *Highly Acclaimed*
49 High East Street, Dorchester DT1 1HU
☎ 01305-264043 Fax 01305-260884

A relaxed, essentially English town house hotel with a modern annex and fine period furnishings, in the heart of Wessex.

14 bedrs, all ensuite, TCF TV P 4 SB £34-£45 DB £50-£70
CC MC Visa Amex DC JCB

Yalbury Cottage
Lower Bockhampton, Dorchester DT2 8PZ
☎ 01305-262382 Fax 01305-266412
Closed 28 Dec-22 Jan

Peaceful 17th century thatched cottage hotel with oak beams and inglenooks in a tranquil hamlet in Hardy's Wessex. Friendly, attentive staff. Excellent wines and cuisine.

8 bedrs, all ensuite, TCF TV P 18 SB £46 DB £72
HB £336-£364 D £19 CC MC Visa JCB

DORKING Surrey 4C3

Pilgrim *Listed*
Station Road, Dorking RH4 1HF
☎ 01306-889951 Fax 01306-889951
6 bedrs, 3 TV P 12 CC MC Visa Amex DC

DOVER Kent 5F3

East Lee *Highly Acclaimed*
108 Maison Dieu Road, Dover CT16 1RT
☎ 01304-210176 Fax 01304-210176

Non-smokers welcomed. Conveniently situated for the docks and town centre. Channel tunnel is a ten minute drive. Traditional English, vegetarian or continental breakfasts.

4 bedrs, all ensuite, TCF TV P 4 DB £36-£42 CC MC Visa

Number One *Highly Acclaimed*
1 Castle Street, Dover CT16 1QH
☎ 01304-202007

Georgian town house with the atmosphere and hospitality of bygone years. Extra touches, such as breakfast served in your room, ensure a comfortable stay. Garage parking. Convenient for Channel port and tunnel.

5 bedrs, all ensuite, TCF TV P 4 DB £36-£42

Ardmore *Acclaimed*
18 Castle Hill Road, Dover CT16 1QW
☎ 01304-205895 Fax 01304-208229
Closed Christmas-New year
4 bedrs, all ensuite, TCF TV DB £35-£48 CC MC Visa

Cleveland *Acclaimed*
2 Laureston Place, Off Castle Hill Road, CT16 1QX
☎ 01304-204622
5 bedrs, 2 ensuite, 2

CLEVELAND GUEST HOUSE

Situated in a quiet street, close to the town centre and with Dover Castle as a picturesque backdrop, this beautiful grade II listed building offers high standards and a warm welcome. The charming en-suite bedrooms have a comprehensive range of facilities that afford this establishment RAC, AA and English Tourist Board Awards.

**2 LAURESTON PLACE,
OFF CASTLE HILL ROAD, DOVER,
KENT CT16 1QX
Tel: 01304 204622**

Gateway Hovertel *Acclaimed*
Snargate Street, Dover CT17 9BZ
☎ 01304-205479 Fax 01304-211504
Closed Jan
27 bedrs, all ensuite, TCF TV P 27 DB £22-£30 CC MC Visa Amex DC JCB

Hubert House *Acclaimed*
9 Castle Hill Road, Dover CT16 1QW
☎ 01304-202253
8 bedrs, all ensuite, 1 TCF TV P 7 SB £26-£28 DB £36-£42 CC MC Visa JCB

Penny Farthing *Acclaimed*
109 Maison Dieu Road, Dover CT16 1RT
☎ 01304-205563 Fax 01304-205563

Spacious, comfortable Victorian guest house close to ferries and hoverport.

6 bedrs, 4 ensuite, 2, TCF TV P 6 SB £22-£24 DB £36-£42

DOVER – ENGLAND

Peverell House *Acclaimed*
28 Park Avenue, Dover CT16 1HD
☎ 01304-202573
6 bedrs, 2 ensuite, 2 ♿ TCF TV 🚭 P 6

St Martins *Acclaimed*
17 Castle Hill Road, Dover CT16 1QW
☎ 01304-205938 Fax 01304-208229
Closed Christmas

Close to ferry, hovercraft, cruise liner terminals, Channel Tunnel 10 minutes. Ensuite rooms, CTV, tea/coffee facilities. In lee of Dover Castle. Internationally recommended.

6 bedrs, all ensuite, TCF TV SB £25-£35 DB £35-£45 CC MC Visa

Tower *Acclaimed*
Priory Hill, Dover CT17 0AE
☎ 01304-208212
2 bedrs, both ensuite, TCF TV 🚭 P 2 DB £34-£42

Beulah House *Listed*
94 Crabble Hill, Dover CT17 0SA
☎ 01304-824615

Beulah House is set in one acre of beautiful topiaried gardens. The accommodation is extremely spacious and elegantly furnished, offering a warm and relaxed atmosphere. A short drive to the port of Dover and Channel Tunnel. Garages available.

6 bedrs, 4 ensuite, 2 ♿ TCF TV 🚭 P 8 SB £25-£30 DB £36-£44 CC MC Visa ♿

Elmo *Listed*
120 Folkestone Road, Dover CT17 9SP
☎ 01304-206236

Family run guest house, two minutes from the town centre. Tea making facilities and colour TV in rooms. Private parking and garage. Early departure/late arrivals catered for.

6 bedrs, 2 ♿ TCF TV P 7 SB £12-£17 DB £24-£32 CC MC Visa JCB

St Brelade's *Listed*
82 Buckland Avenue, Dover CT16 2NW
☎ 01304-206126 Fax 01304-211486
E Mail stbrelades@compuserve.com

A charming, attractive establishment with very friendly and attentive personal service. Peace of mind is assured with the added bonus of off street parking.

6 bedrs, 4 ensuite, 2 ♿ TCF TV P 6 SB £20-£32 DB £32-£42 D £12.50 CC MC Visa JCB

Westbank *Listed*
239 Folkestone Road, Dover CT17 9LL
☎ 01304-201061
6 bedrs, all ensuite, 1 ♿ TCF TV 🐾 P 6

RAC Hotel Reservations Service
0870 603 9109
(Calls charged at national call rate)

Whitmore *Listed*
261 Folkestone Road, Dover CT17 9LL
☎ 01304-203080 Fax 01304-240110

Friendly family run guest house with colour TV in all rooms, tea/coffee facilities and private parking. Close to station, docks and hoverport, fifteen minutes from Channel Tunnel.

4 bedrs, 1 ensuite, 1 ⇨ TCF TV ⚲ P 4 SB £14-£18 DB £25-£35 D £9

Beaufort House
18 Eastcliff Marine Parade, Dover CT16 1LU
☎ 01304-216444 Fax 01304-211100

100 metres from the ferry, open 24 hours, breakfast served from 3am. Hotel situated on the seafront. Single, double and family rooms available. Late arrival early departure welcome.

28 bedrs, all ensuite, 3 ⇨ 🛉 P 26 🕭

Wallett's Court
West Cliffe, St Margarets-at-Cliffe, Dover CT15 6EW
☎ 01304-852424 Fax 01304-853430
Closed 24-27 Dec
10 bedrs, all ensuite, TCF TV P 40 SB £50-£70 DB £65-£85 D £23 CC MC Visa Amex 🐾

DOWNHAM MARKET Norfolk   9D3

★★ Castle
Restaurant merit award
High Street, Downham Market PE38 9HF
☎ 01366-384311 Fax 01366-384311
12 bedrs, 10 ensuite, 1 ⇨ ⚲ P 40 SB £39 DB £49 HB £245 D £14.95 CC MC Visa Amex

Crosskeys Riverside *Highly Acclaimed*
Bridge Street, Hilgay, Downham Market PE38 0LD
☎ 01366-387777
5 bedrs, all ensuite, TCF TV ⚲ P 10 SB £36.50 DB £59 HB £235 D £12.50 CC MC Visa 🎵

DRIFFIELD, GREAT East Yorkshire   11E3

White Horse Inn *Acclaimed*
Main Street, Hutton Cranswick, Great Driffield YO25 9QN
☎ 01377-270383

An inn situated by the village pond and green, with proprietors Clive & Mary Tomlinson offering you a warm and friendly welcome. An ideal base for touring the Yorkshire Wolds.

8 bedrs, all ensuite, TCF TV ⚲ P 200 SB £30 DB £45 D £5 CC MC Visa Amex

---

WALLETT'S COURT

Wallett's Court is a Grade 2 Historic Building of Kent with many antique features. It is set in lovely open countryside close to the White Cliffs and St. Margaret's Bay. All rooms are en suite, individual in style and some are located in pretty, farm buildings. The restaurant has 3 Rosettes and is commended in numerous food guides. Enjoy a bracing cliff walk, a day in France or a visit to the historic city of Canterbury.

St. Margarets-at-Cliffe, Dover CT12 6EW
Tel: 01304 852424   Fax: 01304 853430

DUDLEY West Midlands — 7E3

★★ Station
Castle Hill, Dudley DY1 4RA
☎ 01384-253418 Fax 01384-457503
38 bedrs, all ensuite, TCF TV ✱ 🍴 P 70 SB £46.95 DB £59.90 D £7.50 CC MC Visa Amex DC

DUNMOW, GREAT Essex — 5D1

★★ Starr
Restaurant merit award
Market Place, Great Dunmow CM6 1AX
☎ 01371-874321 Fax 01371-876337
Closed 1-7 Jan
8 bedrs, all ensuite, TCF TV ✉ ✱ P 16 SB £60 DB £90 D £22 CC MC Visa Amex DC

DUNSTER Somerset — 3D2

★★ Exmoor House
West Street, Dunster, Minehead TA24 6SN
☎ 01643-821268 Fax 01643-821268
Closed Nov-Jan
7 bedrs, all ensuite, 1 ⇌ TCF TV ✉ ✱ No children under 12 SB £27.50-£30.50 D £16.60 CC MC Visa Amex DC JCB

DURHAM Co. Durham — 11D1

★★ Crossways
Dunelm Road, Thornley, Durham DH6 3HT
☎ 01429-821248 Fax 01429-820034
23 bedrs, all ensuite, TCF TV ✱ P 150 SB £48-£55 DB £65-£80 HB £245 D £14.95 CC MC Visa Amex DC

DYMCHURCH Kent — 5E3

★★ Chantry *Listed*
Sycamore Gardens, Dymchurch TN29 0LA
☎ 01303-873137
6 bedrs, 5 ensuite, 1 ⇌ TCF TV ✱ P 10 CC MC Visa Amex

EAGLESCLIFFE Cleveland — 11D2

★★ Claireville
519 Yarm Road, Eaglescliffe TS16 9BG
☎ 01642-780378 Fax 01642-784109
17 bedrs, all ensuite, TCF TV ✱ P 30 SB £33-£45 DB £44-£58 D £12 CC MC Visa Amex DC

★★ Sunnyside
580-582 Yarm Road, Eaglescliffe TS16 0DF
☎ 01642-780075 Fax 01642-783789
23 bedrs, 21 ensuite, 3 ⇌ TCF TV ✱ P 22 SB £25-£39 DB £40-£59 CC MC Visa Amex JCB

EAST DEREHAM Norfolk — 9E3

★★ Phoenix
Church Street, East Dereham NR19 1DL
☎ 01362-692276 Fax 01362-691752
22 bedrs, all ensuite, TCF TV ✱ P 20 SB £55 DB £65 HB £227.50-£252 D £11.95 CC MC Visa Amex DC

EASTBOURNE East Sussex — 5D4

★★ Congress
Hospitality merit award
31-41 Carlisle Road, Eastbourne BN21 4JS
☎ 01323-732118 Fax 01323-720016
Closed Nov-Feb ex Christmas, New Year
60 bedrs, 58 ensuite, 1 ⇌ TCF TV ✱ 🍴 P 16 SB £29-£36 DB £58-£72 HB £225-£270 D £9 CC MC Visa

★★ Downland Hotel & Restaurant
Hospitality, Restaurant merit awards
37 Lewes Road, Eastbourne BN21 2BU
☎ 01323-732689 Fax 01323-720321
14 bedrs, all ensuite, TCF TV P 10 No children under 10 SB £27.50-£37.50 DB £55-£75 HB £195-£245 D £17.50 CC MC Visa Amex DC JCB

The Congress Hotel

The Congress Hotel is an elegant family run hotel close to the theatres and seafront. We have 2 small car parks and offer an entertainment programme, 2 lifts, night porter. Service is our aim.

31-41 CARLISLE ROAD, EASTBOURNE, EAST SUSSEX BN21 4JS
Tel: (01323) 732118 Fax: (01323) 720016

★★ Farrar's
3/5 Wilmington Gardens, Eastbourne BN21 4JN
📞 01323-723737 Fax 01323-732902
Closed Jan
45 bedrs, all ensuite, TCF TV 🐾 🛗 P 35 SB £27-£32 DB £54-£64 HB £175-£273 D £8 CC MC Visa Amex JCB ♿

★★ Langham
Royal Parade, Eastbourne BN22 7AH
📞 01323-731451 Fax 01323-646623
Closed Dec-Jan
87 bedrs, all ensuite, 1 ⇔ TCF TV 🐾 🛗 P 4 SB £26-£34 DB £52-£68 HB £190-£275 D £11.50 CC MC Visa Amex JCB

★★ Lathom
Howards Square, Eastbourne BN21 4BG
📞 01323-641986 Fax 01323-416405
45 bedrs, all ensuite, TCF TV 🛗 P 10 SB £25-£30 DB £50-£60 HB £200-£240 D £8.75 CC MC Visa JCB

★★ New Wilmington
Hospitality merit award
25 Compton Street, Eastbourne BN21 4DU
📞 01323-721219 Fax 01323-728900
Closed Jan-Feb
40 bedrs, all ensuite, TCF TV 🐾 🛗 P 2 SB £31-£37 DB £50-£62 HB £235-£275 D £13 CC MC Visa Amex

★★ Oban
King Edwards Parade, Eastbourne BN21 4DS
📞 01323-731581 Fax 01323-721994
Closed Jan-Feb
30 bedrs, all ensuite, TCF TV 🐾 P 10 SB £24-£28 DB £48-£56 HB £242-£291 D £12 CC MC Visa ♿

★★ Stanley House
9-10 Howard Square, Eastbourne BN21 4BQ
📞 01323-731393 Fax 01323-738823
24 bedrs, all ensuite

★★ West Rocks
Grand Parade, Eastbourne BN21 4DL
📞 01323-725217 Fax 01323-720421
Closed mid Nov-mid Mar
44 bedrs, all ensuite, 5 TCF TV 🛗 No children under 3 SB £30-£40 DB £36-£70 HB £160-£346 D £10.50 CC MC Visa Amex DC JCB ♿

★★ York House
14/21 Royal Parade, Eastbourne BN22 7AP
📞 01323-412918 Fax 01323-646238
97 bedrs, all ensuite, 2 ⇔ TCF TV 🐾 🛗 SB £38 DB £76 HB £224-£280 D £12.50 CC MC Visa Amex DC JCB 🛗 🐾

Don't forget to mention the guide
When booking direct, please remember to tell the hotel that you chose it from RAC Bed & Breakfast 1998.

Bay Lodge *Acclaimed*
61-62 Royal Parade, Eastbourne BN22 7AQ
📞 01323-732515 Fax 01323-735009

Small, centrally situated, family run seafront hotel with a large sun lounge, overlooking the Redoubt Gardens. Take the A22 to the seafront, turn right towards the pier and the hotel is 200 yards on the right.

12 bedrs, 9 ensuite, 2 ⇔ TCF TV P 2 No children under 7 SB £19-£23 DB £36-£45 HB £169-£212 D £9 CC MC Visa

Beachy Rise *Acclaimed*
Beachy Head Road, Eastbourne BN20 7QN
📞 01323-639171
6 bedrs, all ensuite, TCF TV 🐾 SB £22-£24 DB £44-£48 HB £200-£210 D £10 CC MC Visa

Flamingo *Acclaimed*
20 Enys Road, Eastbourne BN21 2DN
📞 01323-721654
12 bedrs, all ensuite, TCF TV No children under 5 SB £21-£23 DB £42-£45 HB £175-£186 D £9 CC MC Visa Amex ♿

Mandalay *Acclaimed*
16 Trinity Trees, Eastbourne BN21 3LE
📞 01323-729222 Fax 01323-431494

Chalk Farm *Listed*
Cooper's Hill, Willingdon, Eastbourne BN20 9JD
📞 01323-503800 Fax 01323-520331
9 bedrs, 6 ensuite, 1 ⇔ TCF TV 🐾 P 21 SB £30-£37.50 DB £43-£49.50 D £13.95 CC MC Visa Amex DC

Courtlands *Listed*
68 Royal Parade, Eastbourne BN22 7AQ
📞 01323-726915
10 bedrs, 2 ensuite, 4 🛏, 4 ⇔ TCF TV P 1 SB £21-£23 DB £42-£46 HB £185-£210 D £7 CC MC Visa Amex

Sherwood *Listed*
7 Lascelles Terrace, Eastbourne BN21 4BJ
📞 01323-724002
12 bedrs, 11 ensuite, 2 ⇔ TCF TV 🐾 SB £15-£22 DB £29-£42 HB £130-£145 D £6.50

Meridale
91 Royal Parade, Eastbourne BN22 7AE
📞 01323-729686

Seafront guest house, all rooms ensuite with central heating, TV, coffee and tea. Unrestricted parking, own keys, family, twin and double rooms. Friendly atmosphere.

6 bedrs, all ensuite, 1 🛏 TCF TV 🐕 SB £15-£17.50
DB £30-£35 HB £35-£110

ECCLESHALL Staffordshire 7E2

Offley Grove Farm *Listed*
Adbaston, Eccleshall ST2 0QB
📞 01785-280205
3 bedrs, 1 🛏 TCF SB £16 DB £32 D £6

EGHAM Surrey 9D3

Runnymede Hotel & Spa
Windsor Road, Egham TW20 0AG
📞 01784-436171 Fax 01784-436340

Privately owned on the banks of the River Thames with extensive conference and spa facilities. Modern hotel with a reputation for quality and service.

ELY Cambridgeshire 9D3

★★ Lamb
2 Lynn Road, Ely CB7 4EJ
📞 01353-663574 Fax 01353-662023
31 bedrs, all ensuite, TCF TV 🐕 P 20 SB £58 DB £80
HB £320 D £14.95 CC MC Visa Amex DC

★ Nyton
7 Barton Road, Ely CB7 4HZ
📞 01353-662459 Fax 01353-1666217
10 bedrs, all ensuite, TCF TV 🐕 P 26 SB £38 DB £60
D £15 CC MC Visa Amex DC ♿

Quarterway House *Listed*
Ely Road, Little Thetford, Ely CB6 3HP
📞 01353-648964
3 bedrs, all ensuite, TCF TV ✗ P 9 No children under 7 SB £20-£30 DB £35 D £8.50 CC MC Visa

EMSWORTH Hampshire 4C4

Jingles *Acclaimed*
77 Horndean Road, Emsworth PO10 7PU
📞 01243-373755 Fax 01243-373755

Fully modernised Victorian house, furnished in an appropriate style. Situated between the South Downs and Chichester Harbour.

13 bedrs, 7 ensuite, 1 🛏 TCF TV 🐕 P 14 SB £23-£25
DB £40-£42 D £10 CC MC Visa Amex 🔟

Merry Hall
73 Horndean Road, Emsworth PO10 7PU
📞 01243-431377

Merry Hall Hotel is a modern hotel with a cosy relaxed atmosphere. The rooms are well equipped and some overlook the large private gardens and fields beyond.

9 bedrs, 6 ensuite, 3 🛏 TCF TV 🐕 P 12 SB £24-£30
DB £45-£50 CC MC Visa DC ♿

ENFIELD Middlesex — 5D2

★★ Holtwhites
92 Chase Side, Enfield EN2 0QN
☎ 0181-363 0124 Fax 0181-366 9089
Closed Christmas
30 bedrs, 28 ensuite, 2 ⌂, 1 ⇌ P 20 No children under 6 CC   MC Visa DC

EPSOM Surrey — 4C3

Epsom Downs *Acclaimed*
9 Longdown Road, Epsom KT17 3PT
☎ 01372-740643 Fax 01372-723259
15 bedrs, 13 ensuite, 2 ⌂, TCF TV P 10 SB £35–£52.88 DB £45–£59 D £12.50 CC   MC Visa DC

EPWORTH Lincolnshire — 11E4

★★ Red Lion
Market Place, Epworth DN9 1EU
☎ 01427-872208 Fax 01427-875214
20 bedrs, 19 ensuite, 1 ⇌ TCF TV P 40 SB £49.50 DB £69.50 D £2 CC   MC Visa Amex DC 🛌 ♿

ESHER Surrey — 4C3

★★ Haven
Portsmouth Road, Esher KT10 9AR
☎ 0181-398 0023 Fax 0181-398 9463
20 bedrs, all ensuite, 1 ⇌ TCF TV P 20 CC   MC Visa Amex DC

Lakewood House *Acclaimed*
Portsmouth Road, Esher KT10 9JH
☎ 01932-867859 Fax 01932-867142
12 bedrs, 6 ensuite, 1 ⇌ TV ⌂ ▣ P 50 SB £35.25 DB £82.25 D £12 🛌 ♿

ETON Berkshire — 4C2

★★ Christopher
110 High Street, Eton, Windsor SL4 6AN
☎ 01753-852359 Fax 01753-830914
33 bedrs, all ensuite, TCF TV ⇌ P 20 CC   MC Visa Amex DC

ETWALL Derbyshire — 8A2

Blenheim House *Acclaimed*
56 Main Street, Etwall DE6 6LP
☎ 01283-732254
11 bedrs, all ensuite

EVERCREECH Somerset — 3E2

★★ Pecking Mill Inn
A371, Evercreech BA4 6PG
☎ 01749-830336 Fax 01749-831316
Closed 25-26 Dec
6 bedrs, all ensuite, TCF TV ⇌ P 26 CC   MC Visa Amex DC

EVERSHOT Dorset — 3E3

Rectory House *Highly Acclaimed*
Fore Street, Evershot DT22 0JW
☎ 01935-83273 Fax 01935-83273
Closed Dec-Jan
5 bedrs, all ensuite, TCF TV ✉ P 6 No children SB £35–£60 DB £70–£80 HB £318–£346 D £18 CC   MC Visa

EVESHAM Worcestershire — 7F4

★★ Mill at Harvington
Hospitality, Comfort, Restaurant merit awards
Anchor Lane, Harvington, Evesham WR11 5NR
☎ 01386-870688 Fax 01386-870688
Closed 24-28 Dec
21 bedrs, all ensuite, TCF TV P 55 No children under 10 SB £58 DB £92 HB £360 D £22 CC   MC Visa Amex DC JCB 🛌 ♿ ▣

RECTORY HOUSE

Rectory House is an 18th Century listed building of great charm offering utmost comfort, fragrant rooms and antique furniture, a friendly atmosphere and delicious food.

Rectory House, Fore Street, Evershot, Dorset DT2 0JW
Tel: 01935 83273   Fax: 01935 83273

Church House *Highly Acclaimed*
Greenhill Park Road, Evesham WR11 4NL
📞 01386-40498

Classically elegant Victorian home overlooking historic Evesham. Affectionately run, offering antique furnishings combined with modern ensuite facilities. TV, tea and coffee making facilities, central heating, private parking. French and Spanish spoken.

3 bedrs, all ensuite, TCF TV ✱ P 3 SB £26-£35 DB £38-£46

Croft *Highly Acclaimed*
54 Greenhill, Evesham WR11 4NF
📞 01386-446035
3 bedrs, 2 ensuite, 1 ➥ TCF TV ✱ P 6 SB £30-£36 DB £40-£46

Park View *Listed*
Waterside, Evesham WR11 6BS
📞 01386-442639
E Mail mike.spiers@btinternet.com
Closed Christmas-New Year
26 bedrs, 7 ➥ ✱ P 30 SB £19-£23 DB £34-£39 CC MC Visa Amex DC JCB

EXEBRIDGE Somerset   3D2

★★ Anchor Inn
Exebridge TA22 9AZ
📞 01398-323433 Fax 01398-323808
8 bedrs, all ensuite, TCF TV ✱ P 150 SB £37 DB £60-£70 HB £295-£320 D £20 CC MC Visa

EXETER Devon   3D3

★★ Fingle Glen Hotel, Golf & Country Club
Old Tedburn Road, Tedburn St Mary, Exeter EX6 6AF
📞 01647-61817 Fax 01647-61135
7 bedrs, all ensuite, 2 ➥ TCF TV P 200 SB £39.50 DB £56.50 D £5.50 CC MC Visa Amex DC

★★ Great Western
St David's Station Approach, Exeter EX4 4NU
📞 01392-274039 Fax 01392-425529
41 bedrs, 30 ensuite, 6 ➥ TCF TV ✱ P 24 CC MC Visa Amex DC

★★ Red House
2 Whipton Village Road, Exeter EX4 8AR
📞 01392-256104 Fax 01392-435708

Why not mix business with pleasure? Lounge bar, carvery restaurant. All rooms ensuite with TV and welcome tray. Friendly atmosphere. Quality cuisine and service. Large car park.

12 bedrs, all ensuite, TCF TV ✱ P 28 SB £30-£35 DB £46-£50 D £7.95 CC MC Visa Amex DC ♿

★★ St Andrews
28 Alphington Road, Exeter EX2 8HN
📞 01392-276784 Fax 01392-250249
Closed 24 Dec-1 Jan
16 bedrs, all ensuite, TCF TV P 20 SB £39-£47 DB £49.50-£63 D £12 CC MC Visa Amex DC ♿

Gledhills *Acclaimed*
32 Alphington Road, Exeter EX2 8HN
📞 01392-430469 Fax 01392-430469
Closed Christmas

Family run, licensed hotel, close to the city, river and leisure centre. All modern comfortable bedrooms with full facilities. Own car park.

12 bedrs, 10 ensuite, 2 🚿, 1 ➥ TCF TV P 12 SB £20-£23 DB £40-£44 CC MC Visa

Park View *Acclaimed*
8 Howell Road, Exeter EX4 4LG
📞 01392-271772 Fax 01392-253047

Family run, listed Georgian building. Overlooking the park, close to the city centre, university and stations. From M5 follow B3183 into centre to clock tower roundabout. Take third exit into Elm Grove Road, at end turn left into Howell Road, hotel 100m.

15 bedrs, 8 ensuite, 2 🛏, 2 ➡ TCF TV 🐕 P 6
SB £20-£30 DB £35-£45 CC MC Visa Amex

Braeside *Listed*
21 New North Road, Exeter EX4 4HF
📞 01392-256875
7 bedrs, 2 🛏, 2 ➡ 🐕

Regent's Park *Listed*
Polsloe Road, Exeter EX1 2NU
📞 01392-259749
Closed Christmas
11 bedrs, 3 ➡ P 16

Telstar *Listed*
77 St David's Hill, Exeter EX4 4DW
📞 01392-272466
17 bedrs, 4 ensuite, 4 🛏, 2 ➡ TCF TV 🐕 P 7

Trees Mini *Listed*
2 Queens Crescent, York Road, Exeter EX4 6AY
📞 01392-259531

Blue Ribbon Awards

The highest honour the RAC can bestow on a hotel is to award it Blue Ribbon status. Only hotels who have gained all three merit awards for Hospitality, Comfort and Restaurant are eligible for the award.

Horselake Farm
Cheriton Bishop, Exeter EX6 6HD
📞 01647-24220 Fax 01647-24220

A beautiful 16th century thatched house, set in exquisite mature gardens on the edge of Dartmoor. Self catering accommodation also available in a stylishly converted barn.

3 bedrs, 1 ensuite, 1 ➡ TCF TV P 6 SB £15-£17 DB £36-£40 HB £149-£189 D £8 [3]

Marianne Pool Farm
Clyst St George, Exeter EX3 0NZ
📞 01392-874939
Closed Dec-Feb

Peaceful thatched Devon longhouse down quiet country lane. 2 miles M5 (jnt 30) and midway between Exeter and coast, and Woodbury and Exeter Golf Courses.

2 bedrs, 1 ensuite, 1 ➡ TCF 🐕 P 3 SB £16.50 DB £38

Whitemoor Farm
Doddiscombsleigh, Exeter EX6 7PU
📞 01647-252423
Closed 25 Dec

A 16th century listed thatched farmhouse, surrounded by garden and farmland, with oak beams and doors. Log fires in winter, fully central heated and double glazed.

4 bedrs, 1 ↠ ⊠ ⋔ P 6 SB £17.50-£18.50 DB £35-£36 HB £168.50-£179 D £8 ▣

EXMOUTH Devon 3D3

★★ Manor
The Beacon, Exmouth EX8 2AG
☎ 01395-272549 Fax 01395-225519
Closed 2 weeks Jan
40 bedrs, all ensuite, TCF TV ⊡ P 15 No children under 5 SB £25-£30 DB £45-£55 HB £175-£210 D £7.50 CC MC Visa

★ Aliston House
58 Salterton Road, Exmouth EX8 2EW
☎ 01395-274119
15 bedrs, 12 ensuite, 2 ↠ TCF TV ⋔ P 16 SB £25-£27 DB £50-£54 HB £209-£219 D £8 CC MC Visa ♿

FAKENHAM Norfolk 9E2

★★ (Inn) Crown
Market Place, Fakenham NR21 9BP
☎ 01328-851418 Fax 01328-862433
11 bedrs, all ensuite, TCF TV P 25 SB £45 DB £62 D £15.95

★★ Wensum Lodge
Bridge Street, Fakenham NR21 9AY
☎ 01328-862100 Fax 01328-863365
9 bedrs, all ensuite, 9 ☜, TCF TV P 20 SB £45 DB £60 HB £210 D £10 CC MC Visa Amex DC JCB ▣

FALMOUTH Cornwall 2A4

Prospect House *Highly Acclaimed*
1 Church Road, Penryn, Falmouth TR10 8DA
☎ 01326-373198 Fax 01326-373198

Prospect House is a late Georgian 'gentleman's residence', appropriately decorated and furnished. It is well situated for visiting all central and west Cornwall, including Roseland.

3 bedrs, all ensuite, 1 ↠ ⋔ P 3 No children under 12 SB £30-£35 DB £50-£55 CC MC Visa

Bosanneth *Acclaimed*
Gyllyngvase Hill, Falmouth TR11 4DW
☎ 01326-314649 Fax 01326-314649
8 bedrs, all ensuite, TCF TV P 8 No children under 5 SB £22-£25 DB £44-£50 HB £155-£183 D £8

Chellowdene *Acclaimed*
Gyllyngvase Hill, Falmouth TR11 4DN
☎ 01326-314950
6 bedrs, all ensuite, TCF TV P 6 No children under 13 SB £40-£46 DB £160-£190

Cotswold House *Acclaimed*
49 Melvill Road, Falmouth TR11 4DF
☎ 01326-312077 Fax 01326-319181

Once a Victorian private house, now extensively converted and tastefully furnished. Set among trees and palms with attractive hanging baskets and shrubs.

10 bedrs, 9 ensuite, 1 ☜, TCF TV P 8 No children under 4 SB £18-£19 DB £36-£38 HB £150-£180 D £7

Four Seasons *Acclaimed*
43 Melvill Road, Falmouth TR11 4DG
☎ 01326-311465 Fax 01326-311465
9 bedrs, 6 ensuite, 1 ↠ TCF TV P 7 No children under 5

Gyllyngvase House *Acclaimed*
Gyllyngvase Road, Falmouth TR11 4DJ
☎ 01326-312956 Fax 01326-316166
Closed Nov-Mar
15 bedrs, 12 ensuite, 2 ↠ TCF TV ⋔ P 15 SB £24.50-£28.50 DB £49-£57 HB £220-£265 D £11.50 CC MC Visa Amex DC

Hawthorne Dene *Acclaimed*
12 Pennance Road, Falmouth TR11 4EA
☎ 01326-311427
Closed Sep-Apr
9 bedrs, all ensuite, TCF TV P 9 SB £19-£22 DB £38-£44 HB £145-£178

RAC Hotel Reservations Service
0870 603 9109
(Calls charged at national call rate)

FALMOUTH – ENGLAND

Ivanhoe *Acclaimed*
7 Melvill Road, Falmouth TR11 4AS
☎ 01326-319083

Charming Edwardian house near beaches and town. Comfortable rooms with all facilities. Pleasant lounge. Parking. Tempting breakfast menu. ETB 2 crown commended.

7 bedrs, 4 ensuite, 2 ⇌ TCF TV P 2 SB £18-£22 DB £36-£44 CC MC Visa Amex DC JCB

Rathgowry *Acclaimed*
Gyllyngvase Hill, Falmouth TR11 4DN
☎ 01326-313482
Closed Oct-May
10 bedrs, all ensuite, TV ⚥ P 10 SB £16-£22 DB £32-£44 HB £155-£180 D £7

Trevaylor *Acclaimed*
8 Pennance Road, Falmouth TR11 4EA
☎ 01326-313041
E Mail melsan@globalnet.co.uk
8 bedrs, 7 ensuite, TCF TV P 8 No children SB £20-£22 DB £32-£36 HB £145.25-£164.50

Tudor Court *Listed*
55 Melvill Road, Falmouth TR11 4DF
☎ 01326-312807 Fax 01326-312807

Family owned, licensed, eleven bedroomed mock Tudor hotel, set within pleasant gardens and ideally situated for Falmouths three beaches, the town and harbour.

11 bedrs, 10 ensuite, TCF TV P 13 No children under 6 SB £18.50-£20 DB £36-£39 HB £169.50 D £7.50 CC MC Visa Amex DC

FALMOUTH BEACH RESORT HOTEL
FALMOUTH

Situated at the beach with panoramic views the hotel boasts 127 en suite rooms. 'The Beach Club' (pool, sauna, jacuzzi spa, fitness suite) is free to residents. Our restaurants offer carvery or A la Carte dining and our conference rooms suit all occasions.

TEL: 01326 318084
FAX: 01326 319147

Falmouth Beach Resort
Gyllyngvase Beach, Falmouth TR11 4NA
☎ 01326-318084 Fax 01326-319147
127 bedrs, all ensuite, TCF TV ⚥ 🌐 P 100 SB £42-£49 DB £66-£80 HB £273-£322 CC MC Visa Amex DC 🛎 🏨 🍽 ♿

FAREHAM Hampshire — 4B4

★★ Maylings Manor
Highland Road, Fareham PO16 7XJ
☎ 01329-286451 Fax 01329-822584
24 bedrs, all ensuite, 1 ⇌ TCF TV ⚥ P 87 SB £39-£48 DB £45-£58 D £10.45 CC MC Visa Amex DC

Avenue House *Acclaimed*
22 The Avenue, Fareham PO14 1NS
☎ 01329-232175 Fax 01329-232196
17 bedrs, all ensuite, TCF TV ⚥ P 17 SB £30-£45 DB £40-£55 CC MC Visa Amex DC ♿

FARINGDON Oxfordshire — 4A2

★★ Faringdon
Market Place, Faringdon SN7 7HL
☎ 01367-240536 Fax 01367-243250
20 bedrs, all ensuite, TCF TV ⚥ P 5
SB £47 DB £57 D £8 CC MC Visa Amex DC

White Horse *Highly Acclaimed*
Woolstone, Faringdon SN7 7GL
☎ 01367-820726 Fax 01367-820566
6 bedrs, all ensuite, TCF TV ⚥ P 80 SB £40 DB £55-£60 D £15.95 CC MC Visa Amex DC JCB ♿

FARMBOROUGH Somerset 3E1

Streets *Acclaimed*
The Streets, Farmborough BA3 1AR
☎ 01761-471452 Fax 01761-471452
8 bedrs, all ensuite, **P** 14 No children under 5 **SB** £44
DB £56 **D** £15 **CC** MC Visa Amex

FARNHAM Surrey 4C3

★★ Bishop's Table
*Hospitality, Comfort,
Restaurant merit awards*
27 West Street, Farnham GU9 7DR
☎ 01252-710222 Fax 01252-733494
Closed 29 Dec-3 Jan
18 bedrs, all ensuite, **TCF TV SB** £77 **DB** £93 **D** £18 **CC**
MC Visa Amex DC

FARTHING CORNER Kent 5E3

Travelodge *Lodge*
Granada Medway, M2, Farthing Corner, Gillingham
ME8 8PW
☎ 01634-377337 Fax 01634-360848
56 bedrs, all ensuite, **TCF TV P** 200 **SB** £42.95 **CC** MC
Visa Amex DC

FELIXSTOWE Suffolk 9F4

★★ Waverley
2 Wolsey Gardens, Felixstowe IP11 7DF
☎ 01394-282811 Fax 01394-670185
19 bedrs, all ensuite, **TCF TV P** 35 **SB** £63.45
DB £89.95 **D** £15.95 **CC** MC Visa Amex DC

Dolphin *Listed*
41 Beach Station Road, Felixstowe IP11 8EY
☎ 01394-282261
3 bedrs, 2 ensuite, 2 **TCF TV P** 35 **CC** MC Visa Amex

FERNDOWN Dorset 3F3

★★ Coach House Inn
79 Wimborne Road East, Ferndown
BH22 9NW
☎ 01202-861222 Fax 01202-894130
24 bedrs, all ensuite, **P** 100 **SB** £47-£53 **D** £53-£60
D £10 **CC** MC Visa Amex DC

FILEY North Yorkshire 11E2

★★ Sea Brink
The Beach, Filey YO14 9LA
☎ 01723-513257 Fax 01723-514139
Closed Jan

Traditional sea front hotel overlooking Filey Bay. Delightful ensuite bedrooms with all facilities, many with magnificent views. Licensed restaurant/coffee shop. German spoken.

9 bedrs, 7 ensuite, 2 **TCF TV SB** £30 **DB** £50
HB £218 **D** £10 **CC** MC Visa JCB

Downcliffe House *Highly Acclaimed*
The Beach, Filey YO14 9LA
☎ 01723-513310 Fax 01723-516141
Closed 2-17 Jan
10 bedrs, all ensuite, **TCF TV P** 10 No children under 5
SB £30-£35 **DB** £60-£70 **HB** £210-£250 **D** £12 **CC** MC
Visa

Seafield *Acclaimed*
9-11 Rutland Street, Filey YO14 9JA
☎ 01723-513715
13 bedrs, all ensuite, 1 **TCF TV P** 9 **SB** £18.50-£20.50
DB £37-£41 **HB** £160-£174 **D** £5.50 **CC** MC Visa

FINCHINGFIELD Essex 5D1

Finchingfield House *Acclaimed*
Finchingfield CM7 4JS
☎ 01371-810289 Fax 01371-810289
3 bedrs, 1 ensuite, 1 **TV P** 6 No children under
16 **SB** £28-£35 **DB** £40-£48 **HB** £160-£185

FINEDON Northamptonshire 8C4

★★ Tudor Gate
High Street, Finedon, Wellingborough NN9 5JN
☎ 01933-680408 Fax 01933-680745
27 bedrs, all ensuite, **TCF TV P** 45 **SB** £44-£80
DB £55.50-£100 **D** £12 **CC** MC Visa Amex DC

FLEETWOOD Lancashire 10B3

★★ New Boston
41-43 The Esplanade, Fleetwood FY7 6QE
☎ 01253-874796
35 bedrs, 18 ensuite, 6 **TCF TV P** 8
SB £20-£24.50 **DB** £39-£49 **HB** £140 **D** £8.95

FORDINGBRIDGE Hampshire 4A4

★★ Ashburn
Hospitality, Restaurant merit awards
Station Road, Fordingbridge SP16 1JP
☎ 01425-652060 Fax 01425-652150
20 bedrs, all ensuite, TCF TV 🐕 P 60 CC MC Visa Amex JCB 🏊

FORDWICH Kent 5F3

★★ George & Dragon
Fordwich CT2 0BN
☎ 01227-710661
12 bedrs, 7 ensuite, 2 🛏 🐕 P 40

FOWEY Cornwall 2B4

★★ Cormorant
Golant, Fowey PL23 1LL
☎ 01726-833426 Fax 01726-833426

Small family run hotel, all bedrooms enjoying spectacular views over the Fowey Estuary to timbered slopes beyond. Chef proprietor ensures highest quality food. Indoor pool. Log fire.

11 bedrs, all ensuite, TCF TV 🐕 P 20 SB £37-£54 DB £72-£88 D £18 CC MC Visa Amex JCB 🏊

★ Old Quay House
Fore Street, Fowey PL23 1AQ
☎ 01726-833302
9 bedrs, 7 ensuite, 1 🛏 TCF TV 🐕 SB £26-£36 DB £42-£52 HB £220-£255 D £12 CC MC Visa

Carnethic House *Highly Acclaimed*
Lambs Barn, Fowey PL23 1HQ
☎ 01726-833336 Fax 01726-833336
Closed Dec-Jan
8 bedrs, 5 ensuite, 3 🛁, 2 🛏 TCF TV 🐕 P 20 SB £30-£40 DB £46-£64 HB £250-£310 D £15 CC MC Visa Amex DC 🏊 🎾 🎱 ♿

FOWNHOPE Herefordshire 7E4

★★ Green Man Inn
Comfort merit award
Fownhope HR1 4PE
☎ 01432-860243 Fax 01432-860207
20 bedrs, all ensuite, TCF TV 🐕 P 75 SB £33-£34 DB £52.50-£54 HB £250-£262.50 D £15 CC MC Visa Amex DC 📺 ♿

FRINTON-ON-SEA Essex 5F1

★★ Maplin
Restaurant merit award
Esplanade, Frinton-on-Sea CO13 9EL
☎ 01255-673832
Closed Jan
12 bedrs, 10 ensuite, 1 🛏 TCF TV 🐕 P 12 SB £40-£57.50 DB £70-£100 HB £300-£355 D £19 CC MC Visa 🏊

★★ Rock
Hospitality merit award
Esplanade, Frinton-on-Sea CO13 9EO
☎ 0800-0187194 Fax 01255-675173
Closed Jan

A small luxury hotel, situated on The Esplanade, facing the greensward. Uninterrupted views of the sea and sands of the coastline from many of the rooms.

6 bedrs, all ensuite, 2 🛏 TCF TV 🐕 P 12 SB £50-£60 DB £75-£82 D £17 CC MC Visa Amex DC

FRODSHAM Cheshire 7D1

★★ Old Hall
Comfort merit award
Main Street, Frodsham WA6 7AB
☎ 01928-732052 Fax 01928-739046
21 bedrs, all ensuite, 🐕 P 31 CC MC Visa Amex DC

GAINSBOROUGH Lincolnshire 8C1

★★ Hickman Hill
Cox's Hill, Gainsborough DN21 1HH
☎ 01427-613639 Fax 01427-677591
8 bedrs, 6 ensuite, 1 🛏 TCF TV P 30 SB £39 DB £51 D £11 CC MC Visa

GARBOLDISHAM Norfolk　　　　　　　　9E3

Ingleneuk Lodge *Highly Acclaimed*
Hopton Road, Garboldisham IP22 2RQ
☎ 01953-681541 Fax 01953-681633
Closed Christmas & New Year
7 bedrs, all ensuite, 1 ⚑ TCF TV ✠ P 20 SB £33 DB £53
HB £250-£270 D £15 CC MC Visa Amex JCB ♿

GATWICK AIRPORT West Sussex　　　　5D3

★★ Langshott Manor
Langshott, Horley RH6 9LN
☎ 01293-786680 Fax 01293-783905
9 bedrs, all ensuite, TCF TV P 30 No children under 7
SB £98.50 DB £125-£155 D £23
CC MC Visa Amex DC JCB

Vulcan Lodge *Highly Acclaimed*
27 Massetts Road, Horley RH6 7DQ
☎ 01293-771522
4 bedrs, 3 ensuite, 1 ⚑ TCF TV P 10 SB £25-£31 DB £42-£44 CC MC Visa

Barnwood *Acclaimed*
Balcombe Road, Pound Hill, Crawley RH10 7RU
☎ 01293-882709 Fax 01293-886041
E Mail reception@barnwood.co.uk
Closed 25 Dec-3 Jan
35 bedrs, all ensuite, TV P 55 SB £40 DB £50 D £9 CC MC Visa Amex DC JCB 🍴

Corner House *Acclaimed*
72 Massetts Road, Horley RH6 7ED
☎ 01293-784574 Fax 01293-784620
E Mail the corner house@btinternet.com
Closed Christmas

Family run hotel offering quality accommodation. 24 hour transport to and from Gatwick. Situated only minutes from the airport. Restaurant, bar and holiday parking.

8 bedrs, 25 ensuite, 2 ⚑ TCF TV ✠ P 45 SB £29-£35 B £41-£49 CC MC Visa Amex DC

Gainsborough Lodge *Acclaimed*
39 Massetts Road, Horley RH6 7DT
☎ 01293-783982 Fax 01293-785365
18 bedrs, 16 ensuite, 2 ⚑ TCF TV P 20 SB £32.50
DB £42.50 CC MC Visa Amex DC JCB

Lawn *Acclaimed*
30 Massetts Road, Horley RH6 7DE
☎ 01293-775751 Fax 01293-821803

Luxury Victorian house set in a mature garden, four minutes to Gatwick, two minutes to the centre of Horley and close to mainline rail station. Holiday parking. No smoking.

7 bedrs, all ensuite, TCF TV ✉ ✠ P 15 DB £35-£45 CC MC Visa Amex

Massetts Lodge *Acclaimed*
28 Massetts Road, Horley RH6 7DE
☎ 01293-782738 Fax 01293-782738
10 bedrs, 8 ensuite, 2 ⚑ TCF TV P 15 CC MC Visa Amex DC JCB ♿

Mill Lodge *Acclaimed*
25 Brighton Road, Salfords RH1 6PP
☎ 01293-771170
10 bedrs, 2 ensuite, 2 ⚑ 🅿 P 34

Melville Lodge *Listed*
15 Brighton Road, Horley RH6 7HH
☎ 01293-784951 Fax 01293-785669
6 bedrs, 3 ensuite, 1 ⚑ TCF TV ✠ P 15 SB £25 DB £35-£40 CC MC Visa Amex DC JCB

Prinsted *Listed*
Oldfield Road, Horley RH6 7EP
☎ 01293-785233 Fax 01293-820624
6 bedrs, 4 ensuite, 1 ⌂, 1 ⚑ TCF TV ✠ SB £30 DB £37-£42 CC MC Visa Amex

Short Breaks

Many hotels provide special rates for weekend and mid-week breaks - sometimes these are quoted in the hotel's entry, otherwise ring direct for the latest offers.

Woodlands *Listed*
42 Massetts Road, Horley RH6 7DS
☎ 01293-782994 Fax 01293-776358

A non-smoking family run guest house, half a mile north of Gatwick Airport, off A23. Courtesy car. Long term car parking. English Breakfast. Tariff £30 - £42.

5 bedrs, all ensuite, 1 ⇌ TCF TV ✕ P 20 SB £28-£30 DB £38-£40

GISLINGHAM Suffolk   9E4

Old Guildhall *Highly Acclaimed*
Mill Street, Gislingham, Eye IP23 8JT
☎ 01379-783361
Closed Jan
4 bedrs, all ensuite, TCF TV ✕ ✕ P 5 DB £55 HB £220 D £12.50

GLASTONBURY Somerset   3E2

Cradlebridge Farm *Listed*
Glastonbury BA16 9SD
☎ 01458-831827
2 bedrs, all ensuite, P 10 SB £30 DB £40 ♿

GLOSSOP Derbyshire   10C4

Wind in the Willows *Highly Acclaimed*
Derbyshire Level, Off Sheffield Road (A57), SK13 9PT
☎ 01457-868001 Fax 01457-853354
Closed Christmas

Peace, quiet and tranquillity, log fires, oak panelling, antiques, all ensuite magnificent bedrooms overlooking the Peak District National Park and golf course. Relieve your stress.

12 bedrs, all ensuite, TCF TV ✕ P 20 No children under 8 SB £65-£83 DB £80-£105 D £19 CC MC Visa Amex DC

George *Listed*
34 Norfolk Street, Glossop SK13 9QU
☎ 01457-855449 Fax 01457-857033
9 bedrs, 6 ensuite, 1 ⇌ TCF TV CC MC Visa Amex DC ♿

Snake Pass Inn *Listed*
Nr Ashopton Woodlands, Glossop SK30 2BJ
☎ 01433-651480 Fax 01433-651480
7 bedrs, all ensuite, TCF TV P 38 SB £25 DB £45 D £11 CC MC Visa Amex ♿

GLOUCESTER Gloucestershire   7E4

Gilbert's *Highly Acclaimed*
Gilbert's Lane, Brookthorpe, Gloucester GL4 0UH
☎ 01452-812364 Fax 01452-812364
E Mail j.beer@gilbertsbb.demon.co.uk

This 400 year old Listed gem lies beneath the Cotswolds, central to Bath, Oxford, Stratford, etc. The organic smallholding contributes to the delicious British breakfast.

4 bedrs, all ensuite, TCF TV P 6 SB £25-£37 DB £48-£57

Rotherfield House *Highly Acclaimed*
5 Horton Road, Gloucester GL1 3PX
☎ 01452-410500 Fax 01452-381922

Elegant, detached Victorian property tastefully extended and sympathetically decorated to a high standard throughout. Neat and tidy.

13 bedrs, 8 ensuite, 2 ⇌ TCF TV ✕ P 11 SB £30-£32 DB £44-£46 HB £210-£240 D £10 CC MC Visa Amex DC

Pembury *Acclaimed*
9 Pembury Road, St Barnabas, Gloucester GL4 9UE
☎ 01452-521856 Fax 01452-303418

Licensed family run detached house, close to ski-slope and golfing facilities. Ideal base for Cotswolds, Gloucester docks and cathedral.

10 bedrs, 5 ensuite, 2 ⛉, 1 ⚐ TCF TV P 10 SB £18 DB £32 D £5 CC MC Visa

Edgewood House
Churcham, Gloucester GL2 8AA
☎ 01452-750232

Family run country house in two acres of lovely gardens, four miles from Gloucester. Bedrooms decorated and furnished to a high standard, comfortable beds, hearty breakfasts.

3 bedrs, 2 ensuite, 1 ⚐ TCF ☒ P 6 No children under 8 SB £27-£29 DB £36-£45

GOATHLAND North Yorkshire 11E2

Heatherdene *Acclaimed*
Near Whitby, Goathland YO22 5AN
☎ 01947-896334
8 bedrs, 7 ensuite, 1 ⚐ TCF TV ⚑ P 10
SB £30 DB £58-£70 D £13 ♿

GODALMING Surrey 4C3

★★ Squirrel at Hurtmore
Hurtmore, Godalming GU7 2RN
☎ 01483-860223

Meads *Listed*
65 Meadrow, Godalming GU7 3HS
☎ 01483-421800 Fax 01483-429313
15 bedrs, 6 ensuite, 3 ⛉, 2 ⚐ TCF TV ⚑ P 14 SB £26-£42 DB £40-£50 CC MC Visa Amex

GOOLE Lincolnshire 11E4

★★ Clifton
1 Clifton Gardens, Boothferry Road, DN14 6AR
☎ 01405-761336 Fax 01405-762350
E Mail clifton@globalnet.co.uk.
Closed Christmas
9 bedrs, 8 ensuite, 1 ⚐ TCF TV ⚑ P 8 SB £39 DB £47
D £7.95 CC MC Visa Amex DC JCB

GORLESTON-ON-SEA Norfolk 9F3

★★ Pier
Harbour Mouth, Gorleston-on-Sea NR31 6PL
☎ 01493-662631 Fax 01493-440263
20 bedrs, all ensuite, ⚑ P 20 CC MC Visa Amex DC

Avalon *Acclaimed*
54 Clarence Road, Gorleston-on-Sea NR31 6DR
☎ 01493-662114 Fax 01493-661521
9 bedrs, 4 ensuite, 2 ⚐ TCF TV SB £15-£18 DB £30-£36
HB £128-£136 D £7 CC Amex DC

Squirrel's Nest *Acclaimed*
71 Avondale Road, Gorleston-on-Sea NR31 6DJ
☎ 01493-662746 Fax 01493-662746
9 bedrs, all ensuite, 1 ⚐ TCF TV ⚑ P 5
SB £23-£30 DB £46-£60 HB £130-£230 D £10.95 CC MC Visa Amex ♿

GOSPORT Hampshire 4B4

Royal Navy Submarine Museum

Climb aboard the post-war submarine Alliance, and then discover the stories of lives dedicated to service under the seas, through fascinating exhibits and crew members' personal effects.

Free car park, Jolly Roger Café, Picnic Areas and Gift Shop.

Haslar Jetty Road, Gosport, Hampshire PO12 2AS
Tel: (01705) 529217

Manor *Acclaimed*
Brewers Lane, Bridgemary, Gosport PO13 0JY
☎ 01329-232946 Fax 01329-220392
12 bedrs, all ensuite, TCF TV P 45 SB £38 DB £55 D £9
CC MC Visa Amex JCB

GRANGE-OVER-SANDS Cumbria　　10B3

Elton *Highly Acclaimed*
Windermere Road, Grange-over-Sands LA11 6EQ
☎ 01539-532838

Our small, family run, licensed hotel prides itself in good food and hospitality. Set in peaceful surroundings, with the advantage of ground floor accommodation.

7 bedrs, 5 ensuite, TCF TV ✻ SB £20-£29 DB £40-£48 HB £210-£218 D £11 ♿

GRANTHAM Lincolnshire　　8C2

Lanchester *Acclaimed*
84 Harrowby Road, Grantham NG31 9DS
☎ 01476-574169
3 bedrs, 1 ensuite, 1 ✻ TV P 3 SB £20 DB £30 D £15

Garden *Listed*
86 Barrowby Road, Grantham NG31 8AF
☎ 01476-62040
10 bedrs, 6 ensuite, 3 ✻ TCF TV P 23 ✻

GRASMERE Cumbria　　10B2

★★ Grasmere
Hospitality, Comfort merit awards
Broadgate, Grasmere LA22 9TA
☎ 01539-435277 Fax 01539-435277
Closed Jan

A Victorian country house hotel situated in an acre of informal gardens running down to the River Rothey and close to the centre of Wordsworth's Grasmere.

12 bedrs, all ensuite, TV ✻ P 20 No children under 8
SB £35-£42 DB £70-£80 HB £180-£200 D £13 CC MC Visa JCB ♿

★★ Moss Grove
Grasmere LA22 9SW
☎ 01539-435251 Fax 01539-435691
E Mail martinw@globalnet.co.uk
Closed Dec-Jan
14 bedrs, 13 ensuite, 1 ✻ TCF TV P 16 SB £26-£45 DB £52-£90 HB £272-£370 D £14 CC MC Visa JCB

★★ Oak Bank
Hospitality, Restaurant merit awards
Broadgate, Grasmere LA22 9TA
☎ 01539-435217 Fax 01539-435685
Closed Jan
15 bedrs, all ensuite, TCF TV ✻ P 16
SB £25-£45 DB £50-£80 HB £266-£320 D £17 CC MC Visa JCB

Bridge House *Highly Acclaimed*
Stock Lane, Grasmere LA22 9SN
☎ 01539-435425 Fax 01539-435523
Closed Jan
12 bedrs, all ensuite, TCF TV P 20 No children under 8
CC MC Visa

Fairy Glen *Listed*
Swan Lane, Grasmere LA22 9RH
☎ 01539-35620
3 bedrs, 2 ✻, 1 ✻ TCF P 3 No children DB £34-£40

Forest Side
Grasmere, Near Ambleside LA22 9RN
☎ 015394-35250
Closed mid Jan-mid Feb

An impressive Victorian mansion, nestling at the base of wooded fells, just a ten minute stroll from the picturesque village of Grasmere.

32 bedrs, 24 ensuite, TCF P 30 SB £19.50 DB £39 D £9.35 CC MC Visa

Titteringdales
Pye Lane, Grasmere LA22 9RQ
☎ 01539-435439 Fax 01539-435439

Small, family owned and run guest house situated in a quiet village location, only five minutes from the centre with ample off-road parking. Good breakfasts.

8 bedrs, all ensuite, TCF TV P 8 No children under 12
SB £17.50-£22.50 DB £35-£45

GREAT LANGDALE Cumbria   10B2

★★ Eltermere
Elterwater, Ambleside LA22 9HY
☎ 01539-437207
18 bedrs, 15 ensuite, 3 ↵ P 25 SB £28-£39.50 DB £56-£79 HB £245-£322 D £17

GROBY Leicestershire   8B3

★★ Brant
Leicester Road, Groby LE6 0DU
☎ 0116-2872703 Fax 0116-2321255
8 bedrs, all ensuite, TCF TV ↑ P 100 SB £25-£37.50
DB £35-£49.95 D £9 CC MC Visa DC

GUILDFORD Surrey   4C3

Carlton *Listed*
36 London Road, Guildford GU1 2AF
☎ 01483-575158 Fax 01483-534669
36 bedrs, 19 ensuite, 4 ↵ TCF TV P 40
SB £36 DB £46
CC MC Visa Amex

Harrow *Listed*
The Street, Compton, Guildford GU3 1EG
☎ 01483-810379
4 bedrs, all ensuite, TCF TV ☑ P 35
CC MC Visa Amex

Blanes Court
Albury Road, Guildford GU1 2BT
☎ 01483-573171 Fax 01483-32780
Closed 2 weeks at Christmas

Tastefully decorated ensuite rooms and holiday apartment. Large peaceful garden and heated pool. 10 minutes walk to town/country. Cosy bar, easy access to airports, ample parking.

15 bedrs, 12 ensuite, 1 ↵ TCF TV ↑ P 20 SB £30-£48.50
DB £65-£68.50 HB £240 CC MC Visa

GUISBOROUGH Cleveland   11D2

★★ Fox & Hounds
Hospitality merit award
Slapewith, Guisborough TS14 6PX
☎ 01287-632964 Fax 01287-610778
15 bedrs, all ensuite, ↑ P 50 CC MC Visa Amex DC

HAILSHAM East Sussex   5D4

★★ Old Forge
Hospitality, Restaurant merit awards
Magham Down, Hailsham BN27 1PN
☎ 01323-842893 Fax 01323-842893
Closed Christmas-New Year
8 bedrs, 1 ensuite, 5 ⌂, 2 ↵ TCF TV ↑ P 12 SB £40
DB £50-£60 D £15 CC MC Visa Amex DC

HALESWORTH Suffolk   9F3

Valley Farm B & B and Vineyards
Rumburgh Road, Wissett, Halesworth IP19 0JJ
☎ 01986-785216 Fax 01986-785521

Beautiful farmhouse with an operating vineyard. Large, peaceful gardens. Fresh local food cooked to the highest standards. Comfortable rooms and cosy log fires.

4 bedrs, 2 ensuite, 2 ↵ TCF TV P 10 No children under 5 SB £16-£18 DB £22-£24 D £10.95 CC MC Visa

HALIFAX West Yorkshire 10C4

★★ Hobbit
Hospitality, Comfort, Restaurant merit awards
Hob Lane, Norland, Halifax HX6 3QL
☎ 01422-832202 Fax 01422-835381
22 bedrs, all ensuite, **TCF TV P** 100 **SB** £32-£59 **DB** £49-£73 **D** £11 **CC** MC Visa Amex DC

HALSTOCK Dorset 3E2

Halstock Mill
Halstock BA22 9SJ
☎ 01935-891278
Closed Christmas

Off the beaten track, 17th century Halstock Mill ensures tranquillity, surrounded by 400 acres of pasture land. Dedicated cook provides excellent home grown/locally produced food.

4 bedrs, all ensuite, **TCF TV P** 20 No children under 5
CC MC Visa Amex

HAMPTON IN ARDEN West Midlands 8A3

Cottage Listed
Kenilworth Road, Balsall Common, Hampton in Arden B92 0LW
☎ 01675-442323 Fax 01675-443323

A beautiful cottage with individually decorated ensuite bedrooms, offering the best of facilities, the highest standards of service and a full breakfast of your choice. Located on the A452, 2½ miles from the NEC, Birmingham Airport and railway station.

10 bedrs, 7 ensuite, 2 ⇌ **TCF TV** ⌇ **P** 15 **SB** £20-£25 **DB** £36-£44

Hollies Listed
Kenilworth Road, Balsall Common, Hampton in Arden B92 0LW
☎ 01675-442941 Fax 01675-442941
8 bedrs, 6 ensuite, 1 ⇌ **TCF TV** ⌇ **P** 12 **SB** £20 **DB** £40

THE HOLLIES
Bed & Breakfast

ETB ☆☆ Commended   RAC Listed

The Only Guest House In The Area Recommended By "WHICH"

Excellent accommodation in a rural location offering quality accommodation with –

• Private car parking • Colour TV • Coffee and tea making facilities • En-suites • Visitors lounge with Sky TV • Prize winners of the Food Hygiene Award • Fire Safety Certification

AMENITIES DISTANCE APPROXIMATELY

National Exhibition Centre	2.5 miles	Royal Agricultural Centre	6 miles
Birmingham International Airport	3 miles	International Convention Centre	9 miles
National Motorcycle Museum	2.5 miles	Birmingham City Centre	9 miles
Birmingham Business Park	3 miles	International Train Station	2.5 miles

LOCAL GOLF COURSES

Forest of Arden	2 miles	Copt Heath	4 miles
Belfry	8 miles	Stonebridge	1 mile

• A warm friendly atmosphere welcoming families and businessmen alike.

• Local shops, pubs and restaurants within one and a half miles.

Kenilworth Road, (A452 to Balsall Common), Hampton-in-Arden, Solihull B92 0LW
Tel: (01675) 442681   Fax: (01675) 442941

HAREWOOD West Yorkshire   11D3

★★ Harewood Arms
Comfort merit award
Harrogate Road, Harewood LS17 9LH
☎ 0113-288 6566 Fax 0113-288 6064
24 bedrs, all ensuite, TCF TV 🐕 P 80 SB £68 DB £80
D £17 CC MC Visa Amex DC

HARROGATE North Yorkshire   11D3

★★ Ascot House
Hospitality, Comfort merit awards
53 Kings Road, Harrogate HG1 5HJ
☎ 01423-531005 Fax 01423-503523
Closed New Year & early Feb
18 bedrs, all ensuite, TCF TV 🐕 P 14 SB £48.50
DB £69.50-£80 HB £270-£300 D £14 CC MC Visa Amex DC

★★ Bay Horse
Comfort merit award
Burnt Yates, Harrogate HG3 3EJ
☎ 01423-770230
16 bedrs, all ensuite, P 70 SB £40 DB £55 HB £250
D £15 CC MC Visa ♿

★★ Gables
Hospitality merit award
2 West Grove Road, Harrogate HG1 2AD
☎ 01423-505625 Fax 01423-561312
9 bedrs, 8 ensuite, 1 🛏, TCF TV 🐕 P 9 CC MC Visa

★★ Grafton
1-3 Franklin Mount, Harrogate HG1 5EJ
☎ 01423-508491 Fax 01423-523168

A comfortable and friendly family run hotel, quietly situated yet only a few minutes stroll from the town centre and international conference centre.

17 bedrs, all ensuite, TCF TV P 3 SB £30-£36 DB £54-£65
HB £210-£260 D £13.50 CC MC Visa Amex DC

★★ Low Hall
Hospitality, Comfort merit awards
Ripon Road, Killinghall, Harrogate HG3 2AY
☎ 01423-508598 Fax 01423-560848
7 bedrs, all ensuite, TCF TV P 40 SB £45-£75 DB £55-£85
D £12.95 CC MC Visa Amex DC

★ Alvera Court
Hospitality, Comfort merit awards
76 Kings Road, Harrogate HG1 5JX
☎ 01423-505735 Fax 01423-507996
Closed Christmas
12 bedrs, all ensuite, TCF TV P 8 SB £33-£39 DB £66-£78
D £16 CC MC Visa

★ Scotia House
66 Kings Road, Harrogate HG1 5JR
☎ 01423-504361 Fax 01423-526578
14 bedrs, 12 ensuite, 2 🛏 TCF TV 🐕 P 7 No children under 7 SB £27-£28.50 DB £52-£56 HB £230 D £12 CC MC Visa

Ruskin *Highly Acclaimed*
1 Swan Road, Harrogate HG1 2SS
☎ 01423-502045 Fax 01423-506131

A small Victorian hotel beautifully furnished with antiques and situated only five minutes walk from town. Fourposter bed, residents' lounge and delightful bar/restaurant. Private car park.

7 bedrs, all ensuite, TCF TV P 9 No children under 3
SB £40-£59 DB £60-£89 D £17.95 CC MC Visa

Shannon Court *Highly Acclaimed*
65 Dragon Avenue, Harrogate HG1 5DS
☎ 01423-509858 Fax 01423-530606
Closed Christmas-New Year
8 bedrs, all ensuite, TCF TV 🚭 P 3 SB £22.50-£29.50
DB £44-£55 HB £227-£245 D £15

Abbey Lodge *Acclaimed*
31 Ripon Road, Harrogate HG1 2JL
☎ 01423-569712 Fax 01423-530570

Ideally situated for York, the Dales and Moors. Enjoy a relaxing break in well appointed accommodation with fine cuisine in the award winning restaurant.

19 bedrs, 14 ensuite, 2 🛏 TCF TV 🐕 P 24 SB £28-£49
DB £49-£59 D £11.25 CC MC Visa Amex

Alexa House *Acclaimed*
26 Ripon Road, Harrogate HG2 2JJ
☏ 01423-501988 Fax 01423-504086

A fine old Victorian house retaining all its former charm and splendour, offering fully equipped ensuite bedrooms. The former stable block has been converted to provide ground floor accommodation.

13 bedrs, all ensuite, **TCF TV P** 12 **SB** £45 **DB** £52-£60 **D** £13 **CC** MC Visa Amex DC &

Arden House *Acclaimed*
69/71 Franklin Road, Harrogate HG1 5EH
☏ 01423-509224 Fax 01423-561170
E Mail arden@harrogate.com
Closed Christmas
14 bedrs, all ensuite, **TCF TV ✝ P** 9 **SB** £29.50 **DB** £54 **HB** £220 **D** £15 **CC** MC Visa DC

Ashley House *Acclaimed*
36-40 Franklin Road, Harrogate HG1 5EE
☏ 01423-507474 Fax 01423-560858
E Mail ashleyhousehotel@btinternet.com

Three Victorian town houses converted into a comfortable, friendly, family run hotel. Completely refurbished in 1997. Cosy bar.

18 bedrs, all ensuite, **TCF TV ✝ P** 6 **SB** £30-£35 **DB** £50-£65 **HB** £250-£280 **D** £15 **CC** MC Visa Amex DC

Cavendish *Acclaimed*
3 Valley Drive, Harrogate HG2 0JJ
☏ 01423-509637
9 bedrs, all ensuite, **TCF TV SB** £28-£40 **DB** £50-£65 **D** £10 **CC** MC Visa

Delaine *Acclaimed*
17 Ripon Road, Harrogate HG1 2JL
☏ 01423-567974 Fax 01423-561723
Closed 25 Dec
10 bedrs, all ensuite, 1 ⇌ **TCF TV P** 12 **SB** £35-£37 **DB** £50-£58 **D** £13.95 **CC** MC Visa Amex

Glenayr *Acclaimed*
19 Franklin Mount, Harrogate HG1 5EJ
☏ 01423-504259 Fax 01423-504259

On a peaceful tree-lined avenue this spacious Victorian townhouse is just five minutes from the town centre. Comfortable and welcoming, with really good Yorkshire breakfasts.

6 bedrs, 5 ensuite, 1 ⇌ **TCF TV P** 4 **SB** £20-£21 **DB** £40-£48 **HB** £205-£225 **D** £13 **CC** MC Visa Amex DC

Mrs Murray's *Acclaimed*
67 Franklin Road, Harrogate HG1 5EH
☏ 01423-505857 Fax 01423-530027
14 bedrs, 9 ensuite, 3 ⇌ **TCF TV ✝ P** 5 **SB** £20-£25 **DB** £40-£50 **HB** £188-£210 **CC** MC Visa DC

Wharfedale House *Acclaimed*
28 Harlow Moor Drive, Harrogate HG2 0JY
☏ 01423-522233

Situated overlooking the beautiful Valley Gardens, Wharfedale House is quiet and spacious with every room offering every comfort and where Yorkshire hospitality is at its best.

8 bedrs, all ensuite, **TCF TV ✝ P** 3 **SB** £27 **DB** £48 **HB** £203 **D** £10

HASTINGS & ST LEONARDS – ENGLAND

Anro *Listed*
90 Kings Road, Harrogate HG1 5JX
☎ 01423-503087
7 bedrs, 4 ensuite, 1 ➡ TCF TV No children under 7
SB £22 DB £44 D £12

Gillmore *Listed*
98 King's Road, Harrogate HG1 5HH
☎ 01423-503699 Fax 01423-503699

Small, recently extended, family run hotel, close to the conference centre. King's Road is off Ripon Road.

19 bedrs, 4 ensuite, 1 ⌂, 6 ➡ TV ⋆ P 10 SB £23
DB £38 HB £193 D £8.50 ⌧

HARROW Middlesex 4C2

★★ Lindal
2 Hindes Road, Harrow HA1 1SJ
☎ 0181-863 3164 Fax 0181-427 5435
19 bedrs, all ensuite, TCF TV ⋆ P 17 SB £40 DB £50
D £10 CC MC Visa

Hindes *Acclaimed*
Hindes Road, Harrow HA1 1SJ
☎ 0181-427 7468 Fax 0181-424 0673
14 bedrs, 7 ensuite, 2 ➡ TCF TV P 25 SB £31 DB £44
D £10 CC MC Visa Amex DC JCB

Central *Listed*
6 Hindes Road, Harrow HA1 1SJ
☎ 0181-427 0893 Fax 0181-427 0893
13 bedrs, 4 ensuite, 1 ⌂, 5 ➡ TCF TV P 13 SB £29
DB £39 CC MC Visa

Crescent Lodge *Listed*
58-62 Welldon Crescent, Harrow HA1 1QR
☎ 0181-863 5491 Fax 0181-427 5965
21 bedrs, 13 ensuite, 3 ➡ ⌧ ⋆ CC MC Visa Amex

HARTFIELD East Sussex 5D3

Bolebroke Mill *Highly Acclaimed*
Perry Hill, Edenbridge Road (B2026), Hartfield TN7 4JP
☎ 01892-770425 Fax 01892-770425
Closed Dec-Jan
5 bedrs, all ensuite, TCF TV ⌧ P 8 No children under 7
SB £50 DB £55 CC MC Visa Amex

HARWICH Essex 5F1

★★ Cliff
Marine Parade, Dovercourt, Harwich CO12 3RE
☎ 01255-503345 Fax 01255-240358
26 bedrs, all ensuite, 1 ➡ TCF TV ⋆ P 60 SB £51 DB £60
D £14 CC MC Visa Amex DC

★★ Pier At Harwich
Hospitality, Restaurant merit awards
The Quay, Harwich CO12 3HH
☎ 01255-241212 Fax 01255-551922
6 bedrs, all ensuite, TCF TV P 12 SB £52.50-£67.50
DB £75-£85 D £18 CC MC Visa Amex DC

★★ Tower
Main Road, Dovercourt, Harwich CO12 3PJ
☎ 01255-504952 Fax 01255-504952
14 bedrs, all ensuite, TCF TV P 50 SB £45 DB £55 D £10
CC MC Visa Amex DC ♿

HASTINGS & ST LEONARDS East Sussex 5E4

Eagle House *Highly Acclaimed*
12 Pevensey Road, Hastings TN38 0JZ
☎ 01424-430535 Fax 01424-437771
19 bedrs, all ensuite, 2 ➡ TCF TV P 14 No children under 5 SB £29-£32 DB £44.50-£49 D £9.75 CC MC Visa Amex DC

EAGLE HOUSE HOTEL

A Victorian family house furnished in period style with large car park. All ensuite bedrooms, bar and restaurant overlooking large garden. Near main London Road but in a quiet residential area.

12 Pevensey Road, St. Leonards-on-Sea, East Sussex TN38 0JZ
Tel: Hastings (01424) 430535/441273
Fax: (01424) 437771

HASTINGS & ST LEONARDS – ENGLAND

Highlands Inn *Acclaimed*
1 Boscobel Road, St Leonards on Sea TN38 0LU
☎ 01424-420299 Fax 01424-465065
9 bedrs, all ensuite, **TV** No children **CC** MC Visa

Beechwood *Listed*
59 Baldslow Road, Hastings TN34 2EY
☎ 01424-420078
12 bedrs, 5 ensuite, 1 ⇌ ⊁ **P** 6 **SB** £15–£27 **DB** £28–£45
HB £153–£225 **D** £8

Gainsborough *Listed*
5 Carlisle Parade, Hastings TN34 1JG
☎ 01424-434010
12 bedrs, 8 ensuite, 1 🐾, 1 ⇌ **TCF TV** ☒ ⊁ **SB** £19–£24
DB £36–£48 **HB** £183–£218 **D** £7.50

Argyle
32 Cambridge Gardens, Hastings TN34 1EN
☎ 01424-421294

Twenty years of hospitality assures a warm welcome. A homely guest house offering B&B only. Situated near all amenities. Well furnished rooms with colour TV. Beverage making facilities. Three double rooms ensuite. Open access. Sorry no pets.

8 bedrs, 3 ensuite, 2 ⇌ **TCF TV** No children under 4
SB £16–£20 **DB** £28–£36

HAWES North Yorkshire 10C2

★★ Simonstone Hall
Hawes DL8 3LY
☎ 01969-667255 Fax 01969-667741
10 bedrs, all ensuite, **TCF TV** ⊁ **P** 24 **SB** £35 **DB** £70
HB £346.50 **D** £15 **CC** MC Visa JCB

HAWKHURST Kent 5E3

★★ Queens Head
Rye Road, Hawkhurst TN18 4EY
☎ 01580-753577 Fax 01580-754241
8 bedrs, all ensuite, **TCF TV P** 50 **SB** £35 **DB** £50 **D** £12.50

HAWKSHEAD Cumbria 10B2

★★ Grizedale Lodge
Hospitality, Restaurant merit awards
Grizedale LA22 0QL
☎ 01539-436532 Fax 01539-436572
Closed 2 Jan–8 Feb

A comfortable and elegant former shooting lodge tucked away in the heart of the magnificent Grizedale Forest Park, midway between Coniston Water and Windermere.

9 bedrs, all ensuite, **TCF TV** ⊁ **P** 20 **SB** £39–£48 **DB** £65–£75 **HB** £265–£325 **D** £22.50 **CC** MC Visa Amex JCB ♿

★★ Highfield House Country
Hospitality, Comfort merit awards
Hawkshead Hill, Hawkshead LA22 0PN
☎ 015394-36344 Fax 015394-36793
Closed Christmas & 3–31 Jan
11 bedrs, all ensuite, 2 ⇌ **TCF TV** ⊁ **P** 15 **SB** £40 **DB** £74–£87 **HB** £385 **D** £18 **CC** MC Visa JCB

Buckle Yeat *Highly Acclaimed*
Buckle Yeat, Hawkshead LA22 0LF
☎ 015394-36446 Fax 015394-36446

Tastefully furnished guest house, all rooms ensuite with tea and coffee making facilities. Centrally heated and log fires. Ideally situated for walking and touring. Open all year.

7 bedrs, all ensuite, **TV** ⊁ **P** 8 **SB** £22–£25 **DB** £44–£50
CC MC Visa Amex

HAYWARDS HEATH – ENGLAND 117

Ivy House *Highly Acclaimed*
Ambleside, Hawkshead LA22 0NS
☎ 015394-36204
Closed Nov-Feb

Ivy House is a fine, Grade II Listed hotel, located in the centre of an attractive village.

11 bedrs, all ensuite, 2 🛏 TCF TV 🐕 P 16 SB £29-£31 DB £58-£62 HB £252-£266 D £12 📇

Greenbank House *Acclaimed*
Ambleside, Hawkshead LA22 0NS
☎ 015394-36497
12 bedrs, 6 ensuite, 3 🛏 TCF 🐕 P 12 SB £21-£25 DB £42-£50 HB £210-£231 D £11

Don't forget to mention the guide
When booking direct, please remember to tell the hotel that you chose it from RAC Bed & Breakfast 1998.

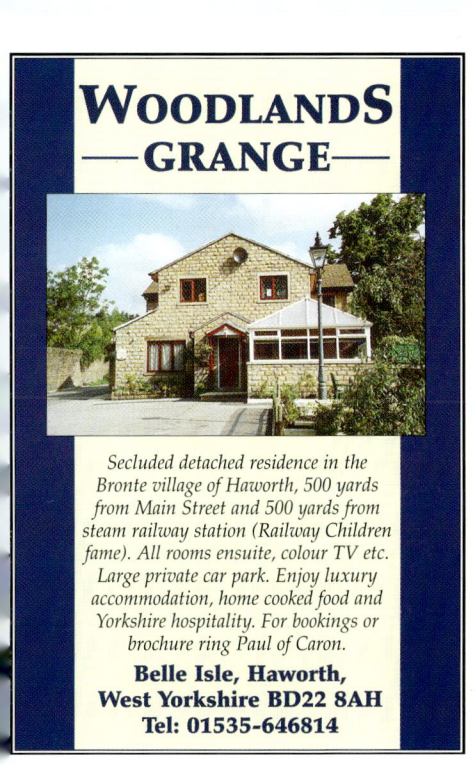

WOODLANDS GRANGE

Secluded detached residence in the Bronte village of Haworth, 500 yards from Main Street and 500 yards from steam railway station (Railway Children fame). All rooms ensuite, colour TV etc. Large private car park. Enjoy luxury accommodation, home cooked food and Yorkshire hospitality. For bookings or brochure ring Paul of Caron.

**Belle Isle, Haworth, West Yorkshire BD22 8AH
Tel: 01535-646814**

HAWORTH West Yorkshire   10C3

Ferncliffe *Acclaimed*
Hebden Road, Keighley, Haworth BD22 8RS
☎ 01535-643405
6 bedrs, all ensuite, TCF TV 🐕 P 12 SB £20-£25 DB £39 HB £207 D £10 CC MC Visa

Woodlands Grange
Belle Isle, Haworth BD22 8AH
☎ 01535-646814
7 bedrs, all ensuite, TCF TV 🐕 P 10 SB £20-£22 DB £32-£37 HB £168 D £7.50 CC MC Visa

HAYDON BRIDGE Northumberland   13E4

Hadrian Lodge *Listed*
Hindshield Moss, North Road, Haydon Bridge NE47 6NF
☎ 01434-688688
5 bedrs, 2 ensuite, 3 🛏 TCF TV P 30 No children under 2 SB £16 DB £32-£35 HB £140 D £6 📇 ♿

HAYLING ISLAND Hampshire   4B4

Cockle Warren Cottage *Highly Acclaimed*
Restaurant merit award
36 Seafront, Hayling Island, Portsmouth PO11 9HL
☎ 01705-464961 Fax 01705-464838

A pretty seaside cottage hotel ideally located between Portsmouth and Chichester, offering a large garden, swimming pool, fourposter beds and log fires. Good food, wine and home-made bread.

5 bedrs, all ensuite, TV 🐕 P 7 No children under 12 SB £55-£65 DB £68-£108 D £27.50 CC MC Visa Amex 📇

HAYWARDS HEATH West Sussex   5D3

★★ Hilton Park
Cuckfield, Haywards Heath RH17 5EG
☎ 01444-454555 Fax 01444-457222
10 bedrs, all ensuite, 1 🛏 TCF TV 🐕 P 50 SB £55-£60 DB £75-£80 D £19 CC MC Visa Amex DC JCB

HELMSLEY – ENGLAND

HELMSLEY North Yorkshire   11D2

★★ Crown
Market Place, Helmsley YO6 5BJ
☎ 01439-770297 Fax 01439-771595

A 16th century former coaching inn run by the same family for 37 years with great character and a warm and friendly atmosphere. Traditional country cooking served in Jacobean dining room. Dogs welcome.

14 bedrs, 12 ensuite, 1 ⇌ TCF TV ⌂ ☎ P 14 SB £30-£35 DB £60-£70 HB £285-£295 D £16 CC MC Visa

★★ Feathers
Market Place, Helmsley YO6 5BH
☎ 01439-770275 Fax 01439-771101
Closed 23 Dec-3 Jan
17 bedrs, 13 ensuite, 2 ⇌ TV ⌂ P 20 SB £30-£35 DB £50-£60 CC MC Visa Amex DC

Barn Close Farm
Rievaulx, Helmsley YO6 5HL
☎ 01439-798321

A luxurious farmhouse set in a valley of oustanding beauty in TV's 'Heartbeat' country.

2 bedrs, 1 ensuite, 1 ⇌ TCF ⌂ P 6 SB £20-£22 D £12 ♿

Laskill Farm
Hawnby, Nr Helmsley YO6 5NB
☎ 01439-798268

This attractive stone built country farmhouse in the North York Moors National Park, near Rivaulx Abbey makes an ideal centre from which to explore the many surrounding places of interest and scenic beauty. York being only 45 minutes away.

7 bedrs, all ensuite, 1 ⇌ TCF TV ⌂ ⌂ P 15 SB £18-£22.50 DB £43-£50 HB £203-£252 D £11 ♿

HELSTON Cornwall   2A4

★★ Gwealdues
Falmouth Road, Helston TR13 8JX
☎ 01326-572808 Fax 01326-561388
17 bedrs, 15 ensuite, 2 ⇌ TCF TV ⌂ P 60
SB £35 DB £50 HB £230 D £15 CC MC Visa Amex

★★ Nansloe Manor
Hospitality, Comfort merit awards
Meneage Road, Helston TR13 0SB
☎ 01326-574691 Fax 01326-564680
7 bedrs, 6 ensuite, 1 ⇌ TCF TV P 30 No children under 10 SB £50-£60 DB £88-£116 D £19 CC MC Visa JCB

HEMEL HEMPSTEAD Hertfordshire   4C2

Southville Listed
9 Charles Street, Hemel Hempstead HP1 1JH
☎ 01442-251387
19 bedrs, 6 ⇌ ⌂ P 10 SB £23.50 DB £33 CC MC Visa

HENFIELD West Sussex   4C4

Tottington Manor Highly Acclaimed
Restaurant merit award
Edburton, Henfield BN5 9LJ
☎ 01903-815757 Fax 01903-879331
Closed 26-30 Dec

A 16th century Sussex town house.

6 bedrs, all ensuite, TCF TV P 100 No children under 5 SB £45-£50 DB £65-£85 D £25 CC MC Visa Amex DC JCB

HENLEY IN ARDEN Warwickshire　8A4

★★ White Swan
100 High Street, Henley-in-Arden B95 5BY
📞 01564-792623 Fax 01564-795886

Attractive Elizabethan inn, recently refurbished, set in the middle of picturesque Henley-in-Arden. 20 minutes by motorway from NEC, 7 miles north of Stratford.

10 bedrs, all ensuite, TCF TV ⚑ P 60 SB £40-£43 DB £57-£60 HB £300 D £4.15 CC MC Visa Amex DC

Lapworth Lodge *Highly Acclaimed*
Bushwood Lane, Lapworth, Henley-in-Arden B94 5PJ
📞 01564-783038 Fax 01564-783635

7 bedrs, all ensuite, TCF TV P 16 CC MC Visa

HENLEY-ON-THAMES Oxfordshire　4B2

Flohr's *Acclaimed*
Restaurant merit award
Northfield End, Henley-on-Thames RG9 2JG
📞 01491-573412 Fax 01491-579721

This listed building is a fine example of a Georgian mansion house dating from around 1750 with a facade virtually unchanged since then. Parts of the house are reputed to date from two centuries earlier.

9 bedrs, 2 🛁, 2 ⚑ TCF TV ⚑ P 5 SB £39-£59 DB £59-£79 D £15 CC MC Visa

Lenwade
3 Western Road, Henley-on-Thames RG9 1JL
📞 01491-573468 Fax 01491-573468

Delightful Victorian home in a quiet road within easy walking distance of town and river. Ideal base when visiting Oxford, Windsor (Legoland), Heathrow, all 40 minutes. French spoken.

3 bedrs, 2 ensuite, 1 ⚑ TCF TV ⚑ P 4 SB £25-£40 DB £38-£45

HENSTRIDGE Somerset　3F2

Quiet Corner Farm
Templecombe, Henstridge BA8 0RA
📞 01963-363045 Fax 01963-363400

Short breaks with country house atmosphere in lovely garden/orchard setting. Home to lots of tiny Shetland Ponies. Wonderful breakfasts, home preserves. First class pubs and restaurants within easy walk. Three days for the price of two (Oct-May).

3 bedrs, 1 ensuite, 1 ⚑ TCF ⚑ P 8 SB £22-£25 DB £38-£42

HEREFORD Herefordshire　7D4

★★ Castle Pool
Hospitality merit award
Castle Street, Hereford HR1 2NW
📞 01432-356321 Fax 01432-356321

27 bedrs, all ensuite, TCF TV ⚑ P 14 SB £38-£52 DB £58-£82 HB £350-£410 D £17 CC MC Visa Amex DC

HEREFORD – ENGLAND

★★ Merton
Commercial Road, Hereford HR1 2BD
📞 01432-265925 Fax 01432-354983
E Mail 106317.2760@compuserve.com

Georgian coaching inn with warm, comfortable atmosphere. Conveniently situated near the town centre.

17 bedrs, all ensuite, **TCF TV** 🐾 **P** 10 **SB** £45 **DB** £65 **HB** £350 **D** £5 **CC** MC Visa Amex DC JCB

★★ Munstone House
Comfort merit award
Munstone, Hereford HR1 3AH
📞 01432-267122
6 bedrs, all ensuite, 🐾 **P** 50 **CC** MC Visa DC

Aylstone Court *Highly Acclaimed*
Aylstone Hill, Hereford HR1 1HS
📞 01432-341891 Fax 01432-267691
11 bedrs, all ensuite, **TCF TV** 🐾 **P** 25 **SB** £35-£42 **DB** £48-£58 **HB** £351 **D** £18 **CC** MC Visa Amex

Hopbine *Listed*
Roman Road, Hereford HR1 1LE
📞 01432-268722 Fax 01432-268722
15 bedrs, all ensuite, 2 🚿 **TCF TV** 🐾 **P** 20 **SB** £20-£25 **DB** £35-£40 **D** £9

Hopbine
Roman Road, Hereford HR1 1LE
📞 01432-268722

Eighteen comfortable rooms, mostly ensuite with tea and coffee making facilities and colour TV in all rooms. Licensed. Safe car parking. Only one mile from the city centre.

18 bedrs, 16 ensuite, 4 🚿 **TCF TV** 🐾 **P** 35 **SB** £25 **DB** £36 **D** £8.50

SALISBURY ARMS HOTEL

Hertford's oldest Hostelry, retaining all the character of a bygone age. Featuring a beam-work frontage, Jacobean staircase and a panelled dining room.

FORE STREET, HERTFORD SG14 1BZ
Tel: 01992-583091
Fax: 01922-552510

HERTFORD Hertfordshire — 5D2

★★ Salisbury Arms
Fore Street, Hertford SG14 1BZ
📞 01992-583091 Fax 01992-552510
29 bedrs, all ensuite, **P** 30 **SB** £35-£58 **DB** £60-£75 **D** £13 **CC** MC Visa Amex DC

HEXHAM Northumberland — 13F4

★★ County
Hospitality merit award
Priestpopple, Hexham NE46 1PS
📞 01434-602030 Fax 01434-603202
9 bedrs, all ensuite, 1 🚿 **TCF TV** 🐾 **P** 2 **SB** £48 **DB** £65 **D** £11 **CC** MC Visa Amex DC

★★ Langley Castle
Langley-on-Tyne, Hexham NE47 5LU
📞 01434-688888 Fax 01434-684019
E Mail langleycastle@dial.pipex.com
16 bedrs, all ensuite, **TCF TV** 🛗 **P** 70 **SB** £74.50 **DB** £95 **HB** £425 **D** £22.50 **CC** MC Visa Amex DC

Rose & Crown *Acclaimed*
Main Street, Slaley, Hexham NE47 0AA
📞 01434-673263 Fax 01434-673305
3 bedrs, all ensuite, **TCF TV P** 32 **SB** £25-£30 **DB** £40-£45 **D** £10 **CC** MC Visa Amex JCB

Westbrooke Listed
Allendale Road, Hexham NE46 2DE
☎ 01434-603818
11 bedrs, 3 ensuite, 2 🛁, 2 🐕 ▣

Rye Hill Farm
Slaley, Nr Hexham NE47 0AH
☎ 01434-673259 Fax 01434-673608

A farm with a difference, deep in the countryside with lots of fresh air, fresh food and family atmosphere. Very comfortable too.

6 bedrs, all ensuite, **TCF TV** 🐕 **P** 8 **SB** £24 **DB** £40 **HB** £189 **D** £10 **CC** MC Visa

HIGH WYCOMBE Buckinghamshire   4C2

Langley Castle

A genuine 14th century fortified castle, with walls 17 feet thick. Set in a private woodland estate with ten acres of rolling lawns. Some suite rooms have a sauna and spa bath.

LANGLEY-ON-TYNE, HEXHAM NE47 5LU
Tel: 01434-688888
Fax: 01434-6844019

Clifton Lodge Acclaimed
210-212 West Wycombe Road, HP12 3AR
☎ 01494-440095 Fax 01494-536322
Situated two miles from the M40 and one mile from High Wycombe on the A40 towards Oxford/Aylesbury.
32 bedrs, 20 ensuite, 2 🛁, 4 🐕 **TCF TV P** 20 **SB** £35-£69 **DB** £58-£80 **D** £14 **CC** MC Visa Amex DC JCB 📺

Bird in Hand Listed
West Wycombe Road, High Wycombe HP11 2LR
☎ 01494-523502 Fax 01494-459449

A family run inn built in the 30's, with original oak panelling and log fire in winter. In summer the patio is popular. There is a fine range of bar meals, snacks and specials. Good choice of cask ales and a large range of fine malt whiskies.

5 bedrs, 4 ensuite, 1 🐕 **TCF TV P** 30 **SB** £35 **DB** £50 **D** £5.80 **CC** MC Visa JCB

Drake Court Listed
141 London Road, High Wycombe HP11 1BT
☎ 01494-523639 Fax 01494-472696
20 bedrs, 3 ensuite, 3 🛁, 4 🐕 **TCF TV** 🐕 **P** 30 **SB** £28.20 **DB** £40 **D** £10 **CC** MC Visa Amex DC JCB 📺

HINCKLEY Leicestershire   8B3

Ambion Court Highly Acclaimed
The Green, Dadlington, Hinckley CV13 6JB
☎ 01455-212292 Fax 01455-213141
E Mail ambion@aol.com

Charming, modernised Victorian farmhouse overlooking tranquil village green. Luxurious ensuite bedrooms and excellent licensed restaurant. Convenient for Leicester, Coventry, Warwick, NEC and main motorways.

7 bedrs, all ensuite, **TCF TV** 🐕 **P** 8 **SB** £35-£45 **DB** £50-£60 **HB** £275-£310 **D** £12 **CC** MC Visa

Kings *Highly Acclaimed*
Restaurant merit award
13-19 Mount Road, Hinckley LE10 1AD
☎ 01455-637193 Fax 01455-636201
7 bedrs, all ensuite, **P** 16 **SB** £45-£70 **DB** £55-£80
HB £350-£450 **D** £17 **CC** MC Visa Amex DC

HINDHEAD Surrey 4C3

★★ Devils Punchbowl
London Road, Hindhead GU26 6AG
☎ 01428-606565 Fax 01428-605713
33 bedrs, all ensuite, **TCF** TV **✱ P** 100 **SB** £50 **DB** £60
D £15 **CC** MC Visa Amex DC

HINDON Wiltshire 4A3

★★ Lamb at Hindon Hotel
High Street, Hindon, Swindon SP3 6DP
☎ 01747-820573 Fax 01747-820605
14 bedrs, all ensuite, **TCF** TV **✱ P** 30 **SB** £38-£43 **DB** £50-£65 **HB** £275-£290 **D** £19 **CC** MC Visa Amex JCB

HITCHIN Hertfordshire 4C1

★★ Firs
83 Bedford Road, Hitchin SG5 2TY
☎ 01462-422322 Fax 01462-432051

Family-run hotel, 30 rooms mostly ensuite, colour TV, telephone, tea/coffee facilities in all rooms. On A600 opposite football ground, walking distance from town centre, 15 minutes to Luton Airport.

30 bedrs, 24 ensuite, 2 **✱ TCF** TV **✱ P** 33 **SB** £31-£49
DB £48-£59 **D** £11 **CC** MC Visa Amex DC JCB

★★ Redcoats Farmhouse
Redcoats Green, Hitchin SG4 7JR
☎ 01463-729500 Fax 01438-723322
E Mail redcoatsfarmhouse@ukbusiness.com
Closed 1 week after Christmas
14 bedrs, 12 ensuite, 1 **✱ TCF** TV **✱ P** 50 **SB** £70-£80
DB £80-£90 **D** £15 **CC** MC Visa Amex DC

HODNET Shropshire 7E2

★★ Bear
Hodnet, Market Drayton TF9 3NH
☎ 01630-685214 Fax 01630-685787
6 bedrs, all ensuite, **TCF** TV **P** 80 **SB** £32.50-£35 **DB** £55-£60 **D** £11 **CC** MC Visa Amex

HOLFORD Somerset 3D2

★★ Alfoxton Park
Holford TA5 1SG
☎ 01278-741211
Closed Dec-Feb
18 bedrs, all ensuite, **TCF** TV **P** 20 **CC** MC Visa Amex DC

★★ Combe House
Hospitality, Comfort, Restaurant merit awards
Holford TA5 1RZ
☎ 01278-741382 Fax 01278-741382
Closed Nov-Mar
18 bedrs, 16 ensuite, 2 **✱ TCF** TV **✱ P** 15 **SB** £33-£44
DB £65-£97 **HB** £273-£339 **D** £18.50 **CC** MC Visa Amex

HOLMFIRTH West Yorkshire 10C4

White Horse Inn *Listed*
Jackson Bridge, Holmfirth HD7 7HF
☎ 01484-683940
5 bedrs, all ensuite, 2 **✱ TCF** TV **P** 12 **SB** £25 **DB** £40
D £6

HOLMROOK Cumbria 10A2

★★ Lutwidge Arms
Holmrook, Holmrook CA19 1UH
☎ 019467-24230 Fax 019467-24100
24 bedrs, all ensuite, **TCF** TV **✱ P** 50 **SB** £29-£40 **DB** £42-£50 **HB** £230 **D** £6 **CC** MC Visa JCB

HOLSWORTHY Devon 2C3

★★ Court Barn Country House
Hospitality, Restaurant merit awards
Clawton, Holsworthy EX22 6PS
☎ 01409-271219 Fax 01409-271309
8 bedrs, all ensuite, 1 **✱ TCF** TV **✱ P** 18 **SB** £38-£45
DB £70-£86 **HB** £315-£396 **D** £18 **CC** MC Visa Amex DC JCB

Bickford Arms *Highly Acclaimed*
Brandis Corner, Holsworthy EX22 7XY
☎ 01409-221318 Fax 01409-221781
5 bedrs, all ensuite, **TCF** TV **P** 47 **SB** £35-£40 **DB** £50-£60
HB £245-£300 **D** £14 **CC** MC Visa

HOLT Norfolk · 9E2

★★ Feathers
6 Market Place, Holt NR25 6BW
☎ 01263-712318 Fax 01263-711774
13 bedrs, 9 ensuite, 1 ⇨ TCF TV P 10 SB £39-£44
DB £56-£61 D £15.95 CC MC Visa

★★ Pheasant
The Coast Road, Kelling, Holt NR25 7EG
☎ 01263-588382 Fax 01263-588101
29 bedrs, all ensuite, TCF TV ⤧ P 80 No children under 10 SB £32-£45 DB £52-£78 D £12 CC MC Visa ♿

Lawn's *Highly Acclaimed*
26 Station Road, Holt NR25 6BS
☎ 01263-713390
11 bedrs, all ensuite, ⤧ CC MC Visa Amex DC

Harsner Rest *Listed*
Coast Road, Cley-next-the-Sea, Holt
☎ 01263-740776
Closed Jan
9 bedrs, 2 ensuite, 1 ⌂, TCF TV ⤧ P 9 SB £24 DB £40
D £9 CC MC Visa

HONITON Devon · 3D3

★★ Greyhound
Fenny Bridges, Honiton EX14 0BJ
☎ 01404-850380

HOOK Hampshire · 4B3

★★ Raven
Comfort merit award
Station Road, Hook RG27 9HS
☎ 01256-762541 Fax 01256-768677
38 bedrs, all ensuite, TCF TV ⤧ P 100 SB £65 DB £75
D £10 CC MC Visa Amex DC ♿

★★ White Hart
Comfort merit award
London Road, Hook RG27 9DZ
☎ 01256-762462 Fax 01256-768351
22 bedrs, all ensuite, TCF TV ⤧ P 60 CC MC Visa Amex

Cedar Court *Listed*
Reading Road, Hook RG27 9DB
☎ 01256-762178 Fax 01256-762178
6 bedrs, 5 ensuite, 1 ⇨ TCF TV P 6 SB £22-£29.50
DB £36 CC MC Visa

Cherry Lodge *Listed*
Reading Road, Hook RG27 9DB
☎ 01256-762532 Fax 01256-762532
6 bedrs, all ensuite, TCF TV ⤧ ⌸ P 30 SB £25 DB £36
D £6 CC MC Visa Amex ♿

HOPE Derbyshire · 8A1

Moorgate
Edale Road, Hope, Sheffield S30 2RF
☎ 01433-621219
Closed mid Jan-mid Feb

Set in the heart of the broad Hope Valley, lovely and remote, with pleasant green dales and magnificent, challenging moorland.

27 bedrs, 11 ensuite, 8 ⇨ TCF P 30 SB £19.50 DB £39
D £9.50 CC MC Visa

HOPE COVE Devon · 2C4

★★ Cottage
Hospitality merit award
Hope Cove TQ7 3HJ
☎ 01548-561555 Fax 01548-561455
Closed 2-30 Jan
35 bedrs, 25 ensuite, 4 ⇨ TCF TV ⤧ P 50 SB £20-£49
DB £40-£97 HB £243-£267 D £17.25

★★ Sun Bay
Inner Hope Cove, Kingsbridge TQ7 3HS
☎ 01548-561371 Fax 01548-561371
Closed Jan
14 bedrs, all ensuite, TCF TV ⤧ P 12 DB £40-£60 D £7.50
CC MC Visa JCB

Hope Cove *Highly Acclaimed*
Kingsbridge, Hope Cove TQ7 3HH
☎ 01548-561233 Fax 01548-561233
7 bedrs, all ensuite, P 19 No children under 7 CC MC Visa

HORNSEA East Yorkshire · 11F3

Merlstead *Listed*
59 Eastgate, Hornsea HU18 1NB
☎ 01964-533068 Fax 01964-536975
6 bedrs, all ensuite, TCF TV ⤧ P 4 SB £30-£33 DB £45-£50 HB £240-£250 D £13 CC MC Visa

HORSHAM West Sussex 4C3

★★ Ye Olde King's Head
Carfax, Horsham RH12 1EG
☎ 01403-253126 Fax 01403-242291
42 bedrs, 41 ensuite, 1 🛏, TCF TV 🐕 P 40 SB £62 DB £73
D £15 CC   MC Visa Amex DC &

HORTON-IN-RIBBLESDALE North Yorkshire 10C3

Crown *Listed*
Horton-in-Ribblesdale, Settle BD24 0HF
☎ 01729-860209 Fax 01729-860444
9 bedrs, 4 ensuite, 5 🛏, 2 ⇌ TCF 🐕 P 20 SB £17–£19
DB £34–£38 HB £118–£136 D £9

HORWICH Lancashire 10B4

★★ Swallowfield
Chorley New Road, Horwich BL6 6HN
☎ 01204-697914 Fax 01204-468900
Closed 21 Dec-1 Jan
32 bedrs, all ensuite, 🐕 P 35 CC   MC Visa Amex DC

HOUNSLOW Middlesex 4C2

Crompton *Listed*
49 Lampton Road, Hounslow TW3 1JG
☎ 0181-570 7090 Fax 0181-577 1975
10 bedrs, all ensuite, 2 ⇌ TCF TV P 12 SB £45–£60
DB £55–£70 CC   MC Visa Amex DC JCB &

CROMPTON GUEST HOUSE

"Hotel Facilities at Guest House Prices"

- All rooms ensuite. • Single, double, triple and family rooms. • Colour/Satellite TV. • Full English Breakfast. • Telephones in all rooms. • Disabled facilities available.• Private car park (short/long term). • Major credit cards accepted. • 10 mins Heathrow, M4/M25. • 20 mins Central London. • 50 yards left of Hounslow Central Underground. • Close to town centre.

Family Business with Personal Touch.
49 LAMPTON ROAD, HOUNSLOW, MIDDLESEX TW3 1JG
Tel: 0181-570 7090 Fax: 0181-577 1975

Kingswood
33 Woodlands Road, Isleworth TW7 6NR
☎ 0181-560 2614 Fax 0181-560 2614

20 minutes by road to Heathrow Airport and 30 minutes by rail to Waterloo. The hotel is 20 minutes from Syon Park and Old Isleworth and local to Brunel University. All rooms have C.H. and colour TV, ensuite and family rooms available.

14 bedrs, 5 ensuite, 4 ⇌ TCF TV P 5 SB £28–£33 DB £33–£42 CC   MC Visa Amex DC

HOVE East Sussex 5D4

★★ Langfords
Third Avenue, Hove BN3 2PX
☎ 01273-738222 Fax 01273-779426
68 bedrs, 54 ensuite, 6 ⇌ 🐕 📺 SB £35–£45 DB £60–£95
HB £297 D £9.50 CC   MC Visa Amex DC

★★ St Catherine's Lodge
Sea Front, Kingsway, Hove BN3 2RZ
☎ 01273-778181 Fax 01273-774949
50 bedrs, 40 ensuite, 5 ⇌ 🐕 📺 P 9 SB £36–£45
DB £60–£65 HB £190–£240 D £13.50 CC   MC Visa Amex DC

HOW CAPLE Herefordshire 7E4

★★ How Caple Grange
How Caple HR1 4TF
☎ 01989-740208 Fax 01989-740301
26 bedrs, 18 ensuite, 4 ⇌ TCF TV 🐕 P 100 📺 📧

HUDDERSFIELD West Yorkshire 10C4

★★ Huddersfield
33-47 Kirkgate, Huddersfield HD1 1QT
☎ 01484-512111 Fax 01484-435262
60 bedrs, all ensuite, TCF TV 🐕 📺 P 75 SB £39 DB £49
D £12 CC   MC Visa Amex DC JCB 📧

HULL East Yorkshire 11E4

★★ Comfort Friendly Inn
Anlaby Road, Hull HU1 2PJ
☎ 01482-323299 Fax 01482-214730
E Mail admin@gb631.u-net.com
59 bedrs, all ensuite, TCF TV 🐕 📺 P 150 SB £44.25–£55.25 DB £50–£61 D £9.75 CC   MC Visa Amex DC 📺 &

Don't forget to mention the guide
When booking direct, please remember to tell the hotel that you chose it from RAC Bed & Breakfast 1998.

Earlsmere *Acclaimed*
76-78 Sunnybank, Off Spring Bank West, Hull HU3 1LQ
☎ 01482-341977 Fax 01482-473714

Here is the original home from home hotel. Most rooms totally re-fitted with the discerning guest in mind. Satisfaction and hospitality is guaranteed.

9 bedrs, 7 ensuite, **TCF TV** 🐕
SB £20-£28 **DB** £30-£40 **HB** £200-£280 **CC** Visa DC ♿

Campanile Hull *Lodge*
Beverley Road, Freetown Way, Hull HU2 9AN
☎ 01482-325530 Fax 01482-587538
50 bedrs, all ensuite, **TCF TV** 🐕 **SB** £41 **DB** £45.50 **D** £10.55 **CC** MC Visa Amex DC ♿

HUNGERFORD Berkshire   4B3

Marshgate Cottage *Acclaimed*
Marsh Lane, Hungerford RG17 0QX
☎ 01488-682307 Fax 01488-685475

A small, friendly, family run hotel in superb countryside, adjoining the Kennet and Avon Canal. M4 (jn 14) just four miles away.

6 bedrs, all ensuite, 1 🛏 **TCF TV** 🐕 **P** 9 **SB** £35.50 **DB** £48.50 **CC** MC Visa ♿

HUNSTANTON Norfolk   9D2

★★ Caley Hall Motel
Comfort merit award
Old Hunstanton, Hunstanton PE36 6HH
☎ 01485-533486 Fax 01485-533348
29 bedrs, all ensuite, **TCF TV** 🐕 **P** 70 **CC** MC Visa 🐾 ♿

★★ Lodge
Old Hunstanton Road, Old Hunstanton PE36 6HX
☎ 01485-532896 Fax 01485-535007
16 bedrs, all ensuite, **TCF TV** 🐕 **P** 70 **SB** £28-£43 **DB** £50-£80 **HB** £217-£310 **D** £18.50 **CC** MC Visa Amex JCB 🐾 ♿

Sunningdale *Highly Acclaimed*
3 Avenue Road, Hunstanton PE36 5BW
☎ 01485-532562
12 bedrs, all ensuite, 1 🛏 **TCF TV P** 2 No children under 10 **SB** £27 **DB** £46 **HB** £230-£260 **D** £12

St Annes
53 Neville Road, Heacham PE31 7HB
☎ 01485-570021

E.T.B. 3 crown commended. Located in quiet village, close to the sea and 10 minute drive to Sandringham and Norfolk Lavender. Bar licence, good home cooking.

8 bedrs, all ensuite, 2 🛏 **TCF TV P** 4 No children under 7 **CC** Visa DC ♿

HUNTLEY Gloucestershire   7E4

King's Head Inn *Acclaimed*
Birdwood, Huntley
☎ 01452-750348

Ideally situated six miles from the city centre of Gloucester, and on the northern fringe of the Forest of Dean on the A40 to Ross-on-Wye. The bedrooms are either double or family, and provide the highest standard of accommodation for visitors.

6 bedrs, all ensuite, **TCF TV P** 50 No children under 3 **SB** £25 **DB** £40 **D** £7

HUTTON-LE-HOLE North Yorkshire 11E2

Hammer & Hand Country Guest House
Acclaimed
Hutton-le-Hole, York YO6 6UA
☎ 01751-417300 Fax 01751-417711

Charming listed property in idyllic village. Tasteful ensuite rooms. Beamed ceilings, antiques. Sitting room with Georgian fireplace and log fire. Oak panelled dining room.

3 bedrs, all ensuite, 1 ⇌ TCF TV ⊠ ⋔ P 4 DB £19-£22 HB £190-£215 D £12

HYDE Cheshire 10C4

Needhams Farm *Listed*
Uplands Road, Werneth Low, Hyde SK14 3AQ
☎ 0161-368 4610 Fax 0161-367 9106

A 500 year old farmhouse, offering a warm welcome to all guests. Views from all rooms. Evening meals from 7:00-9:00 with complementary residential licence.

7 bedrs, 5 ensuite, 1 ⇌ TCF TV ⋔ P 10 SB £18-£20 DB £30-£32 D £7 CC MC Visa

RAC Hotel Reservations Service
0870 603 9109
(Calls charged at national call rate)

ILFRACOMBE Devon 2C2

★★ Arlington
Sommers Crescent, Ilfracombe EX34 9DT
☎ 01271-862002 Fax 01271-862803

Bay-windowed, five storey Victorian hotel overlooking harbour and coast and set in its own small grounds. Family run.

32 bedrs, all ensuite, TCF TV ⋔ ▣ P 30 SB £26-£36 DB £52-£72 HB £190-£250 D £13 CC MC Visa Amex ▣ ▣

★★ Elmfield
Comfort merit award
Torrs Park, Ilfracombe EX34 8AZ
☎ 01271-863377 Fax 01271-866828
Closed Nov-Easter excl Christmas
13 bedrs, all ensuite, 1 ⇌ TCF TV P 14 No children under 8 SB £32-£38 DB £64-£76 HB £225-£245 D £15 CC MC Visa ▣ ▣ ▣

★★ Ilfracombe Carlton
Runnacleave Road, Ilfracombe EX34 8AR
☎ 01271-862446 Fax 01271-865379
Closed Jan-Feb
48 bedrs, all ensuite, 2 ⇌ TCF TV ▣ P 24 SB £27.50-£29.50 DB £50 HB £205-£220 D £12.50 CC MC Visa Amex

★★ St Helier
Hillsborough Road, Ilfracombe EX34 9QQ
☎ 01271-864906 Fax 01271-864906
Closed Oct
16 bedrs, 12 ensuite, 1 ⌂, 2 ⇌ TCF TV ⋔ P 20 SB £25-£26 DB £40-£45 HB £175-£199 D £9 CC MC Visa

★★ Tracy House
Belmont Road, Ilfracombe EX34 8DR
☎ 01271-863933
Closed Oct-Mar
11 bedrs, 9 ensuite, 1 ⇌ ⋔ P 11 CC MC Visa Amex

★ Cairn House
43 St Brannocks Road, Ilfracombe EX34 8EH
☎ 01271-863911

A comfortable small hotel set in its own grounds with superb views of the sea and surrounding hills.

10 bedrs, all ensuite, TCF TV ✱ P 10 SB £16-£20 DB £32-£40 HB £196-£210 D £10 CC MC Visa

★ Torrs
Torrs Park, Ilfracombe EX34 8AY
☎ 01271-862334
14 bedrs, all ensuite, TCF TV ✱ P 14 No children under 5 SB £19.50-£22.50 DB £39-£45 HB £185.50-£206.50 D £7 CC MC Visa JCB

Avalon *Acclaimed*
6 Capstone Crescent, Ilfracombe EX34 9BT
☎ 01271-863325 Fax 01271-866543
11 bedrs, 6 ensuite, 1 🐾, 2 ✱ TCF TV P 10 SB £16-£18 DB £31-£35 HB £140-£165 D £8 CC MC Visa

Collingdale *Acclaimed*
Larkstone Terrace, Ilfracombe EX34 9NU
☎ 01271-863770
Closed 28 Dec-28 Feb
9 bedrs, 8 ensuite, 1 🐾, 2 ✱ TCF ✱ SB £15-£19 DB £30-£37 HB £100-£145 D £8 CC MC Visa

Cresta *Acclaimed*
Torrs Park, Ilfracombe EX34 8AY
☎ 01271-863742

Merlin Court *Acclaimed*
Torrs Park, Ilfracombe EX34 8AY
☎ 01271-862697
13 bedrs, 12 ensuite, 2 ✱ TCF TV ✱ P 15 SB £20-£22 DB £40-£44 HB £170-£182 CC MC Visa Amex

Short Breaks
Many hotels provide special rates for weekend and mid-week breaks - sometimes these are quoted in the hotel's entry, otherwise ring direct for the latest offers.

Southcliffe *Acclaimed*
Torrs Park, Ilfracombe EX34 8AZ
☎ 01271-862958

Charming Victorian mansion set in its own secluded grounds with superb views across the town to the sea. Adjacent to National Trust walks, close to picturesque harbour, seafront and town centre.

14 bedrs, 13 ensuite, 2 ✱ TCF TV P 12 SB £18-£21 DB £36-£42 HB £161-£179 D £6 CC MC Visa JCB

St Brannocks House *Acclaimed*
61 St Brannocks Road, Ilfracombe EX34 8EQ
☎ 01271-863873
16 bedrs, 10 ensuite, 2 ✱ TCF TV ✱ P 20 SB £19.50-£20 DB £39-£40 HB £185-£195 D £9 CC MC Visa Amex

Strathmore *Acclaimed*
57 St Brannocks Road, Ilfracombe EX34 8EQ
☎ 01271-862248 Fax 01271-864044
9 bedrs, 8 ensuite, 1 ✱ TCF TV ✱ P 7 SB £15 DB £32-£40 HB £168-£175 D £9.50 CC MC Visa Amex DC

Trafalgar *Acclaimed*
Larkstone Terrace, Ilfracombe EX34 9NU
☎ 01271-862145 Fax 01271-865193
25 bedrs, 24 ensuite, 1 🐾, TCF TV ✱ P 8 SB £25 DB £46 HB £219 D £10 CC MC Visa Amex DC

Westwell Hall *Acclaimed*
Torrs Park, Ilfracombe EX34 8AZ
☎ 01271-862792 Fax 01271-862792

Quiet and secluded hotel situated in its own grounds with glorious views of the countryside and sea. Ample car parking. Adjacent to National Trust coastal walks. Free phone 0500-60 70 06.

10 bedrs, all ensuite, TCF TV ✱ P 10 SB £18-£23 DB £36-£46 HB £179-£205 D £8 CC MC Visa

Capstone *Listed*
15-16 St James' Place, Ilfracombe EX34 9BJ
☎ 01271-863540 Fax 01271-862277
Closed Nov-Mar
12 bedrs, 11 ensuite, 1 ⇌ TCF TV ⚑ P 4 SB £15-£18
DB £30-£35 HB £150-£175 D £6 CC MC Visa Amex JCB

Combe Lodge *Listed*
Chambercombe, Ilfracombe EX34 9QW
☎ 01271-864518 Fax 01271-867628
Closed Christmas
8 bedrs, 5 ensuite, 2 🛏, 2 ⇌ TCF TV ✉ ⚑ P 7 SB £17.50
DB £35 HB £190 D £11 CC MC Visa

Epchris *Listed*
Torrs Park, Ilfracombe EX34 8AZ
☎ 01271-862751
Closed mid Nov-early Dec

Period hotel in two acres, peaceful and comfortable, with parking, bar, near shops, seafront, NT land and coastal footpath. Ideal touring for beautiful Exmoor and North Devon. Good home cooking.

10 bedrs, 8 ensuite, 1 ⇌ TCF TV P 8 SB £19-£21 DB £38-£42 HB £175-£195 D £8 CC MC Visa 🛏

Lyncott *Listed*
56 St Brannocks Road, Ilfracombe EX34 8EQ
☎ 01271-862425
Closed Nov-Feb
9 bedrs, 3 ensuite, 3 ⇌ TCF ⚑ P 7

Beechwood House
Torrs Park, Ilfracombe EX34 8AZ
☎ 01271-863800 Fax 01271-863800

Small, elegant Victorian mansion peacefully situated in own wooded grounds and gardens bordering spectacular National Trust coastline, splendid views over town to the sea. Described as "a perfect retreat".

10 bedrs, all ensuite, 2 ⇌ TCF TV P 10 No children under 7 SB £22-£25 DB £40-£44 HB £195-£210 D £10 CC MC Visa

INGLETON North Yorkshire 10B3

Pines Country House *Highly Acclaimed*
Via Carnforth, Ingleton LA6 3HN
☎ 015242-41252 Fax 015242-41252
Closed Jan

Delightful, friendly and enthusiastically run country house, we offer comfort and quality in a relaxed atmosphere. Licensed, two lounges, a sauna and a delightful conservatory dinning room.

7 bedrs, all ensuite, TCF TV ⚑ P 14 No children under 10 DB £44-£48 HB £222 D £12.50 CC MC Visa 🛏

Ferncliffe House *Acclaimed*
55 Main Street, Ingleton LA6 3HJ
☎ 015242-42405
Closed Nov-Jan

A lovely detached stone-built house (1897) situated on the edge of the village. Rooms are well equipped and decorated to a high standard.

5 bedrs, all ensuite, TCF TV ⚑ P 5 No children under 12 SB £28 DB £44 HB £230 D £13 CC MC Visa

Springfield *Acclaimed*
Main Street, Via Carnforth, Ingleton LA6 3HJ
☎ 015242-41280
Closed Christmas

A family run detached Victorian villa with a fountain at the front, set in its own grounds backing onto the River Greta with panoramic views.

5 bedrs, all ensuite, 1 ★ TCF TV ★ P 12 SB £21-£22 DB £42-£44 HB £196 D £10 CC MC Visa ▣

Langber Country Guest House *Listed*
Tatterthorne Road, Ingleton, Via Carnforth LA6 3DT
☎ 015242-41587
Closed 22 Dec-3 Jan
7 bedrs, 4 ensuite, 1 ★ TCF ★ P 8 SB £17-£22 DB £32-£44 HB £138-£170 D £7

Lane House Farm
High Bentham, Lancaster LA2 7DJ
☎ 01524-261479
Closed Dec-Feb

You are welcome to relax in our 17th century beamed farmhouse, set in the countryside, overlooking the beautiful Yorkshire Dales, and mountains. Ideal area for walking or touring.

2 bedrs, 1 ensuite, 1 ★ TCF ☒ ★ P 4 SB £16-£17.50 DB £32-£35

INSTOW Devon   2C2

Anchorage *Acclaimed*
The Quay, Bideford, Instow EX39 4HX
☎ 01271-860655 Fax 01271-860767
Closed 12 Jan-1 Mar

Situated on the quay, and only a few yards from Instow's golden sands. The Anchorage Hotel overlooks the calm and sheltered waters of the Taw and Torridge estuary. Cordon-bleu cooking. All rooms ensuite with TV and telephone.

17 bedrs, all ensuite, 1 ★ TCF TV ★ P 24 SB £23-£25 DB £46-£50 HB £222-£234 D £14 CC MC Visa ⚙

IPSWICH Suffolk   5E1

★★ Claydon Country House
Hospitality merit award
16-18 Ipswich Road, Claydon, Ipswich IP6 0AR
☎ 01473-830382 Fax 01473-832476
14 bedrs, all ensuite, TCF TV P 60
SB £48-£54 DB £53-£59 D £12 CC MC Visa Amex

Anglesea *Acclaimed*
Oban Street, Ipswich IP1 3PH
☎ 01473-255630 Fax 01473-255630

A large Victorian house in Suffolk brick, refurbished to a high standard and set in a conservation area.

7 bedrs, all ensuite, TCF TV P 9 No children under 8 SB £35 DB £45 CC MC Visa Amex DC

Highview House *Acclaimed*
56 Belstead Road, Ipswich IP2 8BE
☎ 01473-601620 Fax 01473-688659

Highview is a large Victorian residence converted to create a warm, friendly and relaxed atmosphere. Well equipped to serve the modern business lady or gentleman. Colour brochure available.

11 bedrs, 9 ensuite, 3 ★ TCF TV ★ P 15 SB £30-£33 DB £39.50-£45 D £4.95 CC MC Visa JCB ▣

ISLE OF WIGHT   4B4

★★ Bonchurch Manor
Hospitality, Restaurant merit awards
Bonchurch Shute, Bonchurch PO38 1NU
☎ 01983-852868 Fax 01983-852868
12 bedrs, all ensuite, TCF TV ★ P 11 No children under 7 SB £40 DB £80 HB £285-£320 D £16 CC MC Visa ⑤

ISLE OF WIGHT – ENGLAND

★★ Brunswick
Hospitality merit award
Queens Road, Shanklin PO37 6AM
☎ 01983-863245

★★ Clarendon Hotel & Wight Mouse Inn
Hospitality, Comfort merit awards
Newport Road, Chale PO38 2HA
☎ 01983-730431 Fax 01983-730431

A 17th century coaching inn of immense charm and character. Situated in beautiful sheltered gardens with lovely sea views, excellent food, hospitality and accommodation.

15 bedrs, 12 ensuite, 3 🐕 TCF TV 🐾 P 200 SB £25-£35
DB £50-£70 HB £195-£229 D £12 CC MC Visa JCB

★★ Eversley
Park Avenue, Ventnor PO38 1LB
☎ 01983-852244 Fax 01983-853948
32 bedrs, all ensuite, 1 🐕 TCF TV 🐾 P 23 SB £24-£26
DB £44-£52 HB £175-£225 D £12 CC MC Visa DC

★★ Fernbank
Hospitality merit award
Highfield Road, Shanklin PO37 6PP
☎ 01983-862790 Fax 01983-864412
24 bedrs, all ensuite, TCF TV 🐾 P 22 No children under 7 SB £27-£37 DB £54-£74 HB £245-£294 D £12 CC MC Visa

★★ Fountain
High Street, Cowes PO31 7AW
☎ 01983-292397 Fax 01983-299554
20 bedrs, all ensuite, TCF TV SB £49.50 DB £65 D £12 CC
MC Visa Amex DC

★★ Highfield
Hospitality merit award
Leeson Road, Ventnor PO38 1PU
☎ 01983-852800
11 bedrs, all ensuite, TCF TV 🐾 P 12 No children
SB £26-£28 DB £52-£56 HB £235-£265 D £15 CC MC Visa

★★ Keats Green
Hospitality, Comfort merit awards
3 Queens Road, Shanklin PO37 6AN
☎ 01983-862742 Fax 01983-868572
Closed Oct-Mar
33 bedrs, all ensuite, 1 🐕 TCF TV 🐾 P 30 SB £23-£27
DB £46-£56 HB £195-£245 D £9 CC MC Visa JCB

★★ Luccombe Hall
Luccombe Road, Shanklin PO37 6RL
☎ 01983-862719 Fax 01983-863082
29 bedrs, all ensuite, 🐾 P 26 SB £25-£37 DB £50-£74
HB £224-£298 D £16 CC MC Visa DC JCB

★★ Malton House
8 Park Road, Shanklin PO37 6AY
☎ 01983-865007 Fax 01983-865576
15 bedrs, all ensuite, P 16 SB £22-£25 DB £40-£46
HB £140-£182 D £9 CC MC Visa

★★ Melbourne Ardenlea
Queens Road, Shanklin PO37 6AP
☎ 01983-862283 Fax 01983-862865
Closed Nov-Feb
56 bedrs, all ensuite, TCF TV 🐾 ⓕ P 28 SB £22-£35
DB £44-£70 HB £184-£280 D £11 CC MC Visa Amex

★★ Montrene
Hospitality merit award
Avenue Road, Sandown PO36 8BN
☎ 01983-403722 Fax 01983-405553
Closed Jan
40 bedrs, all ensuite, 2 🐕 TCF TV 🐾 P 35 SB £33-£39
DB £66-£78 HB £265-£305 D £9 CC MC Visa

★★ Old Park
Hospitality merit award
St Lawrence PO38 1XS
☎ 01983-852583 Fax 01983-854920
Closed Nov-Mar ex Christmas
35 bedrs, all ensuite, TCF TV 🐾 P 80 SB £27-£36 DB £54-£72 HB £245-£300 D £12 CC MC Visa

★★ Rocklands
Hospitality merit award
St Lawrence PO38 1XH
☎ 01983-852964
20 bedrs, 16 ensuite, P 22

★★ Sentry Mead
Hospitality, Comfort merit awards
Madeira Road, Totland Bay PO39 0BJ
☎ 01983-753212 Fax 01983-753212

Charming Victorian villa in tranquil location, two minutes walk from beach. Family run with emphasis on guests' comfort and relaxation. Excellent cuisine. Dogs most welcome.

14 bedrs, all ensuite, TCF TV 🐾 P 10 SB £25-£35 DB £50-£70 HB £245-£299 D £12.50 CC MC Visa Amex

ISLE OF WIGHT – ENGLAND

★ Villa Mentone
11 Park Road, Shanklin PO37 6EJ
📞 01983-862346 Fax 01983-862130
27 bedrs, all ensuite, **TCF P** 15 **SB** £22-£28 **DB** £44 **HB** £200-£240 **D** £9.50 **CC** MC Visa

Aqua *Highly Acclaimed*
The Esplanade, Shanklin PO37 6BN
📞 01983-863024 Fax 01983-864841
Closed Nov-Mar
22 bedrs, all ensuite, **TCF TV P** 2 **SB** £21-£27 **HB** £180-£230 **D** £7.95 **CC** MC Visa Amex DC JCB

Bay House *Highly Acclaimed*
8 Chine Avenue, Keats Green, Shanklin PO36 6AG
📞 01983-863180 Fax 01983-866604
E Mail bay-house@netguides.co.uk

Located in a quiet position with one of the finest views over the bay, this family run hotel, serving exceptional cuisine, is just a five minute walk to the old village and beach.

21 bedrs, all ensuite, **TCF TV ⋈ P** 15 **SB** £21-£31 **DB** £42-£62 **HB** £189-£259 **D** £6 **CC** MC Visa

Bondi *Highly Acclaimed*
Clarence Road, Shanklin PO37 7BH
📞 01983-862507 Fax 01983-862326
8 bedrs, all ensuite, **TCF TV ⋈ P** 3 No children under 3 **SB** £20-£28 **DB** £40-£56 **HB** £180-£220 **D** £10 **CC** MC Visa Amex DC

Carlton *Highly Acclaimed*
Eastcliff Promenade, Shanklin PO37 6AY
📞 01983-862517
12 bedrs, all ensuite, 1 ⋈ **TCF TV P** 10 **SB** £20-£25 **DB** £40-£50 **HB** £185-£230 **D** £9.95 **CC** MC Visa ♿

Celebration *Highly Acclaimed*
Avenue Road, Shanklin PO37 7BG
📞 01983-862746 Fax 01983-862746

A unique and romantic hotel, specialising in memorable celebration breaks for any occasion. Perfect for couples looking for somewhere special. Exclusive, intimate. Wedding packages available. Ring Maggie for details.

Hambledon *Highly Acclaimed*
11 Queens Road, Shanklin PO37 6AW
📞 01983-862403 Fax 01983-867894

Our cosy licensed hotel offers you an informal atmosphere in which to enjoy your visit. All bedrooms ensuite with TV, radio and beverage facilities. Choice of menu. Free use of nearby indoor leisure facility. Open all year.

12 bedrs, all ensuite, 1 ⋈ ⋈ **P** 9 **SB** £18.50-£24 **DB** £37-£48 **HB** £160-£205 **CC** MC Visa JCB

Lake *Highly Acclaimed*
Shore Road, Bonchurch PO38 1RF
📞 01983-852613
Closed Nov-Feb
21 bedrs, all ensuite, 3 ⋈ **TCF TV ⋈ P** 21 No children under 3 **SB** £22.50-£27.50 **DB** £45-£55 **HB** £185-£196 **D** £8

Luccombe Chine Country House *Highly Acclaimed*
Luccombe Chine, Bonchurch, Shanklin PO37 6RH
📞 01983-862037
Closed Dec-Jan
6 bedrs, all ensuite, **TCF TV P** 20 No children under 16 **DB** £50-£74 **HB** £266-£297 **D** £15 **CC** MC Visa

Orchardcroft *Highly Acclaimed*
53 Victoria Avenue, Shanklin PO37 6LT
📞 01983-862133
16 bedrs, all ensuite, **TCF TV ⋈ P** 12 No children under 4 **CC** MC Visa

Osborne House *Highly Acclaimed*
Esplanade, Shanklin PO37 6BN
📞 01983-862501 Fax 01983-862501
Closed 15 Oct-2 Jan
12 bedrs, all ensuite, 2 ⋈ **TCF TV** No children under 13 **SB** £30 **DB** £60 **D** £14 **CC** MC Visa

St Catherines *Highly Acclaimed*
1 Winchester Park Road, Sandown PO36 8HJ
☎ 01983-402392 Fax 01983-402399
Closed Christmas-New Year
20 bedrs, all ensuite, TCF TV 🐕 P 8 SB £18-£21 DB £35-£42 HB £179-£194 D £10.50 CC MC Visa

White House *Highly Acclaimed*
7 Park Road, Shanklin PO37 6AY
☎ 01983-862776 Fax 01983-865980
E Mail white-house@netguides.co.uk
Closed Nov-Dec

Situated on the famous cliff walk, with panoramic sea views. Comfortable lounge, bar lounge and attractive dining room offering excellent choice of menu for both breakfast and candlelit dinner. Ample car parking.

11 bedrs, all ensuite, 1 🐕 TCF TV P 11 SB £24-£28 DB £48-£56 HB £204-£245 CC MC Visa Amex DC JCB

Bernay *Acclaimed*
24 Victoria Road, Sandown PO36 8AL
☎ 01983-402205 Fax 01983-402205
10 bedrs, 9 ensuite, 1 🐕 TCF TV 🐕 P 5 SB £15.50-£20.50 DB £31-£41 HB £138-£168 D £7 CC MC Visa

Braemar *Acclaimed*
1 Grange Road, Shanklin PO37 6NN
☎ 01983-863172 Fax 01983-863172
11 bedrs, all ensuite, TCF TV 🐕 P 12 SB £19-£22 DB £38-£44 HB £170-£204 D £10 CC MC Visa

Chester Lodge *Acclaimed*
7 Beachfield Road, Sandown PO36 8NA
☎ 01983-402773
E Mail roger@chesterlodge.demon.co.uk
Closed Oct-Easter
18 bedrs, 14 ensuite, 3 🐕 TCF TV 🐕 P 15 No children under 2 SB £19-£21 DB £28 HB £170-£185 D £7 CC MC Visa ♿

Cranleigh Court *Acclaimed*
15 Clarence Road, Shanklin PO37 7BH
☎ 01983-862393
8 bedrs, 6 ensuite, 1 🐕 TCF TV P 5 CC MC Visa

Crescent *Acclaimed*
21 Hope Road, Shanklin PO37 6EA
☎ 01983-863140

Cygnet *Acclaimed*
58 Carter Street, Sandown PO36 8DQ
☎ 01983-402930 Fax 01983-405112
45 bedrs, 40 ensuite, 4 🐕 TCF TV 🎵 P 30
SB £25-£36.50 DB £50-£73 HB £180-£255 CC MC Visa Amex

Denwood *Acclaimed*
7 Victoria Road, Sandown PO36 8AL
☎ 01983-402980 Fax 01983-40298
15 bedrs, 13 ensuite, 1 🐕 P 10 SB £18-£24.50 DB £36-£49 HB £156-£195 D £8 CC MC Visa

Fernside *Acclaimed*
30 Station Avenue, Sandown PO36 9BW
☎ 01983-402356
Closed Oct-Mar
14 bedrs, 9 ensuite, 1 🐕 TCF TV P 10 No children under 3 SB £22 DB £44 D £6 CC MC Visa

Glen *Acclaimed*
4 Avenue Road, Shanklin PO37 7BG
☎ 01983-862154
Closed Oct-Apr
6 bedrs, 2 ensuite, 1 🐕 TCF P 3 No children under 5 CC MC Visa

Glen Islay *Acclaimed*
St Boniface Road, Ventnor PO38 1NP
☎ 01983-854095
Closed Nov-Feb

Situated at the foot of St. Boniface Down and just a short stroll from the beautiful village of Bonchurch. Off road parking. Excellent cuisine. Four day breaks inc. car ferry.

10 bedrs, 8 ensuite, 1 🐕 TCF TV P 6 No children SB £18-£19 DB £35-£37 HB £123-£259

Grange Hall *Acclaimed*
Grange Road, Sandown PO36 8NE
☎ 01983-403531 Fax 01983-403531
Closed Nov-Feb
29 bedrs, all ensuite, TCF TV P 20 SB £23-£27 DB £43-£51 HB £160-£205 CC MC Visa

Hazelwood *Acclaimed*
14 Clarence Road, Shanklin PO37 7BH
☎ 01983-862824 Fax 01983-862824
10 bedrs, 8 ensuite, 1 🐕 TCF TV 🐾 P 4 SB £16-£20
DB £36-£40 HB £146-£173 D £7 CC MC Visa Amex DC

Heatherleigh *Acclaimed*
17 Queens Road, Shanklin PO37 6AW
☎ 01983-862503 Fax 01983-862503
9 bedrs, 7 ensuite, 1 🐕 TCF TV P 4
SB £18-£22 DB £36-£44 HB £139-£184 D £8 CC MC Visa Amex

Hillside *Acclaimed*
Mitchell Avenue, Ventnor PO38 1DR
☎ 01983-852271 Fax 01983-852271
11 bedrs, all ensuite, TCF TV 🐾 P 12 No children under 5 SB £19.50-£22.50 DB £39-£45 HB £196-£217 D £9 CC MC Visa Amex

Hotel Picardie *Acclaimed*
Esplanade, Ventnor PO38 1JX
☎ 01983-852647
Closed winter
10 bedrs, all ensuite, TCF TV 🖂 🐾 SB £18 DB £36 HB £190 CC MC Visa

Lismore *Acclaimed*
23 The Avenue, Totland Bay PO39 0DH
☎ 01983-752025
5 bedrs, all ensuite, TCF TV 🐾 P 8 No children under 3 SB £18-£20 DB £36-£40 HB £160-£180 D £7 CC MC Visa JCB ♿

Littledene Lodge *Acclaimed*
Granville Road, Totland Bay PO39 0AX
☎ 01983-752411
Closed Nov-Feb

A small, family-run hotel with ensuite facilities in all rooms. Situated between shops and Totland Beach. With friendly staff, good food and relaxed atmosphere.

3 bedrs, all ensuite, TCF 🐾 P 5 No children under 3
DB £38-£41 HB £183-£189 D £10 CC MC Visa

Mount House *Acclaimed*
20 Arthurs Hill, Shanklin PO37 6EE
☎ 01983-862556 Fax 01983-867551
9 bedrs, all ensuite, 1 🐕 TCF TV 🐾 P 8 SB £18-£27.50
DB £36-£44 HB £130-£179 CC MC Visa JCB

Richmond *Acclaimed*
23 Palmerston Road, Shanklin PO37 6AS
☎ 01983-862874 Fax 01983-862874
12 bedrs, 11 ensuite, 1 🐕 TCF TV 🐾 P 5 SB £18-£24
DB £36-£48 HB £159-£199 CC MC Visa

Rooftree *Acclaimed*
26 Broadway, Sandown PO36 9BY
☎ 01983-403175 Fax 01983-407354
E Mail rooftree@netguided.co.uk
9 bedrs, all ensuite, 1 🐕 TV P 10 SB £20-£25 DB £40-£50 HB £160-£195 D £9 CC MC Visa

Roseglen *Acclaimed*
12 Palmerston Road, Shanklin PO37 6AS
☎ 01983-863164 Fax 01983-863164
Closed Dec-Jan
18 bedrs, 13 ensuite, 2 🐕 TCF TV 🐾 SB £20-£25 D £9 CC MC Visa Amex DC 🍴 ♿

Rowborough *Acclaimed*
32 Arthurs Hill, Shanklin PO37 6EX
☎ 01983-866072 Fax 01983-864000
Closed Nov-Feb
8 bedrs, 7 ensuite, 1 🐕 P 5 No children under 5
SB £18-£25.50 DB £36-£51 HB £160-£185 D £8 CC MC Visa DC

Sandford Lodge *Acclaimed*
61 The Avenue, Totland PO39 0DN
☎ 01983-753478
Closed Dec
6 bedrs, 5 ensuite, 1 🐾, TCF TV 🖂 P 5 No children under 6 SB £18-£22 DB £38-£44 HB £189-£205 D £11.50 CC Visa

St Boniface *Acclaimed*
6 St Boniface Road, Ventnor PO38 1PJ
☎ 01983-853109
Closed Nov-Feb

Small friendly, private non-smoking hotel in a nice spot backing onto the down and a nice sea view from the front. Cosy bar and on site parking for 4 cars. Sorry no children or pets.

5 bedrs, all ensuite, TCF 🖂 P 4 No children SB £23
DB £39 HB £169 D £7

Suncliffe *Acclaimed*
8 Hope Road, Shanklin PO37 6EA
☎ 01983-863009 Fax 01983-864868
E Mail sunclif@aol.com
Closed Christmas

Small, friendly, family run hotel, well situated near to beach and shops, offering genuine home cooking and a warm and personal welcome.

11 bedrs, 9 ensuite, 1 ☞, 1 ⚌ TCF TV P 7 SB £19-£24 DB £38-£48 HB £170-£195 D £8 CC MC Visa

Belmore *Listed*
101 Station Avenue, Sandown PO36 8HD
☎ 01983-404189
9 bedrs, 7 ensuite, 2 ☞, 1 ⚌ TCF TV ⚐ P 4 No children under 5 SB £13-£15 DB £25-£29 HB £106-£126 D £6 CC MC Visa

Berry Brow *Listed*
9 Popham Road, Shanklin PO37 6RF
☎ 01983-862825 Fax 01983-865995
Closed Nov-Feb
23 bedrs, 23 ☞, 1 ⚌ TCF TV ▣ P 10 No children under 5 SB £18-£20 DB £35 CC MC Visa

---

MOUNT BROCAS
GUEST HOUSE

Small, friendly Guest House, close to beach and all amenities. Buses to all parts of the island. Some rooms ensuite, tea making in all rooms, keys for access at all times. Choice of breakfast. Please phone for brochure on

(01983) 406276
15 BEACHFIELD ROAD, SANDOWN, ISLE OF WIGHT PO36 8LT

Brackla *Listed*
7 Leed Street, Sandown PO36 9DA
☎ 01983-403648
Closed Oct-Mar
16 bedrs, 9 ensuite, 2 ⚌ TCF P 10 SB £15.50-£19.50 DB £31-£39 HB £129-£172 D £6 CC MC Visa JCB

Brunswick *Listed*
Brunswick House, Ventnor PO38 1ET
☎ 01983-852656
Closed Feb-Oct
7 bedrs, 4 ensuite, 1 ⚌ TCF No children under 5 SB £16-£17 DB £32-£34 D £6

Burlington *Listed*
6 Chine Avenue, Shanklin PO37 6AG
☎ 01983-862090 Fax 01983-862090
Closed Dec-Feb

Large Victorian stone building overlooking the sea, and just a three minute walk to the old village. Turn off the A3055 at Five Ways junction (traffic lights) into Queens Road, proceed to the end into Chine Avenue, and the hotel is on the right.

13 bedrs, 10 ensuite, 3 ☞, 3 ⚌ TCF TV P 8 SB £17-£19 DB £34-£38 HB £156-£170

Channel View *Listed*
Hambrough Road, Ventnor PO38 1SQ
☎ 01983-852230

Channel View *Listed*
4-8 Royal Street, Sandown PO36 8LP
☎ 01983-402347 Fax 01983-404128
Closed early Dec & Jan
48 bedrs, all ensuite, TCF TV ⚐ P 12 SB £16-£21 DB £32-£42 HB £125-£155 D £5.50 ▣ ♿

Llynfi *Listed*
23 Spring Hill, Ventnor PO38 1PF
☎ 01983-852202
Closed Nov-Mar
10 bedrs, 7 ensuite, 2 ⚌ TCF TV P 6 SB £17.50-£22.50 DB £35-£45 HB £182-£192.50 D £6 CC MC Visa

Mount Brocas *Listed*
15 Beachfield Road, Sandown PO36 8LT
☎ 01983-406276
Closed Christmas
8 bedrs, 3 ensuite, 1 ☞, 1 ⚌ TCF TV ⚐ SB £13-£16 DB £26-£32

Nodes Country *Listed*
Alum Bay Road, Totland Bay PO39 0HZ
☎ **01983-752859 Fax 01705-201621**
11 bedrs, all ensuite, 2 ⇌ TCF TV ⇥ P 15 CC   MC Visa

St Leonards *Listed*
22 Queens Road, Shanklin PO37 6AW
☎ **01983-862121**
7 bedrs, all ensuite, 1 ⇌ TCF TV P 6 SB £18-£21 DB £36-£42 HB £145-£175 D £7 CC   MC Visa

St Maur *Listed*
Castle Road, Ventnor PO38 1LG
☎ **01983-852570 Fax 01983-852306**
Closed Dec-Jan
14 bedrs, 13 ensuite, 2 ⇌ P 12 No children under 5
CC   MC Visa Amex DC JCB

Victoria Lodge *Listed*
Alexandra Road, Shanklin PO37 6AF
☎ **01983-862361 Fax 01983-862361**
Closed winter
22 bedrs, 19 ensuite, 1 ⇌ TCF TV P 20 SB £16-£24 DB £32-£48 HB £145-£185 CC   MC Visa

Culver Lodge
Albert Road, Shanklin PO36 8AW
☎ **01983-403819 Fax 01983-403819**
20 bedrs, all ensuite, TCF TV P 20 D £8 CC   MC Visa Amex DC ⌖

RAC Hotel Reservations Service
0870 603 9109
(Calls charged at national call rate)

CULVER LODGE HOTEL

Culver Lodge Hotel is conveniently situated just one hundred and fifty yards from the superb sandy beaches of Sandown. With its pleasant garden and heated outdoor swimming pool, the Culver Lodge is an ideal hotel for the classic family seaside holiday. The hotel has ample free parking should you arrive by car.

**ALBERT ROAD, SANDOWN,
ISLE OF WIGHT, PO36 8AW
Tel: (01983) 403819
Freephone: 0500 121252**

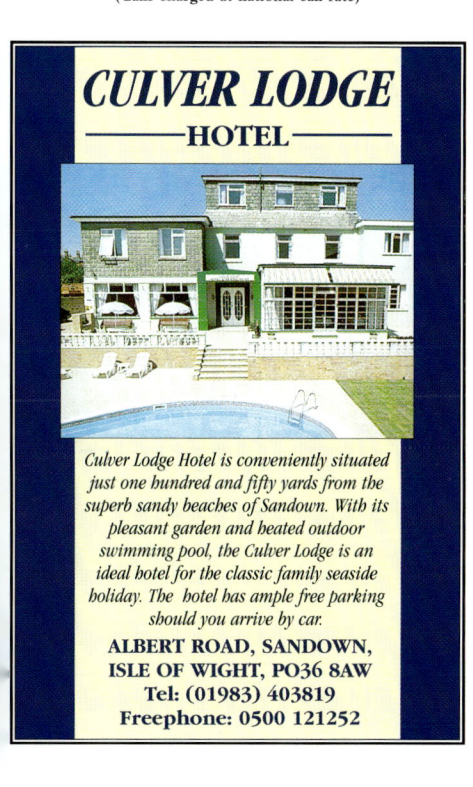

ISLES OF SCILLY   2A3

★★ Godolphin
St Mary's TR21 0JR
☎ **01720-422316 Fax 01720-422252**
Closed 1 Nov-mid Mar
31 bedrs, 28 ensuite, 3 ⇌ TCF TV DB £68-£92 HB £336-£385 D £17 CC   MC Visa

★★ Tregarthen's
Hospitality merit award
Hughtown, St Mary's TR21 0PP
☎ **01720-422540 Fax 01720-422089**
Closed Oct-Mar
33 bedrs, all ensuite, TCF TV No children under 5
SB £51-£67 DB £102-£134 HB £371-£539 D £20 CC   MC Visa Amex DC

Carnwethers Country House *Highly Acclaimed*
Pelistry Bay, St Mary's TR21 0NX
☎ **01720-422415 Fax 01720-422415**
Closed Oct-Apr
9 bedrs, all ensuite, 1 ⇌ TCF TV ⌂ ⇥ P 20 No children under 8 SB £47-£64 DB £70-£104 HB £231-£350 ⌖ ⌖

ISLEWORTH Middlesex   4C2

★★ Osterley
764 Great West Road, Isleworth TW7 5NA
☎ **0181-568 9981 Fax 0181-569 7819**
57 bedrs, all ensuite, TCF TV ⇥ P 140 SB £49-£75 DB £54-£90.90 D £9.95 CC   MC Visa Amex DC

IVYBRIDGE Devon   2C4

★★ Sportsmans Inn
Exeter Road, Ivybridge PL21 0BQ
☎ **01752-892280 Fax 01752-690714**
11 bedrs, 9 ensuite, 1 ⇌ TCF TV P 40 SB £40 DB £50 CC   MC Visa Amex ♿

KEGWORTH Leicestershire   8B2

★★ Kegworth
Packington Hill, Kegworth DE7 2DF
☎ **01509-672427 Fax 01509-674664**
52 bedrs, all ensuite, TCF TV ⇥ P 150 SB £57.50 DB £65 D £11.50 CC   MC Visa Amex ⌖ ⌖ ⌖ ⌖

Short Breaks

Many hotels provide special rates for weekend and mid-week breaks - sometimes these are quoted in the hotel's entry, otherwise ring direct for the latest offers.

KEIGHLEY West Yorkshire — 10C3

★★ Dalesgate
406 Skipton Road, Utley, Keighley BD20 6HP
☎ 01535-664930 Fax 01535-611253

Charming stone-built Victorian house, once a manse, with a modern extension. On the edge of the Dales and Bronte country.

20 bedrs, all ensuite, ⊁ P 30 SB £42 DB £60 HB £210 D £11 CC MC Visa Amex DC ⚒

KENDAL Cumbria — 10B2

★★ Garden House
Fowl-Ing Lane, Kendal LA9 6PH
☎ 01539-731131 Fax 01539-740064
11 bedrs, all ensuite, TCF TV ⊁ P 40 SB £50-£55 DB £70-£75 HB £325-£395 D £18 CC MC Visa Amex DC ⚒

★★ Heaves
Levens, Kendal LA8 8EF
☎ 015395-60396 Fax 015395-60269
Closed 24-29 Dec

A fine family run Georgian mansion set in ten acres of formal gardens and woodland, four miles from Kendal.

15 bedrs, 11 ensuite, 2 ⇌ TCF TV ⊁ P 24 SB £20-£30 DB £40-£64 HB £210-£285 D £12 CC MC Visa Amex DC JCB ⚐

Lane Head House *Highly Acclaimed*
Helsington, Kendal LA9 5RJ
☎ 01539-731283 Fax 01539-721023
7 bedrs, all ensuite, TCF TV ⊁ P 7 SB £35-£40 DB £50-£65 D £16 CC MC Visa Amex DC JCB

Crosthwaite House *Acclaimed*
Crosthwaite, Kendal LA8 8BP
☎ 015395-68264
Closed mid Nov-Feb

Home from home Georgian country house, with superb views over the Lyth valley. Carefully restored, all modern facilities, and a warm and friendly welcome.

6 bedrs, 6 ⌂, TCF TV ⊁ P 10 SB £20-£22 DB £40-£44 HB £210 D £12 CC MC Visa DC JCB

Garnett House Farm *Acclaimed*
Burneside, Kendal LA9 5SF
☎ 01539-724542
Closed Christmas-New Year

A 15th century farmhouse on a dairy/sheep farm, in the countryside but only ½ mile from the A591 Kendal to Windermere Road (leave at Ratherheath crossroads). Some rooms are ensuite.

5 bedrs, 3 ensuite, 2 ⇌ TCF TV P 10 DB £32-£35 D £8.50

Gateside Farm *Acclaimed*
Windermere Road, Kendal LA9 5SE
☎ 01539-722036
Closed Christmas-New Year

Traditional Lakeland farm, with lovely walks, easily accessible for M6 junction 36 on main tourist route through Lakes. 1 night and short stays welcome. Golf & fishing nearby.

5 bedrs, 3 ensuite, 2 ⇌ TCF TV ⊁ P 5 SB £18-£22 DB £33-£40 D £8

KESWICK – ENGLAND

LANE HEAD HOUSE COUNTRY HOTEL

Set in private grounds, formerly 17th Century Manor House. Commanding panoramic views over River Kent Valley to surrounding Fells.
Enter the warmth and ambience of our licensed Country House and just relax, or stroll through our unique Elizabethan Knot garden.

HELSINGTON, KENDAL, CUMBRIA LA9 5RJ
Tel: (Kendal) 01539 731283
Fax: 01539 721023

Martindales *Acclaimed*
9-11 Sandes Avenue, Kendal LA9 4LL
☎ 01539-724028
8 bedrs, all ensuite, TCF TV P 6 No children under 8 CC MC Visa

Jolly Anglers Inn *Listed*
Burneside, Kendal LA9 5QS
☎ 01539-732552
6 bedrs, 1 ensuite, 2 🛁, 6 🐕 SB £20-£25 DB £30-£50 ♿

Roadchef Lodge *Lodge*
Killington Lake Motorway Service Area, M6 Southbound, Nr Kendal LA8 0NW
☎ 01539-621666 Fax 01539-621660
Closed 24 Dec-2 Jan
36 bedrs, all ensuite, TCF TV P 150 **Room only rate** £43.50 D £4.50 CC MC Visa Amex DC ♿

KENILWORTH Warwickshire   8A4

★★ Clarendon House
Old High Street, Kenilworth CV8 1LZ
☎ 01926-857668 Fax 01926-850669
31 bedrs, all ensuite, TCF TV P 31 SB £49.50 DB £75 D £7.25 CC MC Visa

RAC Hotel Reservations Service
0870 603 9109
(Calls charged at national call rate)

KESWICK Cumbria   10B2

★★ Chaucer House
Derwentwater Place, Keswick CA12 4DR
☎ 017687-72318 Fax 017687-75551
Closed Dec-Jan
34 bedrs, 31 ensuite, 4 🛁 TCF TV 🐕 ❄ P 25 SB £29-£38 DB £59-£70 HB £255-£290 D £16 CC MC Visa Amex JCB ♿

★★ Crow Park
The Heads, Keswick CA12 5ER
☎ 017687-72208 Fax 017687-74776
27 bedrs, all ensuite, 1 🛁 TCF TV 🐕 P 27 No children under 2 SB £21.50-£28.50 DB £43-£57 HB £195-£279 D £11 CC MC Visa ♿

★★ Dale Head Hall Lakeside
Hospitality, Comfort, Restaurant merit awards
Lake Thirlmere, Keswick CA12 4TN
☎ 017687-72478 Fax 017687-71070
E Mail daleheadho@aol.com
9 bedrs, all ensuite, TCF P 20 SB £49-£63 DB £49-£75 HB £-£329 D £25 CC MC Visa Amex 🔑

★★ Daleview
Lake Road, Keswick CA12 5DQ
☎ 017687-72666 Fax 017687-75126
14 bedrs, all ensuite, TCF TV P 17 SB £28-£32 DB £50-£60 HB £244-£260.50 D £12.50 CC MC Visa

★★ Grange Country House
Hospitality, Comfort, Restaurant merit awards
Manor Brow, Keswick CA12 4BA
☎ 017687-72500
Closed 6 Nov-9 Mar
10 bedrs, all ensuite, 1 🛁 TCF TV 🐕 P 10 No children under 7 DB £64-£76 HB £325-£339 D £19 CC MC Visa

★★ Highfield
The Heads, Keswick CA12 5ER
☎ 017687-72508

Friendly family-run hotel quietly situated between town and lake with superb views and a relaxed atmosphere. All rooms ensuite with colour TV. Private parking.

17 bedrs, all ensuite, TCF TV P 19 No children under 8 SB £26-£30 DB £48-£60 HB £220-£300 D £12 CC MC Visa

KESWICK – ENGLAND

★★ Lairbeck
Vicarage Hill, Keswick CA12 5QB
☎ 017687-73373
Closed Jan-Feb
14 bedrs, all ensuite, TCF TV P 20 No children under 5
SB £27-£34 DB £54-£68 HB £273-£322 D £14 CC MC Visa

★★ Lyzzick Hall
Hospitality, Comfort, Restaurant merit awards
Underskiddaw, Keswick CA12 4PY
☎ 017687-72277 Fax 017687-72278
Closed Jan-Feb

Victorian manor house clad in traditional Lakeland stone, in spacious grounds on the southern foot of Skiddaw.

25 bedrs, all ensuite, 1 TCF TV P 40 SB £39-£45 DB £78-£90 HB £330-£350 D £19 CC MC Visa Amex

★★ Thwaite Howe
Hospitality merit award
Thornthwaite, Keswick CA12 5SA
☎ 01768-778281 Fax 01768-778529
Closed Nov-Feb
8 bedrs, all ensuite, TCF TV P 12 No children under 12 DB £59.50 HB £294-£310 D £16.50 CC MC Visa

★ Linnett Hill
4 Penrith Road, Keswick CA12 4HF
☎ 017687-73109
10 bedrs, all ensuite, TCF TV P 12 No children under 5 SB £25 DB £46 HB £262.50 D £13.50 CC MC Visa JCB

★ Swinside Lodge
Hospitality, Comfort, Restaurant merit awards
Grange Road, Newlands, Keswick CA12 5UE
☎ 017687-72948 Fax 017687-72948
Closed Dec-Jan
7 bedrs, all ensuite, TCF TV P 12 No children under 10 SB £47-£60 DB £78-£110 D £25

Acorn House *Highly Acclaimed*
Ambleside Road, Keswick CA12 4DL
☎ 017687-72553 Fax 017687-75332
Closed Nov-Feb

A family owned and run large Georgian detached house furnished and decorated to the highest standards. Quietly situated close to the town centre and lake.

10 bedrs, all ensuite, TCF TV P 10 No children under 8 SB £34-£40 DB £50 CC MC Visa

Allerdale House *Highly Acclaimed*
1 Eskin Street, Keswick CA12 4DH
☎ 017687-73891

Pleasantly situated, yet convenient for town, theatre, lakes and parks. Comfort and good food a speciality. Perfect base for a relaxing holiday. Non smokers only please.

6 bedrs, all ensuite, TCF TV P 6 No children under 5 SB £23 DB £46 HB £238 D £11

Applethwaite Country House *Highly Acclaimed*
Applethwaite, Keswick CA12 4PL
☎ 017687-72413 Fax 017687-75706
Closed Christmas-New Year

Victorian Lakeland stone residence in idyllic location off the beaten track, just 1½ miles from Keswick with stunning panoramic views. Friendly relaxed atmosphere. Fresh home cooking, good value wines. Vegetarians welcomed.

KESWICK – ENGLAND

12 bedrs, all ensuite, 1 🛏 TCF TV P 10 No children under 5 SB £30-£34 DB £60-£68 HB £275-£305 D £17 CC MC Visa ✱

Beckside *Highly Acclaimed*
5 Wordsworth Street, Keswick CA12 4HU
📞 017687-73093

Homely guest house with comfortable ensuite facilities and a friendly welcome. Ideally situated for lakes and all amenities. Vegetarians catered for. Special winter rates available.

4 bedrs, all ensuite, TCF TV ✉ DB £30-£37 HB £175-£190 D £11

Charnwood *Highly Acclaimed*
6 Eskin Street, Keswick CA12 4DH
📞 017687-74111
5 bedrs, all ensuite, TCF TV ✉ No children under 5 DB £40-£50 HB £213-£252 D £12.50 CC MC Visa JCB

Dalegarth House *Highly Acclaimed*
Portinscale, Keswick CA12 5RQ
📞 017687-72817 Fax 017687-72817
10 bedrs, all ensuite, TCF TV ✉ P 14 No children under 5 SB £27-£29 DB £54-£58 HB £255-£265 D £18.50 CC MC Visa JCB

Greystones *Highly Acclaimed*
Ambleside Road, Keswick CA12 4DP
📞 017687-73108
Closed Dec

Traditional Lakeland house, set in a quiet location. Close to town, lake and fells.

8 bedrs, all ensuite, 2 🛏 TCF TV ✉ P 7 No children under 10 SB £23.50-£25 DB £47-£50 CC MC Visa

Lynwood *Highly Acclaimed*
12 Ambleside Road, Keswick CA12 4DL
📞 017687-72081 Fax 017687-75021
E Mail lynwood-hotel@compuserve.com
7 bedrs, 6 ensuite, 1 🛏 TCF TV ✉ SB £19-£24.50 DB £40-£54 HB £230-£260 D £11.70 CC MC Visa

Ravensworth *Highly Acclaimed*
29 Station Street, Keswick CA12 5HH
📞 017687-72476
Closed Dec-Jan
8 bedrs, 7 ensuite, TCF TV P 5 No children under 6 DB £30-£50 CC MC Visa

Shemara *Highly Acclaimed*
27 Bank Street, Keswick CA12 5JZ
📞 017687-73936
Closed Dec-Feb
7 bedrs, all ensuite, TCF TV ✉ P 5 No children under 8 DB £34-£50

Silverdale *Highly Acclaimed*
Blencathra Street, Keswick CA12 4HT
📞 017687-72294
12 bedrs, 9 ensuite, 1 🛏 TCF TV P 5 No children under 3 SB £19-£24 DB £38-£48 HB £190-£205 D £10 CC MC Visa

Skiddaw Grove *Highly Acclaimed*
Vicarage Hill, Keswick CA12 5QB
📞 017687-73324
Closed Christmas
10 bedrs, all ensuite, 1 🛏 TCF TV P 12 SB £24 DB £46 HB £245 D £12 ✉

Stonegarth *Highly Acclaimed*
2 Eskin Street, Keswick CA12 4DH
📞 017687-72436
9 bedrs, all ensuite, TCF TV ✉ 🐕 P 9 No children under 5 SB £17-£25 DB £34-£50 HB £185-£240 D £10 CC MC Visa

Swiss Court *Highly Acclaimed*
25 Bank Street, Keswick CA12 5JZ
📞 017687-72637
7 bedrs, all ensuite

Woodlands Country House *Highly Acclaimed*
Ireby, Carlisle CA5 1EX
📞 01697-371791 Fax 01697-371482

A beautiful Listed house in landscaped gardens, convenient for the Quantock Hills and Somerset location, yet is close to the town centre.

8 bedrs, all ensuite, TCF TV ✉ 🐕 P 12 No children under 5 SB £23-£27.50 DB £45-£55.70 HB £210-£225 D £13 CC MC Visa Amex JCB ♿

Fell House *Acclaimed*
28 Stanger Street, Keswick CA12 5JU
📞 017687-72669
Closed 25 Dec
6 bedrs, 3 ensuite, 1 ⇌ TCF TV P 5 No children SB £14-£17 DB £32-£40

Greystoke House *Acclaimed*
Leonard Street, Keswick CA12 4EL
📞 017687-72603
6 bedrs, 4 ensuite, 2 ⇌ TCF TV 🐾 No children under 10 SB £16 DB £36 HB £164 D £9

Howe Keld Lakeland *Acclaimed*
5/7 The Heads, Keswick CA12 5ES
📞 017687-72417 Fax 017687-72417
Closed Christmas
15 bedrs, 12 ensuite, 2 ⇌ TCF TV 🐾 P 8 SB £20-£25 DB £20-£25 HB £220-£240 D £11.75

Rickerby Grange *Acclaimed*
Portinscale, Keswick CA12 5RH
📞 017687-72344
Closed Dec-Feb
12 bedrs, 11 ensuite, 1 ⇌ TCF TV 🐾 P 15 No children under 5 SB £27 DB £54 HB £250 D £12

Tarn Hows *Acclaimed*
3-5 Eskin Street, Keswick CA12 4DH
📞 017687-73217

Long established and comfortably appointed guest house. Pleasantly situated in quiet residential area yet close to lake, parks, fells and town centre. Private parking.

8 bedrs, 4 ensuite, 2 ⇌ TCF TV ☒ 🐾 P 8 No children under 6 SB £20 DB £32-£40 HB £170-£195 D £9

Sunnyside *Listed*
25 Southey Street, Keswick CA12 4EF
📞 017687-72446
Closed Christmas
8 bedrs, 5 ensuite, 3 ⇌ TCF TV 🐾 P 8 SB £18-£22 DB £36-£44

Glaramara
Borrowdale, Keswick CA12 5XQ
📞 017687-77222
Closed mid Jan-mid Feb

Informal and friendly guest house in Northern Lakes, enjoying a peaceful setting in a picturesque valley, with stunning views of high mountains. Ideal for walking, touring and relaxing.

33 bedrs, 14 ⇌ TCF P 25 SB £19.50 DB £39 D £9.50 CC MC Visa

Grasslees
Portinscale, Keswick CA12 5RH
📞 017687-71313

Luxurious bed and breakfast in quiet village. Keswick 1 mile. Central for walks and amenities. Personal service whilst retaining privacy and freedom. Private parking, peaceful garden, very relaxing.

KETTERING Northamptonshire 8C3

Headlands *Listed*
49-51 Headlands, Kettering NN15 7ET
📞 01536-524624 Fax 01536-83367
12 bedrs, 6 ensuite, 1 🅟, 2 ⇌ TCF TV ☒ 🐾 P 10 CC MC Visa

Pennels *Listed*
175 Beatrice Road, Kettering NN16 9QR
📞 01536-81940 Fax 01536-410798
7 bedrs, 5 ensuite, 1 ⇌ TCF TV 🐾 P 4 SB £18-£20 DB £34-£36 HB £126-£136 D £13 CC MC Visa ♿

KETTLEWELL North Yorkshire 10C3

Langcliffe Country House *Highly Acclaimed*
Kettlewell, Skipton BD23 5RJ
☎ 01756-760243

Detached country house with garden and panoramic views. Conservatory, restaurant with reputation for high standard freshly cooked food. Pretty bedrooms. Logfire in winter.

6 bedrs, 3 ensuite, 3 ⌂, TCF TV ⌘ ⊁ P 7 SB £38 DB £56 HB £295 D £15 CC MC Visa ♿

KEYNSHAM Somerset 3E1

★★ Grange
42 Bath Road, Keynsham BS18 1SN
☎ 0117-986 9181 Fax 0117-986 6373
29 bedrs, all ensuite, TCF TV P 25 SB £46 DB £61 D £9 CC MC Visa ⌘ ♿

Grasmere Court *Highly Acclaimed*
22 Bath Road, Keynsham BS18 1SN
☎ 0117-986 2662 Fax 0117-986 2762
17 bedrs, all ensuite, TCF TV P 18 SB £45-£51 DB £48-£58 D £12 CC MC Visa Amex JCB

KIDDERMINSTER Worcestershire 7E3

Cedars *Highly Acclaimed*
Mason Road, Kidderminster DY11 6AL
☎ 01562-515595 Fax 01562-751103
Closed 2 Dec-2 Jan

Pleasant conversion of a Georgian building with a most charming quiet garden at the rear.

22 bedrs, all ensuite, ⊁ P 22 SB £31.25-£51.30 DB £44-£65 D £15 CC MC Visa DC ♿

KING'S LYNN Norfolk 9D3

★★ Grange
Comfort merit award
Willow Park, Off South Wootton Lane, King's Lynn PE30 3BP
☎ 01553-673777 Fax 01553-673777
Closed Christmas-New Year
9 bedrs, all ensuite, TCF TV ⊁ P 16 SB £36.50-£38 DB £48-£52 D £14.50 CC MC Visa Amex

★★ Russet House
Goodwins Road, Vancouver Avenue, King's Lynn PE30 5PE
☎ 01553-773098 Fax 01553-773098
Closed Christmas

A Victorian house built of warm russet bricks, nestling in lovely gardens.

12 bedrs, all ensuite, TCF TV ⊁ P 14 SB £35-£39 DB £48-£60 D £14.95 CC MC Visa Amex DC JCB

★★ Tudor Rose
St Nicholas Street, Tuesday Market Place, King's Lynn PE30 1LR
☎ 01553-762824 Fax 01553-764894
13 bedrs, 11 ensuite, 2 ⌘ TCF TV ⊁ SB £39 DB £50 D £13 CC MC Visa Amex DC ♿

Beeches *Acclaimed*
2 Guannock Terrace, King's Lynn PE30 5QT
☎ 01553-766577 Fax 01553-776664
7 bedrs, 4 ensuite, 1 ⌘ TCF TV ⊁ P 3 SB £22-£30 DB £36-£43 D £9 CC MC Visa Amex

---

RAC Hotel Reservations Service

Use the RAC Reservations Service and you'll never have another sleepless night worrying about accommodation. We can guarantee you a room almost anywhere in the UK and Ireland. The price of a national call is all it takes. The service is free to RAC Members.

0870 603 9109

Havana *Acclaimed*
117 Gaywood Road, King's Lynn PE30 2PU
☎ 01553-772331
Closed Christmas

Rosemary and Barry offer you a warm welcome to their charming Victorian guest house. Most rooms are ensuite, two of which are on the ground floor.

7 bedrs, 4 ensuite, 1 ⇌ TCF TV P 7 SB £17 DB £30

Guanock *Listed*
South Gates, King's Lynn PE30 5JG
☎ 01553-772959 Fax 01553-772959

Small hotel with roof garden. Situated on the road into town from the A47.

17 bedrs, 5 ⇌ TCF TV P 8 SB £21-£23 DB £33-£34 D £5
CC MC Visa Amex DC JCB

Maranatha *Listed*
115 Gaywood Road, King's Lynn PE30 2PU
☎ 01553-774596
8 bedrs, 3 ensuite, 2 ⇌ TCF TV ⚲ SB £17-£20 DB £28

Twinson Lee *Listed*
109 Tennyson Road, King's Lynn PE30 5PA
☎ 01553-762900 Fax 01553-762900
Closed Christmas
3 bedrs, 1 ⇌ TCF TV ⚲ P 3 SB £16 DB £30 D £7

KINGSBRIDGE Devon 2C4

★★ Oddicombe House
Chillington, Kingsbridge TQ7 2JD
☎ 01548-531234
Closed Oct-Easter
8 bedrs, all ensuite, TCF ⚲ P 15 No children under 7
SB £34 DB £60 D £15

Crabshell Motor Lodge *Lodge*
Embankment Road, Kingsbridge TQ7 1JZ
☎ 01548-853301 Fax 01548-856283

Purpose-built motor-lodge on the banks of the Kingsbridge/Salcombe Estuary, with 24 ensuite rooms with balconies overlooking the estuary. Waterside licensed restaurant. Boat moorings available for guests.

24 bedrs, all ensuite, TCF TV ⚲ P 40 SB £33-£35 DB £52-£55 HB £221-£236 CC MC Visa Amex DC

KINGSDOWN Kent 5F3

Blencathra *Acclaimed*
Kingsdown Hill, Kingsdown CT14 8EA
☎ 01304-373725
5 bedrs, 4 ensuite, 2 ⇌ TCF TV ☒ P 7 SB £17-£25 DB £36-£38

KINGSTON Devon 2C4

Trebles Cottage *Acclaimed*
Kingsbridge, Kingston TQ7 4PT
☎ 01548-810268 Fax 01548-810268
5 bedrs, all ensuite, TCF TV ⚲ P 10 No children under 12 SB £30-£35 DB £50-£54 HB £265-£276 D £16 CC MC Visa Amex

KINGSTON UPON THAMES Surrey 4C2

★★ Hotel Antoinette
26 Beaufort Road, Kingston upon Thames KT1 2TQ
☎ 0181-546 1044 Fax 0181-547 2595
100 bedrs, all ensuite, TCF TV ⊡ P 100 SB £44 DB £58
CC MC Visa Amex

Chase Lodge *Highly Acclaimed*
10 Park Road, Hampton Wick, Kingston upon Thames KT1 4AS
📞 0181-943 1862 Fax 0181-943 9363

A small comfortable private hotel situated in a conservation area close to Hampton Court and Kew. Only 20 minutes to the West End and Heathrow.

10 bedrs, all ensuite, 1 ⇌ TCF TV ⇌ SB £48 DB £62 D £15 CC MC Visa Amex DC JCB

KINGTON Herefordshire   7D3

★★ Burton
Mill Street, Kington HR5 3BQ
📞 01544-230323 Fax 01544-230323
Closed 1st week Jan
15 bedrs, all ensuite, ⇌ P 40 SB £42-£48 DB £55-£60 D £15 CC MC Visa Amex DC

KIRKBY STEPHEN Cumbria   10C2

★★ King's Arms
Market Street, Kirkby Stephen CA17 4QN
📞 017683-71378 Fax 017683-71378
9 bedrs, 5 ensuite, 2 ⇌ TCF ⇌ P 11 SB £25-£33 DB £45-£53 HB £210-£231 D £9 CC MC Visa Amex JCB

KNARESBOROUGH North Yorkshire   11D3

★★ Yorkshire Lass
High Bridge, Harrogate Road, Knaresborough HG5 8DA
📞 01423-862962 Fax 01423-869091
6 bedrs, all ensuite, TCF TV P 32 SB £30-£40 DB £40-£55 D £13 CC MC Visa Amex

Don't forget to mention the guide

When booking direct, please remember to tell the hotel that you chose it from RAC Bed & Breakfast 1998.

Newton House *Highly Acclaimed*
5-7 York Place, Knaresborough HG5 0AD
📞 01423-863539 Fax 01423-869748

Charming, family-run, 17th century former coaching Inn located in picturesque Knaresborough. Two and a half miles from A1. Ideal for York, Harrogate and Dales.

12 bedrs, all ensuite, TCF TV ⇌ P 10 SB £33 DB £50-£60 HB £245-£315 D £14 CC MC Visa JCB ♿

Ebor Mount *Acclaimed*
18 York Place, Knaresborough HG5 0AA
📞 01423-863315 Fax 01423-863315
8 bedrs, 1 ⇌ TCF TV ⊠ P 8 SB £20-£21 DB £40-£42 CC MC Visa Amex JCB

Villa *Acclaimed*
47 Kirkgate, Knaresborough HG5 8BZ
📞 01423-865370 Fax 01423-867740
6 bedrs, 4 ensuite, 1 ⇌ TCF TV ⇌ P 1

KNUTSFORD Cheshire   7E1

★★ Longview
Hospitality merit award
Manchester Road, Knutsford WA16 0LX
📞 01565-632119 Fax 01565-652402
Closed Christmas & New Year

Comfortable, friendly hotel of quality in lovely settings overlooking the towns' common yet only minutes away from jn 19 on M6. The hotel offers 23 ensuite rooms, cellar bar and an excellent period restaurant. We enjoy the Longview and hope you do too.

23 bedrs, all ensuite, TCF TV ⇌ P 26 SB £40-£57 DB £60-£85 D £17 CC MC Visa Amex DC

Dog Inn *Highly Acclaimed*
Well Bank Lane, Over Peover, Knutsford WA16 8UP
📞 01625-861421 Fax 01625-861421
3 bedrs, all ensuite, TCF TV P 80 SB £50 DB £60-£70
D £14 CC MC Visa ♿

Pickmere *Highly Acclaimed*
Park Lane, Pickmere, Knutsford WA16 0JX
📞 01565-733433 Fax 01565-733433

Listed Georgian country house in a rural hamlet, situated two miles west of the M6 (jn 19). Easy access to the airport, Manchester, Chester, Liverpool, Warrington, and close to Tatton Park and Arley Hall

7 bedrs, 6 ensuite, 2 TCF TV P 12 SB £20-£32
DB £42-£45 CC MC Visa

LAKENHEATH Suffolk 9D3

★★ Lakenheath
124 High Street, Lakenheath IP27 9EN
📞 01842-860691 Fax 01842-860691
E Mail lakenhotel@aol.com
10 bedrs, all ensuite, TCF TV P 20 SB £45 DB £58
D £11.95 CC MC Visa Amex JCB

LANCASTER Lancashire 10B3

★★ Hampson House
Hampson Green, Lancaster LA2 0JB
📞 01524-751158 Fax 01524-751779
14 bedrs, all ensuite, TCF TV P 50
SB £40 DB £50 D £13 CC MC Visa Amex

Shakespeare *Highly Acclaimed*
96 St Leonardgate, Lancaster LA1 1NN
📞 01524-841041
Closed Christmas
9 bedrs, all ensuite, TCF TV P 4 SB £20 DB £38

Travelodge *Lodge*
Granada Lancaster, M6 (jn32/33), Lancaster LA2 9DY
📞 0800-850950 Fax 01524-792241
53 bedrs, all ensuite, TCF TV P 350 SB £42.95
DB £39.95 CC MC Visa Amex DC ♿

LANCING West Sussex 4C4

★★ Sussex Pad
Restaurant merit award
Old Shoreham Road, Lancing BN15 0RH
📞 01273-454647 Fax 01273-453010
19 bedrs, all ensuite, TCF TV P 60
SB £56-£60 DB £72-£80 D £16.50 CC MC Visa Amex DC

LAUNCESTON Cornwall 2C3

Hurdon Farm *Listed*
Launceston PL15 9LS
📞 01566-772955
Closed Nov-Apr
6 bedrs, 4 ensuite, TCF P 6

LEAMINGTON SPA Warwickshire 8A4

★★ Abbacourt
40 Kenilworth Road, Leamington Spa CV32 6JF
📞 01926-451755 Fax 01926-886339
24 bedrs, all ensuite, TCF TV P 35 SB £50 DB £70
D £13 CC MC Visa Amex DC

★★ Adams
Comfort merit award
22 Avenue Road, Leamington Spa CV31 3PQ
📞 01926-450742 Fax 01926-313110
14 bedrs, all ensuite, P 14 No children under 12
SB £48-£56 DB £54.50-£65.50 D £18.75 CC MC Visa Amex DC

★★ Beech Lodge
28 Warwick New Road, Leamington Spa CV32 5JJ
📞 01926-422227 Fax 01926-435288
Closed Christmas & New Year
14 bedrs, 12 ensuite, TCF TV P 14 SB £36-£44 DB £47-£60 D £18 CC MC Visa Amex DC

★ Lansdowne
Clarendon Street, Leamington Spa CV32 4PF
📞 01926-450505 Fax 01926-421313
15 bedrs, 12 ensuite, 1 TCF TV P 11 No children under 5 SB £49.95-£54.95 DB £41.90-£69.90 D £18
CC MC Visa ♿

Milverton House *Acclaimed*
1 Milverton Terrace, Leamington Spa CV32 5BE
📞 01926-428335 Fax 01926-428335
10 bedrs, 7 ensuite, 2 TCF TV P 5 SB £20 DB £34
D £10 CC MC Visa

RAC Hotel Reservations Service
0870 603 9109
(Calls charged at national call rate)

Charnwood *Listed*
47 Avenue Road, Leamington Spa CV31 3PF
☎ 01926-831074
Closed Christmas
6 bedrs, 3 ensuite, 2 ⇌ TCF TV ⊁ P 6 SB £17-£27
DB £32-£37 HB £189-£259 D £10 CC   MC Visa

Hedley Villa
31 Russell Terrace, Leamington Spa CV31 1EZ
☎ 01926-424504 Fax 01926-424504

A family run guest house with CTV and video, tea/coffee facilities and central heating in all rooms. Close to the town centre, railway station, NEC, Warwick and Stratford. Great home cooking.

7 bedrs, 1 ensuite, 2 ⇌ TCF TV SB £17-£25 DB £34-£50
D £7.50

Hill Farm
Lewis Road, Radford Semele, Leamington Spa CV31 1UX
☎ 01926-337571
Closed Christmas

Attractive, comfortable farmhouse on a working farm. Central for Birmingham, Stratford-on-Avon, Warwick Castle and touring the Cotswolds.

5 bedrs, 3 ensuite, 1 ⇌ TCF TV ☒ P 6 SB £20 DB £32-£40

LEATHERHEAD Surrey   4C3

★★ Bookham Grange
Little Bookham Common, Bookham, Leatherhead KT23 3HS
☎ 01372-452742 Fax 01372-450080
18 bedrs, all ensuite, TCF TV P 80 SB £60-£65 DB £75
D £13 CC   MC Visa Amex DC

LEDBURY Herefordshire   7E4

★★ Royal Oak
5 The Southend, Ledbury HR8 2EY
☎ 01531-632110 Fax 01531-634761
E Mail rohotel@aol.com
10 bedrs, 7 ensuite, 1 ⇌ TCF TV P 16 SB £24.50-£39.50
DB £55.50 D £6 CC   MC Visa ☒

LEEDS West Yorkshire   11D3

Aragon *Acclaimed*
250 Stainbeck Lane, Leeds LS7 2PS
☎ 0113-275 9306 Fax 0113-275 7166
13 bedrs, 11 ensuite, 2 ⇌ TCF TV ⊁ P 24 SB £27-£40
DB £42-£49 D £11 CC   MC Visa Amex DC

Broomhurst *Acclaimed*
12 Chapel Lane, Off Cardigan Road, Leeds LS6 3BW
☎ 0113-278 6836 Fax 0113-230 7099

A small, comfortable, family run hotel in a quiet, pleasantly wooded, conservation area, one and a half miles from the city centre. Convenient for the university and Yorkshire County Cricket Ground.

18 bedrs, 10 ensuite, 3 ⇌ TCF TV P 10 SB £25 DB £40
HB £245 D £10.50 CC   MC Visa ♿

Pinewood *Acclaimed*
78 Potternewton Lane, Leeds LS7 3LW
☎ 0113-262 2561 Fax 0113-262 2561

A detached Swiss style Victorian gentleman's residence with a warm, friendly atmosphere.

10 bedrs, all ensuite, TCF TV SB £35 DB £42 D £10.50 CC
MC Visa Amex

LEEK Staffordshire 7E1

Choir Cottage & Choir House *Highly Acclaimed*
Osters Lane, Cheddleton, Leek ST13 7HS
☎ 01538-360561
Closed Christmas
2 bedrs, all ensuite, TCF TV P 5 No children under 6 SB £30-£40 DB £50-£55

LEEMING BAR North Yorkshire 11D2

★★ White Rose
Leeming Bar, Northallerton DL7 9AY
☎ 01677-422707 Fax 01677-425123
18 bedrs, all ensuite, TCF TV P 50 SB £31-£32.50 DB £45 D £12 CC MC Visa Amex DC

LEICESTER Leicestershire 8B3

★★ Red Cow
Hinckley Road, Leicester Forest East, LE3 3PG
☎ 0116-238 7878 Fax 0116-238 6539
31 bedrs, all ensuite, TCF TV P 60 CC MC Visa Amex DC

Burlington *Listed*
Elmfield Avenue, Leicester LE2 1RB
☎ 0116-270 5112 Fax 0116-270 4207
Closed Christmas-New Year
16 bedrs, 11 ensuite, 4, 1 TCF TV P 18 SB £30-£40 DB £44-£48 D £10 CC MC Visa Amex

Old Tudor Rectory *Listed*
Main Street, Glenfield, Leicester LE3 8DG
☎ 0116-291 5678 Fax 0116-291 1416
Closed Dec 24-Jan 2
16 bedrs, all ensuite, TCF TV P 37 SB £35-£42 DB £42.40-£60 HB £105-£245 D £10 CC MC Visa Amex DC

Scotia *Listed*
10 Westcotes Drive, Leicester LE3 0QR
☎ 0116-254 9200 Fax 0116-254 9200
11 bedrs, 4 ensuite, 3 TCF TV P 5 SB £22-£27 DB £42-£45 D £8.45

Stoneycroft *Listed*
5-7 Elmfield Avenue, Leicester LE2 1RB
☎ 0116-270 7605 Fax 0116-270 6067
44 bedrs, 25 ensuite, 4, 5 TCF TV P 20 SB £38 DB £45 D £7.95 CC MC Visa Amex DC

LEISTON Suffolk 9F4

★ White Horse
Station Road, Leiston IP16 4HD
☎ 01728-830694
13 bedrs, 11 ensuite, 2 TCF TV P 14 SB £25 DB £52 CC MC Visa Amex DC

LENHAM Kent 5E3

Harrow Inn *Acclaimed*
Warren Street, Lenham ME17 2ED
☎ 01622-858727 Fax 01622-850026
15 bedrs, all ensuite, TCF TV P 75 SB £40 DB £50 CC MC Visa Amex

LEOMINSTER Herefordshire 7D3

★★ Royal Oak
South Street, Leominster HR6 8JA
☎ 01568-612610 Fax 01568-612710
18 bedrs, all ensuite, TCF TV P 25 SB £32-£35 DB £45-£48 HB £207-£263 D £10.25 CC MC Visa Amex DC

★★ Talbot
West Street, Leominster HR6 8EP
☎ 01568-616347 Fax 01568-614880
20 bedrs, 16 ensuite, TCF TV P 20 SB £47 DB £66 HB £309 D £16 CC MC Visa Amex DC JCB

Wharton Bank *Acclaimed*
Wharton, Leominster HR6 0NX
☎ 01568-612575 Fax 01568-616089
4 bedrs, 1 ensuite, 1 TCF P 6 No children under 5 SB £17.50-£25 DB £35-£42

LEWES East Sussex 5D4

Berkeley House *Acclaimed*
2 Albion Street, Lewes BN7 2ND
☎ 01273-476057 Fax 01273-476057

An elegant, Georgian townhouse, centrally but quietly located, with a roof terrace giving views across Lewes to the surrounding hills. All rooms but one have private facilities. Residential licence. Winter breaks available.

6 bedrs, 5 ensuite, 1 TCF TV P 2 SB £32-£48 DB £48-£65 CC MC Visa Amex

LEYBURN North Yorkshire 10C2

★ Golden Lion
Comfort merit award
Market Square, Leyburn DL8 5AS
📞 01969-622161 Fax 01969-623836
Closed 25-26 Dec

Traditional Yorkshire stone, market square hotel, set in the heart of town.

16 bedrs, all ensuite, 2 ➜ TCF TV ★ 🖃 P 130 SB £20-£30 DB £40-£60 HB £182-£249 D £15 CC MC Visa Amex ♿

Low Green House
Leyburn DL8 3SZ
📞 01969-663623

Walk in the beautiful dales and return to lounge before a real log fire in this small guest house offering every comfort. Freshly cooked meals using locally grown produce.

3 bedrs, all ensuite, TCF TV ☒ ★ P 4 SB £28 DB £46 HB £259-£294 D £14

LICHFIELD Staffordshire 8A3

★★ Angel Croft
Comfort merit award
Beacon Street, Lichfield WS13 7AA
📞 01543-258737 Fax 01543-415605
17 bedrs, all ensuite, 1 ➜ TCF TV P 60
SB £45-£57.25 DB £57.25-£69.50 D £11 CC MC Visa DC

Coppers End *Listed*
Walsall Road, Muckley Corner, Lichfield WS14 0BG
📞 01543-372910 Fax 01543-372910
Closed Christmas

Charming, detached guest house. Centrally heated, one ensuite, vanity units, hospitality tray, colour TVs, two ground floor rooms, residential licence, lovely conservatory dining room, large attractive garden, parking.

6 bedrs, 1 ensuite, 1 ➜ TV ★ P 8 SB £23-£30 DB £36-£42 D £8 CC MC Visa Amex DC

LIFTON Devon 2C3

Thatched Cottage *Highly Acclaimed*
Sprytown, Lifton PL16 0AY
📞 01566-784224 Fax 01566-784334

A 16th century thatched cottage houses the restaurant, the accommodation is in a converted coach-house. Set in two and a half acres of garden.

5 bedrs, all ensuite, TCF TV ★ P 14 No children under 12 SB £38.50 DB £77 HB £355.95 D £18.50 CC MC Visa Amex DC ♿

LINCOLN Lincolnshire 8C1

★★ Castle
Westgate, Lincoln LN1 3AS
📞 01522-538801 Fax 01522-575457
19 bedrs, all ensuite, TCF TV ★ P 20 SB £55 DB £65
HB £276.50 CC MC Visa JCB ♿

★★ Hillcrest
Hospitality merit award
15 Lindum Terrace, Lincoln LN2 5RT
☎ 01522-510182 Fax 01522-510182
Closed Christmas-New Year
16 bedrs, all ensuite, TCF TV ⚤ P 10 SB £37-£47 DB £62-£65 D £12 CC MC Visa Amex JCB

★★ Loudor
37 Newark Road, North Hykeham, Lincoln LN6 8RB
☎ 01522-500474 Fax 01522-680403
10 bedrs, all ensuite, 1 ⚤ TCF TV ⚤ P 14 SB £28-£32 DB £38-£40 D £11 CC MC Visa Amex DC

D'Isney Place *Highly Acclaimed*
Eastgate, Lincoln LN2 4AA
☎ 01522-538881 Fax 01522-511321
17 bedrs, all ensuite, TCF TV ⚤ P 5 SB £57 DB £72 CC MC Visa Amex DC JCB ♿

Minster Lodge *Highly Acclaimed*
3 Church Lane, Lincoln LN2 1QJ
☎ 01522-513220 Fax 01522-513220
6 bedrs, all ensuite, TCF TV ⚤ P 6 SB £35-£45 DB £48-£55 CC MC Visa

Tennyson *Highly Acclaimed*
7 South Park Avenue, Lincoln LN5 8EN
☎ 01522-521624 Fax 01522-521624

A personally supervised hotel with a comfortable atmosphere, overlooking the South Park, one mile from the city centre. Leisure breaks available.

8 bedrs, all ensuite, TCF TV P 8 SB £29 DB £40 CC MC Visa Amex DC

Carline *Acclaimed*
1-3 Carline Road, Lincoln LN1 1HL
☎ 01522-530422
Closed Christmas-New Year

A short walk from the historic heart of Lincoln. Gill and John offer warm hospitality in their delightful Edwardian house. Ensuite rooms. Non smoking. Garaging and off street parking.

12 bedrs, 10 ensuite, 1 ⚤ TCF TV ✉ P 10 No children under 3 SB £20 DB £40

Halfway Farm *Acclaimed*
A46 Swinderby, Lincoln LN6 9HN
☎ 01522-868749 Fax 01522-868082
17 bedrs, 15 ensuite, 1 ⚤ TCF TV ⚤ P 25 SB £20-£30 DB £36-£42 CC MC Visa Amex DC ♿

Hollies *Acclaimed*
65 Carholme Road, Lincoln LN1 1RT
☎ 01522-522419 Fax 01522-522419
10 bedrs, 6 ensuite, 10 🛁, 1 ⚤ TCF TV P 7 No children under 6 SB £28 DB £65 HB £224-£260 D £11 CC MC Visa Amex ♿

Short Breaks
Many hotels provide special rates for weekend and mid-week breaks - sometimes these are quoted in the hotel's entry, otherwise ring direct for the latest offers.

Halfway Farm Motel

Ideally situated for Lincoln and Newark, this Georgian house and converted farmstead offers 15 ensuite plus 2 other bedrooms furnished and equipped to a high standard of cleanliness and comfort. All rooms have welcome trays and heating under guests control. Facilities for guests include room telephones, lounge with coal fire and beamed ceilings, unlimited parking and pub with restaurant within walking distance.

RAC Acclaimed

SWINDERBY, LINCOLN LN6 9HN
Tel: 01522 868749 Fax: 01522 868082

Admiral *Listed*
16-18 Nelson Street, Lincoln LN1 1PJ
☎ 01522-544467 Fax 01522-544467

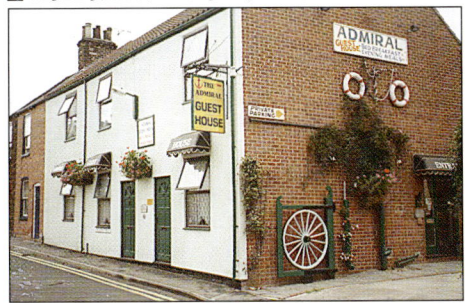

Just off the A57, near the city centre and university. Ensuite rooms, private parking, tea and coffee making facilities, TV in all rooms. Don and Janice offer a warm welcome.

9 bedrs, 7 ensuite, 2 🛏 TCF TV 🐾 P 12 SB £15-£17 DB £32 CC MC Visa ♿

LISKEARD Cornwall   2B3

★★ Colliford Tavern
Colliford Lake, Liskeard PL14 6PZ
☎ 01208-821335 Fax 01208-821335
Closed Oct-Easter
5 bedrs, all ensuite, TCF TV P 50 No children under 14 SB £27.50-£35 DB £35-£50 CC MC Visa Amex JCB

THE LONDON INN

Family owned 17th century coaching inn, adjacent to internationally famous parish church, offers the chance to stay in a warm and welcoming village atmosphere on the edge of Bodmin Moor. Local real ales and home prepared food are our speciality.

ST. NEOT, LISKEARD, CORNWALL PL14 6NG
Tel/Fax: 01579-320263

London Inn *Listed*
St. Neots, Liskeard PL14 6NG
☎ 01579-320263 Fax 01579-320263
3 bedrs, all ensuite, TCF TV P 15 SB £36 DB £48 D £2.25 CC MC Visa

Trewint Farm *Listed*
Menheniot, Liskeard PL14 3RE
☎ 01579-347155 Fax 01579-347155
Closed Christmas & New Year

Wander around our friendly working farm meeting the animals, large and small. Ideal for children, large garden to relax and watch the birds. Enjoy the farmhouse fare home/local produce.

3 bedrs, all ensuite, TCF TV P 4 SB £20-£25 DB £34-£38 HB £160-£182 D £8

LITTLE LANGDALE Cumbria   10B2

★★ Three Shires
Little Langdale LA22 9NZ
☎ 015394-37215
Closed Jan
10 bedrs, all ensuite, 2 🛏 TCF TV P 30 SB £27-£45 DB £54-£70 HB £294-£308 D £18 CC MC Visa

LITTLEHAMPTON West Sussex   4C4

Colbern *Acclaimed*
South Terrace, Sea Front, Littlehampton BN17 5LQ
☎ 01903-714270 Fax 01903-730955
Closed Christmas
9 bedrs, all ensuite, 1 🛏 TCF TV SB £20-£25 DB £40-£50 HB £200 D £10 CC MC Visa Amex DC JCB

Dolphin *Listed*
34 High Street, Littlehampton BN17 5ED
☎ 01903-715789
Closed 25-26 Dec
7 bedrs, 2 🛏 TCF P 15

RAC Hotel Reservations Service
0870 603 9109
(Calls charged at national call rate)

Lamb Inn Listed
The Square, Angmering, Littlehampton BN16 4EQ
☎ 01903-784499

A traditional village country pub. Your hosts Ahad and Mary welcome you. Full bar menu, bed and breakfast, Sky TV.

5 bedrs, 2 ⇌ TCF TV ✝ P 30 No children SB £20 DB £30 D £4.95 ⛔

LIVERPOOL Merseyside 7D1

★★ Green Park
Greenbank Drive, Liverpool L17 1AN
☎ 0151-733 3382 Fax 0151-734 1161
23 bedrs, 21 ensuite, 1 ⇌ P 25 SB £24-£28 DB £36-£38 HB £175 D £6.75 CC MC Visa Amex DC ⛔

Aachen Listed
89-91 Mount Pleasant, Liverpool L3 5TB
☎ 0151-709 3477 Fax 0151-709 1126
Closed Christmas-New Year
17 bedrs, 10 ensuite, 2 ⇌ TCF TV ✝ P 4 SB £22-£30 DB £36-£46 D £6 CC MC Visa Amex DC JCB ⛔ ♿

Blenheim Listed
37 Aigburth Drive, Sefton Park, Liverpool L17 4JE
☎ 0151-727 7380 Fax 0151-727 5833
17 bedrs, 8 ensuite, 4 ⇌ TCF TV P 17 SB £18 DB £29 HB £168 CC MC Visa

Campanile Liverpool Lodge
Chaloner Street, Queens Dock, Liverpool L3 4AJ
☎ 0151-709 8104 Fax 0151-7098725
103 bedrs, all ensuite, TCF TV ✝ P 103 SB £42.50 DB £47 D £10.55 CC MC Visa Amex DC ♿

LIVERSEDGE West Yorkshire 11D4

★★ Healds Hall
Hospitality, Restaurant merit awards
Leeds Road, Liversedge WF15 6JA
☎ 01924-409112 Fax 01924-401895
Closed 1 Jan
25 bedrs, all ensuite, TCF TV ✝ P 80 SB £55 DB £75 HB £350 D £17 CC MC Visa Amex DC ♿

LIZARD Cornwall 2A4

★★ Housel Bay
Housel Cove, Lizard TR12 7PG
☎ 01326-290417 Fax 01326-290359
21 bedrs, all ensuite, TCF TV ⚏ P 25 SB £30-£40 DB £60-£88 HB £275-£360 D £18 CC MC Visa Amex

Parc Brawse House Acclaimed
Penmenner Road, Lizard TR12 7NR
☎ 01326-290466 Fax 01326-290466
7 bedrs, 3 ensuite, 1 🐾, 2 ⇌ TCF TV ✝ P 7 SB £16.50-£24 DB £32-£41 HB £175-£207 D £10 CC MC Visa

LONDON Central London

GRAND TOUR OF LORD'S
Experience the unique atmosphere of Lord's, the home of cricket.

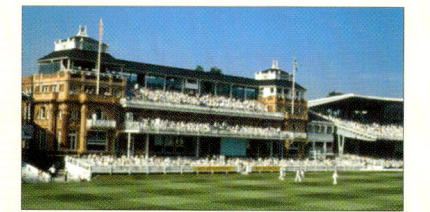

Tours are normally at Noon and 2pm daily — restrictions on some match days.
TELEPHONE 0171-432 1033

★★ Regent Palace
Glasshouse Street, Piccadilly Circus, W1A 4BZ
☎ 0171- 734 7000 Fax 0171-734 6435
950 bedrs, 96 ⇌ TCF TV ⚏ SB £64 DB £101 D £15 CC MC Visa Amex DC JCB

Diplomat Highly Acclaimed
2 Chesham Street, Belgrave Square, SW1X 8DT
☎ 0171-235 1544 Fax 0171-259 6153

The Diplomat is situated in Belgravia, the most exclusive and sought after neighbourhood in London. It is within easy walking distance of Harrods and the fashionable Knightsbridge and Chelsea shops.

27 bedrs, all ensuite, TCF TV ⚏ SB £80 DB £115-£125 D £10 CC MC Visa Amex DC JCB

LONDON – ENGLAND

Windermere *Highly Acclaimed*
142-144 Warwick Way, Victoria, London SW1V 4JE
☎ 0171-834 5163 Fax 0171-630 8831

A small, friendly hotel with well equipped bedrooms. There is a cosy lounge with inviting chesterfields, while English breakfast and dinner are served in the elegant dining room.

23 bedrs, 19 ensuite, 2 ⇌ TCF TV SB £49-£67 DB £59-£92 CC MC Visa Amex JCB

Bickenhall *Acclaimed*
119 Gloucester Place, London W1H 3PJ
☎ 0171-935 3401

An elegant Georgian townhouse situated in the heart of London's West End. Tastefully refurbished, ensuite rooms with colour TV/satellite, tea coffee facilities, hairdryers. Reception open 24 hours.

Bryanston Court *Acclaimed*
50-56 Great Cumberland Place, Marble Arch, London W1H 8DD
☎ 0171-262 3141 Fax 0171-262 7248
54 bedrs, all ensuite, TCF TV SB £60-£73 DB £80-£90 CC MC Visa Amex DC JCB

Short Breaks

Many hotels provide special rates for weekend and mid-week breaks – sometimes these are quoted in the hotel's entry, otherwise ring direct for the latest offers.

Georgian House *Acclaimed*
87 Gloucester Place, London W1H 3PG
☎ 0171-935 2211 Fax 0171-486 7535

Centrally located townhouse type hotel offering clean, comfortable accomodation at reasonable rates. RAC Acclaimed. Same management for 25 years offering real value for money.

19 bedrs, 11 ensuite, 6 ⟨⟩, 2 ⇌ TCF TV ⬚ No children under 5 SB £60-£65 DB £75-£80 CC MC Visa Amex

Hart House *Acclaimed*
51 Gloucester Place, London W1H 3PE
☎ 0171-935 2288 Fax 0171-935 8516
16 bedrs, 11 ensuite, 2 ⇌ SB £49-£60 DB £69-£85 CC MC Visa Amex

Victoria Inn *Acclaimed*
65-67 Belgrave Road, Victoria, London SW1V 2BG
☎ 0171-834 6721
41 bedrs, all ensuite

Wigmore Court *Acclaimed*
23 Gloucester Place, London W1H 3PB
☎ 0171-935 0928 Fax 0171-487 4254

Small, clean, refurbished family hotel with large ensuite rooms, having the usual facilities. Our objective is to be the best value hotel in London.

18 bedrs, 16 ensuite, 2 ⇌ TCF TV SB £45 DB £79 CC MC Visa JCB ♿

Willett Acclaimed
32 Sloane Gardens, Sloane Square, SW1W 8DJ
☎ 0171-824 8415 Fax 0171-730 4830

19 charming bedrooms superbly appointed and decorated. Minutes from Harrods. Excellent night life and shopping.

19 bedrs, all ensuite, 1 ⇒ TCF TV ⌘ SB £72-£82.50 DB £91.65-£99.80 CC MC Visa Amex DC
See advert on page 157

Winchester Acclaimed
17 Belgrave Road, London SW1 1RB
☎ 0171-828 2972 Fax 0171-828 5191
22 bedrs, all ensuite, TV No children under 4 SB £65 DB £65

Blandford Listed
80 Chiltern Street, London W1M 1PS
☎ 0171-486 3103 Fax 0171-487 2786
33 bedrs, all ensuite, TCF TV ▣ SB £60 DB £79 CC MC Visa Amex DC JCB ♿

EDWARD LEAR HOTEL

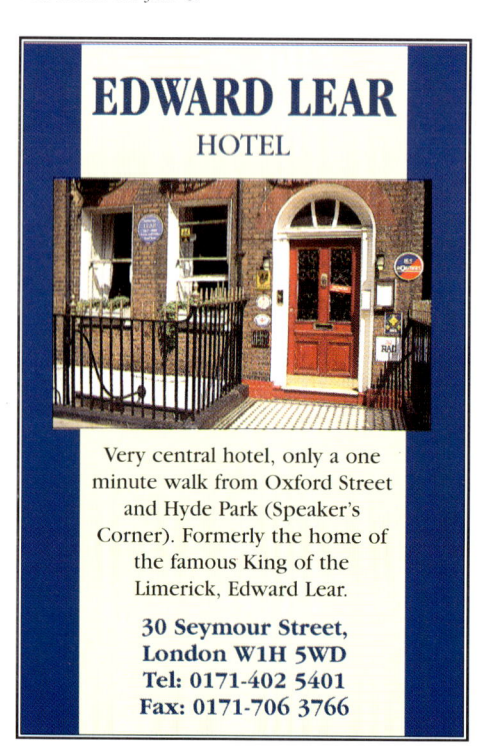

Very central hotel, only a one minute walk from Oxford Street and Hyde Park (Speaker's Corner). Formerly the home of the famous King of the Limerick, Edward Lear.

**30 Seymour Street, London W1H 5WD
Tel: 0171-402 5401
Fax: 0171-706 3766**

Caswell Listed
25 Gloucester Street, London SW1V 2DB
☎ 0171-834 6345
18 bedrs, 7 ensuite, 5 ⇒ TCF TV No children under 5 SB £30-£55 DB £42-£70 CC MC Visa JCB

Concorde Listed
50 Great Cumberland Place, Marble Arch, W1H 7FD
☎ 0171-402 6169 Fax 0171-724 1184
28 bedrs, all ensuite, ▣ P 2 CC MC Visa Amex DC

Edward Lear Listed
30 Seymour Street, London W1H 5WD
☎ 0171-402 5401 Fax 0171-706 3766
31 bedrs, 4 ensuite, 8 ☏, 6 ⇒ TCF TV SB £43.50 DB £60 CC MC Visa JCB

Elizabeth Listed
37 Eccleston Square, London SW1V 1PB
☎ 0171-828 6812

Friendly, private hotel in ideal, central, quiet location overlooking magnificent gardens of stately residential square (c.1835) on fringe of Belgravia, yet within short walking distance of Victoria travel network.

40 bedrs, 34 ensuite, 1 ☏, 3 ⇒ TV ▣ SB £40-£55 DB £62-£80 ⌥

Executive Listed
57 Pont Street, London SW1X 0BD
☎ 0171-581 2424 Fax 0171-589 9456

Upmarket, quality town-house hotel decorated in elegant English designer fabrics and prints.

27 bedrs, all ensuite, TCF TV ▣ SB £81-£86 DB £102-£108 CC MC Visa Amex DC

Hamilton House *Listed*
60 Warwick Way, London SW1V 1SA
☎ 0171-821 7113 Fax 0171-630 0806
40 bedrs, 35 ensuite, 5 ⇌ TCF TV SB £35-£38 DB £50-£68
CC MC Visa

London Continental *Listed*
88 Gloucester Place, London W1H 3HN
☎ 0171-486 8670 Fax 0171-486 8671
25 bedrs, 22 ensuite, TCF TV SB £35-£75 DB £50-£90 CC
MC Visa Amex DC ♿

Stanley House *Awaiting Inspection*
19-21 Belgrave Road, Victoria, London SW1V 1RR
☎ 0171-834 7292 Fax 0171-834 8439
31 bedrs, all ensuite, 6 ⇌ TV No children under 8
SB £28 DB £42 CC MC Visa Amex DC JCB

George
60 Cartwright Gardens, London WC1 H9EL
☎ 0171-387 8777 Fax 0171-383 5044

In a quiet crescent of Georgian town-houses within walking distance of the British Museum and West End. Relaxed and friendly atmosphere at a comparatively low cost. Good value for money.

40 bedrs, 4 ensuite, 9 ⇌ TCF TV SB £39.50-£43.50
DB £49.50-£54.50 CC MC Visa Amex 🔍

LONDON Bayswater, Kensington & Knightsbridge

★★ Delmere
Hospitality, Comfort, Restaurant merit awards
130 Sussex Gardens, Hyde Park, London W2 1UB
☎ 0171-706 3344 Fax 0171-262 1863
E Mail 100255.3347@compuserve.com
38 bedrs, all ensuite, TCF TV 🅿 P 2 SB £78 DB £98
D £12.95 CC MC Visa Amex DC JCB

Five Sumner Place *Town House*
5 Sumner Place, London SW7 3EE
☎ 0171-584 7586 Fax 0171-823 9962

A 'Best Small Hotel' award winner situated in fashionable South Kensington. This family owned and run hotel offers excellent service and personal attention. All rooms are luxuriously appointed.

13 bedrs, all ensuite, 🅿 No children under 7 Unlic CC
MC Visa Amex JCB ♿

Claverley *Highly Acclaimed*
13-14 Beaufort Gardens, Knightsbridge, SW3 1PS
☎ 0171-589 8541 Fax 0171-584 3410
30 bedrs, 29 ensuite, 1 ⇌ TCF TV 🅿 SB £60-£120
DB £110-£195 CC MC Visa Amex DC

LONDON CONTINENTAL HOTEL

88 Gloucester Place, London W1H 3HN
Tel: 0171 486 8670 Fax: 0171 486 8671
Email:reservation@london-continental.com
Website:http://www.london-continental.com

Central London location, off famous Oxford Street. 25 rooms, all en suite, with telephone, satellite TV, radio alarm, tea/coffee making facilities, hairdryer, fridge/ freezer. Singles, doubles, triples and quads. Lift to all floors. Five minutes from Baker Street underground. *Continental breakfast and dining room*

LONDON – ENGLAND

Craven Gardens *Acclaimed*
16 Leinster Terrace, London W2 3ES
☎ 0171-262 3167 Fax 0171-262 2083
43 bedrs, all ensuite, TCF TV 🎵 SB £40-£46 DB £60-£66
D £15 CC MC Visa Amex DC JCB ♿

Henley House *Acclaimed*
30 Barkston Gardens, Earls Court, London SW5 0EN
☎ 0171-370 4111 Fax 0171-370 0026

This charming 'boutique' style hotel offers 20 elegant and beautifully designed rooms. A wonderful place to stay, whether on business or for that special romantic weekend.

20 bedrs, all ensuite, TCF TV No children under 1
SB £60-£70 DB £84-£95 CC MC Visa Amex DC JCB

Kensington Manor *Acclaimed*
8 Emperor's Gate, London SW7 4HH
☎ 0171-370 7516 Fax 0171-373 3163
14 bedrs, 12 ensuite, 1 🛏, 1 🚻 TCF TV SB £40-£60
DB £75-£90 CC MC Visa Amex DC JCB

Mitre House *Acclaimed*
178-184 Sussex Gardens, Hyde Park, W2 1TU
☎ 0171-723 8040 Fax 0171-402 0990

Family run hotel established over 30 years, recently refurbished, renovated and upgraded.

70 bedrs, all ensuite, TV 🎵 P 20 SB £55-£65 DB £70-£75
CC MC Visa Amex DC JCB ♿

Westland *Acclaimed*
154 Bayswater Road, London W2 4HP
☎ 0171-229 9191 Fax 0171-727 1054
30 bedrs, all ensuite, TCF TV 🐕 🎵 P 9 SB £79 DB £95
D £10.50 CC MC Visa Amex DC ♿

Apollo *Listed*
18-22 Lexham Gardens, London W8 5JE
☎ 0171-835 1133 Fax 0171-370 4853
Closed Christmas-New Year
46 bedrs, all ensuite, TV 🎵 SB £58-£65 DB £68-£75 CC
MC Visa Amex DC

One of London's best bed & breakfast hotels

All bedrooms with ensuite bathroom, six band radio, satellite television and direct dial telephone.

Free Car Park ★ Licensed Bar ★ Lift
English Breakfast ★ Reasonable Rates

Centrally located to all major sights, shopping areas and tourist attractions.

One block from Paddington Station and A2 Airbus direct to Heathrow Airport.

Family run hotel for over thirty years.

RAC ACCLAIMED

MITRE HOUSE HOTEL
178-184 SUSSEX GARDENS, HYDE PARK, LONDON W2 1TU
Telephone: 0171-723 8040   Facsimile: 0171-402 0990

ASHLEY HOTEL

A very central, yet quiet hotel, owned and managed by the same Welsh family for over 27 years. Quality ensuite rooms with tea/coffee making facilities and excellent English breakfasts.

15 NORFOLK SQUARE, LONDON W2 1RU
Tel: 0171-723 3375
Fax: 0171-723 0173

Ashley Listed
15 Norfolk Square, London W2 1RU
☎ 0171-723 3375 Fax 0171-723 0173
Closed 24 Dec-Jan
16 bedrs, 11 ensuite, 3 ➡ TCF TV SB £31.50-£32.50
DB £63-£66 CC MC Visa

Averard Listed
10 Lancaster Gate, London W2 3LH
☎ 0171-723 8877 Fax 0171-706 0860
Closed Christmas

Excellently located, friendly family hotel in an interesting Victorian building with original public rooms and period style painting, sculptures and other features.

60 bedrs, all ensuite, ⊟ SB £55-£60 DB £75-£80 CC MC Visa Amex DC

Barry House Listed
12 Sussex Place, London W2 2TP
☎ 0171-723 7340 Fax 0171-723 9775
E Mail bh-hotel@liaison.demon.co.uk

Providing family-like care, this friendly, comfortable B&B has bedrooms with ensuite facilities. English breakfast included in competitive rates. Very central location close to Paddington Station. Web: http://www.hotel.uk.com/barryhouse.

18 bedrs, 14 ensuite, 1 ⌂, 2 ➡ TCF TV SB £32-£50
DB £62-£72 CC MC Visa Amex DC JCB

Blair House Listed
34 Draycott Place, London SW3 2SA
☎ 0171-581 2323 Fax 0171-823 7752
17 bedrs, all ensuite, TCF TV ⊟ SB £70-£85 DB £90-£115
CC MC Visa Amex DC JCB

Dylan Listed
14 Devonshire Terrace, Lancaster Gate, London W2 3DW
☎ 0171-723 3280 Fax 0171-402 2443

A terraced hotel overlooking Queen's Gardens offering a home from home. Centrally heated. All rooms with hot and cold water, tea and coffee making facilities, telephone and TV. Some rooms with full private facilities.

18 bedrs, 8 ensuite, 4 ⌂, 4 ➡ TCF TV ✉ SB £32-£38
DB £48-£58 CC MC Visa Amex DC

Garden Court Listed
30-31 Kensington Garden Square, London W2 4BG
☎ 0171-229 2553 Fax 0171-727 2749
34 bedrs, 15 ensuite, 1 ⌂, 9 ➡ TV ♿ SB £35-£48
DB £50-£75 CC MC Visa

RAC Hotel Reservations Service
0870 603 9109
(Calls charged at national call rate)

Merlyn Court Listed
2 Barkston Gardens, London SW5 0EN
☎ 0171-370 1640 Fax 0171-370 4986
Closed 20-26 Dec

Comfortable, good value, family run hotel in a quiet Edwardian square in Kensington. Family rooms are available. Easy access to Olympia and Earls Court exhibition halls, train stations and motorways.

17 bedrs, 8 ensuite, 1 ⬤, 6 ⬤ TCF TV ⬤ SB £25-£50 DB £45-£60 CC MC Visa JCB

Park Lodge Listed
73 Queensborough Terrace, Bayswater, W2 3SU
☎ 0171-229 6424 Fax 0171-221 4772
29 bedrs, all ensuite, CC MC Visa Amex DC JCB

Parkwood Listed
4 Stanhope Place, London W2 2HB
☎ 0171-402 2241 Fax 0171-402 1574

An attractive town house situated in a quiet residential street just a two minute walk from Oxford Street, Marble Arch and Hyde Park. Excellently managed with spotlessly clean and airy rooms.

18 bedrs, 12 ensuite, 3 ⬤ TCF TV SB £45-£49 DB £80-£88 CC MC Visa

Slavia Listed
2 Pembridge Square, London W2 4EW
☎ 0171-727 1316 Fax 0171-229 0803
31 bedrs, all ensuite, P SB £38-£50 DB £48-£67 CC MC Visa Amex DC

Swiss House Listed
171 Old Brompton Road, South Kensington, SW5 0AN
☎ 0171-373 9383 Fax 0171-373 4983
E Mail recep@swiss-hh.demon.co.uk
15 bedrs, 14 ensuite, 1 ⬤, 1 ⬤ TCF TV ⬤ SB £56-£59 DB £72-£76 CC MC Visa Amex DC

Tregaron Listed
17 Norfolk Square, Hyde Park, London W2 1RU
☎ 0171-723 9966 Fax 0171-723 0173
Closed Christmas-New Year
17 bedrs, 13 ensuite, 3 ⬤ TCF TV SB £31.50-£32.50 DB £63-£66 CC MC Visa

Duke of Leinster
34 Queen's Gardens, Leinster Terrace, Bayswater, London W2 3AA
☎ 0171-258 0079 Fax 0171-262 0741

Former resident of the Duke of Leinster. Our hotel is centrally situated close to all London attractions, 7 minutes from Bayswater underground station. All rooms ensuite with TV, satellite channels, tea/coffee facilities, telephone. Rooms from £45.

42 bedrs, all ensuite, TCF TV SB £49-£54 DB £69-£74 CC MC Visa Amex DC

SWISS HOUSE HOTEL

'Excellent value for money' has always been the motto. The hotel knows guests' priorities and aims to meet them all. Cleanliness, service with a smile, style and comfort come as standard. Best value B&B in London. Award Winner.

171 OLD BROMPTON ROAD, SOUTH KENSINGTON, LONDON SW5 0AN
Tel: 0171-373 9383 Fax: 0171-373 4983

Elegant English Hotels

The *Elegant English Hotels* is a small group of fine townhouse properties located in the cultural areas of South Kensington and Chelsea. These are converted period properties providing elegant charming accommodation amidst period grace and beauty.

The *Gallery Hotel* in South Kensington is a warm place for all business travellers who require the charm of an old English townhouse. With 36 bedrooms uniquely decorated, this is an ideal place for all lovers of culture.

THE GALLERY HOTEL
8-10 QUEENSBURY PLACE, SOUTH KENSINGTON
LONDON SW7 2EA
TEL: +44(0)171 915 0000 FAX: +44(0)171 915 4400
E-mail: gallery@eeh.co.uk

The *Gainsborough Hotel* in South Kensington provides a blend of cultural atmosphere for all travellers.

It is exciting and full of English charm and hospitality. With 49 bedrooms catering for all requirements, this converted Georgian property is as welcoming as it is comfortable.

THE GAINSBOROUGH HOTEL
7-11 QUEENSBURY PLACE, SOUTH KENSINGTON, LONDON SW7 2DL
TEL: +44(0)171 957 0000 FAX: +44(0)171 957 0001
E-mail: gainsborough@eeh.co.uk

The *Willett Hotel* with its 19 bedrooms is a home-from-home. An imposing Victorian property, it is intimate and private and provides a secure environment for guests of all cultures

It is a favourite with travellers from across Europe, North America and Asia.

THE WILLETT HOTEL
32 SLOANE GARDENS, SLOANE SQUARE, LONDON SW1W 8DJ
TEL: +44(0)171 824 8415 FAX: +44(0)171 730 4830
E-mail: willett@eeh.co.uk

Eden Plaza Hotel
68-69 Queensgate, London SW7 5JT
☎ 0171-370 6111 Fax 0171-370 0932

Our hotel is centrally situated close to all London attractions 5 minutes from Gloucester Rd tube station. All rooms ensuite with TV, satellite channels, tea/coffee facilities and telephone. Rooms from £59.

62 bedrs, 62 ⌘, TCF TV SB £64 DB £79 CC MC Visa Amex DC

Gainsborough Hotel
7-11 Queensberry Place, Kensington, SW7 2DL
☎ 0171-957 0000 Fax 0171-957 0001
E Mail gainsborough@eeh.co.uk

Vibrant and alive. 49 uniquely decorated bedrooms. Exclusive night club. Minutes from tube station and the art world. Rooms from £71 inclusive.

49 bedrs
See advert on previous page

RAC Hotel Reservations Service

Use the RAC Reservations Service and you'll never have another sleepless night worrying about accommodation. We can guarantee you a room almost anywhere in the UK and Ireland. The price of a national call is all it takes. The service is free to RAC Members.

0870 603 9109

Gallery
8-10 Queensberry Place, South Kensington, SW7 2EA
☎ 0171-915 0000 Fax 0171-915 4400

Cultured and traditional. Matured and luxurious. In the heart of South Kensington, London's cultural centre. Ideal for business people and individuals. 36 bedrooms embellished with original art.

36 bedrs, all ensuite, TV CC MC Visa Amex DC
See advert on previous page

Kensington Court
33 Nevern Place, London SW5 9NP
☎ 0171-370 5151 Fax 0171-370 3499

Our hotel is centrally situated close to all London attractions, 2 minutes from Earls Court Rd underground & the exhibition. All rooms are ensuite, TV, satellite channels, tea/coffee facilities, direct telephone line. Room price from £59. Free parking.

35 bedrs, all ensuite, TCF TV ▣ P 10 SB £59 DB £75 CC MC Visa Amex

Philbeach Inn
17 Longridge Road, London SW5 9SB
☎ 0171-370 5213 Fax 0171-370 0734
17 bedrs, 4 ⌘ TV SB £25-£30 DB £40-£45 CC MC Visa DC
See advert on back cover

LONDON Bloomsbury & City

Academy *Highly Acclaimed*
17-21 Gower Street, London WC1E 6HG
☎ 0171-631 4115 Fax 0171-636 3442
40 bedrs, 36 ensuite, 2 ⌘ TCF TV SB £100 DB £135 D £17 CC MC Visa Amex DC JCB

Haddon Hall *Listed*
39/40 Bedford Place, Russell Square, WC1B 5JT
☎ 0171-636 2474 Fax 0171-580 4527

Near the British Museum, theatres, shopping (Oxford Street), and tourist attractions. Short walking distances to three tube stations - Russell Square, Holborn and Tottenham Court Road. Euston Station is only a 10-15 minute walk away.

33 bedrs, 12 ensuite, 6 ➡ SB £42-£54 DB £57-£69 CC MC Visa

Crescent
49-50 Cartwright Gardens, London WC1H 9EL
☎ 0171-387 1515 Fax 0171-383 2054

Two Georgian town houses. Part of an attractive, elegant semi circle with private square and tennis courts.

24 bedrs, 18 ensuite, 6 ➡ TCF TV SB £37.50-£55 DB £69-£73 CC MC Visa

Ruskin
23-24 Montague Street, Russell Square, WC1B 5BH
☎ 0171-636 7388 Fax 0171-323 1662

Family run hotel, centrally located, opposite the British Museum, within walking distance of theatreland, Oxford Street and Covent Garden. Near Holborn and Russell Square Underground stations.

33 bedrs, 6 ensuite, 5 ➡ TCF SB £39-£42 DB £55-£70 CC MC Visa Amex DC

LONDON North & West

Dawson House *Highly Acclaimed*
72 Canfield Gardens, London NW6 3ED
☎ 0171-624 0079 Fax 0171-372 3469
E Mail 100712.2636@compuserve.com
15 bedrs, all ensuite, 3 ➡ TCF TV No children under 5
SB £35 DB £52 CC MC Visa Amex ♿

La Gaffe *Acclaimed*
107-111 Heath Street, London NW3 6SS
☎ 0171-435 8965 Fax 0171-794 7595
18 bedrs, all ensuite, TCF TV P 2 D £12.95 CC MC Visa Amex DC

Short Breaks
Many hotels provide special rates for weekend and mid-week breaks - sometimes these are quoted in the hotel's entry, otherwise ring direct for the latest offers.

La Gaffe
La Gaffe Hotel is in quaint Hampstead village, north-west of London and twelve minutes tube ride from the centre of town (West End), close to Hampstead Heath and Hampstead Tube Station (Northern Line).

The hotel boasts an excellent Italian restaurant and a cosy bar.

107-111 HEATH STREET, LONDON NW3 6SS
Tel: 0171-435 8965 Fax: (0171) 794 7592

Langorf *Acclaimed*
20 Frognal, Hampstead, London NW3 6AG
☎ 0171-794 4483 Fax 0171-435 9055

Elegant Edwardian residence offering friendly personalised service in a home from home atmosphere. Situated four minutes walk from Finchley Road Underground station, from where it is 10 minutes to Central London.

31 bedrs, all ensuite, **TCF TV** 🕭 **SB** £68-£78 **DB** £85-£95 **D** £4 **CC** MC Visa Amex DC

Abbey Lodge *Listed*
51 Grange Park, Ealing, London W5 3PR
☎ 0181-567 7914 Fax 0181-579 5350
17 bedrs, 16 ensuite, **TV** 🐕 **SB** £37-£41 **DB** £47-£52 **CC** MC Visa DC JCB

Acton Park *Listed*
116 The Vale, Acton, London W3 7JT
☎ 0181-743 9417 Fax 0181-743 9417
21 bedrs, 20 ensuite, 1 🕭, 🐕 🕭 **P** 20 **SB** £47-£54.05 **DB** £57-£66.97 **D** £10 **CC** MC Visa Amex DC ♿

Anchor *Listed*
10 West Heath Drive, Golders Green, NW11 7QH
☎ 0181-458 8764 Fax 0181-455 3204

A charming, friendly small hotel, great value, two minutes from Golders Green tube station. One stop from Brent Cross shopping centre, 20 minutes from West End. Mostly ensuite rooms, free parking.

11 bedrs, 8 ensuite, 1 🐾 **TCF TV P** 4 **SB** £29-£35 **DB** £40-£49 **CC** MC Visa DC JCB

Central *Listed*
35 Hoop Lane, London NW11 8BS
☎ 0181-458 5636 Fax 0181-455 4792
26 bedrs, all ensuite, 3 🐾 **TV P** 8 No children under 10 **SB** £40-£50 **DB** £55-£65 **CC** MC Visa Amex DC

Colonnade *Listed*
2 Warrington Crescent, London W9 1ER
☎ 0171-286 1052 Fax 0171-286 1057
48 bedrs, all ensuite, 10 🕭, **TCF TV** 🐕 🕭 **P** 4 **SB** £70 **DB** £95 **CC** MC Visa Amex DC JCB ♿

Four Seasons *Listed*
173 Gloucester Place, London NW1 6DX
☎ 0171-724 3461 Fax 0171-402 5594
227 bedrs, all ensuite, 🕭 **P** 80 **CC** MC Visa Amex DC 🍽

Garth *Listed*
64-76 Hendon Way, Cricklewood, London NW2 2NL
☎ 0181-209 1511 Fax 0181-455 4744
46 bedrs, all ensuite, 4 🐾 **TCF TV P** 48 **CC** MC Visa Amex DC JCB

Grange Lodge *Listed*
50 Grange Road, London W5 5BX
☎ 0181-567 1049 Fax 0181-579 5350
14 bedrs, 9 ensuite, 2 🐾 **TV** 🐕 **P** 8 **SB** £37-£40 **DB** £49-£52 **CC** MC Visa DC JCB

Rosslyn House *Listed*
2 Rosslyn Hill, London NW3 1PH
☎ 0171-431 3873 Fax 0171-433 1775
18 bedrs, 17 ensuite, 2 🐾 **TCF TV P** 10 **SB** £39 **DB** £59 **HB** £79 **CC** MC Visa DC

Hazelwood House
865 Finchley Road, Golders Green, London NW11
☎ 0181-458 8884

Whether on holiday or business the friendly atmosphere will enhance your stay. Children and animals welcome. Reasonable terms.

6 bedrs, 2 🐾 **TCF TV** 🐕 **P** 8 No children under 3 **SB** £27.50-£30

LONDON North & East

★★ Spring Park
400 Seven Sisters Road, London N4 2LX
☎ 0181-800 6030 Fax 0181-802 5652
53 bedrs, 36 ensuite, 6 ⇌ TCF TV ✱ P 50 SB £25-£45
DB £40-£60 HB £243-£300 D £10 CC MC Visa Amex JCB

Lakeside *Highly Acclaimed*
51 Snaresbrook Road, Wanstead, London E11 1PQ
☎ 0181-989 6100
Closed Dec-Feb

Imposing residence with large rooms. Two minutes walk from the Central Line for Underground trains to central London.

3 bedrs, all ensuite, TCF TV ✉ P 3 No children under 10 SB £40-£44 DB £45

Cranbrook *Acclaimed*
24 Coventry Road, Ilford IG1 4QR
☎ 0181-554 6544 Fax 0181-518 1463

Conveniently located 7 miles from the City, 20 minutes by train, with the town centre 2 minutes and Gants Hill Underground 5 minutes. All rooms have colour satellite TV, radio and tea and coffee making facilities. Most rooms have a telephone and bathroom.

30 bedrs, 26 ensuite, 1 ⇌ ✱ P 24 CC MC Visa Amex DC ♿

Parkland Walk *Acclaimed*
12 Hornsey Rise Gardens, London N19 3PR
☎ 0171-263 3228 Fax 0171-263 3965
E Mail parkwalk@monomark.demon.co.uk
4 bedrs, 2 ensuite, 1 ⇌ TCF TV ✉ P 6 SB £28-£35
DB £46-£65 CC Amex

Woodville *Acclaimed*
10-12 Argyll Road, Ilford IG1 3BQ
☎ 0181-478 3779
15 bedrs, 7 ensuite, 1 ᛒ, 5 ⇌ TCF TV P 12 SB £22-£30
DB £35-£45 ♿

WOODVILLE GUEST HOUSE

A warm and friendly atmosphere pervades this family run business. The bedrooms are bright, well furnished and comfortable. A beamed dining room, a lovely garden and terrace, make this a delightful place to stay. Rooms on ground floor and first floor and some rooms ensuite. Families with children are particularly welcome. Parking available.

10/12 ARGYLE ROAD, ILFORD, ESSEX
Tel: 0181-478 3779

Aber *Listed*
89 Crouch Hill, Hornsey, London N8 9EG
☎ 0181-340 2847 Fax 0181-340 2847
9 bedrs, 2 ⇌ TCF ✉ SB £24-£26 DB £38-£40 CC MC Visa

ABER HOTEL

A small, friendly bed and breakfast, owned and managed by the Jenkins family for over thirty years. Situated in a leafy suburb of North London but only fifteen minutes from central London by public transport. On a direct route via the Piccadilly line from Heathrow Airport.
Prices include an excellent freshly cooked breakfast. There is a wide selection of restaurants within walking distance. Unrestricted parking outside the hotel.
For further details of the hotel and local area, please phone or fax.

89 CROUCH HILL, HORNSEY, LONDON N8 9EG
Tel: 0181-340 2847 Fax: 0181-340 2847

Forest View Listed
227 Romford Road, Forest Gate, London E7 9HL
📞 0181-534 4884 Fax 0181-543 8959
20 bedrs, 7 ensuite, 3 ♿ TCF TV P 16 SB £38 DB £55
HB £322 D £8 CC MC Visa JCB

Grove Hill Listed
38 Grove Hill, South Woodford, London E18 3JG
📞 0181-989 3344 Fax 0181-530 5286
21 bedrs, all ensuite, 3 ♿ TCF TV 🐾 P 12 SB £25-£36
DB £49 CC MC Visa Amex DC JCB

Redland Listed
418 Seven Sisters Road, London N4 2LX
📞 0181-800 1826 Fax 0181-802 7080

A Victorian town house offering good value, comfortable accomodation with a warm welcome. Just one minute from the tube and ten minutes from West End.

22 bedrs, 1 ensuite, 7 ♿ TCF TV 🍽 P 12 SB £23.50-£27
DB £30-£35 CC MC Visa Amex DC JCB

White Lodge Listed
1 Church Lane, Hornsey, London N8
📞 0181-348 9765 Fax 0181-340 7851

Well maintained family run guest house with 17 bedrooms. The motto is 'cleanliness and friendliness'. Close to all public transport for easy access to central London.

17 bedrs, 8 ensuite, TCF TV SB £26 DB £42 D £15 CC MC Visa

Sleeping Beauty MOTEL

A new purpose-built motel, situated just 20 minutes from Oxford Circus and Covent Garden by car or Underground (Walthamstow Central a ten minute walk), making it an ideal base for business or pleasure.

543 Lea Bridge Road, Leyton, London E10 7EB
Tel: 0181 556 8080
Fax: 0181 556 8080

Sleeping Beauty Motel Lodge
543 Lea Bridge Road, Leyton, London E10 7EB
📞 0181-556 8080 Fax 0181-556 8080
85 bedrs, all ensuite, TCF 🍽 P 75 No children under 4
SB £40-£45 DB £45-£50 D £10 CC MC Visa Amex DC

Mount View GUESTHOUSE

Friendly, clean, privately owned B&B in quiet area. Tastefully individually furnished bedrooms with modern facilities, CTV, tea and coffee. Finsbury Park Station (Piccadilly and Victoria lines). Unrestricted parking. Access A406 North Circular, A1, M1. No smoking. B&B from £20.

31 MOUNT VIEW ROAD, LONDON N4 4SS
Tel: 0181-340 9222 Fax: 0181-342 8494

LONDON – ENGLAND

PARK HOTEL

Acclaimed.
Situated opposite the beautiful Valentine's Park.
Restaurant Mon-Thurs.
Freshly cooked breakfast.
Fully Licensed.
Most rooms ensuite.
All rooms with Sky TV,
tea/coffee making facilities.
Car Park.
5 mins from town centre/Gants Hill Tube.
Easy access M11, M25 & A406.

**327 CRANBROOK ROAD, ILFORD,
ESSEX IG1 4UE**
Tel: 0181-554 9616
Fax: 0181-518 2700

Mount View Guesthouse
31 Mount View Road, London N4 4SS
0181-340 9222 Fax 0181-342 8494
3 bedrs, 1 ensuite, 1 TCF TV SB £30-£40 DB £40-£50
CC Visa

Park
327 Cranbrook Road, Ilford IG1 4UE
0181-554 9616 Fax 0181-518 2700

Situated opposite the beautiful Valentine's Park. Easy access to Underground/BR. Ensuite bedrooms with Sky TV. Freshly cooked breakfast, fully licensed.

20 bedrs, 18 ensuite, 2, 1 TV P 20 SB £40
DB £50 D £12 CC MC Visa

LONDON South & East

★★ Bardon Lodge
15/17 Stratheden Road, Blackheath, London SE3 7TH
0181-853 4051 Fax 0181-858 7387
51 bedrs, 58 ensuite, 1 TCF TV P 30
SB £50-£60 DB £60-£90 D £15 CC MC Visa Amex

★★ Clarendon
8-16 Montpelier Row, Blackheath, London SE3 0RW
0181-318 4321 Fax 0181-318 4378
193 bedrs, 170 ensuite, 10 TCF TV P 60 SB £44
DB £72 HB £392 D £13 CC MC Visa Amex DC

Bedknobs *Listed*
58, Glengarry Road, East Dulwich, London SE22 8QD
0181-299 2004 Fax 0181-693 5611

A guest house which has kept its original Victorian character as a building while adding a warm welcome to its guests.

3 bedrs, 2 TCF TV SB £25-£35 DB £45-£55 HB £160
CC MC Visa JCB

Crystal Palace Tower *Listed*
114 Church Road, Crystal Palace, London SE19 2UB
0181-653 0176
9 bedrs, all ensuite, 1 TV P 10 SB £36-£39
DB £42-£45 CC MC Visa Amex JCB

Weston House *Listed*
8 Eltham Green, Eltham, London SE9 5LB
0181-850 5191 Fax 0181-850 0030

A Victorian villa with modern comforts set in a quiet conservation area of Greenwich Millenium, close to many local attractions and amenities. 18 minutes from central London and convenient for the A2, M20, M25 and A205. An ideal for business and tourists.

9 bedrs, 7 ensuite, 1 TCF TV P 5 SB £30 DB £40-£45
CC MC Visa

LONDON South & West

Worcester House *Acclaimed*
38 Alwyne Road, London SW19 7AE
☎ 0181-946 1300 Fax 0181-785 4058
9 bedrs, all ensuite, TCF TV P 2 SB £46-£53 DB £59-£63
CC MC Visa Amex DC

Trochee *Listed*
21 Malcolm Road, Wimbledon, London SW19 4SW
☎ 0181-946 9425 Fax 0181-785 4058
35 bedrs, 9 ensuite, 5 🚗 TCF TV P 6 SB £37-£47 DB £52-£62 CC MC Visa Amex

Wimbledon *Listed*
78 Worple Road, London SW19 4HZ
☎ 0181-946 9265 Fax 0181-946 9265

A small family run hotel offering a warm comfortable atmosphere for both businessmen and tourist, ideally situated for convenient travel to London or Kingston, Richmond and Hampton Court etc.

14 bedrs, 13 ensuite, 2 🚗 TCF TV P 10 SB £50-£55 DB £60-£65 CC MC Visa Amex DC ♿

LONDON AIRPORT-HEATHROW 4C2

★★ Stanwell Hall
Restaurant merit award
Town Lane, Stanwell Staines, London TW19 7PW
☎ 01784-252292 Fax 01784-245250
Closed 24-30 Dec
19 bedrs, 18 ensuite, 1 ℝ, TCF TV P 50 SB £65-£70 DB £90-£130 D £19 CC MC Visa Amex DC JCB

Heathrow *Acclaimed*
17-19 Haslemere Avenue, Hounslow TW5 9UT
☎ 0181-384 3333 Fax 0181-384 3334

Former private residence in quiet location, only two miles from Heathrow Airport and near the M4 motorway (junction 3).

21 bedrs, 12 ensuite, 2 ℝ, 6 🚗 TCF TV P 10 ♿

Trochee Hotel

- Bed and English Breakfast.
- All rooms centrally heated with hand basin, colour TV, tea and coffee making facility and hairdryers.
- Many rooms have ensuite bathroom and fridge.
- Close to town centre and transport facilities.
- Parking.

**21 MALCOLM ROAD and
52 RIDGEWAY PLACE,
WIMBLEDON SW19 4AS
Tel: 0181-946 1579/9425
Fax: 0181-785 4058**

SHEPISTON LODGE
(GUEST HOUSE)

Shepiston Lodge is a character house, in which the emphasis is on comfort and friendliness. All bedrooms have wall to wall carpeting, full central heating, hot and cold water, colour televisions, and razor points. The majority have private showers, while some have tea and coffee making facilities. A choice of English or continental breakfast is available and is included in room rates

**31 SHEPISTON LANE, HAYES,
MIDDLESEX UB3 ILJ
Tel: 0181-573 0266
Fax: 0181-569 2536**

Shepiston Lodge *Listed*
31 Shepiston Lane, Hayes, London UB3 1LJ
📞 0181-573 0266 Fax 0181-569 2536
13 bedrs, 7 ⚿, 3 ⇌ TCF TV P 20 SB £29-£31.50 DB £42-£44.50 D £4 CC MC Visa Amex DC JCB ♿

Hounslow
41 Hounslow Road, Feltham, London TW14 0AH
📞 0181-890 2358 Fax 0181-751 6103

Easy access to Heathrow Airport (courtesy transport), M3, M4, M25 and central London. Comfortable rooms, all ensuite with colour TV and private telephone. Cosy restaurant and bar. Free off-street parking.

23 bedrs, all ensuite, TCF TV ⇌ P 40 SB £39 DB £49-£52 HB £225-£300 D £5 CC MC Visa DC

LONG EATON Derbyshire 8B2

★★ Europa
20 Derby Road, Long Eaton, Nottingham NG10 1LW
📞 0115-972 8481 Fax 0115-946 0229

Substantial Victorian hotel of pleasing historical appearance. With coffee shop conservation fronting the building.

15 bedrs, 13 ensuite, 1 ⇌ TCF TV ⇌ P 27 SB £35-£37 DB £39.95-£42 HB £300-£315 D £10 CC MC Visa JCB

LONGTOWN Cumbria 13E4

★★ Graham Arms
English Street, Longtown CA6 5SE
📞 01228-791213 Fax 01228-791213
14 bedrs, 10 ensuite, 3 ⚿, 2 ⇌ TCF TV ⇌ P 12 SB £17.50-£19.50 DB £34-£37 CC MC Visa Amex ♪

LOOE Cornwall 2B4

★★ Commonwood Manor
St Martin's Road, Looe PL13 1LP
📞 01503-262929 Fax 01503-262632
E Mail commonwood@compuserve.com
Closed Christmas
11 bedrs, all ensuite, TCF TV ⇌ P 20 No children under 8 SB £33-£39.50 DB £62-£76 HB £311-£343 D £12.40 CC MC Visa Amex JCB ③

★★ Fieldhead
Portuan Road, Hannafore, Looe PL13 2DR
📞 01503-262689 Fax 01503-264114
Closed Jan
14 bedrs, all ensuite, TCF TV P 14 No children under 5 SB £38.50 DB £60-£76 HB £275-£345 D £15.95 CC MC Visa Amex ③

★★ Klymiarven
Restaurant merit award
Barbican Hill, Looe PL13 1BH
📞 01503-262333 Fax 01503-262333
Closed Jan
14 bedrs, all ensuite, TCF TV ⇌ P 16 SB £24-£41 DB £48-£82 HB £258-£377 D £16 CC MC Visa JCB ③

Coombe Farm *Highly Acclaimed*
Widegates, Looe PL13 1QN
📞 01503-240223 Fax 01503-240895
Closed Nov-Feb
10 bedrs, all ensuite, 1 ⇌ TCF TV ⌀ P 20 No children under 5 SB £23-£29 DB £46-£58 HB £238-£294 D £15 CC MC Visa Amex DC ③ ⌀ ♿

Polraen Country House *Highly Acclaimed*
Sandplace, Looe PL13 1PJ
📞 01503-263956 Fax 01503-264389

Situated in the peaceful Looe Valley, an 18th century coaching inn built of Cornish stone and set in two and a half acres of laid out garden.

5 bedrs, all ensuite, 1 ⇌ TCF TV ⇌ P 28 SB £27.50-£30 DB £50-£58 HB £244-£259.50 D £15 CC MC Visa

RAC Hotel Reservations Service
0870 603 9109
(Calls charged at national call rate)

Bucklawren Farm *Acclaimed*
St Martins, Looe PL13 1NZ
☎ 01503-240738 Fax 01503-240481
Closed Nov-Mar

Situated in the countryside by the sea, a delightful farmhouse which enjoys magnificent sea views and provides delicious cooking in a relaxed atmosphere.

5 bedrs, all ensuite, 1 ⇌ TCF TV P 6 No children under 5 SB £19-£21 DB £38-£42 HB £185-£199.50 D £10 CC MC Visa ⚙

Hillingdon *Acclaimed*
Portuan Road, Hannafore, Looe PL13 2DW
☎ 01503-262906
Closed winter
7 bedrs, 4 ensuite, 1 ⇌ TCF TV CC MC Visa Amex

Panorama *Acclaimed*
Hannafore Road, Looe PL13 2DE
☎ 01503-262123 Fax 01503-265654
E Mail panorama@westlooe.avel.co.uk
10 bedrs, all ensuite, 1 ⇌ TCF TV P 7 SB £23 DB £45 HB £195-£205 D £11.75 CC MC Visa Amex DC

Deganwy *Listed*
Station Road, Looe PL13 1HL
☎ 01503-262984
Closed Christmas
9 bedrs, 4 ensuite, 2 ⇌ TCF TV P 6 SB £16-£20 DB £32-£40

LOSTWITHIEL Cornwall 2B4

★★ Lostwithiel Hotel Golf & Country Club
Lower Polscue, Lostwithiel PL22 0HQ
☎ 01208-873550 Fax 01208-873479
18 bedrs, all ensuite, TCF TV ⇌ P 120 SB £38-£40 DB £76-£80 HB £315-£329 D £16 CC MC Visa Amex DC

★★ Royal Oak
Duke Street, Lostwithiel PL22 1AH
☎ 01208-872552
6 bedrs, 5 ensuite, 1 ⇌ TCF TV ⇌ P 14 SB £30 DB £52 D £10 CC MC Visa Amex DC JCB

Ship *Listed*
Lerryn, Lostwithiel PL22 0PT
☎ 01208-872374

LOUGHBOROUGH Leicestershire 8B3

★★ Great Central
Gt Central Road, Loughborough LE11 RW
☎ 01509-263405 Fax 01509-264130

Friendly, family owned, real ale freehouse pub/hotel, five minutes from town centre and university and adjacent to the Great Central Railway. Twenty-two well appointed, but value for money rooms.

22 bedrs, all ensuite, TCF TV ⇌ P 30 SB £30 DB £40 D £7 CC MC Visa

De Montfort *Acclaimed*
88 Leicester Road, Loughborough LE11 2AQ
☎ 01509-216061 Fax 01509-233667
9 bedrs, 7 ensuite, 2 🛁, 2 ⇌ TCF TV SB £23 DB £35 D £5.50 CC MC Visa Amex JCB

De Montfort HOTEL

Refurbished Victorian style family run hotel under new ownership.

88 LEICESTER ROAD, LOUGHBOROUGH LE11 2AQ
Tel: 01509 216061 Fax: 01509 233667

LUDLOW – ENGLAND

Garendon Park *Acclaimed*
92 Leicester Road, Loughborough LE11 2AQ
☎ 01509-236557 Fax 01509-265559

Nine well furnished rooms with radio and satellite TV. Highly recommended a la carte menu. Lounge bar licensed to serve drinks any time of day. Ideally located five minutes walk from the town centre and the Great Central Railway.

9 bedrs, 7 ensuite, 1 🛁 TCF TV 🐕 SB £23-£28 DB £35-£45 D £6 CC MC Visa Amex JCB

LOUTH Lincolnshire 11F4

Priory *Acclaimed*
Eastgate, Louth LN11 9AJ
☎ 01507-602930 Fax 01507-609767

An enchanting Grade II Listed, Gothic building in a lovely garden just five minutes walk from the town centre. Situated on the main road through town next to the police station.

12 bedrs, 9 ensuite, 3 🛁, 1 🛁 TCF TV 🐕 P 20 SB £37.50 DB £52.50 HB £315 D £11 CC MC Visa Amex DC JCB 📧

LOWESTOFT Suffolk 9F3

Albany *Acclaimed*
400 London Road South, Lowestoft NR33 0BQ
☎ 01502-574394
Closed Christmas
7 bedrs, 4 ensuite, 2 🛁, 1 🛁 TCF TV SB £-£16 DB £-£34 HB £-£162 D £6 CC MC Visa DC

Hotel Katherine *Acclaimed*
49 Kirkley Cliff Road, Lowestoft NR33 0DF
☎ 01502-567858 Fax 01502-581341
Closed Jan
10 bedrs, all ensuite, TCF TV 🐕 P 3 SB £35 DB £48 HB £185 D £10.25 CC MC Visa Amex

Rockville House *Acclaimed*
6 Pakefield Road, Lowestoft NR33 0HS
☎ 01502-581011 Fax 01502-574891
E Mail rockvill@interdart.co.uk
Closed Christmas-New Year
5 bedrs, 4 ensuite, 1 🛁 TCF TV No children under 12 SB £22.50 DB £39-£45 D £12 CC MC Visa

---

LOWESWATER Cumbria 10A2

★ Grange Country House
Loweswater CA13 0SU
☎ 01946-861211
Closed Jan-Feb
11 bedrs, 10 ensuite, 2 🛁 TCF TV 🐕 P 20 SB £30-£32 DB £60-£64 HB £290-£305 D £1.50 ♿

LUDLOW Shropshire 7D3

Number Twenty Eight *Highly Acclaimed*
28 Lower Broad Street, Ludlow SY8 1PQ
☎ 01584-876996 Fax 01584-876860
E Mail ross.no28@btinternet.com.
6 bedrs, all ensuite, TCF TV 🐕 SB £35-£60 DB £50-£65
CC MC Visa Amex

THE MOOR HALL

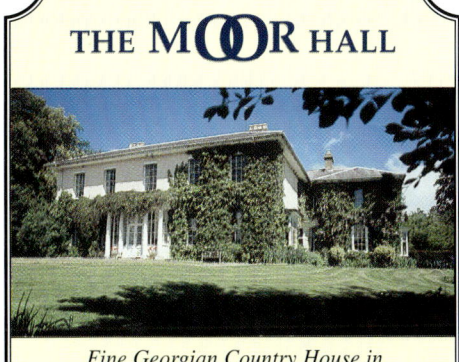

Fine Georgian Country House in outstanding country setting yet only four miles from historic Ludlow. Wonderful gardens. Four posters. Open fires. Informal atmosphere and exceptional hospitality.

RAC Acclaimed
ETB 3 crowns Highly Commended

Contact: Bernie Chivers
THE MOOR HALL,
NR. LUDLOW, SHROPSHIRE SY8 3EG
Tel: 01584 823209
Fax: 01584 823387

Cecil *Acclaimed*
Sheet Road, Ludlow SY8 1LR
☎ **01584-872442** Fax **01584-872442**
9 bedrs, 4 ensuite, 2 ➡ TCF TV ✱ P 8 SB £46-£52
DB £191.70-£235.80 D £12 CC MC Visa

Church Inn *Acclaimed*
Buttercross, Ludlow SY8 1AW
☎ **01584-872174** Fax **01584-877146**
8 bedrs, all ensuite, TCF TV SB £28-£45 DB £45 D £4.75
CC MC Visa

Moor Hall *Acclaimed*
Clee Downton, Ludlow SY8 3EG
☎ **01584-823209** Fax **01584-823387**
3 bedrs, all ensuite, 1 ➡ TCF TV ✱ P 12 SB £27-£35
DB £45-£60 HB £245-£300 D £15 CC MC Visa Amex DC
See advert on previous page

LULWORTH Dorset 3F3

★ Bishop's Cottage
West Lulworth, Lulworth BH20 5RQ
☎ **01929-400261** Fax **01929-400508**
23 bedrs, 18 ensuite, 3 ➡ TCF TV ✱ P 8 SB £21 DB £44-£54 HB £214-£256 D £12.50 CC MC Visa

---

LUSTLEIGH Devon 3D3

Eastwrey Barton
Lustleigh TQ13 9SN
☎ **01647-277338**

17th century farmhouse set in its own grounds with splendid views along the Wrey valley and across to Lustleigh Cleave. A peaceful and restful environment.

6 bedrs, all ensuite, TCF TV ✱ P 8 No children under 12 CC MC Visa

---

LYDFORD Devon 2C3

★★ Lydford House
Comfort merit award
Lydford EX20 4AU
☎ **01822-820347** Fax **01822-820442**
12 bedrs, all ensuite, 2 ➡ TCF TV ✱ P 30 No children under 5 SB £36 DB £72 D £15 CC MC Visa

---

Moor View House
LYDFORD

A small licensed Victorian Country House set in two acres of mature gardens situated on Dartmoor with glorious views over the Devon/Cornish countryside to the west.

Acclaimed

**Moor View House,
Vale Down, Lydford EX20 4BB
Tel: 01822 820220**

Moor View House *Acclaimed*
Vale Down, Lydford EX20 4BB
☎ **01822-820220**
4 bedrs, all ensuite, 1 ➡ TCF TV ✱ P 15 No children under 12 SB £35-£37.50 DB £60-£80 HB £285-£300 D £20

LYME REGIS Dorset 3E3

★★ Bay
Hospitality merit award
Marine Parade, Lyme Regis DT7 3JQ
☎ **01297-442059**
Closed winter
23 bedrs, 20 ensuite, 3, 4 ➡ TCF TV ✱ P 18 SB £28-£31 DB £56-£62 HB £220-£240 D £17 CC MC Visa

★★ Dorset
Silver Street, Lyme Regis DT7 3HX
☎ **01297-442482** Fax **01297-443970**
Closed winter
14 bedrs, 12 ensuite, 1 ➡ P 13 CC MC Visa

★★ Kersbrook
Hospitality, Comfort, Restaurant merit awards
Pound Road, Lyme Regis DT7 3HX
☎ **01297-442596** Fax **01297-442596**
Closed Jan-Feb
10 bedrs, all ensuite, ✱ P 16 SB £50-£60 DB £75-£80 HB £340-£350 D £16.50 CC MC Visa Amex

★★ Mariners
Silver Street, Lyme Regis DT7 3HS
☎ 01297-442753 Fax 01297-442431
14 bedrs, all ensuite, 1 ➡ TCF TV 🐾 P 24 SB £-£34 DB £56-£68 HB £250-£300 D £16.75 CC MC Visa

★★ Orchard Country
Rousdon, Lyme Regis DT7 3XW
☎ 01297-442972
Closed Jan-Feb
12 bedrs, 9 ensuite, 3 ➡ TCF TV 🐾 P 15 No children under 8 SB £33 DB £66 HB £270 D £14 CC MC Visa

★★ Royal Lion
Broad Street, Lyme Regis DT7 3QF
☎ 01297-445622 Fax 01297-445859
Closed Christmas
29 bedrs, all ensuite, TCF TV 🐾 P 36 SD £33-£37 DB £66-£74 HB £241-£294 D £14 CC MC Visa Amex DC JCB 🔲 🈁 🈂

Tudor House *Acclaimed*
Church Street, Lyme Regis DT7 3BU
☎ 01297-442472
Closed Oct-Mar
17 bedrs, 11 ensuite, 3 ➡ TCF TV P 20 SB £17.50 DB £36 CC MC Visa

LYMINGTON Hampshire   4B4

Durlston House *Acclaimed*
Gosport Street, Lymington SO41 9EG
☎ 01590-676908
6 bedrs, all ensuite, 1 ➡ TCF TV 🔲 P 6 SB £20-£25 DB £35-£40 HB £175-£196 D £8 ♿

Efford Cottage *Acclaimed*
Everton, Lymington SO41 0JD
☎ 01590-642315 Fax 01590-642315

Friendly, spacious, Georgian cottage. Award winning guesthouse, four course multi-choice breakfast with homemade bread and preserves. Traditional country cooking, qualified chef, homegrown produce. Good touring location. Parking.

3 bedrs, all ensuite, 1 ➡ TCF TV 🐾 P 3 No children under 12 SB £22 DB £40-£42 HB £203-£245 D £10

Our Bench *Acclaimed*
9 Lodge Road, Pennington, Lymington SO41 8HH
☎ 01590-673141 Fax 01590-673141
E Mail ourbench@newforest.demon.co.uk.
Closed Christmas & New Year
3 bedrs, all ensuite, TCF TV 🔲 P 5 No children SB £20-£26 DB £42-£48 HB £189-£231 D £7 CC MC Visa JCB 🔲 🈁

Brockhills Farm
Sway Road, Tiptoe, Nr Lymington SO41 6FQ
☎ 01425-611280 Fax 01425-611280

A warm welcome awaits in this 250 year old farmhouse, situated between the New Forest and the coast. Driving tuition and stabling in the Shetland Pony breeding and carriage driving centre.

3 bedrs, 1 🚿, 2 ➡ TCF TV 🐾 P 4 SB £16.50-£17 DB £17-£18 HB £-£53 ♿

LYMPSHAM Somerset   3E1

★★ Batch Country House
Batch Lane, Lympsham BS24 0EX
☎ 01934-750371 Fax 01934-750501
Closed Christmas
8 bedrs, all ensuite, TCF TV P 50 SB £37-£39 DB £56-£58 HB £245-£255 D £12 CC MC Visa Amex DC 🔲

LYNDHURST Hampshire   4B4

Knightwood Lodge *Highly Acclaimed*
Southampton Road, Lyndhurst SO43 7BU
☎ 01703-282502 Fax 01703-283730
Closed 25 Dec

Situated on the Southampton road overlooking open forest. Indoor leisure centre with heated pool. Pets welcome in cottage annexe.

18 bedrs, all ensuite, 1 ➡ TCF TV 🐾 P 15 SB £30-£40 DB £55-£70 D £15 CC MC Visa Amex DC JCB 🔲 🈁 🈂

Penny Farthing *Acclaimed*
Romsey Road, Lyndhurst SO43 7AA
☎ 01703-284422 Fax 01703-284488
Closed Christmas

A charming small hotel, recently refurbished and upgraded. Located close to the centre of the village.

15 bedrs, 10 ensuite, 3 ⇌ TCF TV ⋈ P 15 SB £25-£35 DB £49-£70 CC MC Visa Amex JCB

Ormonde House
Southampton Road, Lyndhurst SO43 7BT
☎ 01703-2828066 Fax 01703-283775

Luxurious accommodation at affordable prices. Ideally located set back from the road, opposite open forest. Pretty ensuite rooms, pets welcome. Warm hospitality – relive the delights of total home cooking – our speciality.

17 bedrs, all ensuite, TCF TV ⋈ P 17 SB £21-£31 DB £42-£72 HB £240-£270 D £13 CC MC Visa &

LYNMOUTH Devon   2C2

★★ Bath
Hospitality merit award
Sea Front, Lynmouth EX35 6EL
☎ 01598-752238 Fax 01598-752544
Closed Nov-Feb
24 bedrs, all ensuite, TCF TV ⋈ P 13 SB £28.50-£38.50 DB £57-£77 HB £212-£280 D £16 CC MC Visa Amex DC

★★ Rising Sun
Hospitality, Comfort, Restaurant merit awards
Harbourside, Mars Hill, Lynmouth EX35 6EQ
☎ 01598-753223 Fax 01598-753480
E Mail risingsunlynmouth@easynet.co.uk
16 bedrs, all ensuite, TCF TV No children under 5
SB £45-£48 DB £79 HB £355-£390 D £25 CC MC Visa Amex DC JCB

Bonnicott House *Highly Acclaimed*
Watersmeet Road, Lynmouth EX35 6EP
☎ 01598-753346
Closed Nov-Feb

Built in 1820 as a rectory, the hotel stands in its own gardens overlooking the harbour and Lynmouth Bay. Many superb walks start from the hotel.

8 bedrs, all ensuite, TCF TV ⊠ ⋈ No children under 5
SB £21-£28 DB £42-£56

East Lyn House *Highly Acclaimed*
17 Watersmeet Road, Lynmouth EX35 6EP
☎ 01598-752540 Fax 01598-752540
Closed Dec-Feb
8 bedrs, all ensuite, TCF TV ⋈ P 12 No children under 8 SB £33 DB £56 HB £265 D £15 CC MC Visa

Beacon *Acclaimed*
Countisbury Hill, Lynmouth EX35 6ND
☎ 01598-753268
Closed winter
5 bedrs, all ensuite, TCF TV P 10 No children under 12
SB £20-£22 DB £36-£46

Heatherville *Acclaimed*
Tors Park, Lynmouth EX35 6NB
☎ 01598-752327
Closed winter
9 bedrs, 5 ensuite, 2 ⇌ TCF TV ⋈ P 9 No children under 7 SB £24 DB £48 HB £239 D £14

Shelley's Cottage *Listed*
Watersmeet Road, Lynmouth EX35 6EP
☎ 01598-753219
Closed Dec-Jan
9 bedrs, 7 ensuite, 1 ⇌ TCF TV ⋈ P 2 SB £19-£22 DB £38-£44 CC MC Visa Amex

LYNTON Devon 2C2

★★ Crown
Sinai Hill, Lynton EX35 6AG
☎ 01598-752253 Fax 01598-753311
Closed Jan
15 bedrs, all ensuite, TCF TV ⋈ P 25 ₡₡ MC Visa

★★ Exmoor Sandpiper
Countisbury, Lynton EX35 6NE
☎ 01598-741263 Fax 01598-741358
16 bedrs, all ensuite, TCF TV ⋈ P 70 SB £46.10 DB £92.20 HB £315 D £26.90 ₡₡ MC Visa

★★ Old Rectory
Hospitality, Comfort, Restaurant merit awards
Martinhoe, Parracombe EX31 4QT
☎ 01598-763368 Fax 01598-763567
Closed Nov-Easter
8 bedrs, all ensuite, TCF TV ✉ P 14 No children under 14 DB £80-£90 HB £385 D £25 ♿

★★ Sandrock
Longmead, Lynton EX35 6DH
☎ 01598-753307 Fax 01598-752665
9 bedrs, 7 ensuite, 1 ⋈ TCF TV ⋈ P 9 SB £20-£22 DB £39-£45 HB £196-£225 D £12 ₡₡ MC Visa Amex

★ Chough's Nest
North Walk, Lynton EX35 6HJ
☎ 01598-753315
Closed Nov-Mar
12 bedrs, all ensuite, ✉ P 10 No children under 2 SB £29-£32 DB £58-£64 HB £265-£295 D £18 ₡₡ MC Visa JCB

★ Fairholme
North Walk, Lynton EX35 6ED
☎ 01598-752263 Fax 01598-752263
Closed Oct-Apr
11 bedrs, 8 ensuite, 1 ⋈ TCF TV P 11 No children under 10 SB £23-£25 DB £46-£50 HB £220

★ North Cliff
Hospitality merit award
North Walk, Lynton EX35 6HJ
☎ 01598-752357
Closed Nov-Feb
14 bedrs, all ensuite, TCF TV ⋈ P 15 SB £24-£25 DB £48-£50 HB £240-£245 D £11 ₡₡ MC Visa

★ Seawood
Hospitality, Comfort merit awards
North Walk, Lynton EX35 6HJ
☎ 01598-752272
Closed Nov-Mar
12 bedrs, all ensuite, 2 ⋈ TCF TV ⋈ P 12 No children under 12 SB £27-£30 DB £54-£60 HB £250-£270 D £12

Millslade *Highly Acclaimed*
Restaurant merit award
Brendon, Lynton EX35 6PS
☎ 01598-741322
6 bedrs, 5 ensuite, 1 ⋈ TCF TV ⋈ P 30 ₡₡ MC Visa Amex DC

Victoria Lodge *Highly Acclaimed*
31 Lee Road, Lynton EX35 6BS
☎ 0500-303026 Fax 01598-753203
Closed Dec-Jan
9 bedrs, 3 ensuite, 6 ⋈, 1 ⋈ TCF TV ✉ P 7 SB £21-£32 DB £42-£64 HB £200-£294 D £14 ₡₡ MC Visa

Hazeldene *Acclaimed*
27 Lee Road, Lynton EX35 6BP
☎ 01598-752364 Fax 01598-752364
Closed mid Nov-Jan

Delightful Victorian house situated just off the centre of Lynton, and short walk from cliff railway.

9 bedrs, all ensuite, TCF TV ⋈ P 9 No children under 5 SB £20-£26 DB £36-£44 HB £210-£225 D £13 ₡₡ MC Visa Amex DC

Ingleside *Acclaimed*
Lee Road, Lynton EX35 6HW
☎ 01598-752223
Closed Nov-Feb
7 bedrs, all ensuite, TCF TV P 10 No children under 10 SB £27-£29 DB £50-£54 HB £245-£259 D £13 ₡₡ MC Visa

Mayfair *Acclaimed*
The Lynway, Lynton EX35 6AY
☎ 01598-753227
9 bedrs, 7 ensuite, 2 ⋈, TCF TV P 6 No children under 12 SB £18-£25 DB £36-£50 ₡₡ MC Visa

Rockvale *Acclaimed*
Lee Road, Lynton EX35 6HW
☎ 01598-752279
Closed Nov-Feb
8 bedrs, 6 ensuite, 2 ⋈ TCF TV ✉ P 10 No children under 4 SB £20-£22 DB £44-£48 HB £244-£258 D £14 ₡₡ MC Visa

LYNTON – ENGLAND

St Vincent House *Acclaimed*
Castle Hill, Lynton EX35 6JA
☎ **01598-752244**
Closed Dec-Jan

A charming period guest house with much character, including a Regency spiral staircase. Ideal for walking or touring Exmoor. Pretty bedrooms and excellent food and wines.

6 bedrs, 3 ensuite, 1 ⇌ **TCF TV** ✉ 3 No children under 8 **SB** £17-£18 **DB** £34-£42 **HB** £193-£216 **D** £12.50

Alford House
3 Alford Terrace, Lynton EX35 6AT
☎ **01598-752359**

Elegant Georgian hotel with spectacular views of Exmoor coastline and Devon. Ensuite beds, some fourposter. Relaxing, peaceful, warm hospitality. Outstanding food, fine wines. Non-smoking.

8 bedrs, all ensuite, **TCF TV** ✉ No children under 12 **SB** £22-£26 **DB** £40-£56 **HB** £210-£259 **D** £15 **CC** MC Visa

---

Don't forget to mention the guide
When booking direct, please remember to tell the hotel that you chose it from RAC Bed & Breakfast 1998.

Bear Hotel
Lydiate Lane, Lynton EX35 6AJ
☎ **01598-753391**

A delightful Georgian hotel est.1817. All ensuite rooms, some with exposed beams and sofa or fourposter. Freshly prepared cuisine, log fire on chilly days.

9 bedrs, 8 ensuite, 1 ⇌ **TCF TV** 🐾 **P** 3 **SB** £24 **DB** £20-£27 **HB** £190-£232 **D** £12.50 **CC** MC Visa

---

LYTHAM ST ANNES Lancashire   **10B4**

★★ Lindum
63-67 South Promenade, Lytham St Annes FY8 1LZ
☎ **01253-721534 Fax 01253-721364**
78 bedrs, all ensuite, 4 ⇌ **TCF TV** 🐾 ✉ **P** 20 **SB** £28-£40 **DB** £50-£60 **HB** £250-£260 **D** £11.50 **CC** MC Visa Amex JCB

★★ St Ives
7 South Promenade, Lytham St Annes FY8 1LS
☎ **01253-720011 Fax 01253-722873**
70 bedrs, 64 ensuite, 2 🛁, 1 ⇌ **TCF TV** 🐾 **P** 75 **SB** £29.50-£32.50 **DB** £50-£59 **D** £12 **CC** MC Visa

Endsleigh *Acclaimed*
315 Clifton Drive South, Lytham St Annes FY8 1HN
☎ **01253-725622**
15 bedrs, all ensuite, 1 ⇌ **TCF TV P** 9 **SB** £20-£24 **DB** £40-£48 **HB** £178-£188

Strathmore *Acclaimed*
305 Clifton Drive South, Lytham St. Annes FY8 1HN
☎ **01253-725478**
10 bedrs, 5 ensuite, 1 ⇌ **TCF TV P** 10 No children under 9 **SB** £19-£21 **DB** £38-£42 **HB** £154-£175 **D** £8

MACCLESFIELD Cheshire   **7E1**

Moorhayes House *Listed*
27 Manchester Road, Tytherington, Macclesfield SK10 2JJ
☎ **01625-433228**
9 bedrs, 6 ensuite, 1 ⇌ **TCF TV** 🐾 **P** 13 **SB** £35 **DB** £44 **D** £10 **CC** Visa

MADELEY Staffordshire — 7E1

★★Wheatsheaf Inn at Onneley
Barhill Road, Madeley CW3 9QF
☎ 01782-751581 Fax 01782-751499
5 bedrs, all ensuite, 🐕 P 150 CC MC Visa Amex DC

MAIDENHEAD Berkshire — 4C2

Bell Listed
King Street, Maidenhead SL6 1DP
☎ 01628-24409
7 bedrs, 2 ➥ P 8

Clifton Listed
21 Crauford Rise, Maidenhead SL6 7LR
☎ 01628-23572 Fax 01628-23572
12 bedrs, all ensuite, 3 ➥ TCF TV P 11 SB £35 DB £45 CC MC Visa Amex ♿

MAIDSTONE Kent — 5E3

★★Grangemoor
St Michaels Road, Maidstone ME16 8BS
☎ 01622-677623 Fax 01622-678246
47 bedrs, all ensuite, 4 ➥ TCF TV 🐕 P 60 SB £38-£47 DB £45-£52 D £12.50 CC MC Visa

★★Russell
136 Boxley Road, Maidstone ME14 2AE
☎ 01622-692221 Fax 01622-762084
42 bedrs, all ensuite, TCF TV P 100 SB £50 DB £75 D £14 CC MC Visa Amex DC ♿

Roadchef Lodge Lodge
Maidstone Motorway Service Area, Junction 8 M20, Hollingbourne ME17 1SS
☎ 01622-631100 Fax 01622-739535
Closed 25 Dec, 1 Jan
40 bedrs, all ensuite, TCF TV P 100 CC MC Visa Amex DC ♿

Conway House
12 Conway Road, Maidstone
☎ 01622-688287

Quality accomodation in family home. Ideal touring base near M20 and A20. TV, tea/coffee facilities. Off street parking. Ground floor room available. Guest lounge.

3 bedrs, TCF TV P 5 SB £24-£28 DB £34-£38 CC MC Visa

Court Farm
Village High Street, Aylesford, Maidstone ME20 7AZ
☎ 01622-717293

Beautiful old beamed farmhouse. Lots of character. Antiques. Fourposter. Ensuite. Close to the M2/M20. Parking. Quiet, relaxed. Sorry no children.

3 bedrs, 2 ensuite, TCF TV 🚭 P 6 No children SB £25 DB £40 CC MC Visa JCB

MALDON Essex — 5E2

Swan Listed
73 High Street, Maldon CM9 7EP
☎ 01621-853170 Fax 01621-854490
6 bedrs, 4 ensuite, 1 ➥ TCF TV P 25 SB £35-£45 DB £48-£55 HB £300 D £7 CC MC Visa Amex DC

MALHAM North Yorkshire — 10C3

Buck Inn Acclaimed
Malham, Skipton BD23 4DA
☎ 01729-830317 Fax 01729-830670
10 bedrs, all ensuite, TCF TV P 15 SB £28.50-£33.50 DB £50-£57 HB £-£185 D £10 CC MC Visa

MALMESBURY Wiltshire — 4A2

★★Mayfield House
Crudwell, Malmesbury SN16 9EW
☎ 01666-577409 Fax 01666-577977
20 bedrs, all ensuite, 🐕 P 40
SB £44 DB £65 HB £199 D £16 CC MC Visa Amex DC

RAC Hotel Reservations Service
0870 603 9109
(Calls charged at national call rate)

Widleys Farm
Sherston, Malmesbury SN16 0PY
☎ 01666-840213
Closed Christmas

A Cotswold 200 year old farmhouse. Very peaceful and quiet but within easy driving distance of Bath, Bristol and Westbirt Aboretum. TV, central heating and tea making facilities in all rooms.

3 bedrs, 1 ensuite, 1 ➾ TCF TV SB £18 DB £36 HB £150 D £8

MALPAS Cheshire   7D1

Laurel Farm
Chorlton Lane, Malpas SY14 7ES
☎ 01948-860291 Fax 01948-860291

Rather friendly ducks greet you at this superb farmhouse. Dating from 17th century in glorious countryside bordering Shropshire/North Wales. Full of character - ambience to match.

4 bedrs, all ensuite, TCF TV ✉ No children under 12 SB £36-£42 DB £55-£64 D £8.50

MALTON North Yorkshire   11E3

★★ Talbot
Yorkersgate, Malton YO17 0AA
☎ 01653-694031 Fax 01653-693355
31 bedrs, all ensuite, TCF TV ✠ P 30 SB £42.50-£52.50 DB £85-£105 HB £200-£250 D £16.50 CC MC Visa Amex DC

★ Wentworth Arms
Town Street, Malton YO17 0HD
☎ 01653-692618
Closed Christmas
5 bedrs, 4 ensuite, 1 ➾ TCF TV P 30 No children SB £23 DB £46 D £8 CC MC Visa

Greenacres Country House *Highly Acclaimed*
Amotherby, Malton YO17 0TG
☎ 01653-693623 Fax 01653-693623
Closed Nov-Mar
9 bedrs, all ensuite, TCF TV P 15 SB £28.25 DB £56.50 HB £238 D £12.75 CC MC Visa ⑤

Red House *Acclaimed*
Wharram le Street, Malton YO17 9TL
☎ 01944-768455
Closed Christmas
3 bedrs, all ensuite, TCF TV ✉ ✠ P 8 SB £22.50-£25 DB £45-£50 D £12.70

MALVERN Worcestershire   7E4

★★ Great Malvern
Graham Road, Great Malvern WR14 2HN
☎ 01684-563411 Fax 01684-560514
Closed Christmas
14 bedrs, 13 ensuite, TCF TV ⊞ P 9 SB £50 DB £70-£80 D £6 CC MC Visa Amex DC ♿

★★ Holdfast Cottage
Hospitality, Comfort, Restaurant merit awards
Little Malvern, Malvern WR13 6NA
☎ 01684-310288 Fax 01684-311117
Closed Christmas
8 bedrs, all ensuite, 1 ➾ TCF TV ✠ P 16 SB £42-£44 DB £78-£84 HB £312-£336 D £18 CC MC Visa

★★ Malvern Hills
Wynds Point, Malvern WR13 6DW
☎ 01684-540237 Fax 01684-540327
17 bedrs, 16 ensuite, 1 ➾ TCF TV ✠ P 40 SB £40-£45 DB £65-£70 HB £300-£350 D £15 CC MC Visa

★★ Mount Pleasant
Belle Vue Terrace, Great Malvern WR14 4PZ
☎ 01684-561837 Fax 01684-569968
Closed 25-26 Dec
15 bedrs, 14 ensuite, 1 ➾ TCF TV P 20 SB £50-£52.50 DB £69-£79 HB £250-£305 D £15 CC MC Visa Amex DC

★★ Thornbury House
Avenue Road, Great Malvern WR14 3AR
☎ 01684-572278 Fax 01684-577042
17 bedrs, 14 ensuite, 1 ➾ TCF TV ✠ P 10 SB £38 DB £58 HB £246 D £18 CC MC Visa Amex DC JCB

RAC Hotel Reservations Service
0870 603 9109
(Calls charged at national call rate)

Red Gate *Highly Acclaimed*
32 Avenue Road, Malvern WR14 3BJ
☎ 01684-565013 Fax 01684-565013
Closed Christmas-New Year

A small Victorian hotel well known for its friendliness and decor. All rooms are non-smoking. Vegetarians welcome.

6 bedrs, all ensuite, TCF TV P 7 No children under 10 SB £28-£35 DB £50-£56 CC MC Visa JCB

Wyche Keep *Highly Acclaimed*
22 Wyche Road, Malvern WR14 4EG
☎ 01684-567018 Fax 01684-892304

Historic hilltop country house for discerning travellers, enjoying spectacular 60 mile views. Luxury ensuites including a fourposter. Guests can savour memorable four course candle-lit dinners. Licensed.

3 bedrs, all ensuite, TCF P 6 No children under 12
SB £30-£35 DB £50-£60 HB £301-£336 D £18

Sidney House *Acclaimed*
40 Worcester Road, Malvern WR14 4AA
☎ 01684-574994 Fax 01684-574994
8 bedrs, 5 ensuite, 1 ⇨ TCF TV P 9 SB £20-£40 DB £39-£59 CC MC Visa Amex

Church Farm
Coddington, Ledbury HR8 1JJ
☎ 01531-640271

Working mixed farm with a 16th century Grade II Listed farmhouse, situated in a quiet rural hamlet. Happy relaxed atmosphere with home cooking.

3 bedrs, TCF 🐾
SB £20 DB £39 D £11

Heidelbury
83 Wells Road, Malvern WR14 3PB
☎ 01684-563034
5 bedrs, all ensuite, TCF TV P 5 No children under 8
SB £25 DB £50 D £17.50

Heidelbury

A warm and friendly residence situated on the side of the Malvern Hills, offering spectacular views across the Severn Valley. Bed and Breakfast accommodation. Licensed dining room. Menu carefully prepared and cooked by chef-proprietor. Non-smoking. Parking in grounds. Open all year, including Christmas and New Year.

**83 WELLS ROAD, MALVERN, WORCESTERSHIRE WR14 $PB
Tel: 01684-563034**

MANCHESTER Greater Manchester   10C4

★★ Comfort Friendly Inn
Hyde Road, Birch Street, Manchester M12 5NT
☎ 0161-220 8848
90 bedrs, all ensuite

★★ Crescent Gate
Park Crescent, Victoria Park, Manchester M14 5RE
☎ 0161-224 0672 Fax 0161-257 2822
E Mail cgh@dial.pipex.com
Closed Christmas
24 bedrs, 20 ensuite, 2 ⇔ TCF TV ✻ P 14 SB £39 DB £54
D £12.50 CC   MC Visa Amex DC JCB

★★ Elm Grange
561 Wilmslow Road, Withington, Manchester
☎ 0161-445 3336 Fax 0161-445 3336
31 bedrs, 16 ensuite, 4 ⇔ TCF TV P 30 SB £40-£42
DB £56-£59 D £13 CC   MC Visa Amex ♿

★★ Royals
Altrincham Road, Wythenshawe, Manchester M22 4BJ
☎ 0161-998 9011 Fax 0161-998 4641
32 bedrs, all ensuite, TCF TV P 100 SB £52 DB £66 D £12
CC   MC Visa Amex DC

★ Baron
116 Palatine Road, West Didsbury, M20 9ZA
☎ 0161-434 3688 Fax 01203-520680
16 bedrs, all ensuite, TCF TV P 16 No children under 8
SB £28.50-£33 DB £38-£45 D £7.50 CC   MC Visa

Highbury *Highly Acclaimed*
113 Monton Road, Eccles, Manchester M30 9HQ
☎ 0161-787 8545 Fax 0161-787 9023

A small family run hotel, beautifully decorated and restored to modern standards. Ten minutes from city centre, cricket grounds, football grounds and theatres and 20 minutes from airport. One mile from motorway.

15 bedrs, all ensuite, TCF TV P 19 SB £41 DB £49
HB £280 D £5 CC   MC Visa Amex

Imperial *Listed*
157 Hathersage Road, Manchester M13 0HY
☎ 0161-225 6500 Fax 0161-225 6500
27 bedrs, 21 ensuite, 3 ⇔ TCF TV P 30 SB £30 DB £47
D £13 CC   MC Visa Amex DC ♿

Kempton House *Listed*
400 Wilbraham Road, Chorlton-cum-Hardy, Manchester M21 0UH
☎ 0161-881 8766 Fax 0161-881 8766
Closed Christmas

Small family run business. Well situated for airport, city centre, motorways, G'mex and Trafford Park. On a main bus route two and a half miles from city centre.

13 bedrs, 4 ensuite, 1 ☏, 2 ⇔ TCF TV P 9 SB £24-£29
DB £34-£39 D £5 CC   MC Visa

New Central *Listed*
144-146 Heywood Street, Manchester M8 7PD
☎ 0161-205 2169 Fax 0161-205 2169
10 bedrs, 5 ☏, 2 ⇔ TCF TV ✻ P 5 SB £21 DB £33 D £3.50
CC   MC Visa

Campanile Manchester *Lodge*
55 Ordsall Lane, Salford Quays, Regent Road, Manchester M5 4RS
☎ 0161-833 1845 Fax 0161-833 1847
105 bedrs, all ensuite, TCF TV ✻ P 105 SB £42.50 DB £47
D £10.55 CC   MC Visa Amex DC ♿

Brooklands Luxury Lodge
208 Marsland Road, Sale M33 3NE
☎ 0161-973 3283 Fax 0161-282 0524

'Which' recommended. Gardens and car park. Airport and city centre five miles. Two minutes to Metrolink. Sunbed and jacuzzi. Two miles from M63 junction 8.

9 bedrs, 5 ensuite, 2 ⇔ TCF TV P 9 SB £25-£30 DB £42-£52 HB £210 D £8 CC   MC Visa

MARLOW – ENGLAND

MANNINGTREE Essex — 5E1

Thorn *Listed*
High Street, Mistley, Manningtree CO11 1HG
☎ 01206-392821 Fax 01206-392133
4 bedrs, all ensuite, **TCF TV P** 6 **SB** £30 **DB** £45 **D** £14 **CC** MC Visa

Dimbols Farm
Station Road, Wrabness, Nr Manningtree CO11 2TH
☎ 01255-880328 Fax 01255-880328

A large Georgian farmhouse overlooking the River Stour and open farmland. Situated in a peaceful area, close to the RSPB reserve, Essex Way and Harwich.

2 bedrs, 1 ➡ **TCF TV P** 6 **SB** £21 **DB** £30

MARAZION Cornwall — 2A4

Chymorvah *Highly Acclaimed*
Marazion TR17 0DQ
☎ 01736-710497
Closed Christmas & New Year

Victorian family house built out of granite with access to a private beach. Situated at east end of Marazion overlooking Mount's Bay and St Michael's Mount. A non-smoking hotel.

9 bedrs, all ensuite, 1 ➡ **TCF TV** 🖉 ➡ **P** 12 **SB** £26-£30.50 **DB** £52-£61 **HB** £245-£275 **D** £10 **CC** MC Visa

MARCH Cambridgeshire — 9D3

★★ Olde Griffin Inn
High Street, March PE15 9JS
☎ 01354-652517 Fax 01354-650086
20 bedrs, all ensuite, 1 ➡ **TCF TV P** 30 **SB** £38.50-£42.50 **DB** £55-£60 **D** £9.50 **CC** MC Visa Amex DC ♿

MARGATE Kent — 5F2

Beachcomber *Listed*
3-4 Royal Esplanade, Westbrook, Margate CT9 5DL
☎ 01843-221616
13 bedrs, 5 🛁, 3 ➡ **TCF SB** £16-£16.50 **DB** £30-£33 **HB** £140-£148.50 **D** £9

MARKET HARBOROUGH Leicestershire — 8B3

★★ Sun Inn
Restaurant merit award
Main Street, Marston Trussell LE16 9TY
☎ 01858-465531 Fax 01858-433155
20 bedrs, all ensuite, **TCF TV** ➡ **P** 50 **SB** £38-£45 **DB** £50-£60 **D** £15 **CC** MC Visa Amex 🎵 ♿

MARLBOROUGH Wiltshire — 4A2

Vines *Highly Acclaimed*
High Street, Marlborough SN4 1HJG
☎ 01672-515333 Fax 01672-515338

Six ensuite bedrooms are situated in a character property on the main high street of the delightful town of Marlborough. Guests have full use of the elegant public areas.

6 bedrs, all ensuite, **TCF TV** ➡ **P** 6 **SB** £25 **DB** £51 **D** £19 **CC** MC Visa Amex

Merlin *Listed*
High Street, Marlborough SN8 1LW
☎ 01672-512151 Fax 01672-514656
15 bedrs, 14 ensuite, 1 ➡ **TV** ➡ **SB** £35-£40 **DB** £45-£50 **CC** MC Visa

MARLOW Buckinghamshire — 4C2

Holly Tree House *Highly Acclaimed*
Burford Close, Marlow Bottom, Marlow SL7 3NF
☎ 01628-891110 Fax 01628-481278
5 bedrs, all ensuite, **TCF TV** ➡ **P** 8 **SB** £60 **DB** £70-£75 **CC** MC Visa Amex

---

RAC Hotel Reservations Service
0870 603 9109
(Calls charged at national call rate)

MARTOCK Somerset 3E2

Wychwood *Acclaimed*
7 Bearley Road, Martock TA12 6PG
☎ 01935-825601 Fax 01935-825601
Closed Christmas-New Year

Ideally situated for visiting Wells Cathedral, Glastonbury Abbey, Lyme Regis and the eight 'classic' gardens of South Somerset. Recommended by 'Which?'.

3 bedrs, all ensuite, TCF TV P 4 No children SB £28-£32 DB £38-£42 CC MC Visa JCB

MARYPORT Cumbria 10A1

★ Waverley
Curzon Street, Maryport CA15 6LW
☎ 01900-812115 Fax 01900-817734
20 bedrs, 4 ensuite, 7, 3 TCF TV SB £18 DB £33 D £9.50 CC MC Visa

MASHAM North Yorkshire 11D2

Bank Villa *Listed*
Ripon, Masham HG4 4DB
☎ 01765-689605
Closed Nov-Feb
7 bedrs, 4, 1 P 7 No children under 5 SB £28 DB £38 HB £210 D £16

MATLOCK Derbyshire 8A2

Lane End House *Highly Acclaimed*
Green Lane, Tansley, Matlock DE4 5FJ
☎ 01629-583981 Fax 01629-583981
Closed Christmas & New Year
4 bedrs, 2 ensuite, TCF TV P 6 SB £30-£35 DB £48-£57 D £16 CC MC Visa

Coach House *Listed*
Main Road, Lea, Matlock DE4 5GJ
☎ 01629-534346 Fax 01629-534346
3 bedrs, 1 ensuite, 1 TV P 25 SB £16.50 DB £33-£37 D £9.95 CC MC Visa

Jackson Tor House *Listed*
76 Jackson Road, Matlock DE4 3JQ
☎ 01629-582348 Fax 01629-582348
26 bedrs, 13 ensuite, 7 P 20 SB £15-£30 DB £30-£60 CC MC Visa

Packhorse Farm *Listed*
Tansley, Matlock DE4 5LF
☎ 01629-580950 Fax 01629-580950
Closed Christmas
4 bedrs, 1 ensuite, 1, 1 TCF TV P 10 SB £18-£20 DB £36

Sycamore House
76 High Street, Bonsall, Nr Matlock DE4 2AR
☎ 01629-823903

An attractive 18th century stone house, set in a village and overlooking rolling hills. An ideal base to explore Derbyshire and the Dales.

5 bedrs, all ensuite, TCF TV P 7 SB £27-£35 DB £42-£46 HB £225-£250 D £13

MAWGAN PORTH Cornwall 2B3

★★ Tredragon
Mawgan Porth TR8 4DQ
☎ 01637-860213 Fax 01637-860269
29 bedrs, all ensuite, TCF TV P 35 SB £30-£41 DB £60-£82 HB £259-£423 D £17 CC MC Visa

White Lodge *Listed*
Mawgan Porth TR8 4BN
☎ 01637-860512 Fax 01637-860512
18 bedrs, 13 ensuite, 2 P 18 SB £22-£25 DB £44-£50 HB £180-£210 D £8 CC MC Visa Amex JCB

MAXSTOKE Warwickshire 8A3

Old Rectory *Acclaimed*
Church Lane, Maxstoke BA6 2QW
☎ 01675-462248 Fax 01675-481615
Closed Christmas
3 bedrs, all ensuite, TCF TV P 10 SB £30 DB £46

MELKSHAM Wiltshire 4A3

★★ Conigre Farm
Semington Road, Melksham SN12 6BZ
☎ 01225-702229 Fax 01225 707392
8 bedrs, 7 ensuite, 1 ➥ TCF TV ★ P 14 SB £40 DB £55
HB £329 D £11.95 CC MC Visa &

★★ King's Arms
The Market Place, Melksham SN12 6EX
☎ 01225-707272 Fax 01225-702085

A traditional coaching inn with cobbled forecourt. Log fires, real ale and a warm welcome assured.

13 bedrs, 10 ensuite, 13 ⌂, 2 ➥ TCF TV ★ P 50 SB £47
DB £52 D £13.50 CC MC Visa Amex DC

★★ Shaw Country
Comfort merit award
Bath Road, Shaw, Melksham SN12 8EF
☎ 01225-702836 Fax 01225-790275
Closed 26-28 Dec
13 bedrs, all ensuite, TCF TV ★ P 40 SB £42 DB £63
D £12.50 CC MC Visa Amex DC JCB

MELTON MOWBRAY Leicestershire   8B3

★★ Quorn Lodge
Comfort merit award
46 Asfordby Road, Melton Mowbray LE13 0HR
☎ 01664-66660 Fax 01664-480660
19 bedrs, all ensuite, P 33 SB £45-£49.50 DB £50-£65
D £12 CC MC Visa JCB &

Elms Farm
Long Clawson, Melton Mowbray LE14 4NG
☎ 01664-822395 Fax 01664-8233399

Welcome to our 18th century farmhouse in the beautiful Vale of Belvoir. Enjoy delicious home cooking and attractive, comfortable accommodation in the house or in our renovated self contained cottage.
3 bedrs, 1 ensuite, 1 ➥ TCF TV ⌂ P 6 SB £16-£20
DB £30-£38 HB £140-£190 D £7

MERSHAM Kent   5E3

Farriers Arms *Listed*
Mersham, Ashford TN25 6NN
☎ 01233-720444
3 bedrs, 1 ➥ TCF TV ★ P 22 CC MC Visa ♪

MEVAGISSEY Cornwall   2B4

Mevagissey House *Acclaimed*
Vicarage Hill, Mevagissey PL26 6SZ
☎ 01726-842427 Fax 01726-844327
Closed end Oct-Mar

Just a short walk to Mevagissey, Georgian country house superbly situated with panoramic views across countryside to the sea. B&B only. Comfortable rooms.

4 bedrs, 3 ensuite, 1 ➥ TCF TV P 12 No children under 7 SB £20-£25 DB £44-£54 CC MC Visa

Sharksfin *Acclaimed*
The Quay, Mevagissey PL26 6OU
☎ 01726-843241 Fax 01726-842552
Closed Jan-Feb
11 bedrs, 8 ensuite, 3 ⌂, 1 ➥ TCF TV CC MC Visa Amex DC

Fountain Inn *Listed*
Cliff Street, Mevagissey PL26 6QH
☎ 01726-842320

The Fountain, a 15th century inn situated in the centre of Mevagissey. Two bars, restaurant, ensuite rooms. A warm welcome awaits. Open all year.

3 bedrs, 2 ensuite, 1 ➥ TCF TV ★ No children SB £45
DB £45 D £7.25 CC MC Visa JCB

Headlands *Listed*
Polkirt Hill, Mevagissey PL26 6UX
☎ ff 0500-121298
Closed Dec-Jan
14 bedrs, 9 ensuite, 2 ⇌ TV ⊬ P 11 SB £21-£27
DB £42-£54 HB £238-£280 D £15

Ship Inn *Listed*
Fore Street, Mevagissey PL26 6TU
☎ 01726-843324
6 bedrs, TCF TV CC MC Visa

Steep House
Portmellon Cove, Mevagissey, St Austell PL26 6PH
☎ 01726-843732

Established guest house set in seaside garden. Comfortable bedrooms (share bathroom) or ensuite providing sea views. Beautiful breakfasts served in distinctive dining room. Off road parking, covered swimming pool.

7 bedrs, 1 ensuite, 2 ⇌ TCF TV P 8 No children under 10 SB £20-£25 DB £35-£54 CC MC Visa Amex

---

MIDDLE WALLOP Hampshire   4A3

★★ Fifehead Manor
Hospitality, Restaurant merit awards
Middle Wallop, Salisbury SO20 8EG
☎ 01264-781565 Fax 01264-781400
15 bedrs, all ensuite, TV ⊬ P 30 SB £60-£75 DB £90-£120 D £25 CC MC Visa Amex ♿

MIDDLESBROUGH Cleveland   11D2

Grey House *Highly Acclaimed*
79 Cambridge Road, Linthorpe, TS5 5NL
☎ 01642-817485 Fax 01642-817485
9 bedrs, all ensuite, TCF TV ⊬ P 10 SB £35-£40 DB £46-£50 D £10 CC MC Visa Amex

---

MIDDLETON-IN-TEESDALE Co. Durham   10C2

★★ Teesdale
Market Place, Middleton-in-Teesdale DL12 0QG
☎ 01833-640264 Fax 01833-640651
12 bedrs, 10 ensuite, 1 ⇌ TCF TV ⊬ SB £39.50-£42.50 DB £50-£60 D £19.25 CC MC Visa Amex

Travelodge *Lodge*
Granada Scotch Corner, Middleton-in-Teesdale
☎ 0800-850950 Fax 01325-377890
50 bedrs, all ensuite, TCF TV ⊬ P 100 SB £42.95 CC MC Visa Amex DC ♿

MIDHURST West Sussex   4C3

Redford Cottage
Redford, Midhurst GU29 0QF
☎ 01428-741242 Fax 01428-741242

A comfortable country house in an area of outstanding natural beauty, yet close to Chichester, Goodwood and the South Downs. One hour from Heathrow and Gatwick. TV, tea and coffee making facilities. Parking.

3 bedrs, 2 ensuite, TCF TV ⊬ P 10

MILTON COMMON Oxfordshire   4B2

Three Pigeons Inn
Milton Common OX9 2NS
☎ 01844-279247 Fax 01844-279483
3 bedrs, TCF TV CC MC Visa

MILTON KEYNES Buckinghamshire   4C1

★★ Swan Revived
High Street, Newport Pagnell MK16 8AR
☎ 01908-610565 Fax 01908-210995
40 bedrs, all ensuite, TCF TV ⊬ ▣ P 18 SB £65 DB £72.50 HB £420 D £13 CC MC Visa Amex DC

Swan Inn *Listed*
36 Watling Street, Fenny Stratford, Milton Keynes MK2 2BL
☎ 01908-370100 Fax 01908-270096
10 bedrs, 3 ⇌ TCF TV P 30 CC MC Visa

Haversham Grange
Haversham, Milton Keynes MK19 7DX
☎ 01908-312389 Fax 01908-221554

A most attractive 14th century grange, beautifully furnished in ten acres of gardens and fields, in a quiet situation. No smoking in the bedrooms. Milton Keynes five miles, Oxford / Cambridge one hour away.

3 bedrs, all ensuite, **TCF TV P** 6 No children under 8 **SB** £25 **DB** £46-£50 **HB** £170

MINEHEAD Somerset   3D2

★★ Beaconwood
Church Road, North Hill, Minehead TA24 5SB
☎ 01643-702032 Fax 01643-702032
13 bedrs, all ensuite, **TCF TV ⚑ P** 20
SB £36 **DB** £56 **HB** £180 **D** £14 **CC** MC Visa

★★ Rectory House
Northfield Road, Minehead TA24 5QH
☎ 01643-702611
Closed Nov-Feb
7 bedrs, all ensuite, **TCF TV ⚑ P** 9 **SB** £25 **DB** £50 **HB** £266 **D** £18 **CC** MC Visa

THE THREE PIGEONS INN

An historic coaching inn situated on the A40, adjacent to junction 7 of the M40, approximately 10 miles from the centre of historic Oxford, The Three Pigeons offers ensuite accommodation and a good selection of freshly cooked food, real ales and excellent wines served in its two comfortable bars.

London Road, Milton Common (Nr. Thame), Oxfordshire OX9 2JN
Tel: 01844 279247/279686
Fax: 01844 279483

★★ York House
The Avenue, Minehead TA24 5AN
☎ 01643-705151 Fax 01643-707899
16 bedrs, all ensuite, **TCF TV P** 10 **SB** £28 **DB** £56 **HB** £245 **D** £10 **CC** MC Visa Amex DC

Gascony *Highly Acclaimed*
50 The Avenue, Minehead TA24 5BB
☎ 01643-705939
Closed Mar-Oct

Comfortable and well appointed Victorian house hotel, ideally positioned on the level in the lovely tree lined avenue. All bedrooms ensuite, full central heating, cocktail bar, superb home cooked food. Large private car park.

13 bedrs, all ensuite, 1 ⚐ **TCF TV ⚑ P** 14 No children under 6 **SB** £23-£24 **DB** £44-£46 **HB** £180-£198 **D** £10 **CC** MC Visa

Marston Lodge *Highly Acclaimed*
St Michael's Road, North Hill, Minehead TA24 5JP
☎ 01643-702510
Closed Nov-Feb
12 bedrs, all ensuite, **TCF TV P** 10 No children under 10 **SB** £25-£27 **DB** £50-£54 **HB** £221-£249 **D** £12

Mayfair *Highly Acclaimed*
The Avenue, Minehead TA24 5AY
☎ 01643-702719
Closed winter

A Dutch/English family run hotel of charm and elegance in a delightful Victorian building set in a central position. Fridges in all rooms.

13 bedrs, all ensuite, **TCF TV P** 13 **SB** £25-£28 **DB** £48-£52 **HB** £182-£195 **D** £9 **CC** MC Visa

Marshfield *Acclaimed*
Tregonwell Road, Minehead TA24 5DU
📞 01643-702517
Closed Nov-Feb
11 bedrs, 9 ensuite, 1 ⇌ TCF TV ⊨ P 6 SB £17.50 DB £40
D £10 ♿

Avill House
Townsend Road, Minehead TA24 5RG
📞 01643-704370

A relaxed friendly welcome is assured to all guests. Avill house is a well kept spacious hotel close to town centre and ten minutes walk to seafront.

9 bedrs, 3 ensuite, 2 ⇌ TCF TV ⊞ P 9 No children under 5 SB £18-£19 DB £31-£38

MOLESWORTH Cambridgeshire 8C3

Cross Keys *Listed*
Molesworth, Huntingdon PE18 0QF
📞 01832-710283 Fax 01832-710098
10 bedrs, all ensuite, TCF TV ⊨ P 40 SB £28.50 DB £37
D £7 CC MC Visa Amex ♿

MORECAMBE Lancashire 10B3

★★ Clarendon
Marine Road West, Morecambe LA4 4EP
📞 01524-410180 Fax 01524-421616
31 bedrs, 29 ensuite, 2 🐾, 3 ⇌ TCF TV ⊨ ⊞ CC MC Visa Amex DC

★ Channings
455 Marine Road East, Bare, Morecambe LA4 6AD
📞 01524-417925 Fax 01524-417819
20 bedrs, 18 ensuite, 1 ⇌ TCF TV ⊨ SB £24-£25 DB £39-£40 HB £135-£155 D £8 CC MC Visa Amex DC

Beach Mount *Highly Acclaimed*
395 Marine Road East, Morecambe LA4 5AN
📞 01524-420753
Closed winter
23 bedrs, all ensuite, 2 ⇌ TCF TV ⊨ P 6 SB £-£23 DB £-£43 HB £150-£167.50 D £10 CC MC Visa Amex DC

Hotel Prospect *Highly Acclaimed*
363 Marine Road, Morecambe LA4 5AQ
📞 01524-417819 Fax 01524-417819
Closed winter

Small family run hotel, situated on the promenade overlooking the bay and Lakeland hills.

14 bedrs, all ensuite, 1 ⇌ TCF TV ⊨ P 10 SB £17 DB £34
HB £160 D £8 CC MC Visa DC ♿

Ashley *Acclaimed*
371 Marine Road East, Morecambe LA4 5AH
📞 01524-412034 Fax 01524-421390
13 bedrs, 11 ensuite, 1 ⇌ TCF TV ⊨ P 5 SB £17-£20
DB £32-£38 HB £146-£174 CC MC Visa Amex ♿

New Hazelmere *Acclaimed*
391 Promenade East, Morecambe LA4 5AN
📞 01524-417876 Fax 01524-414488
Closed Nov-Apr
18 bedrs, all ensuite, ⊞ P 3

Wimslow *Acclaimed*
374 Marine Road East, Morecambe LA4 5AH
📞 01524-421947 Fax 01524-417804
14 bedrs, all ensuite, 1 ⇌ TCF TV ⊨ P 10 SB £16-£19
DB £32-£38 HB £168 D £9 CC MC Visa

MORETON-IN-MARSH Gloucestershire 7F4

★★ White Hart Royal
High Street, Moreton-in-Marsh GL56 0BA
📞 01608-650731 Fax 01608-650880
20 bedrs, all ensuite, 1 ⇌ TCF TV ⊨ P 7 SB £40-£55
DB £65-£80 HB £240-£250 D £15.95 CC MC Visa Amex DC ♿

Moreton House *Acclaimed*
High Street, Moreton-in-Marsh GL56 0LQ
📞 01608-650747 Fax 01608-652747

An attractive Cotswold-stone house, family owned and run. Situated on the Fosse Way - the old Roman road linking Bath and Lincoln.

11 bedrs, 7 ensuite, 2 ⇌ TCF TV ♞ P 5 SB £22-£23 DB £40-£60 D £6 CC MC Visa

MORETONHAMPSTEAD Devon 3D3

★★ White Hart
The Square, Moretonhampstead TQ13 8NF
☎ 01647-440406 Fax 01647-440565

Delightful, historic 18th century coaching inn in picturesque market town on edge of Dartmoor. Privately owned with relaxed atmosphere, fine foods and personal attentive service.

20 bedrs, all ensuite, 1 ⇌ TCF TV ♞ P 9 SB £40-£43 DB £63-£70 D £17.50 CC MC Visa Amex DC

Cookshayes *Acclaimed*
33 Court Street, Moretonhampstead TQ13 8LG
☎ 01647-440374
Closed winter

A mid-Victorian villa set in one acre of ornamental gardens with ample secure parking in grounds.

8 bedrs, 6 ensuite, 2 ⇌ TCF TV ♞ P 15 No children under 7 SB £22.50 HB £238 D £16 CC MC Visa

MOULSFORD-ON-THAMES Oxfordshire 4B2

★★ Beetle & Wedge
Hospitality, Comfort, Restaurant merit awards
Ferry Lane, Moulsford-on-Thames OX10 9JF
☎ 01491-651381 Fax 01491-651376
10 bedrs, all ensuite, TCF TV ♞ P 35 SB £90 DB £110-£135 D £35 CC MC Visa Amex DC JCB

MULLION Cornwall 2A4

★★ Mullion Cove
Mullion, Helston TR12 7LJ
☎ 01326-240328 Fax 01326-240998
36 bedrs, 21 ensuite, 5 ⇌ TCF TV ♞ P 30 SB £27-£50 DB £60-£150 HB £231-£525 D £15 CC MC Visa Amex

MUNDESLEY-ON-SEA Norfolk 9F2

★★ Manor
Beach Road, Mundesley-on-Sea NR11 8BG
☎ 01263-720309 Fax 01263-721731
Closed 2-14 Jan
30 bedrs, all ensuite, 2 ⇌ TCF TV ♞ P 50 SB £36-£40 DB £58-£60 HB £160-£240 D £16

MUNGRISDALE Cumbria 10B1

★ Mill
Hospitality, Comfort, Restaurant merit awards
Mungrisdale CA11 0XR
☎ 01768-779659 Fax 01768-779155
Closed Nov-Feb
7 bedrs, 4 ensuite, 1 ⇌ TCF TV ♞ P 15 SB £25-£35 DB £50-£60 D £22.50

NAILSWORTH Gloucestershire 3F1

Apple Orchard House *Highly Acclaimed*
Springhill, Nailsworth GL6 0LX
☎ 01453-832503 Fax 01453-836213

Spacious Cotswold house overlooking the town, surrounded by prettily wooded hills, two minutes walk from Nailsworth centre (7 quality eating/drinking establishments). Home cooking. Disabled guest room. Laundry. Telephone for brochure.

3 bedrs, all ensuite, 1 ⇌ TCF TV ♞ P 4 SB £18-£28 DB £36-£42 HB £198-£223 D £13.50 CC Amex

NANTWICH Cheshire 7E1

★★ Crown
High Street, Nantwich CW5 5AS
☎ 01270-625283 Fax 01270-628047
18 bedrs, all ensuite, **TCF TV** 🐾 **P** 30 **SB** £59.50 **DB** £69
HB £285 **D** £16 **CC** MC Visa Amex DC JCB

★★ Malbank
14 Beam Street, Nantwich CW5 5LL
☎ 01270-626011 Fax 01270-624435
11 bedrs, all ensuite, **TCF TV SB** £32 **DB** £52 **D** £6 **CC** MC Visa Amex DC &

Stoke Grange Farm
Chester Road, Nantwich CW5 6BT
☎ 01270-625525 Fax 01270-625525

An attractive farmhouse on the banks of a picturesque canal side location. Large breakfasts served and vegetarians catered for. Luxurious ensuite rooms, fourposter available. Pets corner and garden with lawns down to the canal. Large car park.

4 bedrs, all ensuite, **TCF TV P** 30 **SB** £20-£25 **DB** £40-£50

NARBOROUGH Leicestershire 8B3

★★ Charnwood
48 Leicester Road, Narborough LE9 5DF
☎ 0116-286 2218 Fax 0116-275 0119
Closed Christmas-New Year
20 bedrs, all ensuite, **TCF TV** 🐾 **P** 18 **SB** £40 **DB** £55
HB £262.50 **D** £13.95 **CC** MC Visa Amex

NEEDHAM MARKET Suffolk 9E4

Pipps Ford *Acclaimed*
Needham Market IP6 8LJ
☎ 01449-760208 Fax 01449-760561
Closed Dec 20-Jan 10
7 bedrs, all ensuite, **TCF** 🚭 **P** 12 No children under 5 **SB** £17-£38 **DB** £45-£65 **HB** £492-£632 **D** £16.50 🏊 &

NELSON Lancashire 10C3

Blacko Laithe Farm *Listed*
Blacko Bar Road, Blacko, Nelson BB9 6LA
☎ 01282-694642 Fax 01282-860822
7 bedrs, 4 ensuite, 2 ➡ **TCF TV** 🐾 **P** 10 &

NETTLEBED Oxfordshire 4B2

White Hart *Highly Acclaimed*
Nettlebed, Henley-on-Thames RG9 5DD
☎ 01491-641245 Fax 01491-641423
6 bedrs, all ensuite, **P** 45 **SB** £50 **DB** £60 **HB** £238 **D** £13 **CC** MC Visa

NEW ALRESFORD Hampshire 4B3

★★ Swan
11 West Street, New Alresford SO24 9AD
☎ 01962-732302 Fax 01962-735274
22 bedrs, all ensuite, 1 ➡ **TCF TV P** 90 **SB** £35-£40 **DB** £45-£55 **D** £11 **CC** MC Visa &

NEW ROMNEY Kent 5E3

★ Broadacre
North Street, New Romney TN28 8DR
☎ 01797-362381 Fax 01797-362381
10 bedrs, all ensuite, **TCF TV** 🐾 **P** 9 **SB** £33-£42 **DB** £45-£60 **D** £12 **CC** MC Visa JCB

NEWARK ON TRENT Nottinghamshire 8C2

★★ Grange
73 London Road, Newark-on-Trent NG24 1RZ
☎ 01636-703399 Fax 01636-702328
Closed Christmas-New Year
15 bedrs, all ensuite, **TCF TV P** 19 **SB** £48 **DB** £63 **D** £13 **CC** MC Visa Amex DC

NEWCASTLE UPON TYNE Tyne & Wear 13F4

★★ Cairn
97-103 Osborne Road, Newcastle upon Tyne NE2 2TA
☎ 0191-281 1358 Fax 0191-281 9031
50 bedrs, all ensuite, **TCF TV** 🐾 **P** 18 **SB** £55 **DB** £68 **D** £9 **CC** MC Visa Amex DC

★★ Whites
Osborne Road, Jesmond, Newcastle upon Tyne NE2 2AL
☎ 0191-281 5126 Fax 0191-281 9953
39 bedrs, 36 ensuite, 3 🚭, **TCF TV P** 30 **SB** £40-£49 **DB** £59-£69 **HB** £300-£390 **D** £12.95 **CC** MC Visa Amex

Chirton House *Acclaimed*
46 Clifton Road, Newcastle upon Tyne NE4 6XH
📞 0191-273 0407
11 bedrs, 5 ensuite, 2 🛏 TCF TV 🐕 P 10 SB £25-£35
DB £35-£45 HB £150 D £10 CC MC Visa

NEWCASTLE UNDER LYME Staffordshire 7E2

★★ Borough Arms
King Street, Newcastle-under-Lyme ST5 1HX
📞 01782-629421 Fax 01782-712388
45 bedrs, all ensuite, TCF TV P 45 SB £39.50-£49 DB £49-£59 D £12.95 CC MC Visa Amex DC

★★ Comfort Friendly Inn
Liverpool Road, Newcastle-under-Lyme ST5 9DX
📞 01782-717000 Fax 01782-713669
E Mail admin@gb617.u-net.com
68 bedrs, all ensuite, TCF TV P 160 SB £47-£59 DB £54-£65 D £9.75 CC MC Visa Amex DC JCB 🅿 ♿

NEWENT Gloucestershire 7E4

Cherry Grove
Cherry Grove Mill Lane, Kilcot, Newent GL18 1NY
📞 01989-720126

Comfortable house in peaceful rural situation one and a half miles from M50 Jct 3, with restaurants and pub grub nearby. Convenient to Wye Valley, Forest of Dean and Gloucester.

3 bedrs, 1 ensuite, 1 🛏 TCF TV 📧 P 6

NEWHAVEN East Sussex 5D4

Old Volunteer *Listed*
1 South Road, Newhaven BN9 9QL
📞 01273-515204 Fax 01273-515204
Closed Christmas New Year
16 bedrs, 7 ensuite, 1 🛏, 3 🛏 TCF TV 🐕 P 3 SB £22-£32 DB £32-£46 CC MC Visa Amex

NEWMARKET Suffolk 9D4

★★ White Hart
High Street, Newmarket CB8 8JP
📞 01638-663051 Fax 01638-667284
23 bedrs, all ensuite, 🐕 P 60

NEWPORT PAGNELL Buckinghamshire 4C1

Thurston *Listed*
90 High Street, Newport Pagnell MK16 8EH
📞 01908-611377 Fax 01908-611394
8 bedrs, all ensuite, TCF TV P 12 SB £33-£42 DB £47-£56 CC MC Visa Amex ♿

NEWQUAY Cornwall 2A3

★★ Beachcroft
Cliff Road, Newquay TR7 1SW
📞 01637-873022 Fax 01637-873022
Closed Oct-Apr
68 bedrs, all ensuite, 6 🛏 TCF TV 🐕 📧 P 50 SB £21-£27 DB £42-£54 HB £149-£228 D £8 CC MC Visa DC JCB 🅿 🅿 🔍 🅿 ♿

★★ Corisande Manor
Riverside Avenue, Pentire, Newquay TR7 1PL
📞 01637-872042 Fax 01637-874557
19 bedrs, 16 ensuite, 4 🛏 TCF TV 🐕 P 19 SB £29-£39 DB £55-£75 HB £220-£290 D £18 CC MC Visa

★★ Great Western
Cliff Road, Newquay TR7 2PT
📞 01637-872010 Fax 01637-874435
72 bedrs, 70 ensuite, 🐕 📧 P 45 SB £28-£30 DB £56-£60 HB £170-£250 D £9 CC MC Visa Amex DC 🅿 ♿

Windward *Highly Acclaimed*
Alexandra Road, Porth, Newquay TR7 3NB
📞 01637-873185 Fax 01637-852436
Closed Nov-Easter
14 bedrs, all ensuite, TCF TV P 14 SB £25-£30 DB £50-£60 HB £140-£209 D £15 CC MC Visa Amex

Copper Beach *Acclaimed*
70 Edgcumbe Avenue, Newquay TR7 2NN
📞 01637-873376
15 bedrs, all ensuite, P 16 ♿

Kellsboro *Acclaimed*
12 Henver Road, Newquay TR7 3BJ
📞 01637-874620
Closed Nov-Easter
16 bedrs, 14 ensuite, 2 🛏, 1 🛏 TV 🐕 P 20 SB £20-£26 DB £38-£50 HB £160-£190 CC MC Visa 🅿 🅿 ♿

RAC Hotel Reservations Service
0870 603 9109
(Calls charged at national call rate)

Pendeen *Acclaimed*
7 Alexandra Road, Porth, Newquay TR7 3ND
☎ **01637-873521 Fax 01637-873521**
Closed Nov-Dec

Beautifully located two minutes from Porth Beach. Tastefully furnished and a high standard of cuisine assured. Friendly, personal and efficient service is our aim. Mid-week bookings accepted. Ideal for the Cornwall coastal path walks.

15 bedrs, all ensuite, **TCF TV P** 15 **SB** £18.50-£26.50 **DB** £37-£48 **HB** £139-£195 **D** £9.50 **CC** MC Visa Amex

Porth Enodoc *Acclaimed*
4 Esplanade Road, Pentire, Newquay TR7 1PY
☎ **01637-872372**
Closed Oct-Mar

Set in its own grounds away from the town, overlooking Fistral beach and Newquay golf course, but within walking distance of the shopping centre.

15 bedrs, all ensuite, **TCF TV P** 15 No children under 2 **SB** £15-£24 **DB** £30-£47 **HB** £129-£189 **D** £9

Priory Lodge *Acclaimed*
30 Mount Wise, Newquay TR7 2BH
☎ **01637-874111 Fax 01637-851803**
Closed 3 Jan-10 Feb

Warm and friendly atmosphere. Set in own grounds with splendid sea views overlooking town and harbour. Entertainment, sauna, solarium, launderette, swimming pool and games room.

26 bedrs, 24 ensuite, 1 **TCF TV P** 27 **SB** £25-£30 **DB** £50-£60 **HB** £160-£225 **D** £10 **CC** MC Visa Amex

Wheal Treasure *Acclaimed*
72 Edgcumbe Avenue, Newquay TR7 2NN
☎ **01637-874136**
Closed Nov-Feb

12 bedrs, all ensuite, 2 **P** 12 **SB** £18-£23 **DB** £36-£46 **HB** £165-£185 **D** £6.50

Arundel *Listed*
Mount Wise, Newquay TR7 2BS
☎ **01637-872481 Fax 01637-850001**

35 bedrs, all ensuite, 2 **TCF TV P** 32 **SB** £15-£25 **DB** £30-£50 **HB** £143-£215 **CC** MC Visa Amex DC

Bedruthan House *Listed*
Bedruthan Steps, St Eval, Nr Wadebridge PL27 7UW
☎ **01637-860346**
Closed Nov

6 bedrs, 5 ensuite, **TCF P** 12 No children under 3 **SB** £17.50-£18.50 **DB** £35-£37 **HB** £162-£168 **D** £8.50 **CC** MC Visa JCB

Brakespear *Listed*
44-46 Edgcumbe Avenue, Newquay TR7 2NJ
☎ **01637-874771**
Closed Dec

10 bedrs, 7 ensuite, 1, 2 **TCF TV P** 8 **SB** £14-£17.50 **DB** £28-£35 **HB** £130-£155 **D** £5

Carlton *Listed*
6 Dane Road, Newquay TR7 1HL
☎ **01637-872658**

Ideally situated on Towan Headland for exploring spectacular coastlines, sandy coves, wild and wonderful seascapes. Magnificent sea views. Convenient for all amenities. Friendly atmosphere.

11 bedrs, 8 ensuite, 1, 1 **TCF TV SB** £17-£20 **DB** £34-£40

Hotel Trevalsa *Listed*
Watergate Road, Porth, Newquay TR7 3LX
☎ 01637-873336 Fax 01637-878843
Closed Nov-Mar
24 bedrs, 20 ensuite, 2 ⇨ TCF TV ✠ P 19 SB £17-£26
DB £34-£52 HB £159-£209 D £8.50 CC MC Visa Amex JCB ♿

Links *Listed*
Headland Road, Newquay TR7 1HN
☎ 01637-873211
Closed Nov-Mar
15 bedrs, 10 ensuite

Philema *Listed*
Esplanade Road, Pentire, Newquay TR7 1PY
☎ 01637-872571 Fax 01637-873188
Closed Nov-Mar
35 bedrs, all ensuite, 2 ⇨ TCF TV ✠ P 37 SB £20-£30
DB £40-£60 HB £147-£230 D £7.50 CC MC Visa 🛎 📺 🐕

Rolling Waves *Listed*
Alexandra Road, Porth, Newquay TR7 3NB
☎ 01637-873236
Closed 25 Dec
9 bedrs, 8 ensuite, 1 ⇨ TCF TV ✠ P 10 SB £18-£27
DB £38-£54 HB £160-£190 D £7 CC MC Visa

Colan Barton
Colan, Newquay TR8 4N
☎ 01637-881388 Fax 01637-881388
Closed Oct-Mar

Secluded 17th century farmhouse set in 11 acres, with lake and waterfowl. Peaceful atmosphere, good food and warm welcome assured from us and our animals.

3 bedrs, 1 ensuite, 1 ⇨ TCF TV ☑ P 6 SB £15-£22
DB £30-£44

NEWTON ABBOT Devon   3D3

★★ Queen's
Queen Street, Newton Abbot TQ12 2EZ
☎ 01626-63133 Fax 01626-64922
22 bedrs, 21 ensuite, 1 ⇨ TCF TV ✠ P 8 SB £45-£50
DB £66 HB £315 D £13.25 CC MC Visa Amex DC 🐕

Lamorna *Listed*
Ideford Coombe, Newton Abbot TQ13 0AR
☎ 01626-65627

The hotel is a friendly family run establishment situated between the South Devon beaches and Dartmoor. Facilities include a 30ft indoor heated swimming pool and a pleasant garden to enjoy.

8 bedrs, 1 ensuite, TCF TV ✠ P 15 SB £19-£20 DB £35-£44 D £6 🛎

NEWTOWN LINFORD Leicestershire   8B3

★★ Johnscliffe
73 Main Street, Newtown Linford LE6 0AF
☎ 01530-242228 Fax 01530-244460
Closed Christmas
15 bedrs, 14 ensuite, TCF TV ✠ P 64 SB £30-£46 DB £50-£69.50 HB £280-£371 D £11.50 CC MC Visa Amex

NORTH NEWNTON Wiltshire   4A3

Woodbridge Inn *Acclaimed*
North Newnton SN9 6JZ
☎ 01980-630266 Fax 01980-630266
Closed 25 Dec
3 bedrs, 2 ensuite, 1 ⇨ TCF TV P 60 SB £27-£32.50
DB £32-£37.50 HB £190-£290 D £9 CC MC Visa Amex DC 🎵

NORTH NIBLEY Gloucestershire   3F1

Burrows Court *Highly Acclaimed*
Nibley Green, North Nibley GL11 6AZ
☎ 01453-546230
6 bedrs, all ensuite, TV ✠ P 20 SB £29-£34 DB £42-£50
HB £210-£220 D £12 CC MC Visa

NORTH WARNBOROUGH Hampshire   4B3

Jolly Miller *Acclaimed*
Hook Road, North Warnborough, Hook RG29 1ET
☎ 01256-702085 Fax 01256-704030
8 bedrs, 4 ensuite, 2 ⇨ TCF TV ✠ P 60 SB £35-£45
DB £45-£55 CC MC Visa Amex DC

NORTHALLERTON North Yorkshire   11D2

Alverton *Acclaimed*
26 South Parade, Northallerton DL7 8SG
📞 01609-776207
Closed Christmas-New Year
5 bedrs, 3 ensuite, 1 🛏 TCF TV 🐾 P 3 SB £18 DB £38
HB £183 D £10

Windsor *Acclaimed*
56 South Parade, Northallerton DL7 8SL
📞 01609-774100
Closed 29-30 Dec
6 bedrs, 2 ensuite, 2 🛏 TCF TV 🐾 P 20 SB £20-£25
DB £34-£40 HB £172-£193 D £10

NORTHAMPTON Northamptonshire   8B4

★★ Aviator
Sywell Airport, Sywell, Northampton NN6 0BT
📞 01604-642111 Fax 01604-790701
51 bedrs, all ensuite, 🐾 P 100 CC MC Visa Amex DC

Poplars *Acclaimed*
Cross Street, Moulton, Northampton NN3 1RZ
📞 01604-643983 Fax 01604-790233

Old Northamptonshire stone-built farmhouse converted into a hotel c.1920.

18 bedrs, 14 ensuite, 2 🛏 TCF TV ⊠ 🐾 P 21 SB £40-£45
DB £50-£55 D £12 CC MC Visa Amex

NORWICH Norfolk   9F3

★★ Annesley House
Hospitality, Comfort, Restaurant merit awards
6 Newmarket Road, Norwich NR2 2LA
📞 01603-624553 Fax 01603-621577

Three listed Georgian buildings, restored and refurbished to a high standard. Set in beautifully landscaped grounds in a conservation area, yet just a short stroll to the city centre.

26 bedrs, all ensuite, TCF TV P 25 SB £58 DB £68 D £17
CC MC Visa Amex DC JCB

Belmonte *Highly Acclaimed*
60-62 Prince Of Wales Road, Norwich NR1 1LT
📞 01603-622533 Fax 01603-760805
9 bedrs, all ensuite, CC MC Visa Amex DC

Gables *Highly Acclaimed*
527 Earlham Road, Norwich NR4 7HN
📞 01603-456666 Fax 01603-250320
Closed 20 Dec-2 Jan

Friendly, family run non-smoking guest house with secluded gardens, very high quality, illuminated car park at rear, snooker table. Close to the city and walking distance to the university.

10 bedrs, all ensuite, 1 🛏 TCF TV ⊠ P 10 SB £35 DB £50-£55 CC MC Visa JCB 🐾 ♿

Wedgewood *Acclaimed*
42 St Stephens Road, Norwich NR1 3RE
📞 01603-625730 Fax 01603-615035

A friendly family run hotel, very close to the bus station and all the city centre places of interest. Car parking. Major credit cards accepted.

13 bedrs, 10 ensuite, 1 🛏 TCF TV P 12 SB £22-£24
DB £40-£44 CC MC Visa Amex DC

Old Corner Shop *Listed*
26 Cromer Road, Hellesdon, Norwich NR6 6LZ
☎ 01603-419000 Fax 01603-419000
Closed Christmas
3 bedrs, all ensuite, TCF TV P 10 SB £23 DB £38 HB £147
CC MC Visa

NOTTINGHAM Nottinghamshire   8B2

★★ Haven
Grantham Road (A52), Whatton NG13 9EU
☎ 01949-850800 Fax 01949-851454
33 bedrs, all ensuite, 1 🛏 TCF TV 🐕 P 72 SB £35 DB £48
D £4 CC MC Visa Amex DC JCB ♿

★★ Rufford
Melton Road, West Bridgford, Nottingham NG2 7NE
☎ 0115-981 4202 Fax 0115-945 5801
Closed Christmas

A 1920s-style residence, conveniently near to Test cricket ground.

34 bedrs, all ensuite, 1 🛏 TCF TV P 35 SB £38-£40
DB £45-£54 D £12 CC MC Visa Amex DC JCB

★★ Stage
Gregory Boulevard, Nottingham NG7 6LB
☎ 0115-960 3261 Fax 0115-969 1040
52 bedrs, all ensuite, TCF TV 🐕 P 70 SB £40-£42 DB £50-£53 D £11.95 CC MC Visa Amex DC JCB

Balmoral *Highly Acclaimed*
55-57 Loughborough Road, West Bridgford, Nottingham NG2 7LA
☎ 0115-955 2992 Fax 0115-955 2991
Closed Christmas-New Year
31 bedrs, all ensuite, P 35 SB £35 DB £45 D £8.50 CC
MC Visa DC

Fairhaven Private Hotel *Acclaimed*
19 Meadow Road, Beeston Rylands, Nottingham NG9 1JP
☎ 0115-922 7509
12 bedrs, 4 ensuite, 3 🛏 TCF TV P 12 SB £20-£30
DB £30-£40 D £8

P & J *Listed*
277-279 Derby Road, Lenton, Nottingham NG7 2DP
☎ 0115-978 3998 Fax 0115-978 3998

Half a mile from city centre, adjacent to Queen's Medical and university. 5.8 miles from M1 exit 25 into Nottingham. Excellent value for money.

20 bedrs, 9 ensuite, 2 🛏, 4 🛏 ▪ CC MC Visa Amex

Royston *Listed*
326 Mansfield Road, Nottingham NG5 2EF
☎ 0115-9622947 Fax 0115-956 5018
14 bedrs, 9 ensuite, 2 🛏, 2 🛏 ▪

St Andrews *Listed*
310 Queens Road, Beeston, Nottingham NG9 1JA
☎ 0115-925 4902 Fax 0115-925 4902

Semi-detached Victorian house.

10 bedrs, 3 ensuite, 3 🛏 TCF TV 🐕 P 7 SB £20 DB £36
D £8.50

NUNEATON Warwickshire   7F3

La Tavola Calda *Listed*
68 & 70 Midland Road, Nuneaton CV11 5DY
☎ 01203-381303 Fax 01203-381816
Closed 25-26 Dec
8 bedrs, all ensuite, TCF TV P 50 SB £18 DB £32 D £8 CC
MC Visa Amex DC

RAC Hotel Reservations Service
0870 603 9109
(Calls charged at national call rate)

OAKAMOOR Staffordshire 7F1

Ribden Farm *Highly Acclaimed*
Oakamoor ST10 3BW
☎ 01538-702830 Fax 01538-702830

An 18th century, stone-built farmhouse, tastefully renovated but retaining natural features like oak beams and uneven floor boards.

5 bedrs, all ensuite, TCF TV P 6 DB £40-£42 CC MC Visa JCB

OKEHAMPTON Devon 2C3

★★ **Oxenham Arms**
South Zeal, Okehampton EX20 2JT
☎ 01837-840244 Fax 01837-840791

Twelfth century inn of immense charm in centre of rural village on edge of Dartmoor National Park. Perfect centre for touring England's West Country.

8 bedrs, all ensuite, TCF TV P 8 SB £40-£45 DB £50-£60 HB £-£280 D £15 CC MC Visa Amex DC

Fairway Lodge
Thorndon Cross, Okehampton EX20 4NE
☎ 01837-52827 Fax 01837-52827

Stone built farmhouse, 10 acre organic smallholding, beautiful large gardens, miniature shetland ponies. Golf, horseriding, deer stalking by arrangement. Large well appointed rooms, beverage facilities, excellent food.

3 bedrs, all ensuite, TCF TV P 8

Higher Coombehead House
Belstone, Okehampton EX20 1QL
☎ 01837-840240

Large thatched country house within Dartmoor National Park. Offering accommodation in a self contained wing which was originally a private chapel. Just of A30. Ideal for touring Devon/Cornwall.

3 bedrs, all ensuite, TCF TV P 10 No children under 10 SB £20-£26 DB £17-£20

OLD SODBURY Gloucestershire 3F1

★★ **Cross Hands**
Tetbury Road, Old Sodbury BS17 6RJ
☎ 01454-313000 Fax 01454-324409
24 bedrs, 20 ensuite, 2 TCF TV P 200 SB £58.45 DB £79.40 CC MC Visa Amex DC JCB

Don't forget to mention the guide
When booking direct, please remember to tell the hotel that you chose it from
RAC Bed & Breakfast 1998.

Sodbury House *Highly Acclaimed*
Badminton Road, Old Sodbury BS17 6LU
☎ 01454-312847 Fax 01454-273105
Closed Christmas-New Year

Former 18th century farmhouse set in extensive grounds on the Cotswold's edge, 12 miles from Bath/Bristol. 13 ensuite bedrooms with colour TV, radio, hairdryer and trouser press.

13 bedrs, all ensuite, **TCF TV ⋈ P** 30
SB £43-£65 **DB** £62-£85 **CC** MC Visa Amex

OLDHAM Lancashire 10C4

★★ High Point
Napier Street, Oldham OL8 1TR
☎ 0161-624 4130 Fax 0161-627 2757
17 bedrs, all ensuite, **TCF TV P** 30 **SB** £35-£40 **DB** £45-£50 **D** £10.95 **CC** MC Visa Amex

OSWESTRY Shropshire 7D2

Sebastian's *Acclaimed*
45 Willow Street, Oswestry SY11 1AQ
☎ 01691-655444 Fax 01691-653452
Closed 25-26 Dec, 1 Jan

A small 16th century hotel and popular restaurant, well known for its innovative French cuisine and the comfort of its ensuite bedrooms. Priced competitively.

3 bedrs, all ensuite, **TCF TV P** 3 **Room only rate** £35-£43 **D** £17.95 **CC** MC Visa Amex

OTTERY ST MARY Devon 3D3

★★ Tumbling Weir
Ottery St Mary EX11 1AQ
☎ 01404-812752 Fax 01404-812752
10 bedrs, all ensuite, **TCF TV ⋈ P** 4 **SB** £38.75 **DB** £58.50 **HB** £285.60-£344.75 **D** £15.75 **CC** MC Visa JCB

Venn Ottery Barton *Listed*
Ottery St Mary EX11 1RZ
☎ 01404-812733 Fax 01404-814713

A 16th century country house hotel, peaceful and relaxing with excellent 'traditional but different' cuisine. Base for walking, visiting the Devon Heritage Coast, Dartmoor and National Trust properties.

17 bedrs, 11 ensuite, 2 ⋈ **TCF TV ⋈ P** 20 **SB** £32-£36 **DB** £60-£68 **HB** £265-£310 **D** £15 **CC** MC Visa JCB

OUNDLE Northamptonshire 8C3

Maltings *Listed*
Main Street, Aldwincle, Oundle NN14 3EP
☎ 01832-720233 Fax 01832-720326
Closed Christmas
3 bedrs, all ensuite, **TCF TV ⊠ P** 10 No children under 10 **SB** £34-£35 **DB** £47-£49 **CC** MC Visa

OXFORD Oxfordshire 4B2

★★ Coach and Horses
Stadhampton Road, Chislehampton, OX44 7UX
☎ 01865-890255 Fax 01865-891995
Closed 26-30 Dec
9 bedrs, all ensuite, **TCF TV ⋈ P** 30 **SB** £47 **DB** £53 **D** £14 **CC** MC Visa Amex DC &

★★ Foxcombe Lodge
Fox Lane, Boars Hill, Oxford OX1 5DP
☎ 01865-326326 Fax 01865-730628
20 bedrs, all ensuite, **TCF TV ⋈ P** 38 **SB** £45-£60 **DB** £60-£80 **D** £15 **CC** MC Visa Amex DC JCB &

★★ Jersey Arms
Restaurant merit award
Middleton Stoney OX6 8SE
☎ 01869-343234 Fax 01869-343565
16 bedrs, all ensuite, **TCF TV P** 50 **SB** £69 **DB** £85 **D** £19.50 **CC** MC Visa Amex DC JCB

BOWOOD HOUSE

Situated on the A4260, 4 miles from Oxford, Bowood offers accommodation of a high standard and a warm friendly atmosphere.
* Private bathrooms * Satellite/Colour TVs
* Direct Dial Telephone
* Tea/Coffee making facilities
* Radio alarms * Residential Licence

BTA Commended
RAC Highly Acclaimed
AA 4 QQQQ

238 OXFORD ROAD, KIDLINGTON, OXFORD OX5 1EB
Tel: Oxford (01865) 842288
Fax: (01865) 841858

★★ Palace
250 Iffley Road, Oxford OX4 1SE
☎ 01865-727627 Fax 01865-200478
8 bedrs, all ensuite, TCF TV P 8 SB £45-£50 DB £60-£67 D £8.50 CC MC Visa

★★ Tree
Church Way, Iffley, Oxford OX4 4EY
☎ 01865-775974 Fax 01865-747554
7 bedrs, all ensuite

★★ Victoria
180 Abingdon Road, Oxford OX1 4RA
☎ 01865-724536 Fax 01865-794909
22 bedrs, 14 ensuite, 3 TCF TV P 20 SB £37.50-£55.50 DB £58.50-£72.50 D £13.50 CC MC Visa

Ascot House *Highly Acclaimed*
283 Iffley Road, Oxford OX4 4AQ
☎ 01865-240259 Fax 01865-727669

A pretty Victorian house offering six beautifully refurbished ensuite rooms with colour TV, radio alarm, hairdryer, tea/coffee, fridge and telephone. Situated half a mile from the university and River Thames.

6 bedrs, all ensuite, TCF TV P 2 No children under 3 SB £30-£40 DB £40-£65 CC MC Visa Amex JCB

Balkan Lodge *Highly Acclaimed*
315 Iffley Road, Oxford OX4 4AG
☎ 01865-244524

Bowood House *Highly Acclaimed*
238 Oxford Road, Kidlington, Oxford OX5 1EB
☎ 01865-842288 Fax 01865-841858
22 bedrs, 20 ensuite, TCF TV P 30 SB £42.50 DB £47.50-£57.50 D £9.95 CC MC Visa Amex

Chestnuts *Highly Acclaimed*
45 Davenant Road, Off Woodstock Road, Oxford OX2 8BU
☎ 01865-553375 Fax 01865-553375
Closed Christmas-New Year
4 bedrs, all ensuite, TCF TV P 4 No children under 10 SB £34-£36 DB £54-£60

Cotswold House *Highly Acclaimed*
363 Banbury Road, Oxford OX2 7PL
☎ 01865-310558 Fax 01865-310558
Closed 10 days at Christmas

Almost 2 miles north of the centre, interesting, modern house offering standards rarely found today. Jim and Anne O'Kane enjoy making their guests feel special.

7 bedrs, all ensuite, TCF TV P 7 No children under 5 SB £37-£40 DB £55-£58

Gables *Highly Acclaimed*
6 Cumnor Hill, Oxford OX2 9HA
☎ 01865-862153 Fax 01865-864054
Closed Christmas-New Year

OXFORD – ENGLAND

Excellent location, five minutes drive from city centre. Warm hospitality combined with a high standard of comfort and service. Ensuite rooms with satellite TV, direct dial telephones, radios, tea/coffee facilities.

6 bedrs, 5 ensuite, 1 ⇌ TCF TV P 6 SB £22-£27 DB £40-£48 CC MC Visa

Marlborough House *Highly Acclaimed*
321 Woodstock Road, Oxford OX2 7NY
☎ 01865-311321 Fax 01865-515329
E Mail enquiries@marlbhouse.win-uk.net
Closed Christmas

Located one and a half miles from the city centre off the M40 (jn 9), this modern purpose-built hotel has immaculate ensuite bedrooms with telephone, TV, fridge, tea/coffee making facilities and minibar. Parking.

16 bedrs, all ensuite, TCF TV P 6 No children under 8 SB £59.50 DB £69.50 CC MC Visa JCB ♿

ELTHAM VILLA Guest House

This friendly well kept guest house with full facilities situated on the A44 between the dreaming spires of Oxford and the historic town of Woodstock, minutes from the magnificent Blenheim Palace, well known for excellent value and a wholesome English breakfast.

148 WOODSTOCK ROAD, YARNTON, OXFORDSHIRE OX5 1PW
Tel/Fax: 01865 376037

Tilbury Lodge *Highly Acclaimed*
5 Tilbury Lane, Botley, Oxford OX2 9NB
☎ 01865-862138 Fax 01865-863700
Closed Christmas

Situated in a tranquil spot in a pleasant lane, but only two minutes walk from buses, tubes, banks and shops, this family run, private hotel has direct dial phones, a jacuzzi and a fourposter, plus ample parking.

9 bedrs, all ensuite, TCF TV P 9 SB £39-£44 DB £52-£64 CC MC Visa

Courtfield *Acclaimed*
367 Iffley Road, Oxford OX4 4DP
☎ 01865-242991 Fax 01865-242991
Victorian town house close to all amenities. Comfortable, prettily decorated ensuite bedrooms with tea/coffee making facilities.
6 bedrs, 4 ensuite, 2 ⇌ P 6 No children under 3 DB £40-£44 CC MC Visa Amex DC JCB

Eltham Villa *Acclaimed*
148 Woodstock Road, Yarnton, Oxford OX5 1PW
☎ 01865-376037 Fax 01865-376037
Closed Christmas-New Year

An immaculately kept small cottage style guest house in countryside village area on the main A44 between the city of Oxford and the historic towns of Woodstock and Blenheim Palace.

7 bedrs, all ensuite, TCF TV P 10 SB £25-£30 DB £40-£50 HB £150-£200 CC MC Visa JCB

Galaxie *Acclaimed*
180 Banbury Road, Oxford OX2 7BT
☎ 01865-515688 Fax 01865-56824
31 bedrs, 25 ensuite, 2, 6 ⇌ TCF TV P 31 CC MC Visa

OXFORD – ENGLAND

Kings *Acclaimed*
363 Iffley Road, Oxford OX4 4DP
☎ 01865-241363

Pickwick *Acclaimed*
17 London Road, Headington, Oxford OX3 7SP
☎ 01865-750487 Fax 01865-742208

A large Georgian guest house that has been fully modernised.

15 bedrs, 9 ensuite, 2 ⇌ TCF TV 🐕 P 17 SB £25-£45 DB £38-£60 CC MC Visa Amex DC ♿

Acorn *Listed*
260 Iffley Road, Oxford OX4 1SE
☎ 01865-247998
Closed Christmas-New Year
6 bedrs, 2 ⇌ TCF TV P 5 SB £20-£25 DB £34-£40 CC MC Visa DC JCB

Bravalla *Listed*
242 Iffley Road, Oxford OX4 1SE
☎ 01865-241326 Fax 01865-250511

A late Victorian house, close to the city centre, river and ring road. Most rooms are ensuite, with TV and beverage facilities. Private parking is available.

6 bedrs, all ensuite, 1 ⇌ TCF TV 🐕 P 4 SB £20-£30 DB £38-£45 CC MC Visa DC

Brown's *Listed*
281 Iffley Road, Oxford OX4 4AQ
☎ 01865-246822 Fax 01865-246822

Tastefully furnished Victorian guest house with comfortable family atmosphere.

9 bedrs, 2 ensuite, 3 ⇌ TCF TV P 4 SB £22-£26 DB £32-£38 CC MC Visa

Conifer *Listed*
116 The Slade, Headington, Oxford OX3 7DX
☎ 01865-63055 Fax 01865-63055
8 bedrs, 3 ensuite, 1 ⇌ TCF TV P 8 SB £21 DB £42 CC MC Visa 🔲

Melcombe House *Listed*
227 Iffley Road, Oxford OX4 1SQ
☎ 01865-249520
Closed Christmas-New Year
9 bedrs, 1 ensuite, 1 🅟, 2 ⇌ TCF TV ✉ 🐕 P 6 SB £20-£25 DB £34-£40

River *Listed*
17 Botley Road, Oxford OX2 0AA
☎ 01865-243475 Fax 01865-724306
Closed Christmas-New Year
21 bedrs, 17 ensuite, 2 🅟, TCF TV P 25 SB £39-£60 DB £60-£75 D £7 CC MC Visa 🔲

OXHILL Warwickshire   8A4

Nolands Farm and Country Restaurant
Acclaimed
Oxhill CV35 0RJ
☎ 01926-640309 Fax 01926-641662
Closed Dec-15 Jan

A working farm situated in a tranquil valley surrounded by fields, woods and a lake. Most bedrooms are on the ground floor overlooking the old stable yard. Romantic fourposters.

9 bedrs, all ensuite, TCF TV P 9 No children under 7 SB £25-£30 DB £36-£44 CC MC Visa 🔲 ♿

PADSTOW Cornwall 2B3

Green Waves *Highly Acclaimed*
Trevone Bay, Padstow PL28 8RD
☏ **01841-520114**

A friendly, family run hotel, superbly situated with sea views in a residential area near the beach.

19 bedrs, all ensuite, 1 ⇌ **TCF TV ⊁ P** 18 No children under 4 **SB** £25-£28 **DB** £50-£198 **HB** £198-£232 **D** £15 **CC** MC Visa

Woodlands *Highly Acclaimed*
Treator, Padstow PL28 8RU
☏ **01841-532426 Fax 01841-532426**
Closed winter
9 bedrs, all ensuite, **TCF TV ⊁ P** 20 No children under 3 **SB** £25-£30 **DB** £40-£48 **HB** £185-£210 &

Old Mill Country House *Acclaimed*
Little Petherick, Padstow PL27 7QT
☏ **01841-540388**
Closed Nov-Feb
7 bedrs, all ensuite, **TCF P** 8 No children under 14 **DB** £50-£61 **CC** MC Visa Amex

PAIGNTON Devon 3D3

★★ Dainton
95 Dartmouth Road, Three Beaches Goodrington, Paignton TQ4 6NA
☏ **01803-550067 Fax 01803-666339**
E Mail dave@dainton.zynet.co.uk
11 bedrs, all ensuite, 1 ⇌ **TCF TV ⊁ P** 20 **SB** £35 **DB** £54 **HB** £235 **D** £9 **CC** MC Visa Amex JCB &

★★ Preston Sands
Marine Parade, Sea Front, Paignton TQ3 2NU
☏ **01803-558718 Fax 01803-522875**
31 bedrs, all ensuite, 1 ⇌ **TCF TV ⊁ P** 24 No children under 10 **SB** £19-£25 **DB** £38-£50 **HB** £185-£240 **D** £13 **CC** MC Visa Amex

★★ Torbay Holiday Motel
Totnes Road, Paignton TQ4 7PP
☏ **01803-558226 Fax 01803-663375**
16 bedrs, all ensuite, **TCF TV ⊁ P** 120 **SB** £30-£33 **DB** £47-£53 **HB** £207-£228 **D** £9 **CC** MC Visa Amex &

Roundham Lodge *Highly Acclaimed*
16 Roundham Road, Paignton TQ4 6DN
☏ **01803-558485 Fax 01803-553090**
Closed Christmas, New Year
8 bedrs, all ensuite, **TCF TV ⊁ P** 9 No children under 2 **SB** £20-£36 **DB** £40-£50 **CC** MC Visa

Channel View *Acclaimed*
8 Marine Parade, Sea Front, Paignton TQ3 2NU
☏ **01803-522432 Fax 01803-528376**

Modern seafront hotel with panoramic views. Turn off the A379 at Seaway Road and continue to sea front, turning left into Marine Parade.

13 bedrs, all ensuite, **TCF TV P** 10 **SB** £20-£25 **DB** £36-£40 **HB** £110-£210 **D** £7.50 **CC** MC Visa

Redcliffe Lodge *Acclaimed*
1 Marine Drive, Paignton TQ3 2NJ
☏ **01803-551394**
Closed Nov-Apr
17 bedrs, all ensuite, **TCF P** 17 **SB** £20-£30 **DB** £40-£60 **HB** £190-£249 **D** £10 **CC** MC Visa

Sattva *Acclaimed*
29 Esplanade, Paignton TQ4 6BL
☏ **01803-557820 Fax 01803-557820**
Closed Oct-Mar excl Christmas
20 bedrs, all ensuite, **TCF TV ⊁ ⬚ P** 10 **SB** £18-£26 **DB** £36-£52 **HB** £170-£199 **CC** MC Visa &

Sea Verge *Acclaimed*
Marine Drive, Preston, Paignton TQ3 2NJ
☏ **01803-557795**
Closed Mar-Nov
12 bedrs, all ensuite, 1 ⇌ **TCF TV P** 14 No children under 9 **SB** £17-£19 **DB** £34-£38 **HB** £119-£133 **D** £8

Sealawn *Acclaimed*
20 Esplanade Road, Paignton TQ4 6BE
☏ **01803-559031**
12 bedrs, all ensuite, **TCF TV P** 12 **SB** £21-£30 **DB** £38-£46 **HB** £168-£196 **D** £8 **CC** MC Visa

St Weonards *Acclaimed*
12 Kernou Road, Paignton TQ4 6BA
☏ **01803-558842**
8 bedrs, 5 ensuite, 2 ⇌ **TCF TV P** 2 **SB** £15-£17 **DB** £30-£34 **HB** £142-£157 **D** £7 **CC** MC Visa

Beresford *Listed*
Adelphi Road, Paignton TQ4 6AW
☎ 01803-551560
Closed Christmas-New Year
8 bedrs, all ensuite, TCF TV P 3 SB £28 DB £46 HB £160

Sunnybank *Listed*
2 Cleveland Road, Paignton TQ4 6EN
☎ 01803-525540 Fax 01803-525540
11 bedrs, 4 ensuite, 4, 2 ⇨ TCF TV ✈ P 8 No children under 3 SB £14-£17 DB £27-£34 HB £120-£150 CC MC Visa

Torbay Sands *Listed*
16 Marine Parade, Preston, Paignton TQ3 2NU
☎ 01803-525568
13 bedrs, 11 ensuite, 2 ⇨ TCF TV ✈ P 6 SB £14-£18 DB £27-£36 HB £125-£152 CC MC Visa

PAINSWICK Gloucestershire 7E4

Hambutts Mynd *Acclaimed*
Edge Road, Painswick GL6 6UP
☎ 01452-812352

A Cotswold house built in 1700 with old beams, open fires and super views. An ideal centre for the Cotswolds, Bath and Stratford-upon-Avon.

3 bedrs, 2 ensuite, 1 ⇨ TV ✈ P 3 No children under 10 SB £21 DB £38-£41

PAPWORTH EVERARD Cambridgeshire 9D4

★★ Papworth
Ermine Street South, Papworth Everard CB3 8PB
☎ 01954-718851 Fax 01954-718069
Closed 25-26 Dec
20 bedrs, all ensuite, TCF TV P 50 SB £30 DB £40 D £7 CC MC Visa Amex DC

PAR Cornwall 2B4

Elmswood House Hotel *Acclaimed*
73 Tehidy Road, Tywardreath, Par PL24 2QD
☎ 01726-814221 Fax 01726-814221
7 bedrs, 6 ensuite, 1 ⇨ TCF TV P 8 SB £26-£27 DB £42-£44 HB £200-£242 D £9

PARBOLD Lancashire 10B4

★★ Lindley
Hospitality merit award
912 Lancaster Lane, Parbold, Wigan WN8 7AB
☎ 01257-462804 Fax 01257-464628
8 bedrs, all ensuite, TCF TV ✈ P 50 SB £33 DB £42 D £12.50 CC MC Visa Amex

PARKGATE Cheshire 7D1

★★ Parkgate
Boathouse Lane, Parkgate L64 6RD
☎ 0151-336 5001 Fax 0151-336 8504
27 bedrs, all ensuite, TCF TV ✈ P 120 SB £30-£49.50 DB £60-£69 HB £280 D £12.95 CC MC Visa Amex

PATELEY BRIDGE North Yorkshire 10C3

Roslyn *Acclaimed*
King Street, Pateley Bridge HG3 5AT
☎ 01423-711374
6 bedrs, all ensuite, TCF TV P 4 SB £16-£29 DB £32-£44 HB £175-£180 D £9

PATTERDALE Cumbria 10B2

★★ Patterdale
Patterdale CA11 0NN
☎ 01768-482231 Fax 01768-482440
Closed Jan & Feb
57 bedrs, all ensuite, 6 ⇨ TCF TV ✈ P 40 SB £25-£30 DB £50-£60 HB £300 D £16 CC MC Visa

PELYNT Cornwall 2B4

★★ Jubilee Inn
Jubilee Hill, Pelynt PL13 2JZ
☎ 01503-220 312 Fax 01503 220 920

A two storey Cornish country inn with old world charm.

9 bedrs, all ensuite, TCF TV ✈ P 50 SB £36 DB £59 D £9 CC MC Visa JCB

PENDOGGETT Cornwall 2B3

★★ Cornish Arms
St Kew, Pendoggett PL30 3HH
☎ 01208-880263 Fax 01208-880335
7 bedrs, 5 ensuite, 1 ⇌ TCF TV ⋔ P 55 SB £35 DB £49
HB £240 D £16.50 CC   MC Visa Amex DC JCB

PENRITH Cumbria 10B1

★★ Brantwood Country
Stainton, Penrith CA11 0AP
☎ 01768-862748 Fax 01768-890164

Early 18th century building with oak beams and log fires (in winter) - very rural with large secure car park in over three acres of private gardens.

11 bedrs, all ensuite, 1 ⇌ TCF TV P 36 SB £38.50-£50
DB £57-£71 HB £280-£298 D £16 CC   MC Visa Amex

★★ Clifton Hill Hotel & Motel
Clifton, Penrith CA10 2EJ
☎ 01768-862717 Fax 01768-867182
62 bedrs, all ensuite, TCF TV SB £35 DB £50 HB £175
D £10.95 ⋔ ♿

Tymparon Hall *Acclaimed*
Newbiggin, Stainton, Penrith CA11 0HS
☎ 01768-483236
Closed Apr-Nov

A cosy summer garden and glorious views are the backdrop against which to enjoy old-fashioned hospitality, home cooked farmhouse breakfasts and three course dinners as well as a cosy interior.

4 bedrs, 2 ensuite, 1 ⇌ TCF ✱ ⋔ SB £18-£25 D £40-£44
HB £210-£215 D £12

Woodland House *Acclaimed*
Wordsworth Street, Penrith CA11 7QY
☎ 01768-864177 Fax 01768-890152
E Mail idavies@id.compulink.co.uk
Closed Nov
8 bedrs, all ensuite, 1 ⇌ TCF TV ✱ P 6 SB £26 DB £42
D £10

Limes Country *Listed*
Redhills, Stainton, Penrith CA11 0DT
☎ 01768-863 343
6 bedrs, all ensuite, 1 ⇌ TCF TV P 7 SB £26-£27 DB £42-£44 HB £220-£230 D £12.50 CC   MC Visa

Brookfield
Shap, Penrith CA10 3PZ
☎ 01931-716397

Renowned for good food, comfort and personal attention, home cooking a speciality. Well stocked bar. Residents' lounge. No pets. Situated one mile from the M6 (jn 39).

6 bedrs, 2 ensuite, 2 ⇌ TCF TV ✱ P 20 SB £17.50-£18
DB £34-£35 D £13.50

PENZANCE Cornwall 2A4

Estoril *Highly Acclaimed*
46 Morrab Road, Penzance TR18 4EX
☎ 01736-362468 Fax 01736-367471
10 bedrs, all ensuite, TCF TV P 4 SB £25-£27 DB £50-£54
HB £252-£266 D £13 CC   MC Visa ♿

Tarbert Hotel & Restaurant *Highly Acclaimed*
Restaurant merit award
11 Clarence Street, Penzance TR18 2NU
☎ 01736-363758 Fax 01736-331336
Closed Christmas-New Year
12 bedrs, all ensuite, 1 ⇌ TCF TV P 5 No children
under 4 SB £28-£30 DB £48-£60 HB £238-£264 D £14 CC
MC Visa Amex

Camilla House *Acclaimed*
12 Regent Terrace, Penzance TR18 4DW
☎ 01736-363771
8 bedrs, 4 ensuite, 2 ⇌ TCF TV ⋔ P 8 SB £15-£20
DB £32-£46 CC   MC Visa

PENZANCE – ENGLAND

Sea & Horses *Acclaimed*
6 Alexandra Terrace, Sea Front, Penzance TR18 4NX
☎ 01736-361961 Fax 01736-330499
11 bedrs, 9 ensuite, 2 ⌂, TCF TV ⚲ P 11 SB £28-£34
DB £56-£68 D £11.50 CC MC Visa Amex DC JCB

Carlton *Listed*
Promenade, Penzance TR18 4NW
☎ 01736-362081
Closed Nov-Feb

A Victorian building overlooking the promenade and Mount's Bay.

10 bedrs, 8 ensuite, 2 ⚲ TCF TV No children under 12
SB £18 DB £40-£50

Carnson House *Listed*
East Terrace, Penzance TR18 2TD
☎ 01736-365589
E Mail rhilder@netcomuk.co.uk

An 18th century, granite built, small private hotel close to the harbour with a friendly atmosphere and excellent food. Ideal for touring the Land's End peninsula. Tours, excursions and car hire arranged.

8 bedrs, 2 ensuite, 1 ⚲ TCF TV No children under 12
SB £16-£19 DB £30-£35 HB £160-£185 D £10 CC MC Visa Amex DC JCB

Keigwin *Listed*
Alexandra Road, Penzance TR18 4LZ
☎ 01736-363930
Closed Christmas
8 bedrs, 5 ensuite, 1 ⚲ TCF TV ⊠ SB £14-£18 DB £28-£36
HB £189-£211 D £14 CC MC Visa

Kimberley House *Listed*
10 Morrab Road, Penzance TR18 4EZ
☎ 01736-362727
9 bedrs, 3 ⚲ TCF TV P 4 No children under 5 SB £13-£16 DB £26-£32 HB £140-£168 D £10

Lynwood *Listed*
41 Morrab Road, Penzance TR18 4EX
☎ 01736-365871 Fax 01736-365871
E Mail lynwood@connexions.co.uk

Comfortable Victorian family run guest house situated in Morrab Road between the promenade and the A30, and close to Morrab Gardens.

6 bedrs, 2 ensuite, 3 ⚲ TCF TV ⚲ No children under 5
SB £12-£16 DB £24-£32 CC MC Visa Amex DC

Mount Royal *Listed*
Chyandour Cliff, Penzance TR18 3LQ
☎ 01736-362233
Closed winter
7 bedrs, 4 ensuite, 2 ⚲ TCF TV ⚲ P 6 SB £17-£26
DB £28-£50

Penmorvah *Listed*
Alexandra Road, Penzance TR18 4LZ
☎ 01736-363711
8 bedrs, all ensuite, TCF TV ⚲ SB £15-£20 DB £30-£40
HB £155-£195 CC MC Visa Amex

Trevelyan *Listed*
16 Chapel Street, Penzance TR18 4AW
☎ 01736-362494
10 bedrs, 6 ensuite, 4 ⌂, 2 ⚲ TCF TV P 6

Woodstock *Listed*
29 Morrab Road, Penzance TR18 4EL
☎ 01736-369049 Fax 01736-369049
E Mail woodstocp@aol.com
8 bedrs, 4 ensuite, 1 ⌂, 1 ⚲ TCF TV No children
SB £12-£18.50 DB £24-£37 CC MC Visa Amex DC JCB ♿

RAC Hotel Reservations Service
0870 603 9109
(Calls charged at national call rate)

PERRANPORTH Cornwall 2A4

★★ Beach Dunes
Ramoth Way, Reen Sands, Perranporth TR6 0BY
☎ 01872-572263 Fax 01872-573824
E Mail beachdunes@thenet.co.uk
Closed Nov-Dec
9 bedrs, all ensuite, **TCF TV** ✉ ♦ **P** 15 No children under 4 **SB** £26.50-£29.50 **DB** £53-£59 **HB** £215-£260 **D** £15 **CC** MC Visa Amex DC JCB

PETERBOROUGH Cambridgeshire 8C3

Aaron Park *Acclaimed*
109-112 Park Road, Peterborough PE1 2TR
☎ 01733-64849 Fax 01733-64849
14 bedrs, all ensuite, **TCF TV** ♦ **P** 11 **SB** £29-£39 **DB** £38-£44 **D** £12 **CC** MC Visa Amex DC JCB

Dalwhinnie Lodge *Acclaimed*
31-33 Burghley Road, Peterborough PE1 2QA
☎ 01733-65968 Fax 01733-890838

Turn of the century building, with the cathedral stonework lovingly cared for by its proprietors.

18 bedrs, 4 ensuite, 4 ⌂, 3 ♦ **TCF TV** ♦ **P** 14 **SB** £16-£23 **DB** £32-£45 **D** £6 **CC** MC Visa Amex DC JCB ♿

Hawthorn House *Acclaimed*
89 Thorpe Road, Peterborough PE3 6JQ
☎ 01733-340608 Fax 01733-440032
8 bedrs, all ensuite, **TCF TV P** 7 **SB** £35-£38.50 **DB** £45-£49.50 **D** £8 **CC** MC Visa Amex DC ♿

Lodge *Acclaimed*
130 Lincoln Road, Peterborough PE1 2NR
☎ 01733-341439 Fax 01733-753437
9 bedrs, all ensuite, **TCF TV** ♦ **P** 6 No children under 10 **SB** £37-£47 **DB** £47-£57 **HB** £210 **D** £15 **CC** MC Visa Amex DC JCB

Thorpe Lodge *Acclaimed*
83 Thorpe Road, Peterborough PE3 6JQ
☎ 01733-348759 Fax 01733-891598
18 bedrs, all ensuite, 2 ♦ **TCF TV P** 20 **SB** £41.12 **DB** £52.87 **D** £12.50 **CC** MC Visa Amex DC JCB

Abbey House

Though mainly Georgian in appearance, the house dates in part from 1190AD having been formerly owned by Burgh Abbey and Peterborough Minster before its later use as a Rectory. Set in pleasant gardens in a quiet village between Stamford and Market Deeping, and offering 7 rooms with private facilities. Abbey House provides an ideal base for touring the Eastern Shires with their abundance of stately homes, abbeys, cathedrals and delightful stone villages.

Proprietors: Mr and Mrs A B Fitton

**Abbey House, West End Road,
Maxey PE6 9EJ
Tel: (01778) 344642**

Formule 1 *Lodge*
Boongate, Eastern Industry, Peterborough PE1 5QT
☎ 01733-894400 Fax 01733-559007
80 bedrs, 16 ♦ **TV** ♦ **P** 80 **SB** £22.50 **DB** £25 **CC** MC Visa Amex ♿

Abbey House
West End Road, Maxey, Peterborough PE6 9EJ
☎ 01778-344642

Set in pleasent gardens in a quiet village between Stamford and Market Deeping and offering 10 rooms with private facilities. A perfect base for touring.

10 bedrs, all ensuite, **TCF TV**

PETERLEE Co. Durham 11D1

★★ Hardwicke Hall Manor
Comfort merit award
Heslenden Road, Blackhall, Peterlee TS27 4PA
☎ 01429-836326 Fax 01429-837676
15 bedrs, all ensuite, ♦ **P** 103 **SB** £47.50-£57.50 **DB** £57.50-£67.50 **D** £15.95 **CC** MC Visa Amex DC

PEVENSEY East Sussex 5D4

★★ Priory Court
Pevensey Castle, Pevensey BN24 5LG
☎ 01323-763150 Fax 01323-768558
11 bedrs, 9 ensuite, 1 ➡ TCF TV ✝ P 60 SB £25 DB £39 D £11.95 CC MC Visa ♿

PICKERING North Yorkshire 11E2

★★ Bean Sheaf
Comfort, Restaurant merit awards
Malton Road, Kirby Misperton, Pickering YO17 0UE
☎ 01653-668614 Fax 01653-668370
20 bedrs, all ensuite, 1 ➡ TCF TV ✝ P 60 CC MC Visa Amex DC JCB 🖼 ♿

★★ Forest & Vale
Malton Road, Pickering YO18 7DL
☎ 01751-472722 Fax 01751-472972
17 bedrs, all ensuite, TCF TV ✝ P 70 SB £45-£49 DB £68-£73 HB £332.50 D £17.75 CC MC Visa Amex

★★ White Swan at Pickering
Hospitality, Restaurant merit awards
The Market Place, Pickering YO18 7AA
☎ 01751-472288 Fax 01751-475554
12 bedrs, all ensuite, TCF TV ✝ P 35 SB £50-£55 DB £70-£90 HB £249-£295 D £15 CC MC Visa Amex

Rawcliffe House Farm *Acclaimed*
Newton-upon-Rawcliffe, Stape, Pickering YO18 8JA
☎ 01751-473292
3 bedrs, all ensuite, P 10 No children under 8 ♿

PICKHILL North Yorkshire 11D2

★★ Nag's Head Country Inn
Restaurant merit award
Pickhill YO7 4JG
☎ 01845-567391 Fax 01845-567212
15 bedrs, all ensuite, TCF TV ✝ P 50 SB £36 DB £50 D £15 CC MC Visa ♿

PIDDLETRENTHIDE Dorset 3F3

Old Bakehouse *Acclaimed*
Piddletrenthide DT2 7QR
☎ 01300-348305
Closed Jan
10 bedrs, all ensuite, ✝ P 16 No children under 10 CC MC Visa 🖼

PLYMOUTH Devon 2C4

★★ Camelot
5 Elliot Street, Plymouth PL1 2PP
☎ 01752-221255 Fax 01752-603660
17 bedrs, all ensuite, TCF TV SB £39 DB £50 D £13 CC MC Visa Amex DC JCB

Forest & Vale Hotel

The ideal base for exploring the beautiful North York Moors, this impressive eighteenth century manor house offers welcoming hospitality, stylish, well equipped bedrooms and award winning cuisine.

Malton Road, Pickering, North Yorkshire YO18 7DL
Tel. 01751-472722
Fax. 01751-472972

Bowling Green Hotel
9-10 Osborne Place,
Lockyer Street,
Plymouth, Devon PL1 2PU
Tel: (01752) 209090
Fax: (01752) 209092

★★ Invicta
11 Osborne Place, Lockyer Street, The Hoe, PL1 2PU
☎ 01752-664997 Fax 01752-664994
Closed 24 Dec-4 Jan
23 bedrs, 21 ensuite, 1 ⇌ TCF TV ⚲ P 10 No children under 12 SB £42 DB £52 HB £196-£228 D £9.50 CC MC Visa Amex

★★ Langdon Court
Down Thomas, Wembury, Plymouth PL9 0DY
☎ 01752-862358 Fax 01752-863428
E Mail langdon@mail.zynet.co.uk
16 bedrs, all ensuite, TCF TV ⚲ P 100 SB £35-£55 DB £62-£75 D £15 CC MC Visa Amex DC JCB

★ Drake
1 Windsor Villas, Lockyer Street The Hoe, Plymouth PL1 2QD
☎ 01752-229730 Fax 01752-255092
Closed Christmas
36 bedrs, 28 ensuite, 5 ⌂, 3 ⇌ TCF TV P 25 SB £42 DB £52 HB £245 D £12 CC MC Visa Amex DC JCB

★ Imperial
Lockyer Street, The Hoe, Plymouth PL1 2QD
☎ 01752-227311 Fax 01752-674986
22 bedrs, 16 ensuite, 3 ⇌ TCF TV P 14 SB £35-£45 DB £45-£58 HB £250-£320 D £13 CC MC Visa Amex DC JCB

Georgian House *Highly Acclaimed*
51 Citadel Road, The Hoe, Plymouth PL1 3AU
☎ 01752-663237 Fax 01752-253953

Set on the Hoe within walking distance of the city centre, seafront, historic Barbican, ferry port, theatre and Plymouth Pavillions. Write for brochure.

10 bedrs, all ensuite, 1 ⇌ TCF TV P 2 SB £25-£29 DB £36-£41 D £6 CC MC Visa Amex DC

Don't forget to mention the guide
When booking direct, please remember to tell the hotel that you chose it from RAC Bed & Breakfast 1998.

Georgian House Hotel

Ideally situated on The Hoe, within walking distance of the city centre, seafront, historic Barbican ferry port, theatre and Plymouth Pavillions.

Ten bedrooms all en-suite with TV, direct dial telephone, tea/coffee making facilities and hairdryer.

Special rates for group or long term stay. Fully Licenced bar and restaurant serving a la carte as well as three course meal for £7.95. Our restaurant serves English and Continental dishes.

Write for brochure to Noel and Virginia Bhadha. All credit cards accepted.

Bristish Hospitality Associate Member RAC Highly Acclaimed Member of the Plymouth Marketing Bureau

51 CITADEL ROAD, THE HOE, PLYMOUTH
Telephone: (01752) 663237 Fax: (01752) 253953

Bowling Green *Acclaimed*
9-10 Osborne Place, Lockyer Street, Plymouth PL1 2PU
📞 01752-209090 Fax 01752-209092
Closed 24-26 Dec

An elegant, family run Georgian hotel overlooking Hoe Gardens, with superbly appointed gardens. Centrally located for the theatre, conference/city centres and ferry port. Enjoy a memorable visit.

12 bedrs, all ensuite, **TCF TV** 🐕 **P** 4 **SB** £36 **DB** £48-£50 **CC** MC Visa Amex DC
See advert on previous page

Drakes View *Acclaimed*
33 Grand Parade, West Hoe, Plymouth PL1 3DQ
📞 01752-221500 Fax 01752-221664
Closed Christmas
9 bedrs, all ensuite, **TCF TV CC** MC Visa

Victoria Court *Acclaimed*
64 North Road East, Plymouth PL4 6AL
📞 01752-668133 Fax 01752-668133
Closed 21 Dec-2 Jan
13 bedrs, 10 ensuite, 2 🐕 **TCF TV P** 6 **SB** £35-£42 **DB** £45-£52 **HB** £227 **D** £12.50 **CC** MC Visa Amex DC

Alexander *Listed*
20 Woodland Terrace, Greenbank, Plymouth PL4 8NL
📞 01752-663247 Fax 01752-225536

A warm welcome awaits you at the Alexander. Centrally located, ideal for business or pleasure. Large car park, ensuite rooms available, licensed bar.

8 bedrs, 2 ensuite, 2 🚭, 2 🐕 **TCF TV P** 6 **SB** £16-£22 **DB** £30-£38

Ashgrove *Listed*
218 Citadel Road, The Hoe, Plymouth PL1 3BB
📞 01752-664046 Fax 01752-664046
10 bedrs, all ensuite, **TCF TV SB** £15-£20 **DB** £30-£35 **CC** MC Visa Amex

Chester *Listed*
54 Stuart Road, Pennycomequick, Plymouth PL3 4EE
📞 01752-663706 Fax 01752-663706
10 bedrs, 3 ensuite, 2 🐕 **TCF TV**

Cranbourne *Listed*
282 Citadel Road, The Hoe, Plymouth PL1 2PZ
📞 01752-263858 Fax 01752-263858
13 bedrs, 7 ensuite, 2 🚭, 2 🐕 **TCF TV** 🐕 **P** 2 **SB** £18 **DB** £40 **CC** MC Visa Amex ♿

Devonia *Listed*
27 Grand Parade, West Hoe, Plymouth PL1 3DQ
📞 01752-665026

Victorian house on sea front overlooking Plymouth Sound and all sailing and shipping activities. Close to the city centre, Pavilions and theatre.

8 bedrs, all ensuite, 1 🐕 **TCF TV** 🐕 No children under 4 **SB** £25 **DB** £40 **CC** MC Visa

Dudley *Listed*
42 Sutherland Road, Mutley, Plymouth PL4 6BN
📞 01752-668322 Fax 01752-673763

Victorian town house situated halfway between Mutley Plain and the railway station.

7 bedrs, 6 ensuite, 1 🐕 **TCF TV** 🐕 **P** 3 **SB** £16-£24 **DB** £28-£34 **HB** £170-£191 **D** £9 **CC** MC Visa Amex

Headland Listed
1a Radford Road, West Hoe, Plymouth PL1 3BY
☎ 01752-660866
Closed Christmas
3 bedrs, all ensuite, 4 ⇨ TCF TV ⇨ CC MC Visa

Oliver's Listed
33 Sutherland Road, Mutley, Plymouth PL4 6BN
☎ 01752-663923

A former Victorian merchant's house situated in a quiet residential part of the town centre. Approved for its hospitality, cuisine and value.

6 bedrs, 4 ensuite, 1 ⇨ TCF TV P 2 No children under 11 SB £19-£30 DB £42-£45 D £11 CC MC Visa Amex DC

Phantele Listed
176 Devonport Road, Stoke, Plymouth PL1 5RD
☎ 01752-561506
Closed Christmas
6 bedrs, 2 ensuite, 2 ⇨ TCF SB £15.50-£25.85 DB £29-£41.80 HB £135-£203.10 D £7

Rosaland Listed
32 Houndiscombe Road, Mutley, Plymouth PL4 6HQ
☎ 01752-664749 Fax 01752-256984

Quiet, Victorian private hotel. Well appointed and well run with the emphasis on quality. Recommended by 'Which?', and all major inspection bodies. Convenient for centre and university.

8 bedrs, 4 ensuite, 1 ⇨, 2 ⇨ TV P 2 SB £17 DB £30 D £8 CC MC Visa Amex DC

Campanile Plymouth Lodge
Marsh Mills, Longbridge Road, Plymouth PL6 8LD
☎ 01752-601087 Fax 01752-223213
50 bedrs, all ensuite, TCF TV ⇨ P 50 SB £41 DB £45.50 D £10.55 CC MC Visa Amex DC ♿

POCKLINGTON East Yorkshire 11E3

★★ Feathers
Market Place, Pocklington YO4 2AH
☎ 01759-303155 Fax 01759-304382
12 bedrs, all ensuite, P 60 CC MC Visa Amex DC

POLPERRO Cornwall 2B4

★ Claremont
The Coombes, Polperro PL13 2RG
☎ 01503-272241 Fax 01503-272241
10 bedrs, all ensuite, ⇨ P 16 No children under 9
DB £34-£54 D £10 CC MC Visa Amex

Penryn House Listed
The Coombes, Polperro PL13 2RG
☎ 01503-272157 Fax 01503-273055

Charming small hotel set in its own grounds in the heart of Polperro offers comfortable ensuite bedrooms, super candlelit dining in the restaurant and parking.

10 bedrs, all ensuite, 1 ⇨ TCF TV ⇨ P 14 DB £40-£56 HB £217-£280 D £13 CC MC Visa Amex

POOLE Dorset 3F3

★★ Norfolk Lodge
1 Flaghead Road, Canford Cliffs, Poole BH13 7JL
☎ 01202-708614 Fax 01202-708614
19 bedrs, 17 ensuite, 2 ⇨ TCF TV ⇨ P 17 SB £35-£40 DB £54-£56 HB £185-£220 D £9 CC MC Visa Amex DC

★★ Quarterdeck
2 Sandbanks Road, Poole BH14 8AQ
☎ 01202-740066 Fax 01202-736780
15 bedrs, all ensuite, TCF TV ⇨ P 32 SB £43 DB £55-£59 HB £248.50-£262.50 D £13.95 CC MC Visa Amex

Avoncourt Listed
245 Bournemouth Road, Parkstone, Poole BH14 9HX
☎ 01202-732025 Fax 01202-732025
6 bedrs, 1 ensuite, 1 ⇨, 1 ⇨ TCF TV ▣ P 6 SB £16-£20 DB £32-£44 HB £133-£160 D £7.50 CC MC Visa Amex DC JCB

Sheldon Lodge *Listed*
22 Forest Road, Branksome Park, Poole BH13 6DA
📞 01202-761186 Fax 01202-769891
14 bedrs, all ensuite, TCF TV 🐾 P 3 SB £20-£29 DB £40-£52 D £8.50 CC MC Visa 🅿 ♿

PORLOCK Somerset   3D2

★★ Oaks
Hospitality, Comfort, Restaurant merit awards
Porlock TA24 8ES
📞 01643-862265 Fax 01643-862265
9 bedrs, all ensuite, TCF TV 🐾 P 12 No children under 8 SB £48 DB £80 HB £350 D £24 CC MC Visa Amex

★ Ship Inn
High Street, Porlock TA24 8QD
📞 01643-862507 Fax 01643-863224
11 bedrs, 7 ensuite, 2 🐾 🐾 P 20 SB £17 DB £45 D £15 CC MC Visa

Lorna Doone *Acclaimed*
High Street, Porlock TA24 8PS
📞 01643-862404
Closed Christmas
15 bedrs, all ensuite, 1 🐾 TCF TV 🐾 P 6 SB £22-£24 DB £40-£50 D £11 CC MC Visa

Doverhay Place
Porlock, Minehead TA24 8EX
📞 01643-862398

A delightful turn-of-the-century country guest house with extensive gardens overlooking the pretty village of Porlock.

27 bedrs, 20 ensuite, 5 🐾 TCF P 30 SB £19.50 DB £39 D £9.50 CC MC Visa

---

PORT ISAAC Cornwall   2B3

Bay *Listed*
1 The Terrace, Port Isaac PL29 3SC
📞 01208-880380
10 bedrs, 4 ensuite, 2 🐾 TCF TV 🐾 P 10 SB £18.50-£22.50 DB £37-£45 HB £173-£195 D £10

Shipwright Inn *Listed*
The Terrace, Port Isaac PL29 3SG
📞 01208-880305 Fax 01208-814405
4 bedrs, all ensuite, TCF TV CC MC Visa

PORTESHAM Dorset   3E3

★★ Millmead Country
Goose Hill, Portesham DT3 4HE
📞 01305-871432 Fax 01305-871884
6 bedrs, all ensuite, 🐾 P 20 No children under 10 SB £42-£47 DB £68-£78 HB £245-£308 D £17.50 CC MC Visa Amex DC ♿

PORTLAND Dorset   3E3

Alessandria *Listed*
71 Wakeham, Easton, Portland DT5 1HW
📞 01305-822270 Fax 01305-820561

Unique Italian hotel with 17 ensuite bedrooms, 3 on ground floor, suitable for slightly disabled people. Exquisite fresh food cooked to order by Giovanni Bisogno, chef proprietor with 30 years, 5-star experience. Efficient, warm & friendly. Free car park.

17 bedrs, 11 ensuite, 1 🛏, 2 🐾 TCF TV P 20 SB £25-£35 DB £45-£55 HB £205-£230 D £15 CC MC Visa Amex ♿

PORTSCATHO Cornwall   2B4

★★ Roseland House
Hospitality merit award
Rosevine, Portscatho TR2 5EW
📞 01872-580644 Fax 01872-580801
15 bedrs, all ensuite, TCF TV P 28 CC MC Visa 🅿 ♿

PORTSMOUTH & SOUTHSEA Hampshire   4B4

★★ Beaufort
Hospitality, Comfort merit awards
71 Festing Road, Portsmouth PO4 0NQ
📞 01705-823707 Fax 01705-870270
19 bedrs, all ensuite, P 10 SB £40-£48 DB £50-£68 HB £180-£265 D £11.90 CC MC Visa Amex

★★ Glendower
22-23 South Parade, Southsea PO5 2JS
📞 01705-827169 Fax 01705-838738
40 bedrs, all ensuite, 🐾 🎬 P 10 CC MC Visa

★★ Red Lion
London Road, Cosham, Portsmouth PO6 3DY
📞 01705-382041 Fax 01705-371981
15 bedrs, all ensuite, TCF TV ⊨ P 40 SB £38 DB £48 D £4
CC MC Visa Amex

★★ Sandringham
Osborne Road, Clarence Parade, Portsmouth PO5 3LR
📞 01705-826969 Fax 01705-822330
45 bedrs, all ensuite, TV ⊟ P 100 SB £25-£35 DB £38-£50 HB £165-£220 D £10 CC MC Visa Amex

★★ Seacrest
Hospitality, Comfort merit awards
12 South Parade, Portsmouth PO5 2JB
📞 01705-875666 Fax 01705-832523
28 bedrs, all ensuite, TCF TV ⊨ ⊟ P 10 SB £38-£50 DB £42-£70 HB £210-£280 D £12 CC MC Visa

★★ Westfield Hall
Comfort merit award
65 Festing Road, Southsea PO4 0NQ
📞 01705-826971 Fax 01705-870200
E Mail joanie@westfield-hall-hotel.co.uk
23 bedrs, all ensuite, TCF TV P 17 SB £40-£48 DB £54-£70 HB £230-£250 D £13.95 CC MC Visa Amex DC

Hamilton House *Acclaimed*
95 Victoria Road North, Southsea, Portsmouth PO5 1PS
📞 01705-823502 Fax 01705-823502

Delightful Victorian town house with bright modern rooms. Centrally located five minutes from the Heritage areas, museums, continental/I.O.W ferryports, stations, centres and university. Breakfast served from 8 am.

8 bedrs, 4 ensuite, 2 ⊨ TCF TV SB £17-£38 DB £34-£45

Saville *Acclaimed*
38-39 Clarence Parade, Southsea PO5 2EU
📞 01705-822491 Fax 01705-737679
45 bedrs, 27 ensuite, 8 ⊨ TCF TV ⊨ ⊟ P 6 SB £18-£20 DB £34-£40 HB £140-£170 D £7 CC MC Visa Amex DC

Upper Mount House *Acclaimed*
The Vale, Clarendon Road, Portsmouth PO5 2EQ
📞 01705-820456

Grade II Listed 19th century hotel standing in its own grounds; close to shops and seafront museums.

11 bedrs, all ensuite, 1 ⊨ TCF TV P 12 SB £25-£28 DB £38-£48 HB £180-£210 D £10 CC MC Visa

Abbeville *Listed*
26 Nettlecombe Avenue, Portsmouth PO4 0QW
📞 01705-826209
11 bedrs, 2 ensuite, 2 ⊨ TCF TV ⊨ P 5

Aquarius Court *Listed*
34 St Ronan's Road, Southsea PO4 0PT
📞 01705-822872 Fax 01705-822872
12 bedrs, 4 ensuite, 2 ⊨ TCF TV P 6 SB £16-£23 DB £31-£38 HB £148-£164 D £7.50 CC MC Visa Amex DC

Bembell Court
HOTEL

Ideally situated in Portsmouth and Southsea's prime holiday area, with an excellent selection of shops, pubs and restaurants nearby.
Single night and midweek bookings accepted.

69 Festing Road, Southsea, Portsmouth, Hampshire PO4 0NQ
Tel: (01705) 735915/750497
Fax: (01705) 756497

PORTSMOUTH & SOUTHSEA – ENGLAND

Bembell Court *Listed*
69 Festing Road, Southsea, Portsmouth PO4 0NQ
☎ 01705-735915 Fax 01705-756497

Friendly family run hotel in prime holiday area. Ideally situated for ferries. An excellent selection of shops, pubs and restaurants nearby. Single night bookings accepted.

14 bedrs, 10 ensuite, 3 🛏 **TCF TV P** 10 **SB** £24-£32 **DB** £42-£46 **HB** £199-£225 **D** £9.95 **CC** MC Visa Amex DC
See advert on previous page

Birchwood *Listed*
44 Waverley Road, Portsmouth PO5 2PP
☎ 01705-811337
E Mail seabeds@aol.com
6 bedrs, 3 ensuite, 1 🛏
SB £15-£18 **DB** £30-£36 **HB** £123.30-£154.35 **D** £6.50 **CC** MC Visa Amex DC

Collingham *Listed*
89 St Ronans Road, Portsmouth PO4 0PR
☎ 01705-821549
Closed 25 Dec
6 bedrs, 2 🛏 **TCF TV** 🐾 **SB** £16-£17 **DB** £30-£32

Dolphins *Listed*
10-11 Western Parade, Portsmouth PO5 3JF
☎ 01705-823823 Fax 01705-820833

Comfortable hotel overlooking the sea and Southsea Common.

33 bedrs, 20 ensuite, 2 🛁, 5 🛏 **TCF TV** 🐾 No children under 1 **SB** £20-£33 **DB** £36-£48 **HB** £196-£235 **D** £12 **CC** MC Visa Amex DC

SOLENT HOTEL
'Hospitality with a smile'

**14-17 South Parade
Southsea,
Hampshire
PO5 2JB**

**Tel: 01705-875566
Fax: 01705-872023**

Refurbished 4 crown sea front hotel with magnificent views of the Solent and Isle of Wight.
Close to all tourist attractions, naval heritage. Lift to all floors, restaurant and public areas. 50 en-suite rooms with coffee/tea facilities, TV and telephone. Disabled guests catered for.

Gainsborough House *Listed*
9 Malvern Road, Portsmouth PO5 2LZ
☎ 01705-822604
7 bedrs, 2 🛏 **TCF TV** No children under 3 **SB** £15-£16 **DB** £30-£31

Salisbury *Listed*
57-59 Festing Road, Southsea PO4 0NQ
☎ 01705-823606 Fax 01705-820955
17 bedrs, 12 ensuite, 6 🛁, 2 🛏 **TCF TV P** 16 **SB** £20-£30 **DB** £38-£48 **HB** £190-£250 **D** £10 **CC** MC Visa

Solent *Awaiting Inspection*
14-17 South Parade, Southsea PO5 2JB
☎ 01705-875566 Fax 01705-872023
50 bedrs, all ensuite, **TCF TV** 🔲 **P** 4 **SB** £37.50-£45 **DB** £47.50-£65 **HB** £225-£275 **D** £12.75 **CC** MC Visa Amex DC JCB 🈯 ♿

PRESTON Lancashire   10B4

★★ Claremont
516 Blackpool Road, Ashton, Preston PR2 1HY
☎ 01772-729738 Fax 01772-726274
14 bedrs, 13 ensuite, 1 🛏 **TCF TV P** 25 **SB** £37.50 **DB** £51 **D** £11.95 **CC** MC Visa Amex DC

★★ Dean Court
Brownedge Lane, Bamber Bridge, Preston PR5 6TB
☎ 01772-35114 Fax 01772-628703
9 bedrs, all ensuite, 1 🛏 **TCF TV P** 35 No children under 10 **CC** MC Visa

Brook House *Highly Acclaimed*
662 Preston Road, Clayton-le-Woods, PR6 7EH
☎ 01772-36403 Fax 01772-36403
E Mail ghhotel@provider.co.uk
Closed Christmas
20 bedrs, all ensuite, 1 ⇌ TCF TV P 28 SB £44 DB £48
D £16.80 CC MC Visa Amex DC JCB

Tulketh *Highly Acclaimed*
209 Tulketh Road, Ashton, Preston PR2 1ES
☎ 01772-728096 Fax 01772-723743
Closed 23 Dec-2 Jan
12 bedrs, all ensuite, 1 ⇌ TCF TV P 12 SB £35 DB £43
D £8 CC MC Visa Amex DC JCB

PRINCES RISBOROUGH Buckinghamshire 4C2

★★ Rose & Crown
Restaurant merit award
Wycombe Road, Saunderton, Princes Risborough HP27 9NP
☎ 01844-345299 Fax 01844-343140
Closed Christmas
17 bedrs, 14 ensuite, 1 ⇌ P 40 SB £62.95 DB £74.25 CC MC Visa Amex DC

George & Dragon *Listed*
74 High Street, Princes Risborough HP17 0AX
☎ 01844-343087 Fax 01844-343087

16th century coaching inn situated in the historic town of Princes Risborough. Once a haunt of The Black Prince, we have an attractive oak-panelled candlelit restaurant. Log fires in the winter and a selection of traditional ales.

8 bedrs, 1 ensuite, 2 ⇌ TV P 20 CC MC Visa ♿

PULBOROUGH West Sussex 4C4

★★ Arun Cosmopolitan
87 Lower Street, Le Petit Cochon Restaurant Francais, Pulborough RH20 2BP
☎ 01798-872162 Fax 01798-872935
6 bedrs, all ensuite, ⇌ P 15 CC MC Visa Amex DC

Don't forget to mention the guide
When booking direct, please remember to tell the hotel that you chose it from RAC Bed & Breakfast 1998.

★★ Chequers
Hospitality, Comfort merit awards
Church Place, Pulborough RH20 1AD
☎ 01798-872486 Fax 01798-872715
11 bedrs, 10 ensuite, 1 ⇌ TCF TV ⇌ P 16 SB £49.50-£59.50 DB £79-£89 HB £309-£344 D £17.95 CC MC Visa Amex DC

White Horse Inn
Sutton, Nr Pulborough RH20 1PS
☎ 01798-869221 Fax 01798-869291

Charming Georgian inn situated in a picture postcard village at the foot of the South Downs. Elegantly furnished bedrooms with private bathrooms.

6 bedrs, all ensuite, TCF TV P 10 SB £48 DB £58-£68 HB £206-£236 D £17 CC MC Visa Amex DC

RADSTOCK Somerset 3E7

Rookery
Wells Road, Radstock, Bath BA3 3RS
☎ 01761-432626 Fax 01761-432626

Set in its own grounds, the Rookery is a homely, family run guest house offering every comfort. Licensed restaurant, ensuite rooms. Situated eight miles from Bath, Wells and the Mendips.

10 bedrs, all ensuite, 1 ⇌ TCF TV ⇌ P 25 SB £30-£40 DB £45-£60 D £6.95 CC MC Visa Amex DC ♿

RAMSGATE Kent 5F3

★★ Savoy
43 Grange Road, Ramsgate CT11 9NA
☎ 01843-592637 Fax 01843-851540
28 bedrs, all ensuite, TCF TV ⇌ P 20 SB £25 DB £40 HB £175 D £12.95 CC MC Visa Amex DC

Morton's Fork
RESTAURANT & HOTEL

A charming 17th century restaurant and hotel, situated in a quiet, historical village, only 5 miles from Ramsgate. Charming ambience with a menu that offers good regional and imaginative dishes. The guest rooms have been attractively refurbished, retaining character yet providing modern conveniences, with additional rooms in 'Durlock Lodge', the nearby annexe.

STATION ROAD, MINSTER, THANET, KENT CT12 4BZ
Tel: (01843) 823000
Fax: (01843) 821224

Mill House Hotel

Charming listed Regency executive hotel, well appointed with beautiful gardens by the River Loddon. Situated south of Reading, three minutes from junction 11 of the M4.

Old Basingstoke Road, Swallowfield, Reading RG7 1PY
Tel: 01734 883124 Fax: 01734 885550

Morton's Fork *Acclaimed*
Station Road, Minster, Ramsgate CT12 4BZ
☎ 01843-823000 Fax 01843-821224
6 bedrs, all ensuite, TCF TV P 7 SB £37-£41 DB £42-£59 HB £217 D £13 CC MC Visa Amex DC

Goodwin View *Listed*
19 Wellington Crescent, Ramsgate CT11 8JD
☎ 01843-591419

Grade II Listed building with uninterrupted views to France, close to town centre and ferry terminal. Ideal base for touring Kent and the South East. A warm and friendly run hotel.

13 bedrs, 4 ensuite, 3 ➡ TCF TV SB £20-£21 DB £32-£35 D £10 CC MC Visa Amex DC JCB

RANGEWORTHY Gloucestershire   3E1

★★ **Rangeworthy Court**
Hospitality merit award
Church Lane, Rangeworthy BS17 5ND
☎ 01454-228347 Fax 01454-228945
14 bedrs, all ensuite, TCF TV ✻ P 30 SB £53-£63 DB £68-£82 D £18 CC MC Visa Amex DC 🛏

RAVENGLASS Cumbria   10A2

Muncaster *Listed*
Muncaster, Ravenglass CA18 1RD
☎ 01229-717693 Fax 01229-717693
Closed Christmas

A welcoming, comfortable guest house, ideally situated for touring, exploring and walking in the Western Lakes, with castle, gardens, miniature railway, coast, lakes and hills nearby.

8 bedrs, 2 ensuite, 2 ➡ TCF ✻ P 20 SB £19-£21 DB £36-£40

RAVENSTONEDALE Cumbria　　　10B2

★★ Black Swan
Hospitality, Comfort merit awards
Kirkby Stephen, Ravenstonedale CA17 4NG
📞 01539-623204 Fax 01539-623604
17 bedrs, all ensuite, 1 🐕 TCF TV 🍴 P 40 SB £50 DB £66-£84 HB £352-£432 D £23 CC MC Visa Amex DC JCB

READING Berkshire　　　4B2

★★ Mill House
Old Basingstoke Road, Swallowfield, Reading RG7 1PY
📞 01734-883124 Fax 01734-885550
10 bedrs, all ensuite, TCF TV 🍴 P 60 SB £56-£61 DB £66-£85 HB £280-£455 D £15 CC MC Visa Amex

★★ Rainbow Corner
132 Caversham Road, Reading RG1 8AY
📞 01189-588140 Fax 01189-586500
22 bedrs, all ensuite, TCF TV 🍴 P 21 SB £38-£65 DB £46-£85 HB £378-£420 D £10 CC MC Visa Amex DC

Abbey House *Acclaimed*
118 Connaught Road, Reading RG30 2UF
📞 0118-959 0549 Fax 0118-956 9299
Closed Christmas
20 bedrs, 16 ensuite, 1 🐾, 2 🐕 TCF TV P 14 SB £47.50 DB £63 CC MC Visa Amex DC

REDCAR Cleveland　　　11D2

★★ Hotel Royal York
27 Coatham Road, Redcar TS10 1RP
📞 01642-486221 Fax 01642-486221
50 bedrs, all ensuite, TCF TV 📺 P 300 SB £27.50-£32.50 DB £45-£55 HB £212.50 D £7.75 CC MC Visa Amex DC

REDDITCH Worcestershire　　　7F3

Campanile Redditch *Lodge*
Far Moor Lane, Winyates Green, Redditch B98 0SD
📞 01527-510710 Fax 01527-517269
50 bedrs, all ensuite, TCF TV 🍴 P 50 SB £41 DB £45.50 D £10.55 CC MC Visa Amex DC

Ardendane Manor
Henley Road, Outhill, Studley B80 7DT
📞 01527-852808
Closed 24 Dec-2 Jan

Stay on business or pleasure in luxurious accommodation. Traditional English breakfast. 25 peaceful acres with commanding views over gardens and orchards to distant hills. Swimming pool available 1999.

2 bedrs, all ensuite, TCF TV P 10 No children SB £40 DB £50 D £25

REDHILL Surrey　　　5D3

Ashleigh House *Acclaimed*
39 Redstone Hill, Redhill RH1 4BG
📞 01737-764763 Fax 01737-780308
8 bedrs, 6 ensuite, 1 🐕 TCF TV P 8 SB £28-£45 DB £45-£55 CC MC Visa

REDRUTH Cornwall　　　2A4

★★ Aviary Court
Hospitality merit award
Mary's Well, Illogan, Redruth TR16 4QZ
📞 01209-842256 Fax 01209-843744
E Mail aviarycourt@connexions.co.uk.
6 bedrs, all ensuite, TCF TV P 30 No children under 3 SB £44 DB £60 HB £258 D £13 CC MC Visa Amex

Lyndhurst *Listed*
80 Agar Road, Redruth TR15 3NB
📞 01209-215146
8 bedrs, 4 ensuite, TCF TV P 8 SB £17 DB £34 D £8.50

Short Breaks
Many hotels provide special rates for weekend and mid-week breaks - sometimes these are quoted in the hotel's entry, otherwise ring direct for the latest offers.

Don't forget to mention the guide
When booking direct, please remember to tell the hotel that you chose it from RAC Bed & Breakfast 1998.

REETH North Yorkshire — 10C2

Arkleside *Highly Acclaimed*
Reeth DL11 6SG
☎ 01748-884200 Fax 01748-884200
Closed Jan

A cosy hotel, all rooms ensuite with spectacular views and friendly service. Renowned for its candle-lit restaurant featuring traditional dishes and an excellent wine list. Ideal for walking, touring or relaxing.

9 bedrs, 8 ensuite, 1 ⇌ TCF TV ✈ P 6 No children under 10 SB £60 D £16.50 CC MC Visa

---

Whashton Springs Farm

A warm welcome awaits you at our delightful Georgian farmhouse on this working family farm set in 400 acres of peaceful countryside just 3 miles from Richmond with its cobbled market square. A perfect centre for touring the dales. Local hospitality of a very high standard with coffee around the log fire on your return.

**RICHMOND,
NORTH YORKSHIRE DL11 7JS
Tel: (01748) 822884**

REIGATE Surrey — 5D3

Cranleigh *Highly Acclaimed*
41 West Street, Reigate RH2 9BL
☎ 01737-223417 Fax 01737-223734
Closed Christmas
9 bedrs, 7 ensuite, 2 ⇌ TCF TV P 6 SB £52-£60 DB £65-£80 D £15 CC MC Visa Amex DC JCB

RICHMOND North Yorkshire — 10C2

★★ Frenchgate
59/61 Frenchgate, Richmond DL10 7AE
☎ 01748-822087 Fax 01748-823596
13 bedrs, 7 ensuite, 3 ⌂, 4 ⇌ TCF TV ✈ P 5 No children under 7 SB £28-£37 DB £53-£60 D £12.50 CC MC Visa Amex DC JCB

★★ King's Head
Hospitality, Comfort merit awards
Market Place, Richmond DL10 4HS
☎ 01748-850220 Fax 01748-850635
30 bedrs, all ensuite, TCF TV ✈ P 25 SB £47-£55 DB £75-£85 HB £297-£369 D £16.95 CC MC Visa Amex DC JCB

Hartforth Hall *Highly Acclaimed*
Gilling West, Richmond DL10 5JU
☎ 01748-825715 Fax 01748-825781

A distinguished Grade II Listed Georgian mansion on earlier foundations, set in a beautiful valley near Richmond. Interior decor of great interest: original cornices and fireplaces.

15 bedrs, all ensuite, 1 ⇌ TCF TV ✈ P 100 SB £30-£45 DB £60-£90 D £10 CC MC Visa Amex ♿

Whashton Springs Farm
Richmond DL11 7JS
☎ 01748-822884 Fax 01748-822884
9 bedrs, all ensuite, TCF TV No children under 5 SB £27 DB £42

Don't forget to mention the guide
When booking direct, please remember to tell the hotel that you chose it from
RAC Bed & Breakfast 1998.

RINGWOOD Hampshire 4A4

★★ Struan Country Inn
Horton Road, Ashley Heath, Ringwood BH24 2EG
☎ 01425-473553 Fax 01425-480529
10 bedrs, all ensuite, TCF TV ⚹ P 72 SB £40-£50 DB £50-£70 HB £245-£280 D £13 CC MC Visa Amex DC ♿

Moortown Lodge *Highly Acclaimed*
244 Christchurch Road, Ringwood BH24 3AS
☎ 01425-471404 Fax 01425-476052
Closed 24 Dec-15 Jan
6 bedrs, 5 ensuite, 1 ⚹ TCF TV P 8 SB £32-£45 DB £50-£80 HB £234-£294 D £17 CC MC Visa Amex

RIPON North Yorkshire 11D3

★★ Unicorn
Market Place, Ripon HG4 1BP
☎ 01765-602202 Fax 01765-690734
Closed Christmas
33 bedrs, all ensuite, TCF TV ⚹ P 19 SB £37 DB £62 HB £222-£258 D £14 CC MC Visa Amex DC JCB

St George's Court
Old Home Farm, High Grantley, Ripon HG4 3EU
☎ 01765-620618

Enjoy the friendly welcome and warm hospitality of St George's Court. You will find us in the beautiful Yorkshire Dales near Fountains Abbey, in twenty acres of secluded farmland including a half acre lake. A sanctury for nature lovers, and ramblers.

5 bedrs, all ensuite, TCF TV ⚹ P 12 SB £23-£30 DB £38-£40 D £12.50 CC MC Visa

ROCHESTER Kent 5F2

★★ Royal Victoria & Bull
16-18 High Street, Rochester ME1 1PX
☎ 01634-846266 Fax 01634-832312
28 bedrs, 21 ensuite, 1 ⚹, 5 ⚹ TCF TV ⚹ P 25 SB £40-£50 DB £65 D £10 CC MC Visa Amex DC

ROCK Cornwall 2B3

★★ Mariners
Slipway, Rock, Nr Wadebridge PL27 6LD
☎ 01208-862312 Fax 01208-863827
Closed Nov-Mar

Situated at the waters edge and enjoying panoramic views over the Camel Estuary to Padstow.

18 bedrs, all ensuite, TCF TV ⚹ P 22 SB £25-£40 DB £40-£70 D £13 CC MC Visa Amex JCB

★★ Roskarnon House
Rock PL27 6LD
☎ 01208-862785
12 bedrs, 10 ensuite, 1 ⚹ TCF TV ⚹ P 14 DB £40 HB £200 D £14 CC Amex

ROMALDKIRK Co. Durham 10C2

★★ Rose & Crown
Hospitality, Comfort, Restaurant merit awards
Barnard Castle, Romaldkirk DL12 9EB
☎ 01833-650213 Fax 01833-650828
Closed 25-26 Dec
12 bedrs, all ensuite, TCF TV ⚹ P 40 SB £58 DB £80 HB £415 D £23 CC MC Visa ♿

ROMSEY Hampshire 4B3

Highfield House
Newtown Road, Awbridge, Romsey SO51 0GG
☎ 01794-340727 Fax 01794-341450

Set in 1½ acres of lovely gardens. Very peaceful location. Old style furnishings and every modern comfort. Guest lounge with log fire. Delicious home cooked food.

3 bedrs, all ensuite, TCF TV P 10 No children under 14

ROSS-ON-WYE Herefordshire 7E4

★★ Bridge House
Hospitality, Restaurant merit awards
Wilton, Ross-on-Wye HR9 6AA
☎ 01989-562655 Fax 01989-567652

Quiet riverside hotel, yet only ten minutes easy walk along the river into Ross-on-Wye. Hospitality, service and quality restaurant meals are our speciality.

9 bedrs, 8 ensuite, 1 ⇌ TCF TV ★ P 15 SB £33.50-£34 DB £54 HB £230 D £15 CC MC Visa

★★ Castle Lodge
Wilton, Ross-on-Wye HR9 6AD
☎ 01989-562234 Fax 01989-768322
10 bedrs, all ensuite, ★ P 5 No children under 5

★★ Chasedale
Walford Road, Ross-on-Wye HR9 5PQ
☎ 01989-562423 Fax 01989-567900
10 bedrs, all ensuite, 1 ⇌ TCF TV ★ P 14 SB £50 DB £59-£62 HB £255-£262 D £13 CC MC Visa DC JCB

★★ Orles Barn
Wilton, Ross-on-Wye HR9 6AE
☎ 01989-562155 Fax 01989-768470
Closed Nov
9 bedrs, all ensuite, TCF TV ★ P 20 SB £30-£45 DB £50-£70 HB £215-£275 D £15 CC MC Visa Amex DC JCB

★★ Pencraig Court
Hospitality merit award
Pencraig, Ross-on-Wye HR9 6HR
☎ 01989-770306 Fax 01989-770040
11 bedrs, all ensuite, TCF TV ★ P 25 SB £45-£50 DB £62.50-£67.50 HB £280-£315 D £20.50 CC MC Visa

★ Rosswyn
High Street, Ross-on-Wye HR9 5BZ
☎ 01989-562733 Fax 01989-562733
8 bedrs, all ensuite, 1 ⇌ TCF TV ★ P 6 SB £35 DB £70 D £15 CC MC Visa Amex

Arches Hotel *Acclaimed*
Walford Road, Ross-on-Wye HR9 5PT
☎ 01989-563348

A Georgian style family run hotel, set in acres of lawns, with all the lovely rooms overlooking the garden. Ideally situated, ten minutes walk from the town centre.

7 bedrs, 4 ensuite, 2 ⇌ TCF TV ✉ P 10 SB £19 DB £44 HB £227 D £7 ♿

Sunnymount *Acclaimed*
Ryefield Road, Ross-on-Wye HR9 5LU
☎ 01989-563880
Closed 21-30 Dec
9 bedrs, 7 ensuite, 1 ⇌ TCF P 7 SB £27-£30 DB £47-£51 HB £215-£230 D £15 CC MC Visa Amex

Brookfield House *Listed*
Overross, Ross-on-Wye HR9 7AT
☎ 01989-562188
8 bedrs, 3 ensuite, 3 ⇌ TCF TV ★ P 15 SB £17-£20 DB £34-£40 CC MC Visa Amex

Radcliffe Guest House *Listed*
Wye Street, Ross-on-Wye HR9 7BS
☎ 01989-563895
6 bedrs, all ensuite, TCF TV SB £20-£22 DB £38-£40 HB £175-£189 D £9

Vaga House *Listed*
Wye Street, Ross-on-Wye HR9 7BS
☎ 01989-563024
Closed Christmas
7 bedrs, 2 ⇌ TCF TV ★ P 6 SB £19-£22 DB £36 HB £186 D £10

ROTHERHAM South Yorkshire 11D4

★★ Brecon
Moorgate Road, Rotherham S60 2AY
☎ 01709-828811 Fax 01709-513030
27 bedrs, 22 ensuite, 5 🛁, 1 ⇌ ★ P 40 SB £39 DB £45 D £11 CC MC Visa Amex DC

Don't forget to mention the guide
When booking direct, please remember to tell the hotel that you chose it from
RAC Bed & Breakfast 1998.

RAC Hotel Reservations Service
0870 603 9109
(Calls charged at national call rate)

★★ Brentwood
Moorgate Road, Rotherham S60 2TY
☎ 01709-382772 Fax 01709-820289
43 bedrs, all ensuite, **P** 60
SB £35-£55 **DB** £40-£68 **HB** £-£312 **CC** MC Visa Amex DC ♿

Stonecroft Residential Hotel *Acclaimed*
Main Street, Bramley, Rotherham S66 2SF
☎ 01709-540922 Fax 01709-540922
8 bedrs, all ensuite, 1 ⇌ TCF TV ⁂ **P** 12 **SB** £31-£36
DB £43-£48 **CC** MC Visa

Regis *Listed*
1 Hall Road, Rotherham S60 2BP
☎ 01709-376666 Fax 01709-513030

Large detached property with private car park, close to town centre. You will be sure of a warm welcome and hearty breakfast.

10 bedrs, 4 ensuite, 2 ⇌ TCF TV ⁂ **P** 6 **SB** £18 **DB** £25
D £5.25 **CC** MC Visa Amex DC

Campanile Rotherham *Lodge*
Lowton Way, off Denby Way, Hellaby Industrial Estate, Rotherham S66 8RY
☎ 01709-700255 Fax 01709-545169
50 bedrs, all ensuite, TCF TV ⁂ **P** 50 **SB** £41 **DB** £45.50
D £10.55 **CC** MC Visa Amex DC ♿

ROTTINGDEAN East Sussex   5D4

Braemar Guest House *Listed*
Steyning Road, Rottingdean BN2 7GA
☎ 01273-304263
15 bedrs, 2 ⁑, 3 ⇌ ⁂ **SB** £15-£18 **DB** £30-£35

RUNCORN Cheshire   7D1

Campanile Runcorn *Lodge*
Lowlands Road, Runcorn WA7 5TP
☎ 01928-581771 Fax 01928-581730
53 bedrs, all ensuite, TCF TV ⁂ **P** 53 **SB** £41 **DB** £45.50
D £10.55 **CC** MC Visa Amex DC ♿

RUSHDEN Northamptonshire   8C4

★★ Rilton
High Street, Rushden NN10 9BT
☎ 01933-312189 Fax 01933-358593
22 bedrs, all ensuite, 1 ⇌ TCF TV ⁂ **P** 60 **SB** £32.50-£35
DB £37.50-£45 **HB** £245-£287 **D** £10 **CC** MC Visa Amex DC

RUSTINGTON West Sussex   4C4

Kenmore *Highly Acclaimed*
Claigmar Road, Rustington BN16 2NL
☎ 01903-784634 Fax 01903-784634
7 bedrs, all ensuite, 1 ⇌ TCF TV ⁂ **P** 7 **SB** £22.50-£25
DB £45-£50 **CC** MC Visa Amex

RYDAL Cumbria   10B2

★★ Glen Rothay
Rydal LA22 9LR
☎ 015394-32524 Fax 015394-31079
11 bedrs, all ensuite, 1 ⇌ TCF TV ⁂ **P** 40 **SB** £27.50-£32.50 **DB** £40-£45 **D** £13.95 **CC** MC Visa Amex DC JCB 📧

★ Rydal Lodge
Hospitality, Restaurant merit awards
Rydal LA22 9LR
☎ 01539-433208
Closed Jan
8 bedrs, 2 ensuite, 3 ⇌ ⁂ **P** 12 **CC** MC Visa

RYE East Sussex   5E3

JEAKE'S HOUSE

In the heart of the Sussex countryside lies the ancient town of Rye. Its medieval houses and cobbled streets make the perfect base for touring Sussex and Kent. Jeakes House originally built in 1689 has a colourful history of its own having been a wool store and later a baptist school. Today it offers a taste of history together with every modern comfort.
Each bedroom has been individually restored to create its own special atmosphere combining traditional elegance and luxury with all modern amenities.

JEAKE'S HOUSE, MERMAID STREET, RYE TN31 7ET
Tel: 01797 222828 Fax: 01797 222623

★ Hope Anchor
Watchbell Street, Rye TN31 7HA
☎ 01797-222216 Fax 01797-223796

Dating from the 17th century in cobbled town centre. Attentive service, panoramic views, excellent food, log fire and car parking. Perfect base for exploring Kent and Sussex.

12 bedrs, 9 ensuite, 3 ⇸ TCF TV No children under 7
SB £25-£35 DB £50-£70 CC MC Visa

Jeakes House *Highly Acclaimed*
Mermaid Street, Rye TN31 7ET
☎ 01797-222828 Fax 01797-222623
E Mail jeakeshouse@btinternet.com

Stylishly restored bedrooms combine traditional elegance with modern comfort. A roaring fire greets you on cold mornings in the galleried breakfast room, while soft chamber music and attentive service provide the perfect start to the day.

12 bedrs, 10 ensuite, 2 ⇸ TCF TV ⼁ SB £24.50 DB £63
HB £220.50 CC MC Visa
See advert on previous page

Old Vicarage *Highly Acclaimed*
15 East Street, Rye TN31 7JY
☎ 01797-225131 Fax 01797-225131
4 bedrs, all ensuite, TCF TV ⼁ DB £64-£88 HB £294-£358
D £14 CC MC Visa Amex JCB

RAC Hotel Reservations Service
0870 603 9109
(Calls charged at national call rate)

White Vine House *Highly Acclaimed*
High Street, Rye TN31 7JF
☎ 01797-224748 Fax 01797-223599

Tudor town house in the heart of ancient Rye with comfortable bedrooms, oak beams, stone fireplaces, books and paintings. Excellent breakfasts. Ideal for antique hunting, castles and gardens. A non-smoking haven for grown ups.

6 bedrs, all ensuite, TCF TV ⊠ ⼁ No children under 12
SB £45 DB £86 CC MC Visa Amex DC JCB

Old Borough Arms *Listed*
The Strand, Rye TN31 7DB
☎ 01797-222128 Fax 01797-222128
9 bedrs, all ensuite, TV ⼁ P 2 No children under 8
SB £25-£40 DB £45-£70 CC MC Visa

Aviemore
28 Fishmarket Road, Rye TN31 7LP
☎ 01797-223052 Fax 01797-223052
Closed Christmas

Overlooking the park and the River Rother, and just two minutes walk from the centre of a beautiful medieval town. Genuinely warm welcome, excellent breakfast, Kenyan coffee.

8 bedrs, 4 ensuite, 2 ⇸ TCF TV SB £18-£21 DB £32-£42
HB £164-£182 D £8 CC MC Visa Amex

SAFFRON WALDEN Essex   5D1

★★ Saffron
Comfort merit award
10 High Street, Saffron Walden CB10 1AY
☎ 01799-522676 Fax 01799-513979
17 bedrs, all ensuite, 1 ⇸ TV ⼁ P 12 SB £45-£60
DB £65-£85 D £14.95 CC MC Visa Amex DC

SALISBURY – ENGLAND

Cross Keys *Listed*
32 High Street, Saffron Walden CB10 1AX
☎ 01799-522207 Fax 01799-526550
5 bedrs, 3 ensuite, 1 ⇌ TCF TV ⋔ P 10 SB £30 DB £39
D £10 CC MC Visa Amex

Wigmores Farm
Debden Green, Saffron Walden CB11 3ST
☎ 01371-830050

A 16th century thatched farmhouse in open countryside and two acres of gardens. TV, radio, tea/coffee facilities in all rooms. Licensed, evening meals by prior arrangement.

3 bedrs, 2 ⇌ TCF TV P 30

SALCOMBE Devon   2C4

★★ Grafton Towers
Moult Road, Salcombe TQ8 8LG
☎ 01548-842882
Closed Nov-Feb
12 bedrs, all ensuite, TCF TV ⋔ P 14 No children under 12 SB £33.50-£36 DB £65-£71 D £16.95 CC MC Visa JCB

★★ Heron House
Thurlestone Sands, Salcombe TQ7 3JY
☎ 01548-560180 Fax 01548-560180
17 bedrs, all ensuite, TCF TV ⋔ P 50 SB £35-£55 DB £70-£130 HB £210-£462 D £20.95 CC MC Visa JCB

★ Sunny Cliff
Cliff Road, Salcombe TQ8 8JX
☎ 01548-842207
18 bedrs, 15 ensuite, 2 ⇌ TV ⋔ P 17 SB £33-£42
DB £66-£84 HB £300-£360 D £14.50 CC MC Visa Amex

Lyndhurst *Highly Acclaimed*
Bonaventure Road, Salcombe TQ8 8BG
☎ 01548-842481 Fax 01548-842481
Closed Dec-Jan
8 bedrs, all ensuite, TCF TV ⋔ P 4 SB £28-£30 DB £56-£60 HB £252-£266 D £15 CC MC Visa JCB

Devon Tor *Acclaimed*
Devon Road, Salcombe TQ8 8HJ
☎ 01548-843106
6 bedrs, 5 ensuite, 1 ⋔, 1 ⇌ TCF TV ⋔ P 5 No children under 8 DB £50-£56 HB £232-£252

Torre View *Acclaimed*
Devon Road, Salcombe TQ8 8HJ
☎ 01548-842633 Fax 01548-842633
Closed Nov-Feb
8 bedrs, 5 ensuite, 3 ⇌ TCF TV ⋔ P 5 No children under 4 SB £25-£28.50 DB £47-£53.50 HB £222-£250
D £12.50 CC MC Visa

Old Porch House *Listed*
Shadycombe Road, Salcombe TQ8 8DJ
☎ 01548-842157 Fax 01548-843750
Closed Christmas
8 bedrs, 6 ensuite, 1 ⇌ ⋔ P 9 CC MC Visa Amex

Penn Torr *Listed*
Herbert Road, Salcombe TQ8 8HN
☎ 01548-842234
Closed Nov-Mar
7 bedrs, 5 ensuite, 1 ⋔, P 9 No children under 4
DB £19-£24

Terrapins *Listed*
Buckley Street, Salcombe TQ8 8DD
☎ 01548-842861 Fax 01548-842265
Closed Nov-Mar
7 bedrs, 6 ensuite, 1 ⇌ ⋔

SALFORD Gtr Manchester   10C4

★★ Hazeldean
467 Bury New Road, Kersall, Salford M7 3NE
☎ 0161-792 6667 Fax 0161-792 6668
21 bedrs, 17 ensuite, 2 ⇌ TCF TV P 21 SB £40 DB £50
D £12 CC MC Visa Amex DC ♿

★ Beaucliffe
254 Eccles Old Road, Salford M6 8ES
☎ 0161-789 5092 Fax 0161-787 7739
21 bedrs, 17 ensuite, 1 ⇌ ⋔ P 25 CC MC Visa ♿

SALISBURY Wiltshire   3F2

Salisbury Cathedral

Superb example of Early English architecture, with the tallest spire in England. An original Magna Carta. Open daily. Guided tours of Cathedral, Tower and West Front. Daily services.

Telephone: (01722) 328726

THE OLD MILL
HOTEL & RESTAURANT
★★ SALISBURY

Beautifully situated on the River Nadder, this historic mill dates back to 1135. Water continues to cascade through the restaurant, adding a unique dimension to our intimate dining room, which specialises in regional English cooking and fresh seafood.
There is a cosy beamed freehouse serving local real ales and inexpensive bar meals.
We have 10 beautiful en-suite bedrooms, all with beautiful river views.

Town Path, Harnham, Salisbury
Tel: 01722 327517
Fax: 01722 333367

★★ King's Arms
9-11 St. Johns Street, Salisbury SP1 2SB
📞 01722-327629 Fax 01722-414246
15 bedrs, all ensuite, 🐕 P 20 CC MC Visa Amex DC

★★ Old Mill
Town Path, West Harnham, Salisbury SP2 8EU
📞 01722-327517 Fax 01722-333367
10 bedrs, all ensuite, TCF TV P 15 SB £40-£45 DB £65-£70 CC MC Visa Amex

★★ Trafalgar
33 Milford Street, Salisbury SP1 2AP
📞 01722-338686 Fax 01722-414496
18 bedrs, all ensuite, TCF TV 🐕 SB £50 DB £65 D £7 CC MC Visa Amex DC JCB

Byways House *Highly Acclaimed*
31 Fowler's Road, Salisbury SP1 2QP
📞 01722-328364 Fax 01722-322146
Closed Christmas-New Year

Short Breaks

Many hotels provide special rates for weekend and mid-week breaks – sometimes these are quoted in the hotel's entry, otherwise ring direct for the latest offers.

Attractive family run Victorian guest house situated close to cathedral in quiet area of city centre. Arriving on A30(A343), take A36 Southampton sign, turn left signposted "city centre service traffic only", immediately right, left at traffic lights.

23 bedrs, 19 ensuite, 1 🛏 TCF TV 🐕 P 15 SB £24-£30.50 DB £39-£51.50 CC MC Visa ♿

Cricket Field Cottage *Acclaimed*
Wilton Road, Salisbury SP2 7HS
📞 01722-322595 Fax 01722-322595
14 bedrs, all ensuite, TCF TV 🚭 P 14 No children under 10 SB £27.50 DB £42.50 ♿

Glen Lyn *Acclaimed*
6 Bellamy Lane, Milford Hill, Salisbury SP1 2SP
📞 01722-327880 Fax 01722-327880
Closed Christmas
6 bedrs, 4 ensuite, 1 🛏 TCF TV 🚭 🐕 P 7 No children under 12 DB £42 HB £210-£230 D £10

Rokeby *Acclaimed*
3 Wain-a-Long Road, Salisbury SP1 1LJ
📞 01722-329800 Fax 01722-329800
7 bedrs, all ensuite, TCF TV P 7 SB £30 DB £40 D £12.50 ⊕

Warren *Acclaimed*
15 High Street, Downton, Salisbury SP5 3PG
📞 01725-510263
Closed 20 Dec-6 Jan

A Grade II Listed village house with parts dating back to Elizabethan times, set in a large walled garden.

6 bedrs, 2 ensuite, 2 🛏 TCF 🐕 P 8 No children under 5 SB £30-£32 DB £44

Hayburn Wyke *Listed*
72 Castle Road, Salisbury SP1 3RL
☎ 01722-412627 Fax 01722-412627

A warm welcome awaits you at this attractive Victorian house. Situated by Victoria Park, a ten minute walk by the River Avon to the city centre and cathedral.

6 bedrs, 2 ensuite, 2 ⇨ TCF TV P 6 SB £24-£37 DB £36-£42 CC MC Visa JCB

Holmhurst *Listed*
Downton Road, Salisbury SP2 8AR
☎ 01722-410407 Fax 01722-323164
6 bedrs, 4 ensuite, 1 ⇨ TCF TV P 8 SB £20-£25 DB £35-£40 CC MC Visa DC JCB

Leena's *Listed*
50 Castle Road, Salisbury SP1 3RL
☎ 01722-335419 Fax 01722-335419
6 bedrs, 5 ensuite, 1 ⇨ TCF TV P 7 SB £19-£22 DB £35-£41

Richburn *Listed*
23-25 Estcourt Road, Salisbury SP1 3AP
☎ 01722-325189
Closed Christmas
10 bedrs, 2 ensuite, 2 ⇨ TCF ⊠ P 10 SB £18-£18.50 DB £32-£42

Newton Farmhouse
Southampton Road (A36), Whiteparish, SP5 2QL
☎ 01794-884416

Family run historic listed 16th century farmhouse, formerly part of Trafalgar Estate. Beamed dining room with flagstone floor. Romantic rooms, three with genuine fourposters. Swimming pool, beautiful breakfasts, home baked bread and free range eggs.

8 bedrs, all ensuite, TCF TV ⊠ P 10 SB £25 DB £35-£45 D £15 ▣

SANDBACH Cheshire   7E1

Grove House *Highly Acclaimed*
Mill Lane, Wheelock, Sandbach CW11 4RD
☎ 01270-762582 Fax 01270-759465
9 bedrs, all ensuite, TCF TV ⇨ P 40 SB £43 DB £55 D £14
CC MC Visa Amex

Poplar Mount *Acclaimed*
2 Station Road, Elworth, Sandbach CW11 3JG
☎ 01270-761268 Fax 01270-761268
7 bedrs, 4 ensuite, 1 ⇨ TCF TV P 9
SB £19 DB £38 D £8 CC MC Visa JCB

SAWREY Cumbria   10B2

★★ Sawrey
Far Sawrey, Ambleside LA22 0LQ
☎ 015394-43425 Fax 015394-43425
Closed Christmas
20 bedrs, 18 ensuite, 1 ⇨ TCF TV ⇨ P 30 SB £24-£29
DB £48-£58 HB £210-£236 D £16 CC MC Visa JCB ♿

Garth Country House *Highly Acclaimed*
Hawkshead, Sawrey LA22 0JZ
☎ 01539-436373
Closed Dec-Jan
8 bedrs, 1 ⇨ TCF TV ⇨ P 12 No children under 5

Sawrey House *Highly Acclaimed*
Sawrey LA22 0LF
☎ 015394-36387 Fax 015394-36010
10 bedrs, all ensuite, TCF TV ⇨ P 20 SB £30-£45 DB £60-£80 HB £300-£360 D £19 CC MC Visa ▣ ♿

West Vale *Highly Acclaimed*
Far Sawrey, Ambleside LA22 0LQ
☎ 015394-42817
Closed Nov-Mar

Situated on the edge of the village and offering splendid views, this excellent family run accommodation provides a warm welcome in a relaxing atmosphere, with home cooking, a log fire and full central heating.

8 bedrs, all ensuite, TCF P 8 No children under 7
SB £23 DB £46 HB £224 D £11

High Green Gate *Acclaimed*
Sawrey, Ambleside LA22 0LF
☎ 01539-436296
5 bedrs, 3 ensuite, 1 ⇌ TCF ⊢ P 7 SB £24-£27 DB £42-£48 HB £190-£210 D £11

SAXMUNDHAM Suffolk　　　　　　　9F4

★ Bell
High Street, Saxmundham IP17 1AE
☎ 01728-602331 Fax 01728-833105
14 bedrs, 9 ensuite, 3 🐾, 2 ⇌ TCF TV ⊢ P 30 SB £25 DB £52 CC MC Visa Amex DC

SCARBOROUGH North Yorkshire　　　11E2

★★ Bradley Court
7-9 Filey Road, Scarborough YO11 2SE
☎ 01723-360476 Fax 01723-376661
40 bedrs, all ensuite, TCF TV ⊢ P 40 SB £35-£40 DB £70-£90 HB £200-£250 D £17.50 CC MC Visa Amex DC

★★ Brooklands
Esplanade Gardens, South Cliff, YO11 2AW
☎ 01723-376576 Fax 01723-376576

The Brooklands Hotel is situated on the South Cliff, less than one minute's walk on level ground to the Esplanade, Spa and Cliff tramway.

63 bedrs, 62 ensuite, 4 🐾, TCF TV ▣ SB £20-£30 DB £40-£60 HB £175-£297 D £9 CC MC Visa

★★ Central
1-3 The Crescent, Scarborough YO11 2PW
☎ 01723-365766
30 bedrs, all ensuite, 2 ⇌ TCF TV ⊢ ▣ P 15 CC MC Visa ♿

★★ Gridleys Crescent
Hospitality, Comfort, Restaurant merit awards
1-2 Belvoir Terrace, Scarborough YO11 2PP
☎ 01723-360929 Fax 01723-354126
20 bedrs, all ensuite, TCF TV ▣ No children under 6 SB £45 DB £75 D £16 CC MC Visa Amex

★★ Lynton
104 Columbus Ravine, Scarborough YO12 7QZ
☎ 01723-374240
8 bedrs, all ensuite, TCF TV P 8 No children under 3 SB £22-£23 DB £44-£46 D £10 CC MC Visa

★★ Red Lea
Prince Of Wales Terrace, South Cliff, Scarborough YO11 2AJ
☎ 01723-362431 Fax 01723-371230
67 bedrs, all ensuite, TCF TV ▣ SB £33-£34 DB £66-£68 HB £290-£295 D £12 CC MC Visa Amex

★★ Ryndle Court
47 Northstead Manor Drive, Scarborough YO12 6AF
☎ 01723-375188 Fax 01723-375188
Closed Nov-Jan excl Christmas

Comfortable hotel near the sea and leisure parks. All rooms ensuite, TV, radio and tea facilities. Residents bar, private parking, overnight stays welcome.

14 bedrs, all ensuite, TCF TV P 10 SB £27-£29 DB £54-£56 HB £190-£210 D £9 CC MC Visa JCB

★★ Southlands
15 West Street, Scarborough YO11 2QW
☎ 01723-318614 Fax 01723-376035
58 bedrs, all ensuite, TCF TV ⊢ ▣ P 30 SB £20-£30 DB £36-£56 HB £195-£252 D £13 CC MC Visa Amex DC

★ La Baia
24 Blenheim Terrace, Scarborough YO12 7HD
☎ 01723-370780
Closed Nov-Feb
11 bedrs, all ensuite, TCF TV SB £30 DB £44 HB £196 D £9 CC MC Visa JCB

★ Tudor House
164-166 North Marine Road, Scarborough YO12 7HZ
☎ 01723-361270
16 bedrs, 7 ensuite, 2 ⇌ TCF TV ⊢

Premier *Highly Acclaimed*
66 Esplanade, South Cliff, Scarborough YO11 2UZ
☎ 01723-501062
19 bedrs, all ensuite, TV ⊢ ▣ P 6 SB £32-£34 DB £54-£58 HB £250-£264 D £12 CC MC Visa

Anatolia *Acclaimed*
21 West Street, South Cliff, Scarborough YO11 2QR
☎ 01723-503205
9 bedrs, all ensuite, TCF TV ⌧ SB £20 DB £36-£40
HB £154-£168

Ash-Lea *Acclaimed*
119 Columbus Ravine, Scarborough YO12 7QU
☎ 01723-361874
8 bedrs, all ensuite, TCF TV SB £19 DB £38 HB £182 D £7
CC MC Visa DC

Ashcroft *Acclaimed*
102 Columbus Ravine, Scarborough YO12 7QZ
☎ 01723-375092
7 bedrs, 6 ensuite, 1 ⌘ TCF TV P 7 SB £17-£18 DB £34-£36 D £6 CC MC Visa

Mount House *Acclaimed*
33 Trinity Road, Scarborough YO11 2TD
☎ 01273-362967
Closed Nov-Feb
7 bedrs, all ensuite, 1 ⌘ TV P 4
CC MC Visa

Parade *Acclaimed*
29 Esplanade, Scarborough YO11 2AQ
☎ 01723-361285
Closed Dec-Mar
17 bedrs, all ensuite, 1 ⌘ TCF TV ⌘ No children under 2 SB £22-£26 DB £44-£52 HB £196-£210 D £9 CC MC Visa

Paragon *Acclaimed*
123 Queens Parade, Scarborough YO12 7HU
☎ 01723-372676 Fax 01723-372676
Closed Nov-Jan
15 bedrs, all ensuite, TCF TV ⌘ P 6 No children under 3 SB £22-£22.50 DB £44-£45 HB £188-£202 D £9.25 CC MC Visa

Parmella *Acclaimed*
17 West Street, South Cliff, Scarborough YO11 2QN
☎ 01723-361914
Closed Nov-Feb
15 bedrs, 12 ensuite, 2 ⌘ TCF TV ⌧

Phoenix *Acclaimed*
157 Columbus Ravine, Scarborough YO12 7QZ
☎ 01723-368319 Fax 01723-368319
Closed Dec-Feb
8 bedrs, 4 ensuite, 1 ⌘ TCF TV SB £13-£16 DB £26-£32
HB £133-£154 D £6 CC MC Visa ⌧

Pickwick Inn *Acclaimed*
Huntriss Row, Scarborough YO11 2ED
☎ 01723-375787 Fax 01723-374284
Closed Christmas
10 bedrs, all ensuite, ⌧ No children under 13 SB £23-£32 DB £35-£55 CC MC Visa Amex DC

Ramleh *Acclaimed*
135 Queen's Parade, Scarborough YO12 7HY
☎ 01723-365745 Fax 01723-365745

Conveniently situated for town and countryside, the Ramleh offers well equipped ensuite bedrooms with a relaxed homely atmosphere and a high standard of catering.

9 bedrs, 7 ensuite, 1 ⌘ TCF TV P 5 SB £18-£19 DB £36-£38 HB £161-£168 D £6 CC MC Visa Amex DC JCB

Boundary *Listed*
124-126 North Marine Road, Scarborough YO12 7HZ
☎ 01723-376737
12 bedrs, all ensuite, 1 ⌘ TCF TV SB £17-£19 DB £34-£38 HB £119-£133 D £6 CC MC Visa

Geldenhuis *Listed*
143-147 Queen's Parade, Scarborough YO12 7HU
☎ 01723-361677
Closed 1 Dec-31 Jan
28 bedrs, 16 ensuite, 6 ⌘ TCF TV P 25 SB £17-£21
DB £34-£42 HB £154-£182 D £5 CC MC Visa JCB

Glywin *Listed*
153 Columbus Ravine, Scarborough YO12 7QZ
☎ 01723-371311
7 bedrs, 2 ensuite, 3 ⌘ TCF TV SB £14-£15 DB £28-£30
HB £147-£154 D £7 CC MC Visa

Granby *Listed*
Queen Street, Scarborough YO11 1HL
☎ 01723-373031 Fax 01723-373031

Centrally positioned and convenient for parking, both bays, all amenities and town centre. Licensed, generous home cooking, friendly atmosphere, informal entertainment, child reductions. Freephone 0500 131229.

25 bedrs, 17 ensuite, 9 ⌘ TCF TV SB £17-£19 DB £34-£38
HB £158-£175 D £6 CC MC Visa

Sefton Listed
18 Prince Of Wales Terrace, South Cliff, Scarborough YO11 2AL
☎ 01723-372310
14 bedrs, 10 ensuite, 7 ⇌ ▣ No children under 12
SB £21-£22 **DB** £42-£44 **HB** £168-£175 **D** £6

Selbourne Listed
4 West Street, South Cliff, Scarborough YO11 2QL
☎ 01723-372822
Closed Christmas-New Year

Three crown family run hotel situated on the South Cliff close to all amenities. Reductions for senior citizens, children and weekly bookings. Telephone for a brochure.

13 bedrs, 9 ensuite, 2 ⇌ **TCF SB** £20 **DB** £47 **HB** £165-£173 **D** £5.50 **CC** MC Visa &

Tamarind Listed
155 Columbus Ravine, Scarborough
☎ 01723-370191

West Lodge Listed
38 West Street, Scarborough YO11 2QP
☎ 01723-500754
7 bedrs, 6 ensuite, 1 ⇌ **TCF TV** ⚹ **P** 7 **CC** MC Visa Amex DC

Wheatcroft Motel Lodge
156 Filey Road, Scarborough YO11 3AA
☎ 01723-374613
Closed Christmas
7 bedrs, all ensuite, **TCF TV P** 9 **SB** £17-£19 **DB** £34-£37

SCOTCH CORNER North Yorkshire   11D2

★★ Vintage
Scotch Corner DL10 6NP
☎ 01748-824424 Fax 01748-826272
Closed Christmas-New Year
8 bedrs, 5 ensuite, 1 ⇌ **TCF TV P** 50 **SB** £29.50-£42.50 **DB** £36.50-£55 **D** £15 **CC** MC Visa Amex DC

SEAHOUSES Northumberland   13F3

★★ Bamburgh Castle
Hospitality, Comfort merit awards
Seahouses NE68 7SQ
☎ 01665-720283 Fax 01665-720848
20 bedrs, all ensuite, **TCF TV** ⚹ **P** 25 **SB** £33-£39 **DB** £66-£74 **HB** £280-£315 **D** £19 ✠

★★ Beach House
Comfort merit award
Seafront, Seahouses NE68 7SR
☎ 01665-720337 Fax 01665-720921
Closed Nov-Mar
14 bedrs, all ensuite, 1 ⇌ **TCF TV** ⚹ **P** 26 **SB** £30-£37 **DB** £59-£74 **D** £19 **CC** MC Visa Amex JCB

★★ Olde Ship
Hospitality, Comfort merit awards
9 Main Street, Seahouses NE68 7RD
☎ 01665-720200 Fax 01665-721383
Closed Dec-Jan
16 bedrs, all ensuite, **TCF TV P** 14 No children under 10
SB £30-£37 **DB** £60-£73 **HB** £270-£320 **D** £13 **CC** MC Visa JCB

★★ St Aidans
Sea Front, Seahouses NE68 7SR
☎ 01665-720355 Fax 01665-830333
Closed mid Nov-mid Feb
9 bedrs, all ensuite, **TCF TV** ⚹ **P** 16 **DB** £50-£70 **D** £13
CC MC Visa Amex DC &

SEATON Devon   3E3

Mariners Acclaimed
The Esplanade, Seaton EX12 2NP
☎ 01297-20560
10 bedrs, all ensuite, **TCF TV** ⚹ **P** 10 **SB** £23-£28 **DB** £38-£42 **HB** £118-£132 **D** £10 **CC** MC Visa Amex

SEDGEFIELD Cleveland   11D1

★★ Crosshill
The Square, Sedgefield TS21 2AB
☎ 01740-620153 Fax 01740-621206
8 bedrs, all ensuite, **TCF TV** ⚹ **P** 9 **SB** £37-£40 **DB** £43-£48 **HB** £329-£361 **D** £12 **CC** MC Visa Amex JCB

SELBY North Yorkshire   11D3

Hazeldene Listed
34 Brook Street, Doncaster Road, Selby YO8 0AR
☎ 01757-704809 Fax 01757-709300
8 bedrs, 3 ensuite, 2 ⇌ **TCF TV** ▣ **P** 5 No children under 10 **SB** £18-£27 **DB** £34-£42

SENNEN Cornwall 2A4

★★ Old Success
Sennen Cove TR19 7DG
📞 01736-871232 Fax 01736-788354
12 bedrs, 10 ensuite, ⚹ P 15 CC MC Visa

Sunny Bank *Listed*
Seaview Hill, Sennen TR19 7AR
📞 01736-871278
Closed Dec
11 bedrs, 2 ☂, 2 ⚹ TCF P 20 SB £14-£16 DB £28-£36
HB £140-£165 D £7

SETTLE North Yorkshire 10C3

Golden Lion *Listed*
Duke Street, Settle BD24 9DU
📞 01729-822203 Fax 01729-824103

A traditional 17th century coaching inn with log fire situated in the heart of Settle's busy market place, offering simply furnished accommodation. Ideally located for Yorkshire Dales and five minutes from Settle-Carlisle Railway.

14 bedrs, 2 ensuite, 2 ⚹ TCF TV P 12 SB £23-£28.50
DB £46-£55 D £8 CC MC Visa

SEVENOAKS Kent 5D3

Moorings *Acclaimed*
97 Hitchen Hatch Lane, Sevenoaks TN13 3BE
📞 01732-452589 Fax 01732-456462
E Mail theryans@mooringshotel.demon.co.uk
24 bedrs, 21 ensuite, 2 ⚹ TCF TV P 22 SB £34 DB £49
HB £295 D £12 CC MC Visa Amex JCB ♿

SHAFTESBURY Dorset 3F2

★★ Grove House
Hospitality merit award
Ludwell, Shaftesbury SP7 9ND
📞 01747-828365 Fax 01747-828365

A small country village with beautiful panoramic views of Cranborne Chase, and overlooking a large delightful garden where badgers are regularly fed at night.

10 bedrs, 5 ensuite, 5 ☂, TCF TV ⚹ P 12 SB £28.50
DB £57 HB £258 D £18 CC MC Visa

SHEERNESS Kent 5E2

Victoriana *Listed*
103-109 Alma Road, Sheerness ME12 2PD
📞 01795-665555 Fax 01795-580633
20 bedrs, 7 ensuite, 3 ⚹ TCF TV ⚹ P 8 SB £16 DB £32
D £8.50 CC MC Visa Amex

SHEFFIELD South Yorkshire 8B1

Cooke House *Highly Acclaimed*
78 Brookhouse Hill, Sheffield S10 3TB
📞 0114-230 8186 Fax 0114-623 0241
Closed 21 Dec-3 Jan

The highest standard of accommodation and sustenance are provided in an elegantly renovated Victorian dwelling situated on the edge of the Peak National Park. Offering international cuisine, complemented by an excellent selection of wines and beers.

3 bedrs, all ensuite, 1 ⚹ TCF TV P 3 SB £39-£45 DB £55-£60 D £12 CC MC Visa

SHEFFIELD – ENGLAND

Westbourne House *Highly Acclaimed*
25 Westbourne Road, Broomhill, Sheffield S10 2QQ
☎ 0114-266 0109 Fax 0114-266 7778

Inexpensive country house style hotel near the centre, university and hospitals. All rooms furnished with antiques, includes Chinese, Venetian, French, Indian bedrooms. Beautiful terraced gardens.

10 bedrs, 9 ensuite, 1 TCF TV P 7 SB £31-£55 DB £48-£75 CC MC Visa Amex

Hunter House *Acclaimed*
Ecclesall Road, Sheffield S11 8TG
☎ 0114-266 2709 Fax 0114-268 6370
24 bedrs, 11 ensuite, 4 TCF TV P 9 SB £24-£40 DB £40-£48 D £9 CC MC Visa Amex JCB

Lindrick *Acclaimed*
226 Chippinghouse Road, Sheffield S7 1DR
☎ 0114-258 5041 Fax 0114-255 4758

The hotel is a converted Victorian property situated in the quiet, tree-lined residential area of Nether Edge, yet only one and a half miles from the city centre.

23 bedrs, 15 ensuite, 2 TCF TV P 20 SB £21-£28 DB £42-£48 D £4 CC MC Visa Amex

Etruria House *Listed*
91 Crookes Road, Broomhill, Sheffield S10 5BD
☎ 0114-266 2241 Fax 0114-267 0853
11 bedrs, 7 ensuite, 2 TCF TV P 9 SB £26-£35 DB £40-£49 CC MC Visa

RAC Hotel Reservations Service
0870 603 9109
(Calls charged at national call rate)

Millingtons *Listed*
70 Broomgrove Road, Sheffield S10 2NA
☎ 0114-266 9549 Fax 0114-269 2576
6 bedrs, 1 ensuite, 2 TCF TV P 4 No children under 12 SB £23 DB £42

Cutlers Inn *Lodge*
George Street, Sheffield S1 2PF
☎ 0114-273 9939 Fax 0114-276 8332
Closed Christmas
50 bedrs, all ensuite, TCF TV P 500 SB £35.90-£45.90 DB £46.85-£56.85 D £6 CC MC Visa JCB

SHEPTON MALLET Somerset   3E2

★★ Crossways Inn
North Wootton, Shepton Mallet BA14 4EU
☎ 01749-890237 Fax 01749-890476
17 bedrs, all ensuite, TCF TV P 150 SB £25 DB £35 D £8.50 CC MC Visa

Belfield *Acclaimed*
34 Charlton Road, Shepton Mallet BA4 5PA
☎ 01749-344353
7 bedrs, 2 ensuite, 2 TCF TV P 6 SB £20-£27 DB £38-£42.50

SHERBORNE Dorset   3E2

Ashclose Farm
Charlton-Horethorn, Sherborne DT9 4PG
☎ 01963-220360

Comfortable farmhouse with super views, friendly welcome and quiet, relaxed atmosphere with large garden and parking. Children welcome. Close to A303 and Sherbourne nearby (A30).

3 bedrs, 2 TCF SB £15-£17 DB £30-£34 HB £160 D £8

SHERINGHAM Norfolk   9E2

Fairlawns *Highly Acclaimed*
26 Hooks Hill Road, Sheringham NR26 8NL
☎ 01263-824717 Fax 01263-824717
Closed Dec-Jan
5 bedrs, all ensuite, TCF TV P 6 No children under 12 SB £32 DB £42 HB £225 D £13

Olivedale *Acclaimed*
20 Augusta Street, Sheringham NR26 8LA
☎ 01263-825871
Closed Christmas-New Year

A charming Victorian house in a quiet residential area only two minutes walk from the sea and town centre. Ideal location for exploring the attractions of North Norfolk.

5 bedrs, 2 ensuite, 1 ➥ TCF TV ✗ P 3 No children under 11 SB £20-£24 DB £36-£46

SHIPLEY West Yorkshire   10C3

Southgate House
145 Bradford Road, Shipley BD18 3TH
☎ 01274-585549

A clean and friendly large Victorian house with two twins and one double ensuite. Evening meal available.

3 bedrs, TCF TV P 3 DB £32-£35 D £4

SHREWSBURY Shropshire   7D2

★★ **Lion and Pheasant**
49-50 Wyle Cop, Shrewsbury SY1 1XJ
☎ 01743-236288 Fax 01743-244475
Closed 25-30 Dec
19 bedrs, 17 ensuite, 2 ➥ TCF TV ➤ P 20 SB £45 DB £60 D £15

★★ **Mermaid**
Atcham, Shrewsbury SY5 6QG
☎ 01743-761220 Fax 01743-761292
16 bedrs, all ensuite, TCF TV ➤ P 100 SB £35-£45 DB £45-£65 D £17.95 CC MC Visa Amex DC JCB

★★ **Nesscliffe**
Hospitality, Comfort merit awards
Nesscliffe, Shrewsbury SY4 1DB
☎ 01743-741430 Fax 01743-741104
8 bedrs, all ensuite, TCF TV SB £45 DB £55 CC MC Visa Amex

★★ **Shelton Hall**
Shelton, Shrewsbury SY3 8BH
☎ 01743-343982 Fax 01743-241515
Closed 26-27 Dec
9 bedrs, all ensuite, 1 ➥ TCF TV P 50 SB £45-£49 DB £62-£68 HB £260-£280 D £17 CC MC Visa Amex JCB

Abbots Mead *Highly Acclaimed*
9-10 St Julians Friars, Shrewsbury SY1 1XL
☎ 01743-235281 Fax 01743-369133

A Grade II Listed property situated between the river and town walls, a few minutes walk from the town centre, Abbey and Quest.

14 bedrs, all ensuite, 1 ➥ TCF TV P 10 SB £34-£37 DB £48-£54 D £13 CC MC Visa Amex JCB

SIDMOUTH Devon   3D3

★★ **Abbeydale**
Hospitality merit award
Manor Road, Sidmouth EX10 8RP
☎ 01395-512060 Fax 01395-515566
Closed 30 Nov-1 Feb
17 bedrs, all ensuite, TCF TV ⊡ P 24 No children under 4 SB £25-£41 DB £50-£82 HB £245-£343 D £13 CC MC Visa

★★ **Brownlands**
Hospitality, Comfort, Restaurant merit awards
Sid Road, Sidmouth EX10 9AG
☎ 01395-513053 Fax 01395-513053
Closed end Nov-begin Mar
14 bedrs, all ensuite, TCF TV ➤ P 25 No children under 8 SB £45-£48 DB £75-£96 HB £320-£383 D £19

SIDMOUTH – ENGLAND

★★ **Byes Link**
Sid Road, Sidmouth EX10 9AA
☎ 01395-513129

★★ **Hotel Elizabeth**
Esplanade, Sidmouth EX10 8AT
☎ 01395-513503
Closed Dec-Jan
28 bedrs, all ensuite, 1 ➥ TCF TV ⊠ ⊟ P 10 SB £22-£44 DB £44-£90 HB £191-£403 CC MC Visa

★★ **Littlecourt**
Comfort merit award
Seafield Road, Sidmouth EX10 8HF
☎ 01395-515279
20 bedrs, 19 ensuite, 1 ➥ TCF TV ⊢ P 17 SB £28-£34 DB £56-£72 HB £243-£356 D £15 CC MC Visa Amex DC JCB ⊡

★★ **Royal York & Faulkner**
Hospitality merit award
Esplanade, Sidmouth EX10 8AZ
☎ 0800-220714 Fax 01395-577472
Closed Jan
68 bedrs, all ensuite, 4 ➥ TCF TV ⊢ ⊟ P 18 SB £25.75-£43 DB £51.50-£86 HB £210-£315 D £13 CC MC Visa JCB ⊞ ⊞ ⊞

★★ **Swallow Eaves**
Hospitality, Comfort, Restaurant merit awards
Colyford, Colyton EX13 6QJ
☎ 01297-553184 Fax 01297-553574
Closed Jan
8 bedrs, all ensuite, TCF TV ⊠ P 10 No children under 12 SB £38-£48 DB £56-£76 HB £290-£340 D £19 CC MC Visa

★★ **Westbourne**
Manor Road, Sidmouth EX10 8RR
☎ 01395-513774
Closed Nov-Feb
12 bedrs, 11 ensuite, 1 ☏, 4 ➥ TCF TV ⊢ P 14 SB £23-£33 DB £45-£66 HB £210-£297 D £11 ♿

★★ **Woodlands**
Cotmaton Cross, Sidmouth EX10 8HG
☎ 01395-513120

Groveside *Acclaimed*
Vicarage Road, Sidmouth EX10 8UQ
☎ 01395-513406
10 bedrs, 7 ensuite, 1 ➥ TCF TV P 7

Short Breaks

Many hotels provide special rates for weekend and mid-week breaks – sometimes these are quoted in the hotel's entry, otherwise ring direct for the latest offers.

Southcombe *Acclaimed*
Vicarage Road, Sidmouth EX10 8UQ
☎ 01395-513861 Fax 01395-513861

Well established family run guest house, half a mile from seafront via town centre. Ensuite rooms with TV/radio and beverage facilities. Large quiet garden.

6 bedrs, 5 ensuite, 1 ☏, 1 ➥ TCF TV P 7 No children under 12 SB £17-£18 DB £34-£36 HB £160-£177 D £8

Willow Bridge *Acclaimed*
1 Mill Ford Road, Sidmouth EX10 8DR
☎ 01395-513599

Canterbury House *Listed*
Salcombe Road, Sidmouth EX10 8PR
☎ 01395-513373
Closed Dec-Feb
8 bedrs, 7 ensuite, 1 ➥ TCF TV ⊢ P 6 SB £16-£19 DB £32-£38 HB £165-£180 D £8 CC MC Visa Amex DC ♿

SITTINGBOURNE Kent   5E3

Hempstead House *Highly Acclaimed*
London Road, Bapchild, Sittingbourne ME9 9PP
☎ 01795-428020 Fax 01795-428020
13 bedrs, all ensuite, TCF TV ⊢ P 25 SB £62 DB £72 HB £372 D £19.50 CC MC Visa Amex DC JCB ⊡

SKEGNESS Lincolnshire   9D2

★ **Crawford**
South Parade, Skegness PE25 3HR
☎ 01754-764215
20 bedrs, all ensuite, 1 ➥ ⊟ CC MC Visa

South Lodge *Acclaimed*
147 Drummond Road, Skegness PE25 3BT
☎ 01754-765057
7 bedrs, all ensuite, TCF TV P 6 SB £15-£18 DB £30-£36 CC MC Visa

Royal Oak *Listed*
73 High Street, Wainfleet, Skegness PE24 4BZ
☎ 01754-880328

Woolpack *Listed*
39 High Street, Wainfleet, Skegness PE24 4BJ
☎ 01754-880353

Abbey
North Parade, Skegness PE25 2UB
☎ 01754-763677 Fax 01754-763677
Closed Jan-Feb

Family-run seafront hotel; some fourposter beds. Live entertainment in season.

25 bedrs, 21 ensuite, 2 ⇌ ⊠ ⋔ P 8

SKIPTON North Yorkshire   10C3

Highfield *Acclaimed*
58 Keighley Road, Skipton BD23 2NB
☎ 01756-793182
Closed Christmas
10 bedrs, 9 ensuite, 1 ⇌ TCF TV ⋔ CC   MC Visa Amex

Skipton Park Guest'otel *Acclaimed*
2 Salisbury Street, Skipton BD23 1NQ
☎ 01756-700640
7 bedrs, all ensuite, ⋔ P 2

SMALLFIELD Surrey   5D3

Chithurst Farm
Chithurst Lane, Horne, Smallfield RH6 9JU
☎ 01342-842487

Attractive 16th century farmhouse with views of garden and surrounding farmland. Ideal for walking/ N.T. Surrey, Kent, Sussex. Convenient for Gatwick/motorways.

3 bedrs, 1 ⇌ TCF ⊠ P 4 SB £15-£18 DB £30-£36

SOLIHULL West Midlands   8A3

★★ Flemings
141 Warwick Road, Olton, Solihull B92 7HW
☎ 0121-706 0371 Fax 0121-706 4494
78 bedrs, all ensuite, TCF TV ⋔ P 70 SB £32-£45 DB £45-£56 D £5 CC   MC Visa Amex DC JCB ⌘

Cedarwood House *Acclaimed*
347 Lyndon Road, Solihull B92 7QT
☎ 0121-743 5844

A family run substantial house. All rooms are ensuite and tastefully decorated, with colour TV and tea/coffee facilities. Easy access to the NIA and NEC/Solihull centres.

5 bedrs, all ensuite, TCF TV P 5 No children under 5
SB £27.50-£40 DB £40-£50

SOUTH BRENT Devon   2C3

★★ Glazebrook House
South Brent TQ10 9JE
☎ 01364-73322 Fax 01364-72350
10 bedrs, all ensuite, P 40 CC   MC Visa Amex ♿

SOUTH MOLTON Devon   2C2

★★ Whitechapel Manor
Comfort, Restaurant merit awards
Whitechapel, South Molton EX36 3EG
☎ 01769-573377 Fax 01769-573797
11 bedrs, all ensuite, TV P 40 SB £70 DB £110 HB £545
D £34 CC   MC Visa DC JCB

Heasley House *Acclaimed*
Heasley Mill, South Molton EX36 3LE
☎ 01598-740213 Fax 01598-740677
E Mail heasleyhouse@enterprise.net
Closed Feb

Bygone hospitality and environment rarely experienced in todays world. Exmoor tranquillity, set in a uniquely peaceful, wooded river valley hamlet. Informal, Georgian hotel, country cooking. Dogs welcome.

8 bedrs, 5 ensuite, 2 ⇌ TCF ⋔ P 11 SB £25.50 DB £51
HB £224 D £14.50

SOUTHAMPTON Hampshire 4B4

★★ Avenue
Lodge Road, Southampton S014 0QR
☎ 01703-229023 Fax 01703-334569
48 bedrs, all ensuite, TCF TV 🐕 🍴 P 48 CC MC Visa Amex DC JCB

★★ Elizabeth House
43-44 The Avenue, Southampton SO17 1XP
☎ 01703-224327 Fax 01703-224327
24 bedrs, 20 ensuite, TCF TV 🐕 P 22 SB £30 DB £40 CC MC Visa Amex DC

★★ Star Hotel & Restaurant
26 High Street, Southampton SO14 2NA
☎ 01703-339939 Fax 01703-335291
Closed 24-28 Dec
44 bedrs, 37 ensuite, 4 🛏 TCF TV 🐕 🍴 P 30 SB £40-£50 DB £50-£65 D £14 CC MC Visa Amex DC JCB

Hunters Lodge *Acclaimed*
25 Landguard Road, Shirley, Southampton SO1 5DL
☎ 01703-227919 Fax 01703-230913

A friendly, family run hotel. Ensuite bedrooms with colour satellite TV, tea and coffee making facilities and direct dial telephones. Resident's bar. Ample car parking.

16 bedrs, 15 ensuite, 1 🛏 TCF TV 🐕 P 18 SB £25-£33 DB £44-£53 HB £125-£167 D £10 CC MC Visa Amex

Villa Capri *Acclaimed*
50/52 Archers Road, Southampton SO1 2LU
☎ 01703-632800 Fax 01703-630100
15 bedrs, 11 ensuite, 2 🛏 TCF TV 🐕 P 14 No children under 3 SB £19-£21 DB £36-£38 D £6 CC MC Visa

Banister House *Listed*
11 Brighton Road, Banister Park, SO15 2JJ
☎ 01703-221279 Fax 01703-221279
Closed Christmas
23 bedrs, 14 ensuite, 3 🐾, 5 🛏 TCF TV 🐕 P 14 SB £22.50-£26.50 DB £30.50-£35 D £6 CC MC Visa Amex

Landguard Lodge *Listed*
21 Landguard Road, Southampton SO15 5DL
☎ 01703-636904 Fax 01703-636904
10 bedrs, all ensuite, TCF TV P 3 No children under 5 SB £20-£25 DB £40 HB £150-£175 CC MC Visa Amex DC

Linden *Listed*
51/53 The Polygon, Southampton SO15 2BP
☎ 01703-225653
Closed Christmas
13 bedrs, 3 🛏 TCF TV P 7 SB £13-£16 DB £26-£31

Nirvana *Listed*
386 Winchester Road, Bassett, Southampton SO16 7DH
☎ 01703-790087 Fax 01703-790575
10 bedrs, 7 ensuite, 3 🛏 TCF TV 🐕 P 18 No children under 14 SB £22 DB £40 HB £210 D £11.95 CC MC Visa Amex

Roadchef Lodge *Lodge*
M27 Westbound, Rownhams, Southampton SO16 8AP
☎ 01703-741144 Fax 01703-740204
Closed 24-27 Dec
39 bedrs, all ensuite, TCF TV P 120 **Room only rate** £43.50 D £4.50 CC MC Visa Amex DC ♿

Baytree House
Blind Lane, Curdridge, Southampton SO32 2BL
☎ 01489-784656

Peaceful, warm, friendly, spacious and relaxing large country house set amidst idyllic rural surroundings. Convenient for the south coast, M27, New Forest, Winchester, Portsmouth and Southampton.

4 bedrs, 1 ensuite, 1 🐾, TCF TV P 9

SOUTHEND-ON-SEA Essex 5E2

★★ Tower
146 Alexandra Road, Southend-on-Sea SS1 1HE
☎ 01702-348635 Fax 01702-433044
32 bedrs, all ensuite, 2 🛏 TCF TV 🐕 3 SB £33-£43 DB £45-£55 HB £220-£275 D £7 CC MC Visa Amex DC

Ilfracombe House *Highly Acclaimed*
11-13 Wilson Road, Southend-on-Sea SS1 1HG
☎ 01702-351000
14 bedrs, all ensuite, ♿

Argyle *Listed*
12 Cliff Town Parade, Southend-on-Sea SS1 1DP
☎ 01702-339483
11 bedrs, 1 🐾, 3 🛏 TCF TV 🐕 No children under 5 SB £18-£19 DB £37

Mayflower *Listed*
6 Royal Terrace, Southend-on-Sea SS1 1DY
📞 **01702-340489**
Closed Christmas
24 bedrs, 4 ensuite, 5 ⇌ TCF TV ⋔ SB £21 DB £32

Terrace *Listed*
8 Royal Terrace, Southend-on-Sea SS1 1DY
📞 **01702-348143 Fax 01702-348143**
9 bedrs, 3 ensuite, 2 ⇌ TCF TV ⋔ SB £20 DB £32

SOUTHPORT Lancashire 10B4

★★ **Balmoral Lodge**
41 Queens Road, Southport PR9 9EX
📞 **01704-544298 Fax 01704-501224**
15 bedrs, all ensuite, 1 ⇌ TCF TV P 10 SB £26-£30
DB £52-£55 HB £235-£265 D £13 CC MC Visa Amex DC JCB 🖼 ♿

★★ **Bold**
583 Lord Street, Southport PR9 0BE
📞 **01704-532578 Fax 01704-532528**
23 bedrs, all ensuite, TCF TV ⋔ P 16 CC MC Visa

★★ **Metropole**
Portland Street, Southport PR8 1LL
📞 **01704-536836 Fax 01704-549041**

One of Southport's finest family run hotels offering traditional standards of comfort and courtesy. Central location ideal for business or leisure breaks. Golf holidays arranged.

24 bedrs, 22 ensuite, 1 ⇌ TCF TV ⋔ P 12 SB £25-£35
DB £40-£60 HB £259 D £12 CC MC Visa Amex JCB 🖼

Don't forget to mention the guide
When booking direct, please remember to tell the hotel that you chose it from RAC Bed & Breakfast 1998.

★ **Sidbrook**
14 Talbot Street, Southport PR8 1HP
📞 **01704-530608 Fax 01704-531198**

A town centre hotel with free parking. All ensuite rooms have telephones, Sky movies, hospitality tray, hairdryers. Select accommodation at a reasonable price.

8 bedrs, all ensuite, 1 ⇌ TCF TV ⋔ P 9 SB £22-£25
DB £35-£44 HB £165-£185 D £15 CC MC Visa Amex DC JCB 🖼 🖼

★ **Talbot**
Portland Street, Southport PR8 1LR
📞 **01704-533975 Fax 01704-530126**
24 bedrs, 18 ensuite, 2 ⇌ TCF TV ⋔ P 30 CC MC Visa Amex

Ambassador *Highly Acclaimed*
13 Bath Street, Southport PR9 0DP
📞 **01704-543998 Fax 01704-536269**
Closed 16 Dec-14 Jan

Delightful small licensed hotel with ensuite bedrooms. 200 yards from Promenade, Conference Centre and Theatre. Adjacent to Lord Street and Victorian Shopping Arcades.

8 bedrs, all ensuite, 2 ⇌ TCF TV ⋔ P 6 No children under 3 SB £30 DB £50 HB £190 D £10 CC MC Visa Amex

Oakwood *Acclaimed*
7 Portland Street, Southport PR8 1LJ
📞 **01704-531 858**
Closed Oct-Easter
6 bedrs, 4 ensuite, 1 ⇌ 🍽 P 10 No children under 5

White Lodge *Acclaimed*
12 Talbot Street, Southport PR8 1HP
📞 **01704-536320** Fax **01704-536320**
8 bedrs, 4 ensuite, 1 🚭, 2 🐕 TCF TV P 6 SB £19-£24
DB £38-£48 HB £135-£185

Edendale *Listed*
83 Avondale Road, Southport PR9 0NE
📞 **01704-530718**
8 bedrs, all ensuite, 1 🐕 TCF TV P 10 No children under 5 SB £18-£22.50 DB £34-£40 CC MC Visa Amex DC

Lake *Listed*
55-56 Promenade, Southport PR9 0DY
📞 **01704-530996**
20 bedrs, all ensuite, 1 🐕 TCF TV 🐕 ▣ P 14 No children under 8 CC MC Visa

Leicester *Listed*
24 Leicester Street, Southport PR9 0EZ
📞 **01704-530049** Fax **01704-530049**
E Mail leicester.hotel@mail.cybas.co.uk
7 bedrs, 3 ensuite, 2 🐕 TCF TV 🐕 P 6 No children
SB £16 DB £32 D £7 CC MC Visa DC

Lyndhurst *Listed*
101 King Street, Southport PR8 1LQ
📞 **01704-537520**
7 bedrs, 3 🐕 TV P 3 No children under 5 SB £15
DB £30 D £6

Rosedale *Listed*
11 Talbot Street, Southport PR8 1HP
📞 **01704-530604** Fax **01704-530604**
Closed Christmas
10 bedrs, 7 ensuite, 1 🐕 TCF TV P 7 SB £18.50-£22
DB £37-£44 D £7.50 CC MC Visa JCB

Whitworth Falls *Listed*
16 Lathom Road, Southport PR9 0JH
📞 **01704-530074** Fax **01704-530074**
13 bedrs, 8 ensuite, 3 🐕 TCF TV P 9 SB £18 DB £35
HB £149-£159 D £7

Windsor Lodge *Listed*
37 Saunders Street, Southport PR9 0HJ
📞 **01704-530070**
10 bedrs, 5 ensuite, 2 🐕 TCF TV P 9 SB £14-£16 DB £27-£31 HB £144-£158 D £7 ♿

Facilities for the disabled ♿
Hotels do their best to cater for disabled visitors. However, it is advisable to contact the hotel direct to ensure it can provide a particular requirement. For further information on accommodation facilities for the disabled why not order a copy of *RAC On the Move – The Guide for the Disabled Traveller*.

| SOUTHWOLD Suffolk | 9F3 |

★★ Pier Avenue
Station Road, Southwold IP18 6LB
📞 **01502-722632** Fax **01502-722632**
13 bedrs, all ensuite, TCF TV 🐕 P 8 SB £45 DB £65
HB £270 D £15 CC MC Visa Amex DC

| SPALDING Lincolnshire | 8C2 |

★★ Cley Hall
22 High Street, Spalding PE11 1TX
📞 **01775-725157** Fax **01775-710785**
11 bedrs, 4 ensuite, TCF TV 🐕 P 15 SB £30-£48 DB £50-£65 D £10 CC MC Visa Amex DC JCB

★★ Woodlands
Hospitality, Comfort, Restaurant merit awards
80 Pinchbeck Road, Spalding PE11 1QF
📞 **01775-769933** Fax **01775-711369**
17 bedrs, all ensuite, TCF TV 🐕 P 40 SB £55 DB £65
D £10 CC MC Visa Amex DC ♿

Travel Stop *Lodge*
Cowbit Road, Spalding PE11 2RJ
📞 **01775-767290** Fax **01775-767716**

Special weekend break for two, £65 for two nights. On the riverside half a mile from the centre of Spalding on B1173. Open fires, bar, breakfast restaurant.

10 bedrs, all ensuite, 1 🐕 TCF TV 🐕 P 34 SB £25-£35
DB £45-£70 CC MC Visa Amex ♿

| ST AGNES Cornwall | 2A4 |

★★ Rosemundy House
8 Rosemundy, St Agnes TR5 0UF
📞 **01872-552101** Fax **01872-552101**
Closed Nov-Mar
44 bedrs, all ensuite, TCF TV 🐕 P 40 SB £25-£41 DB £50-£82 HB £190-£275 D £12.50 CC MC Visa

Porthvean *Acclaimed*
Churchtown, St Agnes TR5 0QP
☎ 01872-552581 Fax 01872-5523773
Closed 20 Dec-20 Jan

The original 18th century village hostelry - oak beams, granite wall, log fires. Rooms furnished with antiques, but all modern comforts.

7 bedrs, all ensuite, 1 🐕 TCF TV P 8 SB £35-£45 DB £50-£75 CC MC Visa

Penkerris *Listed*
Penwinnick Road (B3277), St Agnes TR5 0PA
☎ 01872-552262 Fax 01872-552262
6 bedrs, 3 ensuite, 3 🐕 TCF TV P 9 SB £15-£30 DB £27-£35 HB £135-£160 D £8.50 CC MC Visa Amex DC

ST ALBANS Hertfordshire 4C2

★★Avalon
260 London Road, St Albans AL1 1TJ
☎ 01727-856757 Fax 01727-856750
15 bedrs, all ensuite, TCF TV P 14 SB £50 DB £65 D £11 CC MC Visa Amex JCB

RAC Hotel Reservations Service
0870 603 9109
(Calls charged at national call rate)

PENKERRIS

Situated in an unspoilt Cornish village with dramatic cliff walks and beaches nearby, an enchanting Edwardian residence with garden. Beautiful rooms, superb home cooking.

**PENWINNICK ROAD (B3277),
ST AGNES TR5 0PA
TEL. 01872-552262
FAX. 01872-552262**

★★Lake
234 London Road, St Albans AL1 1JQ
☎ 01727-840904 Fax 01727-862750
43 bedrs, all ensuite, TCF TV P 75 SB £34.50-£68 DB £69-£79 D £12.95 CC MC Visa Amex DC

★★White Hart
25 Hollywell Hill, St Albans AL1 1EZ
☎ 01727-853624 Fax 01727-840237
11 bedrs, 8 ensuite, 3 🐾, 1 🐕 TCF TV 🍴 P 10 CC MC Visa Amex

Ardmore House *Highly Acclaimed*
54 Lemsford Road, St Albans AL1 3PR
☎ 01727-859313 Fax 01727-859313
E Mail 106376.2353@compuserve.com
26 bedrs, all ensuite, TCF TV P 25 SB £45-£49.50 DB £59.50-£75 D £10 CC MC Visa Amex

---

ST AUSTELL Cornwall 2B4

★★Boscundle Manor
Hospitality, Comfort, Restaurant merit awards
Tregrehan, St Austell PL25 3RL
☎ 01726-813557 Fax 01726-814997
Closed Nov-Mar
10 bedrs, all ensuite, TCF TV 🍴 P 15 SB £70-£75 DB £120-£130 HB £525-£560 D £25 CC MC Visa Amex JCB

★★White Hart
Church Street, St Austell PL25 4AT
☎ 01726-72100 Fax 01726-74705
Closed 25-26 Dec
18 bedrs, all ensuite, 🍴 SB £40 DB £63 HB £255 D £11 CC MC Visa Amex DC

Nanscawen Country House *Highly Acclaimed*
Prideaux Road, St Blazey, Par, St Austell PL24 2SR
☎ 01726-814488 Fax 01726-814488
E Mail 101756.2120@compuserve.com
Closed 25-26 Dec

Nanscawen House stands in 5 acres of grounds and gardens. Three luxury ensuite rooms with spa baths. An ideal base for touring all of Cornwall.

3 bedrs, all ensuite, TCF TV P 5 No children under 12 SB £40-£58 DB £68-£78 CC MC Visa JCB

ST AUSTELL – ENGLAND

Wheal Lodge *Highly Acclaimed*
91 Sea Road, Carlyon Bay, St Austell PL25 3SH
☎ 01726-815543 Fax 01726-815543
Closed Christmas

Superb position just above the sea and opposite the golf course. Set in delightful grounds with spacious parking, this character residence offers superior accommodation and peace and quiet.

6 bedrs, all ensuite, TCF TV P 20 No children under 10 SB £30-£40 DB £60-£70 CC MC Visa

Alexandra *Listed*
52-54 Alexandra Road, St Austell PL25 4QN
☎ 01726-66111 Fax 01726-74242
Closed Christmas
12 bedrs, 4 ensuite, 3 TCF TV P 20 SB £24 DB £42 HB £180 D £9.75 CC MC Visa Amex DC JCB

Lynton House *Listed*
48 Bodmin Road, St Austell PL25 5AF
☎ 01726-73787
Closed winter
5 bedrs, 1 P 6

ST BRIAVEL'S Gloucestershire 7E4

George Inn *Acclaimed*
High Street, St Briavel's GL15 6TA
☎ 01594-530228 Fax 01594-530260
3 bedrs, all ensuite, TCF TV P 12 SB £25 DB £40-£50 D £5 CC MC Visa JCB

ST IVES Cornwall 2A4

★★ Chy-an-dour
Trelyon Avenue, St Ives TR26 2AD
☎ 01736-796436 Fax 01736-795772
23 bedrs, all ensuite, TCF TV P 23 No children under 5 SB £29-£32 DB £58-£64 HB £265-£280 D £17 CC MC Visa JCB

RAC Hotel Reservations Service
0870 603 9109
(Calls charged at national call rate)

Dean Court *Highly Acclaimed*
Trelyon Avenue, St Ives TR26 2AD
☎ 01736-796023 Fax 01736-796233
Closed Nov-Feb

Set in own grounds overlooking Porthminster Beach, St Ives Bay and harbour. Comfortably furnished, all rooms ensuite, excellent cuisine, ample parking. Sorry, no children.

12 bedrs, all ensuite, TCF TV P 12 No children under 14 SB £28-£36 DB £54-£72 HB £220-£280 D £8 CC MC Visa JCB

Longships *Acclaimed*
2 Talland Road, St Ives TR26 2DF
☎ 01736-798180 Fax 01736-798180
Closed Mar-Nov
25 bedrs, all ensuite, TCF TV P 20 SB £17-£25 DB £34-£50 D £8 CC MC Visa

Trewinnard *Acclaimed*
4 Parc Avenue, St Ives TR26 2DN
☎ 01736-794168
Closed Nov-Mar

Trewinnard is a four storey, granite-built Victorian house situated in an elevated position with superb views, yet only a three minute walk into town.

7 bedrs, 6 ensuite, 1 TCF TV P 4 No children under 6 SB £19-£25 DB £36-£50 CC MC Visa

Dunmar *Listed*
1-3 Pednolver Terrace, St Ives TR26 2EL
📞 01736-796117 Fax 01736-796117
17 bedrs, 13 ensuite, 2 🛏 TCF TV 🐕 P 22 SB £18-£29
DB £35-£58 HB £147-£236 CC MC Visa Amex JCB

Hollies *Listed*
Talland Road, St Ives TR26 2DF
📞 01736-796605
10 bedrs, all ensuite, TCF TV P 12 SB £15-£20 DB £30-£40

Primrose Valley *Listed*
Primrose Valley, St Ives TR26 2ED
📞 01736-794939
Closed Dec-Feb
10 bedrs, all ensuite, TV P 12 SB £20-£35 DB £20-£35
HB £150-£290 D £8.50 CC MC Visa

St Margarets *Listed*
3 Park Avenue, St Ives TR26 2DN
📞 01736-795785

St Merryn *Listed*
Trelyon, St Ives TR26 2PF
📞 01736-795767 Fax 01736-797248
Closed Nov-Feb
19 bedrs, all ensuite, TV P 20 SB £20.25-£27.75 DB £36-£46 HB £160-£195 CC MC Visa

ST MAWES Cornwall 2B4

★★ St Mawes
The Seafront, St Mawes TR2 5DW
📞 01326-270266
Closed Dec-Jan
7 bedrs, 5 ensuite, 2 🛏 TCF TV 🐕 P 7 No children under 5 D £18 CC MC Visa JCB

ST NEOTS Cambridgeshire 8C4

★★ Wyboston Lakes
Great North Road, Wyboston, St Neots MK44 3AL
📞 01480-212625 Fax 01480-223000
102 bedrs, all ensuite, TCF TV 📺 P 200 CC MC Visa Amex 🅿 📋 🍽 ♿

STAFFORD Staffordshire 8A2

★★ Abbey
Hospitality merit award
65-68 Lichfield Road, Stafford ST14 4LW
📞 01785-258531 Fax 01785-246875
17 bedrs, ensuite, TCF TV 🐕 P 21 SB £32-£35 DB £46-£50 D £8 CC MC Visa Amex JCB

★★ Albridge
Wolverhampton Road, Stafford ST17 4AW
📞 01785-54100
Closed 25-26 Dec
11 bedrs, 7 ensuite, 1 🛏 TCF TV 🐕 P 20 SB £22-£27
DB £30-£38 D £5 CC MC Visa Amex DC

Leonards Croft *Listed*
80 Lichfield Road, Stafford ST17 4LP
📞 01785-223676
Closed Christmas

Large Victorian house with beautiful gardens, a few minutes walk from the town centre. Ideally situated, with easy access to Shugborough Hall, Alton Towers, County Showground and M6 (jn 13).

11 bedrs, 4 ensuite, 4 🛏 TCF TV 🐕 P 12 SB £18-£25
DB £36-£45 D £3 ♿

STAINES Surrey 4C2

Swan *Acclaimed*
The Hythe, Staines TW18 3JB
📞 01784-452494 Fax 01784-461593
11 bedrs, 5 ensuite, 2 🛏 TCF TV SB £41-£68 DB £59-£82
D £3.95 CC MC Visa Amex DC

STALHAM Norfolk 9F2

★★ Kingfisher
Hospitality, Restaurant merit awards
High Street, Stalham NR12 9AN
📞 01692-581974 Fax 01692-582544
18 bedrs, all ensuite, TCF TV 🐕 P 40 SB £39-£45 DB £50-£69 HB £276-£294 D £15 CC MC Visa

STAMFORD Lincolnshire 8C3

★★ Crown
All Saints Place, Stamford PE9 2AG
📞 01780-763136 Fax 01780-756111
Closed Christmas
17 bedrs, all ensuite, 4 🛏 TCF TV 🐕 P 40 SB £42 DB £55
D £11 CC MC Visa Amex DC

Candlesticks *Acclaimed*
1 Church Lane, Stamford PE9 2JU
📞 01780-764033 Fax 01780-756071

Small Victorian hotel set in the oldest part of Stamford.

8 bedrs, all ensuite, TCF TV P 6 SB £30 DB £45 D £15 CC MC Visa JCB

STANDISH Lancashire   10B4

★★ Beeches
School Lane, Wigan, Standish WN6 0TD
📞 01257-426432 Fax 01257-427503
11 bedrs, all ensuite, TCF TV P 75 CC MC Visa Amex DC

STANTON DREW Avon   3E1

Valley Farm
Sandy Lane, Stanton Drew, Nr Bristol BS18 4EL
📞 01275-332723

Modern farmhouse in quiet position, fully central heated, TV and with double glazing. Three rooms (two ensuite). Near Bath, Bristol and Cheddar.

3 bedrs, 2 ensuite, **TV**

STEEPLE ASTON Oxfordshire   4B1

Westfield Farm Motel *Acclaimed*
The Fenway, Steeple Aston, Bicester OX6 3SS
📞 01869-340591 Fax 01869-347594

A converted stable block surrounded by beautiful gardens with own natural spring and stream. Good home cooking with locally grown vegetables and locally produced meats.

7 bedrs, all ensuite, TCF TV ⛔ P 18 SB £38-£42 DB £55-£65 D £15 CC MC Visa Amex JCB ♿

STEYNING West Sussex   4C4

Springwells *Highly Acclaimed*
High Street, Steyning BN4 3GG
📞 01903-812446 Fax 01903-879823
Closed Christmas & New Year

Sympathetically converted Georgian merchant's house, in secluded gardens at the foot of the South Downs. Turn off the A283 and follow High Street to the bottom where the hotel is located on the right-hand side.

10 bedrs, 8 ensuite, 1 ⇨ TCF TV ⛔ P 6 SB £28-£38 DB £49-£79 CC MC Visa Amex DC

Nash *Acclaimed*
Horsham Road, Steyning BN44 3AA
📞 01903-814988
4 bedrs, 1 ensuite, 3 ⇨ TCF TV ⛔ P 50 SB £30 DB £48 HB £252

CARBERY

Delightfully situated, two minutes walk to the centre of the attractive old market village of Stockbridge, in one acre of landscaped gardens and lawns overlooking the River Test.

Heated outdoor pool, games room, lounge

**SALISBURY HILL,
STOCKBRIDGE SO20 6EZ
TEL. 01264-810771
FAX. 01264-811022**

STOCKBRIDGE Hampshire   4B3

Carbery *Acclaimed*
Salisbury Hill, Stockbridge SO20 6EZ
☎ 01264-810771 Fax 01264-811022
11 bedrs, 8 ensuite, 1 🛁 TCF TV P 12 SB £25-£32 DB £48-£51 D £12 ③

Old Three Cups *Acclaimed*
High Street, Stockbridge SO20 6HB
☎ 01264-810527 Fax 01264 810527
Closed 24 Dec-6 Jan
8 bedrs, 3 ensuite, 1 🛁 P 8 CC MC Visa

STOCKTON-ON-TEES Cleveland   11D2

Edwardian *Acclaimed*
72 Yarm Road, Stockton-on-Tees TS18 3PQ
☎ 01642-615655
6 bedrs, all ensuite, TCF TV P 8 SB £25-£30 DB £42 D £6
CC MC Visa

Formule 1 *Lodge*
Teesway, North Tees Industrial Estate, Stockton-on-Tees TS18 2RT
☎ 01642-606560
64 bedrs, 16 🛁 TV 🐾 P 64 SB £22.50 DB £25 CC MC Visa Amex ♿

STOKE-ON-TRENT Staffordshire   8A2

Hanchurch Manor Country House *Highly Acclaimed*
Hanchurch, Stoke-on-Trent ST4 8SD
☎ 01782-643030 Fax 01782-643035
Closed Christmas-New Year
4 bedrs, all ensuite, TCF TV P 60 No children under 14
SB £65 DB £75 D £12.50 CC MC Visa Amex 📧 ♿

Bank House
Farley Lane, Oakamoor
☎ 01538-702810 Fax 01538-702810

Peaceful, elegantly furnished home with beautiful views, open log fires and excellent cooking including home made breads. Close to Alton Towers, the Peak District and the Potteries.

3 bedrs, 2 ensuite, TCF TV 🐾 P 8 SB £39-£40 DB £52-£72
D £20 CC MC Visa

STONY STRATFORD Buckinghamshire   4C1

Bull *Listed*
64 High Street, Stony Stratford MK11 1AQ
☎ 01908-567104 Fax 01908-563765
14 bedrs, 11 ensuite, 3 🛁, TCF TV 🐾 P 28 CC MC Visa Amex DC

Blue Ribbon Awards

The highest honour the RAC can bestow on a hotel is to award it Blue Ribbon status. Only hotels who have gained all three merit awards for Hospitality, Comfort and Restaurant are eligible for the award.

STOW-ON-THE-WOLD – ENGLAND

STOW-ON-THE-WOLD Gloucestershire 4A1

★★ Grapevine
Sheep Street, Stow-on-the-Wold GL54 1AU
☎ 01451-830344 Fax 01451-832278
E Mail enquiries@vines.co.uk

A 17th century town hotel in mellow Cotswold stone with an historic Black Hamburg grapevine crowning its conservatory restaurant.

22 bedrs, all ensuite, TCF TV P 23 SB £60-£100 DB £120-£160 HB £350-£610 D £24
CC MC Visa Amex DC JCB

★★ Stow Lodge
Comfort merit award
The Square, Stow-on-the-Wold GL54 1AB
☎ 01451-830485 Fax 01451-831671
Closed Christmas & January
21 bedrs, all ensuite, TCF TV P 30 No children under 5
SB £45-£95 DB £65-£105 HB £230-£375 D £16 CC MC Visa DC JCB

Limes *Acclaimed*
Tewkesbury Road, Stow-on-the-Wold GL54 1EN
☎ 01451-830034
Closed Christmas
5 bedrs, 4 ensuite, 1 ⓡ, TCF TV ⌇ P 4 SB £33-£34 DB £38-£39

Royalist *Acclaimed*
Digbeth Street, Stow-on-the-Wold GL54 1BN
☎ 01451-830670 Fax 01451-870048
Closed Christmas
12 bedrs, all ensuite, TCF TV ⌇ P 10 CC MC Visa Amex

Short Breaks

Many hotels provide special rates for weekend and mid-week breaks – sometimes these are quoted in the hotel's entry, otherwise ring direct for the latest offers.

Corsham Field Farmhouse
Bledington Road, Stow-on-the-Wold GL54 1JH
☎ 01451-831750

7 bedrs, 5 ensuite, 1 ⇨ TCF TV ⌇ P 10 SB £15-£25
DB £30-£40

STRATFORD-UPON-AVON Warwickshire 7F3

★★ Coach House
16-17 Warwick Road, Stratford-upon-Avon CV37 6YW
☎ 01789-204109 Fax 01789-415916
E Mail kiwiauon@aol.com.uk
Closed Christmas
23 bedrs, 12 ensuite, 8 ⓡ, 1 ⇨ TCF TV P 24 SB £30-£58
DB £48-£98 HB £287-£395 D £12 CC MC Visa Amex DC

SEQUOIA HOUSE HOTEL

51-53 Shipston Road,
Stratford-upon-Avon
CV37 7LN

Superbly situated in prime location just across the Avon for you to park and enjoy the delightful walk through the hotel garden and along the tramway to the Bancroft Gardens, Theatres and town centre. A spacious Victorian house with original period features, decorated and furnished with flair and style, affords excellent facilities and modern comforts. Home cooking and friendly service, all situated in three-quarters of an acre of grounds and gardens.

Your accommodation arranged with pleasure by resident proprietors:
JEAN and PHILIP EVANS
Telephone: Reservations (01789) 268852
Fax: (01789) 414559 Guests: (01789) 204805
http://www.stratford-upon-avon.co.uk/sequoia.htm

MELITA
Private Hotel

37 SHIPSTON ROAD,
STRATFORD-UPON-AVON,
WARWICKSHIRE CV37 7LN
Tel: 01789 292432 Fax: 01789 204867

The Melita has over many years established itself as one of the Premier Private Hotels in Stratford-upon-Avon.

Stratford Visitor Satisfaction Business Award Winner.

This beautifully appointed Victorian house offers a friendly welcome, cheerful service and an excellent breakfast menu. Guests can enjoy a drink in the cosy lounge or simply relax in the hotel's beautiful gardens. There is ample car parking and the theatres and town centre are a pleasant seven minutes walk away. All bedrooms are non smoking, have private facilities, direct dial telephones, TV, tea/coffee. Ground floor rooms are available.

Visa, Mastercard and American Express accepted.

RAC Highly Acclaimed.

RAC Hotel Reservations Service
0870 603 9109
(Calls charged at national call rate)

VICTORIA SPA LODGE
RAC Highly Acclaimed

Victoria Spa Lodge is an elegant English home. Seven beautiful and comfortable en-suite bedrooms. Princess Victoria, later to become Queen, stayed when it was a Spa. She gave it her name, and her coat of arms can still be seen built into the gables. All rooms have colour TV, radio, hairdryer and hostess tray. Completely non-smoking. Open all year. Ample car parking. Full fire certificate. Visa and Mastercard accepted.

RAC Best Small Hotel 1995 Midland Region.
Your hosts are Paul and Dreen Tozer.

Bishopton Lane, Stratford-upon-Avon, Warwickshire CV37 9QY
Telephone: (01789) 267985 Fax: (01789) 204728

★★ Stratford Court
Hospitality, Comfort, Restaurant merit awards
Avenue Road, Stratford-upon-Avon CV37 6UX
📞 01789-297799 Fax 01789-262449

An elegant Edwardian house set in an extensive garden.

11 bedrs, all ensuite, **CC** MC Visa

Hardwick *Highly Acclaimed*
1 Avenue Road, Stratford-upon-Avon CV37 6UY
📞 01789-204307 Fax 01789-296760
Closed Christmas

A large Victorian house set in a quiet, mature, tree lined avenue, a few minutes walk from the town centre. Non smoking bedrooms. Large car park.

14 bedrs, 13 ensuite, 1 ⇌ **TCF TV P** 12 **SB** £28-£38 **DB** £38-£56 **CC** MC Visa Amex JCB

Melita *Highly Acclaimed*
37 Shipston Road, Stratford-upon-Avon CV37 7LN
📞 01789-292432 Fax 01789-204867
Closed Christmas
12 bedrs, all ensuite, **TCF TV** ⌛ ⇸ **P** 12 **SB** £32-£45 **DB** £49-£75 **CC** MC Visa Amex JCB
See advert on previous page

Sequoia House *Highly Acclaimed*
51-53 Shipston Road, Stratford-upon-Avon CV57 7LN
📞 01789-268852 Fax 01789-414559
Closed 21-27 Dec
24 bedrs, all ensuite, **TCF TV** ⌛ **P** 28 No children under 5 **SB** £32-£55 **DB** £42-£72 **CC** MC Visa Amex DC
See advert on previous page

Twelfth Night *Highly Acclaimed*
Evesham Place, Stratford-upon-Avon CV37 6HT
📞 01789-414595

Somewhere special - once owned for a quarter of a century by the Royal Shakespeare Co., this beautifully restored Victorian villa provides nostalgia and luxurious accommodation for the discerning.

6 bedrs, all ensuite, **TCF TV** ⌛ **P** 6 No children under 14 **DB** £44-£58 **CC** MC Visa

Victoria Spa Lodge *Highly Acclaimed*
Bishopton Lane, Bishopton, Stratford-upon-Avon CV37 9QY
📞 01789-267985 Fax 01789-204728

An elegant English house dating back to 1837. Situated in a green area overlooking Stratford Canal, not far from the town centre. Best Small Hotel 1995 Midland Region.

7 bedrs, all ensuite, 1 ⇌ **TCF TV** ⌛ **P** 12 **SB** £40-£45 **DB** £45-£55 **CC** MC Visa
See advert on previous page

Ambleside *Acclaimed*
41 Grove Road, Stratford-upon-Avon CV37 6PB
📞 01789-297239 Fax 01789-295670

STRATFORD-UPON-AVON – ENGLAND

Ideal base for exploring the wealth of history and culture both in and around the town, all the Shakespeare properties and the Royal Shakespeare Theatre, etc.

7 bedrs, 4 ensuite, 1, 1 TCF TV P 8 SB £22-£25 DB £40-£48 CC MC Visa JCB

Nando's *Acclaimed*
18 & 19 Evesham Place, Stratford-upon-Avon CV37 6HT
01789-204907 Fax 01789-204907
20 bedrs, 17 ensuite, 2 TCF TV P 8 SB £21-£30 DB £30-£45 D £8 CC MC Visa Amex DC JCB

Virginia Lodge *Acclaimed*
12 Evesham Place, Stratford-upon-Avon CV37 6HT
01789-292157 Fax 01789-414 872
Closed 23-31 Dec
7 bedrs, all ensuite, TCF TV P 6

Avon View *Listed*
121 Shipston Road, Stratford-upon-Avon CV37 9LQ
01789-297542

Broadlands *Listed*
23 Evesham Place, Stratford-upon-Avon CV37 6HT
01789-299181
Closed Christmas

A warm welcome awaits you at our family run guest house. Within 10 minutes walk from town centre, theatres and station. Parking for five. £14 to £25 per person.

5 bedrs, 4 ensuite, 1 TCF TV P 5 No children under 2 SB £14-£25 DB £28-£50

Cymbeline House *Listed*
24 Evesham Place, Stratford-upon-Avon CV37 6HT
01789-292958 Fax 01789-292958
5 bedrs, 3 ensuite, 1, 1 P 2 SB £16-£22 DB £32-£44

Dylan *Listed*
10 Evesham Place, Stratford-upon-Avon CV37 6HT
01789-204819
5 bedrs, all ensuite, TCF TV P 5 No children under 4 SB £20-£24 DB £36-£44

Marlyn *Listed*
3 Chestnut Walk, Stratford-upon-Avon CV37 6HG
01789-293752 Fax 01789-293752

The Marlyn with Andrew or Rosie welcome you to Stratford just five minutes away from the centre and theatre. We offer a long, comfortable stay.

8 bedrs, 4 ensuite, 1 TCF TV SB £18 DB £34-£44 D £7 CC MC Visa

Minola *Listed*
25 Evesham Place, Stratford-upon-Avon CV37 6HT
01789-293573
5 bedrs, 2 ensuite, 2, 1 TCF TV 1

Parkfield *Listed*
3 Broad Walk, Stratford-upon-Avon CV37 6HS
01789-293313 Fax 01789-293313
7 bedrs, 5 ensuite, 1 TCF TV P 7 No children under 5 SB £19 DB £42 CC MC Visa DC JCB

Penryn *Listed*
126 Alcester Road, Stratford-upon-Avon CV37 9DP
01789-293718
8 bedrs, 6 ensuite, 2 TCF TV P 8 SB £17-£36 DB £17-£50 CC MC Visa Amex DC

Courtland
12 Guild Street, Stratford-upon-Avon CV37 6RE
01789-292401 Fax 01789-292401

Spacious Georgian house with antique furniture. Town centre situation at rear of shakespeare's birthplace. 3 minutes theatre, station collection on request, super breakfasts with home made preserves,

7 bedrs, 3 ensuite, 2 TCF TV P 3 SB £22-£27.50 DB £40-£55 CC MC Visa Amex

STRATFORD-UPON-AVON – ENGLAND

Hunters Moon
150 Alcester Road, Stratford-upon-Avon CV37 9DR
☎ 01789-292888

Close to Ann Hathaways cottage and an ideal base for visiting the Cotswold villages, Warwick Castle and all other Shakespearean properties. English Tourist Board 2 Crowns.

7 bedrs, all ensuite, TCF TV P 6 CC MC Visa

Linhill
35 Evesham Place, Stratford-upon-Avon
☎ 01789-292879 Fax 01789-292879

Diana and her family assure you of a warm welcome, comfortable accommodation and excellent home cooked food. Situated 5 minutes walk into Stratford town centre.

8 bedrs, 2 ensuite, 2 ⇌ TCF TV SB £14-£19 DB £14-£24 HB £140-£160 D £6.50

Penshurst
34 Evesham Place, Stratford-upon-Avon CV37 6HT
☎ 01789-205259 Fax 01789-295322

A prettily refurbished Victorian townhouse five minutes walk from the centre. Totally non-smoking. Delicious breakfasts served from 7am right up until 10.30am. Excellent value for money. ETB commended.

8 bedrs, 2 ensuite, 2 ⇌ TCF TV ✉ SB £16-£20 DB £30-£42 HB £150-£206 D £8.50 ♿

Thornton Manor
Ettington, Stratford-upon-Avon CV37 7PN
☎ 01789-740210

Enjoy a quiet relaxed atmosphere in a 16th century stone built manor house overlooking fields with sheep and horses. Convenient for the Cotswolds, Warwick, Stratford, NEC and M40.

3 bedrs, 2 ensuite, TCF P 4 No children under 5

Travellers Rest
146 Alcester Road, Stratford-upon-Avon CV37 9DR
☎ 01789-266589

Small friendly guest house within walking distance of the town and Anne Hathaway's cottage. Lovely ensuite bedrooms with your comfort in mind. A choice of breakfast including vegetarian. Private parking.

STROUD Gloucestershire   7E4

★★ Bell
Wallbridge, Stroud GL5 3JA
☎ 01453-763556 Fax 01453-758611
12 bedrs, 10 ensuite, 1 ⇌ TV ♣ P 30 SB £30 DB £40 HB £275 D £11.95 CC MC Visa DC ♿

★★ Imperial
Station Road, Stroud GL5 3AP
☎ 01453-764077 Fax 01453-751314
25 bedrs, all ensuite, TCF TV 🐕 P 17 SB £42.50 DB £55
D £9.95 CC MC Visa Amex DC

★★ London
30-31 London Road, Stroud GL5 2AJ
☎ 01453-759992 Fax 01453-753363
12 bedrs, 8 ensuite, 1 🛏 TCF TV P 10 CC MC Visa Amex

Downfield *Acclaimed*
134 Cainscross Road, Stroud GL5 4HN
☎ 01453-764496 Fax 01453-753150
Closed Christmas

An imposing Georgian house in a quiet location offering comfort and a relaxed atmosphere, while maintaining professional standards.

21 bedrs, 11 ensuite, 3 🛏 TCF TV 🐕 P 21 SB £23-£29 DB £33-£39 D £8 CC MC Visa Amex DC JCB

Rose & Crown *Listed*
Nympsfield, Stonehouse, Stroud GL10 3TU
☎ 01453-860240 Fax 01453-860900
E Mail roseandcrowninn@btinternet.com

A 300 year old Cotswold-stone inn of character situated in a peaceful village near the Cotswold edge, within easy reach of the M4 and M5.

4 bedrs, 3 ensuite, 1 🛏 TCF TV P 30 SB £33 DB £56
D £10 CC MC Visa Amex DC JCB

STUDLAND Dorset   3F3

★★ Manor House
Studland Bay, Swanage BH19 3AU
☎ 01929-450288 Fax 01929-450288
Closed Christmas-mid Jan
20 bedrs, all ensuite, 1 🛏 TCF TV 🐕 P 80 No children under 5 SB £33-£43 DB £66-£116 HB £270-£370 D £19
CC MC Visa Amex

STURMINSTER NEWTON Dorset   3F2

DOWNFIELD
HOTEL

An imposing Georgian house in a quiet location offering a comfortable atmosphere. One mile from the centre of Stroud and 5 miles from M5 junction 13/A419. 21 bedrooms. Majority include ensuite facilities, colour TV inc. Sky, direct dial telephones, tea/coffee units. Some ground floor rooms. Families and pets welcome. Excellent food, bar, separate TV lounge. Large car park. RAC Acclaimed. Mastercard, Visa, Eurocheque accepted.

Bed and Breakfast from £16.50 per person.

**134 CAINSCROSS ROAD,
STROUD GL5 4HN**
Tel: (01453) 764496 Fax: (01453) 753150

Stourcastle Lodge

Scrumptious food and well equipped bedrooms overlooking the delightful south facing garden, enhanced by the courteous service from Jill and Ken, the owners of the 17th century Stourcastle Lodge.

**GOUGH'S CLOSE,
STURMINSTER NEWTON,
DORSET DT10 1BU
Tel: 01258-472320
Fax: 01258-473381**

Stourcastle Lodge *Acclaimed*
Gough's Close, Sturminster Newton DT10 1BU
☎ 01258-472320 Fax 01258-473381
5 bedrs, all ensuite, TCF TV P 10 SB £33-£42 DB £53-£68
HB £267-£315 D £16 CC MC Visa
See advert on previous page

SUDBURY Suffolk   9E4

Old Bull Hotel & Restaurant *Acclaimed*
Church Street, Sudbury CO10 6BL
☎ 01787-374120 Fax 01787-379044

Family run 16th century hotel and a la carte restaurant. Two minutes from ancient water meadows and Quay Theatre. Easy access to Constable country.

9 bedrs, 3 ensuite, 4, TCF TV P 16 SB £30-£38
DB £40-£49 D £10 CC MC Visa Amex DC JCB

SURBITON Surrey   4C3

Pembroke Lodge *Listed*
35 Cranes Park, Surbiton KT5 8AB
☎ 0181-390 0731 Fax 0181-390 0731
10 bedrs, 2 ensuite, 3, 2 P 10 SB £29 DB £38

SUTTON Surrey   5D3

★★ Thatched House
135 Cheam Road, Sutton SM1 2BN
☎ 0181-642 3131 Fax 0181-770 0684
32 bedrs, 28 ensuite, 1, 3 TCF TV P 20 SB £40-£45 DB £60-£75 D £15 CC MC Visa DC JCB

Ashling Tara *Acclaimed*
50 Rosehill, Sutton SM1 3EU
☎ 0181-641 6142 Fax 0181-644 7872
17 bedrs, 15 ensuite, 1 TCF TV P 18 SB £45-£58
DB £56-£65 HB £280-£350 D £12 CC MC Visa Amex JCB

Dene *Listed*
39 Cheam Road, Sutton SM1 2AT
☎ 0181-642 3170 Fax 0181-642 3170
28 bedrs, 12 ensuite, 4, 4 TCF TV P 18 SB £21-£40 DB £40-£50

Eaton Court *Listed*
49 Eaton Road, Sutton SM2 5ED
☎ 0181-643 6766 Fax 0181-642 4580
Closed Christmas
12 bedrs, 6 ensuite, 2 TCF TV P 6 SB £30 DB £42
CC MC Visa Amex

SUTTON IN THE ELMS Leicestershire   8B3

★★ Mill On The Soar
B4114 Coventry Road, Sutton in the Elms LE9 6QD
☎ 01455-282419 Fax 01455-285937
20 bedrs, all ensuite, P 200 CC MC Visa

SUTTON-ON-SEA Lincolnshire   9D1

Athelstone Lodge *Acclaimed*
25 Trusthorpe Road, Sutton-on-Sea LN12 2LR
☎ 01507-441521
6 bedrs, 5 ensuite, 1, 1 TCF TV P 6 SB £17-£19
DB £34-£38 HB £147-£160 D £10 CC MC Visa JCB

SWAFFHAM Norfolk   9E3

★★ Lydney House
Norwich Road, Swaffham PE37 7QS
☎ 01760-723355 Fax 01760-721410
12 bedrs, all ensuite, TCF TV P 80 SB £39.50-£41.50
DB £53-£55.50 D £15 CC MC Visa Amex

Horse & Groom *Highly Acclaimed*
Restaurant merit award
40 Lynn Street, Swaffham PE37 7AX
☎ 01760-721567
14 bedrs, 11 ensuite, 3, 1 TCF TV P 10 SB £25-£35 DB £35-£50 D £8 CC MC Visa Amex DC JCB

SWANAGE Dorset   3F3

★ Suncliffe
1 Burlington Road, Swanage BH19 2AD
☎ 01929-423299

Havenhurst *Acclaimed*
3 Cranborne Road, Swanage BH19 1EA
☎ 01929-424224 Fax 01929-424224
17 bedrs, all ensuite, TCF TV P 20 SB £18-£29 DB £36-£58 HB £180-£245 D £12 CC MC Visa

Sandringham *Acclaimed*
20 Durlston Road, Swanage BH19 2HX
☎ 01929-423076 Fax 01929-423076
11 bedrs, 9 ensuite, 1 TCF P 8 SB £23-£27 DB £46-£54
HB £198-£222 D £10 CC MC Visa

Chines *Listed*
9 Burlington Road, Swanage BH19 1LR
📞 01929-422457
Closed Oct-Mar
12 bedrs, 9 ensuite, 2 🛁 TCF TV P 10 SB £18-£22.50
DB £36-£45 HB £213.50-£245 D £12.50 ⌘

Eversden *Listed*
5 Victoria Road, Swanage BH19 1LY
📞 01929-423276

Firswood *Listed*
29 Kings Road, Swanage BH19 9HF
📞 01929-422306
Closed Christmas
6 bedrs, 5 ensuite, 1 🛁 TCF TV P 7 No children under 5 SB £15.50-£16 DB £32-£35

Glenlee *Listed*
6 Cauldon Avenue, Swanage BH19 1PQ
📞 01929-425794
Closed Nov-Mar
7 bedrs, all ensuite, TCF TV 🐕 P 6 DB £38-£50 HB £178-£208 D £8 CC MC Visa

St Michaels *Listed*
31 Kings Road, Swanage BH19 1HF
📞 01929-422064
5 bedrs, all ensuite, 1 🛁 TCF TV 🐕 P 5 No children under 5 DB £30-£35 HB £158-£178 D £8

SWINDON Wiltshire   4A2

Fir Tree Lodge *Highly Acclaimed*
17 Highworth Road, Stratton St Margaret, Swindon SN3 4QL
📞 01793-822372
11 bedrs, all ensuite, TCF TV 🐕 P 14 SB £25-£30 DB £35-£40 ♿

King's Arms
Wood Street, Old Town, Swindon SN1 4AB
📞 01793-522156 Fax 01793-432736

Well situated in Old Town area of Swindon with comfortable rooms and high standards of food and service. Close to motorway, railway and bus stations.

17 bedrs, 15 ensuite, TCF TV 🐕 P 17 SB £35-£45 DB £40-£50 D £25 CC MC Visa Amex JCB

SYMONDS YAT Herefordshire   7E4

★★ Old Court
Symonds Yat West HR9 6DA
📞 01600-890367 Fax 01600-890964
E Mail oldcourt@aol.com
20 bedrs, 14 ensuite, 2 🛁 TCF TV 🐕 P 50 No children under 12 SB £45 DB £70 D £19 CC MC Visa Amex DC ⌘

Saracens Head Inn *Highly Acclaimed*
Symonds Yat East, Ross-on-Wye HR9 6JL
📞 01600-890435 Fax 01600-890034
Closed weekdays Dec & Jan
9 bedrs, all ensuite, TCF P 30 SB £28 DB £50 HB £170 D £15 CC MC Visa DC ⌘

Garth Cottage *Acclaimed*
Symonds Yat East, Ross-on-Wye, Symonds Yat HR9 6JL
📞 01600-890364
Closed winter
4 bedrs, all ensuite, 1 🛁 TCF P 9 No children under 12 DB £46 HB £248 D £15.70 ⌘

Woodlea *Acclaimed*
Symonds Yat West, Ross-on-Wye HR9 6BL
📞 01600-890206 Fax 01600-890206
8 bedrs, 6 ensuite, 2 🛁 TCF 🐕 P 9 SB £25 DB £50 HB £241-£250 D £14.95 CC MC Visa

TAMWORTH Staffordshire   7F2

★★ Castle
Ladybank, Tamworth B79 7NB
📞 01827-57181 Fax 01827-54303
36 bedrs, all ensuite, TCF TV SB £32.50-£67.50 DB £49.95-£87.50 D £12.50 CC MC Visa Amex DC

Victoria Court
42 Victoria Road, Tamworth B79 7HU
📞 01827-64698 Fax 01827-312368

A licensed hotel with ensuite and budget rooms, and an Italian restaurant. Within walking distance of Tamworth railway station, shops and ski centre.

9 bedrs, 5 ensuite, 3 🛏, 1 🛁 TCF TV P 20 SB £18-£35 DB £35-£40 HB £133-£208 D £4 CC MC Visa Amex DC JCB

TAUNTON Somerset   3D2

★★ Corner House
Restaurant merit award
Park Street, Taunton TA1 4DQ
☎ 01823-284683 Fax 01823-323464
Closed Christmas week
29 bedrs, all ensuite, TCF TV P 40 SB £52 DB £72.25
D £17 CC MC Visa Amex JCB

★★ Falcon
Hospitality merit award
Taunton TA3 5DM
☎ 01823-442502 Fax 01823-442670
11 bedrs, all ensuite, TCF TV ✱ P 30
SB £45-£55 DB £55-£65 D £15 CC MC Visa Amex DC

Meryan House *Highly Acclaimed*
Bishops Hull, Taunton TA1 5EG
☎ 01823-337445 Fax 01823-322355
12 bedrs, all ensuite, TCF TV ✱ P 17 SB £40-£50 DB £50-£58 D £17 CC MC Visa JCB ♿

Brookfield *Acclaimed*
16 Wellington Road, Taunton TA1 4EQ
☎ 01823-272786
8 bedrs, 6 ensuite, 2 ✱ TCF TV ✱ P 7 SB £19-£22
DB £34-£40

Old Manor Farmhouse *Acclaimed*
Norton Fitzwarren, Taunton TA2 6RZ
☎ 01823-289801 Fax 01823-289801
7 bedrs, all ensuite, 1 ✱ P 12 CC MC Visa Amex DC

Acorn Lodge *Listed*
22 Wellington Road, Taunton TA1 4EQ
☎ 01823-337613
6 bedrs, 2 ✱ TCF TV P 4 SB £17.50 DB £30 HB £178.50

Queens Arms *Listed*
Pitminster, Taunton TA3 7AZ
☎ 01823-421529 Fax 01823-421635
4 bedrs, 2 ensuite, 2 ✱ TCF TV ✱ P 20 SB £30 DB £40
D £6.95 CC MC Visa

Roadchef Lodge *Lodge*
Taunton Deane Motorway Service Area, M5
Southbound, Trull TA3 7PF
☎ 01823-332228 Fax 01823-338131
Closed 24 Dec-2 Jan
39 bedrs, all ensuite, TCF TV P 150 **Room only rate**
£43.50 D £4.50 CC MC Visa Amex DC ♿

Don't forget to mention the guide
When booking direct, please remember to
tell the hotel that you chose it from
RAC Bed & Breakfast 1998.

Prockters Farm
West Monkton, Taunton TA2 8QN
☎ 01823-412269 Fax 01823-412269

A lovely 17th century farmhouse, full of character with exposed oak beams and log fires. Ideally placed to explore the Exmoor and Quantock Hills and the nearby coastline, yet is only 2 miles from Taunton and 10 minutes from the M5 (jn 25).

6 bedrs, 2 ensuite, 2 ✱ TCF TV ✱ P 6 SB £18-£25
DB £36-£42 ▣ ♿

TEBAY Cumbria   10B2

Carmel House *Acclaimed*
Carmel House, Mount Pleasant, Tebay CA10 3TH
☎ 01539-624651
7 bedrs, all ensuite, TCF TV P 7 SB £17-£18 DB £33-£35
CC Amex

TEIGNMOUTH Devon   3D3

Beachley
3 Brunswick Street, Teignmouth TQ14 8AE
☎ 01626-774249

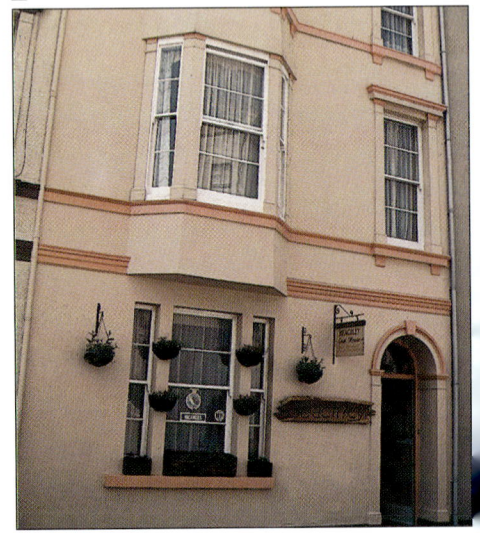

Bed & breakfast, evening meal with good home cooking - your every satisfaction assured. One minute to sea front and shops. Level position. Open all year.

TELFORD Shropshire 7E2

THE IRONBRIDGE GORGE MUSEUM

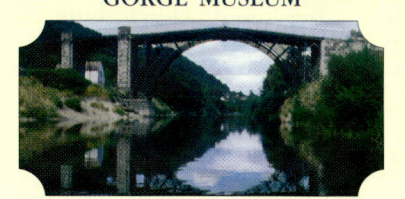

The Ironbridge Gorge in Shropshire is ideal for a short break in stunning scenery with marvellous Museums and Heritage.

IRONBRIDGE GORGE MUSEUMS
Open Daily 10.00-17.00
Tel: 01952 433522/432166 Fax: 01952 432204

★★ White House
Hospitality merit award
Wellington Road, Muxton, Telford TF2 8NG
☎ 01952-604276 Fax 01952-670336
30 bedrs, all ensuite, TCF TV ⚑ P 100 SB £45-£55 DB £55-£66 D £13 CC MC Visa Amex JCB ♿

TENTERDEN Kent 5E3

★★ Little Silver
Hospitality, Comfort, Restaurant merit awards
St Michaels, Tenterden TN30 6SP
☎ 01233-850321 Fax 01233-850647
10 bedrs, all ensuite, TCF TV ⚑ P 100 SB £65 DB £85-£110 D £15 CC MC Visa Amex ▶ ♿

TETBURY Gloucestershire 3F1

Tavern House *Highly Acclaimed*
Willesley, Tetbury GL8 8QU
☎ 01666-880444 Fax 01666-880254

A 17th century, Cotswold stone, Grade II Listed, former staging post, with leaded windows. Charming secluded walled gardens. Close to Westonbirt Arboretum. Excellent base from which to explore the Cotswolds.

4 bedrs, all ensuite, TCF TV P 6 No children under 10 SB £45-£48 DB £57-£66 CC MC Visa

TEWKESBURY Gloucestershire 7E4

★★ Tudor House
High Street, Tewkesbury GL20 5BH
☎ 01684-297755 Fax 01684-290306
21 bedrs, 15 ensuite, TCF TV ⚑ P 20 CC MC Visa Amex DC

Corner Cottage
Stow Road, Alderton, Tewkesbury GL20 8NH
☎ 01242-620630

Originally two farm cottages, now a family home where guests are assured of a warm welcome and a hearty breakfast. An ideal location for touring the Cotswolds.

3 bedrs, 1 ⚑ TCF TV P 6

THAME Oxfordshire 4B2

Essex House *Highly Acclaimed*
Chinnor Road, Thame OX9 3LS
☎ 01844-217567 Fax 01844-216420
13 bedrs, 11 ensuite, 1 ⚑ TCF TV P 15 SB £35 DB £45 CC MC Visa Amex DC

THETFORD Norfolk 9E3

★★ Woodland Comfort Inn
Thetford Road, Northwold, Thetford IP26 5LQ
☎ 01366-728888 Fax 01366-727121
E Mail admin@gb632.u-net.com
34 bedrs, all ensuite, TCF TV ⚑ P 250 SB £47-£59 DB £54-£65 D £9.75 CC MC Visa Amex DC ✈ ♿

THIRSK North Yorkshire 11D2

★★ Angel Inn
Hospitality, Comfort merit awards
Long Street, Topcliffe, Thirsk YO7 3RW
☎ 01845-577237 Fax 01845-578000
15 bedrs, all ensuite, 1 ⚑ TCF TV P 150 SB £39 DB £55 D £15 CC MC Visa

★★ Sheppard's
Hospitality, Comfort, Restaurant merit awards
Church Farm, Front Street Sowerby, Thirsk YO7 1JF
📞 01845-523655 Fax 01845-524720
Closed 1st week in Jan
8 bedrs, all ensuite, TCF TV P 30 No children under 10
SB £55-£60 DB £70-£80 D £18.50 CC MC Visa

THORNE South Yorkshire 8B1

★★ Belmont
Horse Fair Green, Thorne, Doncaster DN8 5EE
📞 01405-812320 Fax 01405-740508
24 bedrs, all ensuite, P 20 SB £48.95-£55.95
DB £64.95-£85 D £11 CC MC Visa Amex DC

THORNTHWAITE Cumbria 10A2

★★ Ladstock Country House
Thornthwaite CA12 5RZ
📞 01768-778210 Fax 01768-778088
22 bedrs, 18 ensuite, 2 P 60 CC MC Visa JCB

THORNTON CLEVELEYS Lancashire 10B3

★★ Regal
Victoria Road West, Thornton Cleveleys FY5 1AG
📞 01253-852244 Fax 01253-859153
41 bedrs, all ensuite, TCF TV P 15 SB £30 DB £53-£54 HB £196-£204 D £8 CC MC Visa

THURGARTON Norfolk 9E2

Grange
Harmers Lane, Thurgarton NR11 7PF
📞 01263-761588

Fine country house situated in secluded grounds of two acres, offering peace and tranquillity in friendly, comfortable surroundings, close to coast and central for local attractions and National Trust properties.

2 bedrs, 2, TCF

TINTAGEL Cornwall 2B3

★★ Bossiney House
Bossiney, Tintagel PL34 0AX
📞 01840-770240 Fax 01840-770501
Closed Dec-Jan
20 bedrs, 18 ensuite, TCF TV P 40 DB £56-£60
HB £280-£296 D £12 CC MC Visa Amex DC JCB

★★ Port William Inn
Trebarwith Strand, Tintagel PL34 0HB
📞 01840-770230 Fax 01840-770936

Probably the best location in Cornwall, romantically situated 50 yards from the sea, beach and cliffs at Trebarwith Strand.

6 bedrs, all ensuite, TCF TV P 50 SB £50-£72 DB £150-£225 D £5 CC MC Visa Amex

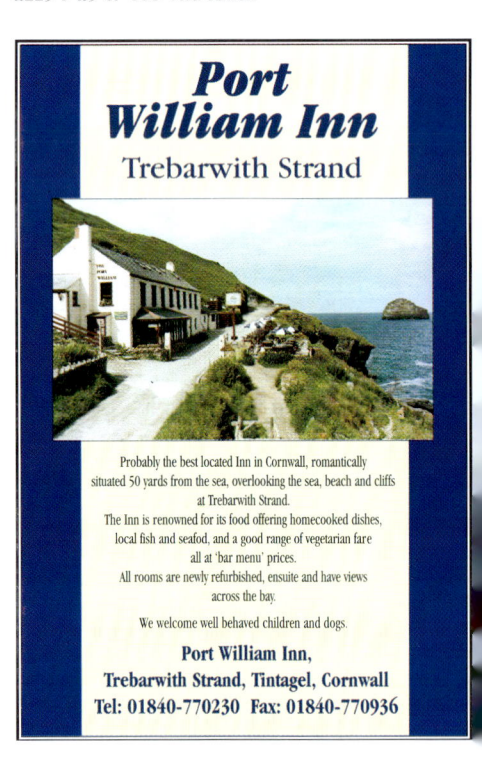

Port William Inn
Trebarwith Strand

Probably the best located Inn in Cornwall, romantically situated 50 yards from the sea, overlooking the sea, beach and cliffs at Trebarwith Strand.
The Inn is renowned for its food offering homecooked dishes, local fish and seafood, and a good range of vegetarian fare all at 'bar menu' prices.
All rooms are newly refurbished, ensuite and have views across the bay.
We welcome well behaved children and dogs.

Port William Inn,
Trebarwith Strand, Tintagel, Cornwall
Tel: 01840-770230   Fax: 01840-770936

TIVERTON Devon 3D2

Bickleigh Cottage *Acclaimed*
Bickleigh Bridge, Tiverton EX16 8RJ
☎ 01884-855230
Closed winter
9 bedrs, 7 ensuite, 2 ⇌ TCF P 10 No children under 14
SB £29 DB £46 D £12 CC MC Visa

Bridge *Acclaimed*
23 Angel Hill, Tiverton EX16 6PE
☎ 01884-252804 Fax 01884-253949

Attractive Victorian town house on the banks of the River Exe with a pretty riverside tea garden. Ideal for touring the heart of Devon.

9 bedrs, 5 ensuite, 2 ⇌ TCF TV ⇌ P 6 SB £18-£19
DB £38-£46 HB £190-£220 D £10

Lodge Hill Farm *Listed*
Tiverton EX16 5PA
☎ 01884-252907 Fax 01884-242090
8 bedrs, all ensuite, 1 ⇌ TCF TV ⇌ P 12 SB £18 DB £36
HB £172 D £10.50 CC MC Visa Amex

Old Rectory
Withleigh, Tiverton EX16 8JG
☎ 01884-243846 Fax 01884-258088
Closed Christmas & Easter

Gracious accommodation in unspoilt mid-Devon. In spring/summer you can hear the birds sing in parklike gardens or relax in our magnificent conservatory.

2 bedrs, all ensuite, TCF TV ⇌ P 4 No children SB £18-£20 DB £34-£36

TIVETSHALL ST MARY Norfolk 9E3

★★ Old Ram Coaching Inn
Comfort, Restaurant merit awards
Ipswich Road, Tivetshall St Mary NR15 2DE
☎ 01379-676794 Fax 01379-608399
Closed 25-26 Dec
11 bedrs, all ensuite, TCF TV P 120 SB £49 DB £68 D £8
CC MC Visa

TONBRIDGE Kent 5D3

Vauxhall Premier Lodge *Lodge*
Pembury Road, Tonbridge TN11 0NA
☎ 01732-773111 Fax 01732-771534
39 bedrs, all ensuite, TCF TV P 120 SB £49.95 DB £49.95
D £11 CC MC Visa Amex DC JCB &

TORCROSS Devon 3D4

★ Greyhomes
Torcross TQ7 2TH
☎ 01548-580220
7 bedrs, 5 ensuite, TCF TV P 15 No children under 4
SB £32-£34 DB £52-£56 HB £238-£250 D £14 CC MC Visa

TORMARTON Gloucestershire 3F1

★★ Compass Inn
Comfort merit award
Badminton, Tormarton GL9 1JB
☎ 01454-218242 Fax 01454-218741
Closed 25-26 Dec
26 bedrs, all ensuite, TCF TV ⇌ P 160 SB £69-£85.50
DB £79.95-£99.95 D £15 CC MC Visa Amex DC JCB &

TORPOINT Cornwall 2C4

★★ Whitsand Bay
Portwrinkle, Crafthole, Torpoint PL11 3BU
☎ 01503-230276 Fax 01503-230329
36 bedrs, all ensuite, 2 ⇌ TCF TV ⇌ P 50 SB £20-£35
DB £40-£60 HB £210-£310 D £15 CC MC Visa

TORQUAY Devon 3D3

★★ Abbey Court
Falkland Road, Torquay TQ2 5JR
☎ 01803-297316 Fax 01803-297316
Closed Jan-Feb
25 bedrs, 22 ensuite, 3 ⇌ TCF TV P 16 SB £19-£29
DB £38-£58 HB £168-£214 D £8 CC MC Visa DC

TORQUAY – ENGLAND

★★ Ansteys Lea
Babbacombe Road, Torquay TQ1 2QJ
☎ 01803-294843 Fax 01803-214333
Closed Jan-Feb
24 bedrs, all ensuite, TCF TV P 20 No children under 2 SB £23-£29 DB £46-£58 HB £172-£220 D £9 CC MC Visa DC JCB

★★ Apsley
Torwood Gardens Road, Torquay TQ1 1EG
☎ 01803-292058 Fax 01803-215105
33 bedrs, 32 ensuite, 1, 1 TCF TV P 20 SB £23-£30 DB £46-£60 HB £187-£230 D £7.50 CC MC Visa Amex

★★ Bancourt
Avenue Road, Torquay TQ2 5LG
☎ 01803-295077 Fax 01803-201114
40 bedrs, all ensuite, TCF TV P 40 SB £18-£30 DB £36-£60 HB £126-£245 D £12.50 CC MC Visa DC

★★ Burlington
462-466 Babbacombe Road, Torquay TQ1 1HN
☎ 01803-294374 Fax 01803-200189
E Mail burlington.hotel@virgin.net
55 bedrs, all ensuite, TCF TV P 20 SB £30-£35 DB £50-£60 HB £175-£199 D £10 CC MC Visa

★★ Bute Court
Hospitality merit award
Belgrave Road, Torquay TQ2 5HQ
☎ 01803-293771 Fax 01803-213429
45 bedrs, all ensuite, 3 TCF TV P 37 SB £19-£32 DB £38-£63 HB £145-£265 D £9 CC MC Visa Amex DC

★★ Cavendish
Belgrave Road, Torquay TQ2 5HN
☎ 01803-293682 Fax 01803-292802
46 bedrs, all ensuite, 3 TCF TV P 20 SB £20-£34 DB £36-£64 HB £165-£225 D £12.95 CC MC Visa DC

★★ Coppice
Barrington Road, Torquay TQ1 2QJ
☎ 01803-297786
Closed Dec-Feb
40 bedrs, 39 ensuite, 1 P 32

★★ Court
Lower Warberry Road, Torquay TQ1 1QS
☎ 01803-212011 Fax 01803-292648
Closed Nov-Feb excl Christmas
16 bedrs, all ensuite, 2 TCF TV P 15 SB £22-£28 DB £44-£55 HB £192-£227 D £12 CC MC Visa JCB

★★ Crofton House
Croft Road, Torquay TQ2 5TZ
☎ 01803-293761 Fax 01803-211796
36 bedrs, all ensuite, 3 TCF TV P 14 DB £26-£37 D £13 CC MC Visa JCB

★★ Gresham Court
Babbacombe Road, Torquay TQ1 1HG
☎ 01803-293007 Fax 01803-215951
Closed Dec-Mar
30 bedrs, all ensuite, TCF TV P 14 SB £22-£29 DB £44-£58 HB £180-£220 D £9 CC MC Visa JCB

★★ Hotel Balmoral
Meadfoot Beach, Torquay TQ1 2LQ
☎ 01803-299224 Fax 01803-293381
24 bedrs, all ensuite, TCF TV P 18 SB £25-£28 DB £50-£56 HB £174-£204 D £11.50 CC MC Visa Amex

★★ Howden Court
23 Croft Road, Torquay TQ2 5UD
☎ 01803-294844 Fax 01803-211350
Closed Nov-Mar
35 bedrs, all ensuite, TCF TV P 35 SB £25.50-£29.50 DB £51-£59.50 HB £178.50-£203 D £12.50 CC MC Visa

★★ Meadfoot Bay
Meadfoot Sea Road, Torquay TQ1 2LQ
☎ 01803-294722 Fax 01803-214473
Closed Jan-Feb
22 bedrs, all ensuite, 1 TCF TV P 20 No children under 2 SB £18-£33 DB £36-£66 HB £179-£220 D £10 CC MC Visa

★★ Morningside
Sea Front, Babbacombe Downs, Torquay TQ1 3LG
☎ 01803-327025 Fax 01803-328820
14 bedrs, all ensuite, P 16 CC MC Visa Amex DC

★★ Norcliffe
Babbacombe Downs Road, Torquay TQ1 3LF
☎ 01803-328456 Fax 01803-328023
27 bedrs, all ensuite, TCF TV P 20 SB £16-£25 DB £32-£50 HB £190-£240 D £11 CC MC Visa

★★ Roseland
Warren Road, Torquay TQ2 5TT
☎ 01803-213829 Fax 01803-291266
36 bedrs, all ensuite, 2 TCF TV SB £25-£30 DB £50-£60 HB £195-£199 D £8 CC MC Visa

★★ Shedden Hall
Shedden Hill, Torquay TQ2 5TX
☎ 01803-292964 Fax 01803-295306
Closed Jan
25 bedrs, all ensuite, TCF TV P 30 No children under 4 SB £20-£28 DB £40-£56 HB £186-£240 D £11 CC MC Visa Amex DC JCB

★★ Sydore
Meadfoot Road, Torquay TQ1 2JP
☎ 01803-294758 Fax 01803-294489
13 bedrs, all ensuite, TCF TV P 17 CC MC Visa Amex JCB

TORQUAY – ENGLAND

★ Ashley Rise
18 Babbacombe Road, Torquay TQ1 3SJ
📞 01803-327282
Closed Jan-Mar
25 bedrs, all ensuite, 🐾 P 14 SB £16-£18 DB £32-£36
HB £130-£175 D £12

★ Fairmount House
Hospitality, Restaurant merit awards
Herbert Road, Chelston, Torquay TQ2 6RW
📞 01803-605446 Fax 01803-605446
Closed Nov-Feb

Beautifully restored Victorian family home, with lovely gardens overlooking quiet residential valley near Cockington Country Park. Mouth watering menu and excellent home cooking.

8 bedrs, all ensuite, 1 🛌 TCF TV 🐾 P 9 SB £25-£32
DB £50-£64 HB £239-£288 D £12 CC MC Visa Amex ♿

★ Hotel Fluela
15/17 Hatfield Road, Torquay TQ1 3BW
📞 01803-297512 Fax 01803-296261
13 bedrs, all ensuite, 1 🛌 TCF TV P 20 SB £17.50-£21.50
DB £33-£41 HB £155-£184 D £8 CC MC Visa JCB

★ Shelley Court
Croft Road, Torquay TQ2 5UD
📞 01803-295642 Fax 01803-215793
28 bedrs, 24 ensuite, 1 🛌 TCF TV P 20 CC MC Visa ♿

★ Sunleigh
Livermead Hill, Torquay TQ2 6QY
📞 01803-607137
Closed Nov-Mar excl Christmas
20 bedrs, all ensuite, 1 🛌 TCF TV 🐾 P 17 SB £16-£26
DB £32-£52 HB £170-£225 D £10.95 CC MC Visa Amex DC

★ Tormohun
Newton Road, Torquay TQ2 5BZ
📞 01803-293681 Fax 01803-213860

Barn Hayes Country *Highly Acclaimed*
Brim Hill, Maidencombe, Torquay TQ1 4TR
📞 01803-327980 Fax 01803-327980
Closed Jan

Friendly and comfortable hotel with lovely gardens in an area of outstanding natural beauty overlooking countryside and sea. Prestigious award from the RAC for 1997.

12 bedrs, 10 ensuite, 1 🛌 TCF TV 🐾 P 14 SB £25-£28
DB £50-£56 HB £245-£266 D £13.50 CC MC Visa

Blue Haze *Highly Acclaimed*
Seaway Lane, Torquay TQ2 6PS
📞 01803-607186 Fax 01803-607186
Closed Nov-Mar

Small, attractive hotel with spacious rooms, set in a quiet leafy lane near the sea in three quarters of an acre of grounds including lovely gardens.

10 bedrs, all ensuite, TCF TV P 20 DB £56-£60 D £15 CC MC Visa Amex JCB

Glenorleigh *Highly Acclaimed*
26 Cleveland Road, Torquay TQ2 5BE
📞 01803-292135 Fax 01803 292135
16 bedrs, 9 ensuite, 4 🛌 TCF P 10 No children under 4
SB £16-£25 DB £36-£56 HB £160-£255 D £10 CC MC Visa

Haldon Priors *Highly Acclaimed*
Meadfoot Sea Road, Torquay TQ1 2LQ
📞 01803-213365
Closed Oct-Easter
8 bedrs, 7 ensuite, TCF P 7 SB £28-£31 DB £56-£76
See advert on next page

Kingston House *Highly Acclaimed*
75 Avenue Road, Torquay TQ2 5LL
📞 01803-212760
6 bedrs, all ensuite, TCF TV P 6 No children under 8
SB £17.50-£19.50 DB £29-£39 CC MC Visa DC

Newton House *Highly Acclaimed*
31 Newton Road, Torre, Torquay TQ2 5DB
📞 01803-297520

Norwood *Highly Acclaimed*
60 Belgrave Road, Torquay TQ2 5HY
📞 01803-294236 Fax 01803-294236
Closed Christmas
12 bedrs, 11 ensuite, 1 🛏 TCF TV P 3 SB £15-£20
DB £34-£43 HB £145-£184 D £9 CC MC Visa

Robin Hill *Highly Acclaimed*
Braddons Hill Road East, Torquay TQ1 1HF
📞 01803-214518 Fax 01803-291410
Closed winter

An impressive Victorian villa standing in its own terraced grounds offering visitors the elegance and service of yesteryear with all the comforts of today.

18 bedrs, all ensuite, TCF TV 🐕 P 12
SB £20-£28 DB £40-£56 HB £190-£246 D £12 CC MC Visa JCB

Haldon Priors
Meadfoot Sea Road, Torquay, Devon TQ1 2LQ
Tel: 01803 213365

Upmarket small hotel with a touch of luxury and nostalgic air of times past. Delightful setting in own grounds and Meadfoot Valley, with beach 200 yards away.
Recommended in 'Holiday Which' Jan '94. All bedrooms ensuite. Superb dining room, Victorian-style conservatory lounge. Swimming pool approx. 83°F. Renowned food and service. Secure parking.
Complimentary Devon cream tea upon arrival.
Your hosts Marion and Eric Grant.
Highly Acclaimed

Bahamas *Acclaimed*
17 Avenue Road, Torquay TQ2 5LB
📞 0500-526022 (free)
E Mail 101625.1626@compuserve.com
11 bedrs, all ensuite, TCF TV P 12 SB £19-£23 DB £38-£46 HB £190-£213 D £9.50 CC MC Visa Amex DC ♿

Belmont *Acclaimed*
66 Belgrave Road, Torquay TQ2 5HY
📞 01803-295028 Fax 01803-211668
13 bedrs, 9 ensuite, 1 🛏 TCF TV 🐕 P 3 No children under 5 CC MC Visa Amex DC

Chesterfield *Acclaimed*
62 Belgrave Road, Torquay TQ2 5HY
📞 01803-292318 Fax 01803-293676
11 bedrs, all ensuite, 1 🛏 TCF TV P 3 SB £18-£26
DB £28-£40 HB £145-£200 D £8 CC MC Visa

Colindale *Acclaimed*
20 Rathmore Road, Torquay TQ2 6NY
📞 01803-293947
8 bedrs, 2 ensuite, 2 🛏 TCF P 5 No children under 5
SB £14.50-£16.50 DB £29-£35 HB £142-£149 CC MC Visa

Craig Court *Acclaimed*
10 Ash Hill Road, Torquay TQ1 3HZ
📞 01803-294400
10 bedrs, 5 ensuite, 3 🛏 TCF TV 🐕 P 10 SB £16.50-£19.50 DB £33-£45 HB £154-£196 D £10 ♿

Cranborne *Acclaimed*
58 Belgrave Road, Torquay TQ2 5HY
📞 01803-298046 Fax 01803-298046
Closed Christmas-New Year
12 bedrs, 11 ensuite, 1 🛏 TCF TV P 3 SB £15-£24
DB £30-£48 HB £135-£187 CC MC Visa

Cranmore *Acclaimed*
89 Avenue Road, Torquay TQ2 5LH
📞 01803-298488

A friendly welcome awaits you at this comfortable family run hotel offering delicious, plentiful food. Close to all amenities with a level walk to the sea front and conference centre.

8 bedrs, all ensuite, TCF TV P 4 SB £14-£16 DB £28-£32
HB £144-£158 D £6.50 CC MC Visa Amex DC

Elmdene *Acclaimed*
Rathmore Road, Torquay TQ2 6NZ
☎ 01803-294940 Fax 01803-294940
11 bedrs, 7 ensuite, 1 ⇌ TCF TV ⌂ P 10 SB £18-£20.50 DB £36-£41 HB £175-£205 D £9.50 CC MC Visa

Everglades *Acclaimed*
32 Marychurch Road, Torquay TQ1 3HY
☎ 01803-295389 Fax 01803-214357
11 bedrs, all ensuite, TCF TV P 8 No children under 5 SB £19-£21 DB £38-£42 HB £155-£180 D £8 CC MC Visa JCB

Exmouth View *Acclaimed*
St Albans Road, Babbacombe, Torquay TQ1 3LG
☎ 01803-327307 Fax 01803-329967
Closed New Year
29 bedrs, 27 ensuite, 1 ⇌ TCF TV P 16 SB £17.60-£28.60 DB £35.20-£57.20 HB £155-£258 D £8 CC MC Visa ♿

Glenwood *Acclaimed*
Rowdens Road, Torquay TQ2 5AZ
☎ 01803-296318 Fax 01803-296318
11 bedrs, 9 ensuite, 1 ⇌ TCF TV ⌂ P 10 No children under 5 SB £20-£30 DB £36-£50 HB £178-£208 D £8.50 CC MC Visa JCB

Hotel Concorde *Acclaimed*
26 Newton Road, Torquay TQ2 5BZ
☎ 01803-292330

RAC Hotel Reservations Service
0870 603 9109
(Calls charged at national call rate)

Red Squirrel Lodge
10th Anniversary

A beautiful furnished Victorian villa with separate spacious gardens and forecourt set in Chelston, one of Torquay's most attractive and peaceful areas. The hotel is within 300 yards of the beach, the local shops and Torquay station, also close by is Cockington Village with its well known parks, gardens and wooded walks. The Red Squirrel Lodge has been established as one of Torquay's most distinctive hotels for many years where you can be sure of a welcome from your hosts.

CHELSTON ROAD, TORQUAY TQ2 6PU
Tel: 01803 605496 Fax: 01803 690170

Hotel Patricia *Acclaimed*
Belgrave Road, Torquay TQ2 5HY
☎ 01803-293339
10 bedrs, all ensuite, 1 ⇌ TCF TV P 9 No children under 5 SB £18-£24 DB £36-£48 HB £157-£189 D £9 CC MC Visa JCB

Ingoldsby *Acclaimed*
1 Chelston Road, Torquay TQ2 6PT
☎ 01803-607497
15 bedrs, 12 ensuite, 1 ⇌ TCF TV ⌂ P 12 SB £15-£21 DB £30-£42 HB £142-£179 CC MC Visa ♿

Lindens *Acclaimed*
31 Bampfylde Road, Torquay TQ2 5AY
☎ 01803-212281
7 bedrs, all ensuite, TCF TV ⌂ P 7 No children under 5 SB £15-£22 DB £30-£44 HB £144-£190 D £9

Rawlyn House *Acclaimed*
Rawlyn Road, Chelston, Torquay TQ2 6PL
☎ 01803-605208
Closed winter
17 bedrs, 14 ensuite, 1 ⇌ TCF TV P 17 ▣

Red Squirrel Lodge *Acclaimed*
Chelston Road, Torquay TQ2 6PU
☎ 01803-605496 Fax 01803-605496
14 bedrs, 10 ensuite, 4 ♺, TCF TV ⌂ P 10 No children under 7 SB £20-£25 DB £40-£50 HB £170-£200 CC MC Visa Amex ♿

Richwood *Acclaimed*
20 Newton Road, Torquay TQ2 5BZ
☎ 01803-293729 Fax 01803-213632
20 bedrs, all ensuite, TCF TV ⌂ P 14 SB £12-£22 DB £24-£44 HB £130-£187 D £8 CC MC Visa Amex JCB ▣ ▣

Seaway *Acclaimed*
Chelston Road, Torquay TQ2 6PU
☎ 01803-605320 Fax 01803-605320

A family run licensed hotel with a reputation for comfort and quality food, situated 200 metres from the sea in a conservation area. Colour TV and tea-making facilities in all rooms.

14 bedrs, 11 ensuite, 1 ⇌ TCF TV ⌂ P 17 SB £16-£22.50 DB £32-£45 HB £144-£199 CC MC Visa Amex

TORQUAY – ENGLAND

Shirley *Acclaimed*
Braddons Hill Road East, Torquay TQ1 1HF
📞 01803-293016
Closed Jan
14 bedrs, 11 ensuite, 1 🛏 TCF TV P 4 No children under 12 SB £16-£21 DB £32-£42 HB £130-£160 D £10 CC MC Visa 🖹 🖼

Trelawney *Acclaimed*
48 Belgrave Road, Torquay TQ2 5HS
📞 01803-296049 Fax 01803-296049
14 bedrs, all ensuite, 1 🛏 TCF TV P 2 DB £34-£44 CC MC Visa

Avron *Listed*
70 Windsor Road, Torquay TQ1 1SZ
📞 01803-294182
Closed Oct-Apr
14 bedrs, 6 ensuite, 2 🛏, 2 🛏 TCF TV 🍴 P 8 SB £15-£25 DB £30-£50 HB £115-£160 CC MC Visa

Briarfields *Listed*
84-86 Avenue Road, Torquay TQ2 5LF
📞 01803-297844
Closed 15 Nov-13 Jan
12 bedrs, 8 ensuite, 1 🛏, 1 🛏 🍴 P 10 SB £15-£18 DB £24-£34 CC MC Visa Amex

Lindum *Listed*
Abbey Road, Torquay TQ2 5NP
📞 01803-292795 Fax 01803-299358
E Mail lindum@mail.zynet.co.uk
20 bedrs, 14 ensuite, 3 🛏 TCF TV 14 SB £16-£27 DB £32-£54 HB £165-£230 D £8.50 CC MC Visa JCB ♿

Morley *Listed*
16 Bridge Road, Torquay TQ2 5BA
📞 01803-292955
Closed Nov-Mar
10 bedrs, 6 ensuite, 1 🛏 TCF TV P 4 No children under 5 SB £14-£17 DB £26-£36 HB £139-£169 D £8 CC MC Visa

Sherwood *Listed*
Belgrave Road, Torquay TQ2 5HP
📞 01803-294534 Fax 01803-294534
64 bedrs, all ensuite, 2 🛏 TCF P 35 SB £23.50-£30.50 DB £47-£61 HB £198-£240 CC MC Visa 🖹 🖼

Skerries *Listed*
25 Morgan Avenue, Torquay TQ2 5RR
📞 01803-293618 Fax 01803-293618
11 bedrs, 7 ensuite, 1 🛏 TCF TV 🍴 P 7 SB £14.50-£17.50 DB £29-£35 HB £116-£145 D £7 CC DC

Torbay Rise *Listed*
Old Mill Road, Chelston, Torquay TQ2 6HL
📞 01803-605241
15 bedrs, all ensuite, 1 🛏 TCF TV 🍴 P 10 No children under 5 CC MC Visa 🖹

Trafalgar House *Listed*
30 Bridge Road, Torquay TQ2 5BA
📞 01803-292486
12 bedrs, 7 ensuite, 3 🛏 TCF TV P 10 No children under 5 SB £14-£16 DB £28-£32 HB £135-£159

Silverlands
27 Newton Road, Torquay TQ2 5DB
📞 01803-292013

Situated on a main route to the town and beach (approx ½ mile), a superb family run guest house with 11 superior rooms, mostly ensuite, furnished and decorated to a high standard.

11 bedrs, 8 ensuite, 1 🛏 TCF TV 🍴 P 13 SB £14-£15 DB £20-£26 CC MC

TORRINGTON Devon   2C2

Smytham Manor *Acclaimed*
Little Torrington EX38 8PU
📞 01805-622110
Closed Nov-Feb
7 bedrs, 5 ensuite, 1 🛏 TCF TV 🍴 P 14 SB £15-£17 DB £32-£44 D £10 CC MC Visa 🖹 🖼

TOTNES Devon   3D3

★★ Old Church House Inn
Torbryan, Ipplepen, Totnes TQ12 5UR
📞 01803-812372 Fax 01803-812180
11 bedrs, all ensuite, TCF TV P 30 SB £45-£55 DB £75-£85 D £15 CC MC Visa ♿

★★ Royal Seven Stars
The Plains, Totnes TQ9 5DD
📞 01803-862125 Fax 01803-867925
18 bedrs, 12 ensuite, 3 🛏 TCF TV 🍴 P 20 SB £44-£52 DB £54-£62 HB £245-£395 D £17 CC MC Visa DC

★★ Watermans Arms Inn
Bow Bridge, Tuckenhay, Totnes TQ9 7EG
📞 01803-732214 Fax 01803-732214
15 bedrs, all ensuite, TCF TV 🍴 P 60 SB £36 DB £40-£70 D £15 CC MC Visa Amex 🖹

★ Sea Trout Inn
Hospitality, Restaurant merit awards
Staverton, Totnes TQ9 6PA
📞 **01803-762274 Fax 01803-762506**

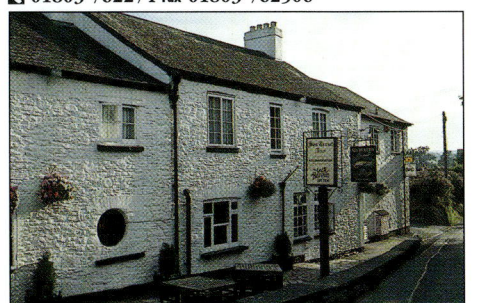

Attractive beamed country inn situated in the peaceful village of Staverton by the River Dart. Pleasant cottage style rooms with good food and service. Choice of restaurant, two bars and patio gardens.

10 bedrs, all ensuite, **TV 🐕 P** 50 **SB** £42.50-£45 **DB** £55-£66 **HB** £275-£290 **D** £18.95 **CC** MC Visa Amex

Old Forge at Totnes
Seymour Place, Totnes TQ9 5AY
📞 **01803-862174 Fax 01803-865385**

Delightfully converted 600 year old stone building, with working forge, in almost rural setting, yet close to the town centre and riverside. Huge choice of breakfast menu - traditional, vegetarian, continental. Licensed. Leisure lounge, whirlpool spa.

10 bedrs, all ensuite, 1 ➡ **TCF TV** 🖂 **P** 10 **SB** £38-£48 **DB** £50-£66 **CC** MC Visa ♿

TROWBRIDGE Wiltshire   4A3

★★ Hilbury Court
Hilperton Road, Trowbridge BA14 7JW
📞 **01225-752949 Fax 01225-777990**
13 bedrs, 10 ensuite, 3 🏠, 1 ➡ **TCF TV P** 20 **SB** £45-£50 **DB** £55-£65 **D** £10.50 **CC** MC Visa ♿

Old Manor *Highly Acclaimed*
Trowle, Trowbridge BA14 9BL
📞 **01225-777393 Fax 01225-765443**
Closed Christmas
14 bedrs, all ensuite, **TCF TV** 🖂 **P** 20 **SB** £48.50-£58 **DB** £55-£85 **D** £15 **CC** MC Visa Amex DC JCB ♿

Gordons *Listed*
65 Wingfield Road, Trowbridge BA14 9EG
📞 **01225-752072 Fax 01225-755902**
Closed Christmas
13 bedrs, 6 🏠, 2 ➡ **TCF TV P** 20 **SB** £24 **DB** £38 **HB** £154
CC MC Visa

Brook House
Semington, Trowbridge BA14 6JR
📞 **01380-870232 Fax 01380-871431**

This Georgian Listed family house is set in extensive grounds, including tennis and croquet lawns, swimming pool and brook. Conveniently placed for Stonehenge, Avebury, Bath, Glastonbury, Longleat and Stourhead.

3 bedrs, 1 ensuite, 1 ➡ **TCF TV** 🐕 **P** 6 **SB** £20 **DB** £42 📷 📧

TRURO Cornwall   2B4

★★ Carlton
Falmouth Road, Truro TR1 2HL
📞 **01872-272450 Fax 01872-223938**
Closed 24 Dec-5 Jan
31 bedrs, 28 ensuite, 1 ➡ **TCF TV** 🐕 **P** 31 **SB** £34-£39 **DB** £45 **HB** £219-£256 **D** £9 **CC** MC Visa Amex DC 📷

★★ Polsue Manor
Ruan High Lanes, Truro TR2 5LU
📞 **01872-501270 Fax 01872-501270**
Closed 31 Oct-mid March
12 bedrs, 10 ensuite, 1 ➡ **TCF TV** 🐕 **P** 20 **SB** £25-£32 **DB** £50-£64 **HB** £277-£305 **D** £17 **CC** MC Visa JCB

Rock Cottage *Acclaimed*
Blackwater, Truro TR4 8EU
📞 **01872-560252 Fax 01872-560252**
Closed Christmas-New Year
3 bedrs, all ensuite, **TCF TV** 🖂 **P** 3 No children under 18 **DB** £41

Trevispian-Vean Farm *Acclaimed*
St Erme, Truro TR4 9BL
📞 **01872-279514**
Closed Oct-Mar
12 bedrs, 10 ensuite, 2 ➡ **TCF** 🖂 **P** 40 **SB** £19-£21 **DB** £34-£38 **HB** £111-£125 **D** £8 📷 ♿

MARCORRIE HOTEL
TRURO, CORNWALL

APPROVED
RAC LISTED

20 Falmouth Road,
Truro TR1 2AX
Tel: +44 1872 277374
Fax: +44 1872 241666

Victorian family house in city conservation area. Close to cathedral and shops. Comfortable ensuite rooms, parking, central for touring Cornwall.

Bedrooms: Single 4, Double 4, Twin 3, Family 1, Ensuite 12
Prices: Single £32, Double £42, Family £60
Open: All year

Marcorrie Listed
20 Falmouth Road, Truro TR1 2HX
01872-277374 Fax 01872-241666
12 bedrs, all ensuite, 1 TCF P 15 SB £32-£35
DB £42-£45 D £9 CC MC Visa Amex DC JCB

Penhale Farm
Grampound Road, Truro TR2 4ER
01726-882324

A lovely old farmhouse on a working farm. Central for touring, beaches and visiting National Trust properties and gardens.

3 bedrs, 1 TCF P 6

Polglaze
St Erme, Truro TR4 9BD
01872-510504

Friendly house in very rural and peaceful setting on a farm with attractive views overlooking fields and woods. Truro city 7 minutes, northcoast 25 minutes.

1 bedrs, all ensuite, TCF TV P 2 SB £15.50-£17.50
DB £30-£35

TUNBRIDGE WELLS Kent — 5D3

★★ Russell
80 London Road, Tunbridge Wells TN1 1DZ
01892-544833 Fax 01892-515846
E Mail russell-hotel@globalnet.co.uk
26 bedrs, all ensuite, TCF TV P 20 SB £68 DB £82 D £18
CC MC Visa Amex DC JCB

TURVEY Bedfordshire — 4C1

★★ Laws
High Street, Turvey MK43 8DB
01234-881213 Fax 01234-888864
19 bedrs, all ensuite, TCF TV P 30 SB £42-£44 DB £55
D £15 CC MC Visa Amex

TWO BRIDGES Devon — 2C3

★★ Two Bridges
Two Bridges, Nr Yelverton, Dartmoor PL20 6SW
01822-890581 Fax 01822-890575

Historic 18th century hotel with a beautiful riverside location at the heart of Dartmoor. Award winning restaurant, cosy bars and comfortable lounges. Warmest welcome guaranteed.

25 bedrs, all ensuite, 2 TCF TV P 150 SB £43-£44.50 DB £66-£69 HB £336 D £17.50 CC MC Visa Amex DC

UTTOXETER – ENGLAND

Cherrybrook *Listed*
Two Bridges PL20 6SP
☎ 01822-880260 Fax 01822-880260
Closed Christmas-New Year

A small friendly, family run hotel set in the middle of Dartmoor National Park. Comfortably furnished with a cosy beamed lounge and bar. Wonderful fresh local foods.

7 bedrs, all ensuite, 1 ⇔ TCF TV ⚹ P 7 SB £26-£27.50 DB £52-£55 HB £245-£280 D £15

TYNEMOUTH Tyne & Wear   13F4

Hope House *Highly Acclaimed*
47 Percy Gardens, Tynemouth NE30 4HH
☎ 0191-257 1989 Fax 0191-257 1989
Elegantly furnished and decorated double-fronted Victorian house with superb coastal views.

3 bedrs, 2 ensuite, 1 ⇔ TCF TV P 3 SB £37.50-£49.50 DB £49.50-£65 D £17.50 CC MC Visa Amex DC

UCKFIELD East Sussex   5D3

Hooke Hall *Highly Acclaimed*
250 High Street, Uckfield TN22 1EN
☎ 01825-761578 Fax 01825-768025
Closed Christmas

9 bedrs, all ensuite, TCF TV P 8 No children under 12 SB £50-£55 DB £70-£75 D £20 CC MC Visa Amex

UMBERLEIGH Devon   2C2

★★ Rising Sun
Umberleigh EX37 9DU
☎ 01769-560447 Fax 01769-560764

13th century sporting inn, overlooking the River Taw, close to Rosemoor Garden, North Devon coast and Exmoor. Traditional hospitality, comfortable bedrooms, excellent food, fine wines.

9 bedrs, all ensuite, TCF TV P 30 SB £40 DB £77 HB £350 D £14 CC MC Visa

UPPINGHAM Rutland   8C3

★★ Crown Inn
High Street East, Uppingham LE15 9PY
☎ 01572-822302 Fax 01572-822942
7 bedrs, all ensuite, TCF TV ⚹ P 15 SB £35 DB £45 D £10 CC MC Visa Amex

★★ Lake Isle
Hospitality, Comfort, Restaurant merit awards
High Street East, Uppingham LE15 9PZ
☎ 01572-822951 Fax 01572-822951
12 bedrs, all ensuite, ⚹ P 6 SB £45-£59 DB £65-£79 D £21.50 CC MC Visa Amex DC

Old Rectory *Listed*
Belton-in-Rutland, Oakham LE15 9LE
☎ 01572-717279 Fax 01572-717343

Mid 19th century rectory and guest annex on the edge of a conservation village, overlooking the Eyebrook Valley. Shop and pub in village. Breakfast from 7am. Located half a mile off the A47, three miles west of Uppingham.

8 bedrs, 6 ensuite, 1 ⇔ TCF TV ⚹ P 10 SB £27-£29 DB £38-£42 CC MC Visa ♿

UTTOXETER Staffordshire   7F2

★★ Bank House
Church Street, Uttoxeter ST14 8AG
☎ 01889-566922 Fax 01889-567565
14 bedrs, all ensuite, TCF TV ⚹ P 16
SB £54.50 DB £69.50 D £10.95 CC MC Visa Amex DC

Hillcrest *Acclaimed*
3 Leighton Road, Uttoxeter ST14 8BL
☎ 01889-564627
Closed 25 Dec
7 bedrs, all ensuite, 1 ⇔ TCF TV P 12 SB £28-£30 DB £38-£40 D £8.50 CC MC Visa

WADEBRIDGE Cornwall 2B3

Hendra Country House *Acclaimed*
St Kew Highway, Wadebridge PL30 3EQ
☎ 01208-841343 Fax 01208-841343
Closed Dec-Jan excl Christmas

A friendly welcome awaits you at this Listed Georgian manor house set in rural tranquillity. Superb countryside views, yet close to beautiful North Cornwall coast.

5 bedrs, all ensuite, 1 ⇌ TCF TV ✈ P 8 SB £22-£27 DB £44-£54 HB £248-£278 D £15 CC MC Visa Amex 🅁

WAKEFIELD West Yorkshire 11D4

Campanile Wakefield *Lodge*
Monkton Road, Wakefield WF2 7AL
☎ 01924-201054 Fax 01924-201055

The hotel combines excellent value for money with the comforts you would expect from a large modern hotel, including Sky TV, direct dial telephones and en suite bathrooms. Opened in 1992, the Campanile boasts a French Bistro restaurant. Free parking.

77 bedrs, all ensuite, TCF TV ✈ P 77 SB £41 DB £45.50 D £10.55 CC MC Visa Amex DC ♿

WALLASEY Merseyside 10B4

★★ Grove House
Hospitality, Comfort, Restaurant merit awards
Grove Road, Wallasey L45 3HF
☎ 0151-639 3947 Fax 0151-639 0028

Twin gabled Victorian building with modern extentions, set in wooded gardens.

14 bedrs, all ensuite, TCF TV ✈ P 40 SB £51-£55 DB £57-£61 D £15 CC MC Visa Amex

Clifton *Listed*
293 Seabank Road, Wallasey L45 5AF
☎ 0151-639 6505

Sea Level *Listed*
126 Victoria Road, New Brighton, Wallasey L45 9LD
☎ 0151-639 3408 Fax 0151-639 3408
Closed Christmas-New Year
15 bedrs, 1 ensuite, 2 🛁, 3 ⇌ TCF TV ✈ P 10 SB £19 DB £35 HB £140 D £7 CC MC Visa JCB

WALSALL West Midlands 8A3

★★ Abberley
29 Bescot Road, Walsall WS2 9AD
☎ 01922-27413 Fax 01922-720933
28 bedrs, all ensuite, ✈ P 30 CC MC Visa Amex DC ♿

★★ Royal
Ablewell Street, Walsall WS1 2EL
☎ 01922-24555 Fax 01922-30028
28 bedrs, all ensuite, TCF TV ✈ 📺 P 40 CC MC Visa Amex DC

WAREHAM Dorset 3F3

★★ Cromwell House
Lulworth Cove, Wareham BH20 5RJ
☎ 01929-400253 Fax 01929-400566

Set in secluded gardens, just 200 yards from Lulworth Cove, with spectacular sea views. Fourteen bedrooms all ensuite. Secluded gardens. Swimming pool (May - October). Fish specialities. Bar/wine list. Groups welcome.

14 bedrs, all ensuite, **TV** ★ **P** 15 **SB** £26-£31 **DB** £51-£61 **HB** £210-£245 **D** £12 **CC** MC Visa Amex

★★ Worgret Manor
Worgret, Wareham BH20 6AB
☎ **01929-552957 Fax 01929-554804**
Closed 1-14 Jan
13 bedrs, 11 ensuite, 2 ★ **TCF TV** ★ **P** 50 **SB** £50 **DB** £40-£70 **D** £14 **CC** MC Visa Amex DC &

★ Black Bear
14 South Street, Wareham BH20 4LT
☎ **01929-553339 Fax 01929-552846**
15 bedrs, all ensuite, ★ **SB** £25 **DB** £40 **CC** MC Visa

WARKWORTH Northumberland   13F3

★★ Warkworth House
16 Bridge Street, Warkworth NE65 0XB
☎ **01665-711276 Fax 01665-713323**
14 bedrs, all ensuite, ★ **P** 14 **SB** £49 **DB** £75 **HB** £275 **D** £16 **CC** MC Visa Amex DC &

North Cottage *Acclaimed*
Birling, Warkworth NE65 OXS
☎ **01665-711263**
Closed Christmas & 1-14 Nov

Welcome to this ground floor, ensuite accommodation. Private parking. Beautiful beaches, many castles and golf courses nearby. Ideal for bird watchers and walkers.

4 bedrs, 3 ensuite, 1 ★ **TCF TV** ⊠ **P** 4 No children **SB** £18.50-£19.50 **DB** £37-£39

WARMINSTER Wiltshire   3F2

★★ Old Bell
Market Place, Warminster BA12 9AN
☎ **01985-216611 Fax 01985-217111**
20 bedrs, 14 ensuite, 2 ★ **TCF TV** ★ **P** 20 **SB** £46 **DB** £58-£65 **D** £12 **CC** MC Visa Amex

WARRINGTON Cheshire   7E1

★★ Paddington House
514 Manchester Road, Warrington WA1 3TZ
☎ **01925-816767 Fax 01925-816767**
37 bedrs, all ensuite, **TCF** ★ ⊡ **P** 150 **SB** £40 **DB** £50 **HB** £398 **D** £17.95 **CC** MC Visa Amex DC &

★★ Rockfield
Hospitality, Comfort merit awards
Alexandra Road, Warrington WA4 2EL
☎ **01925-262898 Fax 01925-263343**
12 bedrs, all ensuite, **TCF TV** ★ **P** 25 **SB** £30-£48 **DB** £45-£58 **D** £15 **CC** MC Visa Amex JCB

Birchdale *Acclaimed*
Birchdale Road, Appleton, Warrington WA4 5AW
☎ **01925-263662 Fax 01925-860607**
Closed Christmas-New Year
16 bedrs, 7 ensuite, 3 ★ **TCF TV P** 40 **CC** MC Visa

Kenilworth *Acclaimed*
2 Victoria Road, Warrington WA4 2EN
☎ **01925-262323 Fax 01925-262323**
14 bedrs, all ensuite, **TCF TV P** 18 **SB** £42 **DB** £54 **D** £12.50 **CC** MC Visa Amex

WARWICK Warwickshire   8A4

★★ Globe
Theatre Street, Warwick CV34 4DP
☎ **01926-492044 Fax 01926-407170**
10 bedrs, all ensuite, **TCF TV SB** £60 **DB** £64 **D** £6.95 **CC** MC Visa Amex DC

Park Cottage *Highly Acclaimed*
113 West Street, Warwick CV34 6AH
☎ **01926-410319 Fax 01926-410319**
Closed 24-26 Dec

An early 16th century Grade II Listed building situated alongside the entrance drive to Warwick Castle, offering completely refurbished accommodation. One mile from town centre.

5 bedrs, all ensuite, **TCF TV** ⊠ **P** 8 No children under 12 **SB** £38-£45 **DB** £40-£55 **CC** MC Visa

Croft *Acclaimed*
Haseley Knob, Warwick CV35 7NL
☎ 01926-484447 Fax 01926-484447

Modern, friendly house in the picturesque village of Haseley Knob, convenient for the National Exhibition Centre, Birmingham Airport, Stratford and Coventry.

5 bedrs, all ensuite, 2 ⇌ TCF TV 🐾 P 8 SB £20-£30 DB £40-£45 D £12 CC MC Visa JCB

High House *Listed*
Old Warwick Road, Rowington, Warwick CV35 7AA
☎ 01926-843270 Fax 01203-257943
3 bedrs, all ensuite, TCF TV P 20 SB £26-£30 DB £50-£60

Hither Barn *Listed*
Star Lane, Claverdon, Warwick CV35 8LW
☎ 01926-842839
3 bedrs, 2 ensuite, 1 ⇌ P 5 SB £29 DB £45 D £13.50 CC DC

WASDALE Cumbria	10A2

★★ Wasdale Head Inn
Restaurant merit award
Wasdale Head CA20 1EX
☎ 01946-726229 Fax 01946-726334
9 bedrs, all ensuite, TCF 🐾 P 50 SB £34 DB £68 D £15.50 CC MC Visa Amex JCB

Church Stile Farm *Acclaimed*
Nether Wasdale, Nr Gosforth CA20 1ET
☎ 019467-26252
Closed 3 Nov-20 Dec
3 bedrs, all ensuite, TCF TV P 3 SB £18-£19 DB £40-£42 D £12.50

WASHINGTON Tyne & Wear	13F4

Campanile Washington *Lodge*
Emerson Road, Washington NE37 1LE
☎ 0191-416 5010 Fax 0191-4165023
77 bedrs, all ensuite, TCF 🐾 P 77 SB £42.50 DB £47 D £10.55 CC MC Visa Amex DC ♿

WATCHET Somerset	3D2

West Somerset *Listed*
Swain Street, Watchet TA23 0AB
☎ 01984-634434 Fax 01984-634434

Small family run hotel in quaint coastal town. Follow the A39 from Minehead or A358 from Taunton.

9 bedrs, 5 ensuite, 2 ⇌ TCF TV 🐾 SB £18 DB £35 HB £158 D £4 CC MC Visa

WATERMILLOCK Cumbria	10B2

Land Ends Country Lodge
Watermillock, Watermillock CA11 0NB
☎ 01768-486438 Fax 01768-486959

Charming 18th century former farmhouse in 7 acre gardens with 2 small lakes offering peace and tranquillity in a fellside location. Warm, cosy, ensuite rooms. Excellent, varied breakfasts.

9 bedrs, all ensuite, TCF TV P 20 SB £28 DB £52 ♿

WEEDON BEC Northamptonshire	8B4

★★ Globe
Comfort merit award
High Street, Weedon Bec NN7 4QD
☎ 01327-340336 Fax 01327-349058
17 bedrs, all ensuite, TCF TV 🐾 P 40 SB £32-£45 DB £45-£55 D £14 CC MC Visa Amex DC ♿

WELLESBOURNE Warwickshire 8A4

Chadley House
Loxley Road, Wellesbourne CV35 9JL
☎ 01789-840994

In its own grounds, surrounded by countryside Chadley is the ideal hotel for visiting Stratford, Warwick and the Cotswolds. Small restaurant, relaxing lounges and ensuite rooms.

WELLINGBOROUGH Northamptonshire 8C4

★★ Columbia
19 Northampton Road, Wellingborough NN8 3HG
☎ 01933-229333 Fax 01933-440418
Closed Christmas
29 bedrs, all ensuite, TCF TV ✼ P 25 SB £50 DB £65 D £14 CC   MC Visa Amex &

★★ High View
156 Midland Road, Wellingborough NN8 1NG
☎ 01933-278733 Fax 01933-225948
Closed Christmas-New Year
14 bedrs, all ensuite, TCF TV P 10 No children under 5 SB £29-£46 DB £44-£53 D £6 CC   MC Visa Amex DC JCB

Oak House *Listed*
9 Broad Green, Wellingborough NN8 4LE
☎ 01933-271133 Fax 01933-271133
Closed Christmas

A white rendered old world building on the edge of the town centre with enclosed car parking. Double glazed.

16 bedrs, 15 ensuite, 1 ✼ TCF TV ✼ P 12 SB £28-£32 DB £38-£42 D £9 CC   MC Visa Amex DC

WELLS Somerset 3E2

★★ Star
18 High Street, Wells BA5 2SQ
☎ 01749-670500 Fax 01749-672654
12 bedrs, all ensuite, 2 ✼ TCF TV ✼ CC   MC Visa Amex DC

★★ White Hart
Sadler Street, Wells BA5 2RR
☎ 01749-672056 Fax 01749-672056
E Mail whitehart@wells.demon.co.uk
13 bedrs, all ensuite, TCF TV ✼ P 15 SB £45-£55 DB £60-£70 D £15 CC   MC Visa Amex

Bekynton *Acclaimed*
7 St Thomas Street, Wells BA5 2UU
☎ 01749-672222 Fax 01749-672222
Closed Christmas

A charming, historic period house with well furnished, comfortable, non smoking rooms and views to the cathedral. An ideal touring centre for Bath to Longleat and the coast.

6 bedrs, 4 ensuite, 1 ✼ TCF TV ✼ P 6 No children under 5 SB £28-£36 DB £43-£48 CC   MC Visa

Double-Gate Farm *Acclaimed*
Godney, Wells BA5 1RZ
☎ 01458-832217 Fax 01458-835612
Closed Dec-Jan

Lovely Georgian farmhouse on a working farm. Excellent ensuite accommodation including a fully equipped games room. Pretty garden. Two golden retrievers and a loving moggy. Home from home!

5 bedrs, 4 ensuite, 1 ✼ TCF TV ✼ P 6 SB £25 DB £40

Tor House *Acclaimed*
20 Tor Street, Wells BA5 2US
☎ 01749-672322 Fax 01749-672322

Historic, sympathetically restored 17th century guest house now a Grade II Listed building, set in delightful grounds overlooking the cathedral and three minutes walk to the town centre.

8 bedrs, all ensuite, 2 ⇨ TCF TV ⌧ P 12 No children under 3 SB £25-£40 DB £38-£55 CC MC Visa ⊞

Littlewell Farm
Coxley, Wells, Somerset BA5 1QP
☎ 01749-677914

Delightful 18th century farmhouse enjoying extensive rural views over beautiful countryside. Charming individually presented ensuite bedrooms with lovely antique furniture. Coxley is one mile south-west from Wells.

8 bedrs, 5 ensuite, TCF TV ⌧ ⊁ P 10 SB £21-£25 DB £37-£46

WELLS-NEXT-THE-SEA Norfolk   9E2

★★ Crown
Hospitality, Restaurant merit awards
Buttlands, Wells-next-the-Sea NR23 1EX
☎ 01328-710209 Fax 01328-711432
14 bedrs, 10 ensuite, 1 ⇨ TCF TV ⊁ SB £40-£55 DB £58-£68 HB £280-£336 D £19.50 CC MC Visa Amex DC

WEM Shropshire   7D2

Lowe Hall Farm
Wem SY4 5UE
☎ 01939-232236 Fax 01939-232236

Historically famous 16th century Listed farmhouse. Delightfully furnished ensuite bedrooms, all with colour TV and tea/coffee making facilities. Highest standard of food, decor & accommodation guaranteed. Large garden, ample parking, ideal touring centre.

3 bedrs, all ensuite, 1 ⇨ TCF TV ⌧ P 6 SB £18 DB £35

WEMBLEY Middlesex   4C2

Elm *Highly Acclaimed*
Elm Road, Wembley HA9 7JA
☎ 0181-902 1764 Fax 0181-903 8365
31 bedrs, 21 ensuite, 5 ⇨ ⊁ P 7 CC MC Visa ♿

ARENA HOTEL

Friendly, private and spacious accommodation with ensuite, TV and satellite in every room.
Comfortable single, double, twin and family rooms. New refurbishment.
Only 1800 yards from Wembley Stadium Complex. Ideally situated, easy access.
Parking for 15 cars.

6 FORTY LANE, WEMBLEY, MIDDLESEX HA9 9EB
Tel: 0181-908 0670/0181-904 0019
Fax: 0181-908 2007

Aaron *Acclaimed*
8 Forty Lane, Wembley HA9 9EB
☎ 0181-904 6329 Fax 0181-385 0472

A family-run bed and breakfast, convenient for the Wembley complex, London's West End and all major routes. All bedrooms ensuite with TV. Free parking.

9 bedrs, 8 ensuite, 1 ➡ **TCF TV P** 15 **CC** MC Visa Amex DC ♿

Adelphi *Acclaimed*
4 Forty Lane, Wembley HA9 9EB
☎ 0181-904 5629 Fax 0181-908 5314

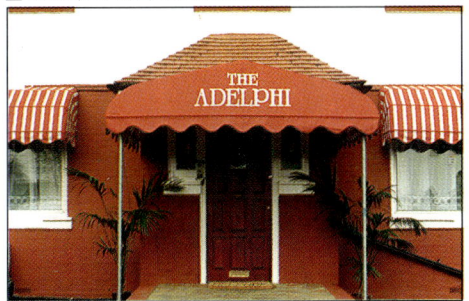

Clean and tidy, pleasant to the eye - noticeable from quite some distance, enjoying a prominent position in Wembley, near major landmarks, yet set back and in a reserved position.

11 bedrs, 7 ensuite, 4 ➡ **TV P** 10 **SB** £28-£35 **DB** £38-£45 **HB** £160-£175 **D** £7 **CC** MC Visa Amex DC

Arena *Acclaimed*
6 Forty Lane, Wembley HA9 9EB
☎ 0181-908 0670 Fax 0181-908 2007

Newly refurbished, friendly, private and spacious accommodation with comfortable single, double, twin and family rooms. Ensuite rooms available. Satellite TV in every room. Ideally situated with easy access to the Wembley Stadium complex only 1 mile away.

13 bedrs, all ensuite, 2 ➡ **TCF TV P** 15 **SB** £30-£39 **DB** £45-£49 **HB** £170-£200 **CC** MC Visa Amex DC JCB

Brookside *Listed*
32 Brook Avenue, Wembley HA9 8PH
☎ 0181-904 3333 Fax 0181-908 3333

Excellent accommodation at reasonable prices. Situated a stones throw from Wembley stadium, Arena, conference centre and opposite Wembley Park Underground station. 15 minutes from central London.

12 bedrs, 8 ensuite, 2 ➡ **TCF TV P** 10 **SB** £38 **DB** £58 **CC** MC Visa Amex DC JCB ♿

WEST MALLING Kent   5D3

Scott House *Acclaimed*
37 High Street, West Malling ME19 6QH
☎ 01732-841380 Fax 01732-870025
Closed Christmas
3 bedrs, all ensuite, **TCF TV** No children **SB** £39 **DB** £55 **CC** MC Visa Amex JCB

WEST MERSEA Essex   5E2

Victory
92 Coast Road, West Mersea CO5 0LS
☎ 01206-382907
3 bedrs, all ensuite, **TCF TV P** 25 **SB** £19.50 **DB** £35.50 **D** £10 **CC** MC Visa Amex 🐾

WEST WITTON North Yorkshire   10C2

★★ Wensleydale Heifer
Restaurant merit award
Wensleydale, West Witton DL8 4LS
☎ 01969-622322 Fax 01969-624183
15 bedrs, 14 ensuite, 2 🛏, **TCF TV** 🐾 **P** 50 **SB** £50-£54 **DB** £70-£90 **D** £23 **CC** MC Visa Amex DC JCB

WESTBURY Wiltshire 4A3

★★ Cedar
Hospitality merit award
114 Warminster Road, Westbury BA13 3PR
☎ 01373-822753 Fax 01373-858423
Closed 26-29 Dec
16 bedrs, all ensuite, TCF TV ✻ P 35 SB £45 DB £55
D £12 CC MC Visa Amex

WESTCLIFF-ON-SEA Essex 5E2

★★ Balmoral
Comfort merit award
34-36 Valkyrie Road, Westcliff-on-Sea SS0 8BU
☎ 01702-342947 Fax 01702-337828
29 bedrs, all ensuite, TCF TV ✻ P 20 SB £39 DB £58
HB £252 D £10 CC MC Visa Amex ♿

Cobham Lodge *Acclaimed*
2 Cobham Road, Westcliff-on-Sea SS0 8EA
☎ 01702-346438 Fax 01702-346438
29 bedrs, 23 ensuite, 3 ⇌ TV SB £29.50-£32 DB £40-£45
HB £165-£200 D £11 CC MC Visa 🐕

Rose House *Listed*
21 Manor Road, Westcliff-on-Sea SS0 7SR
☎ 01702-341959 Fax 01702-390918
21 bedrs, 13 ensuite, 3 ⇌ TCF TV ✻ P 15 SB £20-£25
DB £38-£40 HB £175-£180 D £5 CC MC Visa ♿

WESTERHAM Kent 5D3

Clacket Lane Roadchef Lodge *Lodge*
M25 Westbound, Westerham TN16 2ER
☎ 01959-565577 Fax 01959-561311
Closed 24-27 Dec
58 bedrs, all ensuite, TCF TV P 100 **Room only rate**
£43.50 D £4 CC MC Visa Amex DC ♿

WESTGATE-ON-SEA Kent 5F2

★★ Ivyside
25 Sea Road, Westgate-on-Sea CT8 8SB
☎ 01843-831082 Fax 01843-831082
72 bedrs, 70 ensuite, 3 ⇌ TV ✻ P 45 SB £28-£32
DB £68-£76 HB £196-£252 D £10 CC MC Visa Amex 🛗
♿

WESTON-SUPER-MARE Somerset 3E1

★★ Arosfa
Lower Church Road, Weston-super-Mare BS23 2AG
☎ 01934-419523 Fax 01934-636084
46 bedrs, all ensuite, TCF TV ✻ ⚹ P 16 SB £38.50-
£42.50 DB £55-£60 HB £-£252 D £15 CC MC Visa Amex
DC ♿

★★ Bay
60 Knightstone Road, Seafront, Weston-super-Mare
BS23 2BE
☎ 01934-624137 Fax 01934-626969
11 bedrs, all ensuite, TCF TV ✻ P 8 SB £35 DB £52
HB £235-£276 D £11.50 CC MC Visa Amex

★★ Beachlands
17 Uphill Road North, Weston-super-Mare BS23 4NG
☎ 01934-621401 Fax 01934-621966
Closed Christmas-New Year
23 bedrs, all ensuite, 1 ⇌ TCF TV ✻ P 26 SB £32.50-
£42.50 DB £65-£85 HB £259-£329 D £15 CC MC Visa
Amex 🛗 ♿

★★ Dauncey's
Claremont Crescent, Weston-super-Mare BS23 2EE
☎ 01934-621144 Fax 01934-620281

Family run terraced Victorian hotel with pleasant gardens and good sea views from bar, patio and garden across Weston Bay.

80 bedrs, 69 ensuite, 5 ⇌ TCF TV ✻ ⚹ SB £28-£30
DB £55-£60 HB £224-£260 D £10.50 CC MC Visa JCB

★★ Dorville
Madeira Road, Weston-super-Mare BS23 2EX
☎ 01934-621522 Fax 01934-645585
Closed Dec-Feb
41 bedrs, 27 ensuite, 6 ⇌ TV ⚹ P 10 No children
SB £25-£33 DB £48-£60 HB £137-£210 D £9 🐕 ♿

★★ Queenswood
Hospitality, Comfort, Restaurant merit awards
Victoria Park, Weston-super-Mare BS23 2HZ
☎ 01934-416141 Fax 01934-621759
17 bedrs, all ensuite, TCF TV ✻ P 6
SB £40-£43 DB £65-£70 HB £266-£280 D £14.50 CC MC
Visa Amex DC JCB

Ashcombe Court *Highly Acclaimed*
17 Milton Road, Weston-super-Mare
☎ 01934-625104 Fax 01934-625104
6 bedrs, all ensuite, TCF TV P 6 DB £30-£38 HB £165
D £9

Braeside *Highly Acclaimed*
2 Victoria Park, Weston-super-Mare BS23 2HZ
☎ 01934-626642 Fax 01934-626642

A delightful family-run hotel close to the seafront. All bedrooms are ensuite, with colour TV and tea/coffee making facilities. Some have sea views.

9 bedrs, all ensuite, **TCF TV** 🐾 **SB** £24 **DB** £48 **HB** £196 **D** £10

Milton Lodge *Highly Acclaimed*
15 Milton Road, Weston-super-Mare BS23 2SH
☎ 01934-623161
Closed Oct-Feb
6 bedrs, all ensuite, **TCF TV P** 6 No children **SB** £20-£25 **DB** £32-£36 **HB** £154-£164 **D** £8

Wychwood *Highly Acclaimed*
148 Milton Road, Weston-super-Mare BS23 2UZ
☎ 01934-627793
Closed Christmas
8 bedrs, all ensuite, 1 ⇌ **TCF TV P** 12 **SB** £26 **DB** £42 **HB** £185 **D** £9 **CC** MC Visa

L'Arrivee *Acclaimed*
75 Locking Road, Weston-super-Mare BS23 3DW
☎ 01934-625328 Fax 01934-625328

A Victorian building with spacious rooms, run by resident owners. Located near places of interest, both in town and the surrounding area.

12 bedrs, 10 ensuite, 1 ⇌ **TV** 🐾 **P** 12 **SB** £19.50-£25 **DB** £38 **HB** £192.50 **D** £8 **CC** MC Visa Amex DC ♿

Oakover *Acclaimed*
25 Clevedon Road, Weston-super-Mare BS23 1DA
☎ 01934-620125
8 bedrs, 7 ensuite, **TCF TV P** 8 **SB** £15-£18 **DB** £30-£36 **CC** MC Visa JCB

Saxonia *Acclaimed*
95 Locking Road, Weston-super-Mare BS23 3EW
☎ 01934-633856 Fax 01934-623141

Saxonia is central for beaches, shops and entertainment. Our dining room has air-conditioning and we also offer door to door travel service. Please phone for details.

9 bedrs, 8 ensuite, 1 ⓕ, **TCF TV P** 4 **SB** £18-£23 **DB** £32-£42 **HB** £140-£175 **D** £8 **CC** MC Visa Amex DC JCB ♿

Baymead *Listed*
19-23 Longton Grove Road, BS23 1LS
☎ 01934-622951 Fax 01934-628110
32 bedrs, 27 ensuite, 3 ⓕ, 2 ⇌ **TCF TV** 🐾 📶 **P** 8 **SB** £18-£23 **DB** £35-£40 **HB** £140-£185 **D** £7 🛗

Sandringham *Listed*
1 Victoria Square, Weston-super-Mare BS23 1LS
☎ 01934-624891 Fax 01934-624891
47 bedrs, all ensuite, **TCF TV SB** £36 **DB** £47 **HB** £122-£175 **CC** MC Visa

Vaynor *Listed*
346 Locking Road, Weston-super-Mare BS22 8PD
☎ 01934-632332
3 bedrs, 1 ⇌ **TCF TV** 🐾 **P** 3 **SB** £12-£13 **DB** £24-£25 **HB** £119-£123 **D** £5.50

WESTWARD HO! Devon — 2C2

Buckleigh Lodge *Acclaimed*
Bay View Road, Westward Ho! EX39 1BJ
☎ 01237-475988

A friendly welcome awaits you at our fine Victorian country house with sea views, ensuite rooms, central heating, lounge bar and home cooked food.

6 bedrs, 4 ensuite, 1 ⓕ, 1 ⇌ **TCF TV P** 6 **SB** £18-£19 **DB** £36-£38 **HB** £186 **D** £10

WEYBOURNE Norfolk 9E2

★★ Maltings
The Street, Weybourne NR25 7SY
☎ 01263-588731 Fax 01263-588240
20 bedrs, all ensuite, ✻ P 150 CC MC Visa Amex DC

WEYMOUTH Dorset 3E3

★★ Bay Lodge
Hospitality, Comfort merit awards
27 Greenhill, Weymouth DT4 7SW
☎ 01305-782419 Fax 01305-782828
Closed Nov
12 bedrs, all ensuite, 12 ⇌ TV SB £29 DB £50 HB £230
CC MC Visa Amex DC JCB

★★ Central
15 Maiden Street, Weymouth DT4 8BB
☎ 01305-760700 Fax 01305-760300
Closed Dec-Feb
28 bedrs, all ensuite, TCF TV ✻ P 10 SB £25-£30 DB £45-£54 HB £140-£203 D £7.50 CC MC Visa Amex ♿

★★ Crown
51/52 St Thomas Street, Weymouth DT4 8EQ
☎ 01305-760800 Fax 01305-760300
86 bedrs, all ensuite, TCF TV ✻ P 8 SB £28-£36 DB £54-£62 HB £156-£223 D £10 CC MC Visa Amex DC ♿

★★ Fairhaven
37 The Esplanade, Weymouth DT4 8DH
☎ 01305-760200 Fax 01305-760300
Closed Nov-Feb
76 bedrs, all ensuite, TCF TV ✻ P 18 SB £25-£30 DB £45-£54 HB £147-£224 D £7.50 CC MC Visa Amex ✻

★★ Glenburn
Hospitality merit award
42 Preston Road, Weymouth DT3 6PZ
☎ 01305-832353 Fax 01305-835610
13 bedrs, all ensuite, TCF TV P 30 No children under 3
SB £25-£34 DB £50-£58 HB £225-£245 D £5 CC MC Visa

RAC Hotel Reservations Service

Use the RAC Reservations Service and you'll never have another sleepless night worrying about accommodation.
We can guarantee you a room almost anywhere in the UK and Ireland.
The price of a national call is all it takes.
The service is free to RAC Members.

0870 603 9109

★★ Hotel Rex
Hospitality merit award
29 The Esplanade, Weymouth DT4 8DN
☎ 01305-760400 Fax 01305-760500

A Georgian town house, once the Duke of Clarence's summer residence, situated on the Esplanade, close to shops, beach and harbour.

31 bedrs, all ensuite, TCF TV ✻ ⟡ P 8 SB £42-£52
DB £68-£95 HB £236-£300 D £12 CC MC Visa Amex DC

★★ Moonfleet Manor
Moonfleet, Weymouth DT3 4ED
☎ 01305-786948 Fax 01305-774395
38 bedrs, all ensuite, TCF TV ⟡ P 100 SB £30-£37
DB £60-£74 HB £245-£280 D £13.50 CC MC Visa Amex
✻ ✻ ✻ ✻ ✻ ✻ ✻ ♿

★★ Prince Regent
139 The Esplanade, Weymouth DT4 7NR
☎ 01305-771313 Fax 01305-778100
E Mail hprwey.aol.co.uk
Closed Christmas
50 bedrs, all ensuite, TCF TV ⟡ P 18 SB £63-£67 DB £84-£88 HB £290-£300 D £12 CC MC Visa Amex DC

★ Alexandra
27/28 The Esplanade, Weymouth DT4 8DN
☎ 01305-785767
20 bedrs, 14 ensuite, 2 ⇌ ✻ P 7 SB £15-£27.50
DB £30-£50 CC MC Visa

Kenora *Acclaimed*
5 Stavordale Road, Westham, Weymouth DT4 0AD
☎ 01305-771215
E Mail kenora.hotel@wdi.co.uk
Closed Oct-Easter
15 bedrs, 13 ensuite, 1 ⇌ TCF TV P 15 SB £23-£32
DB £46-£60 HB £184-£215 D £10 CC MC Visa

Tamarisk *Acclaimed*
12 Stavordale Road, Weymouth DT4 0AB
☎ 01305-786514
Closed Nov-Easter
16 bedrs, 12 ensuite, 3 ⇌ TCF TV P 19 SB £20-£23
DB £40-£46 HB £160-£185

WHITBY – ENGLAND

Westwey *Acclaimed*
62 Abbotsbury Road, Weymouth DT4 0BJ
☎ 01305-784564

Birchfields *Listed*
22 Abbotsbury Road, Weymouth DT4 0AE
☎ 01305-773255
Closed Oct-1 Mar
9 bedrs, 3 ensuite, 2 ⇌ TCF TV ★ P 3 SB £15-£20
DB £30-£40 HB £131-£160 D £7

Greenhill *Listed*
8 Greenhill, Weymouth DT4 7SQ
☎ 01305-786026
17 bedrs, 12 ensuite, 2 ⇌ TCF TV P 14 CC MC Visa

Hazeldene *Listed*
16 Abbotsbury Road, Weymouth DT4 0AE
☎ 01305-782579 Fax 01305-761022
6 bedrs, 1 ensuite, 3 ⇌ TCF TV P 7 SB £14-£19 DB £28-£38 HB £90-£120

Hotel Concorde *Listed*
131 The Esplanade, Weymouth DT4 7EY
☎ 01305-776900
16 bedrs, 12 ensuite, 1 ⇌ TCF TV ★ P 4 SB £21-£24 DB £42-£48 HB £155-£190 D £7

Sou West Lodge *Listed*
Rodwell Road, Weymouth DT4 8QT
☎ 01305-783749
Closed Christmas
8 bedrs, all ensuite, TCF TV ★ P 10 SB £22-£24 DB £44-£48 HB £149-£198 D £7 ♿

Sunningdale *Listed*
52 Preston Road, Weymouth DT3 6QD
☎ 01305-832179 Fax 01305-832179

A 'country-style' hotel just 600 yards from the sea. Outdoor swimming pool and gardens. A family run business for thirty five years.

18 bedrs, 12 ensuite, 2 ⌂, 3 ⇌ TCF TV ★ P 18 SB £22-£28 DB £44-£58 HB £159-£217 D £7 CC MC Visa

Trelawney *Listed*
1 Old Castle Road, Weymouth DT4 8QB
☎ 01305-783188 Fax 01305-783181
10 bedrs, all ensuite, 1 ⇌ TCF TV P 13 SB £26-£30 DB £52-£58 HB £185-£230 D £10 CC MC Visa

WHEDDON CROSS Somerset 3D2

Rest & Be Thankful Inn *Acclaimed*
Wheddon Cross, Minehead TA24 7DR
☎ 01643-841222 Fax 01643-841222

Early 19th century coaching inn, painted cream and brown, with building additions over the years. 'L' shaped with a skittle alley and large car park.

5 bedrs, all ensuite, 1 ⇌ TCF TV P 60 No children under 11 SB £26.50 DB £53 HB £245 D £12 CC MC Visa Amex

WHITBY North Yorkshire 11E2

★★ Dunsley Hall
Dunsley, Whitby YO21 3TL
☎ 01947-893437 Fax 01947-893505
18 bedrs, all ensuite, TCF TV ★ P 20 SB £59.50
DB £99.90 D £20.95 CC MC Visa Amex ♿

★★ Old West Cliff
42 Crescent Avenue, Whitby YO21 3EQ
☎ 01947-603292 Fax 01947-821716
12 bedrs, all ensuite, TCF TV ★ SB £27 DB £44 D £9.50
CC MC Visa Amex DC

★★ Saxonville
Ladysmith Avenue, Whitby YO21 3HX
☎ 01947-602631 Fax 01947-820523
Closed 31 Oct-31 March
24 bedrs, all ensuite, TCF TV P 20 SB £33-£38 DB £66-£76 HB £270-£305 D £16.95 CC MC Visa

★★ White House
Hospitality merit award
Upgang Lane, Whitby YO21 3JJ
☎ 01947-600469 Fax 01947-821600
E Mail 101745.1440@compuserve.com
11 bedrs, 9 ensuite, 1 ⇌ ★ P 30 SB £26.50-£30.50
DB £53-£61 HB £250-£295 D £11 CC MC Visa JCB

York House *Highly Acclaimed*
Back Lane, High Hawsker, Whitby YO22 4LW
☎ 01947-880314
Closed Nov-Jan
4 bedrs, all ensuite, 1 ⇌ TCF TV P 6 No children under 16 SB £24-£25 DB £48-£50 HB £217-£224 D £12

WHITBY – ENGLAND

Corra Lynn *Acclaimed*
28 Crescent Avenue, Whitby YO21 3EW
☎ 01947-602214
Closed Nov-Mar
5 bedrs, all ensuite, TCF TV ⚹ P 4 No children under 4
DB £42-£50 D £13

Sandbeck *Acclaimed*
2 Crescent Terrace, West Cliff, Whitby YO21 3EL
☎ 01947-604012
Closed Nov-Feb
16 bedrs, all ensuite, TCF TV No children under 7
CC MC Visa

Seacliffe *Acclaimed*
West Cliff, Whitby YO21 3JX
☎ 01947-603139 Fax 01947-603139
20 bedrs, all ensuite, 1 ⚹ TCF TV ⚹ P 8
SB £30-£38 DB £57-£61 HB £266-£273 D £15 CC MC Visa Amex DC

Waverley *Acclaimed*
17 Crescent Avenue, Whitby YO21 3ED
☎ 01947-604389
Closed Nov-Feb
6 bedrs, 5 ensuite, 2 ⚹ TCF TV No children under 5
SB £17 DB £38 HB £170 D £9

Banchory *Listed*
3 Crescent Terrace, West Cliff, Whitby YO21 3EL
☎ 01947-821888 Fax 01947-821888

Glendale *Listed*
16 Crescent Avenue, Whitby YO21 3ED
☎ 01947-604242
Closed Nov

A comfortable family run guest house, with a pleasant atmosphere, on the West Cliff close to all amenities.

6 bedrs, 5 ensuite, 2 ⚹ TCF TV ⚹ P 6 SB £18-£19 DB £38-£40 D £10

Abbey House
East Cliffe, Whitby YO22 4TJ
☎ 01947-600557
Closed mid Jan-mid Feb

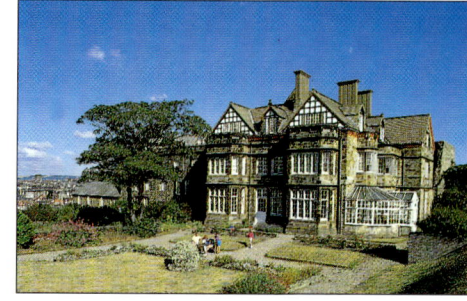

Comfortable, informal and welcoming guest house on the headland, next to the historic Abbey overlooking the bustling fishing port. Ideal for walking, touring or relaxing.

31 bedrs, 11 ⚹ TCF P 30 SB £19.50 DB £39 D £9.50 CC MC Visa

Flask Inn
Robin Hoods Bay, Fylingdales, Whitby YO22 4QH
☎ 01947-880305 Fax 01947-880592

17th century monk's hostelry situated in the North York Moors National Park between Whitby and Scarborough on the A171. 6 bedrooms all en suite, TV, hairdryers, tea/coffee, central heating.

6 bedrs, all ensuite, TCF TV P 30

WHITCHURCH Hampshire   4B3

★★ White Hart
Newbury Street, Whitchurch RG28 7DN
☎ 01256-892900
20 bedrs, 10 ensuite, 4 ⚹ 6 ⚹ TCF TV ⚹ P 20 SB £20-£46 DB £30-£56 D £4 CC MC Visa Amex DC

WHITCHURCH Shropshire   7D2

★★ Redbrook Hunting Lodge
Wrexham Road, Whitchurch SY13 3ET
☎ 01948-780204 Fax 01948-780533
13 bedrs, all ensuite, ⚹ P 100 CC MC Visa Amex ♿

WHITEHAVEN Cumbria — 10A2

★★ Chase
Corkickle, Whitehaven CA28 8AA
☎ 01946-693656 Fax 01946-590807
11 bedrs, all ensuite, TCF TV ♿ P 50
SB £39 DB £49 D £12 CC MC Visa

WHITLEY BAY Tyne & Wear — 13F4

★★ Seacrest
North Parade, Whitley Bay NE26 1PA
☎ 0191-253 0140 Fax 0191-253 0140
23 bedrs, 19 ensuite, 2 ♿ TCF TV ♿ P 4 SB £30-£50
DB £40-£55 HB £165-£280 D £8 CC MC Visa Amex DC JCB ♿ ♿

York House *Acclaimed*
30 Park Parade, Whitley Bay NE26 1DX
☎ 0191-252 8313 Fax 0191-251 3953
E Mail yorkhousehotel@bt.int
16 bedrs, 15 ensuite, 1 ♿, TCF TV ♿ P 5 SB £30-£35
DB £45-£50 HB £250-£280 D £9.95 CC MC Visa Amex ♿

WHITTINGTON Shropshire — 7D2

★ Ye Olde Boot
Castle Street, Whittington SY11 4DF
☎ 01691-662250
6 bedrs, all ensuite, TCF TV ♿ P 100 SB £23 DB £38 CC MC Visa

WIGAN Lancashire — 10B4

★★ Bel Air
Hospitality merit award
236 Wigan Lane, Wigan WN1 2NU
☎ 01942-241410 Fax 01942-243967
Closed 26-30 Dec

A 2 star RAC award winning hotel. Twelve ensuite rooms with all facilities. Elegant restaurant, superb food and wine. Situated on the A49, from M6 (jn 27) and M61 (jn 6).

12 bedrs, all ensuite, TCF TV ♿ P 10 SB £33-£43 DB £43-£53 D £5.95 CC MC Visa Amex

★★ Grand
Dorning Street, Wigan WN1 1ND
☎ 01942-243471 Fax 01942-824583
38 bedrs, all ensuite, ♿ P 40
CC MC Visa Amex DC ♿

Aalton Court *Acclaimed*
23 Upper Dicconson Street, Wigan WN1 2AG
☎ 01942-322220 Fax 01942-517721
15 bedrs, 11 ensuite, TCF TV P 6 SB £30 DB £40 HB £290
D £10 CC MC Visa

Charles Dickens *Listed*
14 Upper Dicconson Street, Wigan WN1 2AD
☎ 01942-323263
16 bedrs, 8 ensuite, TCF TV ♿ P 8 SB £22 DB £32
D £7.50 CC MC Visa ♿

WIGTON Cumbria — 10A1

★★ Kelsey
Comfort merit award
Mealsgate, Wigton CA5 1SP
☎ 01697-371229 Fax 01697-371372
Closed 24-28 Dec
6 bedrs, all ensuite, TCF TV ♿ P 20 SB £30 DB £49
HB £217 D £9 CC MC Visa Amex JCB

★★ Wheyrigg Hall
Wigton CA7 0DH
☎ 01697-361242 Fax 01697-361020
13 bedrs, all ensuite, TCF TV SB £-£33 DB £-£48 D £7.50
♿ ♿

WILLITON Somerset — 3D2

★★ White House
Hospitality, Comfort, Restaurant merit awards
Long Street, Williton TA4 4QW
☎ 01984-632306
Closed Early Nov-mid May
12 bedrs, 9 ensuite, 2 ♿ TCF TV ♿ P 15
SB £41-£54 DB £72-£90 HB £422-£486 D £29.50 ♿

Fairfield House *Acclaimed*
51 Long Street, Williton TA4 4QY
☎ 01984-632636
Closed Nov-Feb
5 bedrs, all ensuite, TCF P 8 No children under 11
SB £25 DB £45 HB £231 D £10 CC MC Visa

Short Breaks

Many hotels provide special rates for weekend and mid-week breaks - sometimes these are quoted in the hotel's entry, otherwise ring direct for the latest offers.

WIMBORNE MINSTER Dorset 3F3

★★ Beechleas
17 Poole Road, Wimborne Minister BH21 1QA
☎ 01202-841684 Fax 01202-849344
Closed 24 Dec-23 Jan

Beautifully restored Grade II Listed Georgian building with its own small walled garden. An award winning hotel with luxury double ensuite bedrooms, and a restaurant with a delightful ambiance.

9 bedrs, all ensuite, **TV ✝ P** 11 **SB** £65-£85 **DB** £78-£98 **D** £20 **CC** MC Visa Amex

Homestay *Acclaimed*
22 West Borough, Wimborne Minister BH21 1NF
☎ 01202-849015
3 bedrs, all ensuite, **TCF TV** No children **SB** £25 **DB** £40-£50

SHAWLANDS

An attractive house and large garden in a peaceful area overlooking farmland.

Children accepted.

46 KILHAM LANE, WINCHESTER, HAMPSHIRE SO22 5QD
Tel: 01962 861166
Fax: 01962 861166

WINCANTON Somerset 3F2

★★ Holbrook House
Hospitality merit award
Holbrook, Wincanton BA9 8BS
☎ 01963-32377 Fax 01963-32681
19 bedrs, all ensuite, 2 ✝ **TV ✝ P** 70 **SB** £50 **DB** £75-£80 **D** £17.50 **CC** MC Visa Amex DC

WINCHELSEA East Sussex 5E4

Strand House *Acclaimed*
The Strand, Winchelsea TN36 4JT
☎ 01797-226276 Fax 01797-224806

Fine old 15th century house with oak beams and inglenook fireplaces. Ensuite rooms with TV and drinks tray. Romantic fourposter available. Residents' bar and lounge.

10 bedrs, 9 ensuite, 1 ✝ **TCF TV ✝ P** 12 **SB** £28-£34 **DB** £40-£58 **CC** MC Visa JCB

WINCHESTER Hampshire 4B3

Wykeham Arms *Highly Acclaimed*
75, Kingsgate Street, Winchester SO23 9PE
☎ 01962-853834 Fax 01962-854411

An 18th century coaching inn/hostelry tucked away in the quiet backstreets of historic Winchester.

7 bedrs, all ensuite, **TCF TV ✝ P** 12 No children under 14 **SB** £69.50 **DB** £79.50 **D** £18 **CC** MC Visa Amex DC

Shawlands *Acclaimed*
46 Kilham Lane, Winchester SO22 5QD
☎ 01962-861166 Fax 01962-861166
5 bedrs, 1 ensuite, 3 ⇌ TCF TV ⌚ ⊣ P 4 SB £24-£25 DB £36-£42 CC MC Visa JCB ♿

WINDERMERE Cumbria   10B2

★★ Cedar Manor
Hospitality merit award
Ambleside Road, Windermere LA23 1AX
☎ 015394-43192 Fax 015394-45970
12 bedrs, all ensuite, TCF TV ⊣ P 16 SB £32-£49 DB £64-£75 HB £220-£319 D £19 CC MC Visa

★★ Crag Brow Cottage
Hospitality, Comfort, Restaurant merit awards
Helm Road, Bowness, Windermere LA23 3BU
☎ 015394-44080 Fax 015394-46003
11 bedrs, all ensuite, TCF TV ⊣ P 30 SB £35-£49.50 D £16 CC MC Visa JCB

★★ Glenburn
New Road, Windermere LA23 2EE
☎ 015394-42649 Fax 015394-88998
16 bedrs, all ensuite, 1 ⇌ TCF TV ⌚ P 17 No children under 5 DB £50-£90 HB £259-£389 D £16 CC MC Visa Amex DC JCB

★★ Grey Walls
Elleray Road, Windermere LA23 1AG
☎ 015394-43741 Fax 015394-47546
14 bedrs, all ensuite, TCF TV ⊣ P 20 SB £25-£30 DB £36-£60 HB £210-£240 D £11 CC MC Visa Amex DC JCB

★★ Hideaway
Hospitality merit award
Phoenix Way, Windermere LA23 1DB
☎ 015394-43070 Fax 015394-43070
Closed Jan
15 bedrs, all ensuite, TCF TV ⊣ P 16 SB £30-£45 DB £60-£100 HB £210-£365 D £15 CC MC Visa Amex JCB

★★ Knoll
Lake Road, Bowness, Windermere LA23 2JF
☎ 015394-43756 Fax 015392-88496
12 bedrs, 9 ensuite, 1 ⇌ TCF TV P 20 No children under 3 SB £30-£36 DB £64-£72 HB £315 D £15 CC MC Visa JCB

★★ Lindeth Fell
Hospitality, Comfort, Restaurant merit awards
Windermere LA23 3JP
☎ 015394-43286 Fax 015394-47455
15 bedrs, 13 ensuite, 2 ⌂ TCF TV P 20 No children under 7 SB £45-£65 DB £90-£130 HB £385-£450 D £19 CC MC Visa ▨ ▨ ♿

★★ Lindeth Howe
Comfort merit award
Longtail Hill, Storrs Park, Windermere LA23 3JF
☎ 015394-45759 Fax 015394-46368
E Mail lindeth.howe@dialin.net
13 bedrs, all ensuite, TCF TV P 25 SB £48.50 DB £68 HB £325 D £17.50 CC MC Visa JCB ▨ ♿

★★ Quarry Garth Country House
Hospitality, Comfort merit awards
Troutbeck Bridge, Windermere LA23 1LF
☎ 015394-88282 Fax 015394-46584
12 bedrs, all ensuite, 1 ⇌ TCF TV ⊣ P 50 SB £35-£60 DB £70-£150 HB £290-£365 D £23.50 CC MC Visa Amex

---

The Beaumont Hotel

The Beaumont is an elegant Victorian Villa occupying an enviable position for all the amenities of Windermere/Bowness and is an ideal base from which to explore Lakeland. The highest standards prevail and the lovely ensuite bedrooms (3 superb Four Poster Rooms) are immaculate, offering all modern comforts – quality beds, colour TVs, hairdryers and welcome trays. Freshly cooked hearty breakfasts are served in the delightful dining room and the charming sitting room is a restful place to relax with a book.

Jim and Barbara Casey assure you of a warm welcome and invite you to experience quality accommodation at a realistic price.

Excellent Private Car Park.
Children over 10 years.
Non Smoking.

Please phone or write for full colour brochure.

HOLLY ROAD, WINDERMERE, CUMBRIA LA23 2AF
Tel/Fax: 015394 47075
Email: thebeaumonthotel@btinternet.com

★★ Ravensworth
Ambleside Road, Windermere LA23 1BA
☏ 015394-43747 Fax 015394-43903
14 bedrs, all ensuite, TCF TV P 17 SB £30-£37 DB £59-£75 HB £256-£276 D £13 CC MC Visa

Beaumont *Highly Acclaimed*
Holly Road, Windermere LA23 2AF
☏ 015394-47075 Fax 015394-47075
E Mail thebeaumonthotel@btinternet.com
10 bedrs, all ensuite, TCF TV P 10 No children under 10 SB £28-£38 DB £48-£72 HB £130-£189 CC MC Visa Amex
See advert on previous page

Blenheim Lodge *Highly Acclaimed*
Restaurant merit award
Brantfell Road, Bowness on Windermere, Windermere LA23 3AE
☏ 015394-43440 Fax 015394-43440
E Mail geoff@twicom.demon.co.uk

Set amongst idyllic countryside yet close to local attractions, this beautiful hotel makes a perfect base for the Lakes.

10 bedrs, all ensuite, TCF TV P 14 No children under 6 SB £27-£32 DB £48-£70 HB £155-£240 D £20 CC MC Visa Amex JCB

Boston House *Highly Acclaimed*
4 The Terrace, Windermere LA23 1AJ
☏ 015394-43654 Fax 015394-43654

Delightful Victorian Listed building, on edge of village with panoramic views and/or romantic fourposters. Superb cooking. Non-smoking. Private parking. Ideal centre for touring, walking or just relaxing.
5 bedrs, all ensuite, 1 ⚌ TCF TV P 6 DB £39-£52 HB £199-£245 D £11 CC MC Visa

Broadoaks Country House *Highly Acclaimed*
Bridge Lane, Troutbeck, Windermere LA23 1LA
☏ 015394-45566 Fax 015394-88766
10 bedrs, all ensuite, TCF TV P 30 SB £49.50-£65 DB £75-£150 D £29.95 CC MC Visa

Cranleigh *Highly Acclaimed*
Kendal Road, Bowness on Windermere LA23 3EW
☏ 015394-43293
15 bedrs, all ensuite, TCF TV P 17 DB £36-£64 HB £162-£246 D £10.50 CC MC Visa JCB

Eastbourne *Highly Acclaimed*
Biskey Howe Road, Windermere LA23 2JR
☏ 015394-43525

Situated in a quiet area of Bowness, a traditionally built, Lakeland house, located below Biskey Howe viewpoint and within easy walking distance of lake, amenities and restaurants.

8 bedrs, 6 ensuite, 1 ⚌ TCF TV P 6 SB £18-£26 DB £34-£54 CC MC Visa

Fairfield Country House *Highly Acclaimed*
Brantfell Road, Windermere LA23 3AE
☏ 015394-46565 Fax 015394-46565
E Mail ray&barb@fairfield.dial.lakesnet.co.uk
Closed Dec-Jan excl New Year

An attractive 200 year old house set in a quiet, secluded, well matured garden, close to the village, lake, fells and Dales Way.

9 bedrs, all ensuite, TCF TV P 14 SB £23-£30 DB £46-£60 HB £291.50-£321.50 D £19.50 CC MC Visa

BLENHEIM LODGE HOTEL

Set amongst idyllic countryside yet close to the local attractions, this beautiful hotel makes a perfect base for the Lakes.

Highly Acclaimed Restaurant Award

BRANTFELL ROAD,
BOWNESS ON WINDERMERE,
WINDERMERE LA23 3AE
Tel/Fax: 01539 443440

Fir Trees *Highly Acclaimed*
Lake Road, Windermere LA23 2EQ
015394-42272 Fax 015394-42272

RAC Hotel Reservations Service
0870 603 9109
(Calls charged at national call rate)

A well situated Victorian guest house of considerable charm and character, furnished with antiques and fine prints throughout.

8 bedrs, all ensuite, TCF TV P 9 SB £26-£32 DB £42-£54 CC MC Visa Amex

Glencree *Highly Acclaimed*
Lake Road, Windermere LA23 2EQ
015394-445822
Closed Nov-Feb
5 bedrs, all ensuite, TCF TV P 6 No children under 7
SB £29-£39 DB £39-£70 CC MC Visa

KIRKWOOD Guest House

Kirkwood provides an excellent base on which to tour the Lakes. A comfortable Victorian house, with spacious rooms, honeymoon suites and four poster beds, all with TV, tea/coffee, and private facilities. The proprietors Carol and Neil do all they can to give friendly, personal service. Help with planning a route, or booking a tour, after serving you with a home-cooked breakfast of your choice.

RAC Highly Acclaimed

**PRINCES ROAD, WINDERMERE,
CUMBRIA LA23 2DD
Tel: 015394 43907**

HAWKSMOOR

A charming licenced Guest House situated mid-way between Windermere and Bowness and backed by unspoilt woodland. All bedrooms have private bath/shower rooms ensuite, colour televisions and complimentary tea/coffee facilities. Some ground floor bedrooms with level access to all public areas. Superb private car park.

LAKE ROAD, WINDERMERE, CUMBRIA LA23 2EQ
Tel: (015394) 42110

Glenville *Highly Acclaimed*
Lake Road, Windermere LA23 2EQ
☏ 015394-43371

Set in its own grounds, the Glenville is perfectly positioned for access to all amenities and within walking distance of the lake. The hotel retains original features which give added character.

8 bedrs, all ensuite, 1 ♿ TCF TV P 10 SB £18-£27 DB £35-£50 D £12 CC MC Visa ♿

Don't forget to mention the guide
When booking direct, please remember to tell the hotel that you chose it from RAC Bed & Breakfast 1998.

Haisthorpe *Highly Acclaimed*
Holly Road, Windermere LA23 2AF
☏ 01539-443445 Fax 015394-43445
E Mail haisthorpe@aol.com

Family run Victorian guest house offering a high standard of accommodation at reasonable prices. Situated in a quiet central location. Phone for full colour brochure.

6 bedrs, 5 ensuite, 1 ♿ TCF TV ⚑ P 3 SB £15-£21 DB £26-£38 HB £137.50-£173 D £7.50 CC MC Visa

Hawksmoor *Highly Acclaimed*
Lake Road, Windermere LA23 2EQ
☏ 01539-442110
Closed 25 Nov-26 Dec
10 bedrs, all ensuite, TCF TV P 12 No children under 6
SB £25-£35 DB £44-£55 D £11.50 CC MC Visa JCB ♿

Holly Park House *Highly Acclaimed*
1 Park Road, Windermere LA23 2AW
☎ 015394-42107

Handsome stone built Victorian house, with original pine woodwork and stained glass. Quiet area but close to village.

6 bedrs, all ensuite, **TCF TV** 🐾 **P** 4 **SB** £26-£30 **DB** £36-£44 **D** £9 **CC** MC Visa Amex DC

Kirkwood *Highly Acclaimed*
Princes Road, Windermere LA23 2DD
☎ 015394-43907 Fax 015394-43907
7 bedrs, all ensuite, **TCF TV** ✉ 🐾 **P** 1 **DB** £42-£55 **CC** MC Visa JCB
See advert on previous page

Newstead *Highly Acclaimed*
New Road, Windermere LA23 2EE
☎ 015394-44485

Elegant detached Victorian house, totally refurbished - high quality ensuite bedrooms, lovely woodwork and original Victorian fireplaces. Large garden and secure car park. Superb lounge and spacious dining room. Scrumptious food.

7 bedrs, all ensuite, **TCF TV** ✉ **P** 10 No children under 7 **DB** £40-£48

Orrest Close *Highly Acclaimed*
3 The Terrace, Windermere LA23 1AJ
☎ 015394-43325 Fax 015394-43325

Conveniently situated within easy reach of buses, trains and village, our listed Victorian guest house offers every comfort including fourposter beds and excellent home cooking. ETB 3 crown commended.

6 bedrs, 4 ensuite, 2 ♿ **TCF TV** ✉ **P** 6 **DB** £36-£46 **HB** £180-£200 **D** £12 **CC** MC Visa JCB

St John's Lodge *Highly Acclaimed*
Lake Road, Windermere LA23 2EQ
☎ 015394-43078
Closed Nov-Feb

A Lakeland stone Victorian building located by the lake, midway between Windermere village and Bowness. Close to all amenities.

14 bedrs, all ensuite, **TCF TV** 🐾 **P** 10 No children under 3 **SB** £20-£28 **DB** £37-£52 **HB** £205-£245 **D** £11 **CC** MC Visa

RAC Hotel Reservations Service
0870 603 9109
(Calls charged at national call rate)

WINDERMERE – ENGLAND

HOLLY-WOOD GUEST HOUSE

A comfortable Victorian guest house, central for touring the Lake District, Dales and Morecambe Bay. Offering traditional breakfasts, friendly atmosphere and high standards.

Holly Road, Windermere, Cumbria LA23 2AF
Tel: 015394-42219

RAC Hotel Reservations Service
0870 603 9109
(Calls charged at national call rate)

Westbourne *Highly Acclaimed*
Biskey Howe Road, Bowness-on-Windermere LA23 2JR
☎ 015394-43625
Closed 24-25, 31 Dec, 1 Jan

Situated in a peaceful area of Bowness close to shops, restaurants and the lake. All rooms are ensuite. Bar lounge. Pets welcome. Private parking

9 bedrs, all ensuite, **TCF TV** ⚲ **P** 11 **SB** £26-£42 **DB** £40-£56 **CC** MC Visa Amex

Westlake *Highly Acclaimed*
Lake Road, Windermere LA23 2EQ
☎ 015394-43020
7 bedrs, all ensuite, **TCF TV P** 7 No children under 5 **SB** £20-£25 **DB** £38-£48 **CC** MC Visa

WOODLANDS

A very comfortable small hotel, family owned and run, offers friendly, attentive service. Bedrooms are well equipped, there is a delightful lounge and good home cooking is provided.

NEW ROAD, WINDERMERE LA23 2EE
Tel: (015394) 43915 Fax: (015394) 48558

Woodlands *Highly Acclaimed*
New Road, Windermere LA23 2EE
☎ 015394-43915 Fax 015394-48558
Closed Christmas

The secret to a truly wonderful holiday is the right hotel. Experience our delightful surroundings, renowned breakfasts and a warm welcome from resident proprietors Juliet and Andrew Wood who take great pride in maintaining high standards throughout.

14 bedrs, all ensuite, **TCF TV P** 14 No children **SB** £22-£29 **DB** £44-£58 **D** £14 **CC** MC Visa JCB

Aaron Slack *Acclaimed*
48 Ellerthwaite Road, Windermere LA23 2BS
☎ 015394-44649
E Mail s.townsend@aaronslack.demon.co.uk

This Victorian terraced house built of local stone is in a quiet part of Windermere but within walking distance of trains, buses, shops and restaurants.

3 bedrs, all ensuite, **TCF TV** No children under 12 **SB** £16-£22 **DB** £32-£42 **CC** MC Visa Amex JCB

Green Gables *Acclaimed*
37 Broad Street, Windermere LA23 2AB
☎ 015394-43886
Closed Christmas-New Year
8 bedrs, 3 ensuite, 2 **TCF TV P** 2

Holly-Wood *Acclaimed*
Holly Road, Windermere LA23 2AF
☎ 015394-42219
Closed Nov-Feb
6 bedrs, 3 ensuite, 2 **TCF TV P** 3 **SB** £16-£21 **DB** £30-£40

Lynwood *Acclaimed*
Broad Street, Windermere LA23 2AB
☎ 015394-42550 Fax 015394-42550
9 bedrs, all ensuite, **TCF TV**

Mylne Bridge House *Acclaimed*
Brookside, Lake Road, Windermere LA23 2BY
☎ 015394-43314 Fax 015394-48052

Ideal tranquil location for your Lakeland break. Family run guest house offering comfortable, well appointed rooms and excellent full English breakfast. Large private car park.

8 bedrs, 7 ensuite, 1 **TCF TV P** 10 No children under 2 **SB** £20-£23 **DB** £38-£44 **CC** MC Visa JCB

Oakthorpe *Acclaimed*
High Street, Windermere LA23 1AF
☎ 015394-43547

Oldfield House *Acclaimed*
Oldfield Road, Windermere LA23 2BY
☎ 015394-88445 Fax 015394-43250
Closed Jan

A double-fronted Lakeland stone residence located off the busy main road, only a short walk from the village.

8 bedrs, all ensuite, 1 **TCF TV P** 7 **SB** £19-£30 **DB** £38-£58 **CC** MC Visa Amex JCB

Rockside *Acclaimed*
Ambleside Road, Windermere LA23 1AQ
☎ 015394-45343 Fax 015394-45343
Closed Christmas

Superb accommodation 100 yards from Windermere village, train and bus station. Most rooms ensuite with remote TV, telephone, clock, radio, hair dryer, etc. Parking for 12 cars. Tours arranged if required.

15 bedrs, 10 ensuite, 2 🐕 TCF TV P 12 SB £16-£23 DB £31-£45 CC MC Visa JCB

Rosemount *Acclaimed*
Lake Road, Windermere LA23 2EQ
☎ 015394-43739 Fax 015394-48978
Closed Dec-Jan

A small, distinctive immaculately decorated, Lakeland stone guest house approximately 120 years old, situated midway between Bowness and Windermere.

8 bedrs, 5 ensuite, 1 🛁, TCF TV 🚭 P 8 SB £19 DB £38-£52 CC MC Visa

Winbrook House *Acclaimed*
30 Ellerthwaite Road, Windermere LA23 2AH
☎ 015394-44932

Located in a quiet part of Windermere, Winbrock House offers immaculate accommodation and excellent breakfasts. All bedrooms have TV and tea/coffee, some with ensuite. Private car park.

6 bedrs, 3 ensuite, 1 🐕 TCF TV P 6 No children under 8 SB £18-£25 DB £33-£40

Elim Bank *Listed*
Lake Road, Windermere LA23 2JJ
☎ 015394-44810

9 bedrs, 6 ensuite, TCF TV 🍴 P 9 SB £21-£27.50 DB £38-£55 HB £205-£260 D £12 CC MC Visa Amex JCB

Royal Lodge *Lodge*
Royal Square, Bowness, Windermere LA23 3DB
☎ 015394-43045 Fax 015394-44990

Standing in the centre of Bowness village, only two minutes walk to Lake Windermere. All rooms are ensuite, most with spectacular fell or lake views.

29 bedrs, all ensuite, TCF TV 🍴 P 15 SB £31 DB £59.50 CC MC Visa Amex DC JCB

Don't forget to mention the guide
When booking direct, please remember to tell the hotel that you chose it from RAC Bed & Breakfast 1998.

Oakbank House
Helm Road, Bowness on Windermere LA23 3BU
☎ 015394-43386

An elegant Victorian house with spacious ensuite rooms, colour TV and tea and coffee making facilities. Superb views of Lake Windermere from most rooms. Close to all amenities.

11 bedrs, 4 ensuite, 7 🅿, TCF TV ⚭ P 11 SB £25-£30 DB £44-£60 CC MC Visa

South View
Cross Street, Windermere LA23 1AE
☎ 015394-42951

Unique in Windermere Village, a guest house with own swimming pool and spa pool. One of Windermere's oldest buildings (1845). Relaxed, friendly atmosphere. Very quiet yet central. Private parking. Licensed. Excellent choice of breakfast.

6 bedrs, 5 ensuite, TCF TV P 6 CC MC Visa Amex 🛏

WINDSOR Berkshire 4C2

★★ Aurora Garden
Hospitality, Comfort merit awards
Bolton Avenue, Windsor SL4 3JF
☎ 01753-868686 Fax 01753-831394
14 bedrs, all ensuite, TCF TV ⚭ P 20 CC MC Visa Amex DC

★★ Royal Adelaide
Kings Road, Windsor
☎ 01753-830683 Fax 01753-841980

Netherton *Highly Acclaimed*
96-98 St Leonards Road, Windsor SL4 3DA
☎ 01753-855508 Fax 01753-621267

A three storey, red-brick hotel, ten minutes from the centre of Windsor.

11 bedrs, all ensuite, TCF TV P 14 SB £45 DB £55 CC MC Visa ♿

Melrose House *Acclaimed*
53 Frances Road, Windsor SL4 3AQ
☎ 01753-865328 Fax 01753-865328
9 bedrs, all ensuite, 🛁 ⚭ P 9 SB £38-£40 DB £45-£50
CC MC Visa JCB

Clarence *Listed*
9 Clarence Road, Windsor SL4 5AE
☎ 01753-864436 Fax 01753-857060

A comfortable hotel close to the town centre, Windsor Castle, Eton College and the Thames. Convenient for Heathrow Airport.

21 bedrs, all ensuite, 1 ⇨ TCF TV ⚭ P 4 SB £33-£42
DB £42-£54 CC MC Visa Amex DC JCB 📺

Oxford Blue *Listed*
Crimp Hill Road, Old Windsor, Windsor SL4 2DY
☎ 01753-861954

WINSFORD Somerset 3D2

Karslake House *Acclaimed*
Halse Lane, Winsford TA24 7JE
☎ 01643-851242 Fax 01643-851242
Closed Nov-Mar
7 bedrs, 5 ensuite, 2 🅿, 1 ⇨ TCF TV 🛁 ⚭ P 10 No children under 10 SB £30.50-£38 DB £45-£60
HB £234.50-£276.50 D £15.50

WINSLOW Buckinghamshire 4C1

★★ Bell
Market Square, Winslow MK18 3AB
☎ 01296-714091 Fax 01296-714805
21 bedrs, all ensuite, TCF TV 🐾 P 100 CC MC Visa Amex ♿

WISBECH Cambridgeshire 9D3

★★ Crown Lodge
Hospitality, Comfort, Restaurant merit awards
Downham Road, Outwell, Wisbech PE14 8SE
☎ 01945-773391 Fax 01945-772668

For business or pleasure, a warm and attentive atmosphere with a high level of personal service, excellent accommodation and supported by delightful, imaginative home-made food.

10 bedrs, all ensuite, TCF TV 🐾 P 60 SB £41-£45 DB £55-£60 D £13.50 CC MC Visa Amex DC

★★ Rose & Crown
Market Place, Wisbech PE13 1DG
☎ 01945-589800 Fax 01945-474610
20 bedrs, all ensuite, 1 🐾 TCF TV 🐾 P 20 SB £42-£53 DB £53-£64 D £11 CC MC Visa Amex DC

WITHAM Essex 5E1

★ Spread Eagle
Newcand Street, Witham CM8 2BD
☎ 01376-511097 Fax 01376-521033
14 bedrs, 2 ensuite, 1, 4 TCF TV P 40 SB £25 DB £35 CC MC Visa Amex

WITHYPOOL Somerset 3D2

★★ Royal Oak Inn
Withypool TA24 7QP
☎ 01643-831506 Fax 01643-831659
Closed 25-26 Dec
8 bedrs, 7 ensuite, 1 🐾 TCF TV 🐾 P 20 No children under 10 SB £30-£34 DB £68-£76 HB £364-£392 D £22 CC MC Visa Amex DC JCB

WITNEY Oxfordshire 4B2

★★ Marlborough
28 Market Square, Witney OX8 7BB
☎ 01993-776353 Fax 01993-702152
22 bedrs, all ensuite, TCF TV 🐾 P 20 CC MC Visa Amex DC JCB

Hawthorn House *Acclaimed*
79 Burford Road, Witney OX8 5DR
☎ 01993-772768
3 bedrs, all ensuite, TCF TV P 5 SB £20-£25 DB £40 CC MC Visa Amex JCB

WITTERSHAM Kent 5E3

Isle of Oxney Shetland Centre *Highly Acclaimed*
Oxney Farm, Moons Green, Wittersham TN30 7PS
☎ 01797-270558 Fax 01797-270558
3 bedrs, all ensuite, TCF P 6 No children SB £25-£27.50 DB £50-£55 HB £230-£260 D £15

WIX Essex 5E1

New Farm *Acclaimed*
Spinnells Lane, Wix, Manningtree CO11 2UJ
☎ 01255-870365 Fax 01255-870837
12 bedrs, 7 ensuite, 2 🐾 TCF TV 🐾 P 20 SB £22-£26 DB £42-£48 HB £315-£337 D £13 CC MC Visa Amex ♿

WOKING Surrey 4C3

★★ Wheatsheaf
Chobham Road, Woking GU21 4AL
☎ 01483-773047 Fax 01483-740904
30 bedrs, all ensuite, 1 🐾 TCF TV P 72 CC MC Visa Amex DC ♿

WOLVERHAMPTON West Midlands 8A3

Travelodge *Lodge*
Granada Birmingham (N), M6 (btw jn 10-11), Wolverhampton WV11 2DR
☎ 0800-850950 Fax 01525-878451
42 bedrs, all ensuite, TCF TV 🐾 P 400 SB £42.95 CC MC Visa Amex DC ♿

Short Breaks

Many hotels provide special rates for weekend and mid-week breaks - sometimes these are quoted in the hotel's entry, otherwise ring direct for the latest offers.

Fox Hotel International
118 School Street, Wolverhampton WV3 0NR
☎ 01902-21680 Fax 01902-711654

Discover a haven of individual attention and welcoming hospitality located in Wolverhampton town centre. Ideally placed for exploring the many attractions in the Black Country and the beautiful countryside of Shropshire. Conference suite. Wedding package.

32 bedrs, all ensuite, 4 ⇌ **TCF TV P** 20 **SB** £29 **DB** £45 **HB** £135 **D** £6 **CC** MC Visa Amex DC JCB

WOODBRIDGE Suffolk 9F4

Grange Farm
Dennington, Woodbridge IP13 8BT
☎ 01986-798388
Closed 10 Dec-30 Jan

Exceptional moated farmhouse dating from 14th century. Superbly situated, spacious grounds, all weather tennis court, relaxed atmosphere, log fires in winter. Homemade bread and marmalade.

3 bedrs, 1 ⇌ **TCF** ✉ **P** 6 No children under 12 **SB** £20 **DB** £40 **HB** £130-£260 **D** £12.50 ⊠

WOODHALL SPA Lincolnshire 8C2

★★ Eagle Lodge
The Broadway, Woodhall Spa LN10 6ST
☎ 01526-353231 Fax 01526-352797

Twenty three ensuite bedrooms, a la carte menu, bar snacks and real ales. Ideally placed for golfing, walking, touring or as a business base.

23 bedrs, all ensuite, **TCF TV ↳ P** 60 **SB** £24-£40 **DB** £44-£60 **D** £10 **CC** MC Visa Amex DC JCB ♿

Claremont
9-11 Witham Road, Woodhall Spa LN10 6RW
☎ 01526-352000

Homely B&B in unspoilt traditional Victorian guest house in the centre of Woodhall Spa, Lincolnshire's unique resort. An ideal centre for exploring the area and its heritage.

10 bedrs, 2 ensuite, 2 ⇌ **TCF TV ↳ P** 4 **SB** £15-£20 **DB** £30

WOODSTOCK Oxfordshire 4B1

★★ Marlborough Arms
Oxford Street, Woodstock OX20 1TS
☎ 01993-811227 Fax 01993-811657
15 bedrs, 11 ensuite, 1 ⛌, 2 ⇌ **TCF TV ↳ P** 20 **SB** £35-£45 **DB** £55-£60 **D** £12.95 **CC** MC Visa Amex ♿

Gorselands *Listed*
Gorselands, Boddington Lane, Woodstock OX8 6PU
☎ 01993-881895 Fax 01993-882799
6 bedrs, all ensuite, **TV** ✉ **↳ P** 8 **SB** £29-£40 **DB** £40-£50 **HB** £198 £260 **D** £14 **CC** MC Visa Amex JCB ⊠

Star Inn *Listed*
22 Market Place, Woodstock OX20 1TA
☎ 01993-811373 Fax 01993-812007
4 bedrs, all ensuite, **TCF TV ↳ SB** £40 **DB** £50 **D** £5 **CC** MC Visa Amex

WOOLACOMBE Devon 2C2

★★ Headlands
Hospitality merit award
Beach Road, Woolacombe EX34 7BT
☎ 01271-870320 Fax 01271-870320
Closed Nov-Feb
14 bedrs, 10 ensuite, 2 ⇌ TCF TV ✱ P 16 No children under 4 **SB** £26-£30 **DB** £52-£60 **HB** £216-£240 **D** £10 **CC** MC Visa

★★ Little Beach
Hospitality, Comfort merit awards
The Esplanade, Woolacombe EX34 7DJ
☎ 01271-870398
Closed winter
10 bedrs, 8 ensuite, 1 ⇌ TCF TV ✱ P 7 No children under 6 **SB** £27.50-£29.50 **DB** £55-£60 **HB** £220-£295 **CC** MC Visa

★ Crossways
Hospitality, Comfort merit awards
The Esplanade, Woolacombe EX34 7DJ
☎ 01271-870395 Fax 01271-870395
Closed Nov-Feb
9 bedrs, 6 ensuite, 1 ⌂, 1 ⇌ TCF TV ✱ P 9 **SB** £20-£27 **DB** £40-£54 **HB** £170-£213 **D** £5

Sunnycliffe *Highly Acclaimed*
Mortehoe, Woolacombe EX34 7EB
☎ 01271-870597 Fax 01271-870597
Closed Dec-Feb

A small hotel set above a sandy cove in an unspoilt coastal village between Mortehoe and Woolacombe.

8 bedrs, all ensuite, TCF TV P 12 No children under 12 **SB** £25-£32 **DB** £50-£64 **HB** £245-£275 **D** £15

Don't forget to mention the guide
When booking direct, please remember to tell the hotel that you chose it from RAC Bed & Breakfast 1998.

Caertref *Acclaimed*
Beach Road, Woolacombe EX34 7BT
☎ 01271-870361
Closed Dec-Feb

Family run hotel two minutes from sandy beach. Home cooking, friendly atmosphere, bar, colour TV's in all rooms. Own private car park. Children welcome.

13 bedrs, 7 ensuite, 1 ⌂, 2 ⇌ TCF TV ✱ P 13 **SB** £17-£22 **DB** £34-£44 **HB** £170-£205 **D** £8

Lundy House *Awaiting Inspection*
Chapel Hill, Mortehoe, Woolacombe EX34 7RZ
☎ 01271-870372 Fax 01271-871001
E Mail walkinharmony@msn.com
Closed Jan
9 bedrs, 6 ensuite, 1 ⇌ TCF TV ✱ P 9 No children under 6 **SB** £17.50-£20 **DB** £35-£54 **HB** £115-£179 **D** £9.99 **CC** MC Visa

WOOLER Northumberland 13F3

★★ Tankerville Arms
Cottage Road, Wooler NE71 6AD
☎ 01668-281581 Fax 01668-281387
16 bedrs, all ensuite, TCF TV ✱ P 100 **SB** £47 **DB** £76 **HB** £336 **D** £17 **CC** MC Visa

WORCESTER Worcestershire 7E3

★★ Ye Olde Talbot
Friar Street, Worcester WR1 2NA
☎ 01905-23573 Fax 01905-612760
29 bedrs, all ensuite, TCF TV ✱ P 8 **SB** £45-£50 **DB** £60 **D** £14 **CC** MC Visa Amex DC

★ Maximillian
Hospitality merit award
Shrub Hill Road, Worcester WR4 9EF
☎ 0500-829145 Fax 01905-724935
17 bedrs, 13 ensuite, 1 ⇌ TCF TV P 20 **SB** £38.50 **DB** £51 **HB** £253.75 **D** £15 **CC** MC Visa Amex DC

★ Park House
Comfort merit award
12 Droitwich Road, Worcester WR3 7LJ
☎ 01905-21816 Fax 01905-612178
7 bedrs, 4 ensuite, 2 ⇌ TCF TV ✱ P 8 **SB** £26-£30 **DB** £36-£42 **HB** £248-£276 **D** £10 **CC** MC Visa

YARMOUTH, GREAT – ENGLAND

Loch Ryan *Highly Acclaimed*
119 Sidbury, Worcester WR5 2DH
01905-351143 Fax 01905-351143
10 bedrs, all ensuite, **TCF TV P** 10 **SB** £40-£45 **DB** £55-£60 **D** £18 **CC** MC Visa Amex DC

WORKINGTON Cumbria 10A1

Morven *Highly Acclaimed*
Siddick Road, Workington CA14 1LE
01900-602118 Fax 01900-602118

Relaxed, informal atmosphere. Ensuite bedrooms for the business visitor to commercial West Cumbria. Ideal stopover for 'Coast to Coast' participants, near the start. Car park and secure cycle storage.

7 bedrs, 6 ensuite, **TCF TV P** 12 **SB** £28-£32 **DB** £38-£48 **HB** £190-£210 **D** £12

WORTHING West Sussex 4C4

★★ Cavendish
115-116 Marine Parade, Worthing BN11 3QG
01903-236767 Fax 01903-823840
15 bedrs, all ensuite, 1 **TCF TV P** 6 **SB** £45 **DB** £60-£75 **HB** £260-£290 **D** £13 **CC** MC Visa Amex DC

Moorings *Highly Acclaimed*
4 Selden Road, Worthing BN11 2L
01903-208882 Fax 01903-236878
8 bedrs, all ensuite, **P** 3 **SB** £18.50-£26 **DB** £36.50-£48 **D** £12.50 **CC** MC Visa Amex

Bonchurch House *Acclaimed*
1 Winchester Road, Worthing BN11 4DJ
01903-202492
7 bedrs, 6 ensuite, 1 **TCF TV P** 6 No children under 4 **SB** £19-£20 **DB** £36-£40 **HB** £200-£230 **D** £14.50 **CC** MC Visa JCB

Delmar *Acclaimed*
1-2 New Parade, Worthing BN11 2BQ
01903-211834 Fax 01903-219052
12 bedrs, all ensuite, **TCF TV P** 5 **SB** £28.50-£29.50 **DB** £55-£75 **HB** £283.50-£296.10 **D** £17.50 **CC** MC Visa Amex DC JCB

WROXHAM Norfolk 9F3

★★ Broads
Station Road, Wroxham NR12 8UR
01603-782869 Fax 01603-784066
28 bedrs, 21 ensuite, 7, **TCF TV P** 40 **SB** £35 **DB** £50-£60 **HB** £234 **D** £10.50 **CC** MC Visa Amex DC

WYMONDHAM Norfolk 9E3

★★ Wymondham Consort
Hospitality, Comfort merit awards
28 Market Street, Wymondham NR18 0BB
01953-606721 Fax 01953-601361

Award winning hotel and restaurant ideally situated in the centre of an historic market town. Excellent touring base for Norfolk Broads, the Norfolk coast, countryside and Norwich City.

20 bedrs, all ensuite, **TCF TV P** 14 **SB** £45-£55 **DB** £60-£65 **HB** £255-£270 **D** £15.95 **CC** MC Visa Amex DC JCB

YARMOUTH, GREAT Norfolk 9F3

★★ Burlington
North Drive, Great Yarmouth NR30 1EG
01493-844568 Fax 01493-331848
Closed Jan
27 bedrs, all ensuite, 1 **TCF TV P** 30 **SB** £45-£60 **DB** £60-£80 **HB** £220-£270 **D** £16 **CC** MC Visa Amex DC

★★ Palm Court
North Drive, Great Yarmouth NR30 1EF
01493-844568 Fax 01493-331848
Closed Jan
43 bedrs, 42 ensuite, 2 **TCF TV P** 50 **SB** £40-£55 **DB** £55-£70 **HB** £164-£275 **D** £16 **CC** MC Visa Amex DC JCB

★★ Regency
5 North Drive, Great Yarmouth NR30 1ED
01493-843759 Fax 01493-330411
15 bedrs, all ensuite, **TV P** 10 No children under 7 **SB** £25-£32 **DB** £52-£58 **HB** £182-£210 **D** £11 **CC** MC Visa Amex DC JCB

★★ Royal
Marine Parade, Great Yarmouth NR30 3AE
📞 01493-844215 Fax 01493-331921
68 bedrs, 63 ensuite, 34 ⇨ TCF TV ♁ 🍽 SB £22 DB £48
D £9 CC MC Visa 🖼 ♿

★★ Sandringham
74-75 Marine Parade, Great Yarmouth NR30 2BU
📞 01493-852427 Fax 01493-852336
Closed Nov-Christmas
24 bedrs, all ensuite, ♁ CC MC Visa

★★ Two Bears
Restaurant merit award
South Town Road, Great Yarmouth NR31 0HW
📞 01493-603198 Fax 01493-440486
11 bedrs, all ensuite, 2 ⇨ TCF TV P 75 CC MC Visa
Amex DC JCB 🖼

Corner House *Highly Acclaimed*
Albert Square, Great Yarmouth NR30 3JH
📞 01493-842773
Closed Nov-Feb
8 bedrs, all ensuite, 1 ⇨ TCF TV P 8 SB £20-£25 DB £40-£50 D £7

Georgian House *Highly Acclaimed*
17 North Drive, Great Yarmouth NR30 4EW
📞 01493-842623
Closed Nov-Easter

Handsome detached marine mansion designed by Paxton Hood-Watson, an arts/craft architect and situated in prominent corner sea front position with magnificent sea views.

19 bedrs, 17 ensuite, 2 ⇨ TCF TV P 19 No children under 5 DB £35-£50

Trotwood *Highly Acclaimed*
2 North Drive, Great Yarmouth NR30 1ED
📞 01493-843971
Closed Christmas-New Year

Opposite bowling greens on seafront, giving unrivalled sea views. Close to Britania Pier and all amenities. Bedrooms ensuite, licenced bar, own car park.

9 bedrs, 8 ensuite, 1 ⇨, TCF TV ♁ P 11 SB £27-£32 DB £42-£54 CC MC Visa

Winchester *Highly Acclaimed*
12 Euston Road, Great Yarmouth NR30 1DY
📞 01493-843950 Fax 01493-843950
Closed Dec-Mar

Conveniently located for all central attractions, secure private parking at rear, your hosts ensure that the hotel is immaculately maintained. All rooms ensuite, separate dinning tables.

14 bedrs, all ensuite, TCF TV P 14 No children under 5 SB £16-£21 DB £29-£39 HB £117-£157.50

Andover *Acclaimed*
28-30 Camperdown, Great Yarmouth NR30 3JB
📞 01493-843490
Closed Nov-Mar
25 bedrs, all ensuite, TCF TV SB £20-£23 DB £36-£44 HB £120-£183 🖼 🖼

Bramalea Balmoral *Acclaimed*
114-115 Wellesley Road, Great Yarmouth NR30 2AR
📞 01493-844722
Closed Nov-Apr
15 bedrs, all ensuite, 1 ⇨ TCF TV SB £13-£17 DB £26-£34 HB £95-£155 D £5

Chequers *Acclaimed*
27 Nelson Road South, Great Yarmouth NR30 7JA
📞 01493-853091
8 bedrs, all ensuite, TCF TV P 7 SB £15-£20 DB £30-£40 HB £115-£179 D £5

Edwardian *Acclaimed*
18-20 Crown Road, Great Yarmouth NR30 2JN
📞 01493-856482
E Mail eaglemont@compuserve.com
18 bedrs, all ensuite, TV P 12 SB £19.50-£24.50 DB £33.50-£37.50 HB £149.50-£169.50 D £8.50 CC MC Visa ♿

Kingsley House *Acclaimed*
68 King Street, Great Yarmouth NR30 2PP
📞 **01493-850948**
7 bedrs, all ensuite, **TCF TV** No children under 2 **SB** £-£18 **DB** £-£36 **HB** £118-£150 **D** £7 **CC** MC Visa Amex DC JCB

Malcolm *Acclaimed*
6 Norfolk Square, Albemarle Road, NR30 1EE
📞 **01493-842381**
15 bedrs, all ensuite, 1 🛏 **TCF TV P** 12 No children under 5 **SB** £18-£26 **DB** £36-£44 **HB** £21-£29

Midland *Acclaimed*
7-9 Wellesley Road, Great Yarmouth NR30 2AP
📞 **01493-330046**
35 bedrs, 26 ensuite, 3 🛏 **TCF TV** 🐕 **P** 25 **CC** MC Visa

Ravenswood *Acclaimed*
5/6 Nelson Road South, Great Yarmouth NR30 3JA
📞 **01493-844117**
Closed late Sept-Easter
19 bedrs, 16 ensuite, 1 🛏 **TCF TV P** 15 **SB** £15-£20 **DB** £30-£40 **HB** £105-£140 **D** £6

Redruth *Acclaimed*
21-24 Nelson Road South, Great Yarmouth NR30 2JR
📞 **01493-844017 Fax 01493-844052**
48 bedrs, all ensuite, **TCF TV** **SB** £15-£20 **DB** £30-£40 **HB** £120-£160 **D** £4

Rhonadean *Acclaimed*
110-111 Wellesley Road, Great Yarmouth NR30 2AR
📞 **01493-842004**
18 bedrs, all ensuite, **TCF TV SB** £15 **DB** £30 **HB** £100

Richmond House *Acclaimed*
113 Wellesley Road, Great Yarmouth NR30 2AR
📞 **01493-853995**
8 bedrs, 6 ensuite, 2 🛏 **TCF TV** No children under 2 **SB** £12-£15 **DB** £24-£30 **HB** £85-£140 **D** £5 **CC** MC Visa Amex

Russell *Acclaimed*
26 Nelson Road South, Great Yarmouth NR30 3TL
📞 **01493-843788**
Closed Nov-Easter
10 bedrs, all ensuite, **TCF TV SB** £16-£23 **DB** £32-£40 **HB** £99-£170 **D** £6 **CC** MC Visa Amex

Sedley House *Acclaimed*
5 St Georges Road, Great Yarmouth NR30 2JR
📞 **01493-855409**
7 bedrs, 2 ensuite, 2 🛏, 1 🛏 **TCF TV P** 6 No children under 15 **SB** £13-£17 **DB** £26-£34

Shemara *Acclaimed*
11 Wellesey Road, Great Yarmouth NR30 2AR
📞 **01493-844054**
9 bedrs, all ensuite, **TCF TV**
SB £12-£20 **DB** £24-£40 **HB** £99-£140

Sienna Lodge *Acclaimed*
17-18 Camperdown, Great Yarmouth NR30 3JB
📞 **01493-843361**
Closed Nov
14 bedrs, all ensuite, **TCF TV** 🐕 **SB** £19-£24 **DB** £38-£48 **HB** £95-£160 **D** £8

Southern *Acclaimed*
46 Queens Road, Great Yarmouth NR30 3JR
📞 **01493-843313**

This family run hotel is situated a few minutes walk from all seafront amenities and town centre. Private car park.

21 bedrs, 15 ensuite, 4 🛏, 3 🛏 **TV P** 10 **SB** £15-£20 **DB** £30-£35 **HB** £110-£155 **D** £6.50 **CC** MC Visa

Sunnydene *Acclaimed*
83 North Denes Road, Great Yarmouth NR30 4LW
📞 **01493-843554 Fax 01493-332391**
16 bedrs, 12 ensuite, 1 🛏 **TCF TV** 🐕 **P** 9 **SB** £13.50-£19.50 **DB** £27-£39 **HB** £65-£130 **D** £6 **CC** MC Visa Amex DC ♿

Baron's Court *Listed*
5 Norfolk Square, Albemarle Road, NR30 1EE
📞 **01493-843987 Fax 01493-843987**
Closed Christmas

Baron's Court has an excellent location with open aspect both front and rear. Quietly situated yet close to the beach and main tourist area.

19 bedrs, 18 ensuite, 2 🛏 **TCF TV P** 12 **SB** £17-£23 **DB** £32-£42 **HB** £105-£175 **D** £6 **CC** MC Visa Amex DC ♿

YARMOUTH, GREAT – ENGLAND

Briglands *Listed*
12 Wellesley Road, Great Yarmouth NR30 2AR
📞 01493-843485
8 bedrs, 6 ensuite, 1 ➡ TCF TV No children under 12
SB £12-£14 DB £24-£36 HB £110-£140

Britannia *Listed*
119 Wellesley Road, Great Yarmouth NR30 2AP
📞 01493-856488 Fax 01493-856488
7 bedrs, 1 ensuite, 1 ➡ TCF TV No children under 4
SB £11.50-£16 DB £23-£32 HB £115.50-£147 D £5

Cairne *Listed*
29 Victoria Road, Great Yarmouth NR30 3BH
📞 01493-855069 Fax 01493-85069

Quietly just off the sea front, close to all amenities including theatres and cinemas. At the Cairne we have a comfortable lounge and dining room, where we offer an excellent and varied menu with good home cooked food.

9 bedrs, 7 ensuite, 2 ➡ TCF TV SB £15.50 DB £32 HB £77-£105 D £4 ♿

Chatsworth *Listed*
32 Wellesley Road, Great Yarmouth NR30 1EU
📞 01493-842890
Closed Nov-Apr
17 bedrs, all ensuite

Dene *Listed*
89 North Denes Road, Great Yarmouth NR30 4LW
📞 01493-844181
Closed Oct-Easter
8 bedrs, 3 ensuite, 2 ➡ TCF TV P 7 SB £15-£18 DB £28-£42 HB £99-£150

Gai-Sejour *Listed*
21 Princes Road, Great Yarmouth NR30 2DG
📞 01493-843371
11 bedrs, 5 ensuite, 2 ➡ TCF TV SB £13-£16 DB £26-£32 HB £95-£130 D £5 CC MC Visa Amex

Lea-Hurst *Listed*
117 Wellesley Road, Great Yarmouth NR30 2AP
📞 01493-843063
Closed Nov-Apr
8 bedrs, 5 ensuite, 1 ➡ TCF TV 🐾 SB £10-£16 DB £20-£32 HB £84-£120 D £5

Little Emily *Listed*
18 Princes Road, Great Yarmouth
📞 01493-842515
11 bedrs, 6 ensuite, 1 🐾, 1 ➡ TV SB £14-£18 DB £28-£36 HB £99-£140 D £6

Merivon *Listed*
6 Trafalgar Road, Great Yarmouth NR30 2LD
📞 01493-844419
7 bedrs, 4 ensuite, 1 ➡ TCF TV No children under 12
SB £12-£15 DB £24-£36 HB £130-£150

Sandholme *Listed*
12 Sandown Road, Great Yarmouth NR30 1EY
📞 01493-300001 Fax 01493-300001
10 bedrs, 6 ensuite, 2 ➡ TCF TV SB £15-£20 DB £21-£35 HB £70-£100 D £6 CC MC Visa Amex

Spindrift *Listed*
36 Wellesley Road, Great Yarmouth NR30 IEU
📞 01493-858674 Fax 01493-858674
Closed Christmas week
7 bedrs, 5 ensuite, 2 ➡ TCF TV SB £18-£25 DB £30-£44 CC MC Visa Amex

Ivinghoe *Awaiting Inspection*
12a Wellington Road, Great Yarmouth NR30 3AQ
📞 01493-384593

Marine Lodge *Awaiting Inspection*
1 Evston Road, Great Yarmouth NR30 1DY
📞 01493-331210 Fax 01493-332040
Closed Nov-mid Feb
39 bedrs, all ensuite, TCF TV P 37 SB £25 DB £34 CC MC Visa Amex ♿

YATTENDON Berkshire   4B2

★★ Royal Oak

The Square, Yattendon RG18 OUG
📞 01635-201325 Fax 01635-201926
5 bedrs, all ensuite, TCF TV 🐾 SB £75-£84.50 DB £90-£109 D £30 CC MC Visa Amex DC

YELVERTON Devon   2C3

Harrabeer Country House *Acclaimed*
Harrowbeer Lane, Yelverton PL20 6EA
📞 01822-853302
Closed 25-26 Dec
7 bedrs, 5 ensuite, 1 ➡ TCF TV 🐾 P 7 SB £20 DB £48
HB £210 D £11 CC MC Visa Amex DC

RAC Hotel Reservations Service
0870 603 9109
(Calls charged at national call rate)

YEOVIL Somerset   3E2

★ Preston
64 Preston Road, Yeovil BA20 2DL
☎ **01935-74400 Fax 01935-410142**
15 bedrs, all ensuite, 6 ⇌ **TCF TV** 🐕 **P** 20 **SB** £39 **DB** £49
D £12.50 **CC** MC Visa Amex DC JCB ♿

Wyndham *Listed*
142 Sherbourne Road, Yeovil BA21 4HQ
☎ **01935-421468**
Closed Christmas
6 bedrs, 1 ⇌ **TCF TV P** 8 **SB** £17-£19 **DB** £34-£38

YORK North Yorkshire   11D3

★★ Abbots Mews
Marygate Lane, Bootham, York YO3 7DE
☎ **01904-634866 Fax 01904-612848**
50 bedrs, all ensuite, **TCF TV P** 30 **SB** £30-£50 **DB** £51
D £10 **CC** MC Visa Amex DC ♿

★★ Alhambra Court
31 St Marys, Bootham, York YO3 7DD
☎ **01904-628474 Fax 01904-610690**
24 bedrs, all ensuite, **TCF TV** 🐕 🍴 **P** 20 **SB** £31.50-
£39.50 **DB** £45-£62 **D** £11.50 **CC** MC Visa

★★ Ashcroft
Comfort merit award
294 Bishopthorpe Road, York YO2 1LH
☎ **01904-659286 Fax 01904-640107**
Closed Christmas
15 bedrs, all ensuite, 🐕 **P** 40 No children under 5
SB £42-£48 **DB** £50-£80 **D** £14.50 **CC** MC Visa Amex DC
JCB ♿

★★ Beechwood Close
19 Shipton Road, York YO3 6RE
☎ **01904-658378 Fax 01904-647124**
E Mail bch@dial.pipex.com
Closed 25 Dec
14 bedrs, all ensuite, **TCF TV P** 36 **SB** £44-£45 **DB** £65-
£75 **HB** £296-£359 **D** £14 **CC** MC Visa Amex DC JCB

★★ Cottage
3 Clifton Green, York YO3 6LH
☎ **01904-643711 Fax 01904-611230**
Closed Christmas
20 bedrs, all ensuite, **TCF TV** 🐕 **P** 12 **SB** £30-£45 **DB** £45-
£70 **D** £26 **CC** MC Visa Amex DC

★★ Elmbank
The Mount, York YO2 2DD
☎ **01904-610653 Fax 01904-627139**
48 bedrs, all ensuite, **TCF TV** 🐕 **P** 20
SB £69-£79 **DB** £95-£105 **D** £16 **CC** MC Visa Amex DC

★★ Heworth Court
Hospitality, Restaurant merit awards
76-78 Heworth Green, York YO3 7TQ
☎ **01904-425156 Fax 01904-415290**
E Mail heworth@btinternet.com

This family-run hotel is a brick built, two storey building with an attractive courtyard and well-maintained gardens. Situated close to the city centre.

25 bedrs, all ensuite, **TCF TV P** 25 **SB** £42-£44 **DB** £42-
£60 **HB** £136.50-£168 **D** £16.95 **CC** MC Visa Amex DC
♿

★★ Holgate Bridge
106-108 Holgate Road, York YO2 4BB
☎ **01904-635971 Fax 01904-670049**
Closed Christmas
14 bedrs, 11 ensuite, 1 ⇌ **TCF TV** 🐕 **P** 11 **SB** £22-£38
DB £38-£40 **D** £7.80 **CC** MC Visa Amex DC JCB

★★ Knavesmire Manor
302 Tadcaster Road, York YO2 2HE
☎ **01904-702941 Fax 01904-709274**

Once a Rowntree family home (c.1833), this Georgian hotel close to the city centre overlooks York racecourse. Walled gardens and car park. Tropical indoor pool and spa.

21 bedrs, all ensuite, **TCF TV** 🐕 🍴 **P** 26 **SB** £40-£59
DB £49-£75 **HB** £210-£280 **D** £12.50 **CC** MC Visa Amex
DC JCB

★★ Newington
147 Mount Vale, York YO2 2DJ
☎ **01904-625173 Fax 01904-679937**
40 bedrs, all ensuite, **TCF TV** 🍴 **P** 35 **SB** £38-£40 **DB** £56-
£66 **HB** £269 **D** £14 **CC** MC Visa Amex

★★ Savages
St Peters Grove, Clifton, York YO3 6AQ
📞 01904-610818 Fax 01904-627729
Closed 25-26 Dec
20 bedrs, all ensuite, TCF TV P 15 SB £28-£38 DB £50-£68 D £12 CC MC Visa Amex DC ♿

Arndale *Highly Acclaimed*
290 Tadcaster Road, York YO2 2ET
📞 01904-702424

Delightful Victorian house, directly overlooking the racecourse with beautiful enclosed walled gardens giving a country atmosphere within the city. Antiques, fresh flowers, fourposter beds. Enclosed gated car park.

10 bedrs, all ensuite, TCF TV P 20 No children under 7 SB £39-£49 DB £47-£69 CC MC Visa

Byron House *Highly Acclaimed*
7 Driffield Terrace, The Mount, York YO2 2DD
📞 01904-632525 Fax 01904-638904
Closed Christmas
10 bedrs, 7 ensuite, 1 🛏 TCF TV 🐕 P 6 SB £25-£28 DB £52-£70 D £18.50 CC MC Visa Amex DC

Curzon Lodge & Stable Cottages *Highly Acclaimed*
23 Tadcaster Road, Dringhouses, York YO2 2QG
📞 01904-703157

A delightful 17th century former farmhouse and stables within historic city overlooking the racecourse. Country antiques, cottage style bedrooms, fourposter and brass beds. Cosy and informal. Parking in grounds. Restaurants nearby.

10 bedrs, all ensuite, TCF TV P 16 No children under 7 SB £30-£42 DB £45-£62 CC MC Visa JCB

Byron House

An elegant, Georgian end-of-terrace property with spacious and comfortable interior.

Within walking distance of the city centre

Closed Christmas

7 DRIFFIELD TERRACE, THE MOUNT, YORK YO2 2DD
Tel. 01904-632525 Fax. 01904-638904

Easton's
Fine Period Bed & Breakfast

"Yorkshire Tourist Board's Bed and Breakfast of the Year 1996"

300 yards from the city walls. William Morris decor. Period furniture. Marble fireplaces. Original paintings. Victorian sideboard breakfast menu, kedgeree, kidneys and more. Ensuite bedrooms. Non smoking. Car Park. Brochure.

90 BISHOPTHORPE ROAD, YORK YO2 1JS
Tel: 01904 626646

HOLMWOOD HOUSE HOTEL

Situated close to the city walls, the hotel comprises two recently refurbished, Grade II Listed, Victorian town houses furnished with antiques.

Highly Acclaimed

114 HOLGATE ROAD, YORK YO2 4BB
Tel: 01904-626183 Fax: 01904-670899

Don't forget to mention the guide
When booking direct, please remember to tell the hotel that you chose it from RAC Bed & Breakfast 1998.

Ascot House
80 East Parade · York · YO3 7YH
Tel: (01904) 426826
Fax: (01904) 431077

★ En-suite rooms of character
★ 4-Poster & Canopy Beds
★ 15 mins. walk to city centre
★ Private car park ★ Sauna
★ Residential Licence

Contact Mrs J. Wood for colour brochure

Eastons *Highly Acclaimed*
90 Bishopthorpe Road, York YO2 1JS
☎ 01904-626646

A pair of late Victorian town residences.

10 bedrs, all ensuite, 1 ⇌ TCF TV ⌘ P 8 No children under 5 SB £34-£48 DB £39-£65

Holmwood House *Highly Acclaimed*
114 Holgate Road, York YO2 4BB
☎ 01904-626183 Fax 01904-670899
E Mail holmwood.house@dial.pipex.com
11 bedrs, all ensuite, TCF TV ⌘ P 10 No children under 8 SB £45-£60 DB £55-£70 CC MC Visa Amex

Acorn *Acclaimed*
1 Southlands Road, York YO2 1NP
☎ 01904-620081 Fax 01904-613331
6 bedrs, 3 ensuite, 1 ⇌ TCF TV SB £13-£17.50 DB £24-£33 CC MC Visa Amex

Ascot House *Acclaimed*
80 East Parade, York YO3 7YH
☎ 01904-426826 Fax 01904-431077

An attractive, family run Victorian villa with rooms of character, some with fourposter or canopy beds. Within easy walking distance of the city centre.

15 bedrs, 12 ensuite, 2 ⇌ TCF TV ⚲ P 12 SB £18-£22 DB £38-£46 CC MC Visa DC

Ashbourne House *Acclaimed*
139 Fulford Road, York YO1 4HG
☎ 01904-639912 Fax 01904-631332
Closed Christmas & New Year

A most charming and comfortable family run hotel situated on the A19 southern approach to York, but within walking distance of the city. Licensed.

6 bedrs, all ensuite, **TCF TV** P 6 **SB** £34-£38 **DB** £40-£50 **HB** £245-£315 **D** £15 **CC** MC Visa Amex DC

Avimore House *Acclaimed*
78 Stockton Lane, York YO3 0BS
☎ 01904-425556 Fax 01904-415352
Closed Christmas
6 bedrs, all ensuite, 6 **TCF TV P** 6 **SB** £18-£25 **DB** £32-£44 **CC** MC Visa

Bedford *Acclaimed*
108 Bootham, York YO3 7DG
☎ 01904-624412

Family run licensed hotel, short walk to the Minster and city centre. Guaranteed space in private car park. Winter mini breaks available November to March.

17 bedrs, all ensuite, **TCF TV P** 14 **SB** £33-£38 **DB** £46-£56 **D** £9 **CC** MC Visa Amex

Beech House *Acclaimed*
6-7 Longfield Terrace, York YO3 7DJ
☎ 01904-634581
Closed Christmas & New Year
10 bedrs, all ensuite, **TCF TV P** 3 No children under 10 **SB** £25-£30 **DB** £40-£50

Bloomsbury *Acclaimed*
127 Clifton, York YO3 6BL
☎ 01904-634031 Fax 01904-634031

An elegantly appointed large Victorian town house, recently refurbished, centrally situated with large private car park. Completely non-smoking.

9 bedrs, all ensuite, 1 **TCF TV** P 9 No children under 7 **SB** £40-£55 **DB** £50-£65 **CC** MC Visa JCB

Derwent Lodge *Acclaimed*
Low Catton, Stamford Bridge, York YO4 1EA
☎ 01759-371468
Closed Dec-Jan
5 bedrs, all ensuite, **TCF TV** P No children under 8 **SB** £31.50 **DB** £47 **HB** £224 **D** £10.50

Field House *Acclaimed*
2 St George's Place, York YO2 2DR
☎ 01904-639572

Fourposter Lodge *Acclaimed*
68-70 Heslington Road, off Barbican Road, York YO1 5AU
☎ 01904-651170
10 bedrs, all ensuite, 1 **TCF TV** P 4 **SB** £30-£37 **DB** £51-£56 **D** £12.70 **CC** MC Visa Amex

Hazelwood *Acclaimed*
24-25 Portland Street, York YO3 7EH
☎ 01904-626548 Fax 01904-628032

Situated in the centre of York, only 400 yards from Minster yet in an extremely quiet location. Elegant Victorian town house with private car park. Non smoking.

13 bedrs, all ensuite, **TCF TV** P 11 No children under 6 **SB** £25-£49 **DB** £39-£59 **CC** MC Visa

Free yourself

RAC Hotel Reservations will find you a room in the UK or Ireland and if you're an RAC Member, the service is absolutely free.
Phone 0870 603 9109.

If you're travelling in Europe, RAC Motoring Assistance provides rapid help in the event of breakdown, fire, accident, theft or illness.
In addition, our **Personal Travel Insurance** covers you for lost luggage, theft of personal belongings, personal injury or cancellation.
Call us on 0800 550 055.

RAC

www.rac.co.uk

Holly Lodge *Acclaimed*
204-206 Fulford Road, York YO1 4DD
☎ 01904-646005

Beautifully appointed Grade II Listed building, a pleasant riverside stroll from the centre. Convenient for all of York's attractions. On site parking. All rooms ensuite overlooking garden or terrace.

5 bedrs, all ensuite, **TCF TV P** 5 **SB** £30-£40 **DB** £40-£60 **CC** MC Visa

Linden Lodge *Acclaimed*
6 Nunthorpe Avenue, Scarcroft Road, York YO2 1PF
☎ 01904-620107 Fax 01904-620985

A small hotel recently upgraded, providing comfortable accommodation in pleasant surroundings. Situated in a quiet cul de sac with unrestricted parking and only ten minutes walk from the historic centre.

12 bedrs, 9 ensuite, 1 ⇌ **TCF TV** ⊠ **SB** £20-£30 **DB** £36-£50 **CC** MC Visa Amex JCB

Midway House *Acclaimed*
145 Fulford Road, York YO1 4HG
☎ 01904-659272 Fax 01904-659272

Charming family run hotel offering 12 individually styled ensuite bedrooms. Self catering annex also available. Own grounds and private car park. Conveniently located south of the city centre.

12 bedrs, 11 ensuite, 1 ⇌ **TCF TV** ⊠ **P** 14 **SB** £25-£37 **DB** £36-£55 **HB** £231-£280 **D** £15 **CC** MC Visa Amex

Priory *Acclaimed*
126 Fulford Road, York YO1 4BE
☎ 01904-625280 Fax 01904-625280
20 bedrs, all ensuite, **TCF TV P** 26 **SB** £35-£40 **DB** £48-£50 **CC** MC Visa Amex DC

St Georges House *Acclaimed*
6 St Georges Place, York YO2 2DR
☎ 01904-625056 Fax 01904-625009

Small Victorian hotel, situated in a quiet cul-de-sac near the racecourse in a select area ten minutes walk from the city walls. All rooms recently renovated to a high standard, including family and fourposter rooms.

10 bedrs, all ensuite, **TCF TV** ⇌ **P** 7 **SB** £25-£30 **DB** £35-£50 **D** £5 **CC** MC Visa Amex DC ♿

Bootham Bar *Listed*
4 High Petergate, York YO1 2EH
☎ 01904-658516
14 bedrs, 11 ensuite, 2 ⇌ **TCF TV P** 6 **DB** £50-£58 **CC** MC Visa

Carlton House *Listed*
134 The Mount, York YO2 2AS
☎ 01904-622265 Fax 01904-637157
E Mail carltonuk@aol.com
Closed Christmas-New Year

Georgian terraced home on the Royal entry to the historic city of York. Run by the same family for more than 45 years and retains a real sense of the 'Upstairs, Downstairs' lifestyle.

13 bedrs, all ensuite, 1 ⇨ TCF TV P 6 SB £27-£28 DB £48-£50

Crescent *Listed*
77 Bootham, York YO3 7DQ
☎ 01904-623216 Fax 01904-623216
10 bedrs, all ensuite, 1 ⇨ TCF TV P 4 SB £18.50-£25 DB £32-£50 HB £199.50-£231 D £10 CC MC Visa Amex DC JCB

Georgian *Listed*
35 Bootham, York YO3 7BT
☎ 01904-622874 Fax 01904-635379
14 bedrs, 8 ensuite, 1 🐾, 2 ⇨ TCF TV P 10 No children under 5 SB £18-£35 DB £14-£48 CC MC Visa

Greenside *Listed*
124 Clifton, York YO3 6BQ
☎ 01904-623631
8 bedrs, 3 ensuite, 2 ⇨ TV 🐾 P 5
SB £16 DB £24-£30 D £10 ♿

Don't forget to mention the guide
When booking direct, please remember to tell the hotel that you chose it from RAC Bed & Breakfast 1998.

Ivy House Farm *Listed*
Hull Road, Kexby YO4 5LQ
☎ 01904-489368

Situated on the A1079 east of York with easy access to the Yorkshire wolds, dales, moors and east coast. Comfortable accommodation with lounge, dining room and gardens, with TV and hot and cold water.

4 bedrs, 1 ⇨ TCF TV P 10 SB £17-£19 DB £30-£32

St Denys *Listed*
St Denys Road, York YO1 1QD
☎ 01904-622207 Fax 01904-624800
10 bedrs, all ensuite, 1 ⇨ TV 🐾 P 9 SB £25-£30 DB £40-£50 CC MC Visa

St Raphael's *Listed*
44 Queen Annes Road, Bootham, York YO3 7AF
☎ 01904-645028 Fax 01904-658788
8 bedrs, 5 ensuite, 2 ⇨ TV 🐾 CC MC Visa

Acer
52 Scarcroft Hill, The Mount, York YO2 1DE
☎ 01904-653839 Fax 01904-677017
A small, friendly, Victorian hotel close to York racecourse.
6 bedrs, all ensuite, TCF TV 🐾 P 4 CC MC Visa Amex

Aldwark Bridge House
Boat Lane, Ouseburn YO5 9SJ
☎ 01423-331097 Fax 01423-331097
Closed Christmas, New Year

18th century country residence, adjacent 18 hole golf course, with mooring and fishing on River Ure. Local village shop / PO, inns and restaurants. Historic area, York, Ripon, Thirsk, Harrowgate within 15 miles.

2 bedrs, 1 ensuite, 1 ⇨ TCF TV 📺 P 2 No children under 12 SB £25 DB £35 HB £105 D £10 ▶ 📺

Burton Villa
22 Haxby Road, York YO3 7JX
📞 01904-626364 Fax 01904-626364

We provide those instances of delight' that make your holiday. Excellent location, choice of hearty breakfasts. Car parking. Quality comfort and value for money.

11 bedrs, 8 ensuite, 1 ➡ TCF TV 🐕 P 7 SB £16-£20 DB £32-£50 CC MC Visa

Coppers Lodge
15 Alma Terrace, Fulford Road, York YO1 4DQ
📞 01904-639871

Once a police station, Copper's Lodge now offers friendly accommodation with guest lounge, breakfast room, colour TV and hot and cold water in all rooms, plus tea and coffee making facilities. Located half a mile from the city walls.

8 bedrs, 1 ensuite, 3 ➡ TCF TV 🐕 SB £15-£18 D £7.50

Limes
135 Fulford Road, York YO1 4HE
📞 01904-624548 Fax 01904-624548

A family run hotel, close to university and golf course and a short walk from the city centre. Ground floor rooms available. Licensed bar. Private car park.

8 bedrs, all ensuite, TCF TV 🐕 P 10 SB £30-£40 DB £40-£55 D £12.50 CC MC Visa ♿

Burton Villa

We provide those "instances of delight" that make your holiday. Excellent location, choice of hearty breakfasts. Car parking. Quality comfort and value for money.

ETB Commended   AA Commended

22 HAXBY ROAD, YORK YO3 7JX
Tel: 01904 626364

Scotland

Top: Columba Hotel, Tarbert

Right: Arran Lodge, Callander

Below: Newton Lodge, Kylesku

RAC

ABERDEEN Aberdeenshire 15F4

Craiglynn *Highly Acclaimed*
36 Fonthill Road, Aberdeen AB11 6UJ
📞 01224-584050 Fax 01224-212225
E Mail craiglynn_hotel_aberdeen@compuserve.com
Closed 25-26 Dec

Craiglynn provides modern comforts whilst retaining Victorian elegance. All bedrooms are non-smoking. There are two comfortable lounges where smoking is permitted. 'Taste of Scotland' featured.

9 bedrs, 7 ensuite, 2 ⇨ TCF TV **P** 8 **SB** £35-£60 **DB** £50-£70 **D** £15.50 **CC** MC Visa Amex DC JCB

Jays *Highly Acclaimed*
422 King Street, Aberdeen AB24 3BR
📞 01224-638295 Fax 01224-638295
E Mail jaysguesthouse@clara.net.
Closed Aug & Dec-Jan

10 bedrs, all ensuite, TCF TV ⊠ **P** 8 No children under 16 **SB** £30-£40 **DB** £50-£70

Belhaven *Acclaimed*
152 Bon Accord Street, Aberdeen AB11 6TX
📞 01224-588384 Fax 01224-588384
8 bedrs, 4 ensuite, 4 ⇨ TCF TV 🐾 **P** 1
SB £20-£30 **DB** £30-£40

Cedars *Acclaimed*
339 Great Western Road, Aberdeen AB10 6NW
📞 01224-583225 Fax 01224-585050
13 bedrs, 10 ensuite, 3 👥, 1 ⇨ TCF TV **P** 13 **SB** £38-£45 **DB** £52-£54 **CC** MC Visa Amex

Short Breaks

Many hotels provide special rates for weekend and mid-week breaks - sometimes these are quoted in the hotel's entry, otherwise ring direct for the latest offers.

Fourways *Acclaimed*
435 Great Western Road, Aberdeen AB1 6NJ
📞 01224-310218 Fax 01224-310218

Centrally situated in a residential area of the city on the main tourist route to Royal Deeside. All rooms ensuite, tea/coffee making facilities, car parking at rear.

6 bedrs, all ensuite, 1 ⇨ TCF TV **P** 5 **SB** £25 **DB** £40 **CC** MC Visa Amex

Bimini *Listed*
69 Constitution Street, Aberdeen AB2 IET
📞 01224-646912 Fax 01224-646912

Personally run with homely atmosphere. Ideally situated for walking to all city centre and seafront attractions, Universities, RGIT and golf courses. Private off road parking.

7 bedrs, 3 ensuite, 2 ⇨ TV ⊠ **P** 6 **SB** £20-£22 **DB** £40-£48 **CC** MC Visa

Klibreck *Listed*
410 Great Western Road, Aberdeen AB10 6NR
☎ 01224-316115
Closed Christmas-New Year
6 bedrs, 1 ensuite, 2 ⇌ TCF TV ⊠ P 3 SB £20 DB £30

Strathboyne *Listed*
26 Abergeldie Terrace, Aberdeen AB1 6EE
☎ 01224-593400
Closed 24 Dec-1 Jan
5 bedrs, 4 ensuite, 1 ⇌ TCF TV No children under 10
SB £25-£27 DB £40-£42

Abbotswell
28 Abbotswell Crescent, Kincorth, Aberdeen AB1 1AR
☎ 01224-871788 Fax 01224-891257

A family run guest house with excellent off road parking. Snacks also available. Restricted licence.

11 bedrs, 5 ensuite, TCF TV P 12 No children under 5

ABERFELDY Perthshire 13D1

★★ Weem
Hospitality merit award
Weem, Aberfeldy PH15 2LD
☎ 01887-820381 Fax 01887-829720
E Mail weem@compuserve.com
12 bedrs, all ensuite, TCF TV ⋈ P 20 SB £24-£40 DB £36-£70 D £10 CC MC Visa

ABERLADY East Lothian 13E2

★★ Kilspindie House
Main Street, Aberlady EH32 0RE
☎ 01875-870682 Fax 01875-587504
26 bedrs, all ensuite, ⋈ P 30
SB £38-£44 DB £54-£64 CC MC Visa JCB ♿

ABINGTON Lanarkshire 13D3

★★ Abington
Carlisle Road, Abington ML12 6SD
☎ 01864-502467 Fax 01864-502223
25 bedrs, all ensuite, TCF TV P 30 SB £37-£47 DB £40-£66 HB £210-£280 D £10 CC MC Visa Amex DC

ABOYNE Aberdeenshire 15E4

Arbor Lodge *Highly Acclaimed*
Ballater Road, Aboyne AB34 5HY
☎ 013398-86951 Fax 013398-86951
E Mail arborlodge@aol.com
Closed Nov-Feb

Spacious luxury accommodation set in a woodland garden. All bedrooms have ensuite bathrooms, tea making facilities and TV. Ideally located for touring Royal Deeside.

3 bedrs, all ensuite, TCF TV P 4 No children under 12
SB £24 DB £48 CC MC Visa

ACHNASHEEN Ross-shire 14C3

★★ Ledgowan Lodge
Hospitality, Comfort, Restaurant merit awards
Achnasheen IV22 2EJ
☎ 01445-720252 Fax 01445-720240
Closed Jan-Mar, Nov-Dec
12 bedrs, all ensuite, TCF TV P 20 SB £35-£39 DB £59-£95 D £15 CC MC Visa Amex DC JCB

AIRDRIE Lanarkshire 12C2

Rosslee
107 Forrest Street, Airdrie ML6 7AR
☎ 01236-765865
Closed 4-23 Sep

A family run guest house one mile from Airdrie town centre on the A89. The M8, M80 and M74 are all nearby. A friendly welcome awaits.

6 bedrs, 4 ensuite, 2 ⇌ TCF TV ⋈ P 12 SB £18-£24 DB £36-£48 D £9.50

ANNAN Dumfriesshire   13D4

★ Corner House
78 High Street, Annan DG12 6DL
☎ 01461-202754
31 bedrs, 1 ensuite, 8 ⇌ TCF TV 🐕 P 45 SB £25 DB £42
CC MC Visa Amex DC

ANSTRUTHER Fife   13E1

★★ Smugglers Inn
High Street East, Anstruther KY10 3DQ
☎ 01333-310506 Fax 01333-312706
9 bedrs, all ensuite, TCF TV 🐕 P 12 No children under 5 SB £32 DB £64 D £15 CC MC Visa Amex DC

Spindrift *Highly Acclaimed*
Pittenweem Road, Anstruther KY10 3DT
☎ 01333-310573 Fax 01333-310573
Closed 20 Nov-10 Dec
8 bedrs, all ensuite, TCF TV ⊠ P 10 SB £35-£50 DB £53-£63 HB £238-£350 D £13.30 CC MC Visa

ARBROATH Angus   13E1

★★ Seaforth
Dundee Road, Arbroath DD11 1QF
☎ 01241-872232 Fax 01241-877473
21 bedrs, 19 ensuite, 🐕 P 50 SB £38-£42 DB £60-£62 D £16 CC MC Visa Amex DC 🛏 🍽

Kingsley House *Acclaimed*
29/31 Market Gate, Arbroath DD11 1AU
☎ 01241-873933 Fax 01241-873933
15 bedrs, 9 ensuite, 4 ⇌ TV 🐕 P 4
SB £16-£21 DB £26-£34 CC MC Visa JCB

Scurdy *Acclaimed*
33 Marketgate, Arbroath DD11 1AU
☎ 01241-872417 Fax 01241-872417
10 bedrs, 3 ensuite, 3 ⇌ TCF TV 🐕 P 2 SB £16-£20
DB £30-£40 HB £147-£150 D £7.50 CC MC Visa Amex ♿

Maulesbank *Listed*
Maules Street, Arbroath DD11 1JJ
☎ 01241-870926
4 bedrs, 2 ensuite, 1 ⇌ TCF TV ⊠ P 6 DB £27-£32

ARISAIG Inverness-shire   14B4

★★ Arisaig
Arisaig PH39 4NH
☎ 01687-450210 Fax 01687-450310
Closed 25-26 Dec
13 bedrs, all ensuite, TCF TV 🐕 P 30
SB £31 DB £62 D £17 CC MC Visa 🍽

AUCHTERARDER Perthshire   13D1

★★ Cairn Lodge
Comfort, Restaurant merit awards
Orchil Road, Auchterarder PH3 1LX
☎ 01764-662634 Fax 01764-664866
7 bedrs, all ensuite, TCF TV P 40 SB £45-£55 DB £80-£102 D £20 CC MC Visa Amex ♿

AUCHTERMUCHTY Fife   13D1

Ardchoille Farmhouse *Highly Acclaimed*
Dunshalt, Auchtermuchty KY14 7ER
☎ 01337-828414 Fax 01337-828414
3 bedrs, all ensuite, TCF TV 🐕 P 3 No children under 10 CC MC Visa

AULTBEA Ross-shire   14B2

★★ Aultbea
Comfort merit award
Aultbea IV22 2HX
☎ 01445-731201 Fax 01445-731214
11 bedrs, all ensuite, TCF TV 🐕 P 30 SB £32-£36 DB £64-£72 HB £340-£365 D £21 CC MC Visa Amex JCB

★★ Drumchork Lodge
Aultbea IV22 2HU
☎ 01445-731242 Fax 01445-731242
Closed Nov-Feb
9 bedrs, all ensuite, TCF TV 🐕 P 50 SB £28-£29 DB £56-£58 HB £260-£295 D £20 CC MC Visa 🛏

AVIEMORE Inverness-shire   15D3

Ravenscraig *Acclaimed*
141 Grampian Road, Aviemore PH22 1RP
☎ 01479-810278 Fax 01479-811800

Feel at home in informal and comfortable surroundings. A full Highland breakfast served.

14 bedrs, all ensuite, TCF TV 🐕 P 16 SB £18-£22 DB £36-£44 CC MC Visa

AYR Ayrshire 12C3

★★ Ayrshire and Galloway
1 Killoch Place, Ayr KA7 2AE
☎ 01292-262626
25 bedrs, 8 ensuite, 5 ⇌ ✦ P 20 ₡ MC Visa Amex

★★ Chestnuts
52 Racecourse Road, Ayr KA7 2UZ
☎ 01292-264393 Fax 01292-264393
14 bedrs, 11 ensuite, 1 ☞, 2 ⇌ ✦ P 50 SB £32.40-£36
DB £61.80-£68 HB £255 ₡ MC Visa Amex ♿

★★ Old Racecourse
2 Victoria Park, Ayr K17 1HT
☎ 01292-262873 Fax 01292-267598
10 bedrs, 8 ensuite, 2 ⇌ ✦ P 30 ₡ Visa ♿

Brenalder Lodge *Highly Acclaimed*
39 Dunure Road, Doonfoot, Ayr KA7 4HR
☎ 01292-443939
3 bedrs, all ensuite, TCF TV ⌧ ✦ P 9 No children under 7 SB £30-£38 DB £50 D £18 ♿

Windsor *Highly Acclaimed*
6 Alloway Place, Ayr KA7 2AA
☎ 01292-264689
10 bedrs, 8 ensuite, 1 ⇌ TCF TV ✦ SB £20 DB £44
HB £195 D £10 ₡ MC Visa ♿

RAC Hotel Reservations Service
0870 603 9109
(Calls charged at national call rate)

FERN VILLA
GUEST HOUSE

The ideal location for walking, climbing or touring amongst spectacular West Highland loch and mountain scenery. A warm welcome, home cooking and comfortable accommodation make a memorable holiday. Non-smoking.

LOANFERN, BALLACHULISH, ARGYLL PA39 4JE
Tel: 01855-811393
Fax: 01855-811727

Belmont
15 Park Circus, Ayr KA7 2DJ
☎ 01292-265588 Fax 01292-265588

Hospitality is assured in this traditional Scottish townhouse, situated in a quiet tree lined conservation area within easy walking distance of the town centre and beach.

5 bedrs, all ensuite, TCF TV ✦ P 5 SB £17.50-£22
DB £35-£37

Dunduff Farm
Dunure KA7 4LH
☎ 01292-500225 Fax 01292-500222
Closed Dec-Jan

A 17th century farmhouse offering two ensuite rooms with private bathrooms and full facilities. Coastal views across to Holy Isle and the Mull of Kintyre. Self catering cottages available.

3 bedrs, 2 ensuite, TCF TV P 10 SB £28-£32 DB £40-£50 ⌧

BALLACHULISH Argyll 14C4

Lyn-Leven *Acclaimed*
West Laroch, Ballachulish PA39 4JP
☎ 01855-811392 Fax 01855-811600
12 bedrs, all ensuite, 1 ⇌ TCF TV ✦ P 14 SB £20-£25
DB £39-£42 HB £190-£205 D £9 ₡ MC Visa ♿

Fern Villa
Loanfern, Ballachulish PA39 4JE
☎ 01855-811393 Fax 01855-811727
5 bedrs, all ensuite, TCF TV ⌧ P 9 DB £36-£40 HB £184-£196 D £10

BALLATER Aberdeenshire 15E4

★★ Monaltrie
5 Bridge Square, Ballater AB35 5QJ
☎ 013397-55417 Fax 013397-55180
24 bedrs, all ensuite, TCF TV ⊁ P 40 CC MC Visa Amex DC

Glen Lui Highly Acclaimed
Invercauld Road, Ballater AB3 5RP
☎ 013397-55402 Fax 013397-55545

Friendly country house hotel in beautiful Highland countryside overlooking Ballater Golf Course towards Lochnagar. The Glen Lui offers a superb setting for visitors for all reasons.

19 bedrs, all ensuite, TCF TV ⊁ P 30 SB £35 DB £70
HB £294 D £15 CC MC Visa Amex

Auld Kirk
Braemar Road, Ballater AB35 5RQ
☎ 013397-55762 Fax 013397-55707

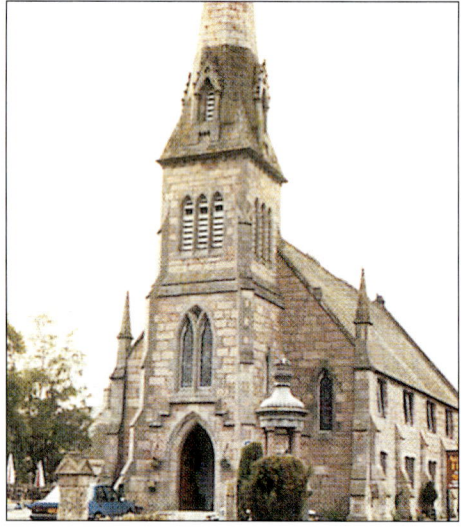

Relax in comfort and warmth; all rooms have ensuite shower and tea/coffee making facilities, TV and direct dial telephone. Our licensed dining room offers an excellent range of home cooking throughout the day.

6 bedrs, all ensuite, TCF TV ⊁ P 15 CC MC Visa

Dee Valley
26 Viewfield Road, Ballater AB35 5RD
☎ 01339-755408 Fax 01339-755408

Detached Victorian granite house with four letting bedrooms on the first floor, one ensuite. Quiet location, central for touring, walking, golf and whisky trails.

4 bedrs, 1 ensuite, 2 ⇨ TCF TV P 3 SB £20-£25 DB £31-£36

Moorside
Braemar Road, Ballater AB35 5RL
☎ 01339-755492 Fax 01339-755492
Closed Nov-Mar

Centrally situated, very comfortable house, furnished to a high standard, offering excellent accommodation at an affordable price. All rooms ensuite. Many excellent restaurants nearby.

9 bedrs, all ensuite, TCF TV P 10 SB £25-£35 DB £38-£40
CC MC Visa

BALLOCH Dunbartonshire 12C2

★★ Balloch
Balloch G83 8LQ
☎ 01389-752579 Fax 01389-755604
14 bedrs, all ensuite, TCF TV ⊁ P 30 SB £42 DB £63
D £15 CC MC Visa Amex DC

BALMACARA Ross-shire 14B3

★★ Balmacara
Balmacara IV40 8DH
☎ 01599-566283 Fax 01599-566329
29 bedrs, all ensuite, ⊁ P 60 SB £30-£39 DB £50-£59
D £16.50 CC MC Visa ♿

BANCHORY Kincardineshire 15F4

★★ Burnett Arms
25 High Street, Banchory AB31 5TD
📞 01330-824944 Fax 01330-825553

An 18th century coaching inn, fully modernised and yet retaining the character and atmosphere of olden times. Situated in the town centre.

16 bedrs, all ensuite, **TCF TV** 🐕 **P** 40 **SB** £48-£50 **DB** £65-£68 **HB** £280-£294 **D** £15 **CC** MC Visa Amex DC

BEATTOCK Dumfriesshire 13D3

★★ Beattock House
Beattock DG10 9QB
📞 01683-300402 Fax 01683-300403
7 bedrs, 3 ensuite, 2 🛁 **TCF TV** 🐕 **P** 30 **SB** £30 **DB** £55 **D** £13 **CC** MC Visa Amex DC 📧

BEAULY Inverness-shire 15D3

Chrialdon *Acclaimed*
Station Road, Beauly IV4 7EH
📞 01463-782336
8 bedrs, 6 ensuite, 1 🛁 **TCF TV** 🐕 **P** 20 **CC** MC Visa

Heathmount *Listed*
Station Road, Beauly IV4 7EQ
📞 01463-782411
5 bedrs, 2 🛁 **TCF TV** 🐕 **P** 6 **SB** £18 **DB** £36

BLAIRGOWRIE Perthshire 13D1

★★ Angus
Blairgowrie PH10 6NQ
📞 01250-872455 Fax 01250-875615
86 bedrs, all ensuite, 🐕 📺 **P** 60 **SB** £30-£40 **HB** £245-£315 **D** £12 **CC** MC Visa Amex DC 💲 ♿

Rosebank House *Highly Acclaimed*
Balmoral Road, Blairgowrie PH10 7AF
📞 01250-872912
Closed Nov-Dec
7 bedrs, 6 ensuite, 1 🛁 **TCF P** 12 No children under 10 **SB** £22-£24 **DB** £44-£48 **HB** £205-£215 **D** £11

Duncraggan *Acclaimed*
Perth Road, Blairgowrie PH10 6EJ
📞 01250-872082 Fax 01250-872098

Beautiful house, furnished to a high standard, built in 1902 by a local architect and set in a one acre garden. Small putting green and outdoor table tennis.

4 bedrs, 2 ensuite, 2 🛁 **TCF TV** 📧 **P** 6 **SB** £18.50 **DB** £37 **D** £8.50

BO'NESS West Lothian 13D2

Kinglass Farm *Acclaimed*
Bo'ness EH9 5RW
📞 01506-822861 Fax 01506-824433
6 bedrs, 2 ensuite, 2 🛁 **TCF TV** 🐕 **P** 20 **SB** £18 **DB** £36 **D** £10

BOAT OF GARTEN Inverness-shire 15D3

Moorfield House *Acclaimed*
Deshar Road, Boat of Garten PH24 3BN
📞 01479-831646
4 bedrs, all ensuite, **TCF TV** 📧 🐕 **P** 8 No children under 12 **SB** £24 **DB** £38 **HB** £210

BONAR BRIDGE Sutherland 15D2

Kyle House *Listed*
Dornoch Road, Bonar Bridge IV24 3EB
📞 01863-766360
Closed Nov-Dec

Comfortable old established Scottish house with views over Kyle of Sutherland to Ross-shire hills offering quiet, comfortable accommodation. Ideal highland touring base. Off street parking.

6 bedrs, 2 ensuite, 1 🛁 **TCF P** 6 No children under 4 **SB** £18 **DB** £35

BOTHWELL Lanarkshire 12C2

★★ Silvertrees
Silverwells Crescent, Bothwell G71 8DP
☎ 01698-852311 Fax 01698-852311
26 bedrs, all ensuite, TCF TV ⋈ P 100 SB £55 DB £80 D £15 CC MC Visa Amex DC

BRORA Sutherland 15D2

Lynwood
Golf Road, Brora KW9 6QS
☎ 01408-621226 Fax 01408-621226
Closed Dec-Feb

Enjoy a warm welcome. Comfortable bedrooms, one ground floor, with CTV, tea and coffee. Golf, bowls, fishing or explore the Northern Highlands where life is at a slow pace.

4 bedrs, 3 ensuite, 1 ⋈ TCF TV P 4 SB £23-£36 DB £38-£44 HB £205-£227 D £12 CC MC Visa ♿

Non Smokers Haven
Tigh Fada, Golf Road, Brora KW9 6QS
☎ 01408-621332 Fax 01408-621332
Closed Christmas/ New Year

Guests return year after year to enjoy the fine views, good food, comfortable beds and friendly atmosphere. Four-hole pitch & putt and croquet green.

3 bedrs, 1 ensuite, 1 ⋈ TCF ☒ P 6 SB £17.50-£20 DB £35-£40 HB £122.50-£130

BUCKIE Banffshire 15E3

★★ Cullen Bay
Cullen, Buckie AB5 2XA
☎ 01542-840432 Fax 01542-840900
14 bedrs, all ensuite, TCF TV ⋈ P 150 SB £33-£46 DB £55-£61 HB £165-£186 D £12 CC MC Visa JCB

CALLANDER Perthshire 12C1

Arden House *Highly Acclaimed*
Bracklinn Road, Callander FK17 8EQ
☎ 01877-330235 Fax 01877-330235
6 bedrs, all ensuite, TCF ☒ ⋈ P 12 SB £20-£23 DB £40-£46 HB £200-£210 D £10

Arran Lodge *Highly Acclaimed*
Leny Road, Callander FK17 8AJ
☎ 01877-330976
Closed Nov-Mar

A luxuriously appointed Victorian bungalow. Tranquil riverside gardens, romantic fourposter bedrooms (ensuite) and Robert's cooking. "Scrumptious and sumptuous". STB Deluxe quality. Recommended by Which? Hotel guide. Private parking.

4 bedrs, all ensuite, TCF TV ☒ P 5 No children under 12 SB £54.90-£63 DB £61-£75 HB £409.50-£428.75 D £27.50 ☒ ♿

Highland House *Highly Acclaimed*
South Church Street, Callander FK17 8BN
☎ 01877-330269
Closed Nov-Mar
9 bedrs, 6 ensuite, 2 ⋈ ⋈ CC MC Visa Amex

Annfield House *Listed*
18 North Church Street, Callander FK17 8EG
☎ 01877-330204

Annfield is situated in a quiet spot a few minutes walk from shops and restaurants. Ideal as an overnight stop or for visiting the surrounding area.

7 bedrs, 4 ensuite, 2 ⋈ TCF ⋈ P 9 SB £18-£20 DB £36-£40

CASTLE DOUGLAS – SCOTLAND

Linley *Listed*
139 Main Street, Callander FK17 8BH
☎ 01877-330087
3 bedrs, 2 ensuite, **P** 5

CAMPBELTOWN Argyll 12B3

★★ Seafield
Kilkerran Road, Campbeltown PA28 6JL
☎ 01586-554385 Fax 01586-522741
9 bedrs, all ensuite, 1 ⇌ TCF TV ⊢ P 12
SB £40-£50 DB £60-£65 D £20 CC MC Visa

Westbank *Listed*
Dell Road, Campbeltown PA28 6JG
☎ 01586-553660 Fax 01586-553660
Closed Nov-Feb
8 bedrs, 2 ensuite, 2 ⇌ TCF TV No children under 3
SB £23 DB £36-£46 D £10 CC MC Visa

CARRBRIDGE Inverness-shire 15D3

Fairwinds *Highly Acclaimed*
Carrbridge PH23 3AA
☎ 01479-841240 Fax 01479-841240
Closed 1 Nov-20 Dec
5 bedrs, all ensuite, TCF TV P 8 No children under 12
SB £24-£27 DB £48-£56 HB £260-£280 D £15 CC MC Visa

Fairwinds Hotel

Experience a true Highland welcome. Dine on Scotland's finest produce in our spacious conservatory restaurant – Speyside trout, salmon, venison, cheeses and many others. Vegetarian dishes and packed lunches available by arrangement. Relax in the Ptarmigan lounge bar. Perhaps glimpse a shy Roe Deer from your bedroom – all our rooms ae ensuite and centrally heated.
Many activities locally – walking, golf, birdwatching, and many more, or just relax and enjoy the beauty of the area.
Allow us to make your stay with us memorable.
2 and 3 bedroom self catering Chalets and Studio Apartment available.

Please write or phone for out brochure and prices to Mrs. E. Reed.

**Carrbridge, Invernesshire PH23 3AA
Tel/Fax: 01479 841240**

Carrmoor *Acclaimed*
Carr Road, Carrbridge PH23 3AD
☎ 01479-841244 Fax 01479-841244

A family run, licensed guest house, central for touring the Highlands. Extensive a la carte and table d'hote menus prepared by the chef/proprietor. A warm welcome awaits.

6 bedrs, all ensuite, TCF ⊢ P 6 SB £20.50-£25 DB £36-£40 HB £199.50-£213.50 D £12 CC MC Visa

CASTLE DOUGLAS Kirkcudbrightshire 12C4

★★ Imperial
35 King Street, Castle Douglas DG7 1AA
☎ 01556-502086 Fax 01556-503009
Closed Christmas-New Year
12 bedrs, all ensuite, 1 ⇌ TCF TV ⊢ P 20 SB £32-£36
DB £52-£56 HB £231 D £13 CC MC Visa Amex 🐾

★★ King's Arms
St Andrews Street, Castle Douglas DG7 1EL
☎ 01556-502626 Fax 01556-502097
Closed Christmas-New Year
10 bedrs, 9 ensuite, 2 ⇌ TCF TV ⊢ P 20 SB £32-£35
DB £52-£56 HB £230 D £13 CC MC Visa 🐾

Craigadam
Castle Douglas DG7 3HU
☎ 01556-650233 Fax 01556-650233
Closed 24 Dec-2 Jan

We look forward to welcoming you to our beautiful farmhouse. Venison, pheasant, duck and salmon a speciality, and sweets not for the calorie conscious. Log fires.

4 bedrs, all ensuite, TCF TV ⊢ P 5 SB £28 DB £46 D £15

CONNEL Argyll 12B1

Ards House *Acclaimed*
Connel, Oban PA37 1PT
☎ 01631-710255
Closed mid Nov-end Jan
6 bedrs, all ensuite, **TCF TV P** 12 No children under 12 **DB** £88-£97.90 **HB** £245-£280 **D** £18 **CC** MC Visa

Loch Etive House *Acclaimed*
Connel, Oban PA37 1PH
☎ 01631-710400 Fax 01631-710680
Closed Nov-Mar
6 bedrs, 4 ensuite, 1 **TCF TV P** 7 **SB** £25-£28 **DB** £40-£50 **HB** £227-£246 **CC** MC Visa

Ronebhal *Acclaimed*
Connel PA37 1PJ
☎ 01631-710310
Closed Oct-Mar
6 bedrs, 5 ensuite, 1 **TCF TV P** 6 No children under 5 **SB** £17-£23 **DB** £34-£54 **HB** £119-£182 **CC** MC Visa

CONTIN Ross-shire 14C3

★★ Craigdarroch Lodge
Craigdarroch Drive, Strathpeffer, Contin IV14 9EH
☎ 01997-421265 Fax 01997-421265
Closed Jan-Mar
13 bedrs, all ensuite, **TCF TV P** 20 **SB** £32-£52 **DB** £54-£84 **HB** £245-£392 **D** £18

Coul House *Highly Acclaimed*
Contin, By Strathpeffer IV14 9EY
☎ 01997-421487 Fax 01997-421945
20 bedrs, all ensuite, **TCF TV P** 40 **SB** £47-£61.75 **DB** £70-£99.50 **HB** £276.50-£451.50 **D** £27.50 **CC** MC Visa Amex DC JCB

CRAIL Fife 13E1

★ Croma
33/35 Nethergate Road, Crail KY10 3TU
☎ 01333-450239
8 bedrs, 4 ensuite, 4 **TCF TV SB** £20-£25 **DB** £40-£50 **HB** £150-£165 **D** £11

Short Breaks

Many hotels provide special rates for weekend and mid-week breaks - sometimes these are quoted in the hotel's entry, otherwise ring direct for the latest offers.

Caiplie House
53 High Street, Crail KY10 3RA
☎ 01333-450564 Fax 01333-450564
Closed Dec-Feb

Located near the harbour of this picturesque fishing village, Caiplie is a very comfortable, informal guest house renowned for its home cooking.

7 bedrs, 2 ensuite, 2 **TCF SB** £16-£22 **DB** £32-£44 **HB** £154-£168 **D** £8

CRAWFORD Lanarkshire 13D3

Field End *Acclaimed*
The Loaning (opposite Church), Crawford ML12 6TN
☎ 01864-502276
Closed Christmas & New Year
3 bedrs, all ensuite, **TCF TV P** 5 **SB** £18-£22 **DB** £32-£36 **HB** £140-£160 **D** £7 **CC** MC Visa

CRIANLARICH Perthshire 12C1

Glenardran *Listed*
Crianlarich FK20 8QS
☎ 01838-300236
6 bedrs, 2 ensuite, 1 **TCF TV P** 6 No children **SB** £19.50-£21 **DB** £39-£49 **CC** MC Visa

CRIEFF Perthshire 13D1

★★ Locke's Acre
Comrie Road, Crieff PH7 4BP
☎ 01764-652526 Fax 01764-652526
7 bedrs, 4 ensuite, 2 **TCF TV P** 30 **SB** £25-£28 **DB** £50-£54 **HB** £252-£280 **D** £14 **CC** MC Visa

★★ Murray Park
Hospitality, Comfort merit awards
Connaught Terrace, Crieff PH7 3DJ
☎ 01764-653731 Fax 01764-655311
20 bedrs, all ensuite, **P** 50 **SB** £45-£49 **DB** £65-£70 **HB** £330 **D** £23 **CC** MC Visa Amex DC

Gwydyr House *Acclaimed*
Comrie Road, Crieff PH7 4BP
☎ 01764-653277 Fax 01764-653277

Delightful eight bedroom Victorian house hotel in own quiet grounds. Colour TV, hairdryer, heating and tea/coffee tray in all rooms. Five minutes walk to town centre. Superb views. Residents licence.

8 bedrs, all ensuite, **TCF TV ⊁ P** 8 **SB** £28 **DB** £64 **CC** MC Visa

Leven House *Acclaimed*
Comrie Road, Crieff PH7 4BA
☎ 01764-652529
Closed Dec-Jan
12 bedrs, 8 ensuite, 2 ⇌ **TCF TV ⊁ P** 12 **SB** £22 **DB** £44
HB £220 **D** £12

Heatherville *Listed*
29-31 Burrell Street, Crieff PH7 4DT
☎ 01764-652825
Closed Dec-Jan

Most attractive and well appointed guest house close to town centre. Private parking to rear. High quality decor. Full breakfast menu available and a warm welcome guaranteed.

4 bedrs, 1 ensuite, 2 ⇌ **TCF TV ⊁ P** 5 **SB** £16-£17
DB £33-£38 **D** £8

CROSSMICHAEL Kirkcudbrightshire   12C4

★★ Culgruff House
Crossmichael DG7 3BB
☎ 01556-670230
15 bedrs, 4 ensuite, 1 🛏, 4 ⇌ **TCF TV ⊁ P** 50 **SB** £17-£19
DB £30-£37.50 **HB** £120-£140 **CC** MC Visa Amex DC

CUMNOCK Ayrshire   12C3

★★ Royal
1 Glaisnock Street, Cumnock KA18 1BP
☎ 01290-420822 Fax 01290-425988
11 bedrs, 5 ensuite, 2 ⇌ ⊁ P 6 **CC** MC Visa DC

CUPAR Fife   13E1

Todhall House
Dairsie, Cupar KY15 4RQ
☎ 01334-656344 Fax 01334-656344
Closed Nov-mid Mar

Traditional elegant Scottish country house peacefully located in glorious countryside offering guests maximum comfort and warm hospitality

3 bedrs, all ensuite, 1 ⇌ **TCF TV ⊠ P** 5 No children under 12 **DB** £48-£58 **HB** £455-£525 **D** £17 **CC** Visa ⊡

DALRY Ayrshire   12C2

★★ Dalry Inn
Kilbirnie Road, Dalry KA24 5JS
☎ 01294-835135 Fax 01294-76651
6 bedrs, all ensuite, ⊁ P 50 **SB** £20-£25 **DB** £40-£44
D £7 **CC** MC Visa Amex DC

DENNY Stirlingshire   13D2

Topps *Highly Acclaimed*
Fintry Road, Denny, Falkirk FK6 5JF
☎ 01324-822471 Fax 01324-823099

A chalet farmhouse in a beautiful hillside location with stunning, panoramic views. Family double or twin-bedded rooms available, all ensuite, tea/coffee, shortbread and TV. Food a speciality (Taste of Scotland listed).

8 bedrs, all ensuite, **TCF TV ⊠ ⊁ P** 12 **SB** £25-£32
DB £28-£44 **D** £9 **CC** MC Visa ♿

DINGWALL Ross-shire 15D3

★★ National
High Street, Dingwall IV15 9HA
☎ 01349-862166 Fax 01349-865178
51 bedrs, all ensuite, TCF TV ⊁ P 30 SB £33-£34 DB £61-£62 D £13 CC MC Visa Amex DC

DORNOCH Sutherland 15D2

★★ Burghfield House
Comfort merit award
Dornoch IV25 3HW
☎ 01862-810212 Fax 01862-810404
Closed Nov-Mar
34 bedrs, 30 ensuite, TCF TV ⊁ P 80 SB £30-£48 DB £60-£88 D £15 CC MC Visa Amex DC

★★ Dornoch Castle
Castle Street, Dornoch IV25 3SD
☎ 01862-810216 Fax 01862-810981
Closed Nov-Mar
17 bedrs, all ensuite, TCF TV ⊁ P 16 SB £37.50-£39.50 DB £66-£70 HB £322-£336 D £20 CC MC Visa Amex

Achandean *Acclaimed*
The Meadows Road, Dornoch IV25 3SF
☎ 01862-810413 Fax 01862-810413
Closed mid Oct-Feb

Central, spacious, comfortable bungalow, large ensuite rooms. Suit disabled. Special rates OAP's. Ideal touring beautiful northern Highlands, walks, golf, car drives, Orkneys. Short breaks welcome. Quiet location. Off road parking. Pets accepted.

3 bedrs, all ensuite, TCF TV ⊁ P 4 DB £38-£44 HB £180 D £8

DOUNE Perthshire 12C1

★★ Woodside
Stirling Road, Doune FK16 6AB
☎ 01786-841237
11 bedrs, all ensuite, ⊁ P 100 CC MC Visa

DRUMBEG Sutherland 14C1

★★ Drumbeg
Drumbeg IV27 4NW
☎ 01571-833236 Fax 01571-833333
Closed Nov-Mar
6 bedrs, all ensuite, TCF TV P 30 No children SB £38 DB £66 CC MC Visa

DRUMNADROCHIT Inverness-shire 15D3

Enrick Cottage
Drumnadrochit IV3 6TZ
☎ 01456-450423 Fax 01456-450423
E Mail avisecott.woodcraft@prestel.co.uk
Closed Nov-Feb

A detached cottage in own grounds delightfully furnished with furniture made in its own workshop. Tea/coffee making facilities and ensuite bedrooms. Cosy lounge/diner. Private parking.

2 bedrs, both ensuite, TCF ⊁ P 3 No children under 15 DB £32-£36 CC MC Visa

DUMBARTON Dunbartonshire 12C2

★★ Abbotsford
Stirling Road, Dumbarton G82 2PJ
☎ 01389-733304 Fax 01389-742599
33 bedrs, all ensuite

★★ Dumbuck
Comfort merit award
Glasgow Road, Dumbarton G82 1EG
☎ 01389-734336 Fax 01389-734336
22 bedrs, all ensuite, TCF TV ⊁ P 200 SB £48 DB £68 D £13.95 CC MC Visa Amex DC

DUMFRIES Dumfriesshire 13D4

★★ Hill
18 St. Marys Street, Dumfries DG1 1LZ
☎ 01387-254893 Fax 01387-262553
E Mail acame45046@aol.com
6 bedrs, 5 ensuite, P 50
SB £36-£39 DB £45-£52 D £10 CC MC Visa Amex DC

DUNBAR East Lothian — 13E2

★★ Bayswell
Bayswell Park, Dunbar EH42 1AE
☎ 01368-862225 Fax 01368-862225
13 bedrs, all ensuite, TCF TV ☛ P 20 SB £39-£49 DB £69
D £13 CC MC Visa Amex DC

★★ Redheugh
Bayswell Park, Dunbar EH42 1AE
☎ 01368-862793
Closed Christmas-New Year
10 bedrs, all ensuite, TCF TV ☛ No children under 8
SB £35-£38.50 DB £55-£59 HB £275-£290.50 D £17.50 CC
MC Visa Amex DC

Overcliffe *Listed*
11 Bayswell Park, Dunbar EH42 1AE
☎ 01368-864004
6 bedrs, 3 ensuite, 2 ⇨ TCF TV ☛ P 2 SB £17 DB £34

Springfield *Listed*
42 Belhaven Road, Dunbar EH42 1NH
☎ 01368-862502
Closed Dec
5 bedrs, 1 ensuite, 2 ⇨ TCF TV ☛ P 7 SB £18 DB £33-£34
HB £167-£170 D £10 CC MC Visa

DUNBLANE Central — 12C1

Mossgiel
Doune Road, Dunblane FK15 9ND
☎ 01786-824325
Closed Dec-Feb

Countryside bungalow ideally located as a touring base for central Scotland. All comfortable bedrooms offer private facilities, radios, hospitality trays, ensuring guests have an enjoyable stay.

3 bedrs, 2 ensuite, 1 ⇨ TCF ✍ P 6 SB £25-£30 DB £36-£40 ♿

DUNDEE Angus — 13E1

Beach House *Acclaimed*
22 Esplanade, Broughty Ferry, Dundee DD5 2EN
☎ 01382-776614 Fax 01382-480241
5 bedrs, all ensuite, TCF TV ☛ SB £32-£38 DB £44-£50
D £11 CC MC Visa

DUNFERMLINE Fife — 13D2

★★ Halfway House
Main Street, Kingseat, Dunfermline KY12 0TJ
☎ 01383-731661 Fax 10383-621274

Thirty minutes from Princes Street, within easy reach of Perth, Stirling, Glasgow and St Andrews. Enjoy the relaxing atmosphere of the bars and restaurants.

12 bedrs, all ensuite, TCF TV ☛ P 100 SB £32-£37
DB £37-£47 CC MC Visa Amex

DUNKELD Perthshire — 13D1

★★ Atholl Arms
Bridge Street, Dunkeld PH8 0AQ
☎ 01350-727219 Fax 01350-727219
16 bedrs, 9 ensuite, 4 ⇨ TCF TV ☛ P 20 No children
under 8 SB £30-£40 DB £50-£60 CC MC Visa Amex ♿

DUNNET Caithness — 15E1

★★ Northern Sands
Dunnet KW14 8XD
☎ 01847-85270 Fax 01847-851626
9 bedrs, all ensuite, P 40 SB £40 DB £60 CC MC Visa ♿

DUNOON Argyll — 12B2

★★ Argyll
Argyll Street, Dunoon PA23 7NE
☎ 01369-702059 Fax 01369-704483
30 bedrs, all ensuite, TCF TV ☐ SB £25-£40 DB £50-£65
HB £200-£300 D £9.50 CC MC Visa DC

★★ Esplanade
West Bay, Dunoon PA23 7HU
☎ 01369-704070 Fax 01369-702129
Closed Nov-Apr
51 bedrs, all ensuite, 2 ⇨ TCF TV ☛ ☐ P 20 CC MC
Visa Amex

Anchorage *Highly Acclaimed*
Shore Road, Ardnadam, Sandbank, Dunoon PA23 8O9
☎ 01369-705108 Fax 01369-705108
E Mail ach2811@aol.com
Closed Nov
5 bedrs, all ensuite, TCF TV ✍ P 14 DB £55-£70 HB £241-£252 D £13 CC MC Visa ♿

Ardtully *Acclaimed*
297 Marine Parade, Hunters Quay, PA23 8HN
📞 01369-702478

Come to the Ardtully hotel and enjoy unforgettable views, excellent meals, spacious rooms. Private parking. 15% discount for over 55's (2 sharing) when staying 3 days or more.

9 bedrs, all ensuite, ✝ P 10 No children under 12
SB £25-£30 DB £50-£60 HB £210-£225 D £13

Rosscairn *Acclaimed*
51 Hunter Street, Kirn, Dunoon PA23 8JR
📞 01369-704344 Fax 01369-704344

Friendly Victorian house hotel overlooking golf course. Private parking. Non-smoking bedrooms and dining room. Two video/TV lounges. Central heating. Excellent food. Highly recommended. Free brochure.

8 bedrs, 7 ensuite, TCF P 14 SB £22-£24 DB £40-£44
HB £189-£203 D £12 CC MC

EDINBURGH   13D2

★★ Allison House
15-17 Mayfield Gardens, Edinburgh EH9 2AX
📞 0131-667 8049 Fax 0131-667 5001
23 bedrs, 21 ensuite, 2 ⇌ TCF TV ✝ P 12 No children under 12 SB £25-£45 DB £50-£88 D £9 CC MC Visa Amex DC JCB

★★ Hawes Inn
Newhalls Road, South Queensferry, EH30 9TA
📞 0131-331 1990 Fax 0131-319 1120
8 bedrs, 3 ⇌ TCF TV ✝ P 50
SB £34 DB £55 D £25 CC MC Visa Amex DC

★★ Iona
17 Strathearn Place, Edinburgh EH9 2AL
📞 0131-447 5050/6264 Fax 0131-452 8574
17 bedrs, 10 ensuite, 4 ⌕, 5 ⇌ TCF TV ✝ P 16 SB £25-£33 DB £45-£85 D £13 CC MC Visa ♿

★★ Murrayfield
18 Corstorphine Road, Edinburgh EH12 6HN
📞 0131-337 1844 Fax 0131-346 8159
33 bedrs, all ensuite, TCF TV ✝ P 33 SB £52.50-£57.50
DB £70-£75 D £15 CC MC Visa Amex DC

★★ Orwell Lodge
29 Polwarth Terrace, Edinburgh EH11 1NH
📞 0131-229 1044 Fax 0131-228 9492

Once an elegant Victorian mansion, now offering excellent accommodation. All rooms ensuite and individually decorated with TV, radio, telephone, hairdryer, tea and coffee-making facilities. All rooms are no smoking. Large car park.

10 bedrs, all ensuite, TCF TV ⊠ P 40 SB £45-£49 DB £70-£75 CC MC Visa Amex

★★ Royal Ettrick
13 Ettrick Road, Edinburgh EH10 5BJ
📞 0131 228 6413 Fax 0131 229 7330
12 bedrs, 9 ensuite, 2 ⌕, 3 ⇌ TCF TV ✝ P 14 SB £42-£46 DB £64-£75 D £10 CC MC Visa

★★ Thrums
14 Minto Street, Edinburgh EH9 1RQ
📞 0131-667 8545 Fax 0131-667 8707
Closed Christmas
14 bedrs, 13 ensuite, 2 ⇌ TCF TV ✝ P 10 SB £35-£45
DB £60-£70 D £8.50 CC MC Visa

A Haven *Highly Acclaimed*
180 Ferry Road, Edinburgh EH6 4NS
📞 0131-554 6559 Fax 0131-554 5252

EDINBURGH – SCOTLAND

A Victorian town house close to the city centre completely refurbished in keeping with the period. Secure private parking.

12 bedrs, all ensuite, **TCF TV P** 12 **SB** £30-£50 **DB** £54-£85 **D** £15.50 **CC** MC Visa Amex

Adam *Highly Acclaimed*
19 Lansdowne Crescent, Edinburgh EH12 5EH
☎ 0131-337 1148 Fax 0131-337 1729

Comfortable and friendly family run hotel in Edinburgh's west end, close to Princes Street. Recently refurbished to a high standard, all rooms ensuite with telephones and TVs.

13 bedrs, all ensuite, **TCF TV SB** £35-£45 **DB** £60-£75 **D** £8 **CC** MC Visa

Ashgrove House *Highly Acclaimed*
12 Osborne Terrace, Edinburgh EH12 5HG
☎ 0131-337 5014 Fax 0131-313 5043

A Victorian detached, family-run hotel, situated on the main A8 road within a mile of the city centre.

7 bedrs, 5 ensuite, ⌧ **P** 10

Brunswick *Highly Acclaimed*
7 Brunswick Street, Edinburgh EH7 5JB
☎ 0131-556 1238 Fax 0131-557 1404
Closed Christmas

Georgian town house refurbished to a high standard, centrally located, close to bus and rail stations. Two fourposter bedrooms for honeymooners or romantics. Personal welcome and attention from resident owners.

11 bedrs, all ensuite, **TCF TV** ⌧ No children under 2 **SB** £25-£45 **DB** £50-£90 **CC** MC Visa Amex

Cumberland *Highly Acclaimed*
1 West Coates, Edinburgh EH12 5JQ
☎ 0131-337 1198 Fax 0131-337 1022
E Mail cumberlandhotel@sprynet.co.uk

Within 5 minutes walk from the city centre, a warm welcome awaits you at this elegant family-run hotel. Excellent facilities in spacious ensuite bedrooms. An attractive cocktail bar, residents lounge and sunny garden offer comfort in a relaxed atmosphere.

9 bedrs, all ensuite, **TCF TV P** 14 **SB** £30-£60 **DB** £50-£90 **CC** MC Visa ♿

Dorstan *Highly Acclaimed*
7 Priestfield Road, Edinburgh EH16 5HJ
☎ 0131-667 5138 Fax 0131-668 4644
14 bedrs, 9 ensuite, 3 ⌂, 2 ⌧ **TCF TV P** 6 **SB** £32-£37 **DB** £66-£76 **D** £14 **CC** MC Visa Amex

Grosvenor Gardens *Highly Acclaimed*
1 Grosvenor Gardens, Edinburgh EH12 5JU
☎ 0131-313 3415
8 bedrs, 7 ensuite, 1 ⌂, **TCF TV** ⌧ No children under 5
SB £30-£45 **DB** £55-£95 **CC** MC Visa

Lodge *Highly Acclaimed*
6 Hampton Terrace, West Coates, EH12 5JD
☎ 0131-337 3682 Fax 0131-313 1700
10 bedrs, all ensuite, 1 ⌧ **TCF TV P** 10 **SB** £35-£45 **DB** £50-£80 **CC** MC Visa

Roselea House *Highly Acclaimed*
11 Mayfield Road, Edinburgh EH9 2NG
☎ 0131-667 6115 Fax 0131-667 3556

Tasteful decor and elegant fabrics enhance the period style, while the luxurious bathrooms would grace a top hotel. Each of the bedrooms without ensuites has its own bathroom, and bathrobes are thoughtfully provided. There is a lounge and dining room.

7 bedrs, 5 ensuite, 2 ⇌ 🐕 P 4 SB £30-£45 DB £50-£80 CC MC Visa

Arthurs View *Acclaimed*
10 Mayfield Gardens, Edinburgh EH9 2BZ
☎ 0131-667 3468 Fax 0131-662 4232
12 bedrs, all ensuite, TCF TV 🐕 P 10 CC MC Visa Amex DC 🅿

Ashdene House *Acclaimed*
23 Fountainhall Road, Edinburgh EH9 2LN
☎ 0131-667 6026
5 bedrs, all ensuite, ⌧ P 3 DB £40-£56

Ashlyn *Acclaimed*
42 Inverleith Row, Edinburgh EH3 5PY
☎ 0131-552 2954
8 bedrs, 5 ensuite, 3 ⇌ TCF TV ⌧

Boisdale *Acclaimed*
9 Coates Gardens, Edinburgh EH12 5LG
☎ 0131-337 1134 Fax 0131-313 0048
10 bedrs, all ensuite, TCF TV 🐕
SB £25-£45 DB £50-£90 D £10 CC MC Visa

Buchan *Acclaimed*
3 Coates Gardens, Edinburgh EH12 5LG
☎ 0131-337 1045 Fax 0131-558 7055
12 bedrs, all ensuite, 1 ⇌ TCF TV 🐕 CC MC Visa

Corstorphine Guest House *Acclaimed*
188 St John's Road, Edinburgh EH12 8SG
☎ 0131-539 4237 Fax 0131-539 4945
E Mail rumafowdar@aol.com

A warm and welcoming Victorian house, tastefully decorated and furnished to the highest standard and providing excellent facilities. Conveniently located midway between airport and city centre with private parking and large gardens.

4 bedrs, 3 ensuite, 2 ⇌ TCF TV P 7 SB £20-£50 DB £36-£70 CC MC Visa ♿

Galloway *Acclaimed*
22 Dean Park Crescent, Edinburgh EH4 7PH
☎ 0131-332 3672 Fax 0131-332 3672
10 bedrs, 6 ensuite, 4 ⇌ TCF TV 🐕 SB £25-£45 DB £35-£50

Heriott Park *Acclaimed*
256 Ferry Road, Edinburgh EH5 3AN
☎ 0131-552 6628 Fax 0131-552 6628
6 bedrs, 2 ensuite, 2 ⇌ ⌧ 🐕 SB £20-£30 DB £34-£50

Ivy House *Acclaimed*
7 Mayfield Gardens, Edinburgh EH9 2AX
☎ 0131-667 3411
8 bedrs, 6 ensuite, 2 ⇌ TCF TV 🐕 P 9 SB £20-£40 DB £32-£60

Joppa Turrets Guesthouse *Acclaimed*
1 Lower Joppa, Edinburgh EH15 2ER
☎ 0131-669 5806 Fax 0131-669 5190
5 bedrs, 3 ensuite, 1 ⇌ TCF TV ⌧ SB £15-£25 DB £30-£48 CC MC Visa

Kew *Acclaimed*
1 Kew Terrace, Murrayfield, Edinburgh EH12 5JE
☎ 0131-313 0700 Fax 0131-313 0747

Don't forget to mention the guide
When booking direct, please remember to tell the hotel that you chose it from RAC Bed & Breakfast 1998.

Victorian terraced house, tastefully refurbished to a high standard, within easy walking distance of the city centre, conference centre and Murrayfield rugby stadium. Secure private car park.

6 bedrs, all ensuite, **TCF TV** P 6 **SB** £35-£38 **DB** £55-£68 **CC** MC Visa Amex

Lindsay *Acclaimed*
108 Polwarth Terrace, Edinburgh EH11 1NN
0131-337 1580 Fax 0131-337 1580

Offering warm, comfortable rooms in a quiet area yet very accessible for all main attractions. Easy access from the city by-pass.

8 bedrs, 3, 2 **TCF TV** P 8 **CC** MC Visa Amex

Marchhall *Acclaimed*
14-16 Marchhall Crescent, Edinburgh EH16 5HL
0131-667 2743 Fax 0131-662 0777

A warm and friendly family owned hotel situated on the south side of the city just off the Dalkeith Road (A7), near the Royal Commonwealth Pool and Queens Park in an environmental area.

14 bedrs, 10 ensuite, 2 **TCF TV SB** £20-£37 **DB** £40-£56 **HB** £182-£260 **D** £9 **CC** MC Visa

Newington *Acclaimed*
18 Newington Road, Edinburgh EH9 1QS
0131-667 3356 Fax 0131-667 8307

Situated between the main A7 and A68 routes into Edinburgh and 10 minutes by bus from city centre. It is very convenient for visiting many places of interest, e.g. Castle, Holyrood Palace, museums, university, Royal College of Surgeons and art galleries.

8 bedrs, 5 ensuite, 1, 1 **TCF TV** P 3 **SB** £26-£30 **DB** £40-£60

Salisbury *Acclaimed*
45 Salisbury Road, Edinburgh EH16 5AA
0131-667 1264 Fax 0131-667 1264

Completely non-smoking house, quietly situated, one mile from the city centre. Spacious, comfortable rooms with private facilities. Private car park.

12 bedrs, 9 ensuite, 2 **TCF TV** P 12 **SB** £24-£30 **DB** £44-£54 **CC** MC Visa

Sherwood *Acclaimed*
42 Minto Street, Edinburgh EH9 2BR
0131-667 1200 Fax 0131-667 2344
Closed 22-29 Dec
6 bedrs, all ensuite, 1 **TCF TV** P 3 **DB** £36-£60 **CC** MC Visa

---

SHERWOOD
Guest House

Props: Susan and David Greig

A warm welcome awaits you in our refurbished Georgian house. Set in Europe's most beautiful city. Approx. 1 mile to city centre. View the amazing 'Arthur's Seat' from some bedrooms.
Enjoy a superb breakfast in our friendly lounge.
All rooms ensuite with one private bathroom.
High standards and excellent facilities.

**42 MINTO STREET,
EDINBURGH EH9 2BR
Tel: 0131 667 1200**

Stra'ven *Acclaimed*
3 Brunstane Road North, Edinburgh EH15 2DL
☎ 0131-669 5580

Beautifully maintained Victorian house in peaceful cul-de-sac adjoining lovely beach and promenade. Unrestricted parking. Easy access to city centre. Resident's lounge. Non smoking.

8 bedrs, all ensuite, 1 ✱ **TCF TV** ☒ **SB** £18-£30 **DB** £36-£60

Strathearn *Acclaimed*
19 Strathearn Road, Edinburgh EH9 2AE
☎ 0131-447 1810 Fax 0131-447 1810
8 bedrs, all ensuite, **TCF TV SB** £22.50-£30 **DB** £40-£60

Averon *Listed*
44 Gilmore Place, Edinburgh EH3 9NQ
☎ 0131-229 9932

A comfortable, fully restored townhouse, built in 1770, in central Edinburgh, with the advantage of a private car park and just ten minutes walk to Princes Street and castle. STB (1 Crown) and Les Routiers approved. B&B from £14.

10 bedrs, 3 ✱ **TCF TV P** 10 **SB** £14-£25 **DB** £28-£46 **CC** MC Visa Amex ♿

Broughton *Listed*
37 Broughton Place, Edinburgh EH1 3RR
☎ 0131-558 9792 Fax 0131-5589790

Chalumna *Listed*
5 Granville Terrace, Edinburgh EH10 4PQ
☎ 0131-229 2086 Fax 0131-221 0880
9 bedrs, 5 ensuite, 1 ☏, 1 ✱ **TCF TV P** 4 **SB** £25-£45 **DB** £36-£60 **CC** MC Visa

Glenalmond *Listed*
25 Mayfield Gardens, Edinburgh EH9 2BX
☎ 0131-668 2392 Fax 0131-668 2392

Deb & Dave warmly welcome you to their ten ensuite, ground and fourposter bedroom guest house. It is mostly furnished by Ducal which is of the highest quality. Full Scottish breakfast with porridge and home made scones.

10 bedrs, all ensuite, **TCF TV** 🐾 **P** 8 **SB** £20-£35 **DB** £18-£30 ♿

Kariba *Listed*
10 Granville Terrace, Edinburgh EH10 4PQ
☎ 0131-229 3773
9 bedrs, all ensuite, 3 ✱ **P** 6 No children under 4 **SB** £22-£28 **DB** £40-£50 ♿

Ailsa Craig
24 Royal Terrace, Edinburgh EH7 5AH
☎ 0131-556 6055 Fax 0131-556 6055

City centre hotel situated ten minutes walk from Princes Street and tourist attractions. Tastefully decorated bedrooms with all facilities. Family rooms available. Ample street parking.

18 bedrs, 16 ensuite, 1 ☏, 2 ✱ **TCF TV SB** £22.50-£40 **DB** £45-£70 **HB** £227.50-£350 **D** £10 **CC** MC Visa Amex DC

Anvilla
1a Granville Terrace, Edinburgh EH10 4PC
📞 0131-228 3381

Anvilla is a small family run guest house within walking distance of city centre. Restaurants, theatre and shops nearby.

6 bedrs, 2 ⇌ TCF TV 🐾 P 5 SB £20-£22 DB £36-£40 HB £125-£1,440 CC MC Visa

Avenue
4 Murrayfield Avenue, Murrayfield, Edinburgh EH12 4AX
📞 0131-346 7270 Fax 0131-337 9733

Located a few minutes drive from Princes Avenue, The Avenue offers clean, comfortable accomodation. Hearty Scottish breakfasts. Unrestricted free street parking. Family run.

9 bedrs, all ensuite, TCF TV 🐾
SB £20-£35 DB £40-£70 CC MC Visa

Bonnington
202 Ferry Road, Edinburgh EH6 4NW
📞 0131-554 7610
6 bedrs, 4 ensuite, TCF TV 🐾 P 9 DB £46-£60

Classic House
50 Mayfield Road, Edinburgh EH9 2NH
📞 0131-667 5847 Fax 0131-662 1016

A highly acclaimed traditional house with elegant rooms. Set along a main bus route and perfect for exploring the capital. Delicious breakfasts. Non smoking throughout.

5 bedrs, all ensuite, TCF TV ⊠ SB £20-£45 DB £40-£60 CC MC Visa

---

RAC Hotel Reservations Service
0870 603 9109
(Calls charged at national call rate)

BONNINGTON
GUEST HOUSE

Eileen and David Watt assure you of a warm welcome at their interestingly furnished guest house, most bedrooms ensuite. Superb breakfast menu to suit all diets. Private car parking.

**202 FERRY ROAD,
EDINBURGH EH6 4NW
Tel: 0131-554 7610**

Greenside
9 Royal Terrace, Edinburgh EH7 5AB
📞 0131-557 0022 Fax 0131-557 0022

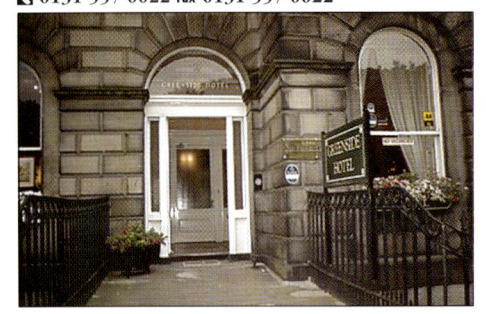

An elegant Georgian town house hotel. Tastefully decorated rooms with all facilities. Family rooms available. Ten minutes walk from Princes Street and Waverley station. Parking available.

14 bedrs, all ensuite, **TCF TV SB** £25-£40 **DB** £40-£70 **HB** £280-£295 **D** £9.95 **CC** MC Visa Amex DC

Parklands
20 Mayfield Gardens, Edinburgh EH9 2BZ
📞 0131-667 7184 Fax 0131-667 2011

Parklands is an attractive stone-built Victorian house, conveniently located one and a half miles south of the famous Princes Street and all the attractions of the capital.

6 bedrs, 5 ensuite, **TCF TV P** 2 **DB** £19-£28

Rowan
13 Glenorchy Terrace, Edinburgh EH9 2DQ
📞 0131-667 2463 Fax 0131-667 2463

Elegant Victorian house with comfortable well equipped bedrooms in a quiet, leafy area, ten minutes by bus from the centre. Within easy reach of the castle, Royal Mile, university and restaurants. Breakfast includes porridge and freshly baked scones.

Salisbury View
64 Dalkeith Road, Edinburgh EH16 5AE
📞 0131-667 1133 Fax 0131-667 1133
Closed 24-26 Dec

Small private Georgian hotel under the personal supervision of the properties. On the A7/A68 with open aspect to Holyrood Park and five minutes from city centre. Licensed restaurant, car park.

8 bedrs, all ensuite, **TCF TV ⚑ P** 8 **SB** £27-£40 **DB** £52-£64 **HB** £290-£332 **D** £15.50 **CC** MC Visa Amex DC ♿

Parklands
Guest House

Parklands is an attractive stone built Victorian house conveniently located 1.5 miles south of the famous Princes Street and all the attractions of the capital. Parklands offers guests a full Scottish breakfast to prepare them for the day, nearby there are many excellent restaurants. All bedrooms are furnished to a high standard and you are assured of a warm welcome.

20 MAYFIELD GARDENS, EDINBURGH EH9 2BZ
Tel: 0131 667 7184

St Margarets House
18 Craigmillar Park, Edinburgh EH16 5PS
📞 **0131-667 2202 Fax 0131-667 2202**

Victorian terraced villa with many retained features. All rooms have colour TV, tea/coffee, most ensuite. Only minutes to the city centre. Car park.

8 bedrs, 5 ensuite, 1 🐕 **TCF TV P** 7 No children under 7 **SB** £35-£55 **DB** £44-£60 **CC** MC Visa

FALKIRK Stirlingshire   13D2

★★ Comfort Friendly Inn
Manor Street, Falkirk FK1 1NT
📞 **01324-624066 Fax 01324-611785**
E Mail admin@gb626.u-net.com
33 bedrs, all ensuite, **TCF TV** 🐕 🍴 **P** 17 **SB** £47-£59 **DB** £54-£65 **D** £9.75 **CC** MC Visa Amex DC JCB ⛔ ♿

FALKLAND Fife   13D1

Covenanter *Acclaimed*
The Square, Falkland KY15 7BU
📞 **01337-857224 Fax 01337-857163**
8 bedrs, all ensuite, **TCF TV P** 6 **SB** £39 **DB** £48 **HB** £280 **D** £15 **CC** MC Visa Amex DC

FORRES Morayshire   15E3

★★ Park
Victoria Road, Forres IV36 0BN
📞 **01309-672611 Fax 01309-672328**
14 bedrs, 9 ensuite, 4 🐕 **TCF TV** 🐕 🍴 **P** 20 **SB** £39.50 **DB** £55 **HB** £350 **D** £16.50 **CC** MC Visa Amex

★★ Ramnee
Hospitality merit award
Victoria Road, Forres IV36 0BN
📞 **01309-672410 Fax 01309-673392**
20 bedrs, all ensuite, 1 🐕 **TCF TV** 🐕 **P** 50 **SB** £37.50-£55 **DB** £65-£82.50 **HB** £315-£385 **D** £22.50 **CC** MC Visa Amex DC JCB

FORT WILLIAM Inverness-shire   14C4

★★ Grand
Gordon Square, Fort William PH33 6DX
📞 **01397-702928 Fax 01397-702928**
Closed Jan
33 bedrs, all ensuite, **TCF TV** 🐕 **P** 20 **SB** £31-£40 **DB** £26-£35 **HB** £252-£350 **D** £18 **CC** MC Visa Amex DC JCB

★★ Nevis Bank
Belford Road, Fort William PH33 6BY
📞 **01397-705721 Fax 01397-706275**
31 bedrs, all ensuite, **TCF TV** 🐕 **P** 35 **SB** £38-£49 **DB** £50-£70 **HB** £248-£350 **D** £16.95 **CC** MC Visa Amex DC ⛔

Distillery House *Acclaimed*
Nevis Bridge, North Road, Fort William PH33 6LH
📞 **01397-700103 Fax 01397-702980**

This friendly guest house is an ideal base for enjoying a comfortable stay at the end of Glen Nevis, but only five minutes from the town centre.

6 bedrs, all ensuite, **TCF TV** 🐕 **P** 7 **SB** £20-£45 **DB** £40-£64 **CC** MC Visa

Ashburn House
Achintore Road, Fort William PH33 6RA
📞 **01397-706000 Fax 01397-706000**
Closed Dec-Jan

A house of outstanding quality, offering true Highland hospitality, values and home baking. Completely non smoking. Highest accolades achieved. Close to town, yet peaceful. Satisfaction guaranteed.

7 bedrs, all ensuite, 1 🐕 **TCF TV** 🚭 **P** 7 **SB** £30-£35 **DB** £60-£70 **CC** MC Visa

FORTINGALL Perthshire　　　　　　　　12C1

★★ Fortingall
Fortingall PH15 2NQ
☎ 01887-830367 Fax 01887-830367
Closed Nov-Mar
10 bedrs, 9 ensuite, 1 ⌕, 1 ⇌ TCF TV ⚲ P 15 SB £26-£32 DB £44-£56 HB £260-£280 D £16 CC MC Visa

GAIRLOCH Ross-shire　　　　　　　　14B2

★★ Old Inn
Gairloch IV21 2BD
☎ 01445-712006 Fax 01445-712445
14 bedrs, all ensuite, TCF TV ⚲ P 50 SB £28-£37 DB £55-£73 HB £206 CC MC Visa Amex

GALASHIELS Selkirkshire　　　　　　13E3

★★ Abbotsford Arms
63 Stirling Street, Galashiels TD1 1BY
☎ 01896-752517 Fax 01896-750744
14 bedrs, 10 ensuite, 2 ⇌ TCF TV P 10 SB £28-£37 DB £50-£58 D £10 CC MC Visa

GATEHOUSE OF FLEET Kirkcudbrightshire 12C4

Bank O'Fleet *Listed*
47 High Street, Gatehouse of Fleet DG7 2HR
☎ 01557-814302 Fax 01557-814302

An attractive black and white painted front which was once a bank. Very well decorated.

6 bedrs, 5 ensuite, 1 ⇌ ⚲ SB £23-£25 DB £45-£48 CC MC Visa Amex ⌕ ♿

GIRVAN Ayrshire　　　　　　　　　　12B3

★★ Westcliffe
Louisa Drive, Girvan KA26 9AH
☎ 01465-712128 Fax 01465-712128
21 bedrs, 12 ensuite, 4 ⇌
CC MC Visa Amex ♿

GLASGOW　　　　　　　　　　　　　12C2

★★ Argyll
973 Sauchiehall Street, Glasgow G3 7TQ
☎ 0141-337 3313

★★ Belhaven
15 Belhaven Terrace, West End, Dowanhill, Glasgow G12 0TG
☎ 0141-339 3222 Fax 0141-339 2212
17 bedrs, 13 ensuite, 2 ⇌ TCF TV SB £35-£50 DB £65 D £12 CC MC Visa Amex DC

★★ Burnside
East Kilbride Road, Rutherglen, Glasgow G73 5EA
☎ 0141-634 1276

★ Dunkeld
10/12 Queen's Drive, Glasgow G42 8BS
☎ 0141-424 0160 Fax 0141-423 4437
E Mail 106130.2723@compuserve.com
19 bedrs, all ensuite, TCF TV ⚲ P 8 SB £27-£37 DB £37-£55 D £10 CC MC Visa Amex JCB

Albion *Acclaimed*
405 North Woodside Road, Glasgow G20 6NN
☎ 0141-339 8620

Ambassador *Acclaimed*
7 Kelvin Drive, Glasgow G20 8QS
☎ 0141-946 1018

Angus *Acclaimed*
970 Sauchiehall Street, Glasgow G3 7TH
☎ 0141-357 5155 Fax 0141-339 9469
E Mail argyll_angus.hotel@virgin.net

Excellent location ½ mile west of city centre next to Kelvingrove Park. Walk to SECC, Glasgow Galleries/Museum, Glasgow University, Mackintosh sites. Warm Scottish welcome awaits.

18 bedrs, all ensuite, TCF TV SB £34-£42 DB £46-£52 CC MC Visa Amex DC

Rennie Mackintosh *Acclaimed*
218-220 Renfrew Street, Glasgow G3 6TX
☎ 0141-333 9992 Fax 0141-333 9995
24 bedrs, all ensuite, TCF TV SB £25 DB £40 CC MC Visa Amex DC

GLENMORISTON – SCOTLAND

Charing Cross *Listed*
310 Renfrew Street, Charing Cross, Glasgow G3 6UW
☎ 0141-332 2503 Fax 0141-353 3047

Pleasant guest house in Glasgow city centre, 24 modern rooms, colour TV (satellite), tea/coffee, telephone in each room. All amenities on our doorstep.

24 bedrs, 7 ensuite, 9 ⇌ TCF TV SB £17.50-£19.50 DB £32-£37 CC MC Visa Amex

McLays *Listed*
264-276 Renfrew Street, Charing Cross, G3 6TT
☎ 0141-332 4796 Fax 0141-353 0422
E Mail mclaysguesthouse@compuserve.com

Pleasant hotel in the city centre with Sauchiehall street only a minute away. 62 modern rooms, 39 with ensuite facilities. Colour TV (satellite), tea/coffee, telephone in each room.

62 bedrs, 39 ensuite, 11 ⇌ TCF TV ☐ SB £18.50-£21 DB £35-£39 CC MC Visa Amex

Smith's *Listed*
963 Sauchiehall Street, Glasgow G3 7TQ
☎ 0141-339 6363 Fax 0141-334 1892

Terraced house on three floors.
33 bedrs, 8 ⇌ TCF TV SB £23.50 DB £36

GLASGOW AIRPORT Renfrewshire 12C2

Myfarrclan
146 Corsebar Road, Paisley PA2 9NA
☎ 0141-884 8285 Fax 0141 884 8285
E Mail myfarrclan_qwest@compuserve.com

Small family run guest house, nestling in leafy suburb of Paisley, famous for its Pattern & Shawl Museum and Abbey. Comfort, quality and the warmest welcome guaranteed. Natural cooking and produce used for breakfast & dinner menus.

3 bedrs, all ensuite, 1 ⇌ TCF TV ☒ P 2 SB £30.35-£50 DB £50-£65 D £15 CC MC Visa ♿

GLENCAPLE Dumfriesshire 13D4

★★ Nith
Glencaple DG1 4RE
☎ 01387-770213 Fax 01387-770568
10 bedrs, 7 ensuite, 2 ⇌ TCF TV ⚲ P 20 SB £30 DB £55 CC MC Visa ⌧

GLENCOE Argyll 14C4

★★ Holly Tree
Kentallen, Glencoe PA38 4BY
☎ 01631-740292 Fax 01631-740345
Closed Nov
10 bedrs, all ensuite, TCF TV ⚲ P 40 SB £42-£62 DB £75-£90 D £26 CC MC Visa Amex ♿

★★ King's House
Glencoe PA39 4HY
☎ 01855-851259 Fax 01855-851259

GLENMORISTON Inverness-shire 14C3

★★ Cluanie Inn
Glenmoriston, Inverness IV3 6YW
☎ 01320-340238 Fax 01320-340293
13 bedrs, 10 ensuite, ⚲ P 60 SB £30 DB £79 D £19 CC MC Visa ⌧

GLENROTHES Fife   13D1

★★ Albany
1 North Street, Glenrothes KY7 5NA
☎ 01592-752292 Fax 01592-756451
29 bedrs, all ensuite, TCF TV ✱ ☱ SB £25-£45 DB £38-£55 D £4.95 CC MC Visa Amex

★★ Rescobie
Hospitality merit award
Valley Drive, Leslie KY6 3BQ
☎ 01592-742143 Fax 01592-620231

A listed country house hotel in two acres of gardens. All bedrooms are ensuite and fully fitted and the restaurant currently holds awards for its cuisine.

10 bedrs, all ensuite, TCF TV P 20 SB £44-£52 DB £55-£74 HB £-£336 D £17.50 CC MC Visa Amex DC ♿

GOLSPIE Sutherland   15D2

★★ Sutherland Arms
Main Street, Golspie KW10 6SA
☎ 01408-633234
15 bedrs, all ensuite, TCF TV P 25 SB £25-£30 DB £45-£50 D £4 CC MC Visa

GRANTOWN-ON-SPEY Morayshire   15E3

Culdearn House *Highly Acclaimed*
Woodlands Terrace, Grantown-on-Spey PH26 3JU
☎ 01479-872106 Fax 01479-873641
Closed Nov-Feb
9 bedrs, all ensuite, TCF TV P 10 No children under 10 SB £45-£60 DB £90-£120 HB £315-£370 CC MC Visa Amex DC JCB (rates include dinner)

Ravenscourt House *Highly Acclaimed*
Restaurant merit award
Seafield Avenue, Grantown-on-Spey PH26 3JG
☎ 01479-872286 Fax 01479-873260
6 bedrs, all ensuite, 1 ⇥ TCF TV ✱ P 9 SB £39-£45 DB £58-£75 HB £385-£413 D £18 CC MC Visa Amex ♿

Garden Park *Acclaimed*
Woodside Avenue, Grantown-on-Spey PH26 3JN
☎ 01479-873235
Closed Nov-Feb
5 bedrs, all ensuite, TCF TV P 8 No children under 12 SB £21-£23 DB £42-£46 HB £197-£220 D £11

Rosegrove
Skye of Curr, Dulnain Bridge, Grantown-on-Spey
☎ 01479-851335

Mountain views and attractive gardens. Log fire, local venison, salmon and beef. Friendly and relaxed. Ideal centre for exploring the Highlands and all outdoor pursuits.

6 bedrs, 3 ensuite, 2 ⇥, TCF ✱ P 8 SB £15-£25 DB £30-£36 HB £161-£189 D £9

GRETNA Dumfriesshire   13D4

★★ Gretna Chase
Gretna DG16 5JB
☎ 01461-337517 Fax 01461-337766
9 bedrs, 6 ensuite, 3 ⇥, TCF TV ✱ P 40 CC MC Visa Amex

★★ Royal Stewart Motel
Glasgow Road, Gretna CA6 5DT
☎ 01461-338210
12 bedrs, all ensuite, ✱ P 24 CC MC Visa Amex

★★ Solway Lodge
Annan Road, Gretna DG16 5DN
☎ 01461-338266 Fax 01461-337791
10 bedrs, all ensuite, TCF TV ✱ P 30 SB £38 DB £53 CC MC Visa Amex DC

Surrone House *Highly Acclaimed*
Annan Road, Gretna DG16 5DL
☎ 01461-338341
7 bedrs, 6 ensuite, TCF TV P 10 SB £32 DB £46 D £9 CC MC Visa Amex

RAC Hotel Reservations Service
0870 603 9109
(Calls charged at national call rate)

HADDINGTON East Lothian 13E2

Brown's *Highly Acclaimed*
1 West Road, Haddington EH41 3RD
☎ 01620-822254 Fax 01620-822254
5 bedrs, all ensuite, **P** 10 **SB** £60 **DB** £80 **D** £27.50 **CC** MC Visa Amex DC ♿

HALKIRK Caithness 15E1

★★ Ulbster Arms
Halkirk KW12 6XY
☎ 01847-831206 Fax 01847-831206
26 bedrs, all ensuite, **TCF TV ⊁ P** 30 **SB** £33 **DB** £55 **D** £18 **CC** MC Visa JCB

HAMILTON Lanarkshire 12C2

Roadchef Lodge *Lodge*
M74 Northbound, Hamilton ML3 6JW
☎ 01698-891904 Fax 01698-891682
Closed 25-27 Dec
36 bedrs, all ensuite, **TCF TV P** 120 **Room only rate** £43.50 **D** £4.50 **CC** MC Visa Amex DC ♿

HAWICK Roxburghshire 13E3

★★ Elm House
17 North Bridge Street, Hawick TD9 9BD
☎ 01450-372866 Fax 01450-374175

A late Victorian house near the city centre converted into a hotel.

15 bedrs, all ensuite, **⊁ P** 11 **SB** £25-£28 **DB** £35-£42 **D** £11 **CC** MC Visa ♿

★★ Kirklands
Comfort merit award
West Stewart Place, Hawick TD9 8BH
☎ 01450-372263 Fax 01450-370404
9 bedrs, all ensuite, **⊁ P** 20 **SB** £40-£52 **DB** £65-£80 **D** £15 **CC** MC Visa Amex DC

★★ Mansfield House
Weensland Road, Hawick TD9 8LB
☎ 01450-373988 Fax 01450-372007
13 bedrs, all ensuite, 1 ⊷ ⊁ **P** 20 **SB** £45 **DB** £70 **D** £15 **CC** MC Visa Amex DC ♿

Kirkton Farmhouse
Hawick TD9 8QJ
☎ 01450-372421
Closed Christmas

A warm welcome awaits you at this family run farmhouse bed and breakfast. Tasty home cooking, open log fire and private loch fishing all available.

3 bedrs, 1 ensuite, 1 ⊷ **TCF ⊁ P** 6 **SB** £20-£24 **DB** £30 **HB** £150 **D** £7

HELENSBURGH Dunbartonshire 12C2

Kirkton House *Highly Acclaimed*
Darleith Road, Cardross G82 5EZ
☎ 01389-841951 Fax 01389-841868
E Mail kirktonhouse@compuserve.com
Closed Christmas-New Year

Set in a tranquil country setting with panoramic views of the Clyde and easy access to Glasgow Airport (14 miles), Kirkton House offers a relaxed atmosphere with home cooked dinners lit by oil lamp.

6 bedrs, all ensuite, **TCF TV ⊁ P** 12 **SB** £38.50 **DB** £31 **HB** £290.50-£308 **D** £19 **CC** MC Visa Amex

HUNTLY Aberdeenshire 15E3

★★ Old Manse of Marnoch
Hospitality, Comfort, Restaurant merit awards
Bridge of Marnoch, Huntly AB54 7RS
☎ 01466-780873 Fax 01466-780873
E Mail manse.marnoch@nest.org.uk
5 bedrs, all ensuite, TCF TV ✕ P 10 No children under 12 SB £54-£60 DB £81-£90 HB £458.50 D £25 CC MC Visa

Castle
Huntly AB54 4SH
☎ 01466-792696 Fax 01466 - 792641

A magnificent 18th century stone building standing above the ruins of Huntly Castle, one mile outside of Huntly. A perfect location for fieldsports, golf and the Whisky Trail.

21 bedrs, all ensuite, TCF TV P 21 CC MC Visa Amex

INNELLAN Argyll 12B2

Osborne *Acclaimed*
Shore Road, Innellan, Dunoon PA23 7TJ
☎ 01369-830445

INVERARAY Argyll 12B1

★★ Great Inn
Inveraray PA32 8XB
☎ 01499-302466 Fax 01499-302421
25 bedrs, 19 ensuite, 2 ✕ ✕ P 30

INVERGARRY Inverness-shire 14C4

Craigard House *Listed*
Invergarry PH35 4HG
☎ 01809-501258
Closed end Oct
7 bedrs, 3 ensuite, 2 ✕ TCF TV ✕ P 10 No children
SB £18-£22 DB £36-£44 HB £231-£259 D £15

INVERNESS Inverness-shire 15D3

★★ Cumming's
Church Street, Inverness IV1 1EW
☎ 01463-232531 Fax 01463-236541
26 bedrs, 24 ensuite, 4 ✕ ✕ ✕ P 25 SB £39-£45
DB £60-£70 D £12 CC MC Visa JCB ✕

Culduthel Lodge *Highly Acclaimed*
14 Culduthel Road, Inverness IV2 4AG
☎ 01463-240089 Fax 01463-240089

Georgian residence set in attractive gardens in a quiet location near the town centre. Ample parking. All rooms individually furnished to a high standard.

12 bedrs, all ensuite, TCF TV ✕ P 12 No children under 10 SB £42 DB £70-£75 HB £330-£365 D £16.95 CC MC Visa

Brae Ness *Acclaimed*
Ness Bank, Inverness IV2 4SF
☎ 01463-712266 Fax 01463-231732

A Georgian residence built in 1830 on the banks of the River Ness, incorporating modern comforts whilst retaining original character.

10 bedrs, 9 ensuite, 1 ✕ P 6 SB £27-£34 DB £46-£60
HB £231-£280 D £16 CC MC Visa ✕

Four Winds *Acclaimed*
42 Old Edinburgh Road, Inverness IV2 3PG
☎ 01463-230397
Closed Christmas-New Year
5 bedrs, all ensuite, 1 ✕ TCF TV P 15 SB £18-£19
DB £36-£38 HB £114-£120 ✕

St Ann's House *Acclaimed*
37 Harrowden Road, Inverness IV3 5QN
📞 **01463-236157 Fax 01463-236157**
Closed Nov-Feb

Quiet family run hotel a few minutes walk from the town centre. All rooms ensuite with private facilities. Restricted licence.

6 bedrs, all ensuite, **TCF TV P** 4 **SB** £20-£25 **DB** £44 **HB** £210-£230 **D** £12

Sunnyholm *Acclaimed*
12 Mayfield Road, Inverness IV2 4AE
📞 **01463-231336**

Large sandstone bungalow set in a mature, secluded garden, five minutes walk from the town centre.

4 bedrs, all ensuite, 1 **TCF TV P** 6 No children under 3 **SB** £22.50-£27 **DB** £34-£38

White Lodge *Acclaimed*
15 Bishops Road, Inverness IV3 5SB
📞 **01463-230693 Fax 01463-230693**

Victorian sandstone double-fronted property with good parking, ten minutes walk from the town centre along the River Ness by the cathedral and theatre.

7 bedrs, all ensuite, **P** 7 No children under 10 **SB** £42-£50 **DB** £36-£42 **CC** MC Visa Amex

---

INVERURIE Aberdeenshire	15F3

★ Grant Arms
Monymusk, Inverurie AB51 7HJ
📞 **01467-651226 Fax 01467-651494**
17 bedrs, 8 ensuite, **TCF**
SB £35 **DB** £57-£62 **CC** Visa Amex

IRVINE Ayrshire	12C3

★★ Redburn
65 Kilwinning Road, Irvine KA12 8SU
📞 **01294-276792 Fax 01294-76651**
28 bedrs, 13 ensuite, 5 **TCF TV P** 100 **SB** £24-£29 **DB** £46-£62 **D** £7 **CC** MC Visa Amex DC

ISLE OF ARRAN	12B2

★★ Lagg
Kilmory KA27 8PQ
📞 **01770-870255 Fax 01770-870250**
15 bedrs, all ensuite, 1 **TCF P** 40 **SB** £30-£42 **DB** £60-£84 **HB** £270-£330 **D** £16 **CC** MC Visa Amex JCB

Invermay *Acclaimed*
Shore Road, Whiting Bay KA27 8PZ
📞 **017707-700431**
Closed Nov-Mar
7 bedrs, 5 ensuite, 3 **TCF P** 10 **SB** £24 **DB** £48 **HB** £230 **D** £11

ISLE OF BUTE	12B2

★★ Ardmory House
Hospitality, Restaurant merit awards
Ardmory Road, Ardbeg PA20 0PG
📞 **01700-502346 Fax 01700-505596**
E Mail ardmory.house.hotel@dial.pipex.com
5 bedrs, all ensuite, **TCF TV P** 12 **SB** £35 **DB** £60 **HB** £290 **D** £16.50 **CC** MC Visa Amex DC JCB

Ardyne-St Ebba *Highly Acclaimed*
38 Mountstuart Road, Rothesay PA20 9EB
📞 **01700-502052 Fax 01700-505129**
21 bedrs, all ensuite, **TCF TV P** 3 **SB** £26-£28 **DB** £46-£50 **HB** £205-£225 **D** £12 **CC** MC Visa Amex

ISLE OF HARRIS	14A2

★★ Harris
Harris, Isle of Harris H53 3DL
📞 **01859-502154 Fax 01859-502281**
E Mail postmaster@tarbert.abel.co.uk
25 bedrs, 16 ensuite, 5 **TV P** 30 **SB** £28-£30 **DB** £56-£58 **HB** £205-£210 **D** £17 **CC** MC Visa Amex JCB

ISLE OF ISLAY   12A2

★★ Port Askaig
Port Askaig PA46 7RD
☎ 01496-840245 Fax 01496-840295
10 bedrs, 6 ensuite, 2 ⇨ TCF TV ★ P 12 No children under 5 **SB** £35-£39 **DB** £66-£72 **HB** £330-£375 **D** £18 ♿

ISLE OF LEWIS   14B1

Galson Farm *Acclaimed*
South Galson HS2 0SH
☎ 01851-850492 Fax 01851-850492

Be assured of a warm welcome at our 18th century farmhouse on the Atlantic coast. Ten miles from the Butt of Lewis. Home cooking and licensed. A no smoking establishment.

3 bedrs, all ensuite, 1 ⇨ TCF ⊠ ★ P 5 **SB** £29 **DB** £58 **HB** £299 **D** £16 **CC** MC Visa

ISLE OF SKYE   14A3

★★ Ardvasar
Hospitality, Comfort merit awards
Ardvarsar IV48 8RS
☎ 01471-844223
Closed Dec-Mar
9 bedrs, all ensuite, TCF TV P 30 **SB** £35-£40 **DB** £60-£70 **D** £20 **CC** MC Visa

★★ Rosedale
Hospitality, Comfort merit awards
Quay Brae, Portree IV51 9DB
☎ 01478-613131 Fax 01478-612531
Closed Oct-Apr
23 bedrs, all ensuite, TCF TV ★ P 18 **SB** £35-£45 **DB** £70-£90 **HB** £355-£450 **D** £22.50 **CC** MC Visa

★★ Royal
Bank Street, Portree IV51 9BU
☎ 01478-612525 Fax 01478-613198
24 bedrs, all ensuite, TCF TV ★ P 20 **SB** £35-£45 **DB** £55-£70 **D** £18 **CC** MC Visa

★★ Uig
Uig IV51 9YE
☎ 01470-542205 Fax 01470-542308
17 bedrs, all ensuite, TCF TV ★ P 20 **SB** £30-£45 **DB** £60-£90 **D** £20 **CC** MC Visa Amex DC

★ Ferry Inn
Hospitality, Comfort merit awards
Uig IV51 9XP
☎ 01470-542242
Closed 1-2 Jan
6 bedrs, all ensuite, TCF TV ★ P 12 **SB** £25-£30 **DB** £50-£56 **D** £15 **CC** MC Visa

★ Hotel Eilean Iarmain
Hospitality, Comfort, Restaurant merit awards
Sleat IV43 8QR
☎ 01471-833332 Fax 01471-833275
12 bedrs, all ensuite, TCF TV ★ P 30 **SB** £63-£70 **DB** £86-£95 **HB** £580-£645 **D** £28.50 **CC** MC Visa Amex

★ Isles
Somerled Square, Portree IV51 9EH
☎ 01478-612129
Closed Oct-Apr
9 bedrs, 7 ensuite, TCF TV No children **SB** £25-£27 **DB** £56-£70 **CC** MC Visa

Roskhill *Acclaimed*
Rosskill, By Dunvegan IV55 8ZD
☎ 01470-521317 Fax 01470-521761

A traditional Croft house in an ideal location for touring this magical island. Delicious home cooked meals are served in the stone walled dining room with log fire and bar. Your home away from home.

5 bedrs, 1 ensuite, 1 ⇨ TCF ⊠ ★ P 6 No children under 10 **SB** £49-£64 **DB** £273-£325 **D** £14.50 **CC** MC Visa

JEDBURGH Roxburghshire   13E3

Ferniehirst Mill Lodge *Acclaimed*
Jedburgh TD8 6PQ
☎ 01835-863279

Situated two and a half miles south of Jedburgh on the A68, this modern, purpose-built guest house is set in 25 acres overlooking the River Jed.

9 bedrs, all ensuite, 1 🛏 TCF 🐕 P 10
SB £23 DB £46 HB £238 D £14
CC MC Visa 🎵 ⛰

Froylehurst
Friars, Jedburgh TD8 6BN
📞 01835-862477 Fax 01835-862477
Closed Dec-Jan

Detached Victorian house in large garden. Spacious guest rooms. Two minutes from and overlooking town centre in quiet residential area. Private parking. Children over 5 welcome.

5 bedrs, 2 🛏 TCF TV P 5 No children under 5 DB £32-£34

JOHN O'GROATS Caithness 15E1

Bencorragh House *Acclaimed*
Upper Gills, Canisbay KW1 4YB
📞 01955-611449 Fax 01955-611449
Closed Nov-Mar
4 bedrs, all ensuite, TCF 🐕 SB £20-£23 DB £36-£37 D £8
CC MC Visa

KILFINAN Argyll 12B2

★★ Kilfinan
Hospitality, Comfort, Restaurant merit awards
Kilfinan PA21 2EP
📞 01700-821201 Fax 01700-821205
Closed Feb
13 bedrs, all ensuite, TV P 50 No children under 12
SB £48 DB £72 D £26
CC MC Visa Amex 🎵 ⛰

KILMARNOCK Ayrshire 12C3

Muirhouse Farm
Gatehead, Kilmarnock KA2 0BT
📞 01563-523975

Comfortable traditional farmhouse in rural surroundings. Convenient for Kilmarnock, the Ayrshire coast and numerous golf courses. Two rooms ensuite and one with private bathroom.

3 bedrs, 2 ensuite, 1 🛏 TCF TV 🐕 P 5 SB £17 DB £34 ♿

KINCARDINE O'NEIL Aberdeenshire 15F4

Gordon Arms
North Deeside Road, Kincardine O'Neil AB34 5AA
📞 013398-84236 Fax 013398-84401
Closed 1 Jan

Family run hotel in Royal Deeside's oldest village. Extensive menus including lunch, supper, dinner, vegetarian/vegan. Real ales. Family rooms available. Centrally located for touring all of Grampian area.

7 bedrs, 6 ensuite, 2 🛏 TCF TV 🐕 P 7 No children under 1 SB £20-£30 DB £32-£45 HB £195 D £4.15 CC MC Visa Amex

KINGUSSIE Inverness-shire 15D4

★★ Royal
29 High Street, Kingussie PH21 1HX
📞 01540-661898 Fax 01540-661061
54 bedrs, all ensuite, TCF TV 🐕 P 10 SB £20-£32 DB £32-£54 HB £198 D £12 CC MC Visa Amex DC ♿

KINROSS Kinross-shire 13D1

★★ Kirklands
20 High Street, Kinross KY13 7AN
📞 01557-863313 Fax 01577-863313
9 bedrs, all ensuite, TCF TV P 12 SB £39 DB £60-£70
HB £250-£300 D £11 CC MC Visa Amex

KIRKCUDBRIGHT Kirkcudbrightshire 12C4

★★ Selkirk Arms
Restaurant merit award
Old High Street, Kirkcudbright DG6 4JG
☎ 01557-330402 Fax 01557-331639
16 bedrs, all ensuite, TCF TV P 16 SB £49 DB £80
HB £300 D £19.75 CC MC Visa Amex DC JCB &

Gladstone House
48 High Street, Kirkcudbright DG6 4JX
☎ 01557-331734 Fax 01557-331734

Award winning Georgian guest house in a quiet conservation area, close to the harbour, castle and restaurants. Quality accommodation and a warm welcome.

3 bedrs, all ensuite, 1 ⇒ TCF TV ⊠ No children under 12 SB £30-£34 DB £50-£58 CC MC Visa

KIRKMICHAEL Perthshire 15E4

★★ Log Cabin
Kirkmichael PH10 7NB
☎ 01250-881288 Fax 01250-881402
Closed 25-26 Dec
13 bedrs, all ensuite, TCF TV ⇒ P 50 CC MC Visa Amex DC ◻ ▨ &

KYLESKU Sutherland 14C1

Newton Lodge
Kylesku IV27 4HW
☎ 01971-502070
Closed mid Oct-mid Mar

For tranquillity and superb scenery enjoy your stay in this quality guest house. Seafood is the menu speciality. Bring your binoculars as the hotel overlooks a small seal colony.

7 bedrs, all ensuite, TCF TV ⇒ P 10 No children DB £52-£60 D £12 CC MC Visa

LARGS Ayrshire 12B2

★★ Queens
North Promenade, Largs KA30 8QW
☎ 01475-675311 Fax 01475-675313
16 bedrs, 2 ⇒ TCF TV P 30 SB £40 DB £60 CC MC

★★ Springfield
North Bay, Largs KA30 8QL
☎ 01475-673119 Fax 01475-673119
58 bedrs, all ensuite, 4 ⇒ TCF TV ⇒ ▣ P 60 SB £50
DB £69.50 HB £295 D £15 CC MC Visa Amex DC

LAUDER Berwickshire 13E2

Grange
6 Edinburgh Road, Lauder TD2 6TW
☎ 01578-722649 Fax 01578-722649

Large comfortable detached private house in own grounds, overlooking the rolling Lammermuir Hills. Located on the A68 and therefore ideal for visiting Edinburgh and all of the Scottish Border country.

3 bedrs, 1 ⇒ TCF ⊠ P 4 SB £15-£20 DB £30-£32

LERWICK Shetland Islands 13F2

Glen Orchy House
20 Knab Road, Lerwick ZE1 0AX
☎ 01595-692031 Fax 01595-692031

Situated on the south side of Lerwick adjoining 9 hole golf course free to the public. Close to town centre and harbour. Licensed with excellent cuisine. Satellite TV in all rooms.

14 bedrs, all ensuite, TCF TV

LOCHEARNHEAD Perthshire 12C1

★★ Clachan Cottage
Lochearnhead FK19 8PU
☎ 01567-830247 Fax 01567-830300
21 bedrs, all ensuite, TCF ⚡ P 50 SB £27 DB £54 HB £269 D £18 CC MC Visa

LOCHGILPHEAD Argyll 12B2

★★ Stag
Argyll Street, Lochgilphead PA31 8NE
☎ 01546-602496 Fax 01546-603549
17 bedrs, all ensuite, TCF TV ⚡ SB £33-£35 DB £60-£64 D £12.50 CC MC Visa

LOCHMABEN Dumfriesshire 13D4

★★ Balcastle
High Street, Lochmaben DG11 1NG
☎ 01387-810239
5 bedrs, all ensuite, ⚡ P 100 CC MC Visa

LOCHMADDY North Uist 14A2

★★ Lochmaddy
Lochmaddy HS6 5AA
☎ 01876-500331 Fax 01876-500210
15 bedrs, all ensuite, 1 ⚡ TCF TV ⚡ P 30 SB £32.50-£40 DB £60-£75 HB £294-£357 D £14.50 CC MC Visa Amex

LOCKERBIE Dumfriesshire 13D4

★★ Somerton House
Carlisle Road, Lockerbie DG11 2DR
☎ 01576-202583 Fax 01576-204218
7 bedrs, all ensuite, ⚡ P 100

Ravenshill House
Dumfries Road, Lockerbie DG11 2EF
☎ 01576-202882 Fax 01576-202882

A family owned hotel with the chef-proprietor providing comfortable ensuite accommodation. Situated in its own grounds, half a mile from the town centre and the A74M. An ideal touring base.

8 bedrs, all ensuite, 1 ⚡ TCF TV ⚡ P 30 SB £35 DB £50 HB £224 D £10.25 CC MC Visa Amex DC

LOSSIEMOUTH Morayshire 15E2

Skerryhill
63 Dunbar Street, Lossiemouth IV31 6AN
☎ 01343-813035

Modern, centrally heated bungalow near beaches, golf courses and bowling green. Tea and coffee making facilities and colour TV in all rooms. Guests' lounge overlooking Moray Firth.

4 bedrs, 2 ⚡ TCF TV ⚡ SB £14-£16 DB £28-£32 ♿

SOMERTON HOUSE

The elegantly furnished bedrooms comprise single, double and family accommodation. Each bedroom is ensuite, has direct dial telephone, colour television and tea/cofee facilities and most have pleasant views over the gardens and surrounding countryside.

**Carlisle Road, Lockerbie, Dumfriesshire DG11 2DR
Tel: 01576-202583 Fax: 01576-204218**

MALLAIG Inverness-shire　　　　14B4

★★ Marine
Station Road, Mallaig PH41 4PY
☎ 01687-462217 Fax 01687-462821
19 bedrs, all ensuite, TCF TV P 6 SB £25-£35 DB £52-£60 D £17 CC　MC Visa

★★ Morar
Mallaig PH40 4PA
☎ 01687-462346 Fax 01687-462212
28 bedrs, all ensuite, P 100 SB £30-£35 DB £60-£70 D £17 CC　MC Visa

★★ West Highland
Mallaig PH41 4QZ
☎ 01687-462210 Fax 01687-462130
Closed Oct-Mar
34 bedrs, all ensuite, 3 P 40 SB £25-£32 DB £50-£64 HB £287-£308 D £16.50 CC　MC Visa

MAYBOLE Ayrshire　　　　12C3

★★ Ladyburn
Ladyburn, Maybole KA19 7SG
☎ 01655-740585 Fax 01655-740580
Closed Nov-Mar
8 bedrs, 7 ensuite, 1 P 12 No children
CC　MC Visa Amex

MELROSE Roxburghshire　　　　13E3

★★ George & Abbotsford
High Street, Melrose TD6 9PD
☎ 01896-822308 Fax 01896-823363
31 bedrs, all ensuite, 1 TCF TV P 150 SB £44-£48 DB £79-£93 CC　MC Visa Amex DC

King's Arms
High Street, Melrose TD6 9PB
☎ 01896-822143

Situated in the heart of historic Melrose, a former coaching inn, modernised to provide ensuite bedrooms, with superb eating facilities and menus.

7 bedrs, all ensuite, TCF TV P 12 SB £35-£37 DB £55-£65 HB £245-£260 D £12 CC　MC Visa

MEY Caithness　　　　15E1

★★ Castle Arms
Mey, Thurso KW14 8XH
☎ 01847-851244 Fax 01847-851244
8 bedrs, all ensuite, TCF TV P 30 SB £35-£39 DB £52-£58 HB £234-£257 D £16 CC　MC Visa Amex ♿

MOFFAT Dumfriesshire　　　　13D3

★★ Annandale
High Street, Moffat DG10 9HF
☎ 01683-220013 Fax 01683-221395
19 bedrs, 11 ensuite, 2, 2 TCF TV P 70 CC　MC Visa Amex ♿

★★ Balmoral
High Street, Moffat DG10 9DL
☎ 01683-220288 Fax 01683-220451
Closed 25-26 Dec
16 bedrs, 6 ensuite, 3 TCF TV P 12 SB £26-£35 DB £40-£50 D £8.60 CC　MC Visa

★★ Beechwood Country House
Hospitality, Comfort, Restaurant merit awards
Harthope Place, Moffat DG10 9RS
☎ 01683-220210 Fax 01683-220889
Closed Jan-14 Feb
7 bedrs, all ensuite, TCF TV P 12 SB £51 DB £72 HB £-£340 D £22.50 CC　MC Visa Amex

★ Star
44 High Street, Moffat DG10 9EF
☎ 01683-220156 Fax 01683-221524
8 bedrs, all ensuite, 1 TCF TV SB £28-£38 DB £38-£56 D £6 CC　MC Visa

Well View *Highly Acclaimed*
Ballplay Road, Moffat DG1O 9JU
☎ 01683-220184 Fax 01683-220088
6 bedrs, all ensuite, TCF TV P 8 SB £40-£46 DB £58-£78 HB £378-£483 D £26 CC　MC Visa Amex

Arden House *Acclaimed*
High Street, Moffat DG10 9HG
☎ 01683-220220
Closed Mar-Oct
8 bedrs, 4 ensuite, 2 TCF TV P 10 SB £19 DB £32-£38 HB £161-£175 D £8 ♿

Gilbert House *Acclaimed*
Beechgrove, Old Edinburgh Road, Moffat DG10 9RS
☎ 01683-220050

A detached Victorian house in a quiet residential area close to the town centre, and offering comfortably furnished good value accommodation.

6 bedrs, 5 ensuite, 1 ↺, TCF ⚘ P 6 SB £18-£20 DB £36-£40 HB £187-£199 D £10.50 CC MC Visa

Waterside
Moffat DG10 9LF
☎ 01683-220092
Closed Oct-Easter

Victorian country house, tastefully decorated and set in 12 acres of woodland garden, with its own river. Peacocks, poultry (own eggs) and donkeys. Moffat three miles. Open Easter to end September.

4 bedrs, 1 ensuite, 2 ⚘ TCF TV ⌧ P 4 SB £18 DB £36-£40 ⚘

MONIAIVE Dumfriesshire   12C3

★★ Woodlea
Moniaive DG3 4EN
☎ 01848-200209 Fax 01848-200412
Closed Oct-Easter
12 bedrs, 10 ensuite, 1 ⚘ TCF TV ⚘ P 20 ⚘ ⚘ ⚘ ⚘

NAIRN Nairnshire   15D3

★★ Alton Burn
Alton Burn Road, Nairn IV12 5ND
☎ 01667-452051 Fax 01667-456697

Stone-built hotel, with extensions, on edge of town; views over Moray Firth.

25 bedrs, all ensuite, 2 ⚘ TCF TV ⚘ P 30 SB £30-£35 DB £50-£60 HB £245-£280 D £15.75 CC MC Visa Amex ⚘ ⚘ ⚘

NEW ABBEY Kircudbrightshire   13D4

Cavens *Highly Acclaimed*
Kirkbean, New Abbey DG2 8AA
☎ 01387-880234 Fax 01387-880234
6 bedrs, all ensuite, TCF TV ⚘ P 10 SB £27-£35 DB £44-£59 HB £200-£245 D £17 CC MC Visa ⚘ ⚘

NEW GALLOWAY Kirkcudbrightshire   12C4

★ Kenmure Arms
High Street, New Galloway DG7 3RL
☎ 01644-420240

NEWTON STEWART Wigtownshire   12C4

★★ Crown
101 Queen Street, Newton Stewart DG8 6JW
☎ 01671-402727 Fax 01671-402727
11 bedrs, 10 ensuite, 1 ⚘ TCF TV ⚘ P 20 SB £25-£30 DB £50-£60 HB £238-£250 D £14 CC MC Visa ⚘

Belmont
St John Street, Whithorn, Newton Stewart DG8 8PG
☎ 01988-500890

Comfortable family home in beautiful and interesting area. Optional evening meals. French spoken. Welcome Host Certificate held.

3 bedrs, 2 ⚘ TCF TV ⌧ ⚘ P 6 No children under 7
SB £15-£17 DB £30-£34 HB £150.50-£174.50 D £6.50

NEWTONMORE Inverness-shire 15D4

★★ Glen
Main Street, Newtonmore PH20 1DD
📞 01540-673203
9 bedrs, 5 ensuite, 2 🐕 P 15 CC MC Visa Amex DC

★★ Mains
Mains Street, Newtonmore PH20 1DE
📞 01540-673206 Fax 01540-673881
31 bedrs, all ensuite, TV 🐕 P 35 SB £22-£25 DB £34-£40 D £12 CC MC Visa 🐾 ♿

NORTH BERWICK East Lothian 13E2

★★ Nether Abbey
Dirleton Avenue, North Berwick EH39 4BQ
📞 01620-892802 Fax 01620-895298
16 bedrs, 11 ensuite, 3 🛏, 2 🐕 TCF TV 🐕 P 60 SB £35-£46 DB £50-£72 D £14 CC MC Visa ♿

OBAN Argyll 12B1

★★ Argyll
Corran Esplanade, Oban PA34 5PZ
📞 01631-562353 Fax 01631-565472
27 bedrs, all ensuite, 🐕 P 6 SB £30-£35 DB £57-£65 D £15.50 CC MC Visa Amex DC

★★ Falls Of Lora
Connel, Oban PA37 1PB
📞 01631-710483 Fax 01631-710694
Closed Christmas-Jan
30 bedrs, all ensuite, 2 🐕 TCF TV 🐕 P 40 SB £30-£50 DB £39-£99 D £15 CC MC Visa Amex DC ♿

★★ King's Knoll
Dunollie Road, Oban PA34 5JH
📞 01631-562536 Fax 01631-566101
Closed 25 Dec-31 Jan
15 bedrs, 13 ensuite, 1 🐕 TCF TV 🐕 P 20 SB £18-£30 DB £40-£58 HB £225-£260 D £14 CC MC Visa ♿

★★ Lancaster
Hospitality merit award
Corran Esplanade, Oban PA34 5AD
📞 01631-562587 Fax 01631-562587
27 bedrs, 24 ensuite, 3 🐕 TCF TV 🐕 P 20 SB £25-£30 DB £54-£58 HB £157-£189 D £10 CC MC Visa 🛏 📺 🐾

Foxholes *Highly Acclaimed*
Cologin, Lerags, Oban PA34 4SE
📞 01631-564982
Closed Nov-Mar

Situated in its own grounds in a quiet glen three miles from Oban.

7 bedrs, all ensuite, TCF TV P 8 SB £34-£36 DB £50-£54 HB £259-£276 CC MC Visa

Ardblair *Acclaimed*
Dalriach Road, Oban PA34 5JB
📞 01631-562668 Fax 01631-562668
Closed Oct-Apr
14 bedrs, 13 ensuite, 1 🛏, 1 🐕 TCF TV P 10 SB £20-£22.50 DB £40-£45 HB £190-£200 D £9

Briarbank *Acclaimed*
Glencruitten Road, Oban PA34 4DN
📞 01631-566549
Closed 25 Dec

Detached traditional house enjoying a high degree of privacy and offering a friendly ambience. Views from all rooms. Ensuite bedrooms, two fourposter beds. International cuisine. Close to ferries.

3 bedrs, all ensuite, 1 🐕 TCF TV 🚭 P 4 No children under 15 DB £40-£44 D £8

Drumriggend *Acclaimed*
Drummore Road,, Oban PA34 4JL
📞 01631-563330 Fax 01631-563330

Situated in a quiet residential setting only 15 minutes from the city centre. All rooms are ensuite with welcome tray, colour TV, radio alarm and central heating.

3 bedrs, all ensuite, TCF TV 🐾 P 6 DB £32-£40 HB £135-£180 D £7

Glenbervie *Acclaimed*
Dalriach Road, Oban PA34 5JD
📞 01631-564770
8 bedrs, 5 ensuite, 2 🐾 TCF TV P 6 No children under 5 SB £18-£22 DB £18-£22 D £8 ♿

Roseneath *Acclaimed*
Dalriach Road, Oban PA34 5EQ
📞 01631-562929
Closed Nov-Jan
10 bedrs, 6 ensuite, 2 🐾, 2 ⚄ TCF TV ⊠ P 8 No children SB £16-£19 DB £34-£44

Sgeir-mhaol *Acclaimed*
Soroba Road, Oban PA34 4JF
📞 01631-562650 Fax 01631-562650

Family run guest house with dining room, lounge and a bedroom all on the ground floor overlooking a pleasant garden. Large private car park within the grounds.

7 bedrs, 5 ensuite, 1 ⚄ TCF TV P 11 SB £18-£26 DB £36-£42 D £9 ♿

Craigvarran House *Listed*
Ardconnel Road, Oban PA34 5DJ
📞 01631-562686
Closed Dec-Jan
8 bedrs, 2 ⚄ TCF TV 🐾 P 10 SB £16-£18 DB £32-£40 D £8

ONICH Inverness-shire   14C4

★★ Loch Leven
North Ballachulish, Onich PH33 6SA
📞 01855-821236
10 bedrs, all ensuite, TCF TV 🐾 P 60 CC MC Visa

Tigh-a-righ *Listed*
Onich PH33 6SE
📞 01855-821255
Closed Oct-Feb
6 bedrs, 🐾 P 20 ♿

PAISLEY Renfrewshire   12C2

★★ Brabloch
62 Renfrew Road, Paisley PA3 4RD
📞 0141-889 5577 Fax 0141-561 7012
30 bedrs, all ensuite, 🐾 P 140 SB £45-£54 DB £60-£74 D £15 CC MC Visa Amex DC

Ashburn *Listed*
Milliken Park Road, Kilbarchan, Paisley PA10 2DB
📞 01505-705477 Fax 01505-705477
6 bedrs, 2 ensuite, 2 ⚄ CC MC Visa

PEEBLES Peeblesshire   13D2

★★ Venlaw Castle
Edinburgh Road, Peebles EH45 8QG
📞 01721-720384
12 bedrs, 10 ensuite, 2 ⚄ 🐾 P 20 SB £36-£38 DB £48-£70 HB £300-£310 D £11 CC MC Visa Amex DC

PERTH Perthshire   13D1

★★★ Kinfauns Castle
Hospitality, Comfort merit awards
Kinfauns, Perth PH2 7JZ
📞 01738-620777 Fax 01738-620778
16 bedrs, all ensuite, TCF TV SB £70-£150 DB £140-£240
CC MC Visa Amex DC

Kingfauns Castle

An abundance of fascinating Heritage. The Castle stands in 26 acres of Parkland situated near Perth on the A90. The Castle's renovation can clearly be seen in the individually decorated 16 bedrooms all with Verona Rosa Marble bathrooms, EL, Safe, Trouser Press, Bathrobe, Mini Bar, Hair dryers, two direct dial telephones to a room and Gas Log Fires etc.
The cuisine is already renowned and the Library Restaurant is open for Lunch and Dinner.

NR. PERTH PH2 7JZ
Tel: 01738 620777   Fax: 01738 620778

★★ Salutation
South Street, Perth PH2 8PH
📞 01738-630066 Fax 01738-633598
84 bedrs, all ensuite, TCF TV 🐕 SB £59-£63 DB £74-£80
D £15 CC MC Visa Amex

Achnacarry *Acclaimed*
3 Pitcullen Crescent, Perth PH2 7HT
📞 01738-621421 Fax 01738-444110

A Victorian house, tastefully decorated, offering a warm friendly atmosphere. All rooms are ensuite and the breakfast menu has a Scottish flavour. Ten minutes walk from the city centre.

4 bedrs, all ensuite, TCF TV 🐕 P 7 No children under 5 DB £39-£42 CC MC Visa Amex

Clunie *Acclaimed*
12 Pitcullen Crescent, Perth PH2 7HT
📞 01738-623625
7 bedrs, all ensuite, TCF TV 🐕 P 9 SB £16-£20 DB £32-£40 HB £210 D £10 CC MC Visa Amex DC

Iona Guest House *Acclaimed*
2 Pitcullen Crescent, Perth PH2 7HT
📞 01738-627261 Fax 01738-444098
5 bedrs, 3 ensuite, TCF TV 🐕 P 6 SB £16-£20 DB £32-£40 HB £160-£200 D £9 CC MC Visa DC

Pitcullen *Acclaimed*
17 Pitcullen Crescent, Perth PH2 7HT
📞 01738-626506 Fax 01738-628265

An attractive guest house situated in a residential district, yet only minutes away from Perth's city centre and nearby Scone Palace. All bedrooms are ensuite. Private parking is available.

6 bedrs, all ensuite, 1 🛁 TCF TV P 6 SB £22-£28 DB £40-£50 CC MC Visa

Park Lane
17 Marshall Place, Perth PH2 8AG
📞 01738-637218 Fax 01738-643519
Closed Dec-Jan

Elegant old Georgian house overlooking park next to town centre. Rooms are ensuite, TV, hairdryer, tea/coffee, flowers. Parking. Few minutes bus/rail.

6 bedrs, all ensuite, TCF TV P 7 SB £20-£24 DB £40-£48 CC MC Visa Amex

Yarrow House
Moray Street, Blackford, Auchterader PH4 1PY
📞 01764-682358

Small family run B&B in village setting. All rooms have TV, tea/coffee facilities. Guest lounge and private parking available. Ideal base for touring and golfing.

3 bedrs, 1 ensuite, 1 🛁 TCF TV 🐕 P 3 SB £15-£17 DB £30-£34 HB £105-£120

PITLOCHRY Perthshire   15D4

★★ Acarsaid
8 Atholl Road, Pitlochry PH16 5BX
📞 01796-472389 Fax 01796-473952
Closed Jan-Mar
18 bedrs, all ensuite, 2 🛁 TCF TV P 20 No children under 10 SB £25-£39 DB £50-£77 HB £230-£310 D £14 CC MC Visa ♿

★★ Balrobin
Higher Oakfield, Pitlochry PH16 5HT
☎ 01796-472901 Fax 01796-474200
Closed Nov-Feb
16 bedrs, 15 ensuite, 1 ⮕ TCF TV ⛔ P 16 No children under 5 SB £25-£35 DB £48-£64 HB £245-£301 D £15 CC MC Visa

★★ Birchwood
Restaurant merit award
2 East Moulin Road, Pitlochry PH16 5DW
☎ 01796-472477 Fax 01796-473951
Closed Dec-Feb
17 bedrs, all ensuite, TCF TV ⛔ P 25 SB £30-£38 DB £60-£76 HB £335-£365 D £20 CC MC Visa Amex

★★ Moulin
Kirkmichael Road, Pitlochry PH16 5EW
☎ 01796-472196 Fax 01796-474098
16 bedrs, all ensuite, 2 ⮕ TCF TV ⛔ P 30 CC MC Visa

★★ Westlands of Pitlochry
Hospitality, Comfort merit awards
160 Atholl Road, Pitlochry PH16 5AR
☎ 01796-472266 Fax 01796-473994
15 bedrs, all ensuite, TCF TV ⛔ P 30 SB £25-£39 DB £49-£78 HB £288-£381 D £18 CC MC Visa

Knockendarroch House *Highly Acclaimed*
Higher Oakfield, Pitlochry PH16 5HT
☎ 01796-473473 Fax 01796-474068
E Mail knock@dial.pipex.com
Closed mid Nov-1 Mar
12 bedrs, all ensuite, TCF TV ✉ P 15 DB £50-£70 HB £224-£301 D £21 CC MC Visa Amex

Dalnasgadh House *Listed*
Killiecrankie, Pitlochry PH16 5LN
☎ 01796-473237
Closed Oct-Easter

Attractive country house in two acres amidst magnificent Highland scenery. Only seven minutes from Pitlochry. Easy touring distance to Queen's View, Loch Tummel, Balmoral, Braemar, Glamis Castle, Scone Palace and Aviemore.

5 bedrs, 2 ⮕ TCF ✉ P 10 No children under 12 SB £18-£20 DB £36-£37

Craigroyston House
2 Lower Oakfield, Pitlochry PH16 5HQ
☎ 01796-472053 Fax 01796-472053

A Victorian country house set in own grounds, centrally situated with direct access to town centre. All rooms ensuite and equipped to high standard.

8 bedrs, all ensuite, TCF TV P 8 SB £18-£27 DB £36-£54

PORTPATRICK Wigtownshire   12B4

★ Mount Stewart
South Crescent, Portpatrick DG9 8LE
☎ 01776-810291
8 bedrs, 4 ensuite, 2 ⮕ TCF TV ⛔ P 15 SB £18-£24 DB £36-£48 D £15 CC MC Visa

PRESTWICK Ayrshire   12C3

★★ Manor Park
Kilmarnock Road, Monkton By Prestwick Airport, Prestwick KA9 2RJ
☎ 01292-479365 Fax 01292-479365
12 bedrs, all ensuite, ⛔ P 80 CC MC Visa Amex

★★ North Beach
5-7 Links Road, Prestwick KA9 1QG
☎ 01292-479069
12 bedrs, all ensuite, TCF TV ⛔ P 20 CC MC Visa Amex

Golf View *Highly Acclaimed*
17 Links Road, Prestwick KA9 1QG
☎ 01292-671234 Fax 01292-671244

Golf View is a small family run hotel overlooking old Prestwick Golf Course, offering elegantly furnished accommodation and full Scottish breakfast at affordable prices.

6 bedrs, all ensuite, 1 ⮕ TCF TV ⛔ P 8 No children under 12 SB £27-£30 DB £54-£60 CC MC Visa

Fernbank *Acclaimed*
213 Main Street, Prestwick KA9 1LH
📞 **01292-475027 Fax 01292-475027**
E Mail fernbank@btinternet.com
7 bedrs, 4 ensuite, 2 ➡ TCF TV ☒ P 7 No children under 5 **SB** £16-£18 **DB** £35-£39

Kincraig *Acclaimed*
39 Ayr Road, Prestwick KA9 1SY
📞 **01292-479480**
8 bedrs, 7 ensuite, 1 ➡ TCF TV P 8 **CC** MC Visa

Braemar *Listed*
113 Ayr Road, Prestwick KA9 1TN
📞 **01292-475820**

RHU Dunbartonshire   12C2

★★ Ardencaple
Shore Road, Rhu G84 8LA
📞 **01436-820200 Fax 01436-821099**
25 bedrs, all ensuite, TCF TV 🐕 P 50 **SB** £41 **DB** £62.50 **D** £14 **CC** MC Visa Amex DC ♿

ROGART Sutherland   15D2

Benview
Lower Morness, Rogart IV28 3XG
📞 **01408-641222**
Closed 28 Oct

Traditional country farmhouse, offering peace and quiet, comfort, good food and friendly, personal attention. Accommodation comprises smoking lounge, TV lounge and dining room. Ideal base for trips to all coasts, hill walking, golfing and fishing.

3 bedrs, 1 🛁, 1 ➡ TCF No children under 10 **SB** £14-£15 **D** £10

ROSYTH Fife   13D2

★★ Gladyer Inn
10 Heath Road/Ridley Drive, Rosyth KY11 2BT
📞 **01383-419977 Fax 01383-411728**
21 bedrs, all ensuite, TCF TV 🐕 P 97 **SB** £35 **DB** £55 **D** £14 **CC** MC Visa Amex 🚭 ♿

SCOURIE Sutherland   14C1

★★ Scourie
Hospitality merit award
Scourie IV27 4SX
📞 **01971-502396 Fax 01971-502423**
Closed 15 Oct-Mar
20 bedrs, 18 ensuite, 1 ➡ TCF 🐕 P 30 **SB** £32-£44 **DB** £54-£78 **D** £14.50 **CC** MC Visa Amex DC JCB

SHIELDAIG Ross-shire   14B3

★ Tigh An Eilean
Hospitality, Comfort, Restaurant merit awards
Shieldaig IV54 8XN
📞 **01520-755251 Fax 01520-755321**
Closed late Oct-Apr
11 bedrs, all ensuite, 1 ➡ TCF 🐕 P 11 **SB** £45.75 **DB** £100.50 **D** £21.50 **CC** MC Visa 🚭

SPEAN BRIDGE Inverness-shire   14C4

★★ Letterfinlay Lodge
Hospitality merit award
Lochlochy, Spean Bridge PH34 4DZ
📞 **01397-712622**
Closed Nov-Feb
13 bedrs, 9 ensuite, 4 ➡ TCF TV 🐕 P 100 **SB** £23.50-£38.50 **DB** £47-£77 **HB** £300-£375 **D** £18.50 **CC** MC Visa Amex DC 🚭

ST ANDREWS Fife   13E1

★★ Ardgowan
2 Playfair Terrace, St Andrews KY16 9HX
📞 **01334-472970 Fax 01334-478380**
Closed mid Dec-mid Jan
13 bedrs, 11 ensuite, 1 🛁, 1 ➡ TCF TV 🐕 **SB** £25-£40 **DB** £40-£64 **D** £23 **CC** MC Visa

★★ Parkland
Double Dykes Road, St Andrews KY16 9DS
📞 **01334-473620 Fax 01334-473620**
Closed Christmas & New Year
15 bedrs, 8 ensuite, 3 ➡ TCF TV P 15 **SB** £30-£40 **DB** £50-£70 **HB** £308 **D** £16.50 **CC** MC Visa

Amberside *Acclaimed*
4 Murray Park, St Andrews KY16 9AW
📞 **01334-474644**
6 bedrs, 5 ensuite, 1 ➡ TCF TV **SB** £18-£27 **DB** £36-£52 **CC** MC Visa Amex

Argyle *Acclaimed*
127 North Street, St Andrews KY16 9AG
📞 **01334-473387 Fax 01334-474664**

Arran House *Acclaimed*
5 Murray Park, St Andrews KY16 9AW
☎ 01334-474724 Fax 01382-779081

Arran House is a small family run guest house, beautifully appointed between the town centre and golf courses. All rooms have tea/coffee facilities, CTV and hairdryer.

5 bedrs, 3 ensuite, 1 ➥ TCF TV 🅿 SB £18-£40 DB £44-£48 CC MC Visa

Bell Craig *Acclaimed*
8 Murray Park, St Andrews KY16 9HS
☎ 01334-472962 Fax 01334-472962
Closed Nov-Feb
5 bedrs, 3 ensuite, 2 ➥ TCF TV 🐕

Cadzow *Acclaimed*
58 North Street, St Andrews KY16 9AH
☎ 01334-476933
8 bedrs, 6 ensuite, 2 ➥ TV 🐕 SB £20-£25 DB £30-£44

Cleveden House *Acclaimed*
3 Murray Place, St Andrews KY16 9AP
☎ 01334-474212 Fax 01334-474212
6 bedrs, 4 ensuite, 1 ➥ TV SB £18-£23 DB £36-£46

Blue Ribbon Awards

The highest honour the RAC can bestow on a hotel is to award it Blue Ribbon status. Only hotels who have gained all three merit awards for Hospitality, Comfort and Restaurant are eligible for the award.

Fossil House *Acclaimed*
12-14 Main Street, Strathkinness, KY16 9RU
☎ 01334-850639 Fax 01334-850639

Peace and tranquillity just two miles from St Andrews, this deluxe accommodation offers hotel facilities, including all ensuite rooms, at B&B prices. Not to be missed.

4 bedrs, all ensuite, 1 ➥ TCF TV 🅿 4 SB £20-£25 DB £40-£44 D £12 CC MC Visa ♿

Hazelbank *Acclaimed*
28 The Scores, St Andrews KY16 9HS
☎ 01334-472466 Fax 01334-472466
Closed 20 Dec-20 Jan
10 bedrs, all ensuite, TCF TV SB £37.50-£80 DB £50-£90 D £15 CC MC Visa

Lorimer House *Acclaimed*
19 Murray Park, St Andrews KY16 9AW
☎ 01334-476599 Fax 01334-476599

West Park House *Acclaimed*
5 St Mary's Place, St Andrews KY16 9UY
☎ 01334-475933
Closed Dec-Jan
4 bedrs, 3 ensuite, 1 🔥, 2 ➥ TCF TV SB £20-£35 DB £40-£50 CC MC Visa

Yorkston House *Acclaimed*
68-70 Argyle Street, St Andrews KY16 9BU
☎ 01334-472019 Fax 01334-472019
Closed 24 Dec-2 Jan

Close to the town centre. All bedrooms with colour TV and tea and coffee making facilities. Ensuite rooms available. Comfortable lounge and separate dining room.

10 bedrs, 6 ensuite, 2 ➥ TCF TV SB £21-£32 DB £40-£70

Edenside House
Edenside, St Andrews KY16 9SQ
☎ 01334-838108 Fax 01334-838493
E-mail: 106076.222@compuserve.com.
Closed Nov-Mar

Waterfront location on bird sanctuary, two miles from St Andrews. Some ground floor rooms. Non smoking. Ample parking. Golf advice.

9 bedrs, all ensuite, 9 ⓕ, TCF TV ✉ ✞ P 10 No children under 10 DB £40-£50 CC MC Visa

Larches
7 River Terrace, Guardbridge, St Andrews KY16 0XA
☎ 01334-838008 Fax 01334-838008
E Mail thelarches@aol.com

Beautiful old memorial hall, centrally situated for golf, fishing and touring. Full central heating. Separate residents' lounge with satellite TV, video player and films. Wonderful food and welcome.

3 bedrs, 2 ⓕ, 1 ⇨ TCF TV ✞ P 2 SB £18-£26 DB £34-£44 ♿

STANLEY Perthshire   13D1

★★ Tayside
Mill Street, Stanley PH1 4NL
☎ 01738-828249 Fax 01738-827216
16 bedrs, 14 ensuite, TCF TV ✞ P 54 SB £42.50-£45 DB £65-£70 D £17.50 CC MC Visa ▣

STIRLING Stirlingshire   12C2

★★ Garfield
12 Victoria Square, Stirling FK8 2QZ
☎ 01786-473730 Fax 01786-473730
8 bedrs, 5 ensuite, 1 ⇨ TCF TV ✞ P 6 SB £38-£40 DB £48-£56 CC MC Visa

STRATHPEFFER Ross-shire   15D3

White Lodge *Highly Acclaimed*
Strathpeffer IV14 9AL
☎ 01997-421730
Closed Apr, Nov

Situated in the centre of small Highland village, lovingly restored by present owners, each room has an individual charm. A warm welcome awaits you. (No smoking).

3 bedrs, all ensuite, TCF TV ✉ P 3 No children under 10 SB £25 DB £36 D £12

STRONTIAN Argyll   14B4

★★ Strontian
Strontian, Acharacle PH36 4HZ
☎ 01967-402029 Fax 01967-402314
7 bedrs, 5 ensuite, 1 ⇨ TCF TV ✞ P 25 CC MC Visa JCB ▣ ▣

TAIN Ross-shire   15D2

★★ Caledonian
Main Street, Portmahomack, Tain IV20 1YS
☎ 01862-871345 Fax 01862-871757
16 bedrs, all ensuite, TCF TV ✞ P 16 SB £23-£31 DB £46-£50 HB £145-£154 D £11.55 CC MC Visa ▣

TARBERT, LOCH FYNE Argyll　　　12B2

★★ Columba
East Pier Road, Tarbert, Loch Fyne PA29 6UF
☎ 01880-820808
Closed 24-26 Dec

Peaceful lochside position. Log fired bars. Rather special bar meals. Restaurant serving the best of Scottish produce imaginatively prepared. 'Taste of Scotland' recommended. Sauna, gym.

10 bedrs, all ensuite, **TCF TV** 🐕 **P** 10 **SB** £32-£34 **DB** £64-£76 **HB** £246-£315 **D** £19 **CC** MC Visa

TAYNUILT Argyll　　　12B1

★★ Polfearn
Taynuilt PA35 1JQ
☎ 01866-822251
14 bedrs, all ensuite, 1 ➡ **TCF TV** 🐕 **P** 50 **SB** £25-£30 **DB** £30-£70 **D** £16 **CC** MC Visa

THORNHILL Dumfriesshire　　　13D3

★★ Buccleuch & Queensberry
Thornhill
☎ 01848-330215 Fax 01848-330215
12 bedrs, 5 ensuite, 7, 2 ➡ **TCF TV** 🐕 **P** 40 **CC** MC Visa Amex DC

★★ George
103-106 Drumlanrig Street, Thornhill DG3 5LU
☎ 01848-330326
8 bedrs, all ensuite, **TV** 🐕 **P** 12 **SB** £28-£30 **DB** £40-£45 **CC** MC Visa

★★ Trigony House
Hospitality, Comfort, Restaurant merit awards
Closeburn, Thornhill DG3 5EZ
☎ 01848-331211 Fax 01848-331303
Closed 25 Dec
8 bedrs, **TV P** 30 No children under 8 **CC** MC Visa

THURSO Caithness　　　15E1

★★ Pentland
Princes Street, Thurso KW14 7AA
☎ 01847-893202 Fax 01847-892761
48 bedrs, all ensuite, 4 ➡ **TCF TV** 🐕 **SB** £30 **DB** £50 **D** £12.75 **CC** MC Visa JCB

★★ Royal
Traill Street, Thurso KW14 8EH
☎ 01847-893191 Fax 01847-895338
104 bedrs, 100 ensuite, 🐕 **P** 40 **CC** MC Visa Amex DC

★★ St Clair
Sinclair Street, Thurso KW14 7AJ
☎ 01847-896481 Fax 01847-896481
36 bedrs, 29 ensuite, 4 ➡ **TCF TV** 🐕 **SB** £28 **DB** £52 **HB** £240 **D** £13.50 **CC** MC Visa Amex JCB

TONGUE Sutherland　　　15D1

★★ Ben Loyal
Hospitality, Comfort merit awards
Tongue IV27 4XE
☎ 01847-611216 Fax 01847-611212
Closed Nov-Feb
12 bedrs, 9 ensuite, 1 ➡ **TCF TV** 🐕 **P** 19 **SB** £25-£38 **DB** £50-£80 **HB** £240-£371 **D** £19 **CC** MC Visa

TROON Ayrshire　　　12C3

★★ Ardneil
51 St. Meddans Street, Troon KA10 6NU
☎ 01292-311611
9 bedrs, 3 ensuite, 3 ➡ 🐕 **P** 100 **CC** MC Visa Amex

★★ Craiglea
80 South Beach, Troon KA10 6EG
☎ 01292-311366 Fax 01292-311366
20 bedrs, 10 ensuite, 4 ➡ 🐕 **P** 14 **SB** £30 **DB** £50 **D** £13.50 **CC** MC Visa Amex DC

TWEEDSMUIR Peeblesshire　　　13D3

★★ Crook Inn
Tweedsmuir ML12 6QN
☎ 01899-880272 Fax 01899-880294
8 bedrs, 6 ensuite, **P** 80 **SB** £26 **DB** £52 **HB** £140 **D** £15 **CC** MC Visa

---

RAC Hotel Reservations Service
0870 603 9109
(Calls charged at national call rate)

TYNDRUM Perthshire — 12C1

Invervey
Tyndrum, Crianlarich FK20 8RY
☎ 01838-400219 Fax 01838-400280
21 bedrs, 17 ensuite, 2 ⇌ TCF TV ⚹ SB £27 DB £54 CC
MC Visa Amex ⌷ ♿

WEST WEMYSS Fife — 13D2

★★ Belvedere
Coxstool, West Wemyss KY1 4SL
☎ 01592-654167 Fax 01592-655279
21 bedrs, all ensuite, TCF TV ⚹ P 50 SB £45-£55 DB £65-£75 D £13.50 CC MC Visa Amex

WHITEBRIDGE Inverness-shire — 15D3

★★ Whitebridge
Whitebridge IV1 2UN
☎ ff 0800-026 6277 Fax 01456-486413
E Mail whiteb@world-traveler.com
Closed Jan-Mar
12 bedrs, 10 ensuite, 1 ⇌ TV ⚹ P 32 SB £25-£30
DB £50-£60 HB £250 D £14 CC MC Visa Amex DC ⌷

WICK Caithness — 15E1

★★ Mackay's
Union Street, Wick KW1 5ED
☎ 01955-602323 Fax 01955-605930
26 bedrs, all ensuite, 2 ⇌ ⚹ ▣ P 20 CC MC Visa Amex

WIGTOWN Wigtownshire — 12C4

Glaisnock House
20 South Main Street, Wigtown DG8 9EH
☎ 01988-402249

Family run guest house in the heart of a county town, ideally situated for touring, hill walking, golf, fishing, bird watching and shooting. Traditional Scottish meals served in a small select licensed restaurant. Scottish Tourist Board 2 crown commended.

4 bedrs, 2 ensuite, 1 ⌧, 1 ⇌ TCF TV ⚹ SB £16.50-£17
DB £33-£34 HB £171.50 D £8.50 CC MC Visa

Invervey Hotel

The Invervey Hotel on the A82/A85 at Tyndrum snuggling at the feet of some of the finest mountains in Scotland is ideal for hill walkers, climbers and ski enthusiasts (30 mins by car to the ski tows).
The lounge bar is large but cosy and is a wonderful meeting place for guests and locals. The games room, pool table, dart board and juke box provides a separate and lively atmosphere for the young at heart. Most of the bedrooms are ensuite and all have central heating, colour TV and telephone.
The restaurant is open all day and offers freshly prepared Scottish fayre and home baking.
Please phone or write for brochure to John and Barbara Riley.

**TYNDRUM, CRIANLARICH,
PERTHSHIRE FK20 8RY
Tel: 01838 400219 Fax: 01838 400280**

Wales

*Top: Borthnog Hall,
Bontddu*

*Right: Brynafor Hotel,
New Quay*

*Below: Bronwylfa Guest House,
Bala*

RAC

ABERCRAF Powys 6C4

Maes-y-Gwernen *Highly Acclaimed*
School Road, Abercraf SA9 1XD
☎ 01639-730218 Fax 01639-730765
8 bedrs, all ensuite, 1 ⇌ TCF TV ⊷ P 12 SB £33–£39 DB £52–£66 HB £250–£330 D £12.50 CC MC Visa Amex

ABERDARON Gwynedd 6B2

★★ Ty Newydd
Aberdaron LL53 8BE
☎ 01758-760207 Fax 01758-760505
Closed Nov-Feb
17 bedrs, 8 ensuite, 3 ⇌ TCF TV SB £35–£45 DB £64–£70 D £8.50 CC MC Visa Amex JCB

ABERDYFI Gwynedd 6C3

Brodawel *Highly Acclaimed*
Tywyn Road, Aberdyfi LL35 0SA
☎ 01654-767347
Closed Oct-Apr
6 bedrs, all ensuite, TCF TV ⊷ P 7 No children SB £22 DB £44 D £14

Bodfor *Acclaimed*
Sea Front, Aberdyfi LL35 0EA
☎ 01654-767475 Fax 01654-767679
E Mail david.a0009660@infotrade.co.uk
15 bedrs, 10 ensuite, 5 ⊕, 3 ⇌ TCF TV ⊷ P 15 SB £27–£34 DB £47–£61 HB £230–£279 D £15 CC MC Visa JCB

Cartref *Acclaimed*
Aberdyfi LL35 0NR
☎ 01654-767273
7 bedrs, 4 ensuite, 1 ⇌ TV ⊷ P 8 SB £18 DB £38 D £9

ABERGAVENNY Monmouthshire 7D4

Rock & Fountain *Listed*
Main Road, Clydach, Abergavenny NP7 0LL
☎ 01873-830393
9 bedrs, all ensuite, TCF TV P 50 SB £19.50–£25 DB £35–£39.50 HB £170–£190 D £5 CC MC Visa ♿

ABERGELE Conwy 6C1

★★ Kinmel Manor
Hospitality merit award
St Georges Road, Abergele LL22 9AS
☎ 01745-832014 Fax 01745-832014
42 bedrs, all ensuite, ⊷ P 100 SB £49 DB £68 HB £340 D £15 CC MC Visa Amex DC

ABERGYNOLWYN Gwynedd 6C2

Dolgoch Falls *Acclaimed*
Tywyn, Abergynolwyn LL36 9UW
☎ 01654-782258

A warm friendly atmosphere, with genuine, tasty home cooking is offered at this hotel. Set at the foot of Dolgoch Falls in Snowdonia National Park with Tal-y-Llyn light railway, golf and the beach close by.

6 bedrs, 3 ensuite, 1 ⇌ TCF ⊷ P 50 No children under 7 SB £20 DB £39 HB £196 D £14 CC MC Visa

ABERSOCH Gwynedd 6B2

★★ Neigwl
Hospitality merit award
Sarn Road, Abersoch LL53 7DY
☎ 01758-712363 Fax 01758-712363
9 bedrs, all ensuite, 1 ⇌ TV ⊷ P 30 SB £37–£50 DB £60–£80 HB £320–£375 D £18 CC MC Visa DC JCB

★★ Tudor Court
Lon Sarn Bach, Abersoch LL53 7EB
☎ 01758-713354 Fax 01758-713354
8 bedrs, 7 ensuite, 1 ⊕, ⊷ P 16 CC MC Visa DC

ABERYSTWYTH Ceredigion 6B3

★★ Four Seasons
Restaurant merit award
50-54 Portland Street, Aberystwyth SY23 2DX
☎ 01970-612120 Fax 01970-627458
Closed Christmas-New Year
15 bedrs, 14 ensuite, TCF TV P 10 SB £47 DB £68 HB £295 D £16 CC MC Visa

★★ Hafod Arms
Devils Bridge, Aberystwyth SY23 3JL
☎ 01970-890232 Fax 01970-890394
Closed Jan
16 bedrs, 3 ⇌ TCF TV P 200 No children under 12

Glyn Garth *Highly Acclaimed*
South Road, Aberystwyth SY23 1JS
☎ 01970-615050
10 bedrs, 6 ensuite, 1 ⇌ TCF TV P 2 SB £18–£19 DB £42–£48

BALA – WALES

Queensbridge *Acclaimed*
Promenade, Aberystwyth SY23 2DH
☎ 01970-612343 Fax 01970-617452

Situated on the promenade, the Queensbridge boasts a passenger lift and offers superior comfort in 15 spacious ensuite bedrooms, with TV, hospitality tray and telephone.

15 bedrs, all ensuite, **TCF TV** ☒ **SB** £36 **DB** £48-£52 **CC** MC Visa Amex DC JCB

Southgate *Acclaimed*
Anatron Avenue, Penparcau, Aberystwyth SY23 1SF
☎ 01970-611550

Family run licensed hotel, one mile from the town centre, with ensuite double, twin and family rooms offering TV and tea and coffee facilities. Cot and high chair available. Dinner optional. Pool table. Parking in own grounds.

10 bedrs, 9 ensuite, 3 ⇌ **TCF TV** ⚞ **P** 30 **DB** £17.50-£19.50 **HB** £164.50-£178.50 **D** £7 **CC** MC Visa

Garreg Lwyd
Bow Street, Aberystwyth SY24 5BE
☎ 01970-828830
Closed Christmas

Situated in own grounds on the A487, 3 miles north of Aberystwyth. Ample parking space, good food, central heating, lounge with colour TV. All modern conveniences, hot and cold in bedrooms and tea/coffee facilities. Refreshments available all day.

3 bedrs, 1 ⇌ **TCF** ⚞ **SB** £16.50 **DB** £32-£37

AMLWCH Anglesey   6B1

★★ Trecastell
Bull Bay, Amlwch LL68 9SA
☎ 01407-830651 Fax 01407-832114
13 bedrs, 11 ensuite, 2 ⇌ **TCF TV** ⚞ **P** 60 **SB** £30 **DB** £45 **D** £14 **CC** MC Visa Amex

BALA Gwynedd   6C2

★★ Plas Coch
High Street, Bala LL23 7AB
☎ 01678-520309 Fax 01678-521135
Closed 25 Dec
10 bedrs, all ensuite, **P** 20 No children **SB** £39-£57 **DB** £65 **HB** £252 **D** £14.50 **CC** MC Visa Amex DC JCB

★★ White Lion Royal
High Street, Bala LL23 7AE
☎ 01678-520314
Closed Christmas
26 bedrs, 22 ensuite, 2 ☒, ⚞ **P** 30 **CC** MC Visa Amex DC

Bronwylfa *Highly Acclaimed*
Llanderfel, Bala LL23 7HG
☎ 01678-530207 Fax 01678-530207

Victorian manor house and cottage on the edge of a picturesque village, with views of Berwyn Mountain and the River Dee. Ideal for touring Snowdonia, walking and water sports. Relax and unwind in a home away from home

4 bedrs, 3 ensuite, 1 ⇌ **TCF TV** ☒ **P** 10 **SB** £25-£30 **DB** £38-£44 **HB** £200-£225 **D** £10

Erw Feurig Farm
Cefn-ddwysarn, Bala LL23 7LL
📞 01678-530262 Fax 01678-530262

An attractive guest house situated on a working farm with fantastic views of the Berwyn Mountains. Comfortable and spacious bedrooms, some ensuite, yet all have heating and tea/coffee making facilities. 2 Crowns - highly commended.

5 bedrs, 2 ensuite, 2 🛏 TCF P 7 SB £15-£20 DB £30-£36 HB £160-£180 D £10 ♿

Fronddderw
Stryd-y-Fron, Bala LL23 7YD
📞 01678-520301
Closed 1 Dec-28 Feb

A period mansion quietly situated overlooking Bala town and lake. Half the accommodation is ensuite. Evening meal and special diets catered for.

9 bedrs, 4 ensuite, 2 🐾, 2 🛏 TCF P 10 SB £16-£22 DB £32-£44 HB £175-£217 D £10 CC MC Visa

Penbryn
Sarnau, Bala LL23 7LH
📞 01678-530297

A working farm with panoramic views overlooking the lovely Berwyn Mountains. 2 double rooms with ensuite facilities, 1 single and 1 twin with private bathrooms. All with C.H., tea/coffee facilities.

BANGOR Gwynedd — 6B1

Country Bumpkin *Acclaimed*
Cefn Coed, Llandegai, Bangor LL57 4BG
📞 01248-370477 Fax 01248-354166
Closed mid Dec-mid Jan
3 bedrs, all ensuite, TCF TV 🐾 P 10 No children SB £30-£33 DB £40-£45 CC MC Visa

Goetre Isaf Farmhouse *Acclaimed*
Caernarfon Road, Bangor LL57 4DB
📞 01248-364541 Fax 01248-364541

Superb country situation Bangor 3km. Ideal touring centre for Snowdonia. Imaginative farmhouse cooking, vegetarians welcome. Bedrooms with dial-phone facilities. Stabling by arrangement. O/S ref: SH562699.

3 bedrs, 1 ensuite, 2 🛏 🐾 P 10 SB £16 DB £28 D £6

BARMOUTH Gwynedd — 6C2

★★ Bryn Melyn
Panorama Road, Barmouth LL42 1DQ
📞 01341-280556 Fax 01341-280276
E Mail amdc@cipality.u-net.com
Closed Nov-Mar
9 bedrs, 8 ensuite, 1 🛏 TCF TV 🐾 P 9 SB £37 DB £56-£62 HB £252-£269 D £15 CC MC Visa Amex DC JCB

★★ Panorama
Panorama Road, Barmouth LL42 1DQ
📞 01341-280550 Fax 01341-280346
18 bedrs, all ensuite, 🐾 P 40 SB £25-£28 DB £50-£56 D £10.95 CC MC Visa Amex DC

★★ Ty'r Graig Castle
Hospitality, Comfort merit awards
Llanaber Road, Barmouth LL42 1YN
📞 01341-280470 Fax 01341-281260
12 bedrs, all ensuite, 2 🛏 TCF TV 🐾 P 15 SB £38 DB £59 HB £290 D £18.50 CC MC Visa Amex JCB

Plas Bach Country *Highly Acclaimed*
Glandwr, Nr Bontddu, Barmouth LL42 1TG
☎ 01341-281234 Fax 01341-281234
5 bedrs, 3 ensuite, 2 🛁, TCF TV 🐾 6 No children under 15 SB £30-£32.50 DB £60-£70 HB £273-£291 D £15.50

BEDDGELERT Gwynedd   6B1

★★ Tanronnen Inn
Comfort merit award
Beddgelert LL55 4YB
☎ 01766-890347 Fax 01766-890606
7 bedrs, all ensuite, TCF TV 🐾 P 8 SB £36 DB £70
HB £280 D £16 CC MC Visa JCB

Sygun Fawr Country House *Acclaimed*
Beddgelert LL55 4NE
☎ 01766-890258
Closed Jan
8 bedrs, all ensuite, 1 ➥ TCF 🐾 P 15 SB £30 DB £54
HB £280 D £16 CC MC Visa JCB 🖼

BENLLECH BAY Anglesey   6B1

★★ Bay Court
Beach Road, Benllech Bay LL74 8SW
☎ 01248-852573 Fax 01248-852606
19 bedrs, 10 ensuite, 3 ➥ TCF 🐾 P 65 SB £20 DB £40
HB £178 D £9.50 CC MC Visa Amex DC JCB ♿

BETWS-Y-COED Conwy   6C1

★★ Gwydyr
Betws-y-Coed LL24 0AB
☎ 01690-710777 Fax 01690-710777
20 bedrs, all ensuite, 🐾 P 20
CC MC Visa 🎵

★★ Park Hill
Hospitality merit award
Llanrwst Road, Betws-y-Coed LL24 0HD
☎ 01690-710540 Fax 01690-710540
11 bedrs, 9 ensuite, 1 ➥ TCF TV P 14 No children under 6 SB £17.50-£19.50 DB £46-£53 HB £–£266
D £13.50 CC MC Visa Amex DC 🎵 🖼

★★ Ty Gwyn
Hospitality, Restaurant merit awards
Betws-y-Coed LL24 0SG
☎ 01690-710383 Fax 01690-710383
13 bedrs, 9 ensuite, 2 ➥ TCF TV 🐾 P 16 SB £19 DB £34-£80 D £18 CC MC Visa ♿

★ Fairy Glen
Hospitality, Comfort merit awards
Fairy Glen, Betws-y-Coed LL24 0SH
☎ 01690-710269 Fax 01690-710269
Closed Dec-Jan
8 bedrs, 6 ensuite, 2 ➥ TCF TV 🐾 P 10 SB £20 DB £40
HB £220 D £12 CC MC Visa

★ Tan-y-Foel Country House
Capel Garmon, Betws-y-Coed LL26 0RE
☎ 01690-710507 Fax 01690-710681
Closed Jan-mid Dec, Christmas
7 bedrs, all ensuite, TV 🐾 P 14 No children under 7
SB £65-£85 DB £90-£150 HB £896-£1,260 D £25
CC MC Visa Amex DC JCB

Aberconwy House *Highly Acclaimed*
Llanrwst Road, Betws-y-Coed LL24 0HD
☎ 01690-710202 Fax 01690-710800
E Mail clive-muskus@celtic.co.uk
Closed Jan-Feb

Situated in a quiet position and overlooking the picturesque village. Superbly furnished for comfort and relaxation. Beautiful views of the valley, surrounding mountains and rivers.

8 bedrs, all ensuite, TCF TV 🐾 P 10 DB £40-£46

Penmachno Hall *Acclaimed*
Penmachno, Betws-y-Coed LL24 0PU
☎ 01690-760207
Closed Christmas & New Year

Set in the heart of the Snowdonia National Park. Major tourist attractions all within easy reach. Our motto: Good food, good wine, good company.

4 bedrs, all ensuite, No children under 5 SB £30
DB £50 HB £255 D £15 CC MC Visa

Bryn Llewelyn *Listed*
Holyhead Road, Betws-y-Coed LL24 0BN
☎ 01690-710601 Fax 01690-710601
7 bedrs, 4 ensuite, 2 ➥ TCF TV 🐾 P 11 No children under 2 SB £16-£20 DB £29-£39

BETWS-Y-COED – WALES

Summer Hill Non-Smokers *Listed*
Coedcynhelier Road, Betws-y-Coed LL24 0BL
☎ 01690-710306
Closed Christmas

Country weekends, midweek breaks, overnighters. Home cooking, good service, warm comfortable accommodation. Forest walks, touring, mountains, lakes.

7 bedrs, 4 ensuite, 1 ⇌ TCF ⊠ ✈ P 6 No children under 3 SB £18-£21 DB £32-£36 D £9.50

Ferns
Holyhead Road, Betws-y-Coed LL24 0AN
☎ 01690-710587 Fax 01690-710587

Conveniently situated on the level in the village of Betws-y-Coed in the beautiful Snowdonia National Park. Attractively decorated bedrooms and delightful, spacious breakfast room.

9 bedrs, 8 ensuite, TCF TV ⊠ P 9 No children under 4 SB £20-£30 DB £36-£42 HB £212-£219 D £12

Fron Heulog Country House
Betws-y-Coed, LL24 0BL
☎ 01690-710736 Fax 01690-710736

The country house in the village. Elegant Victorian stone built house; peaceful wooded riverside scenery; excellent modern accommodation; comfort, warmth, style.

5 bedrs, all ensuite, TCF TV No children under 12 DB £36-£50

BONCATH Pembrokeshire   6B4

Castellan House *Acclaimed*
Blaenffos, Boncath SA27 0HZ
☎ 01239-841644
6 bedrs, 3 ensuite, 2 ⌂, 5 ⇌ ✈ P 15 SB £18-£20 DB £34-£36 D £12 ⊠ ♿

BONTDDU Gwynedd   6C2

Borthwnog Hall *Highly Acclaimed*
Bontddu, Dolgellau LL40 2TT
☎ 01341-430271 Fax 01341-430682
Closed Christmas

Small Georgian style house in quiet riverside location for either a relaxing or an invigorating short break in southern Snowdonia. Well furnished rooms, table d'hote or a la carte.

3 bedrs, all ensuite, TCF TV ✈ P 8 CC MC Visa

BORTH Ceredigion   6C3

Glanmor *Listed*
High Street, Borth SY24 5JP
☎ 01970-871689
7 bedrs, 2 ensuite, 2 ⇌ TCF TV ✈ P 6 SB £20 DB £39 HB £203 D £9.50

BRECON Powys   7D4

★ Tai'r Bull Inn
Comfort merit award
Libanus, Brecon LD3 8EL
☎ 01874-625849
5 bedrs, all ensuite, TCF TV P 12

BUILTH WELLS – WALES

Coach *Highly Acclaimed*
Orchard Street, Llanfaes, Brecon LD3 8AN
☎ **01874-623803**
6 bedrs, all ensuite, TCF TV P 3 No children DB £40-£42

Beacons *Acclaimed*
16 Bridge Street, Brecon LD3 8AH
☎ **01874-623339** Fax **01874-623339**

Georgian town house, Grade II Listed, close to the River Usk and town centre. Cosy bar.

10 bedrs, 7 ensuite, 2 TCF TV P 16 SB £18 DB £36 HB £175 D £10 CC MC Visa

Maeswalter *Acclaimed*
Heol Senni, Brecon LD3 8SU
☎ **01874-636629**

A warm welcome in this 17th century farmhouse situated in a picturesque sheep-farming valley. Three bedrooms tastefully decorated. The beamed lounge serves as a dinning room.

3 bedrs, 1 ensuite, 2 TCF TV No children SB £20-£25 DB £32-£35 HB £30-£33

Old Rectory *Acclaimed*
Llanddew, Brecon LD3 9SS
☎ **01874-622058**
3 bedrs, 2 ensuite, 1 TCF TV P 6 SB £26 DB £40

Flag & Castle
11 Orchard Street, Llanfaes, Brecon LD3 8AN
☎ **01874-625860**

Single, twin, double and family rooms available in cosy guest house opposite Christ College. Convenient for all National Park and town amenities. Car parking and bicycle storage.

6 bedrs, 1 ensuite, 2 TCF TV P 2 SB £16-£18 DB £30-£38 CC Amex

Lower Rhydness Bungalow
Llyswen, Brecon LD3 0AZ
☎ **01874-754264**

Comfortable, centrally heated bungalow looking across open fields into the Wye Valley, 12 miles from Brecon where there are many places of interest.

2 bedrs, 2 TCF P 2 SB £16 DB £32 HB £160 D £7

BUILTH WELLS Powys 6C3

★★ Greyhound
3 Garth Road, Builth Wells LD2 3AR
☎ **01982-553255**
12 bedrs, all ensuite, 2 TCF TV P 20 SB £16.50-£22.50 DB £45 HB £126 D £10 CC MC Visa

Cedars *Acclaimed*
Hay Road, Builth Wells LD2 3AR
☎ **01982-553356**
7 bedrs, 5 ensuite, 1 TCF TV

BURRY PORT Carmarthenshire 2C1

George *Acclaimed*
Stepney Road, Burry Port SA16 0BH
☎ 01554-832211
Closed Christmas
9 bedrs, 5 ensuite, 4 🛏 TCF TV No children under 8
SB £18-£33 DB £34-£44 D £8

BURTON Pembrokeshire 6A4

★★ Beggar's Reach
Milford Haven, Burton SA73 1PD
☎ 01646-600700/560
10 bedrs, 9 ensuite, TCF TV 🐕 P 30 SB £25 DB £40
HB £126 D £8 CC MC Visa

CAERNARFON Gwynedd 6B1

★★ Menai Bank
North Road, Caernarfon LL55 1BD
☎ 01286-673297 Fax 01286-673297
Closed Christmas
15 bedrs, 11 ensuite, 3 🛏 TCF TV 🐕 P 10 SB £20 DB £33-£58 HB £198-£277 D £15 CC MC Visa Amex

Menai View *Listed*
North Road, Caernarfon LL55 1BD
☎ 01286-674602
Closed Christmas-New Year
8 bedrs, 3 ensuite, 2 🛏 TCF TV 🐕 SB £16-£19 DB £25-£33

Pengwern Farm
Saron, Llanwnda, Caernarfon LL54 5UH
☎ 01286-831500 Fax 01286-831500
Closed Dec-Jan

Charming, spacious farmhouse of character. Beautifully situated between the mountains and sea with unobstructed views of Snowdonia. Well appointed bedrooms, all ensuite. Jane Rowlands has a cookery diploma and provides excellent meals using local produce.

3 bedrs, all ensuite, TCF TV 🅿 P 3 SB £25-£35 DB £40-£50 HB £227.50-£280 D £15

CAPEL CURIG Conwy 6C1

★★ Tyn-y-Coed
Capel Curig LL24 0EE
☎ 01690-720331 Fax 01690-720331
14 bedrs, all ensuite, TCF TV 🐕 P 80 SB £27-£30 DB £40-£50 D £12 CC MC Visa Amex JCB

CARDIFF 3D1

★★ Lincoln
118 Cathedral Road, Cardiff CF1 9LQ
☎ 01222-395558 Fax 01222-230537

Two Victorian town houses converted to a modern hotel, centrally located and backing onto Bute Park.

18 bedrs, all ensuite, TCF TV 🐕 P 20 CC MC Visa Amex DC

★★ Phoenix
Fidlas Road, Llanishen, Cardiff CF4 5LZ
☎ 01222-764615 Fax 01222-747812
45 bedrs, all ensuite, 3 🛏 TCF TV 🐕 P 60 CC MC Visa Amex

★★ Sandringham
21 St Mary Street, Cardiff CF1 2PL
☎ 01222-232161 Fax 01222-383998
28 bedrs, all ensuite, TCF TV
SB £44-£53 DB £49-£59 HB £196-£240 D £5 CC MC Visa Amex DC JCB

Albany *Acclaimed*
191/193 Albany Road, Roath, Cardiff CF2 3NU
☎ 01222-494121
Closed Christmas
11 bedrs, 7 ensuite, 2 🚿, 1 🛏 TCF TV

Clare Court *Acclaimed*
46-48 Clare Road, Cardiff CF1 7QP
☎ 01222-344839 Fax 01222-251511
8 bedrs, all ensuite, TCF TV SB £25 DB £36 D £5 CC MC Visa Amex

Balkan *Listed*
144 Newport Road, Cardiff CF2 1DT
☎ 01222-463673

CARDIGAN – WALES

Domus *Listed*
201 Newport Road, Roath, Cardiff CF2 1AJ
☎ 01222-473311
10 bedrs, 2 ensuite, 5 ⌘, 2 ⇌ TCF TV P 10

Tane's *Listed*
148 Newport Road, Roath, Cardiff CF2 1DJ
☎ 01222-493898 Fax 01222-491755
9 bedrs, 4 ensuite, 2 ⇌ TCF TV P 10 No children under 2 SB £18 DB £32

Campanile Cardiff *Lodge*
Caxton Place, Pentwynn, Cardiff CF2 7MA
☎ 01222-549044 Fax 01222-549900
50 bedrs, all ensuite, TCF TV ⚑ P 50 SB £41 DB £45.50
D £10.55 CC MC Visa Amex DC ♿

Travelodge *Lodge*
Granada Cardiff Services, Pontclun, Cardiff CF7 8SB
☎ 0800-850950 Fax 01222-892497
50 bedrs, all ensuite, TCF TV ⚑ P 250 SB £42.95 CC MC Visa Amex DC ♿

Austins
11 Coldstream Terrace, Cardiff CF1 8LJ
☎ 01222-377148 Fax 01222-377158

Small and friendly in the centre of the city, 300 yards from the castle overlooking the river. Ensuite rooms available. Warm welcome to all nationalities.

11 bedrs, 3 ensuite, 2 ⇌ TCF TV ⚑ SB £16-£25 DB £28-£35 CC MC Visa Amex

Courtfield
101 Cathedral Road, Cardiff CF1 9PH
☎ 01222-227701 Fax 01222-227701

Popular licensed hotel set in a fine Victorian conservation area close to Cardiff Castle and city centre. Brochure and further details on request.

14 bedrs, 5 ensuite, 2 ⇌ TCF TV ⚑ No children under 7 SB £20 DB £35-£45 D £12 CC MC Visa Amex DC

Preste Garden
181 Cathedral Road, Pontcanna, Cardiff CF1 9PN
☎ 01222-228607 Fax 01222-374805

An ex-Norwegian consulate situated in the heart of the city. You will enjoy the modern facilities and informal atmosphere that has led this house to be so widely recommended.

10 bedrs, 7 ensuite, 3 ⇌ TCF TV P 3 SB £22-£26 DB £33-£40 CC Amex

CARDIGAN Ceredigion   6B4

★★ Castell Malgwyn
Hospitality merit award
Llechryd, Cardigan SA43 2QA
☎ 01239-682382 Fax 01239-682382
20 bedrs, all ensuite, 1 ⇌ TCF TV ⚑ P 60 SB £38 DB £66
HB £268 D £15 CC MC Visa Amex DC

★★ Penbontbren Farm
Hospitality, Comfort merit awards
Glynarthen, Cardigan SA44 6PE
☎ 01239-810248 Fax 01239-811129
Closed Christmas
10 bedrs, all ensuite, ⚑ P 50 SB £38-£43 DB £68-£74
HB £303-£318 D £13 CC MC Visa Amex DC JCB ♿

Brynhyfryd *Acclaimed*
Gwbert Road, Cardigan SA43 1AE
☎ 01239-612861 Fax 01239-612861
7 bedrs, 4 ensuite, 2 ⇌ TCF TV SB £16-£17 DB £32-£37
HB £150-£175 D £6

Facilities for the disabled ♿

Hotels do their best to cater for disabled visitors. However, it is advisable to contact the hotel direct to ensure it can provide a particular requirement. For further information on accommodation facilities for the disabled why not order a copy of *RAC On the Move – The Guide for the Disabled Traveller.*

CARMARTHEN Carmarthenshire 6B4

★★ Falcon
Restaurant merit award
Lammas Street, Carmarthen SA31 3AP
☎ 01267-234959 Fax 01267-221277
14 bedrs, all ensuite, TCF TV ⚹ P 8 SB £45-£52.50
DB £55-£59.50 D £14.95 CC MC Visa Amex DC

Farm Retreats *Highly Acclaimed*
Capel Dewi Uchaf Farm, Capel Dewi, Carmarthen SA32 8AY
☎ 01267-290799 Fax 01267-290003
3 bedrs, all ensuite, TCF TV ⌧ P 10 SB £23.50 D £17

Ty Mawr *Highly Acclaimed*
Restaurant merit award
Brechfa, Carmarthen SA32 7RA
☎ 01267-202332 Fax 01267-202437
Closed end Nov-Christmas

16th century 'Big House' next to the river Marlais - set amongst some of the most beautiful countryside in Britain. Immaculately maintained - oak beams; quarry tiled floors; open fires and antiques.

5 bedrs, all ensuite, TCF ⚹ P 20 SB £52 DB £84 HB £441 D £20 CC MC Visa Amex

Cothi Bridge
Pontargothi, Carmarthen SA32 7NG
☎ 01267-290251

A family run hotel with an a la carte restaurant, situated on the banks of the River Cothi, six miles fron Carmarthen.

13 bedrs, all ensuite, P 50 CC MC Visa Amex

FALCON HOTEL

This small, pleasant, privately owned hotel is conveniently situated in the town centre. It provides modern furnished and well equipped accommodation, which is equally suitable for both business people and tourists.

The public areas comprise of a pleasant lounge, a small bar and an attractive restaurant where good choice of both popular favourites and more adventurous dishes available.

Young Head Chef William Noblett is becoming quite well known throughout Wales for both his skills and his keenness to promote traditional Welsh dishes. He uses only the best available fresh produce and goes to great lengths to obtain as much of it as possible locally.

RAC RESTAURANT MERIT AWARD

**LAMMAS STREET, CARMARTHEN SA31 3AP
TEL: (01267) 234959/237152
FAX: (01267) 221277**

CHEPSTOW Monmouthshire 3E1

★★ Beaufort
Beaufort Square, Chepstow NP6 5EP
☎ 01291-622497 Fax 01291-927389
18 bedrs, all ensuite, TCF TV ⚹ P 12 SB £36.75-£43.25
DB £53-£59.50 D £13.70 CC MC Visa Amex DC ♿

★★ Castle View
16 Bridge Street, Chepstow NP6 5PZ
☎ 01291-620349 Fax 01291-627397
13 bedrs, all ensuite, ⚹ SB £43.25-£45.70 DB £61-£66.45 D £13.95 CC MC Visa Amex DC

COLWYN BAY Conwy 6C1

★★ Ashmount
College Avenue, Rhos-on-Sea, Colwyn Bay LL28 4NT
☎ 01492-544582 Fax 014952-545479
Closed 31 Oct-1 Mar
17 bedrs, all ensuite, TCF TV ⚹ P 10 SB £34 DB £52-£64
HB £229-£270 D £13.50 CC MC Visa Amex DC JCB ♿

★★ Edelweiss
Lawson Road, Colwyn Bay LL29 8HD
☎ 01492-532314 Fax 01492-534707
26 bedrs, all ensuite, TCF TV ⚹ P 25 CC MC Visa Amex DC 🐕 ♿

★★ Lyndale
410 Abergele Road, Colwyn Bay LL29 9AB
☎ 01492-515429 Fax 01492-518805
14 bedrs, all ensuite, TCF TV 🐕 P 20 SB £18-£32 DB £35-£48 HB £160-£190 D £12 CC MC Visa Amex DC

★★ Rhos Abbey
111 The Promenade, Rhos-on-Sea, LL28 4NE
☎ 01492-546601 Fax 01492-543056
32 bedrs, all ensuite, TCF TV 🐕 ♿ P 120 CC MC Visa

★★ St Enoch's
West Promenade, Colwyn Bay LL28 4BL
☎ 01492-532031 Fax 01492-533736
Closed Nov, Jan, Feb
18 bedrs, 14 ensuite, 2 🛏 TCF TV 🐕 SB £20 DB £35 HB £125-£140 D £12 CC MC Visa

★★ Whitehall
Cayley Promenade, Rhos-on-Sea, LL28 4EP
☎ 01492-547296
Closed Nov-Mar
14 bedrs, 7 ensuite, 3 🛏 🐕 P 5 CC MC Visa

★ Melfort
Llanerch Road East, Rhos on Sea, Colwyn Bay LL28 4DF
☎ 01492-544390
12 bedrs, 8 ensuite, 3 🛏 TCF TV 🐕 ♿ P 20 SB £17.50 DB £35 HB £161 ♿

★ St Margarets
Hospitality, Comfort merit awards
Princes Drive, Colwyn Bay LL29 8RP
☎ 01492-532718
Closed Nov
10 bedrs, all ensuite, TCF TV 🐕 P 10
SB £22 DB £44 HB £150-£200 D £9.95 CC MC Visa

★ West Point
102 Conwy Road, Colwyn Bay LL29 7LE
☎ 01492-530331
Closed Dec-Jan
9 bedrs, 6 ensuite, 2 🛏 TCF TV 🐕 P 6 SB £16-£19 DB £30-£37 HB £140-£160 D £7.50 CC MC Visa

Cabin Hill *Acclaimed*
College Avenue, Rhos-on-Sea, Colwyn Bay LL28 4NT
☎ 01492-544568
10 bedrs, 7 ensuite, 2 🛏 TCF TV 🐕 SB £15 DB £30-£34 HB £154-£168 D £7

Northwood *Acclaimed*
47 Rhos Road, Rhos-on-Sea, Colwyn Bay LL28 4RS
☎ 01492-549931
12 bedrs, 11 ensuite, 1 🛏 TCF TV 🐕 P 12 SB £20.50 DB £41 HB £153-£161 D £12 CC MC Visa ♿

Grosvenor *Listed*
106-108 Abergele Road, Colwyn Bay LL29 7PS
☎ 01492-531586 Fax 01492-531586
18 bedrs, 2 ensuite, 4 🛏 TCF TV 🐕 P 14 SB £18-£19 DB £36-£38 HB £152-£159 D £8

Sunny Downs *Listed*
66 Abbey Road, Rhos-on-Sea, Colwyn Bay LL28 4NU
☎ 01492-544256 Fax 01492-543223

A 4 crown luxury hotel, 2 minutes from sea front and 5 minutes from Llandudno. All rooms have satellite TV, video, radio, telephone, tea/coffee facilities, hairdryers, mini-bar and refrigerator.

15 bedrs, all ensuite, TCF TV 🐕 P 15 SB £25-£30 DB £44-£50 HB £235-£270 D £15 CC Amex DC

CONWY Conwy   6C1

★★ Castle Bank
Restaurant merit award
Mount Pleasant, Conwy LL32 8NY
☎ 01492-593888 Fax 01492-596466
Closed Jan-Feb
9 bedrs, 8 ensuite, 2 🛏 TCF TV ♿ P 12 SB £27-£33.50 DB £57 HB £265 D £14 CC MC Visa Amex JCB

★★ Deganwy Castle
Station Road, Deganwy, Conwy LL31 9DA
☎ 01492-583555 Fax 01492-583555

A 17th century listed building, originally an old farmhouse, which has been built onto over the years. With its oak beams and log fires it provides an atmosphere of old world charm.

31 bedrs, all ensuite, TCF TV 🐕 P 70 SB £31.50-£33 DB £63-£66 D £16 CC MC Visa Amex DC

★★ Tir-y-Coed Country House
Rowen, Conwy LL32 8TP
☎ 01496-50219
Closed mid Nov-Feb
8 bedrs, all ensuite, TCF TV 🐕 P 8 SB £25.50-£29 DB £47-£54 HB £234-£255 D £12.25 CC Amex

★ Old Rectory

Llanrwst Road, Llansanffraid Glan Conwy, Conwy LL28 5LF
📞 01492-580611 Fax 01492-584555
Closed 30 Nov-1 Feb
6 bedrs, all ensuite, TCF TV P 10
No children under 5 SB £79-£99 DB £99-£139 D £30
CC MC Visa Amex DC JCB

Glan Heulog

Llanrwst Rd, Conwy LL32 8LT
📞 01492-593845

Close to Conwy Castle and mountains, quiet location and good views. Our guests say "Lovely warm welcome", "Best place I've stayed" and "I'll be back".

6 bedrs, 5 ensuite, 1 🐕 TCF TV P 6 SB £15-£20 DB £26-£34 HB £141-£166 D £8.50 CC MC Visa

CORWEN Denbighshire   7D2

Corwen Court

London Road, Corwen LL21 0DP
📞 01490-412854
Closed 30 Nov-6 Jan

Gateway to North Wales. Old police station and courthouse. The cells are now single bedrooms. Lounge and dining room are where magistrates once presided.

10 bedrs, 4 ensuite, 2 🐕 🐾 SB £14-£15 DB £30-£32 HB £139.50-£153 D £8

CRICCIETH Gwynedd   6B2

★★ Gwyndy

Llanystumdwy, Criccieth LL52 0SP
📞 01766-522720
10 bedrs, all ensuite, 🐾 P 14 SB £28 DB £46 HB £205 D £11.75 ♿

★★ Lion

Y Maes, Criccieth LL52 0AA
📞 01766-522460 Fax 01766-523075
45 bedrs, 35 ensuite, 10 🛁, 3 🐕 TCF TV 🐾 ⌨ P 25
SB £25.75-£30 DB £49.50-£58 HB £242-£275 D £16 CC
MC Visa Amex DC JCB ♿

★★ Parciau Mawr

High Street, Criccieth LL52 0RP
📞 01766-522368
Closed Nov-Mar
12 bedrs, all ensuite, TCF TV 🐾 P 30 No children under 5 SB £30-£33 DB £50-£56 HB £220-£260 D £12 CC MC Visa ♿

★★ Plas Isa

Porthmadog Road, Criccieth LL52 0HP
📞 01766-522443 Fax 01766-523423
Closed Christmas-New Year
13 bedrs, all ensuite, TCF TV 🐾 P 15 SB £30 DB £46 HB £210 D £9 CC MC Visa Amex DC

★ Caerwylan
Comfort merit award

Beach Bank, Criccieth LL52 0HW
📞 01766-522547
25 bedrs, all ensuite, TCF TV 🐾 ⌨ P 30 SB £18.50 HB £180 D £10.50 CC MC Visa 🔍

Glyn-y-Coed *Acclaimed*

Portmadoc Road, Criccieth LL52 0HL
📞 01766-522870 Fax 01766-523341
Closed Christmas-New Year

A lovely Victorian house overlooking the sea, mountains and castles. Highly recommended home cooking for most diets. One ground floor bedroom. Senior citizen rates.

11 bedrs, all ensuite, TCF TV 🐾 P 14 SB £20-£25 DB £40-£50 HB £190-£210 D £10 CC MC Visa Amex

DOLGELLAU – WALES

Min-y-Gaer *Acclaimed*
Porthmadog Road, Criccieth LL52 0HP
☎ 01766-522151 Fax 01766-523540
E Mail minygaer.hotel@virgin.net
Closed Nov-Feb

A substantial Victorian building in a convenient position overlooking Criccieth Castle and the Cardigan Bay coastline, 200 yards from the beach. An ideal base for touring Snowdonia and the Lleyn Peninsula.

10 bedrs, 9 ensuite, 1 ⛌ TCF TV ⛯ P 12 SB £20-£22
DB £40-£44 HB £199.50-£206.50 D £10 CC MC Visa Amex

Neptune & Mor Heli *Listed*
Marine Terrace, Criccieth LL52 OEF
☎ 01766-522794
8 bedrs, all ensuite, 5 ⛌ TCF TV ⛯

STABLES HOTEL

CRICKHOWELL

Internationally known country hotel with 30 acres of grounds and gardens, magnificent position in Brecon Beacons National Park, overlooking Black Mountains and Usk Valley. Lounge, dining room, bar/restaurant. All main courses served with six fresh vegetables.

Acclaimed

LLANGATTOCK, CRICKHOWELL, POWYS NP8 1LE
Tel: 01873 810244

CRICKHOWELL Powys   7D4

★★ Dragon House
High Street, Crickhowell NP8 1BE
☎ 01873-810362 Fax 01873-811868
E Mail ghhotel@provider.co.uk
15 bedrs, all ensuite, 1 ⛌ TCF TV P 15 SB £26-£50
DB £52-£59 HB £249-£279 D £16.50 CC MC Visa Amex

★★ Gliffaes Country House
Comfort merit award
Crickhowell NP8 1RH
☎ 01874-730371 Fax 01874-730463
22 bedrs, all ensuite, TCF TV ⛯ P 35 SB £37.75-£72
DB £75-£112 HB £420-£514 D £21.50 CC MC Visa Amex
DC JCB

Stables *Acclaimed*
Llangattock, Crickhowell NP8 1LE
☎ 01873-810244

High class internationally known country hotel. Magnificent position in 30 acres of gardens and grounds. Restaurant with Wales' largest fireplace. All main meals served with six fresh vegetables.

20 bedrs, all ensuite, TCF TV ⛯ P 35 SB £40 DB £50-£55
HB £280-£315 D £15 CC MC Visa Amex

DEGANWY Conwy   6C1

★★ Bryn Cregin
Ty Mawr Road, Deganwy, Conwy LL31 9UR
☎ 01492-585266 Fax 01492-596203
16 bedrs, all ensuite, TCF TV ⛯ P 20 CC MC Visa ♿

DOLGELLAU Gwynedd   6C2

★★ Dolserau Hall
Hospitality, Comfort merit awards
Dolgellau LL40 2AG
☎ 01341-422522 Fax 01341-422400
14 bedrs, 13 ensuite, 1 ⛌ ⛯ P 70 CC MC Visa

★★ George III
Hospitality, Comfort merit awards
Penmaenpool, Dolgellau LL40 1YD
☎ 01341-422525 Fax 01341-423-565
12 bedrs, all ensuite, TCF TV ⛯ P 60 SB £50 DB £88
D £15 CC MC Visa JCB ♿

DOLGELLAU – WALES

★★ Royal Ship
Queens Square, Dolgellau LL40 1AR
☎ 01341-422209 Fax 01341-421027
24 bedrs, 18 ensuite, 5 ➡ TCF TV ✝ ▣ P 8 SB £20-£30
DB £30-£50 D £14 CC MC Visa JCB

★ Clifton House
Restaurant merit award
Smithfield Square, Dolgellau LL40 1ES
☎ 01341-422554
Closed January
6 bedrs, 2 ensuite, 2 ®, 1 ➡ TV P 2 SB £25.50-£32.50
DB £35-£49 HB £234.50-£269.50 D £9.50 CC MC Visa ♿

Fronoleu Farm *Acclaimed*
Tabor, Dolgellau LL40 2PS
☎ 01341-422361 Fax 01341-422361

Secretly secluded, family run farm hotel, combining traditional Welsh warmth with modern excellence. Log fires, licensed restaurant, fourposters, harpist, fishing. All enhance the cosy, friendly atmosphere.

10 bedrs, 6 ensuite, 2 ➡ TCF TV ✝ P 38 ♿

FISHGUARD Pembrokeshire   6A4

★★ Abergwaun
Market Square, Fishguard SA65 9HA
☎ 01348-872077 Fax 01348-875412
11 bedrs, 6 ensuite, 2 ➡ TCF TV
SB £22.50 DB £48 D £4 CC MC Visa Amex DC JCB

★★ Cartref
High Street, Fishguard SA65 9AW
☎ 01348-872430 Fax 01348-872430
12 bedrs, 6 ensuite, 4 ®, 2 ➡ TCF TV ✝ P 3 SB £32
DB £48 HB £218 D £9 CC MC Visa

★ Manor House
Hospitality, Comfort, Restaurant merit awards
Main Street, Fishguard SA65 9HJ
☎ 01348-873260 Fax 01348-873260
Closed 23-28 Dec
6 bedrs, all ensuite, TCF TV ✝ SB £25-£30 DB £48-£52
D £16 CC MC Visa

Tregynon Country Farmhouse *Highly Acclaimed*
Restaurant merit award
Gwaun Valley, Fishguard SA65 9TU
☎ 01239-820531 Fax 01239-820808
E Mail tregynon@compuserve.com
8 bedrs, all ensuite, TCF TV DB £48-£70 HB £270-£350
D £17.95 CC MC Visa JCB

Stone Hall *Acclaimed*
Restaurant merit award
Welsh Hook, Wolfscastle SA62 5NS
☎ 01348-840212 Fax 01348-840815

A 14th century manor house in ten acres of gardens, in a quiet secluded location six miles from the coast. Genuine French cuisine by French chefs.

5 bedrs, 4 ensuite, 1 ➡ TCF TV P 50 SB £46 DB £68
HB £315 D £17 CC MC Visa Amex DC

GANLLWYD Gwynedd   6C2

Tyn-y-Groes *Acclaimed*
Ganllwyd, Dolgellau LL40 2HN
☎ 01341-440275 Fax 01341-440275
E Mail douglas.ruthwell@virgin.net
8 bedrs, 7 ensuite, TCF TV ✝ P 30 No children under 8
SB £23 DB £43-£50 D £12.15 CC MC Visa ▣ ❄

HARLECH Gwynedd   6B2

Castle Cottage *Highly Acclaimed*
Restaurant merit award
Pen Llech, Harlech LL46 2YL
☎ 01766-780479 Fax 01766-780479
Closed Feb
6 bedrs, 4 ensuite, 1 ➡ TCF ✝ SB £25-£26 DB £54-£56
D £18 CC MC Visa Amex

St David's *Acclaimed*
Harlech LL46 2PT
☎ 01766-780366 Fax 01766-780820
60 bedrs, all ensuite, TCF TV ▣ P 60 SB £24-£40 DB £48-£80 D £14 CC MC Visa Amex DC ▣ ❄

Byrdir *Listed*
High Street, Harlech LL46 2YA
☎ 01766-780316 Fax 01766-780316
15 bedrs, 7 ensuite, 3 ➡ TCF TV ✝ P 12 SB £15-£24
DB £30-£38 D £10.75

HAY-ON-WYE – WALES

HAVERFORDWEST Pembrokeshire 6A4

★★ Hotel Mariners
Mariners Square, Haverfordwest SA61 2DU
☎ 01437-763353 Fax 01437-764258
29 bedrs, all ensuite, 1 🛏 TCF TV 🐕 P 50 SB £47.50
DB £67.50 HB £295.75 D £13.50 CC MC Visa Amex DC

★★ Pembroke House
6-7 Spring Gardens, Haverfordwest SA61 2EJ
☎ 01437-763652
21 bedrs, 19 ensuite, 1 🛏 TCF TV 🐕 P 18 SB £38 DB £55
HB £235 D £15 CC MC Visa Amex DC

★★ Wolfscastle Country
Restaurant merit award
Haverfordwest SA62 5LZ
☎ 01437-741225 Fax 01437-741383
Closed Christmas
24 bedrs, all ensuite, TCF TV 🐕 P 60 SB £39-£47 DB £73
HB £343 D £15 CC MC Visa Amex JCB

Cuckoo Mill
St. Davids Road, Pelcomb Bridge, Haverfordwest
SA62 6EA
☎ 01437-762139

A quiet comfortable farmhouse, situated close to beaches, riding stables and a golf course, two miles from Haverfordwest.

3 bedrs, 2 🛏 TCF TV 🐕 P 4 SB £15-£17 DB £30-£34
HB £150-£160 D £10

HAY-ON-WYE Powys 7D4

York House *Highly Acclaimed*
Hardwicke Road, Cusop, Hay-on-wye HR3 5QX
☎ 01497-820705
4 bedrs, all ensuite, TCF TV 🐕 P 6 No children under
8 SB £24 DB £44-£48 HB £224-£236 D £14 CC MC Visa
Amex

RAC Hotel Reservations Service
0870 603 9109
(Calls charged at national call rate)

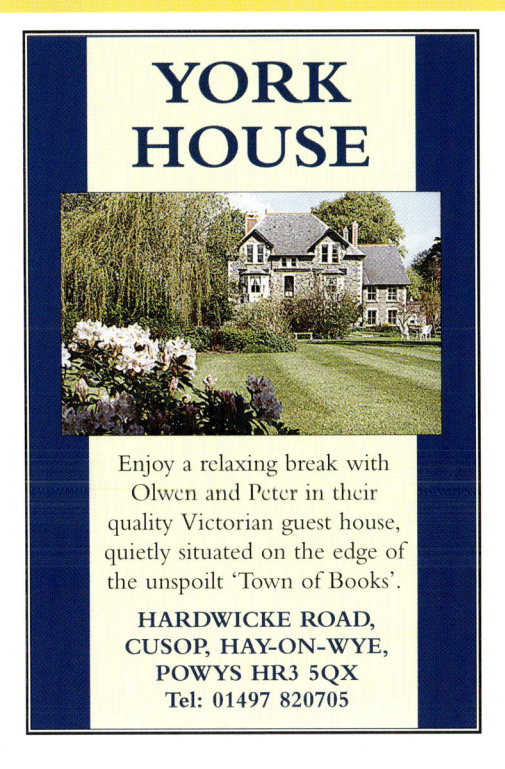

YORK HOUSE

Enjoy a relaxing break with Olwen and Peter in their quality Victorian guest house, quietly situated on the edge of the unspoilt 'Town of Books'.

HARDWICKE ROAD, CUSOP, HAY-ON-WYE, POWYS HR3 5QX
Tel: 01497 820705

La Fosse
Oxford Road, Hay-on-Wye HR3 5AJ
☎ 01497-820613
Closed Christmas

A three storey 18th century cottage rendered in a traditional white stucco design, floral garden and parking area.

5 bedrs, all ensuite, TCF TV 🐕 P 5 No children under
11 SB £20-£25 DB £35-£37 CC MC Visa

HOLYHEAD Anglesey　　　　　　　　6B1

★★ Bull
London Road, Valley LL65 3DP
📞 01407-740351　Fax 01407-742328

Colour washed in cream and green, a small hotel on A5 near centre of village - three and a half miles from Irish Ferry. Bar meals lunch and evening.

14 bedrs, all ensuite, TCF TV 🛏 P 100 SB £33.75 DB £44.75 D £8.95 CC　MC Visa Amex 🅁 ⚿

Valley *Listed*
London Road, Valley, Holyhead LL65 3DY
📞 01407-740203　Fax 01407-740986
19 bedrs, 15 ensuite, 1 🛌 TCF TV 🛏 P 100 SB £20-£33.75 DB £28-£44.75 D £11 CC　MC Visa Amex 🅁

HOLYWELL Flintshire　　　　　　　　7D1

★★ Stamford Gate
Halkyn Road, Holywell CH8 7SJ
📞 01352-712942　Fax 01352-713309
12 bedrs, all ensuite, P 90 SB £38 DB £49 D £15 CC　MC Visa 🅁

LANGLAND BAY Swansea　　　　　　　　2C1

★ Wittemberg
Hospitality, Comfort merit awards
2 Rotherslade Road, Langland, Swansea SA3 4QN
📞 01792-369696　Fax 01792-366995
12 bedrs, all ensuite, 2 🛌 TCF TV 🛏 P 10 SB £30-£36 DB £48-£58 HB £160-£220 D £11 CC　MC Visa Amex

LLANBEDR Gwynedd　　　　　　　　6B2

★★ Ty Mawr
Llanbedr LL45 2NH
📞 01341-241440
Closed 24-25 Dec
10 bedrs, all ensuite, TCF TV 🛏 P 20 SB £20-£29 DB £40-£58 HB £210-£266 D £13

★★ Victoria Inn
Llanbedr LL45 2LD
📞 01341-241213　Fax 01341-241644
5 bedrs, all ensuite, TV 🛏 P 75 SB £28 DB £50 HB £156 D £10 CC　MC Visa JCB

LLANBERIS Gwynedd　　　　　　　　6B1

★★ Lake View
Tan-y-Pant, Llanberis LL55 4EL
📞 01286-870422　Fax 01286-872591
10 bedrs, 9 ensuite, TCF TV CC　MC Visa DC JCB

★★ Padarn Lake
High Street, Llanberis LL55 4SU
📞 01286-870260　Fax 01286-870007
18 bedrs, all ensuite, 🛏 P 20 CC　MC Visa Amex DC

LLANDOGO Monmouthshire　　　　　　　　7D4

Browns *Listed*
Llandogo NP5 4TW
📞 01594-530262

Sloop Inn *Listed*
Llandogo NP5 4TN
📞 01594-530291　Fax 01594-530935
4 bedrs, all ensuite, TCF TV 🛏 P 30 No children SB £25.50 DB £39 D £8 CC　MC Visa

LLANDOVERY Carmarthenshire　　　　　　　　6C4

Llwyncelyn *Listed*
Llandovery SA20 0EP
📞 01550-720566
6 bedrs, 2 🛌 TCF P 12 SB £19-£23 DB £34 HB £199-£218 D £12 📧

LLANDRINDOD WELLS Powys　　　　　　　　6C3

★★ Glen Usk
South Crescent, Llandrindod Wells LD1 5DH
📞 01597-822085　Fax 01597-822964
79 bedrs, all ensuite, TCF TV 🛏 🛗 P 12 SB £35-£65 DB £70-£80 HB £210-£280 D £17.50 CC　MC Visa Amex DC

★★ Severn Arms
Hospitality merit award
Penybont, Llandrindod Wells LD1 5UA
📞 01597-851224　Fax 01597-851693
Closed Christmas

A former coaching inn dating from 1840, with a traditional black and white facade. Conveniently situated on the A44.

10 bedrs, all ensuite, TCF TV ★ P 60 SB £28 DB £50 HB £198 D £14 CC MC Visa Amex DC

Montpellier *Highly Acclaimed*
Temple Street, Llandrindod Wells LD1 5HW
☎ 01597-822388 Fax 01597-825600
12 bedrs, all ensuite, TV P 26 CC MC Visa

Three Wells Farm *Highly Acclaimed*
Chapel Road, Howey, Llandrindod Wells LD1 5PB
☎ 01597-824427 Fax 01597-822484

Working farm overlooking a fishing lake in beautiful countryside. Ideal for rambling and birdwatching.

15 bedrs, all ensuite, 1 ★ TCF TV ★ ⊡ P 20 No children under 8 SB £18-£24 DB £35-£48 HB £180-£210 D £10

Griffin Lodge *Acclaimed*
Temple Street, Llandrindod Wells LD1 5HF
☎ 01597-822432 Fax 01597-825196
8 bedrs, 5 ensuite, 2 ★ TCF TV ★ P 8 SB £19-£25 DB £38-£45 HB £187-£212 D £11 CC MC Visa Amex

Kincoed *Listed*
Temple Street, Llandrindod Wells LD1 5HF
☎ 01597-822656 Fax 01597-824660
10 bedrs, 5 ensuite, 2 ★ TCF TV ★ P 12 CC MC Visa

LLANDUDNO Conwy   6C1

★★ Banham House Hotel & Restaurant
2 St Davids Road, Llandudno LL30 2UL
☎ 01492-875680 Fax 01492-875680
6 bedrs, all ensuite, 1 ★ TCF TV ⊠ P 6 No children under 12 SB £30 DB £46 HB £224 D £9

★★ Bedford
Craig-y-Don Parade, Llandudno LL30 1BN
☎ 01492-876647 Fax 01492-860185
27 bedrs, all ensuite, TCF TV ★ ⊡ P 30 SB £25-£28 DB £40-£50 D £12 CC MC Visa Amex DC &

★★ Branksome
62-64 Lloyd Street, Llandudno LL30 2YP
☎ 01492-875989 Fax 01492-875989
49 bedrs, 42 ensuite, 2 ★ TCF TV ★ P 19 SB £28-£34 DB £36-£48 HB £163-£199 D £10 CC MC Visa JCB

★★ Clarence
Hospitality merit award
Gloddaeth Street, Llandudno LL30 2DD
☎ 01492-860193 Fax 01492-860308
52 bedrs, all ensuite, TCF TV ★ ⊡ SB £32 DB £64 HB £200 D £12 CC MC Visa Amex &

★★ Dunoon
Comfort merit award
Gloddaeth Street, Llandudno LL30 2DW
☎ 01492-860787 Fax 01492-860031
Closed mid Nov-mid Mar
55 bedrs, all ensuite, TCF TV ★ ⊡ P 24 SB £34-£39 DB £50-£54 HB £190-£205 D £12.50 CC MC Visa

★★ Epperstone
Hospitality, Comfort merit awards
15 Abbey Road, Llandudno LL30 2EE
☎ 01492-878746 Fax 01492-871223
Closed Nov-Feb excl Christmas

A small, detached hotel with fine Edwardian features including stained glass and conservatory in its own grounds.

8 bedrs, all ensuite, 1 ★ TCF TV ★ P 8 SB £25-£28 HB £170-£185 D £15 CC MC Visa &

★★ Esplanade
Central Promenade, Llandudno LL30 2LL
☎ 01492-860300 Fax 01492-860418
E Mail esplanade@enterprise.net
59 bedrs, all ensuite, TCF TV ★ ⊡ P 30 SB £29-£42 DB £50-£74 HB £211-£301 D £14 CC MC Visa Amex DC JCB &

★★ Headlands
Hill Terrace, Llandudno LL30 2LS
☎ 01492-877485
Closed Jan-Feb
17 bedrs, 15 ensuite, ★ P 10 No children under 5 SB £28 DB £56 HB £175-£210 D £17 CC MC Visa Amex DC

LLANDUDNO – WALES

★★ Marlborough
South Parade, Llandudno LL30 2LN
☎ 01492-875846 Fax 01492-876529
Closed Jan-Easter
40 bedrs, 39 ensuite, 2 ⇌ TCF TV ⃞ P 3 SB £24-£28
DB £42-£46 HB £217 D £8 CC MC Visa

★★ Ormescliffe
Promenade, Llandudno LL30 1BE
☎ 01492-877191 Fax 01492-860311
Closed Jan-Feb
62 bedrs, all ensuite, TCF TV ⃗ ⃞ P 15 SB £33-£35
DB £66-£70 HB £266-£280.50 D £11 CC MC Visa ⃫

★★ Royal
Church Walks, Llandudno LL30 2HW
☎ 01492-876476 Fax 01492-870210
38 bedrs, all ensuite, TCF TV ⃞ P 30 SB £23-£30 DB £45-£60 HB £195-£225 D £15 CC MC Visa ♿

★★ Sandringham
Hospitality, Comfort merit awards
West Parade, Llandudno LL30 2BD
☎ 01492-876513 Fax 01492-872753
18 bedrs, all ensuite, P 6 SB £25-£29 DB £50-£58
HB £245-£260 D £14 CC MC Visa DC JCB ♿

★★ Somerset
Central Promenade, Llandudno LL30 2LF
☎ 01492-876540 Fax 01492-876540
Closed Jan-Mar
37 bedrs, all ensuite, 1 ⇌ TCF TV ⃗ ⃞ P 25 CC MC Visa ♿

★★ St Tudno
Promenade, Llandudno LL30 2LP
☎ 01492-874411 Fax 01492-860407
20 bedrs, all ensuite, TCF TV ⃗ ⃞ P 12 SB £70-£90
DB £90-£160 HB £415 D £29.50
CC MC Visa Amex DC JCB

★★ Tan Lan
Hospitality, Comfort merit awards
Great Ormes Road, West Shore, Llandudno LL30 2AR
☎ 01492-860221 Fax 01492-870219
Closed Nov-Mar
17 bedrs, all ensuite, 2 ⇌ TCF TV ⃗ P 12 SB £23-£25
DB £46-£50 HB £227-£237 D £13 CC MC Visa ♿

★★ Tynedale
Central Promenade, Llandudno LL30 2XS
☎ 01492-877426 Fax 01492-871213
56 bedrs, all ensuite, TCF TV ⃞ P 35 SB £23-£42 DB £46-£80 HB £199-£339 D £10 CC MC Visa

RAC Hotel Reservations Service
0870 603 9109
(Calls charged at national call rate)

★★ White Court
Hospitality, Comfort merit awards
2 North Parade, Llandudno LL30 2LP
☎ 01492-876719 Fax 01492-871583
Closed Dec-Jan
13 bedrs, all ensuite, TV ⃞ SB £35-£45 DB £48-£50
HB £200-£220 D £13.50 CC MC Visa

★★ Wilton
South Parade, Llandudno LL30 2LN
☎ 01492-876086 Fax 01492-876086
14 bedrs, all ensuite, TV ⃗ P 3 SB £22-£24 DB £44-£48
HB £182-£192 D £8

★ Ambassador
Grand Promenade, Llandudno LL30 2NR
☎ 01492-876886 Fax 01492-876347
63 bedrs, 53 ensuite, 4 ⇌ TCF TV ⃞ P 10 SB £19-£29
DB £44-£58 HB £190-£255 D £11 CC MC Visa Amex ♿

★ Cae Mor
6 Penrhyn Crescent, Central Promenade, Llandudno LL30 1BA
☎ 01492-878101 Fax 01492-878101

A large Victorian building, painted cream and white, situated on the sea front and enjoying panoramic views of the bay.

34 bedrs, 21 ensuite, 6 ⇌ TCF TV ⃗ ⃞ P 30 SB £19.50-£23.50 DB £39-£47 HB £170-£198 D £7.50 ♿

★ Clontarf
Great Ormes Road, West Shore, Llandudno LL30 2AS
☎ 01492-877621
9 bedrs, 5 ensuite, 2 ⇌ P 9 No children under 8

★ Leamore
Hospitality, Comfort merit awards
40 Lloyd Street, Llandudno LL30 2YG
☎ 01492-875552
12 bedrs, 7 ensuite, 2 ⇌ TV ⃗ P 4 SB £23-£25 DB £36-£38 HB £175-£185 D £9

★ Min-y-don
North Parade, Llandudno LL30 2LP
☎ 01492-876511 Fax 01492-878169
28 bedrs, 19 ensuite, 3 ⇌ P 7 SB £19-£21 DB £37-£39
D £7 CC MC Visa

★ Ravenhurst
West Shore, Llandudno LL30 2BB
☎ 01492-875525 Fax 01492-874259
Closed Nov-Feb
25 bedrs, all ensuite, 1 ⇌ TCF TV ↟ P 18 SB £24-£27
DB £48-£52 D £9 CC MC Visa Amex DC ♿

★ Warwick
56 Church Walks, Llandudno LL30 2HL
☎ 01492-876823

Brigstock *Acclaimed*
1 St Davids Place, Llandudno LL30 2UG
☎ 01492-876416 Fax 01492-878184
Closed Dec
10 bedrs, 6 ensuite, 1 ⇌ TCF TV ☒ P 5 No children under 12 SB £21-£25 DB £42 £46 HB £191 £210 D £8

Britannia *Acclaimed*
15 Craig-y-Don Parade, Promenade, Llandudno LL30 1BG
☎ 01492-877185
E Mail 101465.2745@compuserve.com
Closed Nov-Feb
10 bedrs, 8 ensuite, 2 ⇌ TCF TV SB £14.50-£20 DB £29-£40 HB £140-£180

Carmel *Acclaimed*
17 Craig-y-Don Parade, Llandudno LL30 1BG
☎ 01492-877643

Situated in a prime position on the main promenade, with uninterrupted sea views and overlooking the famous Great and Little Ormes.

9 bedrs, 6 ensuite, 2 ⇌ TCF TV ↟ P 6 No children under 4 SB £15.50-£17.50 DB £29-£35 HB £140-£161

Cedar Lodge *Acclaimed*
7 Degawny Lodge, Llandudno LL30 2YB
☎ 01492-877730
Closed Dec-Jan

A small family run guest house centrally situated, car park, good home cooking, ensuite rooms, TV and tea making facilities. Long or short stays welcome.

7 bedrs, 6 ensuite, 1 ⇌ TCF TV P 5 SB £20 DB £36
HB £155 D £6.50

Concord *Acclaimed*
35 Abbey Road, Llandudno LL30 2EH
☎ 01492-875504 Fax 01492-875504
Closed Oct-Easter
11 bedrs, all ensuite, TCF P 11 No children under 5
SB £20-£21 DB £40-£42 HB £164-£176 D £8

Cornerways *Acclaimed*
2 St Davids Place, Llandudno LL30 2UG
☎ 01492-877334
Closed Nov-Feb
7 bedrs, all ensuite, TCF TV P 5 No children SB £23
DB £46-£50 HB £231-£245 D £10

Cranberry House *Acclaimed*
12 Abbey Road, Llandudno LL30 2EA
☎ 01492-879760 Fax 01492-879760
Closed Dec-Feb

A small, select, non-smoking Victorian guest house, all rooms ensuite and of a high standard. Adults only. Conveniently situated for all amenities and Snowdonia National Park.

5 bedrs, all ensuite, TCF TV ☒ P 5 No children SB £22-£25 DB £36-£44 CC MC Visa Amex JCB

LLANDUDNO – WALES

Kinmel *Acclaimed*
Hospitality merit award
Central Promenade, Llandudno LL30 1AR
📞 **01492-876171**
16 bedrs, 14 ensuite, 3 🛏 **TCF TV** 🐕 **SB** £20-£22 **DB** £40-£42 **HB** £169-£176 **D** £7 **CC** MC Visa

Orotava *Acclaimed*
105 Glan-y-Mor Road, Llandudno LL30 3PH
📞 **01492-549780**
6 bedrs, all ensuite, **TCF TV** ✉ **P** 10 No children under 15 **SB** £18.50 **DB** £37 **HB** £179 **D** £7 **CC** MC Visa

Spindrift *Acclaimed*
24 St Davids Road, Llandudno LL30 2UL
📞 **01492-876490**
Closed Christmas-New Year
5 bedrs, all ensuite, **TCF TV** ✉ **P** 4 No children under 14 **SB** £19-£25 **DB** £38-£55 **D** £10

St Hilary *Acclaimed*
16 Craig-y-don Parade, Promenade, Llandudno LL30 1BG
📞 **01492-875551** Fax **01492-875551**
E Mail 106773.1730@compuserve.com
Closed Nov-Feb

Situated on Llandudno's main promenade overlooking the bay and Great Orme headland. Excellent accommodation and great value for money. Brochure/tariff available on request.

11 bedrs, 8 ensuite, 1 🛏 **TCF TV SB** £16-£40 **DB** £31-£42 **HB** £145-£185 **D** £7 **CC** MC Visa JCB

Beach Cove *Listed*
8 Church Walks, Llandudno LL30 2HD
📞 **01492-879638**
Closed 25 Dec
7 bedrs, 5 ensuite, 1 🛏 **TCF TV SB** £13 **DB** £34 **HB** £160 ♿

Brannock *Listed*
36 St David's Road, Llandudno LL30 2UH
📞 **01492-877483**
Closed Nov-Mar
8 bedrs, 5 ensuite, 1 🛏 **TCF TV** 🐕 **P** 5 No children under 4 **SB** £19 **DB** £32-£38 **HB** £135-£155 **D** £6 **CC** MC Visa

Karden House *Listed*
16 Charlton Street, Llandudno LL30 2AN
📞 **01492-879347**

Comfortable accommodation with TV, tea and coffee making facilities and central heating. Idyllic, scenic location. Fresh home cooking with allergy and vegetarian diets catered for. Friendly, caring service, close to all amenities.

10 bedrs, 4 ensuite, 2 🛏 **TCF TV SB** £14-£15 **DB** £32-£34 **HB** £126-£137 **D** £5

Minion *Listed*
21-23 Carmen Sylva, Llandudno LL30 1EQ
📞 **01492-877740**
12 bedrs, all ensuite, **TCF** 🐕 **P** 8
No children under 2 **SB** £15.50-£16.50 **DB** £31-£33 **HB** £154-£171.50

Montclare *Listed*
4 North Parade, Llandudno LL30 2LP
📞 **01492-877061**
15 bedrs, 13 ensuite, 2 🛏, **TCF TV SB** £18 **DB** £36 **HB** £160 **D** £7

Rosaire *Listed*
2 St Seiriols Road, Llandudno LL30 2YY
📞 **01492-877677**
Closed Nov-Feb
10 bedrs, 9 ensuite, 1 🛏 **TCF TV** ✉ 🐕 **P** 7 **SB** £14-£15 **DB** £30-£32 **D** £6

Rosedene *Listed*
10 Arvon Avenue, Llandudno LL30 2DY
📞 **01492-876491**

Seaclyffe *Listed*
11 Church Walks, Llandudno LL30 2HG
📞 **01492-876803** Fax **01492-876803**
Closed Jan-Feb
27 bedrs, all ensuite, 1 🛏 **TCF TV P** 2

Westdale *Listed*
37 Abbey Road, Llandudno LL30 2EH
📞 **01492-877996**
Closed Dec-Jan

A small family run hotel with a relaxing atmosphere, situated on the level in pleasant gardens, overlooking Haulfre Gardens.

12 bedrs, 3 ensuite, 2 ⇌ TCF ⋔ P 5
SB £16 DB £32 HB £154 D £6

LLANDYSUL Carmarthenshire 6B4

Fedwen
Waungilwen, Velindre, Llandysul SA44 5YL
☎ 01559-371421

Peaceful location 3 miles from Newcastle Emlyn. Centrally situated giving access to splendid countryside with many walks and attractions and to the beautiful Welsh coastline.

3 bedrs, 1 ensuite, 1 ⇌ TCF TV ⋔ P 6 SB £15 DB £30
HB £175 D £10 CC MC Visa

LLANELLI Carmarthenshire 2C1

★★ Miramar
158 Station Road, Llanelli SA15 1YH
☎ 01554-773607 Fax 01554-772454
10 bedrs, 8 ensuite, 2 ⇌ TCF TV P 6 CC MC Visa Amex DC

LLANFYLLIN Powys 7D2

★★ Bodfach Hall
Y-parc, Llanfyllin SY22 5HS
☎ 01691-648272 Fax 01691-648272
Closed Nov-Feb
9 bedrs, all ensuite, TCF TV ⋔ P 20 SB £36 DB £72
HB £288 D £14 CC MC Visa Amex DC

LLANGOLLEN Denbighshire 7D2

★★ Hand
Bridge Street, Llangollen LL20 8PL
☎ 01978-860303 Fax 01978-861277
58 bedrs, all ensuite, TCF TV ⋔ P 40 SB £30-£60 DB £60-£75 HB £245-£315 D £14 CC MC Visa Amex DC JCB

★★ Tyn-y-wern
Maes Mawr Road, Llangollen LL20 7PH
☎ 01978-860252
10 bedrs, all ensuite, ⋔ P 80 SB £32 DB £42 D £6 CC MC Visa Amex DC

Hillcrest *Acclaimed*
Hill Street, Llangollen LL20 8EU
☎ 01978-860208 Fax 01978-860508
7 bedrs, all ensuite, TCF TV P 10
SB £30-£32 DB £40-£42 HB £203 D £9

LLANRWST Conwy 6C1

★★ Eagles
Ancaster Square, Llanrwst LL26 0LG
☎ 01492-640454 Fax 01492-640454
12 bedrs, all ensuite, 2, 1 ⇌ TCF TV ⋔ P 50 SB £25-£28 DB £38-£48 HB £195-£240 D £12 CC MC Visa Amex DC JCB

LLANTWIT MAJOR Vale of Glamorgan 3D1

★★ West House Country
Comfort, Restaurant merit awards
West Street, Llantwit Major CF61 1SP
☎ 01446-792406 Fax 01446-796147
21 bedrs, all ensuite, 1 ⇌ TCF TV ⋔ P 50 SB £49.50
DB £62.50 HB £275 D £15.50 CC MC Visa Amex JCB

LLANWRTYD WELLS Powys 6C4

★ Neuadd Arms
Llanwrtyd Wells LD5 4RB
☎ 01591-610236
20 bedrs, 13 ensuite, 4 ⇌ TCF TV ⋔ P 10 SB £21-£23
DB £42 HB £221 D £11.50 CC MC Visa

Lasswade House *Highly Acclaimed*
Station Road, Llanwrtyd Wells LD5 4RW
☎ 01591-610515 Fax 01591-610611
8 bedrs, all ensuite, TCF TV ⋔ P 8 No children SB £35
DB £59 HB £280 D £15 CC MC Visa

Carlton House *Acclaimed*
Restaurant merit award
Dolycoed Road, Llanwrtyd Wells LD5 4RA
☎ 01591-610248 Fax 01591-610242
7 bedrs, 5 ensuite, 2 ⇌ TCF TV ⋔ SB £30 DB £60 HB £295
D £21 CC MC Visa

MACHYNLLETH Powys 6C2

★★ Wynnstay Arms
Heol Maengwyn, Machynlleth SY20 8AE
☎ 01654-702941 Fax 01654-703884

Traditional former coaching hotel in this historic market town. Well appointed rooms (some fourposters), fine foods, cosy bars & lounges. Experience Wales' warmest welcome.

23 bedrs, all ensuite, ⚘ P 30 SB £38 DB £55 HB £263 D £14 CC MC Visa Amex DC JCB

See Blue Ribbon award

★★ Ynyshir Hall
Machynlleth SY20 8TA
☎ 01654-781209 Fax 01654-781366
8 bedrs, 7 ensuite, ⚘ P 20 No children under 9 SB £75-£100 DB £130-£165 HB £610-£700 D £30 CC MC Visa Amex DC JCB

MANORBIER Pembrokeshire 2B1

★★ Castle Mead
Manorbier SA70 7TA
☎ 01834-871358 Fax 01834-871358
8 bedrs, 8 ⚘, TCF ⚘ P 15 SB £30-£31 DB £59-£60 HB £275 D £12 CC MC Visa JCB

MENAI BRIDGE Anglesey 6B1

★★ Gazelle
Glyn Garth, Menai Bridge LL59 5PD
☎ 01248-713364 Fax 01248-713167
9 bedrs, 5 ensuite, 3 ⚘ TCF TV P 50 SB £25-£35 DB £40-£60 D £15 CC MC Visa DC

MERTHYR TYDFIL Merthyr Tydfil 6C4

Tredegar Arms *Listed*
66 High Street, Dowlais Top, Merthyr Tydfil CF48 2YE
☎ 01685-377467 Fax 01685-376540
5 bedrs, all ensuite, TCF TV ⚘ P 5 SB £29 DB £39 D £4 CC MC Visa Amex DC

Travellers Lodge *Lodge*
Dowlais Top, Merthyr Tydfil CF48 2YE
☎ 01685-723362 Fax 01685-377467
Closed 25 Dec
6 bedrs, all ensuite, TCF TV ⚘ P 38 SB £29 DB £32 D £5.45

MILFORD HAVEN Pembrokeshire 6A4

★★ Lord Nelson
Hamilton Terrace, Milford Haven SA73 3AL
☎ 01646-695341 Fax 01646-694026
30 bedrs, all ensuite, TCF TV P 26 SB £25-£42 DB £50-£65 CC MC Visa Amex DC

Belhaven House *Listed*
29 Hamilton Terrace, Milford Haven SA73 3JJ
☎ 01646-695983 Fax 01646-690787
11 bedrs, 2 ensuite, 5 ⚘, 4 ⚘ TCF TV ⚘ P 8 CC MC Visa Amex DC

MOLD Flintshire 7D1

★★ Bryn Awel
Restaurant merit award
Denbigh Road, Mold CH7 1BL
☎ 01352-758622 Fax 01352-758625
Closed Christmas
17 bedrs, 8 ensuite, ⚘ P 40 SB £38-£40 DB £48-£55 D £11.95 CC MC Visa Amex DC

Old Mill *Highly Acclaimed*
Melin y Wern, Denbigh Road, Nannerch, Mold CH7 5RH
☎ 01352-741542 Fax 01352-740254
E Mail guest-services@old-mill.u-net.com

A small friendly comfortable private hotel which forms part of a beautiful water mill conservation area. Chef proprietor. Gardens.

6 bedrs, all ensuite, TCF TV ⚘ P 12 SB £41 DB £60 HB £280 D £13.75 CC MC Visa Amex DC JCB

MONMOUTH Monmouthshire 7D4

Church Farm
Mitchel Troy, Monmouth NP5 4HZ
📞 01600-712176

A spacious and homely 16th century former farm house with oak beams and inglenook fireplaces. Set in a large attractive garden with stream. Easy access to A40 and only 2 miles from historic Monmouth.

8 bedrs, 6 ensuite, 1 ➡ TCF ✉ 🐾 P 12 SB £18-£21 DB £36-£42 HB £196-£217 D £11

MORFA NEFYN Gwynedd 6B2

★★ Woodlands Hall
Edern, Morfa Nefyn LL53 6JB
📞 01758-720425
13 bedrs, 7 ensuite, 2 🅿, 2 ➡ 🐾 P 100 ®

MUMBLES Swansea 2C1

★★ St Anne's
Western Lane, Mumbles SA3 4EY
📞 01792-369147 Fax 01792-360537
28 bedrs, all ensuite, 1 ➡ TCF TV 🐾 P 50 SB £25-£36 DB £40-£58.50 HB £195 D £11.75 CC MC Visa Amex ® ♿

Rock Villa *Acclaimed*
1 George Bank, Southend, Mumbles, Swansea SA3 4EQ
📞 01792-366794
6 bedrs, 3 ensuite, 2 ➡ TCF TV 🐾 No children under 3
SB £16-£19 DB £32-£38

Shoreline *Acclaimed*
648 Mumbles Road, Southend, Mumbles SA3 4EA
📞 01792-366233
14 bedrs, 9 ensuite, 2 🅿, 2 ➡ TCF TV CC MC

NARBERTH Pembrokeshire 6B4

Highland Grange
Robeston Wathen, Narberth SA67 8EP
📞 01834-860952

Excellent base with easy access on A40 in central Pembrokeshire. Welcoming guest house with spacious ground floor accommodation and great lounge. All year round comfort, best of hospitality, delicious meals, residential and restaurant licence.

4 bedrs, 2 ensuite, 2 ➡ TCF TV P 6 SB £14-£18 DB £28-£36 D £8 ♿

NEATH Neath & Port Talbot 2C1

★★ Castle
The Parade, Neath SA11 1RB
📞 01639-641119 Fax 01639-641624
28 bedrs, all ensuite, TCF TV P 20 SB £50 DB £60 HB £180 D £10 CC MC Visa Amex DC

NEW QUAY Ceredigion 6B3

BLACK LION HOTEL

The Black Lion Hotel is situated in the delightful Cardigan Bay resort of New Quay. Sandy beaches, fishing harbour and glorious walks all within a few minutes of the hotel.

Glanmore Terrace, New Quay, Cardiganshire SA45 9PT
Tel: 01545-560209
Fax: 01545-560585

★★ Black Lion
Glanmore Terrace, New Quay SA45 9PT
☎ 01545-560209 Fax 01545-560585
11 bedrs, 7 ensuite, 2 ⚬ TCF TV ⚬ P 25 SB £25-£38
DB £35-£54 D £9 CC MC Visa Amex JCB
See advert on previous page

Brynarfor *Acclaimed*
New Road, New Quay SA45 9SB
☎ 01545-560358 Fax 01545-561204
Closed Nov-Feb

A well run comfortable hotel situated in beautiful gardens with panoramic sea views over Cardigan Bay. Superb area for beaches, cliff walks, bird watching and dolphin spotting.

7 bedrs, all ensuite, TCF TV P 10 SB £23-£29 DB £42-£58
HB £205-£245 D £5 CC MC Visa ⚬ ⚬

NEW RADNOR Powys   7D3

Fforest *Listed*
Llanfihangel-nant-Melan, New Radnor LD8 2TN
☎ 01544-350246
4 bedrs, all ensuite, TCF TV P 30 CC MC Visa Amex JCB

NEWPORT Pembrokeshire   6A4

Springhill Guest House
Parrog Road, Newport SA42 0RH
☎ 01239-820626

Friendly welcome, sea views, 400 yards to coastal path. Rooms have colour TV, wash basins and tea and coffee making facilities. Children and pets welcome. WTB highly commended.

NEWTOWN Powys   7D3

★★ Elephant & Castle
Broad Street, Newtown SY16 2BQ
☎ 01686-626271 Fax 01686-622123
36 bedrs, all ensuite, TCF TV P 40 SB £50 DB £70 D £15
CC MC Visa Amex DC ⚬

PEMBROKE Pembrokeshire   2B1

★★ Bethwaite's Lamphey Hall
Hospitality, Comfort, Restaurant merit awards
Lamphey, Pembroke SA71 5NR
☎ 01646-672394 Fax 01646-672369
10 bedrs, all ensuite, 5 ⚬, TCF TV ⚬ P 35 SB £35 DB £50
HB £339.50 D £15.50 CC MC Visa Amex JCB ⚬

★★ Milton Manor
Milton, Pembroke SA70 8PG
☎ 01646-651398 Fax 01646-651897
19 bedrs, 16 ensuite, 1 ⚬ TCF TV ⚬ P 40 SB £36 DB £48
HB £245 CC MC Visa Amex DC JCB

★★ Wheeler's Old King's Arms
Main Street, Pembroke SA7 4JS
☎ 01646-683611 Fax 01646-682335
20 bedrs, all ensuite, TCF TV ⚬ P 20 SB £33 DB £45 CC
MC Visa Amex JCB

PENARTH Vale of Glamorgan   3D1

★★ Glendale
10 Plymouth Road, Penarth CF64 3DH
☎ 01222-706701
20 bedrs, all ensuite, 3 ⚬ TCF TV SB £29.50 DB £40
D £10.95 CC MC Visa Amex

★ Walton House
Hospitality, Restaurant merit awards
37 Victoria Road, Penarth CF6 2HY
☎ 01222-707782 Fax 01222-711012
12 bedrs, all ensuite, 1 ⚬ TCF TV P 16 SB £30.35 DB £47
D £13.50 CC MC Visa JCB

PENMAEN Swansea   2C1

★★ Nicholaston House
Nicholaston, Penmaen SA3 2HL
☎ 01792-371317 Fax 01792-371317
11 bedrs, all ensuite, ⚬ P 35 CC MC Visa ⚬

PORTHCAWL Brigend   3D1

★★ Seaways
Mary Street, Porthcawl CF36 3YA
☎ 01656-783510
17 bedrs, 11 ensuite, 2 ⚬ TCF TV ⚬ P 2 SB £18-£26
DB £32-£38 D £4.90 CC MC Visa

Penoyre *Acclaimed*
29 Mary Street, Porthcawl CF36 3YN
☏ 01656-784550
6 bedrs, 4 ensuite, 1 ⇄ TCF TV ⊨ SB £15-£20 DB £30-£34 HB £150-£175 D £8

PORTHMADOG Gwynedd — 6B2

Y Wern
Llanfrothen, Penrhyndeudraeth LL48 6LX
☏ 01766-770556 Fax 01766-770556

A 17th century farmhouse within the Snowdonia National Park, 'Y Wern' has oak beams, inglehooks, comfortable bedrooms and delightful views. Excellent for walking, beaches and castles.

5 bedrs, 3 ensuite, 2 ⇄ TCF ⊠ P 6 SB £38-£42 DB £-£120 D £11.50

PRESTATYN Denbighshire — 6C1

★★ Bron y Bryn Country House
Bryniau, Dyserth, Prestatyn LL18 6BY
☏ 01745-570442

RHYL Denbighshire — 6C1

Pier *Listed*
23 East Parade, Rhyl LL18 3AL
☏ 01745-350280
Closed Christmas
8 bedrs, 1 ⇄ TCF TV ⊨ P 3 SB £16-£19 DB £32-£38 HB £130-£160 D £7 CC MC Visa

RUABON Wrexham — 7D2

★★ Wynnstay Arms
Ruabon, Wrexham LL14 6BL
☏ 01978-822187 Fax 01978-820093
8 bedrs, 7 ensuite, TCF TV ⊨ P 80 SB £30 DB £40 D £4 CC MC Visa Amex DC JCB

RUTHIN Denbighshire — 7D1

★★ Castle
St Peters Square, Ruthin LL15 1AA
☏ 01824-702479 Fax 01824-704924
16 bedrs, all ensuite, TCF TV ⊨ P 16 SB £34-£35 DB £44-£48 D £15 CC MC Visa Amex DC

★★ Clwyd Gate Inn and Motel
Comfort merit award
Mold Road, Ruthin LL15 1HY
☏ 01824-704444 Fax 01824-703513
10 bedrs, all ensuite, 1 ⇄ TCF TV ⊨ SB £35.25 DB £49.50 D £4.95 CC MC Visa ⓘ ▣ ⓓ

Eyarth Station
Llanfair DC, Ruthin LL15 2EE
☏ 01824-703643 Fax 01824-707464

Superb, converted old railway station, set in the beautiful Vale of Clwyd, one mile from Ruthin. Medieval banquet. Ideal centre for Chester and Snowdonia. WTB highly commended.

6 bedrs, all ensuite, 1 ⇄ TCF TV ⊨ P 10 SB £21-£23 DB £42-£46 D £14 CC MC Visa ⓘ

SAUNDERSFOOT Pembrokeshire — 6B4

★★ Cambrian
Cambrian Terrace, Saundersfoot SA69 9ER
☏ 01834-812448 Fax 01834-812448
28 bedrs, all ensuite, ⊨ P 70 CC MC Visa Amex

★★ Cwmwennol Country House
Swallow Tree Woods, Saundersfoot SA69 9DE
☏ 01834-813430 Fax 01834-813430
13 bedrs, 3 ensuite, 10 ⓡ, ⊨ P 40 No children under 5 CC MC Visa Amex DC

Don't forget to mention the guide
When booking direct, please remember to tell the hotel that you chose it from
RAC Bed & Breakfast 1998.

SAUNDERSFOOT – WALES

★★ Jalna
Stammers Road, Saundersfoot SA69 9HH
☎ 01834-812282 Fax 01834-812282
Closed Dec 25

On flat ground, close to all the amenities of Saundersfoot harbour and beaches, a well appointed, comfortable, family run, small hotel where personal attention is foremost.

13 bedrs, all ensuite, 1 ♿ TCF TV 🐕 P 14 SB £25-£35 DB £45-£50 HB £195-£215 D £9 CC MC Visa Amex JCB

★★ Merlewood
St Brides Hill, Saundersfoot SA69 9NP
☎ 01834-812421 Fax 01834-812421
Closed Oct
30 bedrs, 28 ensuite, 1 ♿ TCF TV P 20 SB £25-£27 DB £50-£54 HB £195-£245 D £8 CC MC Visa 🎱 ▶ ♿

★★ Rhodewood House
St Brides Hill, Saundersfoot SA69 9NU
☎ 01834-812200 Fax 01834-811863
Closed Jan
44 bedrs, all ensuite, TCF TV P 70 SB £24-£35 DB £38-£60 HB £174-£252 D £10.80 CC MC Visa Amex DC 🎾

Bay View *Acclaimed*
Pleasant Valley, Stepaside, Saundersfoot SA67 8LR
☎ 01834-813417
Closed Oct-Mar
11 bedrs, 8 ensuite, 3 ♿ TCF P 15 SB £15-£19 DB £30-£37 HB £140-£165 D £5 🎱

Gower *Acclaimed*
Milford Terrace, Saundersfoot SA69 9EL
☎ 01834-813452 Fax 01834-813452
21 bedrs, 13 ensuite, 4 ♿ TCF TV 🐕 P 20 SB £18.50-£19.50 DB £42-£44 HB £210-£220 D £9.95 CC MC Visa

Sandy Hill *Acclaimed*
Tenby Road, Saundersfoot SA69 9DR
☎ 01834-813165
Closed Nov-Mar
5 bedrs, 4 ensuite, 1 ♿ TCF TV 🐕 P 7 No children under 5 SB £18-£21 DB £32-£38 HB £168-£189 D £8 🎱

Vine Farm *Acclaimed*
The Ridgeway, Saundersfoot SA69 9LA
☎ 01834-813543
Closed Nov-Feb
5 bedrs, all ensuite, TCF TV 🐕 P 12 SB £22-£24 DB £44-£48 HB £195-£210 ♿

Woodlands *Acclaimed*
St Brides Hill, Saundersfoot SA69 9NP
☎ 01834-813338
Closed Nov-Mar
10 bedrs, all ensuite, 1 ♿ TCF TV P 10 SB £18-£20 DB £32-£38 HB £150-£175 D £8.50 CC MC Visa

SOLVA Pembrokeshire   6A4

Lochmeyler Farm *Highly Acclaimed*
Pen-y-cwm, Solva, Haverfordwest SA62 6LL
☎ 01348-837724 Fax 01348-837622
12 bedrs, all ensuite, 1 ♿ TCF TV 🐕 P 12 SB £15-£30 DB £30-£50 HB £165-£220 D £10 CC MC Visa

ST ASAPH Denbighshire   6C1

★★ Plas Elwy
The Roe, St Asaph LL17 0LT
☎ 01745-582263 Fax 01745-583864
Closed Christmas
13 bedrs, all ensuite, TCF TV P 25 SB £40-£46 DB £58-£68 D £17 CC MC Visa Amex JCB

ST DAVID'S Pembrokeshire   6A4

★★ Old Cross
Cross Square, St David's SA62 6SP
☎ 01437-720387 Fax 01437-720394
Closed Jan-Feb
16 bedrs, all ensuite, TCF TV 🐕 P 18 SB £32-£42 DB £60-£72 HB £260-£330 D £16.25 CC MC Visa JCB

★★ St Non's
Catherine Street, St David's SA62 6RJ
☎ 01437-720239 Fax 01437-721839
Closed Dec
21 bedrs, all ensuite, TCF TV 🐕 P 30 SB £47-£57 DB £74-£90 HB £329-£392 D £17 CC MC Visa

★★ Whitesands Bay
St David's SA62 6PT
☎ 01437-720403 Fax 01473-720403
13 bedrs, all ensuite, 2 ♿ TV 🐕 P 50 CC MC Visa Amex 🎱 🏊 ▶ 🎾

Short Breaks

Many hotels provide special rates for weekend and mid-week breaks – sometimes these are quoted in the hotel's entry, otherwise ring direct for the latest offers.

RAC Hotel Reservations Service
0870 603 9109
(Calls charged at national call rate)

Ramsey House *Highly Acclaimed*
Lower Moor, St David's SA62 6RP
☎ 01437-720321 Fax 01437-720025

Exclusively for non-smoking adults seeking quiet relaxation, with award winning Welsh food and wines. Convenient for the cathedral, coast path, beaches and attractions. Pleasant garden. Easy parking.

7 bedrs, all ensuite, **TCF TV** 🐕 **P** 10 No children under 14 **SB** £25-£31 **DB** £50-£54 **HB** £228-£246 **D** £14 **CC** MC Visa JCB

Y-Gorlan *Highly Acclaimed*
77 Nun Street, St Davids SA62 6NU
☎ 01437-720837 Fax 01437-720837
5 bedrs, all ensuite, **TCF TV P** 2 **SB** £15.50-£19.50 **DB** £29-£37 **D** £6.50 **CC** MC Visa Amex

Y Glennydd *Acclaimed*
51 Nun Street, St David's SA62 6NU
☎ 01437-720576 Fax 01437-720184
Closed Nov-Jan

A comfortable Victorian house with 10 spacious centrally heated rooms, all with H & C, Teasmaid, colour TV, many with splendid views, rooms with ensuite facilities available. Ideal for walking, bird watching and outdoor activity.

10 bedrs, 8 ensuite, 2 🛏 **TV SB** £19-£25 **DB** £36-£40 **D** £13.50 **CC** MC Visa

SWANSEA   2C1

★★ Beaumont
Hospitality, Comfort, Restaurant merit awards
72-73 Walter Road, Swansea SA1 4QA
☎ 01792-643956 Fax 01792-643044
17 bedrs, all ensuite, **TCF TV** 🐕 **P** 14 **SB** £52.75 **DB** £65 **D** £14.75 **CC** MC Visa Amex DC

★★ Oaktree Parc
Birchgrove Road, Birchgrove, Swansea SA7 9JR
☎ 01792-817781 Fax 01792-814542
10 bedrs, all ensuite, 🐕 **P** 40 **CC** MC Visa Amex DC

★★ Oxwich Bay
Oxwich Bay, Gower, Swansea SA3 1LS
☎ 01792-390329 Fax 01792-391254
Closed 25 Dec
13 bedrs, all ensuite, **TCF TV** 🐕 **P** 300 **SB** £30-£55 **DB** £42-£85 **HB** £217-£304.50 **D** £15 **CC** MC Visa JCB

★★ Windsor Lodge
Hospitality, Comfort, Restaurant merit awards
Mount Pleasant, Swansea SA1 6EG
☎ 01792-642158 Fax 01792-648996
18 bedrs, all ensuite, **TV** 🐕 **P** 20 **SB** £47.50 **DB** £62.50 **HB** £380 **D** £17.60 **CC** MC Visa Amex DC JCB

St James *Highly Acclaimed*
Restaurant merit award
76b Walter Road, Swansea SA1 4QA
☎ 01792-649984

Windsor Lodge HOTEL

Windsor Lodge is a Wedgewood blue Georgian building with a bay tree in front of it

**MOUNT PLEASANT,
SWANSEA SA3 1LS
Tel: 01792-642158
Fax: 01792-648996**

Coast House *Acclaimed*
708 Mumbles Road, Mumbles, Swansea SA3 4EH
☎ 01792-368702
Closed Christmas
6 bedrs, 4 ensuite, 1 ⇔ TCF TV ⊁ SB £19-£20 DB £34-£38

Crescent *Acclaimed*
132 Eaton Crescent, Uplands, Swansea SA1 4QR
☎ 01792-466814 Fax 01792-466814
Closed Christmas & New Year
6 bedrs, all ensuite, TCF TV ⊁ P 6 SB £25-£30 DB £40-£48

Grosvenor House *Acclaimed*
Mirador Crescent, Uplands, Swansea SA2 0QX
☎ 01792-461522 Fax 01792-461522

Grosvenor House warmly welcomes businessmen and holiday visitors. Quietly situated providing quality comfort. Convenient for Swansea and Gower. Tourist Board 3 crowns highly commended.

7 bedrs, all ensuite, TCF TV ⊁ SB £25-£28 DB £40-£46 D £9 CC MC DC JCB

Guest House *Acclaimed*
4 Bryn Road, Brynmill, Swansea SA2 0AR
☎ 01792-466947
14 bedrs, 7 ensuite, 2 ⋔, 2 ⇔ TCF TV ⊁ SB £15-£25 DB £30-£40 HB £125-£170 D £7.50 CC MC Visa Amex

---

RAC Hotel Reservations Service

Use the RAC Reservations Service and you'll never have another sleepless night worrying about accommodation.
We can guarantee you a room almost anywhere in the UK and Ireland.
The price of a national call is all it takes.
The service is free to RAC Members.

0870 603 9109

Alexander *Listed*
3 Sketty Road, Uplands, Swansea SA2 0EU
☎ 01792-470045 Fax 01792-476012
Closed 24 Dec-2 Jan

Family run hotel situated on A4118 to Gower Peninsula, close to city centre, university and Grand Theatre. Ensuite bedrooms, TV, radio, telephone, tea/coffee, games room.

7 bedrs, 6 ensuite, 1 ⇔ TCF TV ⊁ No children under 2 SB £30-£33 DB £42-£45 HB £200 CC MC Visa Amex DC

Coynant & Ganol Farm *Listed*
Felindre, Swansea SA5 7PU
☎ 01269-595640
5 bedrs, 3 ensuite, 1 ⋔, TCF TV P 10

Uplands Court *Listed*
134 Eaton Crescent, Uplands, Swansea SA1 4QS
☎ 01792-473046 Fax 01792-473046
8 bedrs, 3 ensuite, 1 ⋔, 3 ⇔ TCF TV SB £18 DB £36 CC MC Visa Amex

Travelodge *Lodge*
Granada Swansea, M4, Junction 47, Swansea SA4 1GT
☎ 0880-850950 Fax 01792-899 8806
50 bedrs, all ensuite, TCF TV ⊁ P 300 SB £42.95 CC MC Visa Amex DC JCB ♿

TAL-Y-LLYN Gwynedd   6C2

★★ Tynycornel
Talyllyn, Tywyn LL36 9AJ
☎ 01654-782282 Fax 01654-782679
17 bedrs, all ensuite, TCF TV ⊁ P 30 SB £47-£57 DB £94-£114 HB £420 D £20 CC MC Visa Amex DC JCB

★ Minffordd
Hospitality, Comfort, Restaurant merit awards
Tal-y-Llyn LL36 9AJ
☎ 01654-761665 Fax 01654-761517
Closed Jan-Feb
6 bedrs, all ensuite, TCF P 12 No children under 5 DB £58-£70 HB £315-£339 D £18.50 CC MC Visa

TALSARNAU Gwynedd 6C2

★★ Maes-y-Neuadd
Talsarnau LL47 6YA
☎ 01766-780200 Fax 01766-780211
E Mail myn@marketsite.co.uk
16 bedrs, 15 ensuite, 1 ⋔, ⋔ P 50 SB £55-£136.50
DB £119-£167 HB £470-£639 D £25
CC MC Visa Amex DC JCB &

TALYBONT-ON-USK Powys 7D4

Llanddetty Hall Farm
Talybont-on-Usk, Brecon LD3 7YR
☎ 01874-676415 Fax 01874-676415

A 17th century farmhouse situated in the Brecon Beacons National Park, overlooking the river Usk with the Brecon to Monmouth canal to the rear.

3 bedrs, all ensuite, TCF ⊠ P 5 No children SB £23
DB £38 D £12

TENBY Pembrokeshire 2B1

★★ Greenhills Country House
St Florence, Tenby SA70 8NB
☎ 01834-871291 Fax 01834-871948
26 bedrs, all ensuite, TV ⋔ P 25 SB £22-£25 DB £44-£50
HB £195-£215 D £12 &

★★ Royal Gate House
North Beach, Tenby SA70 7ET
☎ 01834-842255 Fax 01834-842441
59 bedrs, all ensuite, TCF TV ⋔ ▣ P 35
SB £42-£44 DB £72-£76 HB £300-£320 D £17 CC MC
Visa Amex DC JCB

★★ Royal Lion
High Street, Tenby SA70 7EX
☎ 01834-842127 Fax 01834-842441
Closed Nov-Apr
21 bedrs, all ensuite, TCF TV ⋔ ▣ P 35 SB £35-£42
DB £70-£76 HB £292-£300 D £14 CC MC Visa DC

Broadmead *Highly Acclaimed*
Heywood Lane, Tenby SA70 8DA
☎ 01834-842641 Fax 0814-845757
20 bedrs, all ensuite, TCF TV P 20 SB £27-£33 DB £44-£56 HB £224-£266 D £13 CC MC Visa JCB

Heywood Mount *Highly Acclaimed*
Heywood Lane, Tenby SA70 8BN
☎ 01834-842087 Fax 01834-842087
20 bedrs, all ensuite, 20 ⋔ P 20 SB £21-£28 DB £42-£56 HB £185-£250 D £9 CC MC Visa Amex DC &

Kinloch Court *Highly Acclaimed*
Queens Parade, Tenby SA70 7EG
☎ 01834-842777
Closed winter
12 bedrs, all ensuite, 1 ⋔ TCF TV P 25 No children under 3 SB £26-£28 DB £52-£56 HB £236-£242 D £11 CC MC Visa

Waterwynch Bay *Highly Acclaimed*
Waterwynch Bay, Tenby SA70 8TJ
☎ 01834-842464 Fax 01834-845076
Closed Nov-Mar
17 bedrs, all ensuite, TCF TV ⋔ P 25 No children under 7 SB £34-£46 DB £60-£84 HB £260-£336 D £15 CC MC Visa &

Ashby House *Acclaimed*
24 Victoria Street, Tenby SA70 7DY
☎ 01834-842867
9 bedrs, 8 ensuite, 1 ⋔ TCF TV No children under 3
SB £18-£26 DB £30-£40 CC MC Visa

Castle View *Acclaimed*
The Norton, Tenby SA70 8AA
☎ 01834-842666
10 bedrs, all ensuite, 2 ⋔ TCF TV ⋔ P 8 SB £15-£22
DB £30-£60 CC Visa

Hildebrand *Acclaimed*
29 Victoria Street, Tenby SA70 7DY
☎ 01834-842403 Fax 01834-842403
Closed Nov-Feb

A warm welcome from Veronica and Jim. Excellent fresh home cooked food. Ensuite bedrooms with television, hairdryers, radio and courtesy tray. Near South Beach and car park.

7 bedrs, all ensuite, TCF TV ⋔ No children under 3
SB £17-£20 DB £31-£42 HB £150-£187 D £10 CC MC Visa Amex DC

Just rewards

Join the RAC today and take out **Standard Cover.** If you don't call us out during your membership year, we'll reward you with a **£25 discount** when you renew at the same level of cover. Call us on **0800 029 029**

quote GUIDE 1.

rac

www.rac.co.uk

TINTERN – WALES 363

Ivy Bank *Acclaimed*
Harding Street, Tenby SA70 7LL
☎ 01834-842311
Closed Christmas
5 bedrs, all ensuite, TCF TV SB £16-£19 DB £32-£38
D £8

Marlborough House *Acclaimed*
South Cliff Street, Tenby SA70 7EA
☎ 01834-842961
8 bedrs, 4 ensuite, TCF TV SB £13-£15 DB £25-£30
HB £85-£95 D £7.50 CC MC Visa Amex

Pen Mar *Acclaimed*
New Hedges, Tenby SA70 8TL
☎ 01834-842435

A modern, detached hotel in Pembrokeshire National Park situated between Tenby and Saundersfoot with fine sea views. 'A Touch of Italy' awaits in the restaurant's Anglo/Continental cuisine.

10 bedrs, 6 ensuite, 2 ⇨ TCF TV P 10 SB £16.50-£22.50
DB £33-£45 HB £104-£140 D £10 CC MC Visa Amex DC JCB

Ripley St Mary's *Acclaimed*
St Mary's Street, Tenby SA70 7HN
☎ 01834-842837 Fax 01834-842837
Closed Oct-Easter

Situated in a quiet street in the centre of Tenby, the hotel has won 'Tenby in Bloom' awards for its hanging baskets and window boxes. Situated 100 yards from the sea front and Paragon Gardens.

14 bedrs, 8 ensuite, 3 ⇨ TCF TV ⚑ P 14 SB £20-£22
DB £40-£44 HB £180-£200 D £9 CC MC Visa

CLARENCE HOUSE

Located on the south sea front near the old walled town with superb coastal views to Caldy Island. Sea view restaurant offers excellent cuisine. Auto safety Otis lift to all floors. Quiet olde worlde comfort offering modern amenities at reasonable cost.

ESPLANADE, TENBY SA70 7DU
Tel: 01834-844371
Fax: 01834-844372

Clarence House
Esplanade, Tenby SA70 7DU
☎ 01834-844371 Fax 01834-844372
Closed Oct-Mar
68 bedrs, all ensuite, 5 ⇨ TCF TV ⚑ 🛗 No children under 3 SB £16-£35 DB £26-£68 HB £147-£238 D £9 CC MC Visa ♿

TINTERN Monmouthshire 3E1

★★ Royal George
Hospitality, Restaurant merit awards
Tintern, Chepstow NP6 6SF
☎ 01291-689205 Fax 01291-689448

Set in the beautiful Wye valley, serving the finest local produce in an award winning restaurant with an international wine list. All rooms have refurbished luxury bathrooms. Under the personal supervision of the resident owners.

19 bedrs, 16 ensuite, 1 🅿, 1 ⇨ TCF TV ⚑ P 40 SB £55
DB £77 D £21 CC MC Visa Amex DC ♿

Parva Farmhouse *Highly Acclaimed*
Restaurant merit award
Tintern, nr Chepstow NP6 6SQ
☏ 01291-689411 Fax 01291-689557
9 bedrs, all ensuite, 1 ➡ TCF TV ⛔ P 15 SB £39-£44 DB £58-£64 HB £276 D £17.50 CC MC Visa Amex DC JCB

Valley House *Acclaimed*
Raglan Road, Tintern NP6 6TH
☏ 01291-689652 Fax 01291-689805
Closed Christmas
3 bedrs, all ensuite, TCF TV ✉ ⛔ P 7 CC Amex

TREARDDUR BAY Anglesey   6B1

★★ **Seacroft**
Ravenspoint Road, Trearddur Bay LL65 2YU
☏ 01407-860348

Moranedd *Listed*
Trearddur Road, Trearddur Bay LL65 2UE
☏ 01407-860324
Closed Christmas
6 bedrs, 2 ➡ TCF P 10 SB £15 DB £30

TREGARON Ceredigion   6C3

Talbot *Listed*
The Square, Tregaron SY25 6JL
☏ 01974-298208
14 bedrs, 4 ensuite, 3 ➡ TCF TV ⛔ P 12 SB £26-£32 DB £42-£50 D £11 CC MC Visa

TRESAITH Ceredigion   6B3

Bryn Berwyn *Highly Acclaimed*
Restaurant merit award
Tresaith, Aberporth CA43 2JG
☏ 01239-811126 Fax 01239-811126
7 bedrs, all ensuite, TCF TV P 15 SB £21-£25 CC MC Visa

TYWYN Gwynedd   6B2

★★ **Corbett Arms**
Tywyn LL36 9DG
☏ 01654-710264 Fax 01654-710359
40 bedrs, all ensuite, TCF TV ⛔ ✉ P 60 SB £22-£32 DB £39-£64 HB £196-£245 D £8 CC MC Visa Amex DC

★ **Greenfield**
High Street, Tywyn LL36 9AD
☏ 01654-710354 Fax 01654-710354
Closed Jan
8 bedrs, 5 ensuite, 1 ➡ TCF TV SB £17-£19.50 DB £32-£37 HB £156-£166 D £7 CC MC Visa JCB

WELSHPOOL Powys   7D2

Trefnant Hall Farm *Acclaimed*
Berriew, Welshpool SY21 8AS
☏ 01686-640262
3 bedrs, all ensuite, TCF TV ✉ P 6

Tynllwyn Farm *Listed*
Welshpool SY21 9BW
☏ 01938-553175
Closed Christmas
6 bedrs, 1 ensuite, 2 ➡ TCF TV ⛔ P 20 SB £15 DB £30 HB £140

WHITLAND Carmarthenshire   6B4

Llangwn House *Acclaimed*
Whitland SA34 0RB
☏ 01994-240621 Fax 01994-240621
4 bedrs, all ensuite, TV ⛔ P 10

Northern Ireland & Republic of Ireland

Top: Grovemount House, Ennistymon

Right: Glenn Fia Country House, Killarney

Below: Caireal Manor Guest House, Cushendall

RaC

AGHADOWEY Co. Londonderry 17E1

★★Brown Trout Golf and Country Inn
209 Agivey Road, Near Coleraine BT51 4AD
☎ 01265-868209 Fax 01265-868878
17 bedrs, all ensuite, TCF TV ⚑ 🅿 P 100 SB £45-£60 DB £70-£80 HB £150-£160 D £15 CC MC Visa Amex DC
🎌 ▶ 📼 ♿

ARMAGH Co. Armagh 17E3

★★Drumsill
Comfort merit award
35 Moy Road, Armagh BT61 8DL
☎ 01861-522009 Fax 01861-525624
9 bedrs, all ensuite, TCF TV P 100 SB £50 DB £74 HB £297 D £13 CC MC Visa Amex DC

BELFAST 17F2

★★Balmoral
Blacks Road, Dunmurry, Belfast BT10 0NF
☎ 01232-301234 Fax 01232-601455
44 bedrs, all ensuite, TCF TV ⚑ P 300 SB £45 DB £65 HB £245 D £11 ♿

★★Holiday Inn Express
106 University Street, Belfast BT7 1HP
☎ 01232-311909 Fax 01232-311910
114 bedrs, all ensuite, TCF TV 🅿 SB £54.95 DB £54.95 D £7.95 CC MC Visa Amex DC JCB ♿

BUSHMILLS Co. Antrim 17E1

Craig Park Country House
24 Cranborne Road, Bushmills BT57 8YF
☎ 012657-32496 Fax 012657-32479
Closed Christmas-New Year

A comfortable country house 2 miles from Bushmills and close to the Giant's Causeway. Set in an elevated position facing west with distant views.

3 bedrs, TCF TV

CARNLOUGH Co. Antrim 17F1

★★Londonderry Arms
Hospitality, Restaurant merit awards
Glens of Antrim, Carnlough BT44 0EU
☎ 01574-885255 Fax 01574-885263
35 bedrs, all ensuite, P 50 SB £45 DB £65 D £14.95 CC MC Visa Amex DC

CARRICKFERGUS Co. Antrim 17F2

★Dobbins Inn
Hospitality merit award
Carrickfergus BT38 7AF
☎ 01960-351905 Fax 01960-351905
Closed Christmas

Friendly family owned 16th century hotel with full bar and restaurant facilities and regular evening entertainment. Fully refurbished during 1997.

13 bedrs, all ensuite, TCF TV ⚑ SB £42 DB £62 D £5 CC MC Visa Amex DC

CUSHENDALL Co. Antrim 17F1

Caireal Manor *Highly Acclaimed*
90 Glenravel Road, Glen's of Antrim, Martinstown, Cushendall BT43 6QQ
☎ 012667-58465 Fax 012667-58465

Superior quality luxury accommodation situated on the A43 7 miles north of Ballymena, 5 miles from Cushendall. Ideal for exploring Antrim coast and glens. All rooms ensuite and furnished to a high standard. Close to golf, fishing, swimming, walking.

5 bedrs, all ensuite, TCF TV P 8 SB £25 DB £50 HB £270 D £16 ♿

ENNISKILLEN Co. Fermanagh 17D3

★Railway
Enniskillen BT74 6AJ
☎ 01365-322084 Fax 01365-327480
19 bedrs, 18 ensuite, 2 ⚑ TCF TV SB £28-£32.50 DB £55-£65 D £15 CC MC Visa

Abbeyville Listed
1 Willoughby Court, Portora, Enniskillen BT74 7EE
☎ 01365-327033
3 bedrs, 1 ensuite, 1 ⇌ TCF TV SB £20 DB £30

Riverside Farm Guesthouse
Gortadrehid, Culkey P.O., Enniskillen
☎ 01365-322725

Farmhouse on 65 acre livestock farm. N.T. properties, fishing, shooting, scenic drives, golfing nearby, babysitter. Dogs allowed outside. Fire certificate, small parties catered for (max. 25).

6 bedrs, 1 ensuite, 1 ⇌ TCF SB £16-£17 DB £30 HB £140-£145 D £8

IRVINESTOWN Co. Fermanagh 17D2

★★Mahons
Enniskillen Road, Irvinestown BT74 9GS
☎ 013656-21656 Fax 01365-628344
18 bedrs, all ensuite, TCF TV ⇌ P 50 SB £30-£35 DB £55-£65 D £13 CC MC Visa Amex ♿

LARNE Co. Antrim 17F2

Derrin Acclaimed
2 Prince's Gardens, Larne BT40 1RQ
☎ 01574-273269 Fax 01574-273269
Closed Christmas

Beautifully appointed Grade A guest house, family run since 1964. 'Highly commended' in the 1994 Galtee Breakfast Awards. Full fire certificate. Private car park. Friendly welcoming atmosphere.

7 bedrs, 4 ensuite, 1 ⇌ TCF TV ⇌ P 3 SB £20-£25 DB £30-£36 CC MC Visa Amex

LONDONDERRY Co. Londonderry 17D1

Banks of the Faughan Motel
69 Clooney Road, Londonderry BT47 3PA
☎ 01504-860242 Fax 01504-860242

Beautifully situated overlooking Lough Foyle and the Donegal Hills and within minutes of the City of Derry airport. Private car park, full fire certificate and a friendly welcoming atmosphere.

NEWCASTLE Co. Down 17F3

Briers Country House Highly Acclaimed
39 Middle Tollymore Road, Newcastle BT33 0JJ
☎ 013967-24347 Fax 013967-24347
9 bedrs, all ensuite, TV P 30 No children under 12
SB £35 DB £50 D £16 CC MC Visa Amex ♿

Brook Cottage Acclaimed
58 Bryansford Road, Newcastle BT33 0LD
☎ 013967-22204 Fax 013967-22193
9 bedrs, 7 ensuite, 1 ⇌ TV P 50 SB £40-£42.50 DB £60-£68 D £15 CC MC Visa Amex DC ♿

OMAGH Co. Tyrone 17D2

★★Royal Arms
51 High Street, Omagh BT78 1BA
☎ 01662-243262 Fax 01662-244860
Closed 25 Dec
21 bedrs, all ensuite, TCF TV ⇌ P 100 SB £39 DB £75 D £13 CC MC Visa

PORTADOWN Co. Armagh 17E3

★★Seagoe
Upper Church Lane, Portadown BT63 5JE
☎ 01762-333076 Fax 01762-350210

PORTBALLINTRAE Co. Antrim 17E1

★★Bayview
2 Bayhead Road, Portballintrae BT57 8RZ
☎ 012657-31453 Fax 012657-32360
16 bedrs, all ensuite, TCF TV ⇌ P 60 SB £45 DB £75 HB £262.50 D £13 CC MC Visa ♿

ADARE Co. Limerick 18C2

Adare Lodge *Acclaimed*
Kildimo Road, Adare
☎ 061-396629 Fax 061-395060
6 bedrs, all ensuite, 1 ⇥ TCF TV ⊠ P 6 SB £30 DB £35-£40 CC MC Visa ♿

ARDMORE Co. Waterford 19D3

★★ Cliff House
Ardmore
☎ 024-94106 Fax 024-94496
Closed 1 Nov-28 Feb
13 bedrs, all ensuite, 1 ⇥ TCF P 30 SB £25-£80 DB £64-£80 D £18.50 CC MC Visa Amex DC

Newtown View Farmhouse
Grange, Ardmore
☎ 024-94143 Fax 024-94143
Closed 1 Nov

A working dairy farm with views of the Atlantic Ocean. All rooms ensuite with TV and tea making facilities. Award winning seafood dishes a speciality. Hard tennis court, pony trekking, games room. Ardmore cliff walks.

6 bedrs, all ensuite, TCF TV ⇥ P 10 SB £15-£20 DB £33-£36 HB £175-£189 D £12 CC MC Visa

ATHY Co. Kildare 19E1

★★ Tonlegee House
Hospitality, Restaurant merit awards
Athy
☎ 0507-31473 Fax 0507-31473
9 bedrs, all ensuite, ⇥ P 40 CC MC Visa Amex

AUGHRIM Co. Wicklow 19F2

★★ Lawless's
Aughrim, Arklow
☎ 01402-36146 Fax 01402-36384
Closed 24-26 Dec
10 bedrs, 8 ensuite, 2 ⇥ TV P 30 SB £38.50-£43 DB £56.50-£64.50 HB £295-£325 D £17.75 CC MC Visa Amex DC ♿

BALLINAMORE Co. Leitrim 17D3

Riversdale Farm Guesthouse *Acclaimed*
Ballinamore
☎ 078-44122 Fax 078-44813

The hotel is situated two miles west of the town of Enneskillen, 100 yards from the house is fishing, nearby is a driving range and two 18 hole golf courses.

9 bedrs, all ensuite, P 20 SB £25-£30 DB £44 HB £185-£190 D £12 CC MC Visa

Commercial & Tourist *Listed*
Ballinamore
☎ 078-44675 Fax 078-44679

This family run hotel is located just a few hundred yards from the Ballinamore/Ballyconnell Canal in the heart of the greenest and most uncluttered part of Ireland.

16 bedrs, all ensuite, TCF TV P 30 SB £34 DB £50 HB £190 D £12 CC MC Visa Amex DC

BALLINGEARY Co. Cork 18B3

★★ Gougane Barra
Gougane Barra, Ballingeary
☎ 026-47069 Fax 026-47226
27 bedrs, all ensuite, TCF TV P 25 No children under 11
SB £51-£59 DB £68-£80 D £19 CC MC Visa Amex DC

BALLINROBE Co. Mayo 16B4

Red Door *Listed*
The Neale Road, Ballinrobe
☎ 092-41263
6 bedrs, all ensuite, TCF TV ⇥ P 40 SB £20 DB £35 HB £32 D £12.95 CC MC Visa

BALLYBUNION Co. Kerry　　　18B2

★★ Marine Links
Hospitality, Restaurant merit awards
Sandhill Road, Ballybunion
☎ 068-27139 Fax 068-27666
Closed Nov-10 Mar
11 bedrs, all ensuite, TCF TV ✱ P 100 SB £38-£50
DB £52-£75 HB £285-£336 D £20 CC MC Visa Amex DC

BALLYMACARBRY Co. Waterford　　　19D3

Clonanav Farm Guesthouse *Acclaimed*
Nire Valley, Ballymacarbry
☎ 052-36141 Fax 052-36141
E Mail clonanav@iol.ie
Closed 1 Nov-1 Feb
10 bedrs, all ensuite, P 20 SB £27-£34 DB £46-£54
HB £260-£280 D £10 CC MC Visa Amex DC

BALLYVAUGHAN Co. Clare　　　18C1

Rusheen Lodge *Highly Acclaimed*
Knocknagrough, Ballyvaughan
☎ 065-77092 Fax 065-77152
Closed Nov-Feb
8 bedrs, all ensuite, TCF TV P 12 SB £30-£40 DB £45-£55
CC MC Visa Amex

Rusheen Lodge GUEST HOUSE

Renowned for our friendly, warm welcome and personal service, Rusheen Lodge is family owned by Rita and John McGann. Our individually designed bedrooms are generously apportioned and offer all modern comforts. An ideal base from which to explore the varied attractions of counties Galway and Clare

**Ballyvaughan, Co. Clare,
Republic of Ireland
Tel: 065-77092 Fax: 065-77152**

BANTRY Co. Cork　　　18B4

Eden Crest
Newtown, Bantry
☎ 027-51110 Fax 027-51036
Closed Dec-Feb

Comfortable and tranquil scenic house overlooking Bantry Bay. With golf and parking, golf etc. near by.

4 bedrs, all ensuite, TCF P 6 SB £17-£21 DB £34 CC MC Visa DC

BLESSINGTON Co. Wicklow　　　19F1

★★ Downshire House
Hospitality, Comfort, Restaurant merit awards
Blessington
☎ 045-865199 Fax 045-865335
Closed 22 Dec-6 Jan
25 bedrs, all ensuite, P 30 SB £45 DB £77 D £18 CC MC Visa

BRUFF Co. Limerick　　　18C2

Bridge House Farm
Grange, Bruff
☎ 061-390195
Closed Nov-Feb

200 year old house on a cattle farm by Camogue River on the R512 road, 15 minutes drive south of Limerick City. Archaeology, fishing and golf nearby.

4 bedrs, 2 ensuite, 1 ➜ TCF P 10 No children under 6
SB £15 DB £30 D £14

BUNBEG – REPUBLIC OF IRELAND

BUNBEG Co. Donegal — 16C1

Teach h-Anraoi *Listed*
Magheraclogher, Bunbeg
📞 075-31092

Family run B&B, near golf leisure centre, horse riding centre, beautiful golden beaches, centre of Donegal. Gaeltacht failte roimh gach duine.

7 bedrs, 5 ensuite, 2 🛏 🐾 P 10 SB £15-£18 DB £30-£32.50 HB £130-£140 D £9 CC Visa ♿

BUNRATTY Co. Clare — 18C2

Bunratty View
Cratloe, Bunratty
📞 061-357352 Fax 061-357491
Closed 20 Dec-6 Jan
7 bedrs, all ensuite, 1 🛏 TCF TV P 20 CC MC Visa ♿

AGLISH HOUSE

**AGLISH, CAPPOQUIN,
CO. WATERFORD,
REPUBLIC OF IRELAND**

Tel/Fax: 024 96191

RAC Hotel Reservations Service
0870 603 9109
(Calls charged at national call rate)

BUNRATTY CASTLE & FOLK PARK
Bunratty, Co. Clare

Bunratty Castle is one of the most complete examples of mediaeval castles surviving in Ireland today. Built in 1425, it is wholly intact and houses an exceptional collection of late mediaeval European furniture and tapestries.
The domestic theme at Bunratty is carried into the Folk Park which contains typical nineteenth century rural and urban dwellings.

*Bunratty Castle & Folk Park open daily, year round: 9.30 a.m. – 5.30 p.m.
(Open until 7 p.m. June – Aug.)*

**CENTRAL RESERVATIONS AT
BUNRATTY CASTLE & FOLK PARK**
061-361511

CAPPAGH Co. Waterford   19D3

Castle Farm *Acclaimed*
Millstreet, Cappagh
☎ 058-68049 Fax 058-68049
Closed mid Nov-Feb
5 bedrs, all ensuite, 1 ⇌ TCF TV ⊁ P 20 No children under 5 SB £24 DB £38 HB £210 D £14 CC MC Visa DC

CAPPOQUIN Co. Waterford   19D3

Richmond House *Highly Acclaimed*
Restaurant merit award
Cappoquin
☎ 058-54278 Fax 058-54988
Closed 23 Dec-Jan
9 bedrs, all ensuite, TCF TV P 15 SB £35-£50 DB £60-£90 HB £550 D £25 CC MC Visa DC

Aglish House
Aglish, Cappoquin
☎ 024-96191 Fax 024-96191
4 bedrs, all ensuite, TV ⊁ P 4

CARAGH LAKE Co. Kerry   18A3

Caragh Lodge *Highly Acclaimed*
Caragh Lake
☎ 066-69115 Fax 066-69316
Closed Oct-Easter

Mid Victorian fishing lodge in seven acres. Award winning gardens on shore of Caragh Lake.

15 bedrs, all ensuite, P 20 No children under 10 SB £71.50 DB £49.50-£66 D £28 CC MC Visa Amex

CARLOW Co. Carlow   19E2

Barrowville Town House *Highly Acclaimed*
Kilkenny Road, Carlow
☎ 0503-43324 Fax 0503-41953

Regency town house, with antique furnishing, in its own grounds. Three minutes walk to the town centre with pubs, restaurants, etc. An ideal location for golf, touring the south east, Kilkenny and Mount Juliet and Glendalough Japanese Gardens.

7 bedrs, all ensuite, TCF TV P 11 No children under 12 SB £23.50-£27 DB £40-£45 CC MC Visa Amex

CARRIGANS Co. Donegal   17D1

Mount Royd Country Home *Highly Acclaimed*
Carrigans, Nr Londonderry
☎ 074-40163
4 bedrs, all ensuite, 1 ⇌ TV P 8 SB £19 DB £32 D £12

CASTLETOWN BERE Co. Cork   18B4

★★ Ford Ri
Castletown Bere
☎ 027-70379 Fax 027-70506
Closed Jan-Feb
18 bedrs, all ensuite, P 100

CELBRIDGE Co. Kildare   19F1

Green Acres *Listed*
Dublin Road, Celbridge
☎ 01-627 1163 Fax 01-627 1163

A bungalow set in its own grounds with car park. Dublin 20 minutes, 30 minutes to the airport and ferries. On bus route. Castletown House 2 km. Golf and fishing nearby. Open from 3 January to 23 December.

6 bedrs, TCF P 6 No children under 6 SB £21 DB £17

CLIFDEN Co. Galway 16A4

★★ Erriseask House
Hospitality, Restaurant merit awards
Clifden, Ballyconneely
📞 095-23553 Fax 095-23639
Closed Nov-Easter
12 bedrs, all ensuite, TCF P 20
SB £53-£61 DB £66-£99 HB £289-£319 D £19.50 CC MC Visa Amex DC

Mal Dua *Highly Acclaimed*
Galway Road, Clifden
📞 095-21171 Fax 095-21739
E Mail maldua@iol.ie
Closed Dec

A family run guest house, about a mile from Clifden in the heart of Connemara. Spacious bedrooms all individually designed, with TV, radio, telephone, and tea/coffee facilities.

14 bedrs, all ensuite, TCF TV P 40 SB £30-£50 DB £44-£60 CC MC Visa Amex

Sunnybank *Highly Acclaimed*
Church Hill, Clifden
📞 095-21437 Fax 095-21976
Closed 3 Nov-14 Mar

A period house of character, situated in its own grounds and surrounded by gardens with many interesting features. The house overlooks the picturesque town of Clifton. A warm Irish welcome awaits our guests from the O'Gradys.

11 bedrs, all ensuite, TV P 12 No children under 8
DB £50-£60 CC MC Visa

Dun Ri *Acclaimed*
Clifden
📞 095-21625 Fax 095-21635
Closed Nov-Mar
10 bedrs, all ensuite, TV P 10 No children under 3
SB £20-£35 DB £40-£50 CC MC Visa

Mallmore House *Acclaimed*
Ballyconneely Road, Clifden
📞 095-21460
Closed Nov-Feb
6 bedrs, all ensuite, 1 ⇌ P 15 DB £37

Ben View House *Listed*
Bridge Street, Clifden
📞 095-21256
8 bedrs, 7 ensuite, 🐕

Kingstown House *Listed*
Bridge Street, Clifden
📞 095-21470 Fax 095-21530
Closed 23-27 Dec
8 bedrs, 6 ensuite, 2 ⇌ TCF TV 🐕 SB £18-£25 DB £32-£36 CC MC Visa

Heather Lodge
Westport Road, Clifden
📞 095-21331

A delightful family home with a warm atmosphere, splendid views of the lake and mountains, breakfast menu and home baking. Ideal base for touring Connemara. Area of unspoilt beaches, angling, golf and fishing.

6 bedrs, 5 ensuite

CLONAKILTY Co. Cork 18C4

Duvane Farm
Ballyduvane, Clonakilty
📞 023-33129
Closed 15 Mar-30 Oct
5 bedrs, 2 ⇌ TCF 🐕 SB £20-£25 DB £32-£44 D £13

RAC Hotel Reservations Service
0870 603 9109
(Calls charged at national call rate)

CLONMEL Co. Tipperary 19D3

Amberville
Glenconnor Road, (off Western Road), Clonmel
☎ 052-21470

Spacious bungalow (300M off Western Road, near hospitals) set in own grounds in nice residential area. TV lounge for guests, tea/coffee available, private parking.

5 bedrs, 3 ensuite, 2 🐕 🐾 P 5 SB £15-£17 ♿

CORK Co. Cork 18C3

★★ John Barleycorn Inn
Riverstown, Glanmire
☎ 021-821499 Fax 021-821221
Closed 25-26 Dec
17 bedrs, all ensuite, TCF TV 🐾 P 180 SB £51-£59 D £17
CC MC Visa Amex DC 🅿 ♿

DUVANE FARM

*Elegant Georgian house situated on Beef Farm 2km from Clonakilty, on N71 on the Skibbereen side of town. Comforting, relaxing accommodation with period furniture including brass and canopy beds, TV, tea/coffee facilities in bedrooms.
Galtee Award Winner. All meals from local and home produce. All leisure activities nearby. Ideal base for touring Cork and Kerry. AA listed. 3 QQQ.
Open from March to October. B&B from £18-£22 per person*

Write or phone for brochures:
Noreen McCarthy 023-33129

DUVANE FARM, BALLYDUVANE, CLONAKILTY, CO. CORK

Garnish House *Acclaimed*
Western Road, Cork
☎ 021-275111 Fax 021-273872
E Mail garnish@iol.ie

Renowned for its warm welcome and excellent service from owner/manageress - Hansie Lucey. The city centre is just a stones throw from Garnish House and we are on the gateway to West Cork and Kerry, with excellent off street parking.

14 bedrs, all ensuite, 1 🐕 TCF TV 🐾 P 8 SB £30-£40
DB £45-£50 CC MC Visa Amex DC ♿

Killarney House *Acclaimed*
Western Road (opp U.C.C.), Cork
☎ 021-270290 Fax 021-271010
E Mail killarneyhouse@iol.ie
Closed 25-26 Dec

A family run guest house situated opposite University College, and a short drive from Cork airport and ferry, offering exceptional style and comfort within walking distance of the city.

19 bedrs, all ensuite, 1 🐕 TCF TV P 20 SB £20-£44
DB £20-£55 CC MC Visa Amex

Roscrie Villa *Acclaimed*
Mardyke Walk, Off Western Road, Cork
☎ 021-272958 Fax 021-274087
16 bedrs, all ensuite, 1 🐕 TCF TV P 8 No children under 5 SB £23-£40 DB £40-£60 CC MC Visa Amex DC

Aaran Isle Inn *Awaiting Inspection*
14 Mardyke Parade, Cork
☎ 021-278158 Fax 021-278093
16 bedrs, all ensuite, TCF TV SB £20-£28 DB £18-£24 CC MC Visa Amex DC

COURTMACSHERRY Co. Cork   18C4

★★ Courtmacsherry
Courtmacsherry
📞 023-46198 Fax 023-46137
Closed 1 Oct-30 Apr
13 bedrs, 11 ensuite, 2 🛏 TV 🐕 P 60 SB £50-£58
DB £64-£78 HB £290-£315 D £19 CC MC Visa

CRUSHEEN Co. Clare   18C1

Lahardan House *Acclaimed*
Crusheen
📞 065-27128 Fax 065-27319

Family residence 9.5 miles north of Ennis, 1.5 miles off N18 Ennis/Galway road at Crusheen. Rooms ensuite, direct dial telephones, hairdryers, central heating. Fishing, golf, pitch and putt available locally. Relax in the peace and quiet of Lahardan.

8 bedrs, all ensuite, TV 🐕 P 15 CC MC Visa

DINGLE Co. Kerry   18A3

Alpine House *Highly Acclaimed*
Mail Road, Dingle
📞 066-51250 Fax 066-51966

Family run purpose-built guest house in its own grounds with garden, located at the entrance to the town. All rooms are ensuite and furnished to a high standard.

12 bedrs, all ensuite, TCF TV P 20 No children under 5
SB £17.50-£37 DB £30-£45 CC MC Visa

Ard-Na-Greine *Highly Acclaimed*
Spa Road, Dingle
📞 066-51113 Fax 066-51898
4 bedrs, all ensuite, TCF TV P 4 No children under 7
DB £30-£34 CC MC Visa

Cleevaun House *Highly Acclaimed*
Ladys Cross, Milltown, Dingle
📞 066-51108 Fax 066-51108
Closed Dec-Feb

Galtee Regional Breakfast winner 1994. Cleevaun is set in landscaped gardens overlooking Dingle Bay. Rooms with private bathrooms, TV's, hairdryers, tea/coffee facilities.

9 bedrs, all ensuite, P 9 No children under 8 DB £30-£45 CC MC Visa

Doyles Town House *Highly Acclaimed*
John Street, Dingle
📞 066-51816 Fax 066-51816
Closed mid Nov-mid Mar
8 bedrs, all ensuite, TV SB £44 DB £68 D £15 CC MC Visa DC

Greenmount House *Highly Acclaimed*
Upper John Street, Dingle
📞 066-51414 Fax 066-51974

Luxury guest house, set on a hillside in a peaceful, tranquil location with panoramic views over Dingle town and harbour.

12 bedrs, all ensuite, TCF TV P 15 No children under 8
SB £20-£40 DB £35-£65 CC MC Visa ♿

Milltown House *Highly Acclaimed*
Dingle
📞 066-51372 Fax 066-51095
Closed 15 Nov-15 Mar
10 bedrs, all ensuite, TCF TV 🐕 P 20 No children under 10 SB £25-£40 DB £40-£70 CC MC Visa ♿

Pax House *Highly Acclaimed*
Upper John Street, Dingle
📞 066-51518 Fax 066-51518

Situated half a mile from Dingle Town. Large lounge, dining room, balcony with an uninterrupted panoramic view of Dingle Bay and harbour. A large gourmet breakfast greets guests each morning.

7 bedrs, all ensuite, 2 🛏 TCF TV P 10 SB £30-£35 DB £44-£50 CC MC Visa

Bamburys Guesthouse *Listed*
Mail Road, Dingle
📞 066-51244 Fax 066-51786

Ideally situated new house with half hips and dormer windows, one side overlooking Dingle Harbour.

12 bedrs, all ensuite, 1 🛏 TCF TV P 12 SB £18-£40 DB £26-£50 CC MC Visa ♿

Bolands *Listed*
Goat Street, Dingle
📞 066-51426

House with view of Dingle Bay. Walking distance to all amenities. Sky TV, hairdryers, clock radio, tea/coffee making facilities. Orthopedic beds.

6 bedrs, all ensuite, TV DB £15-£18 CC MC Visa

DONEGAL Co. Donegal   16C2

Ardeevin *Highly Acclaimed*
Lough Eske, Barnesmore, Donegal
📞 073-21790 Fax 073-21790
Closed Nov-Mar

A country residence with magnificent views of Lough Eske and the Bluestack Mountains from all bedrooms. Lake and sea fishing available locally. Lovely mountain walks. Golf nearby.

6 bedrs, all ensuite, 1 🛏 TCF TV 🐕 P 8 SB £21-£22 DB £34

DOOLIN Co. Clare   18B1

Churchfield *Listed*
Doolin
📞 065-74209 Fax 065-74622

DROGHEDA Co. Louth   17E4

Tullyesker Country House *Highly Acclaimed*
Tullyesker, Monasterboice, Drogheda
📞 041-30430 Fax 041-32624
Closed 1 Dec-1 Feb

Award winning luxurious country house with panoramic views, private parking, 4 acre gardens overlooking N1. Extensive breakfast menu, bedrooms with orthopedic beds, tea/coffee facilities, satellite TV, electric blankets, hairdryers and all toiletries.

5 bedrs, all ensuite, TCF TV P 20 No children under 10 SB £32 DB £38

DUBLIN Co. Dublin 19F1

★★ Holly Brook
Holly Brook Park, Clontarf, Dublin 3
☎ 01-833 5456 Fax 01-833 5458
22 bedrs, all ensuite, 2 ⇌ TV ⊁ P 70
SB £45-£50 DB £60 D £13 CC MC Visa Amex ♿

66 Town House *Highly Acclaimed*
66 Northumberland Road, Ballsbridge, Dublin 4
☎ 01-660 0333 Fax 01-660 1051
6 bedrs, all ensuite, TCF TV P 6 SB £40-£55 DB £55-£70
CC MC Visa

Aberdeen Lodge *Highly Acclaimed*
53-55 Park Avenue, Dublin
☎ 01-283 8155 Fax 01-283 7877
16 bedrs, all ensuite, P 16

Ariel House *Highly Acclaimed*
50-52 Lansdowne Road, Ballsbridge, Dublin
☎ 01-668 5512 Fax 01-668 5845
28 bedrs, all ensuite, TV ⊠ P 30 No children under 7
CC MC Visa ♿

Butlers *Highly Acclaimed*
44 Lansdowne Road, Ballsbridge, Dublin
☎ 01-667 4022 Fax 01-667 3960

RAC Hotel Reservations Service
0870 603 9109
(Calls charged at national call rate)

Charleville Lodge *Highly Acclaimed*
268-272 North Circular Road, Phisboro, Dublin
☎ 01-838 6633 Fax 01-838 5854
E Mail charleville@indigo.ie.
Closed Christmas

Completely refurbished to combine old charm and character with all modern facilities, the luxurious premises are located 15 minutes walk from O'Connell Street and are on main bus routes. Large car park.

30 bedrs, 28 ensuite, 1 ⇌ TV P 15 SB £33-£45 DB £55-£75 CC MC Visa Amex DC ♿

Eglinton Manor *Highly Acclaimed*
83 Eglinton Road, Donnybrook, Dublin 4
☎ 01-269 3273 Fax 01-269 7527

· 66 · TOWNHOUSE

- *Refurbished Victorian House*
- *I.T.B./A.A./R.A.C. Approved*
- *Central Heating*
- *All bedrooms have:*
  - Ensuites
  - Direct Dial Phones
  - Hair Dryers
  - Tea/Coffee making facilities
  - Colour TVs
- *10 mins from city centre*
- *Buses: 5, 7, 7a, 8, 45, 46, 84*
- *Adjacent to:*
  - Lansdowne Road
  - RDS, RTE
  - Embassies, Universities
  - Dart
  - Jurys, Berkeley Court, Hibernian, Burlington Hotels
- *Restaurants & Pubs*

66 NORTHUMBERLAND ROAD, BALLSBRIDGE, DUBLIN 4
Tel: 6600333/6600471   Fax: 6601051

Glenogra *Highly Acclaimed*
64 Merrion Road, Ballsbridge, Dublin
☎ 01-668 3661 Fax 01-668 3698

A beautifully appointed Edwardian residence opposite RDS, close to the city centre.

9 bedrs, all ensuite, TCF TV ☒ P 9 SB £45-£60 DB £60-£90 CC MC Visa Amex DC

Merrion Hall *Highly Acclaimed*
54/56 Merrion Road, Ballsbridge, Dublin
☎ 01-668 1426 Fax 01-668 4280

Situated in Dublin's most elegant suburb and within its own secluded grounds, Merrion Hall has recently been refurbished with a homely but refined elegance.

15 bedrs, all ensuite, TCF TV P 10 SB £40-£80 DB £55-£90 CC MC Visa

Raglan Lodge *Highly Acclaimed*
10 Raglan Road, Ballsbridge, Dublin
☎ 01-660 6697 Fax 01-660 6781

A large Victorian residence dating from 1861, carefully restored to its former splendour.

7 bedrs, all ensuite, TCF ⊁ P 20 CC MC Visa Amex

MERRION HALL
RAC Highly Acclaimed

Elegant Victorian House, situated in Ballsbridge, Dublin's most exclusive suburb and centre of Dublin's embassy belt. Beautifully refurbished, the dining room looks out onto gardens. TV and reading rooms are available. An enclosed car park is encompassed within the grounds. Situated 1.5 miles from city centre and adjacent to RDS, American Embassy and Lansdown RFC.

56 MERRION ROAD, BALLSBRIDGE, DUBLIN 4
Tel: 01668 1426 Fax: 01668 4280

Fitzwilliam *Acclaimed*
41 Upper Fitzwilliam Street, Dublin 2
☎ 01-660 0448 Fax 01-676 7488

12 bedrs, all ensuite, TV ⊁ SB £45 DB £60-£80 D £23 CC MC Visa Amex DC

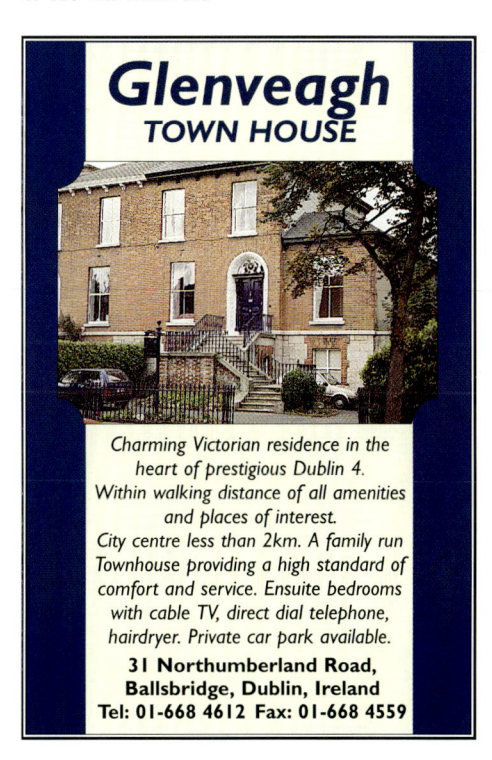

Glenveagh TOWN HOUSE

Charming Victorian residence in the heart of prestigious Dublin 4. Within walking distance of all amenities and places of interest.
City centre less than 2km. A family run Townhouse providing a high standard of comfort and service. Ensuite bedrooms with cable TV, direct dial telephone, hairdryer. Private car park available.

31 Northumberland Road, Ballsbridge, Dublin, Ireland
Tel: 01-668 4612 Fax: 01-668 4559

Glenveagh Town House *Acclaimed*
31 Northumberland Road, Ballsbridge, Dublin 4
☎ 01-668 4612 Fax 01-668 4559
Closed 22-29 Dec
10 bedrs, all ensuite, TCF TV P 10 SB £40-£60 DB £60-£80 CC MC Visa ♿
See advert on previous page

Kingswood *Acclaimed*
Naas Road, Clondalkin
☎ 01-459 2428 Fax 01-459 2428
Closed Christmas & Good Friday
7 bedrs, all ensuite, 2 🛏 TV P 70 SB £61-£80 DB £90 D £22.95 CC MC Visa Amex DC ♿

Mount Herbert *Acclaimed*
Herbert Road, Lansdowne, Dublin
☎ 01-668 4321 Fax 01-660 7077
140 bedrs, all ensuite, TV ▣ P 100 SB £40-£49 DB £65-£75 D £14.50 CC MC Visa Amex DC 🖥 ♿

Talbot *Acclaimed*
95-98 Talbot Street, Dublin 1
☎ 01-874 9202 Fax 01-874 9672

Situated in the heart of the city centre, this modern, purpose built guest house provides an ideal base for visitors to explore Dublin.

48 bedrs, all ensuite, TCF TV ▣ P 8 SB £33-£38 DB £53-£65 CC MC Visa Amex ♿

Uppercross House *Acclaimed*
26-30 Upper Rathmines Road, Dublin
☎ 01-497 5486 Fax 01-497 5486
14 bedrs, all ensuite, TCF TV 🐾 CC MC Visa Amex

Clifden House *Listed*
32 Gardner Place, Dublin 1
☎ 01-874 6364 Fax 01-874 6122
10 bedrs, all ensuite, 2 🛏 TCF TV SB £30-£45 DB £46-£80 CC MC Visa

Herbert Lodge *Listed*
65 Morehampton Road, Donnybrook, Dublin 4
☎ 01-660 3403
7 bedrs, 6 ensuite, 1 🛏 TCF P 4 SB £40 DB £70 CC MC Visa

HERBERT *lodge*

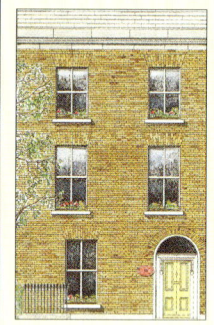

Ideally located in the fashionable Dublin 4 area, close to the RDS, Landsdowne Road Stadium and award winning Pubs and Restaurants. Only a short walk to St. Stephen's Green and Grafton Street. All rooms are en-suite with Cable Television, direct dial telephones and tea/coffee making facilities with Free off-street parking.

65 MOREHAMPTON ROAD, DONNYBROOK, DUBLIN 4
Tel: 660 3403   Fax: 688 8794

Leeson Inn *Listed*
24 Lower Leeson Street, Dublin 2
☎ 01-661 2002 Fax 01-662 1567
E Mail leesonin@iol.ie
13 bedrs, all ensuite, TCF TV P 2 SB £50-£55 DB £60-£65 CC MC Visa Amex

Othello House *Listed*
74 Lower Gardiner Street, Dublin
☎ 01-855 4271 Fax 01-855 7460

Two hundred year old house situated in the city centre. Central bus station 50 metres, direct bus from the airport (number 41) stops outside. O'Connell Street 100 metres. Abbey 100 metres, train station 150 metres.

16 bedrs, all ensuite, 16 🛏, TCF TV P 12 SB £25-£35 DB £22-£30 CC MC Visa Amex DC JCB

Egans House

7-9 Iona Park, Glasnevin, Dublin
☎ 01-830 3611 Fax 01-830 3312
Closed 24-26 Dec

Egans House, a charming guest house away from city traffic, convenient to Dublin airport, ferry, city centre and botanical gardens. 23 bedrooms containing TV, telephone, hairdryer, tea/coffee.

23 bedrs, all ensuite, TCF TV ⚞ P 9 SB £25-£30 DB £54-£61 HB £230.40-£265 D £12.50 CC MC Visa ♿

Windsor Lodge

3 Ilsington Avenue, Sandycove, Dun Laoghaire
☎ 01-284 6952 Fax 01-284 6952

Period home recently refurbished overlooking Dublin Bay, 2 minutes walk from Dart, 10 minutes from ferry. All rooms are ensuite, with off street parking. Irish Tourist Board Recommended.

4 bedrs, all ensuite, TCF TV P 5 SB £25-£30 DB £36-£44 CC MC Visa

DUN LAOGHAIRE Co. Dublin   19F1

★★ Kingston

Adelaide Street, Dun Laoghaire
☎ 01-280 1810 Fax 01-280 1237
38 bedrs, 34 ensuite, 4 🐾, TCF TV P 6 SB £44-£49 DB £68-£75 D £12 CC MC Visa Amex DC

Ferry House *Listed*

15 Clarinda Park North, Dun Laoghaire
☎ 01-280 8301 Fax 01-284 6530
Closed Christmas
6 bedrs, 3 ensuite, 2 ⚞ TV SB £30 DB £42-£46 CC MC Visa

Tara Hall

This newly refurbished Regency style house is ideally situated in Sandycove near the "Joyce Tower", Fitzgerald's pub and Dunlaoghaire Harbour. Only 10 minutes walk from DART Station and on the No. 8 bus route from Trinity College. All rooms have TV and tea/coffee making facilities with Free off-street parking.

**24 SANDYCOVE ROAD,
DUN LAOGHAIRE, CO DUBLIN**
Tel/Fax: 01 280 5120

Tara Hall *Listed*

24 Sandycove Road, Dun Laoghaire
☎ 01-280 5120 Fax 01-280 5120
6 bedrs, 5 ensuite, 1 ⚞ TCF TV ☒ P 6 SB £20-£22 DB £20-£22 CC MC Visa

DUNSHAUGHLIN Co. Meath   17E4

Ye Olde Workhouse *Highly Acclaimed*

Ballinlough, Dunshaughlin
☎ 01-825 9251 Fax 01-668 7279
Closed Christmas & New Year

Striking cut-stone building (c1840), tastefully restored and furnished throughout with antiques. The atmosphere is welcoming and the cooking excellent - don't miss dinner! Ideally situated for touring Boyne Valley heritage sites and award winning gardens.

4 bedrs, all ensuite, 1 ⚞ TCF P 50 SB £35-£40 DB £50-£60 D £22.50 CC MC Visa ♿

ENNIS Co. Clare　　　　　　　　　　18C2

★★ Queens
Abbey Street, Ennis
📞 065-28963 Fax 065-28628
52 bedrs, all ensuite, **TCF TV** 🔲 **SB** £30-£50 **DB** £40-£80
HB £210-£280 **D** £17 **CC** MC Visa Amex DC ♿

Carraig Mhuire *Listed*
Barefield, Ennis
📞 065-27106 Fax 065-27375

Surrounded by beautiful countryside and convenient for Shannon Airport, this is an ideal touring base for Co. Clare.

5 bedrs, 3 ensuite, 1 🛏 **TCF P** 5 **SB** £17-£23 **DB** £32-£34
HB £180 **D** £12 **CC** MC Visa

Brookville House
Clonroadmore, Ennis
📞 065-29802

Tranquil location with large garden. 10 minute walk from the town centre. Ideal touring base for Bunratty Castle, Cliffs of Moher, Burrow. Comfortable rooms with ensuite.

3 bedrs, 2 ensuite

ENNISKERRY Co. Wicklow　　　　　　19F1

★★ Enniscree Lodge
Restaurant merit award
Glencree Valley, Enniskerry
📞 01-286 3542 Fax 01-286 6037
E Mail enniscre@iol.ie
Closed 25 Dec
10 bedrs, all ensuite, **TCF TV P** 20 **SB** £51-£59 **DB** £75-£80 **D** £21 **CC** MC Visa Amex DC

ENNISTYMON Co. Clare　　　　　　　18B1

Grovemount House *Highly Acclaimed*
Lahinch Road, Ennistymon
📞 065-71431 Fax 065-71823
Closed Oct-Apr

Situated on the outskirts of Ennistymon and offering east access to the Burren and Cliffs of Moher. Golfing, fishing and traditional music sessions can be arranged.

8 bedrs, all ensuite, **TCF TV P** 20 **SB** £20-£25 **DB** £34-£40
CC MC Visa ♿

FANORE Co. Clare　　　　　　　　　18B1

Admirals Rest *Listed*
Coast Road, Fanore
📞 065-76105 Fax 065-76161

FEAKLE Co. Clare　　　　　　　　　18C1

★★ Smyth Village
Feakle
📞 061-924000

FERNS Co. Wexford　　　　　　　　　19F2

Clone House
Ferns, Enniscorthy
📞 054-66113 Fax 054-66113

Internationally known for its fresh cuisine and 'house' atmosphere, this award winning period house (five bedrooms with TV) offers angling and shooting on the 300 acre working farm. Located three kilometres south east of Ferns off the N11.

5 bedrs, 4 ensuite, **TV** 🛏 **P** 20 **SB** £25 **DB** £40 **HB** £210
D £14 **CC** Visa

GALWAY & SALTHILL Co. Galway 18C1

Killeen House
Killeen, Bushypark, Galway
📞 091-524179 Fax 091-528065

Built in 1840 the house is set in 25 acres of private gardens and grounds with private access to the shores of Lough Corrib. Situated on the N59 which is the main road to Clifden.

4 bedrs, all ensuite, **TCF TV P** 6 No children under 7 **CC** MC Visa DC

GALWAY & SALTHILL Co. Galway 18C1

★★ Twelve Pins Lodge
Barna, Galway
📞 091-592368 Fax 091-592485
Closed 23-27 Dec
17 bedrs, all ensuite, **TCF TV P** 100 **SB** £32.50-£35 **DB** £55-£70 **D** £18 **CC** MC Visa Amex DC ♿

VILLAGE HOUSE

Family run guest house on the Ring of Kerry. All rooms ensuite with TV and telephone. Central to all golf courses in Kerry. Three miles of sandy beaches near by.

**Glenbeigh, Co Kerry,
Republic of Ireland
Tel: 066-68128
Fax: 066-68486**

GLANDORE Co. Cork 18B4

★★ Marine
Restaurant merit award
Glandore
📞 028-33366

GLENBEIGH Co. Kerry 18A3

Village House *Listed*
Glenbeigh
📞 066-68128 Fax 066-68486
9 bedrs, all ensuite, **TV P** 9 **SB** £18-£25 **DB** £32-£40
CC MC Visa DC

GLENDALOUGH Co. Wicklow 19F1

Carmel's *Acclaimed*
Annamoe, Glendalough
📞 0404-45297

Select family run country home set in peaceful surroundings in the Heath of Wicklow Mountains. Within easy distance of ferry and airport.

4 bedrs, 4 ensuite, 1 **TCF P** 5 **SB** £32 **DB** £34-£36 ♿

GLENGARRIFF Co. Cork 18B4

★★ Casey's
Glengarriff
📞 0127-63010 Fax 0127-63072
Closed Nov-Mar
19 bedrs, all ensuite, **P** 15 **CC** MC Visa Amex DC ♿

Short Breaks

Many hotels provide special rates for weekend and mid-week breaks - sometimes these are quoted in the hotel's entry, otherwise ring direct for the latest offers.

GRAIGUENAMANAGH Co. Kilkenny   19E2

Barleycroft *Acclaimed*
Ballyvarra, Graiguenamanagh
☎ 051-423668 Fax 051-423668
Closed 18 Dec-10 Jan

Highest standards customer care and comfort with acclaimed home cooking in a tranquil rural setting. Dramatic scenery of mountains and river. Central location for golf, fishing, walking, riding and touring southeast. Rosslare 40 miles.

3 bedrs, all ensuite, TCF P 4 No children under 12 SB £18-£20 DB £31-£34 HB £179-£200 D £14

INNISHANNON Co. Cork   18C4

★★ **Innishannon House**
Hospitality, Comfort, Restaurant merit awards
Innishannon
☎ 021-775121 Fax 021-775609
Closed 15 Jan-15 Mar
13 bedrs, all ensuite, TCF TV P 100 SB £50-£75 DB £75-£110 HB £400-£675 D £25 CC MC Visa Amex DC

KENMARE Co. Kerry   18B3

Ardmore House *Acclaimed*
Killarney Road, Kenmare
☎ 064-41406 Fax 064-41406
Closed Dec-Feb

Bungalow in quiet cul-de-sac adjoining farmland, five minutes walk from town centre. Half a mile from Kenmore on N71.
6 bedrs, all ensuite, 1 P 6 SB £22 DB £32-£34 CC MC Visa

Muxnaw Lodge *Acclaimed*
Castletownbere Road, Kenmare
☎ 064-41252

KILKEE Co. Clare   18B2

Halpins *Highly Acclaimed*
Kilkee
☎ 065-56032 Fax 065-56317
12 bedrs, all ensuite

KILKENNY Co. Kilkenny   19E2

Newlands Country House *Highly Acclaimed*
Seven Houses, Danesfort, Kilkenny
☎ 056-29111 Fax 056-29171

Sheer luxury, all bedrooms TV, electric blanket, teasmaid, fridge. Suites have whirlpool baths and 6 foot beds. Delicious freshly prepared food, extensive breakfast served until noon.

4 bedrs, all ensuite, TCF TV P 10 DB £40-£60 D £20 CC MC Visa

Chaplins *Acclaimed*
Castlecomer Road, Kilkenny
☎ 056-52236 Fax 056-63603
Closed 23-29 Dec
6 bedrs, 4 ensuite, 1 TCF TV P 7 SB £18-£20 DB £34 HB £105-£115 CC Visa

Shillogher House *Acclaimed*
Callan Road, Kilkenny
☎ 056-63249 Fax 056-64865
Closed 24-25 Dec

Enjoy a stay in this luxurious home, one kilometre from the castle and city centre. Golf, angling and horse-riding available locally.

5 bedrs, all ensuite, TCF TV P 12 SB £23-£30 DB £34-£37 CC MC Visa

KILLARNEY Co. Kerry   18B3

★★ Arbutus
Comfort merit award
College Street, Killarney
☎ 064-31037 Fax 064-34033
Closed 1 Nov-1 Mar
34 bedrs, all ensuite, **SB** £30-£50 **DB** £56-£90 **HB** £250-£300 **D** £9.95 **CC** MC Visa Amex DC

Castle Oaks House *Highly Acclaimed*
Muckross Road, Killarney
☎ 064-34154 Fax 064-36980
Closed Christmas
16 bedrs, all ensuite, **TV P** 16 **SB** £25-£35 **DB** £40-£50
CC MC Visa DC ♿

Earls Court *Highly Acclaimed*
Woodlawn Junction, Muckross Road, Killarney
☎ 35364-34009 Fax 35364-34366
Closed Nov-10 Mar

A hotel dedicated to offering fine food, superb comfort and individual hospitality. Luxurious bedrooms with private bathrooms, TV, phone, hairdryers. Private parking. Five minutes walk to town centre.

11 bedrs, all ensuite, **TV P** 15 **SB** £25-£55 **DB** £50-£80
CC MC Visa

Foley's Townhouse *Highly Acclaimed*
Restaurant merit award
23 High Street, Killarney
☎ 064-31217 Fax 064-34683
Closed Nov-5 Mar
12 bedrs, all ensuite, **TCF TV P** 25 **CC** MC Visa Amex

Gleann Fia Country House *Highly Acclaimed*
Old Deer Park, Killarney
☎ 064-35035 Fax 064-35000
E Mail gleanfia@iol.ie
Closed 1 Dec-1 Mar

Idyllic secluded setting nestling in 25 acres of mature woodlands with private river walk. Peace and quiet assured. Guest lounge with open fire, conservatory, varied breakfast menu.

17 bedrs, all ensuite, 1 🚭 **TCF TV** 🚭 **P** 25 **SB** £25-£30
DB £36-£56 **CC** MC Visa Amex ♿

Kathleens Country House *Highly Acclaimed*
Tralee Road, Killarney
☎ 064-32810 Fax 064-32340
Closed 14 Nov-7 Mar
17 bedrs, all ensuite, **TV** 🚭 **P** 20 No children under 5
SB £30-£65 **DB** £59-£75 **CC** MC Visa Amex ♿

Lohans Lodge *Highly Acclaimed*
Tralee Road, Killarney
☎ 064-33871 Fax 064-33871
Closed 10 Nov-10 Feb

Modern bungalow situated about 3½ miles from Killarney. Bedrooms are ensuite with colour TV and tea/coffee facilities. Convenient for golfing and touring lakes and gardens. Golf and bus tours arranged.

5 bedrs, all ensuite, **TCF TV** 🚭 **P** 10 No children under 6 **DB** £32-£34

Victoria House *Highly Acclaimed*
Muckross Road, Killarney
☎ 064-35430 Fax 064-35439
Closed Dec
15 bedrs, all ensuite, **TV** 🚭 **P** 15 **SB** £22-£32 **DB** £36-£48
CC MC Visa Amex DC

Cedar Lodge *Acclaimed*
Lissivigeen, Cork Road (N22), Killarney
☎ 064-34754 Fax 064-34754
6 bedrs, all ensuite, **TCF TV P** 6 **SB** £17-£23 **DB** £30-£34
CC MC Visa Amex

Glena House *Acclaimed*
Muckross Road, Killarney
☎ 064-32705 Fax 064-35611
26 bedrs, all ensuite, **TCF TV** 🐾 **P** 20 **SB** £25-£38 **DB** £40-£56 **D** £10 **CC** MC Visa Amex DC ♿
See advert on next page

Killarney Villa *Acclaimed*
Waterford Road (N72), Killarney
☎ 064-31878 Fax 064-31878
Closed Nov-Easter
6 bedrs, all ensuite, 1 🚭 **TCF TV** 🚭 🐾 **P** 8 No children under 6 **SB** £17-£20 **DB** £32-£35 **CC** MC Visa

Park Lodge *Acclaimed*
Cork Road, Killarney
📞 064-31539 Fax 064-34892

In scenic Killarney, County Kerry, a beautiful large homely guest house including top class rooms and private grounds with oak trees and exotic shrubs. Private parking. A delightful stay guaranteed.

20 bedrs, all ensuite, 2 ⇌ **TCF TV P** 22 **SB** £20-£40 **DB** £30-£50 **CC** MC Visa

Riverside Farm *Acclaimed*
Kilgarvan, Killarney
📞 064-85487
Closed end Oct-Feb

Large period farmhouse overlooking Rourty River on main Kenmare-Cork road. Ideal centre for touring. Extensive gardens, private parking. Home cooking and fresh wild salmon.

5 bedrs, 1 ensuite, 2 ⇌ ⇌ **P** 12 No children under 3 **SB** £15 **DB** £30 **D** £12

Purple Heather *Listed*
Gap of Dunloe, Beaufort, Killarney
📞 064-44266 Fax 064-44266

Scenic area, electric blankets, hairdryers, tea/coffee. Pool room, tennis, pony riding, golf, fishing, arranged restaurant, Irish music only 1k.

6 bedrs, 5 ensuite, 1 ⇌, 1 ⇌ **TCF** ⇌ **P** 6 **SB** £17-£22 **DB** £31-£34 **HB** £177-£187 **D** £12 **CC** MC Visa DC

Sliabh Lauchra House *Listed*
Loreto Road, Killarney
📞 064-32012 Fax 064-32012
Closed Sep

A beautiful modern stone house, just over half a mile from Killarney town centre, adjacent to the National Park, golf course and horse riding. Tours may also be arranged.

6 bedrs, all ensuite, **TCF P** 6 No children under 12 **DB** £36

Climbers Inn *Awaiting Inspection*
Glencar, Killarney
📞 066-60101

GLENA HOUSE

An attractive, large guest house, five minutes walk from the town centre. An ideal centre for touring and walking.

MUCKROSS ROAD, KILLARNEY, CO. KERRY, EIRE
Tel: 064-32705 Fax: 064-35611

Gorman's
Tralee Road, Killarney
☎ 064-33149 Fax 064-33149
Closed Christmas

All rooms have satellite TV, video, hairdryers and tea facilities. Breakfast menu. Electric blankets available. Reductions for low season. Killarney 5 miles on N22.

5 bedrs, all ensuite, **TCF TV CC** MC

Nashville
Airport/Tralee Road, Killarney
☎ 064-32924
Closed Dec-Mar

All rooms ensuite with TV, hair dryers and tea/coffee making facilities in bedrooms. ITB approved. Two miles from Killarney on N22.

6 bedrs, all ensuite, **TCF TV P** 10

KILLORGLIN Co. Kerry 18B3

Grove Lodge *Highly Acclaimed*
Killarney Road, Killorglin
☎ 066-61157 Fax 066-62330

Dromin Farmhouse
Miltown, Killorglin
☎ 066-61867
Closed Dec-mid Mar

A dairy/sheep farm in a peaceful scenic location offering superb mountain views, including McGillacuddy Reeks and Irelands highest mountain. A friendly and comfortable atmosphere in the perfect touring base.

4 bedrs, 3 ensuite, 1 🐕 **TCF TV** 🛏 **P** 6 **SB** £20-£22 **DB** £32-£34 **HB** £195-£210 **D** £14 **CC** MC Visa

KINSALE Co. Cork 18C4

Moorings *Highly Acclaimed*
Scilly, Kinsale
☎ 021-772376 Fax 021-772675
Closed Christmas
8 bedrs, all ensuite, 2 🐕 **TV** 🛏 **P** 8 No children
SB £35-£55 **DB** £60-£90 **CC** MC Visa DC ♿

Old Bank House *Highly Acclaimed*
11 Pearse Street, Kinsale
☎ 021-774075 Fax 021-774296
Closed Christmas

A three storey Georgian house, formerly the Munster and Leinster Bank. Antique furniture.

9 bedrs, all ensuite, **TV** 🛏 No children under 8 **SB** £45-£85 **DB** £80-£130 **CC** MC Visa Amex

Rivermount House *Highly Acclaimed*
Knocknabinny, Kinsale
☎ 021-778033 Fax 021-778225
Closed 5 Nov-1 Mar

Modern award winning guest house with panoramic views of Bandon River, yet only 2 miles from Kinsale. Spacious well appointed bedrooms and superb decor throughout.

6 bedrs, all ensuite, 1 🐕 **TCF TV** 🛏 **P** 10 **SB** £20-£25 **DB** £34-£40

LETTERKENNY Co. Donegal 17D1

Hillcrest House *Acclaimed*
Lurgy Brack, Sligo Road, Letterkenny
📞 074-22300 Fax 074-25137
Closed Christmas

Modern bungalow on N13 to Sligo, overlooking town and river. Rooms ensuite with TV and tea-making facilities. Private car park. Ideal touring base for Donegal and Northern Ireland.
6 bedrs, 5 ensuite, 1 ➡ TCF TV **P** 10 **SB** £20-£25 **DB** £32-£35 **CC** MC Visa Amex

LIFFORD Co. Donegal 17D1

Haw Lodge
The Haw, Lifford
📞 074-41397 Fax 074-41985
Closed Nov-Feb

Olde worlde farmhouse enjoying delightful views over the river. On N15 road to Donegal Town. Central for touring or overnight stop. Fishing, golfing, greyhound racing, leisure centre and good restaurants locally.
4 bedrs, 2 ensuite, 1 ➡ TCF TV 🅿 **P** 6 **SB** £15-£20 **DB** £30-£35 **HB** £95-£110 **CC** MC Visa

LIMERICK Co. Limerick 18C2

★★ Woodfield House
Ennis Road, Limerick
📞 061-453022 Fax 061-326755
Closed 25 Dec
21 bedrs, all ensuite, TV **P** 80 **SB** £45-£50 **DB** £74-£80 **D** £17 **CC** MC Visa Amex DC ♿

Clifton House *Acclaimed*
Ennis Road, Limerick
📞 061-451166 Fax 061-451224
210 bedrs, all ensuite, **SB** £22-£28 **DB** £36-£40

LISDOONVARNA Co. Clare 18B1

★★ Sheedy's Spa View
Hospitality, Comfort, Restaurant merit awards
Lisdoonvarna
📞 065-74026 Fax 065-74555
Closed 30 Sep-4 Apr
11 bedrs, all ensuite, **P** 20 **SB** £50.65-£58.50 **DB** £64-£78.25 **CC** MC Visa Amex DC

LONGFORD Co. Longford 17D4

Tivoli
Dublin Road, Longford
📞 043-46898
Closed Christmas

A modern detached house, situated beside the golf links, with a large garden and private car park. Half a kilometre from Longford centre.

11 bedrs, 7 ensuite

MACROOM Co. Cork 18C3

★★ Castle
Restaurant merit award
Macroom
📞 026-41074 Fax 026-41505
Closed 24-27 Dec
42 bedrs, all ensuite, TCF TV **P** 10 **SB** £32-£45 **DB** £55-£80 **HB** £230-£240 **D** £17.50 **CC** MC Visa Amex DC

Mills Inn *Highly Acclaimed*
Ballyvourney N22, Macroom
📞 026-45237 Fax 026-45454
10 bedrs, all ensuite, TCF TV 🐕 **SB** £25-£35 **DB** £50-£60 **D** £16 **CC** MC Visa DC ♿

MALLOW Co. Cork 18C3

Springfort Hall *Highly Acclaimed*
Mallow
📞 022-21278 Fax 022-21557
Closed Christmas-New Year
24 bedrs, all ensuite, TV **P** 200 **SB** £43 **DB** £68 **HB** £338 **D** £20 **CC** MC Visa Amex DC

MOUNTSHANNON Co. Clare	18C1

★★ Mountshannon
Mountshannon
☎ 061-927162

NAAS Co. Kildare	19F1

★★ Harbour View
Hospitality merit award
Limerick Road, Naas
☎ 045-879145 Fax 045-874002
Closed 25-27 Dec
10 bedrs, all ensuite, TCF TV CC MC Visa Amex DC &

NEW ROSS Co. Wexford	19E3

Woodlands House *Highly Acclaimed*
Carrigbyrne, Newbawn, New Ross
☎ 051-428287 Fax 051-428287

On Rosslare/New Ross road (N25), close to Cedar Lodge, just 30 minutes from the Rosslare ferries. Ensuite bedrooms with TV, electric blankets and a complimentry tray. Games room, secure parking. Central to tour Wexford, Waterford and Kilkenny.

4 bedrs, all ensuite, 1 ⇌ TCF TV P 7 No children under 2 SB £16-£18 DB £30-£32 CC MC Visa Amex

NEWMARKET-ON-FERGUS Co. Clare	18C2

Golf View
Latoon Cross, Ennis Road, Newmarket-on-Fergus
☎ 061-368095 Fax 065-28624

Home on N18 overlooking Dromolond Castle and Clare Inn Hotel golf course. Shannon Airport, castles, Ennis 10 minutes. Swimming pool, horse riding, fishing 100 metres. Many golf courses local.

4 bedrs, 3 ensuite, 1 ⇌ P 8 DB £17.50-£18 &

OGONNELLOE Co. Clare	18C2

Lantern House *Acclaimed*
Ogonnelloe
☎ 061-923034 Fax 061-923139
6 bedrs, all ensuite, P 20 CC MC Visa Amex DC

OMEATH Co. Louth	17E3

Granvue House *Acclaimed*
Omeath
☎ 042-75109 Fax 042-75415
9 bedrs, all ensuite, 1 ⇌ TV P 25 SB £22-£25 DB £44 D £12 CC MC Visa

ORANMORE Co. Galway	18C1

Moorings *Acclaimed*
Main Street, Oranmore
☎ 091-790462 Fax 091-790462
6 bedrs, all ensuite, TCF TV P 30 SB £25-£35 DB £45-£50 D £19 CC MC Visa Amex &

PORTLAOISE Co. Laois	19E1

Chez Nous *Highly Acclaimed*
Kilminchy, Portlaiose
☎ 0502-21251
Closed 20 Dec-3 Jan
5 bedrs, all ensuite, ⌘ P 8 No children under 8 SB £23.50 DB £37

PROSPEROUS Co. Kildare	19E1

★★ Curryhills House
Prosperous, Naas
☎ 065-868150 Fax 065-868805
E Mail abi@indigo.ie
Closed 23-31 Dec
10 bedrs, all ensuite, TCF TV ⌘ P 40 CC MC Visa Amex DC

ROOSKEY ON SHANNON Co. Roscommon	16C4

Mount Carmel *Listed*
Rooskey on Shannon
☎ 078-38434 Fax 078-38434
6 bedrs, 3 ensuite, 3 ⇌ TCF TV ⌘ ⌘ P 10 SB £20-£22 DB £44 HB £210-£220 D £12 CC MC Visa Amex

ROSSLARE Co. Wexford 19F3

Rosslare *Acclaimed*
Rosslare Harbour
☎ 053-33110 Fax 053-33386
Closed Christmas
25 bedrs, 22 ensuite, 2 TV P 40 SB £39-£49
DB £58-£78 D £12.50 CC MC Visa Amex DC

Palms *Listed*
Rosslare
☎ 053-32312
3 bedrs, all ensuite, P 3 SB £17 DB £30

ROSSLARE HARBOUR Co. Wexford 19F3

Elmwood *Acclaimed*
Station Rd, Rosslare Harbour
☎ 053-33321
Closed Nov-Feb

Excellent recommendations. Peaceful location, two minutes drive from the ferry. Signposted opposite church. Rooms with TV, hairdryer, tea and coffee making facilities. Early breakfast. Travel agent vouchers accepted.

3 bedrs, all ensuite, TCF TV P 5 SB £21 DB £32 CC Visa

ROUNDSTONE Co. Galway 16A4

★★ Eldons
Hospitality merit award
Roundstone
☎ 095-35933 Fax 095-35871

Situated midst the rugged grandeur of Connemara, the newly constructed Eldons is a haven with magical landscape all around. The seafood restaurant features lobster and seasonal catch from the harbour.

19 bedrs, all ensuite, TCF TV SB £30-£40 DB £40-£60
D £20 CC MC Visa Amex DC

★★ Roundstone House
Roundstone, Connemara
☎ 095-35864 Fax 095-35944
13 bedrs, all ensuite, TV

SKIBBEREEN Co. Cork 18B4

★★ Barleycove Beach
Barley Cove, Skibbereen
☎ 028-35234

SLANE Co. Meath 17E4

★★ Conyngham Arms
Slane
☎ 041-24155 Fax 041-24205
15 bedrs, all ensuite, P 20

SNEEM Co. Kerry 18A3

Tahilla Cove Country House *Highly Acclaimed*
Tahilla, Sneem
☎ 064-45204 Fax 064-45104
Closed mid Oct-Easter
9 bedrs, all ensuite, TV P 20 CC MC Visa Amex DC

TIPPERARY Co. Tipperary 19D2

Bansha Castle *Acclaimed*
Bansha, Tipperary
☎ 062-54187 Fax 062-54294
5 bedrs, all ensuite, P 20

TRAMORE Co. Waterford 19E3

Cliff House *Highly Acclaimed*
Cliff Road, Tramore
☎ 051-381497 Fax 051-381497
6 bedrs, all ensuite, P 10 No children under 6
SB £23-£25 DB £34-£36 CC MC Visa

Glenorney *Highly Acclaimed*
Newrown, Tramore
☎ 051-381056 Fax 051-381103
6 bedrs, all ensuite, 1 TCF TV P 8 SB £18-£22 CC MC Visa

TRIM Co. Meath 17E4

Brogans Guesthouse
High Street, Trim
📞 046-31237 Fax 046-37648
E Mail brogangh@iol.ie

Located in historic, medieval town of Trim, family run Brogans Guesthouse offers superb accommodation and a warm welcome. Close to golf, fishing and all amenities.

14 bedrs, 8 ensuite, 1 🛏 TCF TV P 14 SB £15-£30 DB £30-£40 CC MC Visa ♿

TULLAMORE Co. Offaly 19E1

Moorhill Country House *Highly Acclaimed*
Moorhill, Clara Road, Tullamore
📞 0506-21395 Fax 0506-52424

Mature chestnut trees and manicured lawns form a tranquil setting for the Victorian elegance of Moorhill. Superbly appointed ensuite bedrooms, award winning restaurant and olde worlde bar.

10 bedrs, all ensuite, TCF TV 🛏 P 60 SB £30-£35 DB £50-£60 D £18.95 CC MC Visa Amex ♿

Shepherds Wood *Acclaimed*
Screggan, Tullamore
📞 0506-21499
Closed Oct-Mar
6 bedrs, all ensuite, TCF TV 🛏 P 10 No children under 12 SB £29 DB £44 D £23

TYRRELLSPASS Co. Westmeath 19E1

★★ Village Inn
Tyrrellspass
📞 044-23171

WATERFORD Co. Waterford 19E3

★★ Dooley's
The Quay, Waterford
📞 051-73531 Fax 051-70262
Closed Christmas
35 bedrs, 34 ensuite, 1 🛏 TCF TV CC MC Visa Amex DC JCB

Diamond Hill *Acclaimed*
Milepost, Slieverue, Waterford
📞 051-832855 Fax 051-832254

Family run country guest house set amidst national award winning gardens. Ensuite rooms with TV, phones, tea/coffee facilities, highly commended Galtee Irish breakfast award. Situated off the N25 Rosslare/Waterford road.

10 bedrs, all ensuite, TCF TV 🛏 P 14 No children under 5 SB £25 DB £44-£48 HB £140 CC MC Visa Amex ♿

Coach House
Butlerstown Castle, Butlerstown, Waterford
📞 051-384656 Fax 051-384751

19th century elegant country house situated in rural historical setting just 5 minutes from Waterford Crystal and city. Stunning views, 13th century tower house in grounds. All rooms ensuite, private sauna.

7 bedrs, all ensuite, TCF TV P 15 SB £32.50-£39.50 DB £49-£59 D £16 CC MC Visa Amex DC

WATERVILLE Co. Kerry   18A3

Klondyke House *Acclaimed*
New Line Road, Waterville
📞 066-74119 Fax 066-74666

A spacious detached residence situated on the main Ring of Kerry Road overlooking Waterville championship golf course and the Atlantic Ocean.

6 bedrs, all ensuite, TCF ⌐ P 10 CC MC Visa

O'Gradys *Acclaimed*
Spunkane, Waterville
📞 066-74350 Fax 066-74730
6 bedrs, all ensuite, TCF TV P 7 No children under 7
SB £18-£25 DB £30-£32 CC MC Visa

WEXFORD Co. Wexford   19F3

★★ Wexford Lodge
Wexford Bridge, Wexford
📞 053-23611 Fax 053-23342
24 bedrs, all ensuite, TCF TV P 25 SB £29-£45 DB £55-£70 D £16.50 CC MC Visa Amex DC

Darral House *Highly Acclaimed*
Spawell Road, Wexford
📞 053-24264

Luxury accommodation close to town centre. Beautiful period house renovated to the highest standards in 1995. All rooms ensuite with tea/coffee facilities and television.

4 bedrs, all ensuite, TCF TV P 6 SB £18-£22.50 CC MC Visa

AVONMORE HOUSE
YOUGHAL

18th Century Georgian House in N.25; 3 minutes' walk Youghal's famous Clock Tower and town centre – private parking. Golf, fishing and sandy beaches nearby. Rooms all en-suite, TV, tea/coffee making facilities – credit cards accepted.

SOUTH ABBEY, YOUGHAL, CO. CORK
Tel: 024-92617

YOUGHAL Co. Cork   19D3

★★ Ahernes Seafood Restaurant and Townhouse
Hospitality, Comfort, Restaurant merit awards
Youghal
📞 024-92424 Fax 024-93633
Closed Christmas
12 bedrs, all ensuite, TV P 12 SB £70-£85 DB £100-£120 D £23 CC MC Visa Amex DC ♿

★★ Devonshire Arms
Pearse Square, Youghal
📞 024-92827 Fax 024-92900
10 bedrs, all ensuite, TV ⌐ P 20 CC MC Visa Amex DC ♿

Avonmore House
South Abbey, Youghal
📞 024-92617 Fax 024-92617
Closed Christmas
6 bedrs, all ensuite, 1 ⇌ TCF TV P 9 SB £20-£30 DB £36-£50 CC MC Visa Amex DC

Channel Islands & Isle of Man

Top: *La Bonne Vie,*
St Helier

Right: *Ann-Dawn,*
St Sampsons

Below: *Symphony House*
L'Ancresse

RAC

DOUGLAS   10A4

★★ Rutland
Hospitality merit award
Queens Promenade, Douglas
☏ 01624-621218
Closed winter
65 bedrs, 51 ensuite, TCF TV 🖬 CC MC Visa DC 🖾 ♿

★★ Welbeck
Mona Drive, Douglas
☏ 01624-675663 Fax 01624-661545
E Mail welbeck@isle-of-man.com
25 bedrs, all ensuite, TCF TV 🖬 SB £30 DB £60 HB £259
D £14 CC MC Visa Amex

Melrose *Acclaimed*
14 Loch Promenade, Douglas IM1 2LX
☏ 01624-676269

Modwena *Acclaimed*
39-40 Loch Promenade, Douglas
☏ 01624-675728 Fax 01624-670954
Closed 1 May-30 Sept
32 bedrs, 17 ensuite, 2 🛏, 3 ⛢ TCF TV 🐕 🖬 SB £24.50
DB £46 HB £196 D £5 CC MC Visa DC 🖾

Inglewood *Listed*
Queen Promenade, Douglas IM2 4NF
☏ 01624-674734 Fax 01624-674734
Closed Nov-Feb
15 bedrs, 10 ensuite, 4 ⛢ TCF TV 🐕 SB £16-£19
HB £161-£182 D £7 CC Amex DC

Rio *Listed*
Loch Promenade, Douglas IM1 2LY
☏ 01624-623491 Fax 01624-670966
14 bedrs, 12 ensuite, 1 ⛢ TCF TV SB £25-£26 DB £44-£46
HB £210-£220 D £8 CC MC Visa

PORT ERIN   10A4

★★ Port Erin Imperial
Promenade, Port Erin IM9 6LH
☏ 01624-832122 Fax 01624-835402
51 bedrs, all ensuite, TCF TV 🖬 P 100 SB £33-£38
DB £52-£62 HB £182-£212 D £11.50 CC MC Visa 🖾 🖾
🅿 🆀 ♿

Regent House *Highly Acclaimed*
Promenade, Port Erin
☏ 01624-833454 Fax 01624-833454
6 bedrs, all ensuite, TCF TV 🖾 No children under 10
SB £21-£23 DB £42-£46 D £9

ALDERNEY   2A1

★★ Inchalla
The Vall, St Annes GY9 3UL
☎ 01481-823220 Fax 01481-824045
Closed Christmas/New Year
9 bedrs, all ensuite, **TCF TV P** 9 **DB** £64-£88 **D** £16 **CC**
MC Visa Amex JCB

★★ Rose & Crown
Le Huret GY9 3TR
☎ 01481-823414 Fax 01481-823615
E Mail rosecrwn@alderney.net
Closed mid Nov-mid Mar
6 bedrs, 4 ensuite, 1 **TCF TV** No children under 3
SB £28-£50 **DB** £56-£80 **D** £7.45 **CC** MC Visa Amex DC JCB

GUERNSEY   2A2

★★ Grange Lodge
The Grange, St Peter Port GY1 1RQ
☎ 01481-725161 Fax 01481-724211
Closed 24 Dec-2 Jan
31 bedrs, all ensuite, **TCF TV P** 20 **SB** £23-£34 **DB** £46-£68 **D** £11 **CC** MC Visa

★★ Hougue du Pommier
Restaurant merit award
Castel GY5 7FQ
☎ 01481-56531 Fax 01481-56260
44 bedrs, all ensuite, **TCF TV P** 70 **SB** £28-£44 **DB** £56-£88 **HB** £280-£392 **D** £14.50 **CC** MC Visa Amex DC

★★ Le Carrefour
The Grange, St Peter Port GY1 2QJ
☎ 01481-713965 Fax 01481-714494
Closed 1 Oct-30 Apr
10 bedrs, 9 ensuite, 2 **TCF TV P** 12 **SB** £39.35 **DB** £78.50 **HB** £348.25 **D** £12.50 **CC** MC Visa Amex

★★ Les Rocquettes
Hospitality merit award
Les Gravees, St Peter Port GY1 1RN
☎ 01481-722146 Fax 01481-714543
Closed 24-31 Dec
26 bedrs, all ensuite, **TCF TV** **P** 50 **SB** £25-£45 **DB** £50-£90 **HB** £175-£350 **D** £11.50 **CC** MC Visa

★★ Sunnycroft
Comfort merit award
5 Constitution Steps, St Peter Port GY1 2PN
☎ 01481-723008 Fax 01481-712225
Closed Nov-Mar
13 bedrs, all ensuite, 1 **TCF TV P** 4 No children under 14 **SB** £23.50-£33 **DB** £47-£66 **HB** £213.50-£283.50 **D** £12.50 **CC** MC Visa

Ann-Dawn *Highly Acclaimed*
Route Des Capelles, St Sampsons GY2 49Q
☎ 01481-725606 Fax 01481-725930

Situated in a charming rural area, peaceful hotel with the emphasis on letting guests relax. Excellent cuisine and friendly service.

11 bedrs, all ensuite, 1 **TCF TV P** 11 No children under 12 **SB** £22-£28 **DB** £38-£56 **HB** £198-£231 **D** £8 **CC** MC Visa

La Michele *Highly Acclaimed*
Les Hubits de Bas, St Martins GY4 6NB
☎ 01481-38065 Fax 01481-39492
Closed Nov-Mar
13 bedrs, all ensuite, **TCF TV P** 15 No children under 8
SB £24-£33 **DB** £48-£66 **HB** £203-£273 **D** £9 **CC** MC Visa Amex

Le Galaad *Highly Acclaimed*
Rue Des Francais, Castel GY5 7FH
☎ 01481-57233 Fax 01481-53028
12 bedrs, all ensuite, **TCF TV P** 12 **SB** £22-£28 **DB** £44-£56 **HB** £189-£238 **CC** MC Visa

Marine *Highly Acclaimed*
Well Road, St Peter Port GY1 1WS
☎ 01481-724978 Fax 01481-711729

An old granite-built Guernsey house with a sun-trap patio with sea views.

11 bedrs, all ensuite, **TCF TV SB** £15.50-£25.50 **DB** £31-£51 **CC** MC Visa JCB

Midhurst House *Highly Acclaimed*
Candie Road, St Peter Port GY1 1UP
☎ 01481-724391 Fax 01481-729451
Closed mid Oct-Easter
8 bedrs, all ensuite, TCF TV P 1 No children under 8
DB £50-£68 D £12 CC MC Visa

Symphony House *Highly Acclaimed*
Hacse Lane, L'Ancresse GY3 5DS
☎ 01481-45418 Fax 01481-43581
Closed Jan

Tranquil country house setting, five minutes from the marina, beaches and golf course. Ensuite bedrooms with garden views. Renowned for its fine restaurant and excellent cuisine.

15 bedrs, all ensuite, TCF TV P 40 No children under 5
SB £30-£35 DB £60-£70 HB £273-£308 D £9.95 CC MC Visa JCB

JERSEY 2A2

★★ **Beau Rivage**
Hospitality, Comfort merit awards
St Brelade's Bay JE3 8EF
☎ 01534-45983 Fax 01534-47127
E Mail welcome@jerseyweb.demon.co.uk
Closed Nov-Mar
27 bedrs, all ensuite, 1 ⛶ TCF 🖃 P 12 DB £45-£124
HB £200-£480 D £13 CC MC Visa Amex JCB ♿

★★ **Dolphin**
Hospitality merit award
Gorey Pier, Gorey
☎ 01534-853370 Fax 01534-855343

Overlooking the sandy beach of Grouville and the picturesque Gorey Harbour. The restaurant is renowned for its excellent cuisine. Fisherman's Bar.

All rooms are ensuite with modern facilities. Open all year round. ½m from golf course.

16 bedrs, all ensuite, TCF TV 🐾 SB £33-£44 DB £64-£84
HB £258-£290 D £14.50 CC MC Visa Amex JCB

★★ **Maison Gorey**
Hospitality merit award
Gorey Village, Gorey JE3 9EP
☎ 01534-857775 Fax 01534-857779
Closed Oct-Apr
30 bedrs, all ensuite, TCF TV 🐾 SB £37.50-£55 DB £55-£90 D £9.50 CC MC Visa Amex DC

★★ **Moorings**
Hospitality, Restaurant merit awards
Gorey Pier, Gorey JE3 6EW
☎ 01534-853633 Fax 01534-857618
16 bedrs, all ensuite, TCF TV 🐾 SB £37-£54 DB £72-£104
HB £317-£382 D £18.50 CC MC Visa Amex JCB

★★ **Sarum**
Hospitality merit award
19-21 New St John's Road, St Helier JE2 3LD
☎ 01534-58163 Fax 01534-31340
E Mail welcome@jerseyweb.demon.co.uk
Closed Dec-Feb
49 bedrs, all ensuite, 1 ⛶ TCF TV 🖃 P 6 SB £28-£56
DB £46-£100 HB £204-£400 D £13 CC MC Visa Amex JCB 🛗 🅿 ♿

★★ **White Heather**
Rue de Haut, Millbrook, St Lawrence JE3 1JQ
☎ 01534-20978 Fax 01534-20968
Closed Dec-Feb
33 bedrs, all ensuite, TCF TV P 12 SB £19.60-£29.60
DB £39.20-£59.20 HB £158.20-£228.20 D £8 CC MC Visa DC 🛗

Bon Air *Highly Acclaimed*
Coast Road, Pontac, St Clements JE2 6SE
☎ 01534-855324 Fax 01534-857801
Closed Nov-Feb
18 bedrs, all ensuite, TCF TV P 20 D £8.95 🛗

Hotel Des Pierres *Highly Acclaimed*
Greve de Lecq Bay, St Ouen JE3 2DT
☎ 01534-481858 Fax 01534-485273
Closed 15 Dec-15 Jan
16 bedrs, all ensuite, TCF TV P 15 SB £25-£32 DB £40-£54 HB £196-£245 D £9.75 CC MC Visa 🅿

Millbrook House *Highly Acclaimed*
Rue De Trachy, Millbrook, St Helier JE2 3JN
☎ 01534-33036 Fax 01534 24317
Closed 5 Oct-19 Apr
27 bedrs, all ensuite, 1 ⛶ TCF TV 🖃 P 20 SB £25-£33
DB £50-£66 HB £210-£266 D £8.50 CC MC Visa Amex JCB 🅿

Bryn-y-Mor *Acclaimed*
Route de la Haule, St Aubin's Bay JE3 8BA
☎ 01534-20295 Fax 01534-24262

A large Georgian house set in well-tended gardens with a magnificent view of St Aubins Bay, just 100 yards from three miles of golden sand.

14 bedrs, 12 ensuite, 2 ⇌ **TCF TV** 🐾 **P** 6 **SB** £15-£27 **DB** £30-£54 **HB** £150-£250 **D** £10 **CC** MC Visa Amex DC JCB

Domino *Acclaimed*
6 Vauxhall Street, St Helier
☎ 01534-30360 Fax 01534-31546
13 bedrs, 9 ensuite, 2 ⇌ **TCF TV** No children under 12 **SB** £20-£52 **CC** MC Visa Amex

Mon Desir *Acclaimed*
La Rue des Pres, Grouville, Gorey JE3 9DJ
☎ 01534-854718 Fax 01534-857798
13 bedrs, 12 ensuite, 1 ⇌ **TCF TV P** 13 No children under 3 **SB** £15.50-£24.50 **DB** £35-£53 **CC** MC Visa 🔳 ♿

Alhambra
Roseville Street, St Helier JE2 4PL
☎ 01534-32128 Fax 01534 31771
Closed Nov-Mar

A beautifully decorated 18 bedroom hotel with restaurant and bar. Easy walking distance to town, bus station and beach. Bedrooms have modern facilities, some fourposter beds and all non-smoking.

18 bedrs, all ensuite, 2 ⇌ **TCF TV SB** £16-£35 **DB** £35-£70 **D** £10 **CC** MC Visa Amex

Bromley
7 Winchester Street, St Helier JE2 4TH
☎ 01534-25045 Fax 01534-69712

Small family town guest house open most of the year for B&B. Most rooms ensuite with colour TV, tea/coffee facilities. Inclusive holiday can be arranged. Most credit cards accepted.

La Bonne Vie
Roseville Street, St Helier JE2 4PL
☎ 01534-35955 Fax 01534-33357

Beautiful Victorian guest house, situated one minutes' walk from the beach and five minute's walk from the town. All rooms are ensuite with TV and refreshment trays. Some have fourposter or antique brass beds. Open all year.

10 bedrs, all ensuite, 1 ⇌ **TCF TV** No children under 8 **SB** £17.50-£25 **DB** £35-£50 **CC** MC Visa

Free yourself

Our Hotel Reservations service will find you a room in the UK or Ireland and if you're an RAC Member, it's absolutely free.
Phone 0870 603 9109

If you're travelling in Europe, RAC Motoring Assistance provides rapid help in the event of breakdown, fire, accident, theft or illness. In addition, our Personal Travel Insurance covers you for lost luggage, theft of personal belongings, personal injury or cancellation.
Call us on 0800 550 055

RAC

www.rac.co.uk

Great Britain & Ireland Maps

Key to Maps

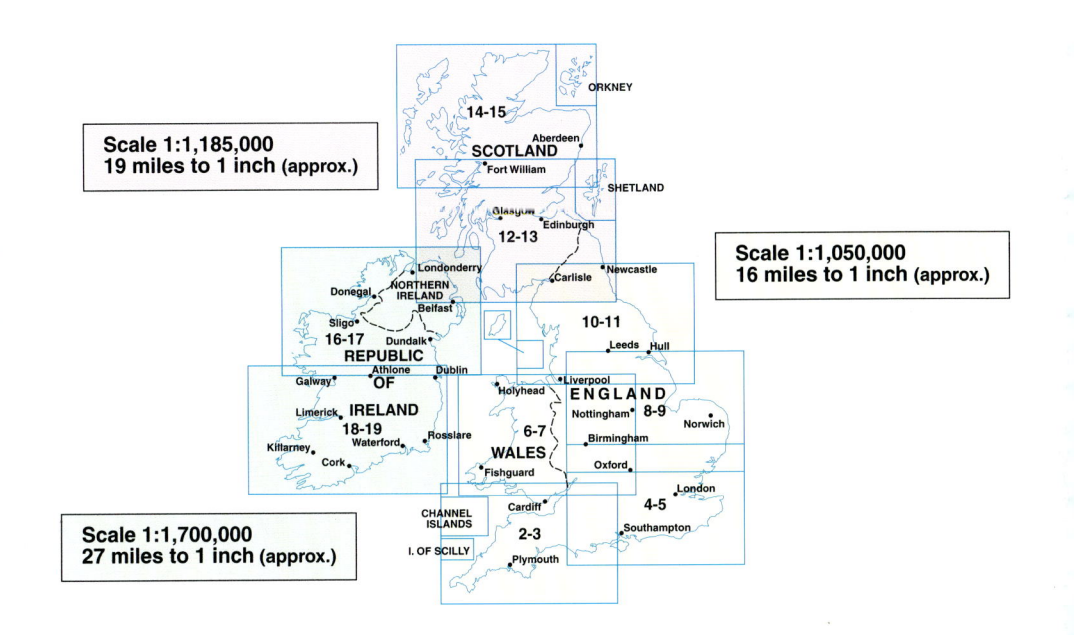

Scale 1:1,185,000
19 miles to 1 inch (approx.)

Scale 1:1,050,000
16 miles to 1 inch (approx.)

Scale 1:1,700,000
27 miles to 1 inch (approx.)

Legend

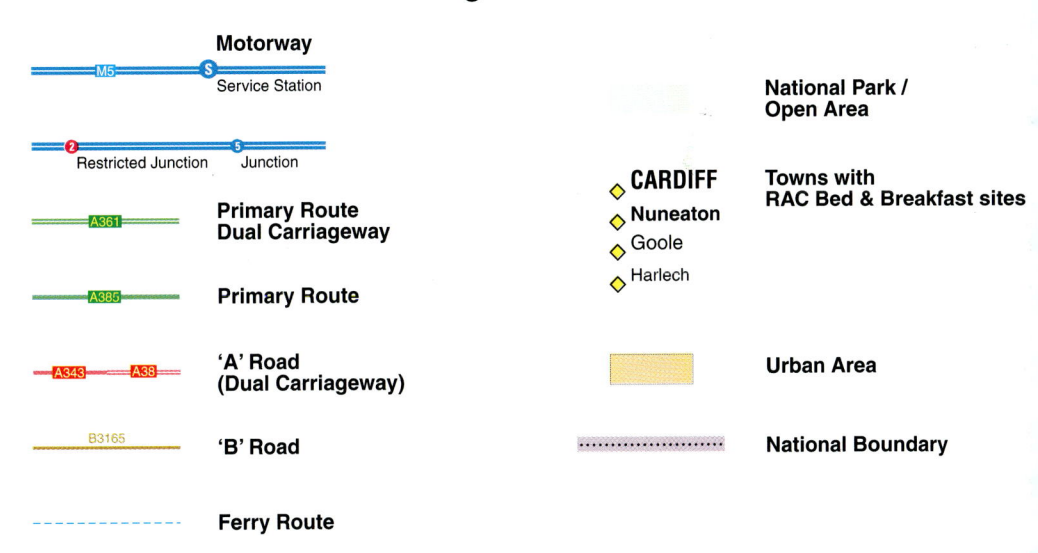

- Motorway
- Service Station
- Restricted Junction / Junction
- Primary Route Dual Carriageway (A361)
- Primary Route (A385)
- 'A' Road (Dual Carriageway) (A343, A38)
- 'B' Road (B3165)
- Ferry Route
- National Park / Open Area
- Towns with RAC Bed & Breakfast sites: CARDIFF, Nuneaton, Goole, Harlech
- Urban Area
- National Boundary

© RAC/LOVELL JOHNS LTD. 1997

2

RAC Hotel Reservations Service 0870 6039109
(Calls charged at the national rate)

RAC Hotel Reservations Service 0870 6039109
(Calls charged at the national rate)

3

4

RAC Hotel Reservations Service 0870 6039109
(Calls charged at the national rate)

RAC Hotel Reservations Service 0870 6039109
(Calls charged at the national rate)

6
RAC Hotel Reservations Service 0870 6039109
(Calls charged at the national rate)

RAC Hotel Reservations Service 0870 6039109
(Calls charged at the national rate)

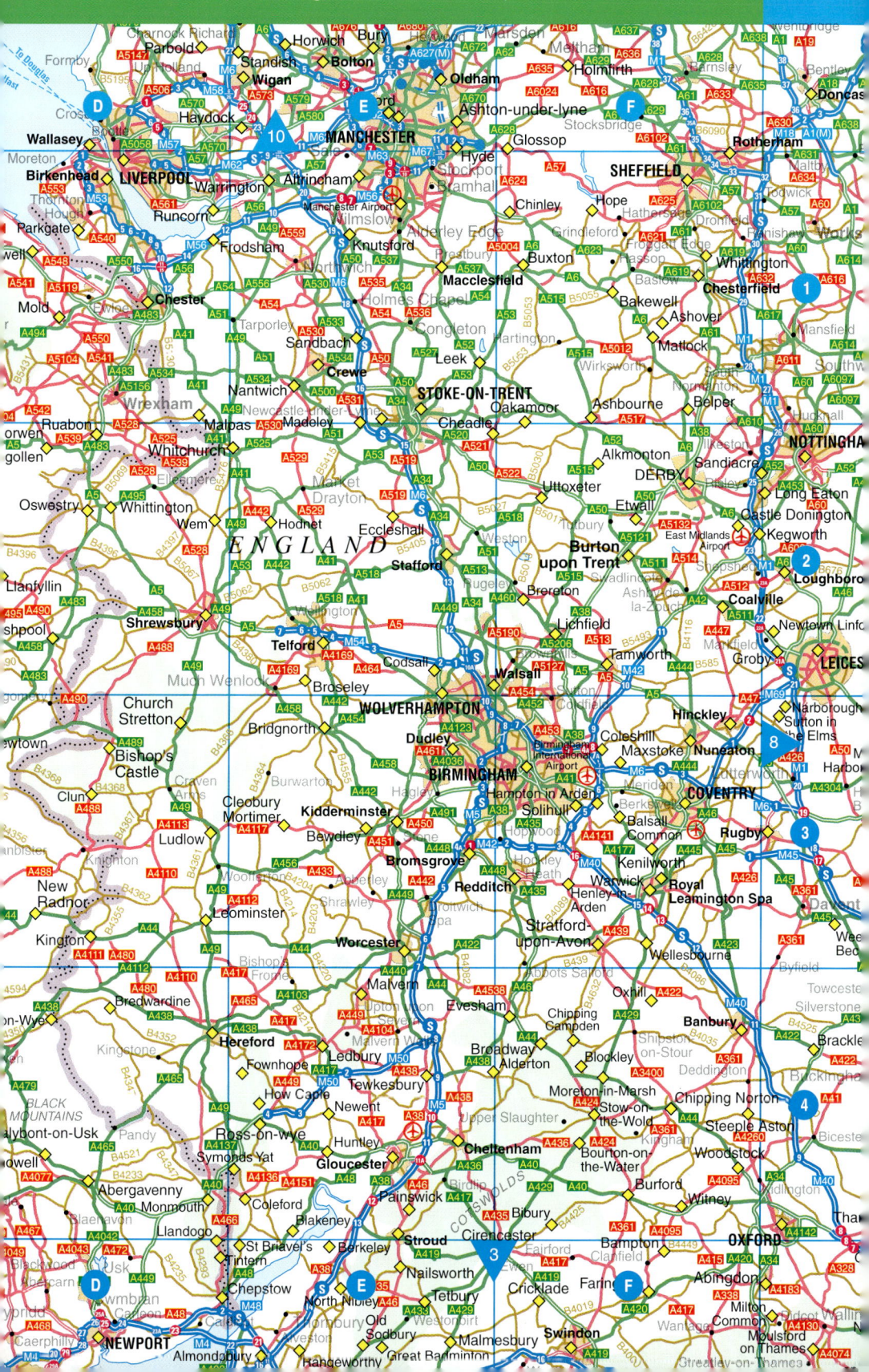

7

RAC Hotel Reservations Service 0870 6039109
(Calls charged at the national rate)

8

RAC Hotel Reservations Service 0870 6039109
(Calls charged at the national rate)

9

10

RAC Hotel Reservations Service 0870 6039109
(Calls charged at the national rate)

RAC Hotel Reservations Service 0870 6039109
(Calls charged at the national rate)

11

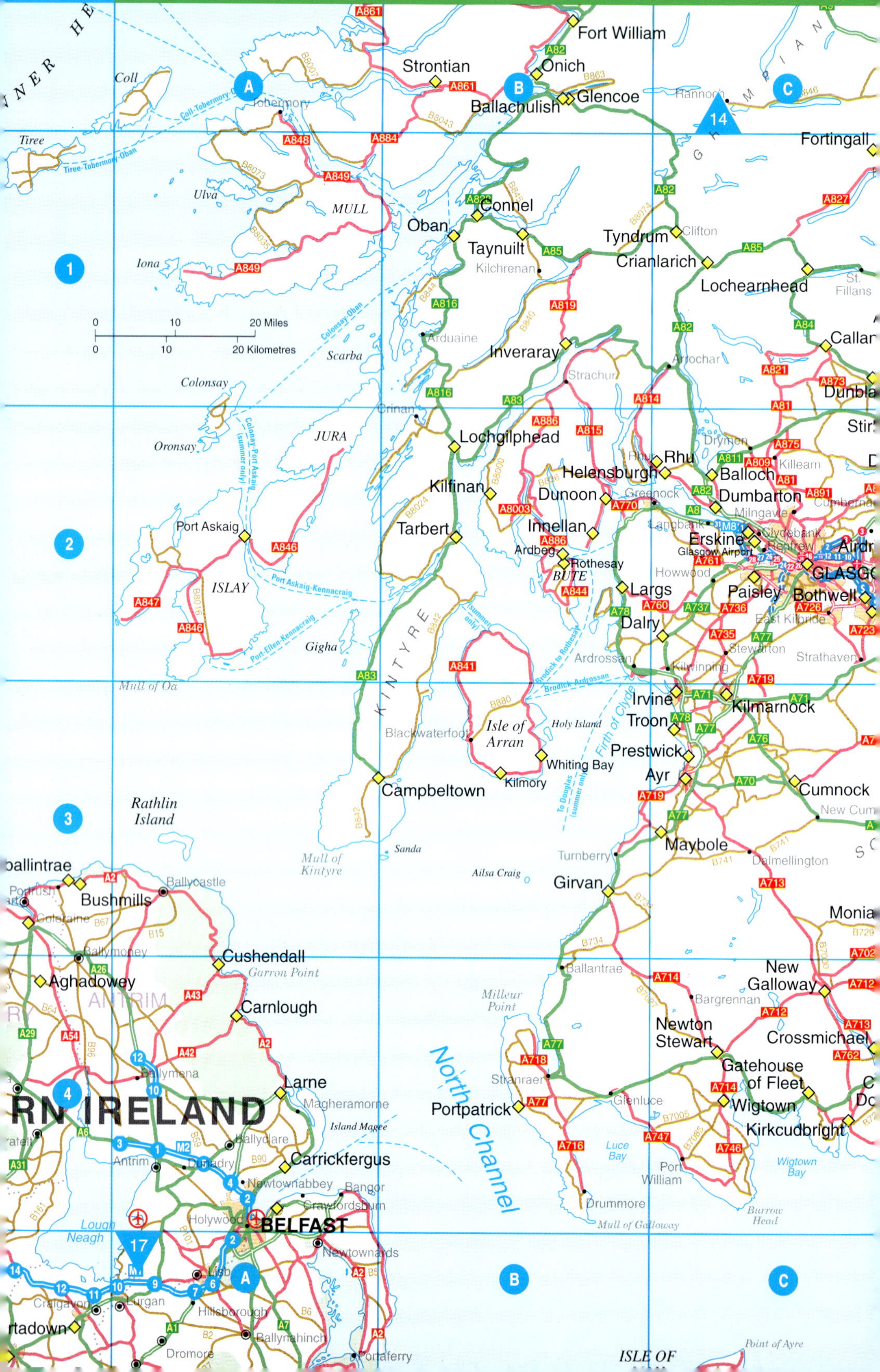
A
B
C
1
2
3
4
14
17
Fort William
Strontian
Onich
Glencoe
Ballachulish
Rannoch
Fortingall
Coll
Tiree
Tobermory
Coll-Tobermory-Oban
Tiree-Tobermory-Oban
MULL
Ulva
Iona
Oban
Connel
Taynuilt
Kilchrenan
Tyndrum
Clifton
Crianlarich
Lochearnhead
St. Fillans
Callander
Arduaine
Inveraray
Arrochar
Strachur
Scarba
Colonsay-Oban
Colonsay
Oronsay
Crinan
JURA
Colonsay-Port Askaig (summer only)
Lochgilphead
Rhu
Helensburgh
Balloch
Drymen
Killearn
Dumbarton
Kilfinan
Dunoon
Greenock
Milngavie
Port Askaig
Tarbert
Innellan
Langbank
Erskine
Clydebank
Renfrew
Glasgow Airport
GLASGOW
Airdrie
ISLAY
Port Askaig-Kennacraig
Ardbeg
Rothesay
BUTE
Howwood
Paisley
Bothwell
Largs
Dalry
East Kilbride
Gigha
Port-Ellen-Kennacraig
KINTYRE
Ardrossan
Stewarton
Strathaven
Brodick to Rothesay
Brodick-Ardrossan
Kilwinning
Mull of Oa
Irvine
Kilmarnock
Troon
Isle of Arran
Holy Island
Firth of Clyde
Blackwaterfoot
Whiting Bay
Prestwick
Kilmory
Ayr
Campbeltown
Cumnock
New Cumnock
To Douglas (summer only)
Rathlin Island
Sanda
Maybole
Mull of Kintyre
Turnberry
Dalmellington
Ailsa Craig
Ballintrae
Portrush
Bushmills
Ballycastle
Girvan
Coleraine
Ballymoney
Cushendall
Garron Point
Aghadowey
ANTRIM
Ballantrae
Milleur Point
New Galloway
Bargrennan
Carnlough
Newton Stewart
Crossmichael
Ballymena
Stranraer
Gatehouse of Fleet
Larne
Glenluce
Wigtown
Magheramorne
Island Magee
North Channel
Portpatrick
Kirkcudbright
NORTHERN IRELAND
Ballyclare
Antrim
Doagh
Carrickfergus
Luce Bay
Port William
Wigtown Bay
Newtownabbey
Bangor
Crawfordsburn
Drummore
Mull of Galloway
Burrow Head
Lough Neagh
Holywood
BELFAST
Newtownards
Lisburn
Craigavon
Lurgan
Hillsborough
Ballynahinch
Portadown
Dromore
Portaferry
Point of Ayre
ISLE OF
0
10
20 Miles
0
10
20 Kilometres

RAC Hotel Reservations Service 0870 6039109
(Calls charged at the national rate)

13

14

RAC Hotel Reservations Service 0870 6039109
(Calls charged at the national rate)

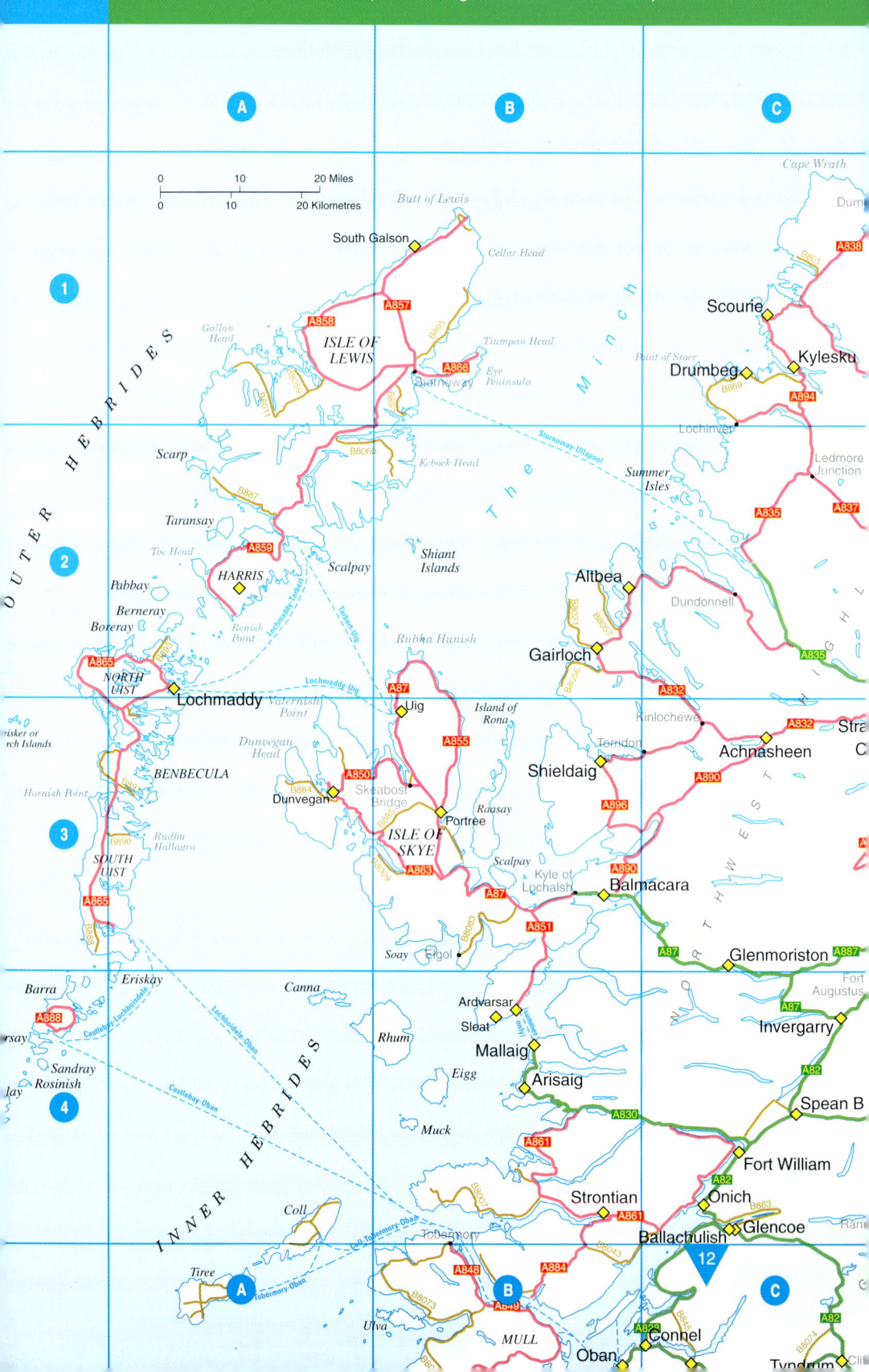

RAC Hotel Reservations Service 0870 6039109
(Calls charged at the national rate)

15

16

RAC Hotel Reservations Service 0870 6039109
(Calls charged at the national rate)

RAC Hotel Reservations Service 0870 6039109
(Calls charged at the national rate)

17

18
RAC Hotel Reservations Service 0870 6039109
(Calls charged at the national rate)

RAC Hotel Reservations Service 0870 6039109
(Calls charged at the national rate)

19